ENGLAND'S LAST WAR AGAINST FRANCE

Also by Colin Smith

Carlos: Portrait of a Terrorist

Cut-Out (novel)

The Last Crusade (novel)

Fire in the Night: Wingate of Burma, Ethiopia and Zion (with John Bierman)

Alamein: War Without Hate (with John Bierman)

Singapore Burning

ENGLAND'S LAST WAR AGAINST FRANCE

Fighting Vichy 1940–1942

COLIN SMITH

Weidenfeld & Nicolson
LONDON

First published in Great Britain in 2009
by Weidenfeld & Nicolson

1 3 5 7 9 10 8 6 4 2

A CIP catalogue record for this book is available from the British Library.

ISBN: 978 0 297 85218 6

Typeset by Input Data Services Ltd,
Bridgwater, Somerset

Printed and bound in the UK by
CPI Mackays, Chatham ME5 8TD

Weidenfeld & Nicolson

Orion Publishing Group Ltd
Orion House, 5 Upper Saint Martin's Lane,
London, WC2H 9EA
An Hachette UK Company

www.orionbooks.co.uk

For Murray Wrobel, my friend and recent translator
of arcane military documents, who last met the
Vichy French in Syria as a member of the
Combined Services Detailed Interrogation Centre.

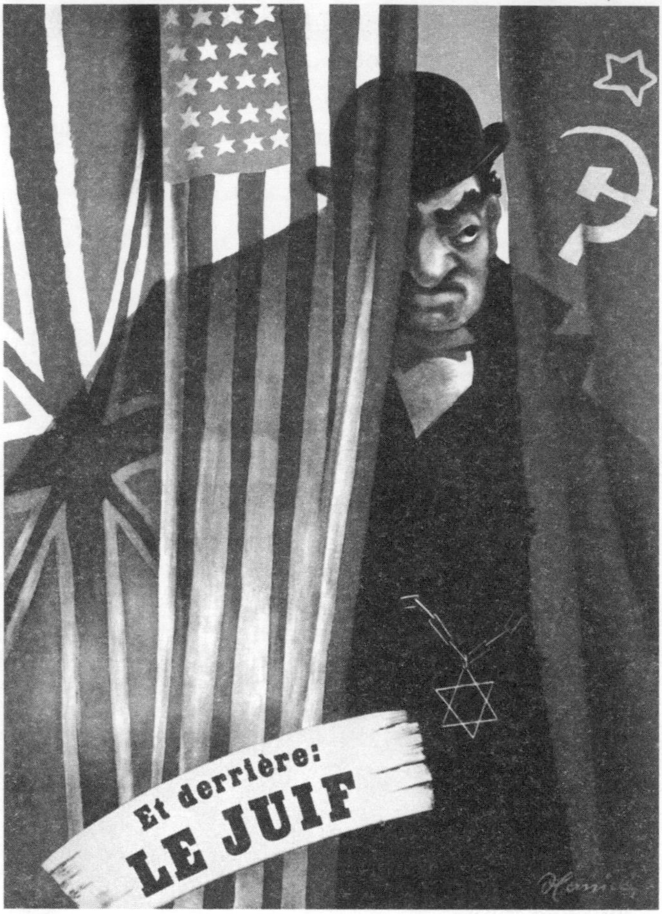

Vichy views its foes: 1942

CONTENTS

LIST OF ILLUSTRATIONS

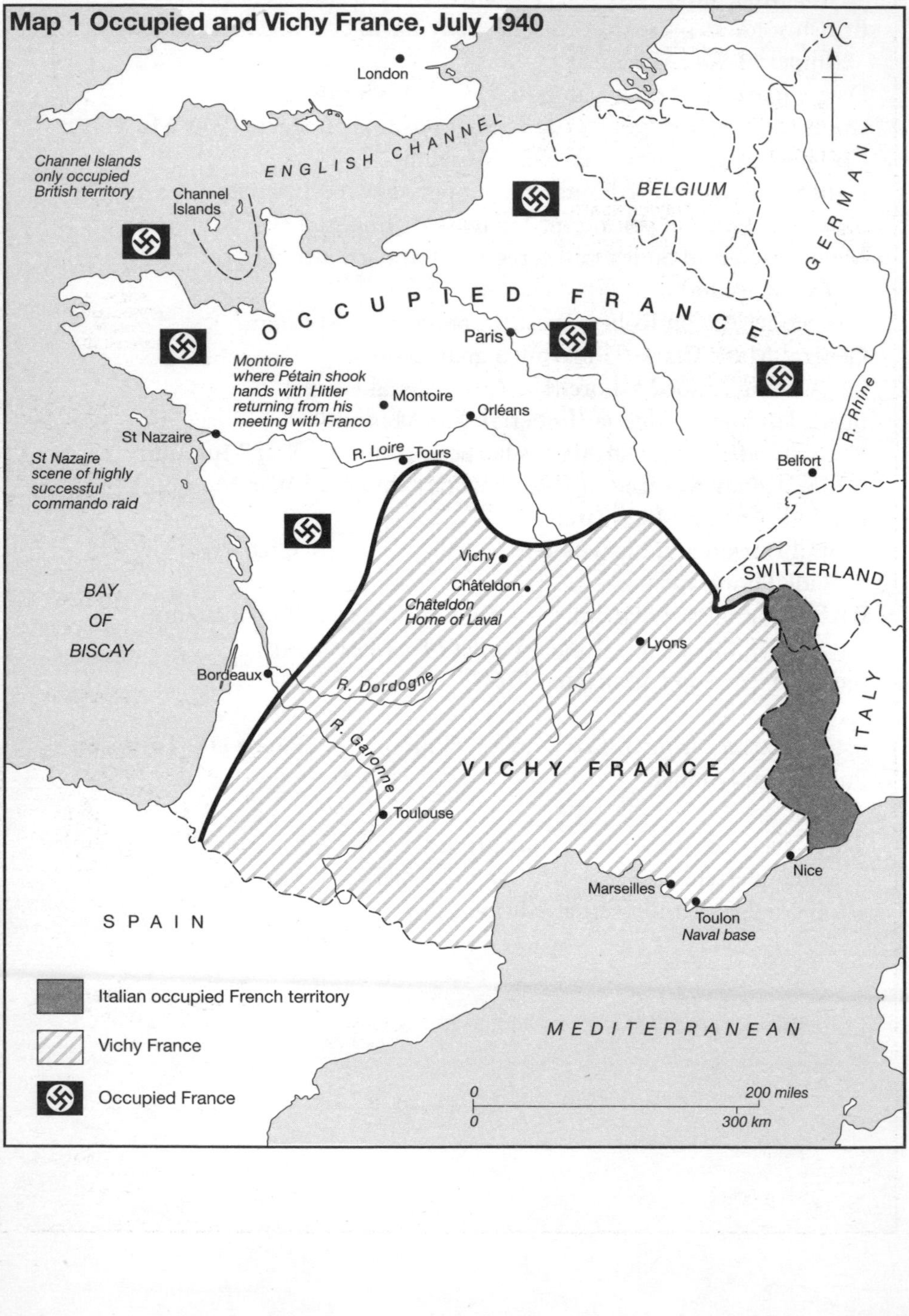
London
ENGLISH CHANNEL
Channel Islands only occupied British territory
Channel Islands
BELGIUM
GERMANY
OCCUPIED FRANCE
Paris
Montoire where Pétain shook hands with Hitler returning from his meeting with Franco
Montoire
Orléans
St Nazaire
St Nazaire scene of highly successful commando raid
R. Loire
Tours
Belfort
R. Rhine
Vichy
Châteldon
Châteldon Home of Laval
SWITZERLAND
BAY OF BISCAY
Lyons
Bordeaux
R. Dordogne
R. Garonne
ITALY
VICHY FRANCE
Toulouse
Nice
Marseilles
Toulon
Naval base
SPAIN
Italian occupied French territory
Vichy France
Occupied France
MEDITERRANEAN
0
200 miles
0
300 km

Map 1 Occupied and Vichy France, July 1940

Map 2 How Africa was divided between the British, French and other European powers, summer 1940

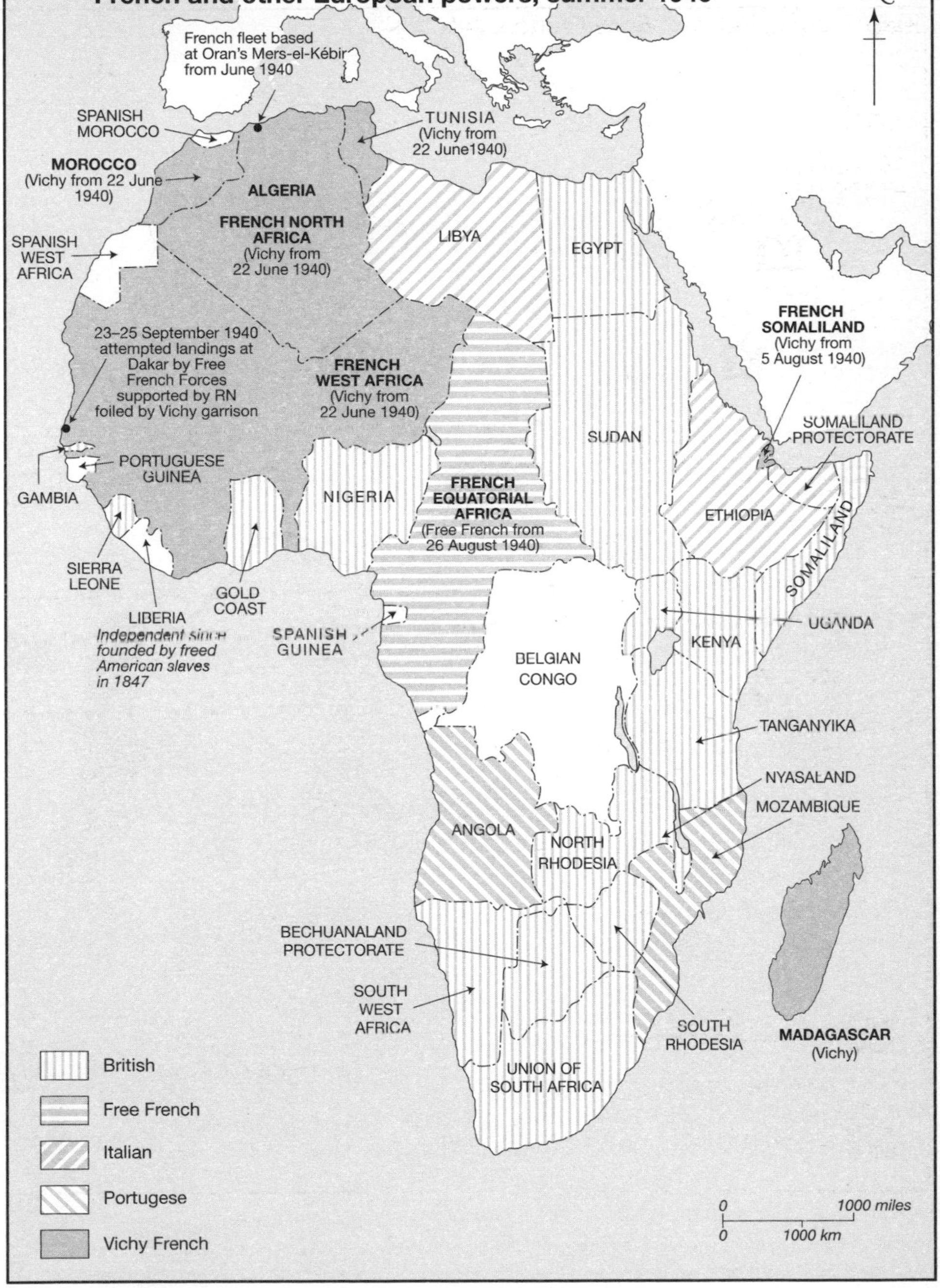
N
French fleet based at Oran's Mers-el-Kébir from June 1940
SPANISH MOROCCO
TUNISIA (Vichy from 22 June1940)
MOROCCO (Vichy from 22 June 1940)
ALGERIA
FRENCH NORTH AFRICA (Vichy from 22 June 1940)
SPANISH WEST AFRICA
LIBYA
EGYPT
FRENCH SOMALILAND (Vichy from 5 August 1940)
23–25 September 1940 attempted landings at Dakar by Free French Forces supported by RN foiled by Vichy garrison
FRENCH WEST AFRICA (Vichy from 22 June 1940)
SUDAN
SOMALILAND PROTECTORATE
PORTUGUESE GUINEA
GAMBIA
NIGERIA
FRENCH EQUATORIAL AFRICA (Free French from 26 August 1940)
ETHIOPIA
SOMALILAND
SIERRA LEONE
GOLD COAST
LIBERIA
Independent since founded by freed American slaves in 1847
SPANISH GUINEA
UGANDA
KENYA
BELGIAN CONGO
TANGANYIKA
NYASALAND
MOZAMBIQUE
ANGOLA
NORTH RHODESIA
BECHUANALAND PROTECTORATE
SOUTH WEST AFRICA
SOUTH RHODESIA
MADAGASCAR (Vichy)
UNION OF SOUTH AFRICA
British
Free French
Italian
Portugese
Vichy French
0 1000 miles
0 1000 km

AUTHOR'S NOTE

Readers may well wonder why this book is not called *Britain's Last War Against France*. After all, large numbers of Scots, Welsh and Irish found themselves fighting the Vichy French. Its title does not reflect any animus against the Union on my part. Far from it. But for the French, perhaps because over the centuries they sometimes acquired Celtic allies, their old enemy is almost always 'the English'. Sometimes – usually when they are very angry with us or we are allied to the Americans or both – we become 'the Anglo-Saxons'. Only rarely, in their eyes, are we 'the British', a people with whom they tend to have a more neutral relationship. CS

PROLOGUE
The Fugitive Fleet

Robert Surcouf was the most famous of France's eighteenth-century privateers who, based on Mauritius in the Indian Ocean, grew rich on English plunder before retiring to his native St Malo. Renowned for his chivalry towards prisoners, in France he is perhaps best remembered for the reply he gave a captive officer who admonished him for fighting for money rather than, as the British did, for honour. 'Each of us fights,' admitted Surcouf, 'for what he lacks most.'

In the 1930s the huge submarine named after him was the largest submersible in the world and seemed a potent symbol of France's growing sea power. Her main armament was the twin long-range guns housed in an enclosed turret of cylindrical design just forward of the conning tower. To spot her prey she even carried a small Marcel-Berson seaplane in a waterproof hangar. Once the aircraft had returned and been winched back aboard, *Surcouf* would stalk her targets submerged until they were within range of her formidable 8-inchers, a calibre not normally found on anything smaller than a cruiser. Her victims might then be finished off with torpedoes.

At least, that was the theory. The reality was that the *Surcouf* was a white elephant, a prototype that had never grown out of her teething problems and spent more time under repair than under water. Towards the end of June 1940, when only the diehards of the French Army were still fighting and the bulk of Britain's small contribution to the land war had been home two weeks from Dunkirk, the submarine was at Brest suffering with another bout of engine trouble and had yet to fire a shot in anger.

As the panzers approached the coast, *Surcouf*'s delicate innards were gathered up and, with three broken connecting rods and powered only by her auxiliary electric motors, she left harbour at dusk on 18 June unable to dive or go any faster than 4 knots. The submarine was heading for England. From the conning tower Bernard Le Nistour, a big athletic man who was the *Surcouf*'s doctor, recalled looking back at the fires that were beginning behind them as the demolitions started. 'All of us hoped to continue the fight,' he said. 'Morale was high; the physical fitness of the crew excellent.'

Shortly after dawn on the 19th an inquisitive Sunderland flying boat, RAF Coastal Command's main anti-submarine aircraft, took a good look at it. Aldis lamps blinked the agreed recognition signals between allies and, satisfied, the big four-engined aircraft flew away. Landfall was in late afternoon: first the hazy outline of the Lizard then Penzance. Here the *Surcouf* dropped anchor while her engineers made some adjustments that enabled the submarine to make 10 knots as she followed the Cornish coast up to Plymouth Sound. On arrival two launches came out and circled slowly around them but kept out of hailing distance. They made Le Nistour feel uneasy. 'Are we prisoners?' he asked himself.

The next day the crew were told to move a couple of miles up the coast to Devonport. En route, holidaymakers who had spotted *Surcouf*'s tricolour rose from their deckchairs waving their hats, towels and what looked like miniature entrenching tools. For those French sailors allowed on deck it was a depressing sight. The Boche were in Paris and, despite Dunkirk, the English were still on the beach.

At Devonport the submarine berthed alongside the *Paris*, a distressed French dreadnought launched in 1912 which made the *Surcouf* look frisky. Bombed in Le Havre, she had been towed to Brest, then tried to get to England under her own power but her engines were not up to it and British tugs pulled her into Plymouth where her crew had now been long enough to start getting irritated with their hosts. They were quick to tell the newcomers that what infuriated them most about the English was the number of young men of military age still in civilian clothes, some of them carrying tennis racquets. You didn't have to look far to see why a fully mobilized France, despite its smaller population, had fielded eighty divisions compared with the British Expeditionary Force's ten. At the end of 1918 there had been almost sixty khaki-clad divisions in France and the English were claiming to have won the war. There was no sign yet of conscription on that scale.

Two days after the *Surcouf*'s arrival in Devonport, at the Compiègne forest some 35 miles north of Paris, history was repeating itself in, as far as the French were concerned, a nightmare mirror image reversing all that was good. It had taken just six weeks of blitzkrieg to reverse the punch-drunk decision reached after four years of fighting and over a million French dead. Now, in the same railway dining car where Maréchal Foch had received Imperial Germany's war-weary emissaries in November 1918, a French delegation under Général Charles Huntzinger had come to hear what price this new Germany would put on an armistice following its amazing victory.

To seal their triumph German engineers had liberated the sacred rolling stock with its polished wood interior by demolishing one side of the little museum where it had been immured since 1927 when France decided to preserve in perpetuity the best known symbol of Germany's humiliation. By the time Huntzinger and his delegation turned up the stage had been set. Hitler, Hess, Goering, Feldmarschal Wilhelm Keitel and Joachim von Ribbentrop, the Foreign Minister, were already seated in the carriage. Outside, a big swastika flag draped over an imposing granite block hid its inscription: 'Here on the 11th November 1918 succumbed the criminal pride of the German people.'

Huntzinger, who had had no idea where the Germans were leading his delegation for the surrender ceremony, was mortified at this gloating tit for tat. 'The historic forest of Compiègne has been chosen in order to efface once and for all by an act of reparative justice a memory resented by the German people as the greatest shame of all time,' lectured Feldmarschal Keitel in a lengthy preamble.

But at least the French could console themselves with the thought that they were not quite offering unconditional surrender. Leading the new government, which had decided to seek an armistice with Germany while it still had something left to bargain with, was the octogenarian national icon Maréchal Philippe Pétain who in 1916 had inspired the sacrifice that had stopped the Germans at Verdun. Pétain had given Huntzinger firm instructions to break off talks if the Germans demanded either of two things: any French colonial territory or the surrender of their fleet. This had not proved necessary.

Hitler, who shared the general astonishment over the French collapse, had decided it would pay to be magnanimous in victory. He did not want France to follow Poland, Norway and Holland (and soon Belgium) who all had governments-in-exile in London from where they could wage a propaganda war, if little else. 'It would be better to permit the existence of a French government in France which would be the sole responsible one,' he told Mussolini when he explained why he was unable to meet Il Duce's demands for an Italian occupation zone east of the Rhône plus Corsica, Tunisia and French Somaliland. All this was to be a reward for Fascist Italy's ten days of fighting following its long-awaited declaration of war against France and Britain on 10 June, the day the French government left Paris.

While Anglo-German hostilities continued, France was to be offered peace on condition that the Wehrmacht occupied about three-fifths of its territory including all its Channel and Atlantic coasts and Paris. If it wished, the French government could operate from its occupied capital or choose a city in the south-eastern unoccupied zone as a temporary seat of government until Churchill gave in and there were proper peace treaties. A spa town like Vichy was an obvious choice, its season curtailed and with lots of empty hotels that could be requisitioned to accommodate government departments and provide living quarters for civil servants.

Unlike the Italians, Hitler had little interest in France's colonial possessions. But he was determined that the French fleet must not fall into British hands. When he met Mussolini in Munich, three days before the armistice talks began, he made it plain that he thought the best option would be to have the French scuttle their ships. The worst, he said, would be to have the world's fourth most powerful fleet amalgamating with the Royal Navy, thereby giving the British the chance of moving large forces 'to all sorts of places' and thus prolonging the war because Germany would find it impossible to deliver a decisive blow.

Hitler's answer to the problem of France's fugitive fleet – by now most of it was either in its African colonies or in Britain – was typical. Without, it seems, a trace of irony the Führer laid on the table a solemn promise of the kind that, one after the other, had been broken so often during all the crises that had led to war. Article Eight of the terms being offered to Huntzinger's delegation at Compiègne – which Hitler had made clear were not negotiable – pledged: 'The German government solemnly declares to the French government that it does not intend to use for its own purposes in the war the French fleet which is in ports under German supervision. Furthermore, they solemnly and expressly declare that they have no intention of raising any claim to the French navy at the conclusion of peace.'

When Général Maxime Weygand, who had been Foch's Chief of Staff during the 1918 ceremony and now commanded what was left of the French Army, heard the terms from Huntzinger on a telephone line laid on by the Germans, he took Hitler at his word. Weygand advised Pétain that the terms were harsh but did not dishonour the 50,000 French soldiers who had fallen during the last six weeks of fighting. France would keep its colonies and the fleet would be immobilized but remain in French ports with skeleton French crews. It could have been a lot worse. All that remained was to get the ships back.

On 3 July 1940 the *Surcouf* was still moored at Devonport where her 140-strong crew could not fail to notice that they were covered by the huge 15-inch guns on the British battleship HMS *Revenge*, which had last fired them in anger at the Battle of Jutland in 1916. It seemed so pointless. It was eleven days since the armistice had been signed. The war was over. Would the English really prevent them going home? They could not possibly continue to fight the most powerful war machine on the planet on their own.

Alongside them aboard the battleship *Paris* were 600 or so similarly minded French sailors under Amiral Jean Cayol. A French destroyer and two submarines were also anchored nearby. Few of their crews doubted that the English would be the next to come to terms with Germany. The hundreds of abandoned trucks and artillery pieces the Wehrmacht's mechanics were now picking over at Dunkirk, from where Lord Gort's army had been so lucky to get home in their socks, were surely proof enough that the British had no real stomach for a fight with Hitler?

In the Compiègne forest some of the Germans present had confided to Huntzinger's delegation that they expected London would sue for peace by mid-August. On 1 July Amiral François Darlan, head of the French Navy he had done so much to modernize, was assuring William Bullitt, the US ambassador to France, that Germany would conquer England within five weeks 'unless she surrendered sooner'.

Pétain had already rejected an extraordinary proposal from Winston Churchill, who was desperate to keep France in the war, that Britain and France unite to form a single confederated state. 'It is not in France's interests to marry a corpse,' declared the maréchal, 84 last birthday.

He had been in Madrid as France's ambassador to Franco's new Spain when Prime Minister Paul Reynaud had invited him to join his government as Deputy Prime Minister with the expectation that the maréchal would stiffen the resolve of the waverers in the Cabinet who wanted to give in. But to his astonishment he soon discovered that the old soldier who had saved Verdun was equally convinced that the game was up.

As far as Pétain and a good many less senior officers were concerned, gallant exceptions apart, the French Army was no longer the army they had once served. The sacrifices of the Verdun generation had been blasphemed by the decadence that had rotted the entire nation for most of the last twenty years. It had reached its disgusting highpoint during the leftist government of Léon Blum's Front Populaire with its anticlericalism and forty-hour weeks for the workers and was reflected in the spinelessness of the army that had collapsed at Sedan. For the British too, he had nothing but contempt. If they had truly possessed the will to fight on they would have met with French demands for massive RAF reinforcements while there was still time to stop the panzers. They might also have sent an army big enough to be worthy of the name; not less than one-tenth of the men France had put in the field.

All Churchill had to counteract Petain's defeatism was another of Paul Reynaud's late appointments to his War Cabinet: Brigadier général Charles de Gaulle, France's foremost exponent of armoured warfare and as such accorded a certain respect by his contemporaries but unknown to most civilians and hardly the man to take on Pétain, a popular figure bringing an end to an unpopular war. Nonetheless, de Gaulle was the best available. The Francophone British Major General Sir Edward Spears, Churchill's special emissary to the French government, spirited him away on an RAF aircraft which took off from a chaotically overcrowded airfield at Bordeaux, where the French government had evacuated after an earlier stop in Tours. The aircraft refuelled in Jersey which, along with the rest of the Channel Islands, would shortly become the only British territory to be occupied by Nazi Germany. It was here, Spears observed, that the martyrdom of the général's exile began when at the airport's canteen he innocently enquired whether what he was drinking was coffee or tea.

Five days later de Gaulle, in his first BBC broadcast, announced: 'France has lost a battle. But France has not lost the war.' His words were primarily intended for the 100,000 or so French military in England who had been evacuated there from Dunkirk and a much smaller contingent from the smaller Anglo-French defeat in Norway. At first these evacuees had expected to be returned to France to fight in the battle being waged on the Somme but now they merely wanted to be back with their families. Very few of them had heard de Gaulle speak. For the most part, homesick *poilus* – the 1914–18 nickname for the formidable French infantry – and sailors cast up on the wrong side of the Channel were not in the habit of listening to the BBC. And even if they had been it is unlikely that it would have made much difference. The war was over. Ever since it began German propaganda had insisted that London wanted to fight it with French soldiers. Now the British had left France and the French wanted to leave Britain.

Spears reflected that as a liaison officer in the 1914–18 war, when the French and the English fell out, he always knew that the will to fight Germany was not eroded and these were passing spats. But this time he sensed some irreconcilable break between the two nations. 'No more perceptible than a crack in crystal but going right through, irreparably. We were no longer one.'

PART ONE

The Making and the Breaking of the Entente Cordiale

Chapter One

In the spring of 1903 a new dish began to appear on the menus of the smarter Parisian restaurants. *Selle de mouton à l'anglaise* was yet another mark of the success of King Edward VII's recent visit. The Welsh mutton chosen by his accompanying English chef for a dinner held at the British Embassy in honour of President Émile Loubet had only added to the affection France felt for this merry monarch. 'French cooks are so fond of cutting up joints into morsels and making what they call, "little dishes" of the meat,' explained the correspondent of the *Belfast Newsletter* to the beef-eating Protestant gentry. 'Now every gourmet in Paris wants to have a saddle of mutton for dinner.'

Edward was no stranger to France or at least to Paris. Queen Victoria's eldest son and Europe's best known royal lothario had often visited it, when possible incognito, during his long apprenticeship as Prince of Wales. Among his mistresses had been the great *tragédienne* Sarah Bernhardt who made her debut at the Théâtre Français.

In those days his presence had been a nightmare for the French police who feared he might be assassinated by Irish Fenians or some other brand of republican. It never happened in France but in April 1900, the year before he took the throne, the Belgians nearly lost him at Brussels railway station when a teenage gunman missed with two shots before he was overpowered. Jean-Baptiste Sipido, aged 16, was infected by the Anglophobia then widespread on the Continent over the cruel war Imperial Britain was waging against southern Africa's Boer republics. These proud descendants of Dutch and other continental European settlers were, it was alleged, being treated as if they were no better than unruly Africans. The anti-war movement, which was also gathering strength in Britain, was incensed by a new British tactic of denying the Boer guerrillas their civilian support by concentrating women and children in wired-off and guarded temporary accommodation. There were reports of them dying in their hundreds from typhoid. Offers from Germany and Holland to send medical assistance to these concentration camps, as they were becoming known, had been refused. So had an American proposal to mediate in the conflict.

Sipido told his interrogators that he wanted to kill the man who would one day wear the crown that was taking so many lives in South Africa. As it happened, the very next day, 5 April 1900, one of the latest casualties was Colonel Comte de Villebois-Mareuil, a French aristocrat and distinguished regular officer who had resigned his commission to command a legion of foreign volunteers to the Afrikaner cause. Nor was his loss felt only in France.

Like many of his class, while the comte's world view was often Anglophobic his style was distinctly Anglophile: he spoke good English, wore Savile Row, hired his daughter an English governess and was acquainted with the London set who regularly visited Paris, including Oscar Wilde and the Prince of Wales. The comte had met Wilde through their mutual friend, the writer and historian John Bodley, whose two-volume contemporary anatomy of France he was translating for a French publisher.

Yet Villebois-Mareuil, a veteran of France's disastrous 1870 war with Prussia as well as colonial triumphs in Morocco and Algeria, had been willing to die for his cause, dug in on a hilltop and rejecting calls for surrender until he was killed by a shell. (Although not before he had shot dead the yeomanry volunteer Sergeant Patrick Campbell whose wife was a famous actress.) Only then did his followers – mostly compatriots in plumed slouch hats who bore themselves as if they were the inventions of Alexandre Dumas – decide they had had enough. Any fears that the English might treat them as little better than mercenaries and have them shot out of hand were soon dispelled. Lord Methuen, the British commander, not only insisted on burying Villebois-Mareuil with full military honours but paid for his headstone and wrote a letter of condolence to his daughter.

Methuen's chivalry was appreciated. 'We are prisoners of an army which is the bravest of the brave,' reported Comte de Bréda, the fallen hero's deputy who joined Boer prisoners of war in Napoleonic exile on the island of St Helena. One senses embarrassment on both sides. After nearly a millennium of intermittent warfare, killing each other was no longer quite the norm. 'For the first time since the Norman Conquest, three generations have gone by without the armies of England and France meeting in battle array,' wrote Bodley in the work the colonel was meant to be translating.

But the years since Waterloo in 1815 had not all been ones of peaceful coexistence. King Edward was 60 and in his lifetime this unaccustomed peace with France had rarely been easy. When he was younger it had taken the older generation a long while to get used to it. Forty years after he lost an arm at Waterloo, the fashionably lisping Lord Raglan, then commanding the British contingent of the Anglo-French army in the Crimea, constantly referred to the enemy as 'the Fwench' when he meant to say 'the Wussians'. Nor had time proved a great healer.

Only five years before Edward's state visit to Paris, Britain and France had seemed on the brink of war over who should possess Fashoda, the site of an old Arab mud-walled slave-trading fort on the brown and crocodiled waters of Sudan's Upper Nile. After his brutal victory over the Dervishes at Omdurman, Lieutenant General Sir Horatio Kitchener pushed on upriver to reclaim territory lost thirteen years before when General Charles Gordon had been beheaded at Khartoum and his Egyptian soldiers massacred. When he arrived at Fashoda he discovered its fort was flying the tricolour.

For the last ten weeks it had been in the hands of about 130 Senegalese soldiers and 8 French officers under the command of the soldier-explorer Commandant Jean-Baptiste Marchand. It had taken Marchand's expedition almost two years to cross most of the continent from west to east starting at Brazzaville in the French Congo. During that time almost thirty of them had died, not only in the skirmishes they had fought with people who knew they must fear white men, but of malaria and in the accidents that come with unexplored terrain. Jungles, mountains and rivers had all taken their toll. Once, they had spent five days and nights wading through a swamp that was often neck-high. For four months Paris had received no word from them at all and it was feared that, one way or another, Africa had consumed them.

It was an achievement made even more remarkable by Marchand's African porters who, with the Nile in mind, had manhandled across their continent the components of a small steam launch, three steel dinghies with sails as well as oars, a hurdy-gurdy that could play the 'Marseillaise' and about 2,000 bottles of claret, champagne, brandy and absinthe. All to wash down a staple diet of Anglo-Saxon stodge: 5 tons of canned corned beef and 10 tons of rice.

For some time both the British and French had the same master plan for their African colonies: where need be this was to expand them until they were contiguous so that one day they could be knitted together by transcontinental railways. Britain wanted to lay its tracks north to south, from Cairo to the Cape via Sudan; France west to east, from Dakar to Somaliland in the Horn of Africa from where a westbound expedition was heading towards Fashoda and what it hoped would be a historic meeting.

When Gabriel Hanatoux, the French Foreign Minister, had secretly given his blessing to all this the eastern Sudan was still a territory in turmoil. The corrupt Egyptian administration had been driven out and, eleven years after Gordon's death, the British seemed in no hurry to avenge him and fill the vacuum. Egypt had been a British protectorate since 1882 but Hanatoux saw a chance for bolder spirits to prosper. To further French influence in the Horn of Africa, he had already begun to undermine Italian attempts to conquer neighbouring Abyssinia by supplying Emperor Menelik with some of the arms he would use to win his surprising victory at Adowa.

And not for the first time Whitehall suspected that France was plotting to restore its influence in Egypt where in November 1869 the Francophile Khedive Ismail had invited Napoléon III's Empress Eugénie to Suez to open the canal built by her distant cousin Ferdinand de Lesseps. There was even talk that Marchand's party were surveying sites for a massive dam that would control the waters of the Nile. But the French had arrived on the scene a little too late. A powerful Anglo-Egyptian army was now on the river and it had tasted blood.

'We were confronted with the fact that a "friendly Power" had, unprovoked, endeavoured to rob us of the fruits of our victory,' wrote Winston Churchill, who had charged with the 21st Lancers at Omdurman, a 25-year-old soldier journalist writing for the *Morning Post* at £15 a column and armed with the latest German automatic pistol. 'While England had been devoting itself to great military operations ... other operations – covert and deceitful – had been in progress designed solely for the mischievous and spiteful object of depriving them of the produce of their labours.'

Fortunately Kitchener, who spoke reasonable French, having served in a volunteer ambulance unit during the 1870 Franco-Prussian War, revealed an unsuspected talent for diplomacy and from the beginning he and Marchand maintained cordial relations. The flags of France, Britain and Egypt flew over Fashoda and for the senior officers there were reciprocal drinks invitations, though Marchand disliked Kitchener's whisky and soda, which he had never sampled before, and thought it a poor exchange for even Nile-cooled champagne.

Kitchener's timely arrival with a battalion or so of infantry, two Maxim guns and some light artillery had undoubtedly saved the French. To the Dervishes all Europeans and their various mercenaries were bad news and they had already obliged these latest intruders to expend far more ammunition than they could afford with a determined assault on Fashoda. When he first sighted Kitchener's paddle boats Marchand, thrice wounded in the service of his country, thought the Muslims had returned in force to finish them off.

Now he found himself playing a gigantic game of bluff with his saviours. There was, of course, no question who would win a shoot-out: the commandant was hopelessly outnumbered. 'An explorer in difficulties upon the Upper Nile,' sniffed Lord Salisbury, and the Foreign Secretary saw that the Royal Navy reinforced its Gibraltar squadron so that the French found themselves outgunned in the Mediterranean as well. 'Great Britain was determined to have Fashoda or fight,' young Churchill, later an ardent Francophile, wrote in his bestselling book *The River War*, first published in 1899 less than a year after the confrontation.

Perhaps the French would not have climbed down had Hanatoux, Marchand's patron, still been in charge of foreign affairs. But he had been replaced by the pragmatic Théophile Delcassé who, not thirty years since the loss of the border provinces of Alsace and Lorraine, saw Germany as the main enemy and Britain as a potential ally. After almost three months of brinkmanship Marchand, who had been obliged to absent himself to British-controlled Cairo to pick up his orders from the French consulate there, departed Fashoda for Abyssinia in the little boats that had come so far. The British troops bade them farewell with an honour guard and a band playing the 'Marseillaise'. Before they left a *sous-officier* uprooted the flagstaff that had borne the tricolour and hurled it to the ground.

In France there was outrage. The pestilential fort with its mosquitoes and crocodiles had monopolized public debate. A newspaper cartoon depicting Marianne as Little Red Riding Hood about to hand over her Fashoda parcel to the haggish wolf Britannia caught the national mood. Charles de Gaulle, the 8-year-old middle son of a monarchist schoolmaster, a veteran of the lost 1870 war against the Prussians, would remember for the rest of his long and eventful life his father's heated discussions and his own brooding boyhood shame at this national humiliation.

Among young French officers disgust with the government knew no bounds and there was talk, encouraged by the newspapers, that only war with England would remove this stain on their honour. Nor did they have the slightest doubt who would win. France would certainly not have waited thirteen years to reconquer Sudan. As allies in the Crimea, British tactics had been comical, none more so than that idiotic charge of a brigade of light cavalry they so gloried in and never mind maréchal Bosquet's polite flattery, for '*magnifique*' it was not. Even the barefoot Zulu had given them a drubbing, among the casualties France's exiled Prince Imperial, the *beau sabreur* the Bonapartists would have made Napoléon IV, abandoned by his bolting English cavalry escort and left dismounted to fight it out alone on foot. Afterwards the Zulus said they suspected he was different because he fought like a lion with a broken assegai pulled from his own body. Every Frenchman knew the English, though not bad sailors, were very bad soldiers. But here lay the rub. Britannia really did rule the waves. The ascendancy of the Royal Navy was such, their native moat so uncrossable, attacks on their colonies so vulnerable to overwhelming maritime interception, it was impossible to get at the drunken and overfed *rosbifs* and give them the thrashing they so richly deserved.

This was frustrating enough. But to make matters worse Fashoda had come at a time when the French Army and much else French was being torn apart by the Dreyfus Affair: a festering, self-inflicted wound that had become an international cause célèbre and so upset Queen Victoria that she had cancelled her annual holiday in France. Capitaine Alfred Dreyfus was that rare thing in most European armies of the 1890s: a Jewish officer. He was a refugee from Alsace, under German rule since the defeat of 1871, where his wealthy family had owned a cotton mill at Mühlhausen. In October 1894 Dreyfus, an artillery officer on a temporary attachment to the General Staff in Paris, was accused of passing secrets to the German Embassy, court-martialled and sentenced to hard labour for life on the nightmarish South American Devil's Island penal colony off French Guiana.

In Paris, where it was rarely hard to fan the embers of its smouldering anti-Semitism, it was a popular verdict. Prior to his transportation to South America in chains, a salivating mob were encouraged to attend a public ceremony at which Dreyfus was stripped of all badges of rank and decorations and his sword snapped in two. Throughout this ordeal Dreyfus's cries that he was innocent were drowned by the taunts from his civilian audience.

The men who convicted Dreyfus were genuinely convinced of his guilt. But four years later, by the time Kitchener and Marchand had met at Fashoda, Dreyfus's innocence – first suggested by British private detectives hired by his family – had been established beyond all reasonable doubt. The real culprit was the high–living Commandant Ferdinand Esterhazy whose outrageous acquittal in January 1898 by a corrupt court martial caused the novelist Émile Zola to write *J'Accuse*, his famous 4,000-word proclamation of Dreyfus's innocence. 'The truth is on the march,' concluded Zola, 'and nothing will stop it.' Shortly afterwards, despite the verdict in his favour, Esterhazy fled to England. An officer who had committed perjury to secure Esterhazy's acquittal then killed himself.

By now it was obvious that there existed among the army's senior ranks a faction far more concerned with covering up their mistakes than righting a shameful miscarriage of justice. First the French officer corps, then it seemed almost the entire nation, was split between the Dreyfusards and their opponents. Some of the latter even conceded that Dreyfus might not be guilty but believed he had to be sacrificed for the greater good. It was a point of view strongly defended by the Catholic Church. The French Army must not be undermined by a plot hatched by Jews and Freemasons, the twin axes of evil as far as many conservative Catholics were concerned.

The scandal dragged on for over a decade. In 1899 an emaciated, fever-ridden Dreyfus was brought back to France only to have his conviction upheld by a new court martial. After international protests, not least from Queen Victoria who in an uncoded telegram to the British Embassy in Paris referred to him as 'the poor martyr Dreyfus', he was 'pardoned' though his supporters insisted that he had done nothing to be pardoned for. Not until 1906 was the artillery officer fully exonerated, restored to the army, promoted and awarded the Légion d'Honneur.

The affair left its mark on a whole generation of French officers. In 1902 the Dreyfusard and secular Radical Party, in which French Freemasonry was strongly represented, was elected to office. Within three years, to the great displeasure of the Vatican, they had repealed the Napoleonic Concordat and separated the Church from the state. Troops found themselves being used to close down illegal convent schools while Masons also began to flourish in the officer corps. Practising Catholics started to feel that when it came to promotion it was no longer how good a soldier you were but who you knew in the Grand Orient Lodge with its large military membership. In the garrison towns of Toulouse, Bastia and Montélimar, Catholics and Freemasons fought duels, sometimes with fatal results.

In a milder way a certain Major Philippe Pétain also became a casualty of this quarrel. Pétain had long ago lapsed from the strict Catholicism of his boyhood and at 50 he had had numerous and sometimes inappropriate love affairs, never married, and was maintaining at least one illegitimate child, the product of a brief relationship with a teenage shop assistant. But Pétain still held the Church in great respect and resented the influence of the anticlerical faction who were now ruling the roost in the army. When a well-known Freemason offered him the command of the prestigious rifle school at Châlons, which would have meant automatic promotion to lieutenant colonel, he turned it down. It would take him another four years to reach that rank and by then he was approaching retirement age.

Pétain looked every inch a soldier and lived up to appearances. The erect bearing, piercing grey-blue eyes and generous blond moustache belonged to an excellent horseman, fencer and rifle shot. And in recent years he had delighted his seniors with the lucid and popular lectures he delivered in his clipped undemonstrative way at the École de Guerre where he was an Assistant Professor of Infantry Tactics. He argued for firepower with accuracy, dismissing the old musketry dictum that marksmanship counted less than delivering rapid volleys. In 1870 the Chassepot rifle had been the best infantry weapon in Europe and he believed that France's failure to exploit its accuracy had made a significant contribution to the Prussian victory.

Pétain had been a 14-year-old boarder at a strict Catholic school in the marshy flatlands of his native Pas de Calais when the Franco-Prussian War – usually referred to as the debacle until the next debacle some seventy years later – persuaded him that his vocation was for the military and not, as he had believed for most of his boyhood, in holy orders. He was from a family of smallholders originally of Flemish stock – the name comes from Piet-heim, meaning Peter's home – whose bit of land and literacy placed them at least a couple of notches above the ordinary peasant farmer and they were always careful to refer to themselves as *cultivateurs*.

Even so, the family's only military experience had been in the ranks. His maternal grandmother's brother, one Philippe-Michel Lefebre, had been about to be ordained when his seminary was closed down and he was press-ganged into the army. During some twenty years' service he campaigned for Napoléon in Italy before he was allowed to resume his theological studies, though later in life Abbé Lefebre enjoyed reminiscing about his soldiering, not least to his great-nephew who was not quite ten when the Abbé died.

The only other Pétain who had worn uniform was his father's elder brother Cyrille, though this was hardly a source of pride. Having had the misfortune to have his conscription number come up, Cyrille, as the law permitted, paid a citizen substitute to march for him, the money coming from the sale of some of his doting parents' land. But not long afterwards, for reasons unknown – perhaps an affair of the heart – Cyrille decided to enlist anyway, signed on for fifteen years and went to Algeria. Then his regiment was shipped to the Crimea. The Russians proved a more efficient foe than Arab rebels and at some point Cyrille decided he would soldier no more and was posted as a deserter. Later it emerged he had settled in the Caucasus where he raised a deracinated sub-clan of the Pétains with whom there was little communication.

Cyrille's entry into the army some twenty years later came at a time when the officer training school at St Cyr was widening a social base which, in the years since Waterloo, had been decidedly aristocratic. Officer cadet Pétain entered the academy in 1876, the year Sitting Bull defeated Custer, at the start of a career that would see some of the most momentous changes in warfare since the invention of gun powder. Two years later he was, in order of excellence, number 229 of the 386 cadets who received their commissions as *sous-lieutenants* and pledged on bended knee their willingness to die for their country.

But for the next thirty-six years Pétain was never given the opportunity to put his oath to the test. Unlike some of his contemporaries he did not elect to join one of the regiments policing the French Empire where, like its British rival, there was always the chance of a skirmish with its less docile subjects. Perhaps Pétain was more hard-headed than some and failed to see the romance of foreign fields, but this was not as unadventurous as it seems. Young French officers expected sooner rather than later to participate in a war of revenge against Germany that would recover Alsace and Lorraine and eradicate the shame of 1870. When the great day came it would be an unspeakable anguish to be marooned in some fever-ridden colonial posting while others won all the glory.

Fashoda had only briefly held out the prospects of war with England, the old enemy. On 8 April 1904, following Edward VII's ground-breaking official visit to Paris the previous year, Britain and France signed the Anglo-French Entente that newspapers on both sides of the Channel began to refer to as the Entente Cordiale. To prevent more Fashodas, it had already been agreed that the British and French spheres of influence in Africa should be divided by the watershed between the Nile and Congo. The Entente was a continuation of this, a desire to settle all the outstanding issues between them which might flare up into a colonial turf war. It took in West Africa, Madagascar, Siam, the Pacific's New Hebrides, Newfoundland's cod fishing banks and Morocco, where it was decided France could do anything it liked except build fortifications that menaced Gibraltar.

Whatever the French thought, as far as the British were concerned at first the Entente was not an alliance and nor was it intended to be anti-German though the Germans thought it was. A treaty of alliance between Britain and France was not signed until shortly after the outbreak of war with Germany in August 1914. At that point Pétain, now a full colonel, had spent the last year commanding a brigade, though, two years away from mandatory retirement at 60, his superiors had not seen fit to promote him to brigadier général. But he could console himself with the thought that many of his contemporaries at St Cyr had not risen above major and had long since left the army. To retire on a colonel's pension was no bad thing for an officer who had never heard or fired a shot in anger.

Before he got his brigade Pétain had commanded the 33rd Infantry Regiment at Arras where in 1913 one of his junior officers, recently hatched from officer school, had been Sous-lieutenant Charles de Gaulle, the monarchist schoolteacher's son who as a child had been so stung by the shame of Fashoda. De Gaulle's entry into the army had not been easy. At St Cyr, where short haircuts accentuated his large nose and protruding ears, he was known as 'The Great Asparagus'. Six foot five inches of uncoordinated endeavour, however hard he tried, his marks for horsemanship, fencing and rifle shooting – all the things Pétain excelled at – were dismal. There was certainly nothing of the *beau sabreur* about de Gaulle. Yet his instructors noticed that this somewhat aloof, difficult young man had other qualities. He won a distinction for his 'practical fieldwork' and praise for something known as 'moral education'. And another asset had been noted: a stubborn refusal to give in.

On the face of it Pétain, still the compulsive womanizer with the piercing blue eyes and magnificent moustache, did not have much in common with this gangling, long-necked and studious subaltern. But, far from stupid himself, one day he would find himself doing a lot to further the career of a clever and dedicated young officer who, by the fortunes of war, would be granted the time to develop some original ideas.

In February 1916 Pétain, by now a général thanks to the mass sacking of incompetent senior officers, got the job that would make him not only a maréchal of France but give him worldwide recognition and a lingering fame for saying something he never actually said. As commander of the 2nd Army he was told to take his men to the fortress of Verdun on the Meuse, the traditional invasion route to Paris, and hold it.

Verdun was the longest battle in history. It lasted for almost ten months and was an attempt by the German commander Erich von Falkenhayn to 'bleed the French white' by making them defend a position that was not only of tactical importance but also a symbol of the national will to defend the capital. (In 1870 Verdun had lasted six weeks.) The battle took place over 4 square miles of pulverized ground and the most conservative estimates put the German dead at 100,000 and the French at 120,000, with a combined total of at least another 700,000 men wounded.

The French casualties might have been much higher but for Pétain's skill at defensive tactics, his insistence on keeping up morale by constantly rotating his front-line troops and his reluctance to mount costly counter-attacks. He may have looked like a lot of other generals but gradually his *poilus* began to realize that here was a soldier's soldier. 'I have a chilling mask,' he confided to the French journalist Henri Lottman at Verdun. But behind this lapidary exterior, and by the standards of that conflict, Pétain cared deeply about the lives of men who had so often come from the same rural background as his own. 'My heart bled when I watched our 20-year-olds going under fire at Verdun,' he would write in his own account of the battle, '... knowing they would quickly lose the enthusiasm aroused by their first battle ... their eyes staring into space as if transfixed by terror.'

Soon the Paris press, Fleet Street and even war correspondents from the neutral countries such as Spain and Switzerland began to give the caring general whose men were putting up such stubborn resistance some attention. Fulsome praise in *The Times*, then very much the voice of the establishment, probably did much to ensure formal British recognition in the award of the Grand Cross of the Order of St Michael and St George. Verdun made Pétain. Yet he was there for scarcely two months of the battle, just long enough to put his indelible mark on it. Above all he was the soldiers' friend, reluctant, as his British biographer Charles Williams puts it, 'to throw warm bodies at barbed wire and machine-guns'.

By the end of April 1916 French Commander-in-Chief Joseph Joffre, impatient with Pétain's reluctance to go on the offensive and perhaps a little jealous of the attention he was getting, kicked him upstairs to command the Centre Army Group. Verdun was the most important of this Army Group's tasks but Pétain would no longer be responsible for the day-to-day running of the battle. His replacement as head of the 2nd Army was the dashing and well-connected Robert Nivelle, whose mother was English. It was Nivelle who uttered the words so often wrongly attributed to Petain: '*Ils ne passeront pas*.' Once the Anglo-French offensive on the Somme, which began at the end of June, had begun to draw the best German troops away from Verdun it was Nivelle who launched the counter-attack that finished the battle by Christmas. As a result he was made Commander-in-Chief and Pétain's star seemed to be on the wane.

But Nivelle did not last very long. In April 1917, in a quagmire caused by unseasonal flurries of snow and sleet and ignoring Pétain's protests, Nivelle launched a massive offensive in the southern sector near Reims. A few days earlier the British had enjoyed some limited though costly success around Arras in the north. But Nivelle's attack along a 25-mile front on the river Aisne, in which for the first time the French Army used the tanks the British had invented, was an unmitigated disaster. A predicted advance of 6 miles was halted after 600 yards with many of the tanks bogged down on their start line. The infantry they should have been supporting were mown down. What was left of a Senegalese regiment being used as first-wave shock troops because of their well-known love of hand-to-hand combat broke and ran. For the first day's fighting it had been estimated that French casualties would be in the region of 15,000; the real figure was 100,000. Morale began to crumble. There were protests. Troops being sent up to the front no longer sang their marching songs. Instead when they spotted senior officers they began to bleat like sheep being sent to the slaughter.

Nivelle was sacked and Pétain was appointed Commander-in-Chief, a position he held until the end of the war. His first task was to deal with the growing unrest in the army. Almost half the front-line divisions were infected by it and in some it had progressed from a partial withdrawal of labour – they would defend but not leave their trenches and attack – to the Bolshevism preached by those Russians who felt that the recent replacement of the Tsar by Karensky's social democrats was not going nearly far enough. At one point Paul Painlevé, the War Minister, estimated that there were no more than two reliable divisions between Paris and no-man's-land 70 miles away. By extraordinary good fortune the Germans had yet to hear about it and, if the French had had their way, the British would have remained equally unaware. But there had already been trouble with unruly conscripts in the capital itself and nothing could control Parisian gossip.

One of the people whose job it was to sift the rumour mill was the bilingual, clever and ambitious Major Edward Spears who had been involved in a secret pre-war project to write the Anglo-French code book that, in theory at least, enabled the Allies to start the conflict with an agreed cypher. A polo-playing Hussar officer of Anglo-Irish and possibly Alsatian Jewish stock, Spears had been on front-line liaison duties since August 1914, was wounded four times and had several British and French decorations for gallantry including a Military Cross and the ribbon of a Chevalier of the Légion d'Honneur.

'A Paladin worthy to rank with the truest knights,' was Winston Churchill's description of Spears. The fighting bard of Omdurman was now Minister for Munitions and had met Spears several times at the front both as a visiting politician and during his short post-Gallipoli penance as a battalion commander. More importantly, the major was admired, though certainly not as effusively, by Pétain and was beginning to add French politicians to his contacts. Aged 30, he had recently been appointed liaison officer between the French and British War Cabinets, a newly created post with a clerical staff from both armies and an office in Les Invalides close to France's new Commander-in-Chief.

But Pétain was not yet ready to reveal to his allies the full extent of the crisis in his army and Spears took himself off to the Aisne sector to investigate. If anything, it was even worse than he suspected. Just behind the front line, he discovered a battalion with red rosettes pinned to their uniforms, who had corralled their officers into a corner of the village they occupied and were busy learning all the words of the 'Internationale'. Not far away another mutinous infantry battalion was being shelled by their own artillery, while cavalrymen, despised by the foot sloggers because they had spent most of the war waiting safely to be inserted into the breakthrough that never came, closed in.

For the moment the British were the stronger ally but they could not possibly fight on without France who, despite its smaller population, continued to make a much larger contribution to the land war against Germany. France manned more than two-thirds of the trench line that divided Europe from the North Sea to Switzerland and had suffered four times the British casualties. One of the reasons for Spears's popularity with the French was that he never ceased reminding his superiors of this or his admiration for the quicksilver qualities of the *poilu* in the attack.

Pétain ended the mutinies, which Spears thought he considered an even greater service to France than his generalship at Verdun, with a judicious mixture of carrot and stick. Part of the carrot was a well-publicized directive explaining that the moment was not right for a breakthrough and that in future their tactics would be to wear down the enemy. 'It is wholly unnecessary to mount huge attacks with distant objectives.' What made this change of heart wholly credible was that in April the United States had declared war on Germany, leading to much joyful speculation that all the Allies had to do was hold the Kaiser and his allies until the arrival of a huge American army so outnumbered them that victory was inevitable. Meanwhile, the soldiers' friend made life easier for his beloved, *poilus* by making home leaves more frequent – seven days every four months – and emulating the British by setting up cheap canteens for soldiers at railway stations.

Stick came in the form of 554 death sentences though only 49 of these were carried out, the rest being commuted to deportation to some Dreyfusian penal hellhole. Those who faced the firing parties at dawn, often refusing a blindfold, were the ringleaders: the Reds, the anticlericalists, who wished to pull down the whole edifice and at both ends of the rifles there were eyes that had seen enough to make it easier than it should have been.

Pétain himself, having tasted battle at such a late and elevated point in his career, had never killed anybody or been in great personal danger for prolonged periods. But like most professionals he realized that it was possible to exploit the basic instinct for self-preservation if soldiers knew that the alternative to the chance of an honourable death was the near certainty of a dishonourable one. In the early part of the Verdun battle he was reported to have cured an epidemic of self-inflicted wounds to hands or feet by posting orders that in future offenders would spend a night tied to stakes in no-man's-land.

One of the early casualties of Verdun was Capitaine Charles de Gaulle who was wounded there for the third time. It happened near Douaumont, one of the forts on the flanks of the salient, when German infantry rushed his position during a snowstorm. In the mêlée that followed he received a bayonet thrust in the left thigh and was taken prisoner.

Given the high percentage of junior officer casualties among all the combatants, to be captured wounded would have been an honourable way to survive had he chosen it. But as well as his burning patriotism de Gaulle had an ambition that would simply not permit it. He could not endure the idea of his luckier and often dimmer classmates from St Cyr climbing the promotion ladder while he rotted in a prison camp. Determined to get back he made several escape attempts, once with the aid of a false moustache, and twice came close to making home runs to neutral Holland or Switzerland. At one point he was interned for a while in 1917's version of Colditz along with British and Russian officers who were also persistent escapers.

Between escapes and during the lengthy spells of solitary confinement he suffered as a result, he developed his theories about mobile warfare and the use of the new tanks as massed cavalry. In the early years of the peace, when he was trying to prove that he had something more to offer than just another good war record, it was these ideas that would bring the young officer who had joined Pétain's last pre-war command back to the maréchal's attention.

Chapter Two

On 14 July 1919, Bastille Day, sixteen days after the signatures on the 230-page Treaty of Versailles had, in theory at least, reduced the German Army to little more than a gendarmerie, a great victory parade was held in Paris. Pétain rode a grey charger some way behind the vanguard that, in sombre and proper contrast to the pomp and circumstance that would follow, was led by representatives of *les grands mutilés:* three young men in their wheelchairs. Immediately behind the paraplegics and spanning the Champs-Elysées shuffled in no particular order some of those who could still just about walk with the aid of crutches and walking sticks and the artificial limbs hidden beneath their trousers.

Among the latter was the hulking and wondrously moustached figure of Sergent Maginot, the former Under-Secretary of State for War who in 1914, though almost 40, had volunteered for the infantry rather than sit out the conflict in Paris. André Maginot had won the Médaille Militaire for courage and devotion to duty, refused to become an officer, then lost half a leg at Verdun.

Total French casualties during the Great War were put at 1.3 million killed, much higher than the British. Only the Germans and the Russians had lost more (1.8 and 1.7 million respectively) but per capita French losses were the highest of any of the major participants – 27 per cent of the 8.3 million they had in uniform. The British Empire had 935,000 killed in action, a little over 10 per cent of the 8.9 million it was estimated to have mobilized. About 743,000 of these came from the United Kingdom where, for the first time in its history, conscription had been introduced in 1915. All the colonial troops who died, including the 49,000 Indians and Gurkhas, were volunteers. Canada lost 60,000, Australia 59,000, New Zealand 16,000 and South Africa 8,000.

After Sergent Maginot and the other maimed had gone by came mounted Republican Guards in all their Napoleonic finery. These were the escort for maréchals Joseph Joffre and Ferdinand Foch. Joffre had saved Paris in 1914. Foch was the steel-nerved genius who, as Supreme Allied Commander, stopped Erich Ludendorff's 1918 spring offensive then turned the tide with his French, British and fresh American formations to win the war in six months. A respectable length behind Foch rode Général Maxime Weygand, his dapper Chief of Staff with his high cheekbones and deep-set eyes. Weygand was said to be the illegitimate offspring of a Mexican dancer and the Emperor Maximilian, the Austrian archduke proclaimed Mexico's Emperor by Napoléon III then abandoned to a revolutionary firing squad when the United States objected and French troops were withdrawn.

For an hour the most decorated infantry companies in the French Army, now without doubt the largest, most powerful and certainly the most victorious army in Europe, followed Pétain down the Champs-Elysées to 'Marche Lorraine' and Rauski's rousing 'Sambre-et-Meuse'. Not only the home-grown foot-sloggers but also breast-plated cavalry, Senegalese warriors with tribal cheek scars, wiry Indochinese in conical hats, turbaned North Africans and inscrutable Foreign Legionnaires moving to their own regimental march, 'Le Boudin', the other martial airs being too fast for their loping desert pace. Then, bringing up the rear, a reminder of how much war had changed since 1914: a squadron of nine FT-17s, Renault's latest refinement of the tank, clattering along at just under 5 miles an hour. The stench of their exhaust fumes lingered in the July heat, tracks flattening the dung deposited by the cavalry that had preceded them under the Arc de Triomphe.

But first, as a kind of warm-up act before the long-awaited appearance of Pétain and his *poilus*, came the foreign contingents. The French had decided that their allies would march in 1,500–strong contingents and in alphabetical order. Since it was *Les Américains* rather than *États-Unis* General John Pershing's Doughboys came first behind a sea of Stars and Stripes and a band playing 'Over There', the ragtime march Paris had taken to its heart. The Americans had suffered 50,300 battle deaths, most of them during the last six months of the war as American reinforcements poured into France. If the war had not ended, Pershing, who started his military career skirmishing with Geronimo's Apaches, would have had over 3 million men under his command by now with more on the way.

Pershing's contingent was followed by the Belgians – 13,800 killed out of the 267,000 who served. Then, faintly at first, came the distant strains of 'Tipperary' and there was Field Marshal Sir Douglas Haig with his British and Dominion troops: Australians, New Zealanders, Canadians, (white) South Africans and Indians all shouldering the ten-shot Lee-Enfield rifles the French had quite envied until they saw the Americans' Springfields, and crunching the pavés with an identical pattern of seventeen studs on the sole of each boot. The Parisians cheered, perhaps not quite as loudly as they had cheered the Americans but loud enough, and some waved paper Union flags along with their Tricolours and Stars and Stripes, while girls in the costume of newly liberated Alsace threw rose petals and the Tommies smiled and tried to keep in step.

Sadly, the senior soldiers and statesmen of Britain and France had not emerged from their hard-won victory over Germany with anything like the mutual affection on display in Paris that Bastille Day. Between the principal Allies the conflict had ended on a high note of bickering which characterized the six months of treaty negotiations with Germany that followed and went on to sour Anglo-French relations for the next twenty years.

During the last twelve weeks of the fighting the British had captured almost as many prisoners as the French, Americans and Belgians put together: 188,700 compared with 196,700. But their own losses had been heavy and Haig counselled accepting Berlin's offer of an armistice, claiming that his soldiers were now doing most of the fighting, normally the French complaint. 'Why expend more British lives?'

But Pétain, along with much of the French officer corps, was against accepting a ceasefire until they had inflicted on Germany the kind of abject military defeat that would leave it bereft of military ambition for generations to come. Instead, the Kaiser's army had been allowed to turn its back on the four years of carnage they had wreaked in France and Belgium and march home in good order, its professional cadre convinced that they had not lost the war but been betrayed by the politicians. 'Deep fear of Germany pervaded the French nation on the morrow of their dazzling success,' wrote Churchill. It was true. France saw Germany as down but not out and was determined not to let it back on its feet.

Foch had at first favoured the armistice because he believed France would get a new frontier on the broad moat of the Rhine behind which the German tribes could bang their swords on their shields as much as they liked without disturbing their neighbours. Düsseldorf, Cologne, Koblenz and Mainz would all be on the eastern edge of a Rhineland transformed into a quasi-independent buffer state under Allied occupation. 'America is far away and protected by the ocean,' argued President Georges Clemenceau who backed his maréchal to the hilt. 'England could not be reached by Napoleon himself. You are sheltered ... we are not.'

But US President Woodrow Wilson and Prime Minister David Lloyd George remained deaf to the entreaties of France's most Anglophile President, whose first wife was an American, convinced that far from preventing another war this would cause one. Alsace-Lorraine went back to France but by a majority of two to one the Treaty of Versailles left Germany's 1870 frontiers almost intact. 'This is not peace,' snapped Foch. 'It's an armistice for twenty years.'

It took almost that long to finish burying the dead. It was not until August 1932 that Albert Lebrun, the French President, inaugurated at Verdun the Ossuary of Douaumont. It is near where de Gaulle was bayoneted and contains the bones of 130,000 unidentified soldiers, French and German, collected from the battlefield. All the British sector's wartime graves were tidied into landscaped cemeteries on land donated to the Imperial War

Graves Commission 'in perpetuity' by the Belgian and French governments. In July 1938 the commission completed its last necropolis in northern France when the Australian memorial at Villers-Bretonneux was unveiled by the newly crowned King George VI who was on a state visit with Queen Elizabeth.

Remembrance of the fallen was very much the theme of their visit that was intended to revive what, when it suited political needs, was fondly supposed to have been the spirit of 1914–18. It started even before the royal yacht HMS *Enchantress* had berthed at Boulogne harbour where the royal party were greeted by a recently completed 30-foot-high Britannia gazing out to sea with raised trident and shield at the ready. The statue, which most locals found remarkably ugly, marked the spot where in August 1914 the Argyll and Sutherland Highlanders had been the first of Sir John French's British Expeditionary Force to disembark. Maréchal Pétain, always wheeled out for these occasions, was at hand to make a pretty speech and be photographed planting a gallant kiss on the young Queen's hand. In his response the King, who was learning to control his dreadful stutter, mentioned, 'Ties that the passing years can never weaken'.

This was about as true as Pétain's kiss and everyone knew it. The passing years had seen them weaken almost to breaking point. Post-war rows about the greedy French being beastly to the Germans, demanding too much in the way of financial reparations, occupying the Saar coalfields, or the British having the effrontery to sign their new naval treaty with Germany on the 120th anniversary of Waterloo, had been bad enough. 'England has always been France's most implacable enemy,' Pétain had told Mussolini's ambassador in Paris and gone on to explain that, though the Germans were enemies too, 'I would favour an alliance with Germans which would guarantee absolute peace in Europe.'

At least the maréchal's little outbursts of Anglophobia, which do not seem to have been all that frequent, were discreet. One of the more distressing signs of the decline of the Entente Cordiale was the public slanging matches some of the less exalted veterans of the recent conflict had indulged in.

'No more wars for me at any price!' declared Edmund Blunden. 'Except against the French. If there's ever a war with them I'll go like a shot.' His fellow war poet Captain Robert Graves quotes Blunden towards the end of his bestselling memoir *Goodbye to All That* which was first published in 1929. Graves, whose mother was German, was one of many young officers resuming their education at Oxford in 1919. 'Anti-French feeling among most ex-soldiers amounted almost to an obsession,' he discovered. 'Some undergraduates even insisted we had been fighting on the wrong side: our natural enemies were the French.'

In France these feelings were amply reciprocated, though sometimes it was emphasized that it was *les Anglais* they objected to and not the other natives of the British Isles or its far-flung colonies. Like Graves, Henri Desagneaux had been an infantry officer. In A *French Soldier's War Diary* he records the contempt reserved for English troops after Ludendorff's 1918 spring offensive, which concentrated its considerable weight on the British sector and took 20,000 prisoners. Paris was threatened and the German advance only came to a halt when Pétain plugged the breach with French divisions and Foch was put in command of all Allied troops.

'The English gave way,' wrote Desagneaux. 'It was our troops, yet again, who saved the situation ... the inhabitants are glad to see the French again. They have no confidence in the English any more ... People have nothing but praise for the Canadians, Australians and Indians – it was they who stopped the enemy advance ... the English are hopeless, it's the Scots, the Australians and Canadians who do all the work.'

Undoubtedly Dominion infantry led the British recovery when, on 8 August 1918, a surprise attack east of Amiens spearheaded by 480 tanks manned by UK British crews crashed through the German lines. Ludendorff called it 'Black Day' and it convinced him that Germany would have to sue for peace. Within seventy-two hours some 16,000 prisoners and more than 400 guns had been captured. Never before had the German Army suffered a defeat of this magnitude. 'Even now, old timers like us relive that feeling of impending doom which overtook us that day,' wrote Heinz Guderian in his *Achtung Panzer*! that was first published in 1937. It was the beginning of Haig's big push and the foundation of his claim that, at the end, it was the British who won the war.

The high point came at the end of September when an English Midlands division breached the Hindenburg line, the enemy's last major defence works. Life belts and rafts from cross-Channel ferries were used to make a surprise crossing of the St Quentin canal. Exploiting a foggy dawn, nine North Staffords dashed across the Riqueval Bridge, bayoneting a man about to detonate a demolition charge. This was an innovative British Army, no longer lions led by donkeys, thinking on its feet in a way the Germans, or the French for that matter, had not seen before.

'I lost all my earthly faculties and fought like an Angel,' a lieutenant in the Manchesters wrote home after being awarded a Military Cross. 'With this corporal, who stuck to me like your prayers, I captured a machine gun and scores of prisoners ... I only shot one man with my revolver (about 30 yards!); the others I took with a smile ...' A month later Wilfred Owen was dead, killed trying to build a pontoon bridge across the Sambre canal under fire. He was 25. Most of his poetry was published posthumously and few of his army contemporaries knew he wrote it. In his battalion he was mourned for being a good officer and, if he had been thought of as being a bit different, it was for his tendency to like the French, the result of a year in Bordeaux as an English language teacher before he joined up. It was not until 1931, when Britain had virtually disarmed, that the Oxford

Francophobe Professor Blunden wrote that Owen's 'genius and premature death' was reminiscent of Keats.

Owen died on 4 November 1918, one of thousands killed in the last week of the war. In the ninety-five days between Ludendorff's Black Day and 11 November the British had about 250,000 men killed or wounded, their highest daily casualty rate since the last bout of fluid fighting in 1914. The French, of course, did not for a single moment accept that *les Anglais* had done more to bring about the final defeat of Germany than they had. Quite the opposite. For them it was the grit of the *poilu* and genius of Foch, particularly his counter-offensive along the Marne, that did the trick. This had been followed by his famous call to arms, '*Tout le monde à la bataille!*': simultaneous attacks along the entire front to which everybody had contributed, even the British, though it was mainly the French, and occasionally the Americans, who made any real headway.

So the war's principal Allies, like opposing drivers in a car crash, clung to their own version of events, each over the years enshrining it into their national mythologies. But for 1938's royal visit to Boulogne these indelible subtexts were decently camouflaged and the events of almost a quarter of a century ago looked at through the rosy prism of the revived Entente. For while they had squabbled Germany had rearmed and re-entered the Rhineland and, like an old loveless couple faced with an outside threat, France and Britain needed each other again. Both countries were determined to make the visit a huge success, the democracies' riposte to the torch-lit pageants in Berlin and Rome.

From the Eiffel Tower fluttered 1,500 square yards of Union flag and a delighted British ambassador assured the Foreign Office, 'No celebration since the Armistice has aroused such deep feeling.' At Versailles the King dressed as an admiral to review a march past of 50,000 troops and afterwards attended a state banquet in the Hall of Mirrors, which was said to be the most august occasion since Clemenceau signed the peace treaty there. Waiters clad in the ornate livery, powdered wigs and knee breeches Louis XVI would have found familiar served thirteen different wines with courses that included caviar, quail stuffed with foie gras, and Périgord truffles. Madame Lebrun even attempted to greet her royal guests with a curtsy, a *génuflexion catastrophé* according to the *Manchester Guardian*'s Alexander Werth and an outrage for those guardians of France's republican flame who felt it was no way for their first lady to behave.

Privately, Édouard Daladier, the French Prime Minister, indulged in a little republican reaction of his own by confiding to the American ambassador William Bullitt that George was 'a moron' and Elizabeth 'ready to sacrifice every other country in the world' in order to remain Queen. But Daladier well understood the uses of constitutional monarchy and in terms of the realpolitik at hand the visit had been as helpful as the arrival of King George's grandfather Edward to Paris in 1903. Then later that year another

Englishman really did win Gallic hearts and a lot of others besides.

In September came the Munich crisis. Hitler, encouraged by the way the appeasing democracies accepted Austria's recent union with the Third Reich, annexed another juicy remnant of the old Austro-Hungarian Empire: Czechoslovakia's Sudetenland with its 3 million German speakers and Pilsen's tank-building Skoda works. France, and to a lesser extent Britain, had guaranteed Czechoslovakia's sovereignty and it looked as if war was inevitable. On both sides of the Channel gas masks were issued to civilians and air-raid shelters dug. The Czechs mobilized and so did the British fleet. In France reservists were called up to reinforce the conscripts manning the foul-smelling concrete subterranean fortresses – there were problems with their septic tanks – along the eastern frontier's Maginot line, named after the Verdun amputee André Maginot, Secretary of State for War when he died in 1932.

But neither France nor Britain really had the stomach for a fight. 'Let's not be heroic,' pleaded the arch-appeaser Georges Bonnet, Daladier's Foreign Minister, and it did not fall on deaf ears. Just like England, where H.G. Wells's 1936 film *Things to Come* had played to packed cinemas, France was obsessed by apocalyptic visions of aerial warfare. Picasso's Guernica at the Spanish government's pavilion had been one of the most talked-about exhibits at 1937's International Exposition in Paris. The Czech crisis packed the capital's railway stations with panic-stricken civilians convinced that Guernica was about to be writ large and traffic jammed the major highways west and south. The Aviation Minister encouraged his colleagues to follow his own example and send their families to the safety of Brittany. Some of those left behind looted Jewish-owned shops and chanted, 'Down with the Jewish war.' Who else would want to take on Hitler?

Then along came the Prince of Peace cunningly disguised as an elderly clerk in a wing-collar and tie, striped trousers and carrying an umbrella. Neville Chamberlain, Britain's septuagenarian Prime Minister, became a hero in both countries when he flew, for the first time in his life, to meet Hitler in Munich and returned with his autograph on a note pledging 'the desire of our two peoples never to go to war with one another again'. In London he appeared on the Buckingham Palace balcony with the King and Queen while the throng below cheered him to the heavens. In Paris Daladier, who also attended the four-power meeting along with Mussolini, got similar treatment including an open-topped car ride from Le Bourget airport through flag-waving, flower-throwing crowds. But the French recognized the real architect of the Munich Agreement which had given Hitler the Sudetenland because he said this was the end of his territorial ambition. In Paris a public appeal was started to buy Chamberlain a house with a trout stream where he could enjoy the fly fishing of which he was said to be so fond; around the Eiffel Tower the souvenir shops had a new line in lucky umbrellas '*à la Chamberlain*'.

Enthusiasm for peace at any price spanned the political spectrum. 'Anything, even the cruellest injustice, was better than war,' wrote the philosopher Simone de Beauvoir, lover and intellectual soundboard of Jean-Paul Sartre, already becoming an icon of the left with that year's publication of his autobiographical novel *La Nausée*. Pétain, whose sympathies, like most senior officers', were with the Catholic right, congratulated the cautious Bonnet for saving his country from certain defeat. 'I know how you have struggled to avoid war,' he said. 'You were right; we would have been beaten.'

De Gaulle, now a full colonel in charge of a tank brigade at Metz, disagreed, declaring that the time gained by the Munich Agreement resembled poor Comtesse du Barry's famous last words beneath the guillotine: 'Another few seconds please Mr Executioner.' It was not his first disagreement with his old mentor. On military theory there had long been a parting of the ways. His belief in offensive tank warfare challenged the maréchal's unshakable faith in the Maginot line as the apogee of a Verdun-style static defence and an unspoken promise that France would never strike first.

De Gaulle's firm anti-appeasement views matched those of an influential politician who had begun to take an interest in his advocacy of a smaller, mechanized, more professional army. Paul Reynaud, a member of the centre-right Alliance Démocratique, got on well with Churchill and this was hardly surprising for he had much in common with Britain's maverick Tory who was four years his senior. Both had held Cabinet office several times then been dropped by their parties for going against the prevailing pacifism and warning of the dangers of paying Hitler's Danegeld. 'Disfigured the smiling landscape with a hideous blot,' in the words of Churchill's supporter and fellow Francophile Duff Cooper who had been the only member of Chamberlain's Cabinet – he was in charge of the Admiralty – to resign over Munich.

Reynaud was, like Churchill, a good parliamentary performer though the Sorbonne-trained lawyer and economist was better known for rapier thrusts of Carthusian logic than grand oratory. In appearance he was as short as de Gaulle was tall and kept himself trim with swimming and cycling. His enemies said he wore lifts and dyed his hair in order to please the Comtesse Hélène de Portes, a petite brunette who did not share his enthusiasm for the English and their desire to fight another war until the last Frenchman. In most accounts of these times the comtesse is described as his mistress but this probably makes their relationship sound rather more racy than it was. They were openly living together in a country where divorce, as in England, was considered even more scandalous than extramarital sex.

Unlike Churchill, who was still relegated to the back benches at the time of Munich, Daladier had put Reynaud back in the Cabinet, first as Justice then as Finance Minister which was the job he wanted. France's economy was stagnating. Even by the standards of the Third Republic, with governments in and out of office like cuckoo clocks, and street cleaners always busy with the detritus of the latest riot, domestic politics had just undergone a particularly volatile spasm.

It had begun almost two years before Munich, in June 1936, when the socialist Léon Blum, a brave and clever velvet-collared dandy, became France's first Jewish Prime Minister as head of the left-wing coalition known as the Popular Front. This had outraged the anti-Semitic Catholic right in the National Assembly. Deputy Xavier Vallat, a pious one-eyed, one-legged war veteran who claimed to speak for the nation's silent majority, described the secular Prime Minister, who had first made his name as a gifted literary and drama critic, as 'a cunning talmudist'. Not long before, some of Vallat's supporters had beaten up Blum who, aged 64, maintained an old-fashioned regard for the rights of the individual, which irritated the various admirers of the decade's dictators.

London had its political street violence too as Sir Oswald Mosley's Black shirts clashed with Communists in the East End. But this was rarely lethal. In France there was the military-booted Solidarité Française in their blue berets and matching shirts and Colonel de la Rocque's Croix de Feu which claimed half a million members. But the right's most extreme reaction to the Popular Front was beyond the wildest dreams of their British equivalent. The terrorists of La Cagoule (the Cowl), whose wealthy backers included Eugène Schueller of L'Oréal cosmetics, had recruited service officers, lawyers, doctors and senior civil servants. Some were Fascist sympathizers, others were monarchists or conservative republicans. Almost all were Jew-hating nationalists who believed that the Bolsheviks were at Christendom's gates and something must be done.

Aircraft flying arms from France to the Spanish republicans, whose left-wing government was also called the Popular Front, were sabotaged. La Cagoule were never able to get to Blum but among their victims were two prominent Italian anti-Fascists who had sought sanctuary in France, and a beautiful prostitute suspected of disclosing their activities to the Sûreté, who was stabbed to death on the Métro. In the hope of provoking a Franco-style military coup against the Popular Front bombs were planted in the kind of exclusive suburb Trotskyite terrorists might target. Despite this, during the twelve months before Blum was forced out of office, the Front managed to introduce the kind of reforms British trade unionists only dreamed about: as well as the forty-hour working week, there were paid holidays, collective bargaining and nationalization of the railways.

'Better Hitler than Blum,' said his opponents and it was not only Les Cagoulards who meant it. Among his critics was Pierre Laval, twice Prime Minister and *Time* magazine's 'Man of the Year 1931' (1930's was Gandhi) where he was lauded, among other things, for his firm hand with the

French economy. Laval, a trade union lawyer who had become a successful entrepreneur owning newspapers and radio stations, was once as left wing as Blum, then took democracy's well-trodden path from a wing to the central place where the most votes live most of the time. Apart from his stints as Prime Minister he had been a key figure in almost all of the reshuffled governments that ruled France, between 1930 and 1936 and as Minister of Labour had succeeded in pushing the Social Insurance Act through the National Assembly.

But his main interest was abroad and during his four terms as Foreign Minister he subscribed to the general view that Germany was France's 'hereditary enemy'. In the spring of 1935, a couple of months before he became premier for the second time, Laval crafted an unlikely pact between Mussolini's Italy, Britain and France intended to curb German ambitions in Austria. Then it fell apart when Italy invaded Ethiopia in 1936 and, much to Laval's disgust, Britain went wobbly on him and quit, partly because it feared an expansionist Fascist Italy on the border of colonial Kenya. It cost him his job. He never forgave the British for it and his newspapers and radio stations began to campaign for a rapprochement with Germany and against Blum's Popular Front with its hard line on all Europe's dictators except the one in Moscow.

Other protests were more extreme and some days it seemed that the country was teetering on the brink of total anarchy. Agitators who wanted revolution not reform made sure the workforce was constantly demanding more. At Renault the dispute was no longer even with the management but against 'union tyranny'. During a transport strike it was Blum who called in the army to deliver food. Then six people were killed by police during a riot in the working-class district of Clichy and a heartbroken Blum, who had just been to the opera, was snapped in white tie and tails as he rushed to the scene with the press and the ambulances. 'Who said this man has no French blood?' enquired a cartoonist in a Paris daily where blatant anti-Semitism might lose a newspaper advertising but rarely circulation.

Foreign correspondents were beginning to speculate that France might be heading for a civil war as frightful as the one next door in Spain where neither side were taking many prisoners. For a while, despite Blum's departure, the Popular Front lingered on: first under Camille Chautemps, who as a young man had played rugby for Paris's Stade Français but was not renowned for his political backbone, then for a month under Blum again, and then Daladier who called the economy 'the fourth arm of defence' and invited Reynaud on board to make it strong.

Despite his impeccable anti-Fascist credentials, Reynaud's liberal economic policies – 'the laws of profits, individual risk, free markets, and growth by competition' – would never have been tolerated by the original Front. One of the first casualties was the famous forty-hour week. An austerity programme cut all government subsidies except to the armament industries. There were strikes and protests but times had changed and they were faced down. In a year Reynaud's reforms had increased the Treasury coffers by 11 billion francs and Hélène de Portes was telling people that many of the Cabinet thought her Paul should replace Daladier as Prime Minister.

By now the lucky umbrellas were gathering dust. Even before Hitler trampled all over the Munich Agreement by marching into Prague, Chamberlain's triumph had been undergoing a reassessment. In April 1939 Britain, France and Poland – which owed its existence to the French desire to have a beholden ally on Germany's eastern border – signed a 'mutual assistance' pact. Hitler now wanted mainly German-speaking Danzig, the Baltic port that under the Versailles Treaty had a League of Nations administrator and Polish customs control. After years of disarmament, with France often branded as an aggressor for its insistence on maintaining a large army, Britain had introduced conscription – a first in peacetime – and accelerated its expansion of the Royal Air Force.

On Bastille Day, July 1939, exactly twenty years after the victory parade, British troops once again marched down the Champs-Élysées when the Grenadier Guards, boiling under their bearskins and ceremonial scarlet, helped celebrate the French Revolution's 150th anniversary. Watching them was Général Maurice-Gustave Gamelin, the French Commander-in-Chief who knew that, if war came soon, he was looking at one of the better parts of the very small number of trained British infantry available. Standing alongside him was the stocky figure of Gamelin's British equivalent, Lord Gort VC, who had inherited an Irish viscountcy at sixteen. The Grenadiers were Gort's old regiment. In the last weeks of the war he had been badly wounded and added a Victoria Cross to three DSOs and an MC, commanding a Grenadier battalion in an attack on the Hindenburg line. Now, as Chief of the Imperial General Staff, Gort was putting together a wartime contingency plan to reinforce France's eighty divisions with an initial four British ones and an armoured brigade. About 160,000 men compared with 1 million. True, more divisions – mostly Territorial Army – would follow but they were so unprepared it was intended that they should complete their training in France while acting as lines of communcations troops. It was Sir John French's 'contemptible little army' all over again, only worse.

As far as Gamelin was concerned, what Westminster had done to its army since the last time they were invited to march down the Champs-Élysées was criminal. At the 1918 armistice the British Army in France had numbered about 1.5 million UK British plus 500,000 Dominion and Indian troops. Two years later the rush to get men out of uniform was such that it had been reduced to 370,000 and, with smaller defence budgets every year since, was in free fall. All this was in accordance with popular feeling. Even during the high unemployment of the early 1930s anti-militarism was so strong there were never enough volunteers to meet the army's shrinking requirements. Nor did successive governments particularly care because for years the prevailing thinking was that the British Army would never need to fight on continental Europe again. Two months after Hitler had come to power, more defence cuts had reduced the army's budget to its nadir. 'Thank God for the French army,' an almost lone voice told the Commons. That was in the spring of 1933 when the warmonger Churchill was an exclusive taste.

Chapter Three

It was not until February 1939, seven months before the start of the war, that Gort, now well into his arrangements for the second British Expeditionary Force in twenty years, felt he could no longer conceal from the French what the British contribution was likely to be. Their reaction was predictable. Size mattered. 'France does not intend England to fight their battles with French soldiers,' snapped Général Henri Dentz, deputy to Commander-in-Chief Gamelin and, at that stage, probably no more Anglophobic than the rest of the French High Command.

French public opinion, the British ambassador in Paris explained to his government, demanded a big British Army on French soil as proof of its commitment to their joint stand against Hitler. 'It's no use pointing out the size of our air force or navy,' he said. US ambassador William Bullitt agreed. 'The only great army on the side of decency is the French army,' he informed President Roosevelt. 'The British have even less of an army than we have.'

As it happened, while Bullitt and the French generals sniffed at Gort's Lilliputian offerings, the sailors were getting on rather well. True, Amiral François Darlan, whose wife Berthe Morgan had some English ancestry, enjoyed reminding the British that his great-grandfather Antoine Darlan had been killed at Trafalgar aboard the *Redoubtable* from whose topsails a sniper shot Nelson on his quarterdeck. But the commander of the French Navy was respected in London as the ambitious little man who was creating the most efficient Marine Française republican France had ever known.

At the beginning of 1937 Darlan had been the surprise appointment to the post, overtaking the favourite because he came from an unusually left-wing background for a senior serving officer and was therefore more acceptable to the ruling Popular Front. The Darlans were a long-established family of seafarers from the village of Podensac in south-west France, some 20 miles up the Garonne river from Bordeaux in the claret country from where the English have long imported their favourite wine.*

For several generations, when they were not serving their country, they

* Although Podensac itself is better known for the bitter orange vermouth marketed as Lillet, a favourite tipple of the Duchess of Windsor; also James Bond's in *Casino Royale*.

made their living working river boats. But Darlan's paternal grandfather, Sabin, had more ambition. When he retired from the navy he acquired some of the seagoing vessels involved in the wine trade and made the fortune that pushed them up the social ladder. Darlan's father, Jean-Baptiste, became a lawyer, his uncle Xavier a doctor. Somewhat unusually even for the tight-knit ways of provincial France, the Darlan brothers married the Espagnac sisters, the daughters of a physician from the village of Nérac, about 60 miles up-stream from Podensac. Distancing themselves even further from the sea, both brothers settled there and this is where François Darlan, the future amiral, was born on 7 August 1881 into a meritocratic family with a strong belief in the egalitarianism that had permitted its own success.

Jean-Baptiste, who became mayor of Nérac and a deputy in the National Assembly, was everything Pétain and the majority of the officer corps detested: a member of the old Dreyfusard Radical Socialist Party, an enthusiastic Freemason and, above all, an anticlericalist who believed in the sanctity of the Third Republic and a Church divorced from politics. How much of this upbringing survived in his son as he approached his sixtieth year is hard to say, though the amiral was not loath to display a certain distance from the cloth. 'I don't have any special respect for the Lord's Day,' he told an old friend when he chose to leave port on a Sunday for a training exercise. But if he could not help his father's politics they could certainly help him when it came to working with the Popular Front.

It paid for senior French officers to be more politically adroit than their British counterparts, especially in the navy where they were unlikely to have acquired the popular recognition of a Pétain or a Foch. Darlan had graduated from the École Navale in 1902 and his peacetime duties took him all over the French Empire, particularly to Indochina waters. Even so, he had little personal experience of sea warfare. In 1914–18 the British had maintained Allied naval supremacy in the Channel and the North Sea. As a result, Darlan was among those French naval officers whose war had mostly been spent on land providing additional artillery support for the army from adapted heavy naval guns. This included a spell in the British Ypres-Passchendaele sector during which he was praised by his allies for spoiling a German counter-attack with a prompt barrage.

Darlan's post-war relations with the British did not start on such a harmonious note. In 1930 he had been technical adviser at the London Naval Conference. For three months America, Britain, France, Italy and Japan wrangled over how much naval tonnage each should be allowed to build depending on their coastlines and colonial commitments. From the start things had not augured well for the French delegation as the conference's opening ceremony was in the House of Lords' Royal Gallery which is dominated by Daniel Maclise's huge paintings of the dying Nelson and Wellington's victorious meeting with Blücher. 'On one of the walls, the Battle of Trafalgar; on the other, Waterloo: charming!' Darlan wrote home to Berthe, who was herself descended from Admiral Sir George Rodney, another scourge of the French and the name of a contemporary British battleship.

Quite apart from having to suffer their hosts' appalling taste in triumphalist art the French also had to put up with their absurd insistence that they should be allowed no more tonnage than the Italians. Darlan produced statistics comparing territory controlled, coastlines and dispersal of colonial possessions that showed, without a shadow of doubt, that France's naval needs were second only to the British Empire's. Italy shared bottom place with Japan. In the end, France and Italy declined to sign the only thing that really mattered to them concerning the building of light ships and all agreed on a five-year moratorium on capital ship construction and restricting submarine warfare which, for the time being, suited everybody's budgets. 'A vast fabric of stupidities,' said Darlan after the meeting broke up.

But by the time the Popular Front had put him in charge of the navy the British were no longer looking at the Italians with such a favourable eye. Mussolini, ignoring all agreements, had expanded his fleet. The Royal Navy could no longer be certain of secure passage across the Mediterranean from Gibraltar to the Suez canal. France was concerned about access to its North African possessions. Darlan saw shared interests that outweighed other considerations.

The Spanish Civil War was now into its second year. In the Mediterranean Il Duce, who had sent thousands of Italian 'volunteers' to fight on the side of General Franco's mostly Fascist-inspired nationalists, was also using his fleet to help blockade the republican government's ports. Italian submarines had sunk British and French merchant ships bound for them and the Admiralty, having cracked the Italian naval code, knew exactly who was responsible. But their political masters wished to avoid a confrontation and, true to the policy of appeasement, declared that the ships were being torpedoed by 'unknown submarines'.

In Paris the *rosbifs* were much ridiculed. It became fashionable to refer to Mussolini as 'The Unknown Statesman' and the Boulevard des Italiens as the 'Boulevard des Inconnus'. Most of Léon Blum's original Popular Front had yearned to intervene in Spain, whose besieged leftist anticlerical republicans also called themselves the Popular Front, but they had not dared for fear of igniting a similar conflagration in France. But here was an opportunity to put overwhelming Anglo-French naval power on the side of the angels. Armed with suggestions from Darlan about how surveillance zones could be policed, the French Foreign Minister persuaded Britain to co-sponsor an international conference on piracy. It took place at Nyon in Switzerland in September 1937. Italy and Germany declined to attend. But among those who did was the Soviet Union, the Spanish republicans' main supplier. The upshot was the Nyon Agreement that gave the Anglo-French fleets carte blanche to patrol the most sensitive areas and hunt down the culprits.

Even before the agreement was signed the Admiralty's code-breakers were reporting that the Italians were withdrawing their submarines. *Figaro* hailed it as a triumph of French diplomacy, which it was, and 'a prelude to a stiffening of Franco-British diplomacy' which – a year before Munich – it was not. But it was the start of an operational Anglo-French naval partnership in the Mediterranean that far exceeded the more notional peacetime arrangements between their armies.

British and French ships could turn up at each other's ports – Toulon or Gibraltar for instance – without giving prior diplomatic notice and expect to be victualled and refuelled. Five of Britain's thirty-five destroyers in the Mediterranean – the French had twenty-eight – operated out of French North Africa. The Royal Navy, which also sent an aircraft carrier, two battleships and three cruisers, became a common sight in Marseilles and there was a good deal of socializing between the two navies: sporting fixtures and the exchanges of cap ribbons for the men; reciprocal wardroom cocktails and dinners for the officers.

The maiden voyage of France's new battle cruiser the *Dunkerque* – faster and bigger gunned than Germany's latest pocket battleships – took her to Britain for King George VI's coronation and naval review at Spithead. *Dunkerque*'s rakish lines were much admired by her hosts (who had nothing quite like it) while her crew, with their distinctive red pom-poms in their caps and attentive Gallic ways, discovered that the enduring French belief that all young Englishwomen had horsey teeth and big feet was exaggerated. The only bad note came at the coronation itself when Darlan, who was a vice-amiral, the highest rank in the French Navy, discovered that at Westminster Abbey protocol placed him behind the admiral in charge of China's ramshackle fleet. A year later, in June 1939, after some determined lobbying by Darlan on the need for the French command structure to be clearly understood by even the most obdurate foreigners, France also had its first Admiral of the Fleet.

When the war started *Dunkerque*, together with her sister ship *Strasbourg* and eight destroyers, was based at Brest as part of Amiral Marcel-Bruno Gensoul's Force de Raid, France's Atlantic fleet. This was the pride of La Marine Français: integrated, powerful, fast and of innovative design. On the two battle cruisers the problem of how to acquire speed while retaining firepower and protective armour plate had been resolved by reducing the normal allocation of gun turrets by half and placing all eight heavy 13.4-inch guns forward in two four-barrel turrets. Some of the destroyers belonged to a new intermediary class of warship the French had developed which they called *contre-torpilleurs*. Their eight 5.5-inch guns made them almost as well armed as a light cruiser, but they were faster than most destroyers. The *Volta*, which had been delivered shortly before

Hitler invaded Poland, had done well over 40 knots in trials.

It was true that Britain then had the world's biggest navy, including fifteen battleships with more on the way because most of the existing ones were over twenty years old. (The first thing young sailors joining the *Renown* were shown was a dent the old Imperial German Navy had made in her armoured deck at Jutland.) There were also seven aircraft carriers, the latest the new *Ark Royal* which had just completed her sea trials. France's only carrier, the *Béarn*, had been launched in 1927 and there was talk of turning her into a seaplane tender, which was a bit like putting an old racehorse between the shafts of a milk float. Nor did the French have the Royal Navy's as yet primitive but rapidly improving shipborne radar. Nor the ASDIC sonar detectors for U-boats, which was strange, for the acronym stood for Allied Submarine Detection Investigation Committee and started out as an Anglo-French 1914–18 research project. After the war, the French dropped out but the offshore islanders, for whom the submarine threat was much more important, tinkered on and by 1938 were installing a working apparatus in their destroyers. Nonetheless, large parts of Darlan's fleet, lacking though it may have been in the latest electronic implants, were every bit as good as they looked.

Gensoul's squadron was ideally placed to protect convoys crossing the Atlantic. During the war's first winter *Dunkerque* was detached and teamed up with HMS *Hood* to hunt the German surface raiders which, by November 1939, had started to sink Allied merchant shipping with impunity. Each warship carried a signals liaison team from the other, had the speed and endurance to cover what Churchill called 'the trackless ocean' and enough firepower to make almost anything they were likely to encounter sorry indeed. All they lacked was the luck to meet up with them.

The next month, bound for Canada with some of France's gold reserves, *Dunkerque* listened to the British radio chatter from the River Plate estuary where Commodore Henry Harwood's cruisers *Exeter*, *Ajax* and *Achilles* were about to bluff the *Admiral Graf Spee* into scuttling. It had been a near thing. *Dunkerque* and *Strasbourg* had been built with German pocket battleships in mind. An Anglo-French group operating out of Dakar included both the *Strasbourg* and the aircraft carrier HMS *Hermes*. Of several hunting parties the Allies had set up in the South Atlantic these British cruisers, two hardly bigger than France's latest destroyers, were the weakest.

But Harwood had guessed he would meet his prey in the waters between Uruguay and Argentina and danced his cruisers in and out of range of the *Spee*'s 11-inch guns to deliver their wounds like picadors. In doing so he lost exactly twice as many men as the thirty-six German dead. *Exeter*, whose 8-inchers were the biggest at Harwood's disposal, was reduced to a disarmed hulk with all her main guns silenced and a nasty list. The *Spee* appeared almost untouched but shell splinters had damaged her fuel cleaning system and neutral Uruguay was pro-British enough to make repairs impossible, even attempting to obstruct her departure until the *Renown* and her 15-inch guns arrived. Hitler wanted Captain Hans Langsdorff to go down with all guns blazing. Langsdorff, unaware that Harwood was still awaiting big gun reinforcements, chose to scuttle his ship and save his men. So the Royal Navy celebrated the first major naval victory of the war and six days before Christmas, Langsdorff, a chivalrous opponent who had always rescued the crews of the merchant ships he sank, shot himself in a hotel room in Buenos Aires. As far as La Marine Française was concerned, it was typical of the undeserved good fortune England so often enjoyed on naval occasions.

On their way back from Halifax, *Dunkerque* and the light cruiser *Gloire* had escorted seven British troopers and freighters taking part of a Canadian infantry division to England. Gensoul, who had the better ships, was in command of the escort. In order to ensure the best possible liaison the British had placed Captain Cedric Holland, who for the last two years had been Britain's naval attaché in Paris, in command of the convoy with the acting rank of vice-admiral. Holland was flying his flag from the Jutland veteran *Revenge* which was 10 knots slower than the French battle cruiser and nothing like as well armoured.

The convoy was a tempting target for German raiders above and below the waves and it had been at sea for only twelve hours when the Admiralty sent Gensoul a warning that the *Graf Spee*'s sister ship *Admiral Scheer* was on the prowl. But Gensoul was not about to get his chance to show the English how to sink a pocket battleship without her captain's assistance. The weather closed in and Christmas Day 1939 was celebrated off Iceland in a Force Nine storm. For some of the prairie boys from Ontario in the packed holds of the troopships it must have been unmitigated hell.

By the 28th the wind had abated. As they approached the Irish coast intercepted British wireless traffic revealed that a U-boat had torpedoed the battleship HMS *Barham*, on patrol to the north of them, killed four of her crew but only inflicted minor damage. The next day the convoy and its French escort parted company: one bound for Southampton and the other for Brest, their Aldis lamps blinking out the customary courtesies and fulsome expressions of mutual admiration.

Amiral Gensoul: HOPE THAT WE MAY HAVE AN OPPORTUNITY OF MEETING AGAIN. I CONGRATULATE YOU ON THE WAY YOU HANDLED THE CONVOY.

Admiral Holland: I LOOK FORWARD HAPPILY TO SERVING UNDER YOU AGAIN.

Only in this case it all appears to have been true. Holland – Hooky to his navy friends because of the shape of his nose – was 51 and married with children. During his time in Paris he had acquired a French mistress and a certain sympathy with the Gallic viewpoint. He had first met Gensoul shortly before the war during an official visit to France's Atlantic naval base at Brest. Gensoul, who happened to be a Protestant, which was rare for a senior French naval officer, was generally well disposed towards the English. 'An infinitely courteous, loyal and able collaborator,' he wrote of Holland in a confidential report to Darlan on the December 1939 Atlantic crossings. Gensoul was close to his boss, one of an inner circle jealous outsiders referred to as the ADD – *Amis de Darlan*.

Shortly afterwards Holland returned to his duties as naval attaché in Paris. Then, at the beginning of May, and on the eve of the Wehrmacht blitzkrieg through France and the Low Countries, he left France to command the aircraft carrier *Ark Royal*. Almost immediately Holland's new ship was embroiled in the closing stages of the Norwegian campaign.

Two months before, the Fleet Air Arm had made naval history, though not the kind most sailors wanted to hear. At the edge of their range, some of its Orkney-based Skua fighter-bombers had become the first aircraft to sink a major warship when they dive-bombed the light cruiser *Koenigsberg* in Norway's Bergen harbour. Holland was ordered to do the same thing to the *Scharnhorst*, licking her wounds in Trondheim after she had taken a torpedo from a dying British destroyer. But by now the Germans had plenty of fighters and anti-aircraft guns in place. Eight of fifteen Skuas *Ark Royal* sent to Trondheim did not come back and the only bomb that found its target failed to explode.

Nobody could dispute the courage of the *Ark Royal*'s air crews who knew they were attacking a strongly defended target, but the Norwegian campaign had shaken French confidence in the Royal Navy to the core. On 9 April, pre-empting an Anglo-French plan to do it first, Germany had the audacity to invade neutral Norway despite the presence of the best part of the Royal Navy's Home Fleet at Scapa Flow not 300 miles away from Bergen. Simultaneously Germany secured a direct line of communication by brushing aside a resistance that was as brave as it was foolish and moving into neighbouring Denmark, a handy stepping stone between the Reich and its ultimate Scandinavian ambitions. An immediate prize was the strategic value of Norway's long coastline with all the additional naval and air bases it could provide for sorties against the British in both the North Sea and the Atlantic. But it also secured the ice-free northern port of Narvik, warmed by the Gulf Stream and a winter outlet for the Swedish iron ore Germany's steel mills craved when the Baltic froze.

The Wehrmacht's Norwegian campaign was a foretaste of all they were about to do in much of the rest of western Europe, a much smaller affair but characterized by what Churchill, with grudging admiration, called 'surprise, ruthlessness and precision'. As the panzers rolled though Jutland and the Kriegsmarine glided unopposed into Copenhagen's harbour, so the world's first airborne assault took place. Paratroopers seized the airfields at Oslo and Stavanger where the British-built Gloster Gladiator biplane fighters that were the core of Norway's minuscule air force were based. Then the Luftwaffe flew in its squadrons complete with logistical back up and soon its Stukas and Messerschmitts had established the kind of air superiority European powers could only normally expect over camel cavalry.

Within thirty-six hours, starting at Oslo, the Germans captured seven Norwegian ports, ending at Narvik 1,400 miles away. At Narvik the assault troops landed from destroyers and were met by units that had infiltrated the harbour in the holds of the innocent-looking German ore carriers lining its quays. These ships were also carrying their artillery, ammunition and other heavy weapons. In the first twenty-four hours the only serious opposition the Norwegians had put up was at Oslo where the heavy cruiser *Blücher* was sunk by the Krupp guns and torpedoes mounted in the Oscarsborg fortress. The first foreigners to come to Norway's assistance were the crew of the British-based Free Polish submarine *Orzel* which torpedoed the German troopship *Rio de Janeiro*. A large number of survivors were picked up by Norwegian fishing boats. They informed their rescuers they had been bound for Bergen to help the Norwegians resist an Anglo-French invasion.

Originally there had been an Allied plan to deny Narvik to the Germans by intervening on the Finnish side in their war against Stalin's Russia which, an accomplice in Hitler's invasion of Poland, proceeded in November 1939 to try to settle its territorial disputes with Finland the same way. The Baltic was a German lake and there was no question of sending men and equipment through Helsinki. It was felt that Norway, which sided with Finland, could hardly object if an Anglo-French military mission planted a big logistical base at Narvik, not 100 miles from the Finnish frontier. Churchill, who as First Lord of the Admiralty oversaw the trade blockade against Germany, was a firm supporter, saying it was 'worth all the rest of the blockade and provides a great chance of shortening the war'.

Two British brigades and one of French Chasseurs Alpins were earmarked for the expedition – 20,000 men – and staff work began. But the Allies were not ready to move until March 1940 by which time the Finns, who had fought doggedly against overwhelming odds, were about to call a ceasefire and concede territory. Force Avonmouth, as it had been codenamed, was then stood down, much to the relief of some senior British officers who had always considered it 'harebrained'.

Nonetheless, both Neville Chamberlain and Paul Reynaud, who at last had replaced Daladier as Prime Minister, wanted to take action in Norway before Germany did. It was decided that the British would mine the approaches to Narvik, thus forcing the German ore boats further out to sea where they would be easy prey for submarines. In response to the German objections and threats that were bound to follow, the Allies would then send troops to take over Narvik and three other ports along the coast: Trondheim, Bergen and Stavanger.

The Narvik operation was postponed from 5 to 8 April, a delay that turned out to be crucial and for which there were mutual recriminations though at the time the British were not unduly concerned because they felt the outnumbered Kriegsmarine would never dare risk making the first move in the North Sea. Thus, only hours before the first German paratroopers dropped among them, the Norwegian government, determinedly neutral against all comers, was far more perturbed by British mines fouling the approaches to its valuable northern port than vague reports of troops massing on the Danish frontier and warships leaving Wilhelmshaven.

When air reconnaissance confirmed that a battle cruiser, two light cruisers, fourteen destroyers and what looked like a troop transport had put to sea, Churchill admitted, 'we found it hard at the Admiralty to believe this force was going to Narvik'. Even so, reinforcements were despatched to back up the battle cruiser *Renown*, the cruiser and eight destroyers already off the Norwegian coast covering the mine-layers. From Scapa Flow went the battleships *Warspite*, *Rodney*, *Valiant* and *Repulse* plus two cruisers and ten destroyers. More cruisers and at least a score of destroyers sailed from Rosyth, though not before some of the cruisers had disembarked the infantry that were to have made unopposed landings at the ports now in German hands.

As it was, these ships arrived twenty-four hours too late to prevent the enemy establishing a firm foothold in Norway. For many of them their first task was to go back and collect the men who would be the first British soldiers to meet the Wehrmacht in open battle in the six months since war had been declared. The result did not impress their allies.

Two Territorial brigades, about 8,000 men, had been selected to garrison the Norwegian ports in what had originally been intended as a kind of police operation. If the Norwegian militia made any difficulties platoon commanders were to be instructed to avoid force and 'use bluff and good humoured determination'. Now the Territorials were landed north and south of German-occupied Trondheim with orders to make a pincer attack on an enemy not easily amused. Apart from naval gunfire the British had no artillery support (owing to a mix-up the gunners arrived *sans* guns), no mobile anti-aircraft weapons, no anti-tank guns and, of course, no air cover and no white camouflage.

From a Messerschmitt cockpit the frozen, khaki-clad figures sprawled on the open snow below looked like a scatter of chocolate buttons on a bedsheet. Amazingly, casualties were mercifully light. When morale crumbled it probably had more to do with exhausting snow marches in sub-zero temperatures while Austrian ski troops harassed their flanks. Napoleonic retreats to the coast began, their trails blazed by discarded Bren light machine guns which weighed twice as much as a rifle, mortars, radios and smallpacks. One brigade was reduced to about 300 officers and men; most of the missing were the cold and disheartened, cut-off stragglers glad to be taken prisoner.

Help in the shape of two fully equipped brigades of regular soldiers, one of them Guards, arrived in time to stop the rot and, backed by artillery denied to the Territorials, handed out some bloody noses to the over-confident. But without air support there was a limit to what they could do. Towards the end of April it was decided to evacuate all the troops involved in the fighting around Trondheim in central Norway and concentrate on the capture of Narvik in the north where the Guards, who were heavily engaged, had just been considerably reinforced. France had sent three battalions of ski-trained Chasseurs Alpins and two of the Foreign Legion, plus four battalions of exiled Poles that had been attached to the French Army. All were under the command of Britain's Lieutenant General Claude Auchinleck who arrived on 11 May. This was twenty-four hours after the Germans had started their offensive in France and Churchill, as a result of the Commons debate on the reverses in Norway, had replaced Neville Chamberlain as Prime Minister of an all-party national coalition with a five-man War Cabinet in which he was Minister of Defence.

The irony of Churchill profiting from Britain's Scandinavian misadventures has often been pointed out. After all, he was as much in favour of intervening in Norway as Chamberlain, probably more so. His conviction that stopping Germany's supply of Swedish iron ore was a war winner was no less deeply held than his belief in 1915's Gallipoli landings which had almost ended his political career and led to a penitential year in the trenches as a battalion commander.

But quite apart from the House of Commons making it plain that, as Germany moved from sitzkrieg to blitzkrieg, they wanted a failed peacemaker replaced by a more warrior breed, Churchill had also been boosted by a brave and reassuring performance by the senior service. 'In their desperate grapple with the Royal Navy the Germans ruined their own,' the Prime Minister would write and it was true that Germany's surface fleet, which to start with was so much smaller than Britain's, would never quite recover. After the Norwegian batteries had opened the score with the *Blücher* off Oslo, the British sank two light cruisers, ten destroyers, eight U-boats, and a torpedo boat. In addition the pocket battleships *Scharnhorst*, *Gneisenau* and *Lützow*, as well as another three light cruisers, were all badly damaged and in need of months of repair.

The Germans, as they usually did, gave as good as they got and the British also suffered heavy losses. Among the last was the only capital ship to go down, the old aircraft carrier *Glorious* (built on the hull of a 1915 cruiser) which was sunk by the *Scharnhorst* on her way home along with her two escort destroyers, though not before one of them, HMS *Acasta*, had got close enough to send the *Scharnhorst* limping back to Trondheim with torpedo damage. Almost 1,500 British sailors died, over half of them from exposure because there was a wireless failure and rescue ships were late on the scene. The only survivor from the *Acasta* turned out to be one of the torpedo men who had hit back.

A measure of the intensity of the naval warfare around Norway in the two months from 9 April to 8 June 1940 may be gauged by the award of the war's first three Victoria Crosses, two of them posthumous, to Royal Navy officers engaged in it. One went to the captain of the destroyer *Glowworm* which met the heavy cruiser *Admiral von Hipper* in stormy weather, missed with her torpedoes then, too badly hit to escape, rammed the heavy cruiser before capsizing with one gun still firing. Captain Hellmuth Heye was so impressed he positioned the *Hipper*, which was holed above the waterline and not seriously damaged, so that an icy swell carried *Glowworm*'s gasping survivors towards her. Her commander, Lieutenant Commander Gerard Roope, aged 35 and a well-known navy cricketer, was almost among the thirty-one Heye saved; but he had spent too long in the freezing water encouraging others and could not keep his grip on a rescue rope.

Narvik, where about 2,000 Germans had held out against, a combined force of British, French, Poles and Norwegians ten times that size, was finally taken on 28 May after a tremendous naval bombardment was followed by an assault by the Foreign Legion and the Poles. Some 400 German prisoners were taken. But, though the Norwegians were the last to be told, it had already been decided that the situation in France – at Dunkirk the evacuation of the BEF had already begun – was far too serious to continue with the Norwegian venture. King Haakon VII and his Cabinet, who had retreated to the Arctic sealing town of Tromso, refused to surrender. Instead, they boarded a British cruiser and set up a government-in-exile in London which brought with them Norway's huge merchant fleet, most of it in foreign waters, which before long would be delivering almost half of Britain's oil imports.

Eleven days after they had captured it all Allied troops had been withdrawn from Narvik. They left its port a wreck, though the Germans had it up and running again in six months – which was more than they could do with their navy.

For the army, the campaign had come as a shock. 'Some of our finest troops, the Scots and Irish Guards, were baffled by the vigour, enterprise and training of Hitler's young men,' admitted Churchill. In France Britain's senior soldiers could (and usually did) blame the French for all that went wrong. In Norway, in both planning and execution, there was nobody to blame but themselves and, if anything, their allies came out looking better. The navy might be satisfied that its crews still had hearts of oak but Churchill was only reflecting the army's own doubts about the quality of some of its infantry. 'By comparison with the French, or the Germans for that matter, our men for the most part seemed distressingly young, not so much in years as in self reliance and manliness generally,' noted General Auchinleck, though British Indian Army officers could be notoriously biased against Home regiments.

The French, usually willing to concede that the English performed better at sea than on land (though not always good enough for Surcouf and his kind), thought that even the Royal Navy had let them down. True, the English had started well enough, subjecting the Kriegsmarine destroyers bottled up in the narrow fjords around Narvik to a Nelsonic harpooning and winning their second VC.* But they had got there too late to prevent troops being unloaded. The number of German ships sunk could not disguise their failure to inflict the devastating defeat expected of an ally who had so often justified its feeble contribution to the land war by reminding France of its naval traditions. From Paris a few weeks later US Ambassador Bullitt reported that Darlan had told him that the British fleet 'had proved to be as great a disappointment as the French Army'. It was, of course, outrageous to compare the rout of the French Army with the fight the Royal Navy had put up in Norwegian waters.

The fault lay in not getting there in time and in Paris there was almost universal agreement among its chattering classes that *they* would have done much better. Norway was not an Allied defeat. It was a British one.

Gensoul's Force de Raid had escorted some of the French troop convoys to Narvik but in June 1940 they were back in the Mediterranean looking for the Italian fleet which wisely kept out of the way. Mussolini had waited for the Germans to enter Paris and then, with what the *New York Times* called 'the courage of a jackal on the heels of a bolder beast of prey', declared war on France and Britain. 'All I need to sit at the peace conference is 2,000 Italian dead,' Mussolini confided to Marshal Baglioni as his mountain troops were mown down in Alpine passes by well-dug-in machine gunners.

Three French divisions held something like ten times that number of Italians on the Franco-Italian border while an Italian incursion into the Côte d'Azur is said to have been repulsed by a sergeant and seven men. But when RAF Wellington bombers attempted to use an airfield near Marseilles to attack northern Italy, French fears of Italian reprisal raids

* The third VC went to Lieutenant Richard Stannard, a 37-year-old Royal Navy Reserve officer from the merchant fleet. His anti-submarine trawler *Arab* was the only one of twelve to survive a campaign in which Stannard had distinguished himself on numerous occasions including a single-handed attempt to put out a fire in a dockside ammunition dump. Already bomb-damaged, almost out of anti-aircraft tracer and limping out of a fjord, Stannard refused to surrender his ship to the pilot of a Junkers 88 who, evidently sickened by the slaughter, flashed a Morse message. When the German lost patience and attacked, Stannard got his Lewis gun crew to hold their fire until the last moment and shot it down. Then he got the *Arab* home.

were such that they blocked the runway with trucks. If *les Anglais* wanted to bomb Turin they could do it from British territory and let the reciprocal bombs that would surely follow fall on them.

Darlan despatched some of his cruisers from Toulon in a 200-mile dash up the Côte d'Azur in a hit-and-run bombardment of the northern Italian naval base at Genoa. There were also plans for French ships to join the British in shelling Italian military positions along the Libyan coast. But by the time Général Huntzinger was signing the armistice in Maréchal Foch's wagon-lit at Compiègne, *Dunkerque* and *Strasbourg* and the rest of Amiral Gensoul's ships anchored in Mers-el-Kébir, the old corsairs' lair across the bay from Oran, had yet to fire a shot with their main armament.

By the ceasefire, at least half of France's fleet, including almost all its heavy units, were in African ports: Bizerte, Algiers, Oran, Casablanca and Dakar. The *Richelieu* and the *Jean Bart*, the bigger gunned successors to the *Dunkerque* class with the same forward turret design, were so new they had not been quite finished when they escaped. The *Richelieu*, which was the most complete, fled to Dakar in French West Africa. The *Jean Bart*, which was far less ready having never even started her engines, found sanctuary in the Moroccan port of Casablanca, arriving there with only one of her two four-gun turrets in place.

This dispersal suited Darlan. The armistice permitted France to maintain vessels in its colonies for their protection and if they were already in situ it would be easier to negotiate their numbers and whereabouts rather than try to extract them from a pool of mothballed vessels in Toulon. Having rejected several invitations to sail his fleet to British ports, what did not suit Darlan at all was the number of his ships still under the control of France's erstwhile ally.

In the Egyptian port of Alexandria, surrounded by the Royal Navy and not far from where the rotting timbers of an older French fleet lay where Nelson had left it after the Battle of the Nile, was Amiral Godfroy's squadron. This was made up of the battleship *Lorraine* and four cruisers – three of them the 8-inch gun type the Royal Navy was so short of at the Battle of the River Plate – and various support craft. In Britain itself, mostly in Portsmouth and Plymouth, there were 2 battleships, 4 light cruisers, several submarines including the mammoth *Surcouf*, and about 200 smaller vessels, many of them the kind of converted trawlers that were so useful for minesweeping and anti-submarine work.

All of them had sought sanctuary there before the signing of the armistice and Darlan wanted them back or rendered useless. Certainly, he was not going to have the English fighting their hopeless battle with French ships. Among other things, German willingness to release the thousands of recently captured French soldiers almost certainly hinged on a firm display of neutrality. If French warships were not for the Germans they were not for the British either.

Chapter Four

At Devonport, shortly before dawn on Wednesday, 3 July 1940, the radio operator on the *Surcouf*, who was monitoring the long-wave channels, received an 'officer only' signal from French naval headquarters which had moved to Bordeaux and was still out of German hands.

Even an English summer was warming up and the air inside the submarine was stifling. Capitaine de corvette Paul Martin had ordered all but one of *Surcouf*'s four deck hatches to be battened down. Only the hatch nearest the bow was open and that was to enable the two duty sentries, big Lebel revolvers holstered at their waists, to get back inside fast if they had to. One sentry, the duty petty officer, kept an eye out for waterborne intruders by patrolling the hull casing or climbing up into the conning tower and trying to make out if there were any small craft moving between the dim outlines of the ships moored in the blacked-out harbour. The other stood at the submarine's end of the gangplank joining it to one of the lower deck hatchways on the *Paris* whose dark bulk loomed above them like an overhanging cliff. To get to the *Surcouf* from the quay you first had to pass through the old French battleship, which made them doubly secure from that direction.

Ever since the amiable Sir Dunbar-Nasmith, the vice admiral who commanded the Western Approaches, had turned up unannounced a couple of days before, Martin's suspicions that the English had at least made contingency plans to seize his submarine had hardened. Dunbar-Nasmith's entourage, eyes everywhere, had included Lieutenant Patrick Griffiths, his French-speaking liaison officer who was off the mine-laying submarine *Rorqual*, which was presently in the Mediterranean. Martin had little doubt that the admiral's surprise visit was more by way of reconnaissance than social. But there was not much he could do about it except see that his hatches were sealed, his sentries doubled and alert enough to warn him of a boarding party in time to scuttle his ship at her moorings if necessary. Already the torpedoes had been disarmed, their fuses and firing pins removed.

When the officer-only message arrived Lieutenant de vaisseau Émile Crescent, the duty officer, was in the wardroom with its framed print of the doughty Robert Surcouf, cutlass in hand, leading his men onto a fat

English merchantman. He hurried down to the radio cabin with the key to its safe and extracted the relevant code book. Long before he had finished Crescent realized that he was unwrapping the orders they had all been dreading as France's armistice with Germany slipped into its second week and there was still no sign of Britain ending its futile war with Germany.

Surcouf was to be scuttled immediately. It appeared the British were not prepared to accept Darlan's assurances that the fleet would not fall into the hands of the Germans and Italians. Already there were indications that the Royal Navy was poised to attack Amiral Gensoul's squadron at Mers-el-Kébir where the clock was two hours ahead and dawn had long since broken. It was obvious that the 200 or so craft, including coastal patrol boats and converted trawlers, that had found shelter in Britain's southern ports would not be ignored. On *Surcouf* Lieutenant Crescent, the message from Bordeaux decrypted in full, rushed off to tell Commandant Martin, shouting as he went, 'The English are coming.' But he was too late; the English were already there.

Zero hour for all boarding parties in the ports concerned had been set at 4.30 a.m. – almost first light. At Dartmouth they were made up of instructors from its naval college and some of the older officer cadets. In the main, they had enjoyed good relations with the crews of the six minesweepers they were about to seize. Nor did it help that the flotilla's flagship was called *Entente Cordiale*.

At Devonport the *Surcouf* had been allotted sixty boarders. Half of them were sailors from the submarine *Thames*, recently refitted and about to go on patrol in the North Sea, and the rest Royal Marines. Among the sailors were engine room artificers carrying the various tools of their trade including wooden mallets to knock back obstinate control levers set to self-destruct. All of them were under Commander Denis 'Lofty' Sprague, the *Thames*'s lanky captain, whose deputy for the occasion was the liaison officer Griffiths from the *Rorqual*, another experienced submariner and anxious to rejoin his ship and get back into the war.

Almost everybody wore steel helmets and the officer and petty officers were armed with .455 Webley revolvers, as were some of the men who also carried wooden pickaxe helves. A few sailors and all the Royal Marines had rifles and bayonets, though the marines, like almost every other branch of Britain's neglected armed forces, were stretched, and fully trained professionals were thin on the ground. 'All men who had fired a rifle were included and care was taken to detail the maximum number of NCOs and old soldiers to each platoon,' reported Colonel Edward Noyes.

It was hoped that an overwhelming show of forces would lead to bloodless boardings everywhere. Officers had been given a typewritten sheet of four French phrases thought likely to assist. They started with,

'*Nous sommes La Marine Britannique*.' Next came, '*Nous sommes vos camarades*,' followed by '*Montez*' – to indicate that the crew should go up on deck – and the last a distinctly uncomradely, '*Levez vos mains*' ('Raise your hands').

The *Paris* was peacefully occupied by a party led by Dunbar-Nasmith in person. The admiral had armed himself with his own five-paragraph letter, a predictable mixture of flattery and threat, that was to be given to the captains of all the French vessels, big and small, being seized that night. 'The French Nation has fought gallantly to a standstill,' it began generously enough, before spelling out that Hitler could not be trusted and Britain was not going to risk French ships falling into German hands. 'Any resistance can only cause unnecessary bloodshed which would be of advantage to our common enemy.'

While Amiral Cayol, roused from his slumbers by *Paris*'s duty officer and the sound of English voices, was trying to digest this the boarding party spread through the ship and discovered in the officers' cabins 'arms and ammunition readily available'. But nobody had attempted to use them. 'Admiral Cayol was naturally very distressed,' recalled Dunbar-Nasmith, who was by no means unsympathetic. 'He told me that he had considered the question of scuttling his ships but decided not to do it as it would have obstructed the harbour and inconvenienced me.'

Commander Sprague's capture of the neighbouring *Surcouf* did not start down the gangplank from the *Paris*. They arrived – as Capitaine Martin had thought they might – from across the water in three motor launches lying flat between the thwarts so that in the faint light of the new day, all that could be discerned were the silhouettes of the coxswains hunched over their tillers. First man onto the submarine was Lieutenant Francis Talbot of the *Thames* whose men got aboard without a shot being fired and captured one of the sentries. But the other was too fast for them. Talbot watched as he 'ran along the casing for'ard, hammering on the hull by the conning tower and went down the fore hatch which was shut after him'. Sprague's plan had assumed that all four hatches would be open and entered simultaneously. Now they were locked out. There is little on the planet as watertight as a submarine. Talbot climbed the deck ladder into the *Surcouf*'s tall conning tower but his torch revealed that the hatch there was closed too. Then the submariner spotted that its catches looked similar to the new ones on British conning tower hatches which allowed rescue divers to open them from the outside.

Below him Crescent, gripping his decoded message from Bordeaux, got to the Command Post – underwater, the place from where the periscope is operated and the equivalent of the bridge on a ship – when he saw the sentry who had got away lowering himself through the forward hatch, his Lebel still in its holster. He told Crescent that armed Englishmen had landed on the upper deck.

> I ordered him to close the last hatch, which I saw him do, and to sound 'Action Stations'. I rushed to warn the captain and the officers and ran forward to wake the *Premier Maître Électricien* and the *Maître Torpilleur*, telling them to start destroying the equipment we had singled out beforehand. When, about a minute after the alarm, I returned to the Command Post I collided with armed sailors under Commander Sprague, captain of the *Thames*. Our captain then came into the Command Post and spoke to Sprague who handed him a message from the British Admiralty. During this time English sailors spread all over the ship. Later I learned they had been able to open the conning tower hatch from outside.

Dunbar-Nasmith would give Talbot a mention in despatches for his 'most praiseworthy' action in getting into a vessel 'battened down and known to be hostile'. But some of *Surcouf*'s officers were armed and it was far from over.

As more of Sprague's men found their way below deck and the locked hatches were opened, the boarding party tried with varying success to herd the sleepy and reluctant matelots out of their bunks to the upper deck. Some, notably the engine room artificers, glowered at these trespassers and refused to budge. Sprague had more success when he asked all the French officers to muster in their wardroom which was on the deck immediately below the Command Post with the often shared officers' cabins built off it. Once they had gathered there Sprague read them what purported to be a note from Amiral Cayol urging them to join the nascent Free French Navy under Amiral Émile Muselier, an extrovert Marseillais who at that point was the most senior French naval defector to de Gaulle.

Capitaine Martin, who quite rightly did not believe a word of it, demanded to be allowed onto the *Paris* so that he could hear it from Cayol's own lips. Sprague let him go, perhaps thinking that, for whatever reason, the sight of her captain voluntarily leaving his command would deprive the *Surcouf* of leadership and might encourage others to follow. In any case, there was a good chance that the French amiral was no longer aboard *Paris*, for he knew Dunbar-Nasmith wanted him off the old battleship quickly. Before he left, Martin told Capitaine de corvette Pichevin, his second-in-command, to take over.

In the wardroom both sides were standing either side of its long dining table. 'I'm sorry, I have my orders,' said Sprague who, like some of the French officers, was wearing a uniform jacket and tie despite the heat and the hour. Médecin de premiere classe de la Marine Le Nistour, the man who two weeks before had wondered if the circling patrol boats meant they were already prisoners, noted he was 'very pale and constantly wiping his forehead'. Although all the hatches were now open the submarine was still a sticky place, the scents of dark tobacco and coffee breaking through the familiar fug of diesel and body odour to remind the British that this was alien territory.

'Good humour and friendliness are of more value than arms,' Dunbar-Nasmith had advised his boarding parties. It appeared that at least some of the French were of the same mind. When a teenage midshipman somehow contrived to drop his Webley as he climbed out of the engine room one of them pulled him back by the seat of his pants and returned it to his holster. Meanwhile, Talbot managed to persuade the crew in the forward part of the submarine, including the stubborn artificers, to leave peacefully, and Sprague followed him aft to see if he could work the same magic on the other mess deck, which was the larger of the two.

Then Sprague's long legs returned him to the Command Post just in time to catch a glimpse through the hatch into the wardroom below of Pichevin passing a note to a rating who turned out to be an electrician. The lieutenant had decided that the English had no intention of allowing Martin back and they must throw the main power switches and use the blackout to wreck as much as they could. Pleading his bladder, the electrician left the room to be followed by one of Talbot's petty officers, who had a suspicious nature and a mallet. Switches and mallet appear to have connected at about the same time. 'A short fight ensued, which my petty officer won, and the lights were made good again,' reported Talbot.

Even so, there had been enough of a blackout for one man to vanish behind the flapping portière of one of the cabins adjoining the wardroom. Inside the cubicle he shared with Surgeon Commander Le Nistour, Ingénieur mécanicien Daniel was tearing up his engine manuals in preparation for flushing them down a head. While he did this Dr Le Nistour stood guard outside. As far as Sprague was concerned the brief blackout and the man who had run off, evidently intending to do some damage while he could, was the last straw. He began to act like a petulant schoolmaster who feels suddenly let down, his attempts to be reasonable mistaken for weakness. As soon as the lights were back on he ordered all the French officers off the *Surcouf* immediately.

Capitaine de corvette Pichevin, the deputy commander, told Sprague that they would only take orders from their captain and strode off to his cabin where Crescent and the others, who were already armed, arranged themselves so that they shielded him as he picked up a revolver. Perhaps to distract Sprague, Crescent, the duty officer who had decoded the warning message from Bordeaux, announced that he had no intention of leaving and would remain where he was until Capitaine Martin had returned from the *Paris*.

'I have my orders,' repeated Sprague in French, only this time he drew his Webley. 'If you don't leave I'll kill you.' On his right Lieutenant Griffiths and the able seaman, whose name was William Heath, also had their revolvers out.

'Fire if you want,' said Crescent. 'I'm not moving.' At this point Sprague called for reinforcements from the Command Post above him, which contained about ten men under Lieutenant Talbot and Chief Petty Officer Herbert Mott. The petty officer despatched another old salt, the formidable-looking figure of Leading Seaman Albert Webb, the naval equivalent of a sergeant, who had fixed the Lee-Enfield's standard 17-inch bayonet to his rifle and was carrying his ammunition in khaki webbing. Webb took up a position at the foot of the steps he had just descended from the Command Post.

If the French suspected Sprague was bluffing the next thing the Englishman did seemed to confirm it. Instead of shooting, Sprague half turned towards Webb and, pointing to Crescent with his revolver, said loudly in French, 'Shoot this man.' Since Royal Navy officers are not in the habit of giving British sailors orders in a foreign language it seems reasonable to assume that the words were intended for French consumption.

Standing either side of Crescent were Pichevin, who had walked back into the wardroom area from his cabin having finished loading his revolver, and Enseigne de vaisseau Massicot, the French equivalent of a midshipman. A little behind them and leaning against the door of his cabin was Lieutenant de vaisseau Bouillaut, the submarine's gunnery officer in charge of her twin 8-inch guns.

The pipe-smoking Bouillaut, in his late twenties and recently married, was from an old naval family. In a pocket he had stuffed his personal weapon, a small flat .32-calibre nine-shot MAB automatic as carried by French detectives, a pistol naval officers sometimes bought for their personal protection during trips ashore in France's more volatile colonies. Bouillaut decided that Sprague would not tolerate having his bluff called any more than they could 'allow ourselves to be thrown off our ship and threatened with death without reacting'.

The British already had their weapons in their hands but they were there as a reminder of the overwhelming force at their disposal, intended to stop violence rather than start it. It is unlikely that the *Surcouf* boarding party had heard of the firearms discovered in the officers' quarters on the *Paris*. It probably never occurred to them that anybody but the duty officer and his sentries would be armed, which would almost certainly have been the case on a British ship. Above all, it was a good example of the old rule that you should never point a gun at somebody unless you are prepared to use it. When Bouillaut, who seems to have had a duellist's nerve, drew his MAB and started shooting he must have amazed them.

> I took a pace forward and shot at Commander Sprague, Lieutenant Griffiths, the two English sailors and then again on their officers. As I was shooting I had moved to the companionway [the ladder leading up to the Command Post] – that was the moment I was wounded – and I fired at a sailor who,

no doubt kneeling in the Command Post and showing only his steel helmet at the top of the companionway, was shooting at me.

This was Chief Petty Officer Mott, not kneeling but lying on his stomach, looking down into the wardroom and firing .455 bullets as big as musket balls with his 6-inch-barrel revolver which had first been issued to the British Army almost half a century before. These were the first shots exchanged between official representatives of the British and French military in the 125 years since Waterloo.

The sweet scent of cordite filled the *Surcouf*'s stale air and Sprague and Griffiths were both bleeding to death on the wardroom floor. Sprague – who had squeezed off one ineffectual shot as he fell – had collapsed against the door of the captain's cabin after being shot through the neck, in the abdomen and below his right collarbone where a severed main artery was soaking his clothing and the surrounding floor space with blood. Griffiths's fatal wound was in the liver and he had also been shot in a hip and one arm. He had somehow lapsed into unconsciousness almost upright, hanging onto the ladder to the Command Post.

Bouillaut, the man who had started it all, had been lucky. One of Mott's large but low-velocity bullets – possibly made slower by being old ammunition – had travelled down the inside of his right arm, entered his chest and exited off his third rib above his right nipple. Bleeding profusely, he was still able to work both hands and remove his pistol's empty magazine to insert a fresh one. When he looked round he saw, 'there were no English capable of fighting left in the wardroom, and we now all had pistols in our hands.'

But it seems only one other French officer had fired, though, for the moment, he was not visible. In the midst of his own gunfight, Bouillaut had heard more shots, then cries of pain coming from one of the cabins of the Ingénieurs mécaniciens around the wardroom, followed by the clatter of a rifle falling on a steel deck.

Le Nistour had listened as the confrontation between Sprague and Crescent reached boiling point then went into his cabin and picked up his pistol. Daniel was sitting on the edge of his bunk still busy shredding blueprints and manuals. 'Things are getting hot,' said the doctor. The words were hardly out of his mouth when he heard Bouillaut fire the first shots. Perhaps Leading Seaman Webb saw Le Nistour dart back into his cabin and confused him with the man who was doing the shooting; Bouillaut was also standing further back from the other officers and, at the best of times, a submarine's lighting is fairly dim. For whatever reason, Le Nistour had just armed himself when Webb, '*baionette au canon*', charged across the wardroom and burst into his cabin, Able Seaman Heath hard at his heels.

It appears the doctor had a smaller calibre pistol than Bouillaut, possibly one of the popular .25 lady's handbag pistols that Manufacture d'Armes Bayonne made in the inter-war years.

> The English sergeant [Webb] rushes towards us with his fixed bayonet. I fire the whole of my magazine at him. Carried forward by his rush, he falls dead at our feet in front of the washbasin. Unfortunately, he had time to fire and *Ingénieur mécanicien* Daniel, hit in the right shoulder, cries out and collapses. I step over the body of the dead sergeant and go for the English sailor who followed him and seemed to be having trouble with his revolver. I manage to disarm him and with one blow of my fist send him reeling against the curtain which covers the door to *Ingénieur mécanicien* Catherine's cabin. I move forward and with a second, better blow – which dislocates my thumb – I send him rolling at the foot of the companionway to the wardroom, where he lies still.

Le Nistour did not realize it but Heath was not only reeling from his punches. All but one of the eight small-calibre bullets he had pumped at almost touching distance into Webb had passed straight through the leading seaman to hit Heath around his head and shoulders as he crouched behind him struggling to cock his defective Webley. Heath's face was covered in blood from flesh wounds; the only explanation for the lack of serious injury is that the bullets were now so spent they had little force. Meanwhile, in another bizarre example of what can happen when small arms are used at close quarters in the confined space of even a *Surcouf*-sized submarine, it appears that Daniel was not killed by the bullet that hit him in the shoulder but by the dying Webb stabbing him with his bayonet as he fell towards him, still clutching his rifle.

After Daniel and Webb had gone down, all firing ceased and it became apparent to some of the French officers that they had recaptured their wardroom by laying on the kind of carnage that Robert Surcouf himself might have considered pointless.

'I believe you were very wrong to have done that,' Crescent told the bleeding Bouillaut, brushing aside the gunnery officer's protests that if he had not done so Crescent would not be alive to complain about it. But Le Nistour sided with Bouillaut. Only his marksmanship had saved Crescent's life, he said, examining his hero's arm and chest wounds and assuring him that he would live.

The dead and the dying lay where they had fallen amid the blood and the spent cartridge cases. At the end of the wardroom, where they could not be seen from the Command Post, stood Pichevin, the doctor and the other three officers, guns in hand. The enemy would have to venture down if they wished to shoot at them but there was no need to do anything: hopelessly outgunned, the French would be shot to pieces if they tried to get back into the Command Post. Pichevin decided to surrender and shouted up to the English that it was finished. Lieutenant Talbot told them to put their weapons down and come up one at a time as he called them. Only Bouillaut wanted to fight on – 'we can't let them do this to us' – but Pichevin gently prised his MAB police special out of his hand and put it on the wardroom table with the other four pistols. Then he led the way up saying, 'Finis.'

It was not quite over yet. In the Command Post the French officers once again refused to leave the *Surcouf* without receiving a direct order from Capitaine Martin. Since three of the four British casualties had been from the submarine *Thames*, one of them his commander, at this stage Talbot must have been sorely tempted to have these recalcitrants chased up the gangway to the *Paris* with the aid of pickaxe helves and rifle butts. In the end, the impasse was resolved by Crescent suggesting, with Pichevin's consent, that he would go and speak with their captain providing Talbot 'gave his word as an officer' that he could return.

Crescent discovered a resigned Martin on the *Paris*'s rear deck. Shortly afterwards only two French officers remained on the *Surcouf*: Dr Le Nistour was in the sick bay bandaging Bouillaut. 'English sailors kept coming up and asking me to go and see their wounded officers,' he recalled. 'I told them to wait.'

Dunbar-Nasmith and his staff had laid their plans for the seizure of the French ships well. They had even made sure ambulances were available to transport any French seamen discovered in ships' infirmaries to hospital. But they had made one curious omission. Although, in theory at least, they had by no means ruled out resistance to the boarding parties, they had not attached any naval surgeons or medics to deal with casualties. 'After first aid was given it must have been 25 minutes before the doctor reached Commander Sprague,' reported Talbot, obviously incensed by the delay. 'And a further ten minutes to a quarter of an hour before Lieutenant Griffiths was attended to.'

Given the drugs and the surgical procedures of the day, whether more prompt treatment would have saved lives is a moot point. They both had multiple gunshot wounds and were seriously hurt. Dr Le Nistour, who was the last of the French officers to leave the wardroom, thought Griffiths looked dead but he gave Sprague a cursory examination and found him just capable of speech. 'He could only tell me that he had been wounded in the right shoulder. He had also been shot in the abdomen. His lips were beginning to lose colour.'

Talbot's men managed to get Griffiths, who was still alive, up the ladder and into the Command Post where Le Nistour, having attended to Bouillaut, gave the lieutenant a morphine injection and urged his rapid removal to hospital though he knew there was not the slightest hope. He was about to return to the wardroom and see what he could do for Sprague when into the Command Post staggered another British casualty.

Able Seaman Heath, blood streaming from his seven separate bullet wounds in the face, arms and neck, spotted his assailant treating one of the wounded British officers and revealed with a wagging finger and some strong language the doctor's pivotal role in recent events. At first, according to Le Nistour's account, Heath was ignored. Then it became apparent that these were not the ravings of a man in shock. Talbot brusquely ushered the doctor off the submarine and a few minutes later he was replaced by a medical officer from the *Paris*, Dr Adrian Carré.

> An English officer, bareheaded and very agitated, came to the rear deck of the *Paris* calling for a doctor. I went aboard *Surcouf* followed by *Médecin auxiliaire* Caillard. As soon as I reached the bridge I was threatened with a revolver in the very shaky hand of a very agitated midshipman and searched several times. Going below I saw a man I later knew to be Bouillaut, lying on a couch in the infirmary guarded by a sentry holding a revolver. Thinking I had been called for him, I went into the room but could hardly get to say two words before being pushed, revolver against my back, to the Command Post, where I saw on the floor a Lieutenant [Griffiths], clearly on the point of death. I leant over him and saw a bullet's entry hole in the lower costal region. There was nothing I could do. Each time I moved two English officers, who seemed near to panic, threatened me with their guns. 'What do you do? Where do you go?' When I asked where the French doctor was, one of them replied: 'He shot a man.' An English doctor arrived and we were pushed towards the exit, always with a gun in our backs, and carefully searched again before we were able to leave the vessel and get back to *Paris*.

But shortly afterwards Father Buffner, the chaplain on board the old battleship, was allowed onto the *Surcouf* where he gave conditional absolution to Engineer Daniel and Leading Seaman Webb whose bodies were still lying where they had fallen. Three RN doctors were now on board, a surgeon commander and two lieutenant surgeons and they supervised the evacuation of the wounded to Plymouth Naval Hospital. Sprague, who arrived there in the same ambulance as Bouillaut, died the next day. An attempt was made to extract the bullet from Griffiths's liver and he lingered on for another twenty-four hours. Bouillaut would make a complete recovery.

On his way back up the gangplank to the *Paris*, Father Buffner's British escort, visibly moved, whispered to the priest, 'How sad, how sad.'

It was about to get even sadder, for there was no going back.

Chapter Five

Dawn and French Algeria's high summer heat haze hid Oran's headland from the crews of the warships in the sheltered waters of Mers-el-Kébir some 4 miles to the west of the main commercial port. Sleepy young men in white vests stowed their hammocks then, mess tins in hand, lined up for breakfast rolls and coffee. Arab fishing boats painted Spanish-style in gaudy fairground colours headed out to sea. Bugle calls. On a battle cruiser's deck a marine platoon in white gaiters clattered to attention.

Enseigne de vaisseau Jean-Paul Bezard on the new super-destroyer *Volta*, the fastest ship there, was thinking about the day's sporting activities ahead: a water polo match with their sister ship the *Mogador*, then rowing races with teams of gunners, signallers, engine room artificers and stokers taking turns in the skiffs and whalers. Afterwards the more confident swimmers would take a dip and this evening liberty men would go ashore to carouse in the bars of Oran. The important thing was to keep the crew occupied. Some of the reservists were getting restless, especially those who came from the areas the Germans had occupied and had received no recent word from their families. Almost everybody envied the *pieds-noirs* in the crew who had all been discharged on indefinite leave. North Africa's white colonials were already home, last seen stepping ashore with a wave and a cheeky '*Bonnes Vacances*'. At least their absence gave credence to the rumour that the *Volta* would soon be leaving for Toulon because the Germans were insisting that most of the French fleet was gathered there with skeleton crews. Meanwhile, they had their water sports.

Then at about 9.30 a.m. the haze had thinned enough to reveal, anchored about a mile off the jetty, what dozens of binoculars and knowing eyes identified as a British destroyer. Shortly afterwards *Dunkerque* signalled the squadron to general quarters and the rowing teams were called in.

The Royal Navy generally regarded Mers-el-Kébir as a contiguous part of Oran and in speech and despatches rarely bothered to recognize its separate identity. In Arabic it means 'Grand Harbour' and as far as the corsairs were concerned it provided ample room for their slave-oared galleys and galleons and the prizes they seized. In recent years the French had failed to dredge all of it to a depth capable of accommodating twentieth-century warships with easy room to manoeuvre, yet by the second week of the armistice large parts of France's fugitive fleet had gathered there.

Some provision for deeper anchorage had been made by building a high concrete jetty from a spit of land on the western side of the bay, which also served as a breakwater. Along it, at intervals of about 120 yards, Amiral Gensoul had moored by their sterns his five biggest ships, the product of two generations of stylish French naval architecture.

Nearest the shore and the beginning of the jetty was his flagship *Dunkerque*. Next in line was the older battleship *Provence*, in 1918 the flagship of the French fleet, and then *Dunkerque*'s sister ship *Strasbourg* followed by the *Bretagne*, which was the same 1915 vintage as the *Provence* and like her had been extensively refitted. At the seaward end of the jetty was the large seaplane tender *Commandant Teste*,* an alternative to flat-deck aircraft carriers embraced by most major navies in the 1920s. Her float planes had played an important role in the Anglo-French patrols protecting neutral shipping during the Spanish Civil War. Six escort destroyers – *Volta*, *Mogador*, *Terrible*, *Kersaint*, *Tigre* and *Lynx* – were moored from the bows in the shallower waters of Saint Andre, the French name for the old harbour.

Gensoul was not at all happy about the way his ships were deployed but he had no choice. 'The arrangements and the bottom of the Mers-el-Kébir did not lend itself to the mooring of these ships at the front of the jetty, that is to say pointing out to sea,' he would explain in his report to Darlan. This meant that the sixteen 13.5-inch guns of the *Dunkerque* and *Strasbourg*, concentrated in their two forward turrets, were useless because they could not be brought to bear on any threat coming from the open sea. All he could do was order both the *Bretagne* and *Provence* to ensure that one of their two aft turrets was at action stations. That would give him at least four heavy guns pointing in the right direction. In addition there were also coastal batteries at both the western and eastern sides of the bay though, in accordance with the armistice, these were already in the process of removing their breech blocks.

Nonetheless, Gensoul was reluctant to give up all the habits of war acquired over the last ten months of hostilities between France and Germany. Perhaps there were some fears of Italian post-armistice treachery. Rome, despite its tardy and ineffectual appearance on the battlefield, had made no secret of its desire to be tougher on their defeated Mediterranean rival whose virtually intact fleet was a reminder that, even in its shrunken

* Named after Paul Teste, 1917–18 fighter pilot and Aviation Navale pioneer, killed in 1924 flying a prototype single-engined biplane bomber in which he was contemplating an Atlantic crossing.

state, France could be dangerous. Mussolini might yet find a reason to trample over the terms of the armistice, order his navy to take some unilateral action and argue with the Germans about it later. Then there was this other possibility, though so distant, such a small cloud on the horizon that even an experienced sailor might be forgiven for not at first spotting it as the beginning of a storm brewing up from an unseasonal direction.

First came the plight of Vice-amiral René Godfroy's Force X which had been attached to the Royal Navy's Mediterranean fleet under Sir Andrew Cunningham operating out of the British base at Alexandria in Egypt. On the eve of the armistice they were about to participate in an Anglo-French raid on Italian shipping in the Straits of Messina and bombard the Sicilian port of Augusta. Now Godfroy's squadron was stuck in Alexandria. This included the battleship *Lorraine*, his flagship whose 15-inch guns had recently shelled Italian Army positions on the Libyan-Egyptian frontier, three heavy and one light cruiser, three destroyers and a submarine.

Darlan had ordered them to report as soon as possible to Bizerte in French Tunisia but Cunningham, who had a good personal relationship with the widower Godfroy, whose late wife had been a Scot, had sent him an apologetic note explaining that he had been ordered to prevent him sailing. To get out of this impasse they reached a gentleman's agreement: Godfroy promised not to attempt to sail without notifying Cunningham who in turn agreed not to try to seize his ships.

This was not what either of their superiors wanted. On the British side it meant that Cunningham must keep ships either in or just outside Alexandria in order to keep the French bottled up. Darlan was particularly incensed because he feared the Germans would suspect him of trying to finesse conditions and endanger negotiations on the number of ships he might retain in French North African ports. He advised Godfroy that, as a last resort, he should consider fighting his way out, which would have been suicidal, though, apart from more humane considerations, the British might have baulked at the prospect of clogging an important harbour with sunken ships.

There was, or course, no comparison between Gensoul's and Godfroy's position. Gensoul's ships were in Mers-el-Kébir, not a British-controlled port. A recent visit from Admiral Sir Dudley North, who was based in Gibraltar from where he commanded the Royal Navy's North Atlantic Station, had only seemed to emphasize the point. On 24 June, two days after the signing of the armistice with the Germans and the day the whole wretched business had to be gone through again for the benefit of the smirking Italians, North had turned up unannounced at Mers-el-Kébir in the destroyer *Douglas*. Even for Gensoul with his Anglophile sympathies, this was a bit difficult. France was now neutral. It was not supposed to receive the warships of its recent allies in its ports. Nonetheless, Gensoul invited North aboard the *Dunkerque* and gave him twenty minutes.

North had made a blunt request that he should bring his ships to Britain where a warm welcome awaited them and where there was no danger of them being seized by Axis forces. Gensoul gave the same reply that Darlan had already given several times over to Churchill and First Sea Lord Sir Dudley Pound: that French ships would be scuttled rather than allow them to fall into German or Italian hands and that preparations had already been made to blow their bottoms out. Otherwise he must abide by the armistice and there could be no question of his squadron eloping with the Royal Navy.

His amiable visitor had departed, apparently satisfied, and for four days they were left alone. Then twice in the same week a British seaplane flew slow, insolent circles above Gensoul's ships. Once this obvious photo-reconnaissance was done it disappeared towards Gibraltar, Britain's only toehold in a continental Europe that was otherwise hostile, Nazi-occupied or neutral. The French might have chased the trespasser off with a couple of fighters but for the moment the armistice had grounded its aircraft. In any case, La Marine Française was not yet ready to treat British aircraft as hostile intruders.

Then, some forty-eight hours after this seaplane's last appearance, the destroyer HMS *Foxhound* appeared and anchored off the jetty. On board was the Francophile Hooky Holland, Gensoul's 'infinitely courteous, loyal and able collaborator' from their days in the North Atlantic together and, for the last two months, captain of the *Ark Royal*. Holland's aircraft carrier would shortly be coming up behind him on the horizon along with the battleships *Hood*, *Valiant* and *Resolution*, the cruisers *Arethusa* and *Enterprise* and ten destroyers. These ships were all part of Force H, a new formation sent to Gibraltar to plug the yawning gap the French departure had left in the Mediterranean where previously the Royal Navy, with squadrons operating out of Malta and Egypt's Alexandria, had concentrated on its eastern basin.

Force H was under Admiral Sir James Fownes Somerville, whose flagship was named after his ancestor Lord Hood who once burnt down the Toulon dockyard. Somerville's own relations with the French had always been more amicable, most recently at Dunkirk where Admiral Bertram Ramsay and he had worked alongside Amiral Jean Abrial. On the whole, cooperation between the British and French navies, already tried and tested, had been much better than between the two armies where scuffles over alleged queue-jumping were frequent and sometimes reached the point where triggers had already yielded first pressure. When it was all over and 366,000 troops had been landed in England's south coast ports, Darlan praised Ramsay for a 'masterly operation' and the King had received Abrial at Buckingham Palace to offer congratulations and condolences. Seven of the sixteen destroyer-size warships sunk by bombing had been French. The number of British vessels and small craft sunk and damaged was much greater but they were from a much bigger fleet and it was mostly their army they were rescuing.

Dunkirk had marked the beginning of Somerville's return to active service. A month before the outbreak of war it looked as though, aged 57, the admiral's career had come to an end when he was retired with suspected tuberculosis. Admiralty rules were firm. TB was Britain's biggest killer and a carrier on a ship was a time bomb. Regardless of rank you were out. For the navy this was an appalling loss: Somerville was a star, way ahead of his contemporaries in his understanding of radar and naval air power, and had a devoted following among younger officers. Even so, the opinion of two Harley Street specialists that his lung patches were healed had failed at first to impress the Admiralty. Then war brought its own priorities. A vague 'consultancy' role soon saw him in sole charge of the development of naval radar. Still officially on the retired list, he achieved in months what in peacetime would have taken years. If he had done nothing else in the war he would have done enough. But he yearned to get back to sea and the command of Force H was a wonderful prize for a man so recently invalided out of the service.

It was now almost three weeks since, on 13 June, Churchill and his Spitfire escort had taken off from a bomb-cratered airfield at Tours where, on its westward trek from Paris, Paul Reynaud's migrating government had convened the winding-up meeting of the Anglo-French Supreme War Council in the local prefecture. Behind them the British left the Pétainists – united in their scorn and suspicion of the proposed Franco-British Union* – to seal their triumph over the beleaguered Reynaud loyalists who wished to fight on from North Africa. It was about then that Churchill's initial concern over what would happen to the French fleet had started to become an obsession. It was not an unreasonable one.

On the same day that Somerville was preparing to leave Gibraltar, Lieutenant General Sir Alan Brooke had once again been inspecting some of what stood between Britain and a successful German invasion. 'The more I see the nakedness of our defences the more appalled I am!' Brooke, newly knighted for his services at Dunkirk, wrote in his diary. 'Untrained men, no arms, no transport and no equipment... The ghastly part of it is that I feel certain that we can only have a few more weeks left before the Boche attacks.'

As far as Churchill was concerned the fate of Darlan's ships was as crucial to Britain's survival as more barbed wire and land mines on Southern Command's beaches. In the space of a couple of weeks Britain had just suffered the double blow of having the Italians enter the conflict and the

* 'Rarely has so generous a proposal encountered such a hostile reception,' observed Churchill.

French leave it. What if the Germans discovered that, after their losses in Norway, the only way they could pull off an invasion of England would be to requisition all the decent French ships they could find? In the circumstances, French assurances that the Germans had made a solemn pledge not to use its fleet were not all that comforting. Hitler was good at breaking solemn pledges. And the army that had so brilliantly circumvented the Maginot line might well find it even easier to discover a way through Darlan's plans to scuttle his fleet.

Nor, for that matter, were French promises on such matters always kept. There had, for instance, been the question of the Luftwaffe prisoners. Just before the armistice Reynaud had promised Churchill he would send to Britain over 400 shot-down German aircrew in French prison camps, most of them put there by the RAF, according to the Air Ministry. Then suddenly Reynaud was no longer there to keep his promise and, as Churchill put it, 'We had to shoot them down a second time.'

Within the secrecy of a War Cabinet meeting the Prime Minister revealed his current fears with his usual eloquence:

> The addition of the French Navy to the German and Italian Fleets confronted Great Britain with mortal dangers ... who in his senses would trust the word of Hitler after his shameful record and the facts of the hour? ... the Armistice could at any time be voided on any pretext of non-observance. There was in fact no security for us at all. At all costs, at all risks, in one way or another we must make sure that the Navy of France did not fall into the wrong hands.

The Cabinet were in unanimous agreement. 'You are charged with one of the most disagreeable and difficult tasks that a British Admiral has ever been faced with,' Churchill told Somerville as his ships crept out of Gibraltar under cover of darkness. 'But we have complete confidence in you and rely on you to carry it out relentlessly.'

It was a good adieu, carefully worded and equally necessary for both sender and recipient, for it would have been surprising if the Prime Minister's confidence in Somerville was anything like as complete as he said it was. Never in the Royal Navy's long history had one of its admirals gone into battle, certainly not against the French, as reluctantly as this one.

As soon as he arrived in Gibraltar, Somerville's old friend Admiral Sir Dudley North, the last senior officer to have a face-to-face meeting with Gensoul, lost no time in telling him that using force against the French fleet 'should be avoided at all costs'. North arranged a meeting with Holland and the two lieutenant commanders, both lately employed as liaison officers with La Marine Française, who would be working under him as Force H's emissaries when they were lying off Oran and Mers-el-Kébir. They were all convinced that force should be avoided, pointing out that it would transform the French 'from a defeated ally into an active enemy'. Holland, wearing the ribbon of the Légion d'Honneur recently presented to him by Darlan himself for his liaison work, was particularly emphatic.

There can be no doubt that this is exactly what Somerville wanted to hear. He and North and the three former liaison officers were at one in feeling that the politicians in the War Cabinet were asking the Royal Navy to do something that was as dishonourable as it was unnecessary. So much so that he did something that only highly regarded admirals who know their own worth, and don't give a damn, can do on the eve of a major operation: he queried his orders, putting forward the views of his emissaries and proposing that they negotiate without the threat of force. 'I felt that I should be failing in my duty if I did not represent as fully as possible the very strongly expressed views of officers who had been so recently in contact with the French.' Their Lordships at the Admiralty took a long afternoon to digest this then told the distinguished sailor to get on with it.

Its code-name was Operation Catapult and Somerville's orders were simple. He was to deliver Gensoul a note from His Majesty's Government which, after a brief preamble concerning Britain's determination 'to fight to the end' and its need to ensure that 'the best ships of the French Navy are not used against us by our common foe', listed three options:

> (a) Sail with us and continue to fight for victory against the Germans and Italians.
> (b) Sail with reduced crews under our control to a British port. The reduced crews will be repatriated at the earliest moment. If either of these courses is adopted by you, we will restore your ships to France at the conclusion of the war, or pay full compensation if they are damaged.
> (c) Alternatively, if you feel bound to stipulate that your ships should not be used against the Germans or Italians unless these break the Armistice, then sail them with us with reduced crews to some French port in the West Indies – Martinique, for instance – where they can be demilitarised to our satisfaction, or perhaps be entrusted to the United States and remain safe until the end of the war, the crews being repatriated.
>
> If you refuse these fair offers, I must, with profound regret, require you to sink your ships within six hours. Finally, failing the above, I have the orders of His Majesty's Government to use whatever force may be necessary to prevent your ships falling into German or Italian hands.

These orders were far more explicit than 'whatever force may be necessary'. They read: 'It is the firm intention of His Majesty's Government that if the French do not accept one of the alternatives ... their ships must be destroyed.'

*

By the time the mist had cleared and the startled Enseigne de vaisseau Bezard got his first glimpse of *Foxhound*, the British destroyer had already been in the vicinity of the steel mesh torpedo net at the entrance to Mers-el-Kébir harbour since shortly after seven that morning. After they had gone through the preliminaries of identifying themselves and asking permission to enter, Holland had sent a message in French flashed by a Morse signal lamp explaining why he was there. Ostensibly, it was intended for the flagship *Dunkerque* but Holland knew that every duty signaller on every ship in the squadron would pick it up and Gensoul's sailors soon learn what was afoot.

> THE BRITISH ADMIRALTY HAS SENT CAPTAIN HOLLAND TO CONFER WITH YOU – STOP – THE BRITISH NAVY HOPES THAT THEIR PROPOSALS WILL ENABLE YOU AND THE VALIANT AND GLORIOUS FRENCH NAVY TO BE BY OUR SIDE – STOP – IN THESE CIRCUMSTANCES YOUR SHIPS SHOULD REMAIN YOURS AND NO ONE NEED HAVE ANXIETY FOR THE FUTURE – STOP – A BRITISH FLEET IS AT SEA OFF ORAN WAITING TO WELCOME YOU – STOP

This was the message, immediately relayed to Darlan's headquarters, which enabled it – with the time difference – to alert *Surcouf* and the other French warships in southern England that they were likely to be boarded. Meanwhile, at Mers-el-Kébir any hopes Somerville had pinned on the mutual admiration that had developed between Gensoul and Holland during last winter's North Atlantic crossings were soon dashed.

As most British liaison officers were only too aware, formal dealings between the two navies were often dogged by a French awareness that theirs was the smaller fleet with the less successful history and patronizing slights could be detected where none was intended. Gensoul may well have had some affection for Holland but he did not think he was senior enough. 'The first time, they sent me a Vice Admiral [North's visit],' he told one of his staff. 'Today it is a Captain; tomorrow it will be a midshipman.'

Holland knew there would be no tomorrow. They were working against the clock. One way or the other the Admiralty wanted Operation Catapult completed by dusk and Somerville had already decided that, unless they looked on the brink of a breakthrough, his deadline would be 3 p.m.

But Gensoul was as yet unaware of any deadlines and even if he had been it is unlikely to have made any difference. 'I refused to receive Captain Holland and sent a launch with my gunnery officer, *Lieutenant de vaisseau Dufay* who speaks English and, moreover, is a longstanding friend of Captain Holland,' he would tell Darlan.

For the next two and a half hours Holland had to negotiate in an agonizingly slow fashion through Bernard Dufay whom he had got to know well during his time in Paris. Gensoul had given his gunnery officer permission to use his amiral's barge with its polished brass and gilded woodwork. Holland had *Foxhound*'s more workaday destroyer's motor-boat. Their meetings took place at a point between the anti-torpedo boom net and the jetty where the *Dunkerque* was moored with the other big ships.

At their first encounter Dufay read Holland a brief message from Gensoul which repeated the assurances given Admiral North that, 'In no case will French ships fall undamaged into the hands of the Germans and Italians.' For good measure Dufay told Holland that 'in no case' could be read as, 'any time, anywhere, any way and without further orders from the French Admiralty'. However, if this was not good enough, having been presented with an ultimatum, 'French ships will use force to defend themselves.'

According to Dufay, Holland took the last part of Gensoul's reply 'as if it had been addressed to him personally' and confessed that he himself found the British note, 'somewhat maladroit in substance and form'. He gave Dufay the impression that he was unsure of himself, 'hesitant and pale-faced, perspiring heavily' and despite his normal fluency 'unable to find French words'. Diffidence and self-deprecation are perhaps very English traits, especially if the Englishman wants something badly enough, and when Dufay reported back to Gensoul he seems to have misinterpreted them, for it made him think 'there was still a possibility of further negotiations'.

Holland pleaded to be allowed a personal audience with Gensoul, saying it was imperative they met face to face. But Dufay insisted that this was impossible and Holland settled for handing over a sealed envelope and said he would wait for a reply. The envelope contained a typed copy of Somerville's 'three fair offers' and expressed his 'profound regret' for the awful consequences that would follow if none of them was taken up.

The barge went away to return some forty minutes later with a written reply from Gensoul scrawled in pencil on the kind of printed signal pads officers in both navies used for writing radio messages. Gensoul reiterated the assurances given to Admiral North: French warships would not be allowed to fall into German or Italian hands; but he warned that 'this veritable ultimatum' the British had delivered could only be answered by meeting 'force with force'.

Holland responded by crossing over to the barge and asking Dufay to 'discuss the matter as old friends'. Then, once seated around its cabin table, the emissary played what he evidently regarded as his ace in the hole. First he persuaded Dufay to hand over to his amiral a typed copy of what he had intended to say at the audience Gensoul had declined to grant him. It began with a bold assertion that only two days before, the worst suspicions of the British government had been confirmed 'beyond all doubt'. The Axis was preparing – 'as soon as a favourable opportunity occurred' – to seize the French Navy. 'This intended action is a dastardly trick which reacts as much against us as it does against you.' The allegation was quite untrue but so glaringly unsourced that it was probably hoped that the French would assume it was based on decrypts of German naval codes, for they knew the British had enjoyed some success with these during the Norwegian campaign.

Certainly, the second thing Holland had to say to Dufay gave the impression that they had not lost their skills in that department.

> I tackled him on the question of Admiral Darlan's hands being tied . . . then asked when they last had a signal from Darlan? He said a couple of days ago. I asked if it had the special code word on it? He seemed surprised at my knowing this and said that Darlan had not used it for some days. I pointed out the whole of the foregoing pointed to Darlan's hands being tied and begged him to stress this point of view, which was ours, to the Admiral. He was evidently impressed and returned to the *Dunkerque* at 10.50 a.m. with my typescript.

Twenty minutes later Dufay was back, this time accompanied by Capitaine de vaisseau Danbé, Gensoul's Chief of Staff. But if for a moment the sight of this fresh face raised Holland's spirits he was about to be disappointed. Danbé delivered another handwritten note. It made no demands to see proof of Axis plots or dastardly tricks. It made no mention of them whatsoever. It simply said that Amiral Gensoul could only confirm what he had said in his previous note and would defend himself by all the means at his disposal. Meanwhile, he wished to point out to Admiral Somerville that 'the first shot fired against us will have the result of immediately putting the whole French fleet against Great Britain'. As Holland and his team made their way out of the inner harbour and back towards the *Foxhound* deck awnings were being furled, funnel covers brought down and steam raised: the French were preparing to sail. Curious sailors looked at the little boat below them, the large white ensign on its stern beginning to pick up the slight breeze. Most of them, officers included, still had little idea what it was all about.

On the deck of the battleship *Bretagne* Lieutenant Jean Boutron, a merchant navy reservist who was in charge of the forward gunnery control post, encountered his captain for the first time that morning.

'They're mad – absolutely mad,' said Capitaine de vaisseau Le Pivain by way of greeting.

'Who's mad?' enquired Boutron.

Le Pivain said that the English were mad to think that they'd join them and stomped off. It was the first Boutron had heard about it.

He was not surprised Le Pivain had not lingered to discuss the matter. Like most of the senior officers the captain had accepted the armistice. It was a catastrophe but he accepted it: duty and discipline required nothing less. But aboard the *Bretagne*, Boutron was one of its most outspoken critics and Le Pivain thought that, for the sake of morale, he ought to shut up.

'But we are not beaten. Do you feel beaten, with our *Bretagne* intact?' Boutron had asked when they first received Darlan's outline of the armistice terms. 'The *Provence* alongside, is she beaten? And the *Dunkerque* and *Strasbourg* – brand flaming new and full of guns and shells – are they beaten? And the rest of the Navy? In any case, I am not beaten. And I'm not going along with this.'

It was sweltering on deck. After his brush with the captain Boutron went down to the officers' wardroom for lunch. Somebody told him that he had seen a squadron signal from the *amiral* announcing that the English had presented an 'unacceptable ultimatum' and force would be met by force. Nonetheless, *Bretagne* was not yet at her highest state of readiness or they would not have been allowed to gather there, scuttles open and ceiling propeller fans churning the cigarette smoke.

The wardroom was packed. Everybody who was not on duty wanted to be there, for, like a rabbit out of a hat, the mess president had produced an important guest. It was none other than Lieutenant de vaisseau Bernard Dufay, the man who knew almost as much about what was going on as Gensoul himself and normally took his lunch three ships down the jetty at the *Dunkerque*. After a hurried meal Dufay gave them most of what he knew of the morning's events: his comings and goings with his old friend Holland; the British fears that their excellent ships would fall into German hands; their determination to sink them if they did not agree to one of the options on offer. Just before he came to lunch Holland had flashed a message saying that Amiral Godfroy, who commanded the French squadron at Alexandria from the battleship *Lorraine*, had agreed to demobilize his ships in that port.

When Dufay finished speaking there was silence. Then somebody asked when the ultimatum would expire. He told them Somerville had given them until three o'clock, about two hours' time. Originally it had been 1.30. Boutron suggested that scuttling might be worth considering and there was an immediate outcry. Didn't he realize this would contravene the armistice which stated that French ships must return to France? 'The bloody Armistice, we haven't finished paying for it,' Boutron told the table. 'It's only just beginning. If the English behave like swine today, we also behaved like swine by capitulating to Hitler.'

Uproar. Howls of protest and repeated pleas for order from the mess president until the din slowly subsided. Vietnamese stewards from French Indochina began serving coffee. Shortly afterwards came news that might well have brought orders for large *digestifs* to go with them. British aircraft were trying to bottle them up by dropping mines near the harbour entrance.

Ark Royal's Swordfish biplanes had laid five, all of them seabed magnetic mines fused to rupture a ship's nether parts as her steel hull passed over them. This was Somerville's first hostile action against the French and he hoped it would be his last. Somehow he had to convince Gensoul that this outrageous business was not a bluff.

The midday sun had made the guard rails on his flagship the *Hood* untouchable and eyelids heavy. Most of Force H had snatched only three or four hours' uninterrupted sleep since leaving Gibraltar the night before. Nor had they altogether adjusted to July in the Mediterranean. On the *Hood*, hardly two weeks out of Scotland, the officers' wardroom lunch had been a piping-hot stew followed by rock cakes. For the men, served at their action stations, there was hot soup and great doorsteps of sandwiches filled with the canned bully beef they called 'corned dog'. Sailors over twenty could wash it down with their daily tot of free rum British seamen had drunk since well before Nelson's time. The 200 or so teenagers on board got lime juice.

Among these unrummed ones was signaller Ted Briggs who had joined the navy as a 15-year-old boy signaller at the shore establishment HMS *Ganges*, survived its spartan training and after almost a year on the *Hood* was still eight months short of his eighteenth birthday. Briggs, who worked on the flag deck above the bridge where the yeoman of signals jotted down *Foxhound*'s heliographed Morse, was watching Somerville pace up and down like a caged tiger apparently oblivious to the heat. The teenager thought he was looking at a man who was not about to wait much longer.

At 1415 the *Foxhound*'s projector started to relay another message from Gensoul.

> I HAVE NO INTENTION OF PUTTING TO SEA – STOP – I HAVE TELEGRAPHED MY GOVERNMENT AND AM AWAITING A REPLY – STOP – YOU SHOULD NOT BELIEVE THE SITUATION TO BE BEYOND HOPE – STOP

Somerville replied:

> PASS TO GENSOUL – STOP – IF YOU ACCEPT THE TERMS HOIST A LARGE CHEQUERED FLAG AT THE MASTHEAD OTHERWISE I MUST OPEN FIRE AT 1500.

Then twenty minutes before the deadline was due to expire, and about one and a half hours after the mines were dropped, there came another signal from the *Dunkerque*:

AM PREPARED PERSONALLY TO RECEIVE YOUR REPRESENTATIVE FOR HONOURABLE DISCUSSIONS – STOP

Somerville's instincts told him the French were playing for time. 'But I decided that it was quite possible Admiral Gensoul only now realised that it was my intention to use force if necessary.'

So once again, perhaps against his better judgement, the deadline was extended. The new time was 1730. Meanwhile Captain Holland returned to *Foxhound*'s lowered motorboat and set off for Mers-el-Kébir which was now about 7½ miles away because the destroyer's captain, expecting that hostilities were imminent, had thought it prudent not to make it too easy for the harbour's coastal batteries. It was estimated that it would take Holland about an hour to get there.

Gensoul was hoping for the best and preparing for the worst. The best was that Somerville was indeed carrying out an elaborate bluff intended to make him scuttle his ships. All he had to do was keep his nerve and the British would sail away because, however much the armistice had changed the world, they had never intended to sink his squadron regardless of the cost in French lives. But if the worst was the case, it was his intention to spin out the talks long enough 'to gain the advantage of darkness' and escape to Toulon. Already he was in a better position to fight his way out than he had been when *Foxhound* first turned up at at his front door.

For by the end of the morning the breech blocks had been restored to the coastal batteries Santon and Canestal; at the last count forty-two aircraft had been rearmed and were ready for take-off; tugs were standing by to help move his big ships smartly away from the jetty if he ordered them to put out to sea. And with this in mind, some of the big buoys that held up a section of the steel anti-submarine net had been sunk with machine-gun fire in order to widen the passage out of the harbour and their chances of avoiding Somerville's mines.

Everything that could be done had been done. For the 6,000 or so men under his command all that remained was to sit at their action stations and wait. For those among them who had longed for the chance to show what the French Navy could do against the Germans there was an exquisite irony about their plight that made it even more insufferable.

In the engine room of the *Dunkerque*, Ingénieur mécanicien de première classe Xavier Grall had swapped a safe posting with a Brest coastal battery within commuting distance from home for a berth on the battle cruiser where his close friend Albert Borey, another Ingénieur mécanicien, was serving. His wife Herveline had been four months pregnant with their third child when he went away. As it happened, *Dunkerques*'s deployment with Gensoul's Force de Raid had enabled him to be back for the birth of their son Hervé on 30 March 1940. Then he sailed away again. Herveline had known it would be like this when she married him: they both came from naval families living close to Brest in the small port of Landévennec in Brittany's Cape Finistère, a community sustained by patriotism and the Catholic Church.

Since the armistice Grall and Borey both found it hard to believe that the wonderful navy Darlan had built up was about to be put into mothballs before it had even had the chance to use its big guns. For months they had been trying to imagine what it would be like to go into action against the *Scharnhorst* or one of the other German raiders they had been trying to hunt down with HMS *Hood*. If they had ever sighted one of them *Dunkerque*'s speed would have certainly compensated for their slightly smaller guns as they overtook their British ally, a 20-knot plodder from the same era as the *Bretagne*: 100,000 horsepower of beautiful Rateau-Bretagne turbines closing in at 30–plus knots with all eight 13-inch guns blazing over their bows, the enemy presented with the narrowest possible target because, unlike the *Hood* with her old-fashioned two turrets fore and two turrets aft, they did not need to turn to deliver a full broadside.

Of course, they both realized that fate was not always kind to even the best designed ships and when disaster struck it was often the men two decks below in the engine rooms who found themselves in the most trouble. On Sunday, at their last meeting in Borey's slightly roomier cabin, they had found themselves debating whether ingénieurs Mécaniciens should carry side arms at action stations. They agreed that, as a last resort, a concealed weapon might be useful to stem panic. But when Borey suggested that, if all hope had gone, a pistol provided a less painful exit for both himself and others if they chose it, Grall was horrified. 'If God judged that my salvation depended on this final trial,' he told his friend, 'I will kneel down and pray whilst I wait for death.'

Unlike its head, the navy as a whole was still strongly churched. Spiritual adviser aboard the *Bretagne* was Father de Gueuser who was also chaplain for the *Provence*, the two older ships making up one division of Gesoul's Force de Raid and the newer *Strasbourg* and *Dunkerque* the other. The priest was evidently of the liberal kind, for he was friendly with Jean Boutron and equally opposed to the armistice. In the course of the afternoon, seething with excitement, he told Boutron of a row he had just had with Contre-amiral Bouxin who commanded the 2nd Light Squadron of super-destroyers and flew his flag on the *Mogador*.

It was well known that Bouxin did not approve of the armistice either. But as a French amiral, he felt he must obey Gensoul who must obey Darlan who must obey Maréchal Pétain. Personal feelings, Bouxin explained, took second place. He reminded the priest that the navy was the only part of the armed forces that had remained intact, unbeaten and firmly behind its leaders. 'On no account can we break up this unity which could play a large role in averting the disintegration of the country.'

At this point de Gueuser felt he had listened to quite enough platitudes.

'Amiral – what can I say to you – God forgive me – you haven't got the balls.'

Bouxin, struck dumb, had pointed to the door. Then slowly, through a red haze, the power of speech had returned.

'You – priest – fuck off – now!'

And de Gueuser, like some scolded court jester, had scampered away to inform his friend Boutron of Bouxin's foul-mouthed defeat.

Map 3 Mers el-Kébir, 3 July 1940

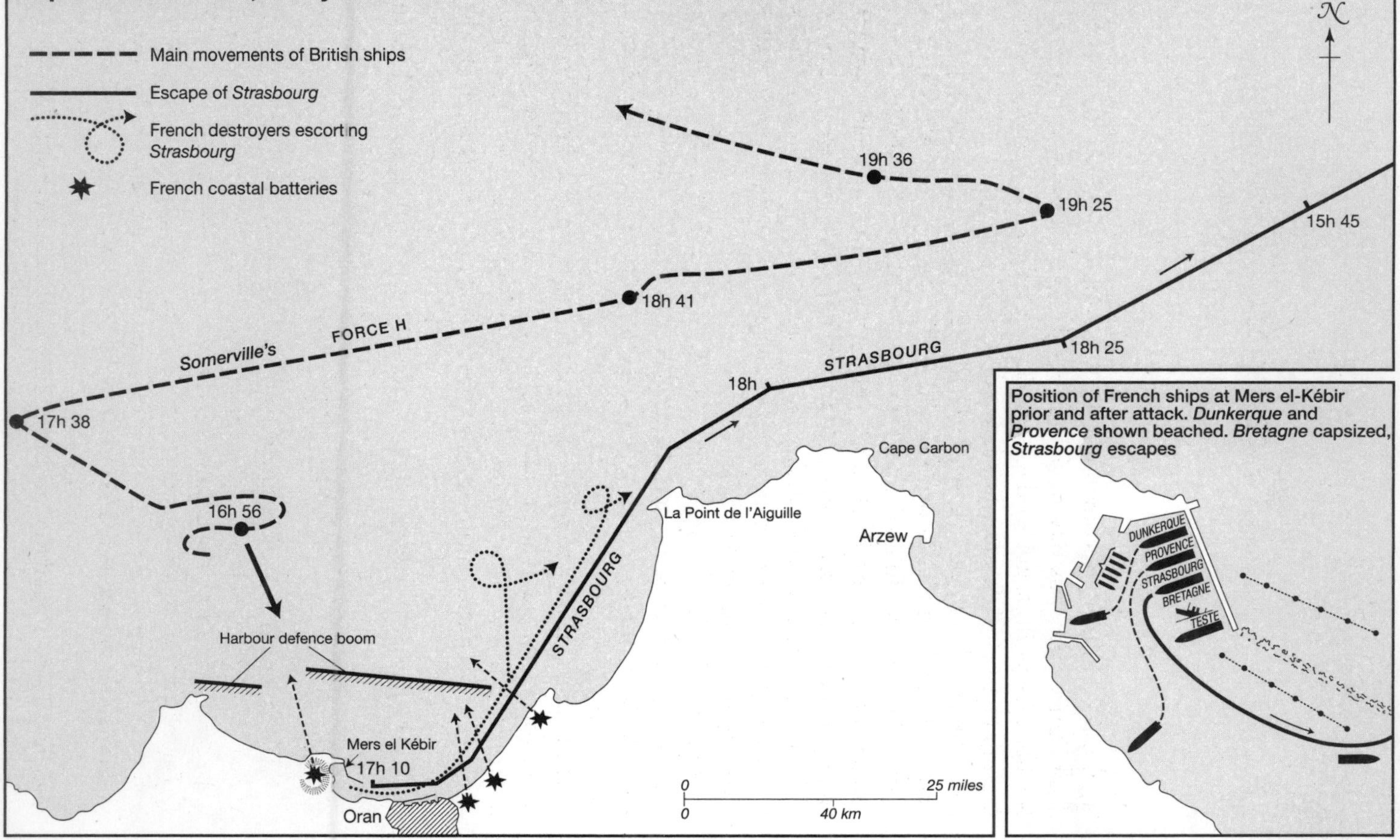

Main movements of British ships
Escape of *Strasbourg*
French destroyers escorting *Strasbourg*
French coastal batteries
N
Somerville's FORCE H
17h 38
16h 56
18h 41
19h 36
19h 25
15h 45
18h 25
18h
STRASBOURG
STRASBOURG
Harbour defence boom
Mers el Kébir
17h 10
Oran
La Point de l'Aiguille
Cape Carbon
Arzew
0
25 miles
0
40 km
Position of French ships at Mers el-Kébir prior and after attack. *Dunkerque* and *Provence* shown beached. *Bretagne* capsized, *Strasbourg* escapes
DUNKERQUE
PROVENCE
STRASBOURG
BRETAGNE
TESTE

Chapter Six

Hooky Holland, accompanied by Lieutenant Commander Geoffrey Davies who was one of the former liaison officers with the French Mediterranean fleet, got to the *Dunkerque* at about 4.15 p.m. : seventy-five minutes before Somerville's latest deadline.

Passing the boom gate vessel they had been smartly saluted by her crew and, just inside the anti-torpedo and mine net, the amiral's barge was waiting for them. Holland and Davies were beckoned aboard and the three-man crew of the *Foxhound*'s motorboat – one of them a signaller equipped with an Aldis lamp – told to remain where they were. It seemed that Gensoul wished to limit the number of prying British eyes admitted to his squadron's inner sanctum. As they approached the flagship, Holland observed that most of the French ships were already in a state of advanced readiness. 'All director range finders in tops of battle ships, with the exception of *Strasbourg*, were trained in the direction of our fleet. Tugs were ready by the sterns of each battleship. Guns were trained fore and aft.'

Holland and Davies were piped aboard the *Dunkerque*, the high-pitched shriek of a bosun's whistle alerting all the crews along the jetty that important persons were visiting the flagship. But once they were aboard Holland noticed that, although there were plenty of ratings on deck, there was 'a marked lack of officers'. Among the few to be seen was a stiff-backed Capitaine de vaisseau Danbé, the Chief of Staff, who led them into the amiral's cabin and a greeting of such *froideur* that Holland was left in no doubt of Gensoul's temper.

> He commenced by stating that he had only consented to see me because the first shot fired would not only alienate the whole French navy but would be tantamount to a declaration of war between France and Great Britain. That if our aim was to ensure that the French fleet was not used against us, the use of force would not achieve this aim. We might sink his ships but we should find the whole of the rest of the French navy actively against us.

Gensoul also argued that mining the harbour entrance had already ruled out any possibility of him accepting any of the options offered other than scuttling. Since he had never intended contravening the armistice, even when he could have reasonably pleaded resisting Somerville's overwhelming force would incur terrible French losses, this was entirely academic. He had not even informed Darlan about the third option to sail to the French West Indies or the United States, saying merely that the British had offered: join us or sink your ships or we'll do it for you.

Now he repeated what he had first told Dudley North and what he had been telling Somerville all day: if the Axis attempted to break the armistice by taking over his squadron then, and only then, would he sink them. To which Holland gave what had become the standard British response:

> I explained most carefully to him that the British government were unable to accept this as a guarantee that the ships would not fall into enemy hands ... Already I said, Admiral Somerville had on his own responsibility disobeyed orders by not taking action within the time laid down, thus showing his desire to avoid the use of force if this were possible. It was at this stage, I think, that Amiral Gensoul began to think that force might really be used.

This must have been the case because Gensoul's next move was to show Holland a message from Darlan dated 24 June 1940 – two days after the signing of the armistice. Almost immediately Holland spotted that among the contingency plans laid down to prevent the French fleet falling into enemy hands it mentioned the possibility of sailing the fleet to the USA or Martinique, France's Caribbean colony. At last Holland glimpsed a ray of hope. This was close to the third option the British had offered if only the French could be persuaded that between scuttling and being destroyed by the British, internment in the Americas was the logical third choice. It was now 5 p.m. – thirty minutes before the deadline expired.

> Admiral Gensoul however remained stubborn, and would not give way any further, except to state that steps had been taken to commence the reduction of crews by demobilising a certain number of reservists. I again pointed out Admiral Somerville must obey his orders and use force unless the terms were accepted to our satisfaction immediately, to which Amiral Gensoul reiterated that the first shot fired would alienate our two navies and do untold harm to us ... Asked if he had received any answer from his government to the message he had sent that morning, he rather unconvincingly replied that the answer was 'resist by force'.

About now Somerville, back on the *Hood*, received a message from the Admiralty in London warning him to 'settle matters quickly or you will have reinforcements to deal with'. Wireless intercepts had indicated that a squadron of cruisers was on its way from Toulon.

Somerville promptly sent a message to Gensoul:

> IF ONE OF THE BRITISH PROPOSALS HAS NOT BEEN ACCEPTED BY 1730, I SAID 1730, IT WILL BE NECESSARY THAT I SINK YOUR SHIPS.

By the time Gensoul was showing Holland this message in his cabin they were fifteen minutes away from the deadline. Holland, desperate for another stay of execution, replied directly through one of the *Dunkerque*'s signallers offering his few crumbs of progress:

> ADMIRAL GENSOUL SAYS CREWS BEING REDUCED AND IF THREATENED BY THE ENEMY WOULD GO TO MARTINIQUE OR USA BUT THIS IS NOT QUITE OUR PROPOSITION – STOP – CAN GET NO NEARER.

Before they parted Gensoul gave Holland another pencil-written note which, though unsigned and undated, was by far the most conciliatory of the day. It listed four points and appeared to be an attempt to back up Holland's last plaintive signal, even starting with a kind of apology.

> 1. The French Fleet cannot do otherwise than apply the clauses of the Armistice – on account of the consequences which would be borne by Metropolitan France. 2. Formal orders have been received, and these orders have been sent to all Commanding Officers, so that if, after the Armistice, there is a risk of the ships falling into enemy hands they would be taken to the USA or scuttled. 3. These orders will be carried out. 4. Since yesterday, 2nd July, the ships now at Oran and Mers-el-Kébir have begun their demobilisation (reduction of crews). Men belonging to North Africa have been disembarked.

The British emissaries left the *Dunkerque* at 5.25 p.m. to farewells from Gensoul which were markedly warmer than their reception had been. 'Even at that stage I do not believe that he was certain that fire would be opened,' recalled Holland.

Before they boarded the amiral's barge he told Danbé, the Chief of Staff, that they had a signaller aboard their motorboat 'if they had anything to communicate'. As they moved away from the flagship buglers were calling action stations but Holland noted that large numbers of sailors were still on the upper decks of the battleships as if they had difficulty in taking it seriously. The officer of the watch on the bow of the *Bretagne*, the last but one ship in line along the jetty, saluted smartly as they went by. In his armoured range-finding eyrie above him Lieutenant Boutron was thinking that the only probable ending was that they would all be massacred.

It was 5.35 p.m. by the time the amiral's barge reached *Foxhound*'s motorboat and Holland and Davies transferred. They were well clear of the net defences and about a mile to seaward when at 5.54 p.m. – twenty-four minutes after Somerville's latest deadline – they heard the first shots.

Almost directly above the *Hood*'s guns on the flag deck a deafened Briggs, who had just helped hoist the red and white open fire signal, felt as if his ears had been 'sandwiched between two manhole covers'. The older battleships *Resolution* and *Valiant*; which had not fired their main armament in earnest since 1918, started the bombardment. Twenty seconds later, with a loud ting-ting of her firing bell, the *Mighty Hood* joined in. In all twenty-four 15-inch guns were hurling shells weighing almost 2,000 pounds: about the same weight as a small car and in 1940 about four times heavier than the most commonly used RAF bomb. Briggs saw 'high cascading water spouts' raised to the north of the harbour. For a moment he wondered if this was all it was going to be, a few warning shots. Then the second salvo fell right among Gensoul's Force de Raid, gouging great chunks of concrete out of the jetty to which they were moored and flinging them onto the nearby decks.

Somerville had positioned Force H north-west of Mers-el-Kébir so that it was firing over the spit of land from where the jetty started and along the line of big ships. This way overshoots, as Briggs had seen, were falling in the sea north of the harbour and reducing the chances of casualties among the white colonialist community whose white stucco homes, cafés and churches made the north African coastline look little different from Mediterranean France. They were at maximum visibility range. Through powerful optics Somerville's crews could just about make out the masts and antennae of Gensoul's ships. On the *Bretagne*, which had the *Strasbourg* and *Commandant Teste* either side of it, Boutron was sweating it out in his fire control turret:

> There is a sudden loud explosion close by. A dull thud; it has not hit us, but I'm sure it was not far away. I take a quick look: salvoes are landing beyond the jetty, there is also a lot of dust; I think the jetty got hit. The shell was ranged on us, but just a little too much to the left as seen from HMS *Hood*. The bastards will correct their aim and then it will be us. The *Strasbourg* is already moving, slowly going forward. I think we shall go last, after the other three battleships. It's going to be a long wait. The shelling is now intense, but it seems to me that it is still falling on the jetty, or beyond it. And, suddenly, it is not the jetty, but us ... our stern got it ... *Bretagne* vibrates all over, trembling under the blow which I felt go through me. Towards the stern – but where? There's no time to start thinking, another blow, even stronger, and an even more violent trembling of the ship – immediately followed by another. Now it is two shells that have hit

us, or something has exploded following the first! It's still towards the back, but perhaps a little closer to me ... I try to think where they could have landed, but from my little hole I can't see much. Enormous white clouds hide the *Strasbourg* from me.

It is not clear whether Boutron's white clouds were the geysers raised by near misses or steam. Perhaps a mixture because *Strasbourg* was beginning to move away. Her commander, Capitaine de vaisseau Collinet, had had his crew standing by so that, without waiting for orders from Gensoul, they could cast off and start engines as soon as he heard the first shot. If *Dunkerque*, her sister ship, was not quite so well prepared it was probably because Gensoul was aboard and for a long time Gensoul had believed that the British were bluffing. It was inevitable that Capitaine de vaisseau Sanguin, like many a commander before him whose vessel has been selected as the squadron's flagship, had to put up with a certain amount of back seat driving from his resident admiral. Now he was waiting for the word to slip his moorings and go.

All the armoured hatches had been sealed. In the engine and boiler rooms, poised for the start signal, Ingénieur mécanicien en chef Egon, Xavier Grall, another ingénieur mécanicien named Quentel and the 120 or so ratings and petty officers they commanded could hear only distant echoes of the gunfire above them. But the vibrations that had begun to shake the ship at regular intervals told them that at least some of their guns had swivelled to starboard and were engaging the English by firing blindly over the Mers-el-Kébir spit.

At last the order came down the voice pipe from the bridge: 'Fifty revolutions both sides.' Four Rateau turbines started up. Then, almost simultaneously, the *Dunkerque* was hit by the first of four 15-inch shells – a half salvo from one of Somerville's three battleships. Whoever had made the final decision on the bridge had left it just too late.

In that semi-automated age, even on a ship as modern as the *Dunkerque*, men were mixed in with machinery in a way that would become unthinkable long before the century ended. The four armour-piercing shells (one of which failed to explode though it still did a great deal of damage) killed 180 men on the battle cruiser including five officers: about 12 per cent of her crew. Well over half the dead were among the artificers, stokers and electricians. In one section those who survived a scalding cloud of steam were incinerated when engine oil spilling from damaged tanks caught fire.

Some, the lucky ones, died instantly in the havoc wreaked by the third shell that exploded in the medical store and blew a gaping hole in the starboard side. En route it had detonated a conveyor belt of shell charges for one of the two smaller 5.1-inch turrets, set fire to the air-conditioning plant that cooled the engine room and plunged the vessel into darkness by shattering the major electricity control panel. 'All the men in that section were shredded to ribbons,' said a damage report, 'their charred remains buried under an enormous heap of ironwork which completely covered the access hatch to the engine room.'

Immediately below this carnage, locked in a dark oven that was warming by the minute, Grall was telling his artificers not to panic. Above them the fire had developed enough heat to start melting down the four large aluminium trunks that delivered cool air to the engine room and even ignited its molten flow. An acrid yellow smoke that watered eyes and smarted throats began to drift into the engine compartment. The only exit not blocked by debris was the port escape hatch but, as they climbed up towards it, the yellow smoke got thicker and breathing harder.

Some gave up and went back down where they could find somewhere that was marginally cooler and lie down. Despair and stubborn courage were in touching distance. A middle-aged quartermaster screamed for his mother while a chief stoker of the same vintage named Pierre Le Gall calmly tended the boiler which allowed *Dunkerque*'s one working engine to take them away from the jetty, perhaps even away from the shells.

About fifteen forced themselves up to the port hatch through the smoke only to discover, in a panic of pounding fists, that it refused to open. Ingénieur mécanicien en chef Egon and Ingénieur mécanicien Quentel restored order and raised the hatch an inch at a time using the emergency pump the others had overlooked. Egon called to Grall to join them. But Grall was surrounded by cursing, sobbing, half-suffocated men, stumbling about the narrow engine room walkways in the dark too disorientated by heat and fumes to try to get back up and begging him not to abandon them. 'No, lad, I won't leave you,' he was heard to tell one young sailor. Then the emergency hatch went down and could only be opened by being pumped up again from the inside. Grall began to climb back up but at some point he lost a shoe which fell to the bottom of the companionway.

The *Bretagne* had taken several more hits and at least one magazine had exploded, but cocooned behind his armour plate and with his communications to the bridge down Boutron had no idea of any of this. He stepped out of his fire control turret for a better look but there was so much black smoke, particularly towards the stern, that it was hard to tell how serious the damage was. Then he noticed people were abandoning ship.

> I look left and see men come up onto the deck and jump into the water ... How will the crew in the engine-rooms, the boilers, manage to get up through the flames and the smoke? ... And then, suddenly, the ship begins to list more rapidly. I feel almost relieved: we'll capsize before we blow up! There will perhaps be fewer casualties because, if we explode, even those already in the water will not survive. The ship is now turning. It appears to

> be cracking, loses its balance ... Holding on tight, almost upright on the guard rail which is falling rapidly, I see to port my range finder being snatched by the water whilst to starboard the deck is turning towards me ... Then it was the bubbling waters which swept me away, and the feeling of being sucked down to the bottom. It was all over. I did not lose consciousness. I could barely see anything, it was completely black in the middle of a sea of fuel oil. I thought I was in a whirlpool and that the *Bretagne*, completely overturned, was pushing me down ... It didn't seem worthwhile to struggle! An immense and complete indifference took hold of me. A quick thought of my mother and my son, that was all.

In the space of ten minutes Somerville's three battleships fired 36 salvos of 15-inch shells – a total of 288 rounds or 96 a ship – after which he called a halt in order to 'give the French an opportunity to abandon their ships and thus avoid further loss of life'. By now Mers-el-Kébir was wreathed in black oil smoke and the crews of the spotting *Swordfish* from *Ark Royal* were finding it difficult to see what the bombardment had done. All Somerville knew for certain was that, three minutes after it began, a tremendous explosion had started a column of smoke several hundred feet high. One of his spotters thought it had been caused by the 'blowing up of a battleship of the *Bretagne** class'. Another, smaller explosion, seemed to mark the destruction of a destroyer.

This would turn out to be the *Mogador*, flagship of Bouxin's 2nd Light Division, her stern amputated by a 15-inch shell which detonated all the depth charges she carried for her anti-submarine role. From her complement of 228 crew thirty-seven were killed and several seriously wounded, though the truncated ship – cut off at a watertight compartment and perfectly afloat – would be towed back to her anchorage at Saint André. Nearby were the *Dunkerque* and *Provence* who had both limped away from the jetty to run themselves aground there. The *Provence*, which had returned fire from her aft 13.5-inch turrets over both the *Dunkerque* and the Mers-el-Kébir spit, was also badly damaged in her stern where a serious fire had only gone out when that part of the ship slipped under water. But unlike the *Dunkerque*, casualties were light: her single fatality the gunnery officer who had supervised the return fire.

The only sign of the *Bretagne* was a large and spreading blot of glutinous fuel oil studded with various bits of wreckage, on some of which the clinging forms of treacled men could be discerned. The old battleship had blown up and then capsized with the loss of 1,079 lives. Among the 180

* A class of warship is named after the first one of that type to be built, in this case the *Bretagne*. It was known that another of her class, the *Provence*, was in Mers-el-Kébir but they were almost identical and it would have been impossible to tell which was which from the air.

survivors was her commander Le Pivain and Lieutenant Jean Boutron, another anonymous tar baby recognized only by his wristwatch by the doctor friend who pumped and pummelled at his unconscious form until Boutron had at last brought up enough of the oil he had swallowed to live.

By an enormous fluke, *Bretagne*'s immediate neighbours along the jetty, the big seaplane carrier *Commandant Teste* and the battle cruiser *Strasbourg* escaped the initial bombardment almost unscathed with only minor damage from shrapnel and nasty bits of concrete. *Strasbourg* then went on to make her own luck.

Bouxin, the amiral the priest had needled for not following the dictates of his heart over the armistice, had been leading the dash for the open sea in the *Mogador* when the 15-inch shell brought his personal participation to an abrupt end and left him marooned on his propellerless flagship. Directly behind the truncated *Mogador* came the other two super-destroyers of the 2nd Light, *Volta* and *Le Terrible*. All Bouxin could do was watch and wave them God speed as they swerved around him like horses in a steeplechase, working their engines up to 40-plus knots.

From the *Volta* Bezard, the officer who had started the day with water sports on his mind, looked across at the *Mogador* and saw her bareheaded second-in-command standing with a fire extinguisher in his hands among the twisted and blackened steel plate that marked his ship's new stern. Life-jacketed corpses were in the water but most of the crew had survived and gave them a cheer as they passed, the dead men bobbing in their wake. From his undamaged bridge Bouxin watched the *Volta* with his heart in his mouth, for he reckoned that, even with the extra leeway gained by Gensoul's bright idea to remove part of the torpedo net, they were too close to the magnetic mine cluster the British had dropped. Sure enough, the water suddenly stirred and welled up under her stern.

'The *Volta*'s done for!' shouted Bouxin and, for a moment, so it seemed. But the mine was too deep and the *Volta* too fast. Undamaged, the destroyer roared on, still under fire and shooting back, as was *Le Terrible* behind her, their combined sixteen 5.5-inch guns firing blindly at the smoke screen the English had laid around their ships. Smoke screens would soon become redundant because there was not much more than two hours' decent light left. As soon as it was dark, *Volta*'s Capitainc dc frégate Jaquinet, temporary commander of the 2nd Light now that Bouxin could do no more than organize a tow for the stricken *Mogador*, planned to double back with *Le Terrible* and empty her thirty-eight torpedo tubes at Somerville's ships.

Then, to his delight, out of the smoke haze behind them, appeared the *Strasbourg*, all eight of her 13.5-inch guns blazing and apparently intact, though making a lot of extra black smoke through a funnel holed by the shrapnel at the jetty. Behind her was the old destroyer *Tigre*, panting to keep up. This changed everything. If *Strasbourg* had to run through a

British gauntlet of combined sea and air attacks she would need every extra gun and depth charge around her she could get.

Somerville was first warned that *Strasbourg* might have escaped by one of *Ark Royal*'s spotters about fifteen minutes after he had ordered the ceasefire, but he chose not to believe it. 'Since the French knew that the entrance to the harbour had been mined, I felt quite positive that no attempt would be made by them to put to sea.'

Furthermore the smoke from burning ships and shells still made it difficult to be sure of anything. He preferred to stick with 'the certainty I entertained that the French would abandon their ships'. The assumption that France's sailors would be as demoralized as its soldiers was in the back of Somerville's mind throughout the Mers-el-Kébir affair, though there had been no defeat at sea and there was great pride in their new and untested ships. Gensoul exploited this because, knowing that *Strasbourg* and the 2nd Light were attempting a sortie, he now ran up the chequered flag Holland had arranged if he wished to renew negotiations. At the same time he sent radio and visual signals to Somerville asking for confirmation of a ceasefire followed by a second message which said that his fighting ships were 'incapable of action' and he was evacuating their crews.

It is perhaps to his credit that, despite the hideous casualties he had just incurred, Gensoul was troubled that his chequered flag ploy was not entirely honourable. He would tell Darlan:

> the conditions required by the English were being met and I did not hesitate to use that signal for a short time ... for these ships the intentions of the English had been achieved ... for the time being ... and as a result we should make every effort to stop the English from reopening fire ... I planned – provided the English did not return to finish us off – to try and put to sea during the night. I knew that *Dunkerque* was unfit to fight, but could, using two boilers and the main engine, reach 18 knots.

Somerville's reply to Gensoul's entreaties was a brutal-sounding: UNLESS I SEE YOUR SHIPS SINKING I SHALL OPEN FIRE AGAIN. But the commander of Force H, more disgusted than ever by his mission, had no intention of doing any such thing if he could possibly avoid it. He had ordered his ships to make smoke and move north-westwards because he wanted to get them away from both the coastal batteries, which had been the first to return fire with their newly restored breech blocks, and any of the bigger guns on Gensoul's Force de Raid that remained in action.

At first most of the French fire had fallen short but they soon got their eye in and, though there had been no direct hits, some of Somerville's ships had experienced narrow escapes as carnival plumes of bright red, yellow and purple sea water rose around them, for La Marine Française dyed its shells so that each vessel could see where her shot was falling and correct accordingly. Several had been straddled by salvos that fell either side of them, including *Hood* where shell splinters had blinded an able seaman in one eye, winged an officer and inflicted minor damage. The destroyer *Wrestler*, detached from the main force to watch for submarines leaving Oran harbour 5 miles up the coast, estimated that at least 100 of the smaller 4-inch and 6-inch shells fired by coastal batteries had landed near her.

When another report from *Ark Royal*'s aerial reconnaissance alerted Somerville to a flurry of activity at the previously moribund Oran airfield, it persuaded him to move even further away from the entrance to Mers-el-Kébir harbour 'to avoid a surprise attack by aircraft under cover of smoke'. Then young Briggs and the others on the *Hood*'s flag deck began to realize that something was wrong. Staff officers were running to and from the admiral's bridge and the compass platform. The *Hood* began to move off towards the east, rapidly building up speed. It had been confirmed, beyond all doubt, that one of the *Dunkerque* class battle cruisers and several destroyers had got out, and that their head start was such that they were already approaching Oran.

'The resultant delay in commencing the chase, though not appreciably affecting the situation, could have been avoided,' confessed Somerville. This must have raised some eyebrows at the Admiralty, for it was obvious that it would not have occurred at all had he continued to cover the harbour mouth and not put the safety of his ships before what he would always call 'this beastly operation'.

Somerville's first move was to divert to the *Strasbourg* six bombed-up Swordfish with a fighter escort of three Blackburn Skuas which had been bound for Mers-el-Kébir to administer any *coup de grâce* required on the wounded ships there. Skuas were the Fleet Air Arm's first all-metal monoplanes with enclosed cockpits and retractable wheels. In Norway they had initially done well as dive bombers, sinking the cruiser *Koenigsberg*, but had fared badly when they came up against Messerschmitts, being neither manoeuvrable nor fast enough (top speed 225 mph) to merit being called fighters.

But before they could get on the trail of the *Strasbourg* the three Skuas found themselves engaged in a series of dogfights with French fighters. First they intervened to save two of the *Ark Royal*'s spotting aircraft which were being attacked by five American-built Curtiss Hawk 75s, the interceptor in which the French had shot down their first Messerschmitt 109s of the war. With its big Pratt and Whitney radial engine, the Curtiss was almost in the same league as the RAF's earliest model of the Spitfire and could fly rings around the slow, two-seater Skua. Soon Petty Officer Airman Tom Riddler's aircraft was sent spinning into the sea and both he and his observer/gunner, Naval Airman Harold Chatterley, were killed.

Then the Curtisses broke off the engagement and went in pursuit of the Swordfish, followed some way behind by the two remaining Skuas under Lieutenant Bill Bruen, a regular who had switched to flying after five years as a ship's officer and now commanded the *Ark Royal*'s Skua squadron. They were not hard to find because the enormous amount of black smoke *Strasbourg* was making through her holed funnel was visible for miles: all the aircraft bent on attacking or defending the French battle cruiser were heading for it.

Bruen and the other Skua, piloted by Sub-Lieutenant Guy Brokensha, the 22-year-old son of a Scots high court judge with a Distinguished Service Cross from the Norwegian campaign, were the third set of aircraft to get to the smoke. They caught up with the Swordfish just in time to ambush their ambushers who now outnumbered the Skuas almost five to one, having been joined by four Morane 406s. Moranes were the mainstay of the French fighter fleet and looked a bit like a stubby Spitfire, though appearances were deceptive for they were under-powered and poorly armed. Even so, in most circumstances they were more than a match for a Skua. But in this case the Fleet Air Arm pilots had the advantage of surprise and the sun behind them and they took it well. Next day the Dublin-born Bruen wrote a short account of this second half of these opening shots of the air war against France for his squadron's war diary.

> At about 1910, while at 12,000 feet, 9 French fighters (Curtiss 75As and Morane 406s) were observed above and astern of the Swordfish. A dog fight ensued during which Brokensha obtained some hits on a Curtiss 75 which broke off the engagement. I was able to get a long burst on a Morane, which was on Brokensha's tail. This aircraft was also engaged by Leading Airman F. Coston. [Coston was Brokensha's rear gunner so the Morane was coming under fire from both front and rear.] Several hits were observed and the machine broke off combat and dived away. Several other aircraft were engaged by both Skuas. Three guns on each Skua jammed during this fight. [This would have left these aircraft with two working guns.] At about 1930 three Curtisses appeared and a dog fight ensued with no apparent results on either side. Shortly after this the Swordfish started their attack and the *Strasbourg* fired a barrage in front of us. We returned towards the carrier. On the way back we met a Berget 'Bizerte' flying boat and carried out attacks on it. During my second attack she dropped some bombs on a destroyer [they missed]. Brokensha put one engine out of action and observed streams of petrol coming out of the tank. We returned to the carrier and landed just after sunset.

Meanwhile, the Swordfish did no better than the French flying boat. All twenty-four of their 250-pound armour piercing bombs and forty-eight anti-personnel bombs missed and the *Strasbourg* proved to have a sting.

Two of the six were shot down by her well-trained anti-aircraft gunners who, their attackers had noticed, had showed commendable restraint by waiting for the first bomb to be dropped before opening fire. Fortunately the Swordfish floated rather better than a Skua and all six aircrew were picked up by the destroyer *Wrestler*, which had spent most of the early evening dodging the coastal battery fire off Oran. The destroyer also went to investigate a small craft flying two flags and heading relentlessly towards Force H. On closer inspection the two flags turned out to be the Royal Navy's White Ensign and a white flag of truce. Hooky Holland and his entourage were retrieved but not *Foxhound*'s motorboat, which was left to drift away.

By the time all the ditched aircrew were safely aboard, Wrestler had been joined by the *Hood* and her escorts, Somerville having decided to leave the slower *Valiant* and *Resolution* behind. Leading the British pursuit, and screening the *Hood*, were the eleven destroyers of the 6th and 13th flotillas. On *Keppel* Captain Francis de Winton, who commanded the 13th and whose five ships included *Wrestler*, had just signalled 30 knots. De Winton had no more desire to hurt the French than Somerville but he was thoroughly enjoying himself.

> It was a fine sight, and must have been rare in the war, to see two destroyer flotillas ahead of a battle squadron in full pursuit of the enemy. It recalled the numerous occasions in fleet exercises between the wars when flotillas proceeded ahead at full speed to fire torpedoes at the 'enemy'. The only thing was, this was the wrong enemy, at the wrong place and the wrong time.

The wrong enemy was building up on its torpedo carriers too. *Strasbourg*'s three escorting destroyers had been joined by the fast frigates *Poursuivante* and *Bordelais* which had slipped out of Oran as soon as *Wrestler*'s back was turned. And from the other direction the Algiers-based squadron of cruisers and destroyers were on their way to join her.

Meanwhile, the protection afforded by *Strasbourg*'s guns briefly tempted another small vessel to leave Oran and join the battle cruiser in her dash for Toulon. For half an hour or so *Rigault de Genouilly*, a shallow-bottomed gunboat named after the amiral who had captured Saigon, also tagged along. But though recent additions included a set of torpedo tubes and mine-laying equipment, she was essentially a colonial police work cutter built with river estuaries and a more tropical pace in mind. Unable to keep up, Lieutenant de vaisseau Louis Frossard had turned back for Oran, hugging the coast, when a couple of miles out to sea along came the *Hood* and her escorts including the cruisers *Arethusa* and *Enterprise*. Frossard could not resist it. Years later Briggs, who watched the French attack unfold from the flag deck of the *Hood*, would describe it as 'the bravest thing I have ever seen'.

> Where there had been six destroyers in our screen on the starboard wing, there was unaccountably a seventh, and this interloper was heading straight for the *Hood* at full speed ... She was close to the shore and making a torpedo run ... From twelve thousand yards the *Arethusa* opened fire; from eighteen thousand yards the *Enterprise* joined in; the *Hood*'s guns roared again, too, at this mosquito which might have a deadly sting ... hits were observed on the lone raider, but before she veered away the *Hood* had to veer, too. The *Rigault de Genouilly* managed to unloose two torpedoes, and we swung 180 degrees off course to port to avoid them. I looked back and saw the bubbles boil by well astern of us.

Although Frossard's attack was futile, in other respects fortune did, at least for the moment, favour the brave. Pursued by 15-inch shells from *Hood* and *Valiant*, which was using her stern guns at long range, his little ship managed to return to the sanctuary of Oran harbour. At least one submarine there was badly hit and had to be beached but no serious damage had been inflicted on the *Rigault de Genouilly*. Briggs's hits must have been near misses.

Now it was Somerville's turn to try torpedoes. Having tried to do it with bombs, *Ark Royal*'s Swordfish were going to make another attempt at least to slow down the *Strasbourg* with what was supposed to be their main weapon. The light was fading fast as the Stringbags, their ordnance set for a depth of 20 feet, wobbled off the carrier, then, keeping about 15 miles offshore, flew in an easterly direction until the battle cruiser's give-away black smoke came into view. They closed up to confirm they had found their target, encountering in the process some surprisingly accurate long-distance anti-aircraft fire, then turned south to be swallowed up by Algeria's gathering gloom.

Sunset was at 8.35. Two Swordfish had already been lost on bombing runs and the low, slow and level approach required for torpedo attacks made them even more vulnerable. Flying up and down the coast, Lieutenant Commander Guy Hodgkinson delayed his squadron's attack for another twenty minutes until he judged the *Strasbourg* was best silhouetted by the afterglow. Only then did Hodgkinson, seated behind his pilot in the observer role and at 37 a bit old for aircrew, let his Swordfish start their torpedo runs at 300-yard intervals and no higher than 20 feet.

Since none of the French ships had the radar that was fast becoming standard in the Royal Navy surprise was complete. Four Swordfish had dropped and gone before the last two attracted some machine-gun fire. None was damaged and all six navigators found their way home for moonlit landings on *Ark Royal*'s gently pitching deck. 'One or two hits were possibly obtained,' reported Hodgkinson. 'Darkness and funnel smoke made definite observation impossible.'

More than one of his aircrews were certain they had seen the orange flash of an explosion but Hodgkinson was right to be cautious. Despite a textbook attack *Strasbourg* was unscathed. One torpedo had almost hit her stern but its track was spotted by *Poursuivante* and a frantic radio warning permitted evasive action. The orange flash came from it exploding just behind the target when its sensitive detonator was activated by the big ship's turning wake, apparently a common enough occurrence with 1940's torpedoes.

This was the last offensive action of the day. As soon as the Swordfish had located and radioed back *Strasbourg*'s latest position, some twenty minutes prior to their actual attack, Somerville had decided to abandon the chase. The battle cruiser was now 25 miles ahead of him and, unless the Swordfish sank it, would have been reinforced by the cruisers from Algiers long before the *Hood* was on the scene. In his report he listed good tactical reasons for not pressing on, his main one being the foolishness of exposing his outnumbered destroyers to a night action before *Hood*'s 15-inch guns were there to back them up. These considerations apart, Somerville made plain his mounting contempt for the operation. 'I did not consider,' he told Their Lordships, 'the possible loss of British ships was justified against the possibility of French ships being allowed to fall into German or Italian hands.'

There was nobody to censor an admiral's mail and in a letter home to Molly Somerville, his wife of twenty-seven years, he poured his rebellious heart out:

> I was quite determined that I would not have any of my destroyers sunk or big ships seriously damaged in this beastly operation and I succeeded. Wonder if anybody will think I had cold feet? Shouldn't be surprised. But the truth is that the action left me quite unmoved. I just felt so damned angry being called on to do such a lousy job. I never thought they would fight in spite of what the French admiral said . . . But the French were furious that we did not trust them . . . We all feel thoroughly dirty and ashamed that the first time we have been in action was an affair like this. I feel I will be blamed for bungling the job and I think I did. But to you I don't mind confessing that I was half-hearted and you can't win an action that way.

So Force H turned back leaving behind them the submarines *Pandora* and *Proteus*, which had been in place for several days, with orders to attack any French ships they encountered along the coast. It was thought *Pandora* might be in a good position to intercept *Strasbourg* off Algiers. Somerville intended to go back to his original plan to launch another air strike at whatever remained intact among the oil and flotsam in

Mers-el-Kébir. Since Gensoul had assured him that he had evacuated his ships he was unlikely to kill many more Frenchmen and perhaps he thought that it was a way of making amends for the lack of due diligence that had allowed the *Strasbourg* to escape. On *Ark Royal* twelve Swordfish and nine Skuas were being readied for take-off at first light. Then a teasing Mediterranean fog came down, swirling around the ships so that one moment the bridge could not see their own bows before it cleared and descended again almost in the space of the same minute, a regular dance of the seven veils. By dawn it had tired of being capricious and settled into something much thicker. Even if the aircraft got off there was not much chance they would get back on. The attack was called off and Somerville set course for Gibraltar.

On the *Dunkerque*, on which Gensoul had left 400 men to start basic clearing up and repairs, they had spent the foggy evening trying to get to the last of the engine room men trapped in the bowels of the ship. The battle cruiser had beached herself in an upright position among the fishing boats in front of the village of Saint André but the shock of running aground had toppled more debris onto the emergency hatches and hampered rescue.

Eight half-crazed artificers were discovered in a compartment that also housed thirty broiled dead. Then the word went round that also among the living was Ingénieur mécanicien Xavier Grall. 'At about eight o'clock the first of the rescuers could get into the engine room,' recalled his friend Albert Borey. 'Xavier was kneeling between the control panel and the signal board, leading towards the gangway which would have let him escape. He was at his last gasp, already unconscious ... For hours three doctors worked desperately, giving their all. Until ten o'clock we still hoped, he was fighting.'

Grall died about an hour later. Borey was convinced that his friend had refused to save himself to stay with his men and drifted into unconsciousness while kneeling in prayer just as he said he would during their discussion the previous Sunday.

Total casualties incurred by the French through British operations on and around Mers-el-Kébir are usually put at 1,297 dead and about 350 wounded. This includes five of the *Strasbourg*'s engine room personnel who, like Grall, died from inhaling poisonous fumes as they kept up the revs during their dash for Toulon which they reached without any encounters with the *Pandora*. Instead the submarine chanced on and torpedoed the gallant Frossard's *Rigault de Genouilly*, making her second attempt to go east towards Algiers, and twelve of her crew went down with her. In the harbour itself, the longest casualty list was inevitably from the capsized *Bretagne* with her 1,079 dead. Another fifty died on the *Mogador* and two tugs which were hit. *Dunkerque* would end up with 210 of her crew killed, the last after a French radio broadcast claiming that the ship had only been slightly damaged resulted in the re-staging of the air attack that had been cancelled by fog.

At sunrise on 6 July, almost exactly three days after Hooky Holland had turned up in the destroyer *Foxhound* to deliver his ultimatum, twelve torpedo-carrying Swordfish fell on Gensoul's crippled flagship, her bows stuck firmly in the mud of Saint André. After various malfunctions in the shallow water it seems that only two of their torpedoes exploded and neither of these hit the *Dunkerque*. But as it turned out, this was quite enough. The first one went off under the stern of the habour patrol boat *Terre Neuve* which sank with the loss of eight lives and forty-four depth charges aboard less than 100 feet from the battle cruiser. Some minutes later the second torpedo, tracking an almost identical path, hit the submerged depth charges which went off as one 7-ton parcel of TNT, tearing a huge hole in the battle cruiser's side and killing another twenty-five of her crew as well as wounding many more.

'And so that filthy job is over at last,' wrote Somerville in another letter home to his wife and in certain company, whenever the subject came up, he would sometimes refer to himself as 'the unskilled butcher of Oran'.

Chapter Seven

At Mers-el-Kébir the French buried their dead as quickly as they could, for it was July and there was not enough mortuary space to cope decently with this shoal of slippery, oil-blackened corpses. Amiral Gensoul wore tropical whites and parade-ground gloves and stood among the files of coffins and the sailors who had borne them there, while photographers and at least one film cameramen took the pictures that French, German and Italian audiences would see but not the British. When he spoke Gensoul addressed both the living and the dead. 'If there is a stain on a flag today,' he assured them, 'it's certainly not on yours.'

Some forty-eight hours before these funerals, Darlan and Pétain had already given the American Ambassador William Bullitt a surprising glimpse of an Anglophobia that Gensoul's casualties were about to fan to furnace heat. Bullitt had these first informal chats with the new regime at Clermont-Ferrand, about 40 miles south-west of Vichy, and what they had to tell him had clearly come as a dreadful shock. At the beginning of an encrypted 2,500-word telegram sent, as usual, directly to President Roosevelt he told him:

> The impression which emerges from these conversations is the extraordinary one that the French leaders desire to cut loose from all that France has represented during the past two generations, that their physical and moral defeat has been so absolute that they have accepted completely for France the fate of becoming a province of Nazi Germany. Moreover, in order that they may have as many companions in misery as possible they hope that England will be rapidly and completely defeated by Germany.

The American journalist William S. Shirer thought it was probably the most disillusioning day in the Francophile Bullitt's life. 'But it produced what must be by far the most enlightening diplomatic dispatch he ever wrote.'

Bullitt, an aristocratic Philadelphian, twice divorced and author of a bestselling novel about the unhappiness high birth, money, charm and good looks can bring, was as dedicated to his work as he was to the pursuit of beautiful and intelligent women. One of his lovers, until she dumped him for King Edward VIII, was Wallis Simpson. In 1938 a *New Yorker* magazine profile had summed him up as: 'Headstrong, spoiled, spectacular, something of a nabob, and a good showman'.

True to form, the ambassador had remained in Paris when the Germans entered on 14 June, defying the wishes of Secretary of State Cordell Hull – his immediate boss – that he remain in close touch with France's government by following them south. Instead Hull had to be content with Bullitt's deputy Anthony Biddle, who was becoming something of an expert on blitzkrieg, having previously been ambassador in Warsaw. One of the reasons Hull wanted Bullitt there rather than at the more operatic occasion in Paris was that even at this stage, three days before Pétain agreed to a ceasefire, neutral America shared Britain's concern that the French fleet might fall into German hands and threaten the western Atlantic. 'Should the French government ... permit the French Fleet to be surrendered to Germany, the French government will permanently lose the friendship and the goodwill of the United States,' he instructed his ambassador.

But Bullitt, aged 49 and at the height of his powers, was much too egocentric to leave centre stage and miss his chance to give a once-in-a-lifetime performance of grace under pressure in the city he loved best. American ambassadors, he reminded Roosevelt, had remained in place when Madame Guillotine was working overtime during the Terror; again in 1870 throughout the Prussian siege and the subsequent horrors of the Commune; most recently in 1914 when, shortly before the Germans were repulsed on the Marne, the US Embassy had demonstrated more faith in Maréchal Foch than his own government which had already departed for Bordeaux. Bullitt was not going to have it said that he was the first to run away.

His decision was much appreciated by Prime Minister Paul Reynaud who, after declaring the capital an open city, asked Bullitt to get in touch with the Germans to ensure an orderly entry. Of particular concern was a clandestine Communist radio station broadcasting from one of the industrial suburbs which was urging the capital's workers, those who remained, to rise up and murder the bourgeoisie. Meanwhile, the State Department had met his request to supply a dozen Thompson sub-machine guns for embassy protection – 'I am fully prepared to pay for them myself' – via neutral Lisbon which the American light cruiser USS *Trenton* was visiting en route for home. Their delivery was accompanied by a message from Hull stressing: 'Every precaution should be taken to avoid publicity.'

This was not always the ambassador's strongest point though it was difficult to keep a low profile when the military government was staying next door in the Prince of Wales suite at the Hôtel Crillon which adjoined the embassy building. When some German linesmen strayed onto the embassy roof while installing secure field telephone connections, Bullitt responded to this gross violation of US turf by threatening to shoot the trespassers himself. The Wehrmacht, who knew the whole world was watching what they did in Paris, beat a hasty retreat from this enraged neutral, probably the first territory they had conceded all summer.

When, at the end of the month, Bullitt had moved his embassy to the unoccupied zone in a caravan of expensive cars the Thompson guns had gone with them. In addition, a French family had delighted the ambassador by entrusting him with the duelling pistols George Washington had presented to the Marquis de Lafayette for his help in the American War of Independence. Bullitt, proud of the Jewish and French Huguenot mix in his predominantly white Anglo-Saxon Protestant genes, was always inclined to favour France over Britain.

'The French at this moment do honor to the human race,' he cabled Hull on the eve of a panic-stricken mass exodus of refugees from Paris. He had persuaded Roosevelt to take the French side in their argument with Churchill over the RAF's failure to send more fighter squadrons to France; he had reported without comment their contention that it was a British collapse that allowed the Germans to punch a hole in the line they were trying to hold on the Somme, though the British had hardly any troops there. But he never shared the strident Anglophobia of Joseph Kennedy, his even richer Irish-American counterpart in London who distrusted Anglo-Saxon Protestants on both sides of the Atlantic. Kennedy's Celtic rapture at the prospect of the old enemy's imminent defeat had Robert Vansittart, an outspoken British diplomat whose indiscretions had annoyed Chamberlain, jotting on the American's Foreign Office file, 'a very foul specimen of double crosser and defeatist'.

By the time he caught up with Darlan at Clermont-Ferrand, the amiral's views were a perfect match for those held by the founder of what would become America's most famous and tragic political dynasty and Bullitt had cabled his scoop to Roosevelt as fast as the journalist he once was. Harvard's Coolidge Professor of History William L. Langer would describe it as, 'one of the most remarkable and revealing documents in the entire annals of this great war'.

> Darlan went on to say that he felt absolutely certain that Great Britain would be completely conquered by Germany within 5 weeks unless Great Britain should surrender sooner ... For his part he did not believe that the British government or people would have the courage to stand against serious German air bombardments and he expected a surrender after a few heavy attacks. I remarked that he seemed to regard this prospect with considerable pleasure and when he did not deny this but smiled I said that it seemed to me that the French would like to have England conquered in order that Germany might have as many conquered provinces to control as possible and that France might become the favored province. He smiled

again and nodded ... It was in his opinion certain that Hitler intended to bring the entire continent of Europe including England into a single customs union and that he desired to make France his leading vassal state.

Darlan's reaction to the news that the spineless English, instead of accepting their gallows fate with what dignity was left to them, had risen far enough off their knees to murder his loyal and defenceless sailors was predictable enough. But even some of the *Amis de Darlan* were unprepared for the new depths of his loathing for Perfidious Albion. Gone was the shrewd and level-headed commander they all admired. Instead, here was a man beside himself with rage, demanding a war of revenge against Britain and announcing that he had already ordered the *Strasbourg* to attack British ships, merchant as well as naval, at will.

Eventually he was calmed down by Foreign Minister Paul Baudouin, the former head of Banque Indochine and one of Reynaud's more surprising appointees because he had always been considered something of an appeaser, a man whose 'soft silky manner' had been noted by Churchill at his last meeting with Reynaud's Cabinet at Bordeaux. 'War with Britain will only weaken France's already pitiful condition,' Baudouin counselled. Instead, it was agreed with Pétain to sever diplomatic relations with London for the first time since 1815 when Napoleon escaped from Elba for his last 100 days as Emperor. 'Little stands between French acts of war against the British except the good sense of Maréchal Pétain,' cabled Bullitt in a despatch saved until he reached the secure wireless communcations available at the US Embassy in Madrid en route to Washington and a new job. Bullitt seems to have been in complete agreement with his political counsellor Robert Murphy, now US chargé d'affaires in Vichy, who thought the British attack was 'unnecessary'. Distraught French naval officers informed Murphy that the English had always envied their ships and had seized their chance to sink the defenceless fleet. Murphy assured them that 'while our interests and sympathies in the war were entirely on the side of Britain ... the American government had no prior knowledge of the naval attack and deplored it'.

This was false. True, Secretary of State Hull thought it was 'a tragic blunder' but Roosevelt did not deplore it at all and did not hesitate to say so. 'Even if there was only the remote possibility of seeing your Fleet pass into German hands, the British government had reason to act as it did. I would not have acted otherwise,' he told Count René Doynel de St Quentin when on 1940's Fourth of July, the day after Mers-el-Kébir, France's ambassador in Washington delivered with his Independence Day congratulations a note from Pétain on this 'hateful aggression'. The President must have enjoyed this exchange, for he disliked St Quentin and had been urging Bullitt to persuade the French to replace him.

What Roosevelt was unable to say, at least in public, were the views being openly espoused by the newly arrived American military attaché in London, General Raymond E. Lee, a descendant of the Confederate leader Robert E. Lee. The general contradicted his ambassador's gleeful forecasts of Britain's imminent collapse with fulsome praise for Operation Catapult. 'After all the defeatism in France and elsewhere,' he said, 'the British mean to win.'

Nor was Lee on his own. Approval, often mingled with astonishment, was widespread. From the Balkans to Brazil, British ambassadors and naval attachés reported favourable reaction. For once the Turks and the Greeks were of the same opinion though the Hellenic Navy thought they would have made a better job of it. A predictable contra was Spain with all its military debts to the Axis; nonetheless there was said to be, within Franco's immediate circle, a grudging admiration for 'the English pirates'. Another exception was Switzerland where editorials in most of the French- and German-language newspapers almost all blamed the British. 'It is a mortal insult to soldiers like Pétain and Weygand,' declared *La Suisse* and predicted it would revive an Anglophobia dormant since Fashoda. 'A monstrous presumption,' pronounced *Bund*. But even in hostile Rome, Mussolini's mercurial son-in-law and Foreign Minister Count Ciano, who was currently inclined to think that Adolf Hitler was a genius (this would change), could not resist a rueful diary entry on the enduring fighting spirit of the Royal Navy which 'still has the ruthlessness of the captains and pirates of the 16th century'.

No doubt Admiral Somerville, the self-styled 'unskilled butcher of Oran', would not have found this flattering. Nor would the eastern Mediterranean commander Cunningham who, by persistent negotiation, had persuaded Amiral Godfroy to accept the hopelessness of his tactical position and mothball his squadron in Alexandria with reduced crews. The surplus personnel were to be repatriated to Vichy France unless they wanted to join de Gaulle which very few did. Neither Somerville nor Cunningham were lacking in fighting spirit. On the contrary, soon they would be making life very miserable indeed for the Italians and obliging the Germans to divert resources needed elsewhere. But brave, hard, practical men that they were, unafraid of new technology, tactically creative, unpretentious yet careful of their honour, they still lacked that slither of ice in their hearts that enabled Churchill to do evil that good might come. In his own account of Mers-el-Kébir his defiance shines from every word. These included some that were first uttered in defence of regicide by Georges Danton, of all France's revolutionary heroes the one whose patriotism, oratory and life-enhancing hedonism matched his own.

> It was Greek tragedy. But no act was ever more necessary for the life of Britain and all that depended upon it. I thought of Danton in 1793: 'The coalesced Kings threaten us, and we hurl at their feet as a gage of battle the

> head of a King.' The whole event was in this order of ideas . . . Here was this Britain which so many had counted as down and out, which strangers had supposed to be quivering on the brink of surrender to the mighty power arrayed against her, striking ruthlessly at her dearest friends of yesterday and securing for a while to herself the undisputed command of the sea. It was made plain that the British War Cabinet feared nothing and would stop at nothing.

Or rather Churchill would stop at nothing. Mers-el-Kébir was the first major triumph of his premiership which was now towards the end of its second month. On 18 June, Waterloo Day as it happens, he had made the speech that ends 'this was their finest hour' and starts, 'The battle of France is over. I expect the battle of Britain is about to begin.' By now the music he made with the English language, the speeches which de Gaulle observed 'stir up the heavy dough of the English', was in full flow.

But until 3 July, as far as the British were concerned, nothing much had happened since the evacuation of the army from Dunkirk ended on 3 June and the Norwegian campaign shortly afterwards. As yet there was no sign of a German invasion and, despite all the dire pre-war predictions of civilians massacred by chemical warfare, not a single gas mask had been used for its intended purpose. To date, air attacks had mostly been limited to shipping strikes in the Channel. The Battle of Britain Churchill had alluded to had still not begun and perhaps it never would.

Nonetheless, there was plenty of apprehension that things might get much worse. Only two weeks before Mers-el-Kébir Duff Cooper's Ministry of Information was warning that defeatism would grow 'unless there was a strong lead from the prime minister'. There was talk of German peace feelers. These went with other rumours that Foreign Secretary Lord Halifax, who had been of the appeasement tendency, was waiting in the wings, ready to take over once Churchill messed up. Certainly, a lot of Conservative MPs still regretted the passing of Chamberlain and would have preferred to have been led by his crony Halifax. Most of the Prime Minister's support in the coalition government came from the Labour and Liberal benches.

Then the day after the attack on the French fleet Churchill spoke to the House, enlarging on the brief and often confused newspaper reports of what had occurred, starting with the boarding of the French ships in British ports before spelling out the implications of the 'melancholy action' at Mers-el-Kébir: 'In itself, sufficient to dispose once and for all of the lies and rumours that we have the slightest intention of entering into negotiations with Germany.' For good measure, he finished by reading 'the admonition' he had sent the day before to the inner circles of all government departments, civil and military, demanding a curb on any defeatist talk.

> The Prime Minister expects all His Majesty's servants in high places to set an example of steadiness and resolution. They should check and rebuke the expression of loose and ill-digested opinions in their circles or by their subordinates. They should not hesitate to remove any persons ... whose talk is calculated to spread alarm and despondency. Thus alone will they be worthy of the fighting men who have already met the enemy without any sense of being outmatched in martial quality.

Pegged as they were to bloody proof that Nazi Germany did not have the monopoly on brutal surprises, Churchill's words must have been beyond the wildest dreams of the 'strong lead' advised by the men from the Ministry of Information. When he had finished speaking old enemies joined with his supporters in giving the Prime Minister a cheering, shouting, order-paper-waving, foot-stomping standing ovation and thus began the process that would soon make his position as Britain's war supremo unassailable. 'It is not often that the House is so deeply moved,' reported *The Times*. With the exception perhaps of the recipient of these praises who, as was his wont, greeted his applause with tears of joy coursing down his cherubic cheeks. He had been in the House for over thirty years and it was, he said, 'a scene unique in my own experience'.

The jubilation with which the Commons greeted the Prime Minister's account of the sinkings at Mers-el-Kébir is sometimes cited as proof of the deep-rooted Francophobia of the English. But it seems to have had much more to do with an immense feeling of relief that Churchill had at last matched the pledge of no surrender he made after Dunkirk with action. Ships that might have fallen into the hands of the enemy had been denied to them and England was safer for it. It was as simple as that. 'The House is at first saddened by this odious attack,' the writer and National Liberal member for Leicester Harold Nicolson noted at the time. 'But is fortified by Winston's speech.'

That a feeling existed that Pétain and the men around him had 'let us down' was true but there was certainly no delight in killing Frenchmen. On the contrary, there was such horror at France's plight, often coupled with guilt that Britain had been no more ready for war with Germany than their ally, that Nicolson was by no means the only one to find the idea of inflicting further suffering odious. 'Horrible but necessary ... to be weak is to be destroyed', declared the editorial in next day's *News Chronicle*, flagship of British liberal opinion. 'There can be little pleasure in contemplating the defeat of enemies whom we believe to be at heart our friends,' lamented *The Times*. 'The Battle of the Brothers', the socialist *Daily Herald* called it though they praised the government for its 'fearless and terrible decision'. The conservative *Daily Telegraph* was in total agreement: 'An Inexorable Duty'. And at the end of the week The *Observer* summed it all up as a case of 'human reluctance and relentless necessity'.

Nor was it quite over. In the early hours of Monday, 8 July, under a pale African half-moon, a wooden-hulled motorboat painted a matt black for the occasion edged alongside the stern of the brand-new battleship *Richelieu* as she lay in shallow waters at Dakar. The boat belonged to the British aircraft carrier *Hermes* which was a few miles offshore, and its nine-man crew, faces boot-polished the same colour as their craft, included two Royal Marines manning a Vickers machine gun in the bow. But that night its main armament was four depth charges, each as big as a 40-gallon oil drum, which had affected the boat's trim so badly there had been times over the last three hours when they feared the heavy Atlantic swell might capsize them.

The previous day Pierre Boisson, the Governor General of French West Africa, had dismissed an ultimatum presented by Acting Rear Admiral Rodney Onslow offering him the same choices for the *Richelieu* that Gensoul had turned down at Mers-el-Kébir. Boisson, who had lost a leg at Verdun under Pétain, said that such demands were 'shameful'. And a few hours later the British had picked up a radio signal ordering all French shipping in the harbour to 'meet attacks from the English enemy with the utmost ferocity'.

Onslow knew Boisson and Amiral Placon, the local naval commander, quite well. Until the armistice *Hermes* had been based in Dakar as part of the Anglo-French squadron deployed there to hunt down German commerce raiders in the South Atlantic. But once his terms had been rejected Onslow did not linger. He took his old ship, Britain's first purpose-built carrier, and her escort of two cruisers – one of them HMAS *Australia* – almost out of range of the *Richelieu*'s eight 15-inchers, which could easily have wreaked revenge for Mers-el-Kébir. Then *Hermes*' motorboat and volunteer crew under Commander Bobby Bristowe, Onslow's executive officer whose idea the raid was, had headed for the harbour with only one of its twin engines working. The other had been wrecked by an unfuzed depth charge when they were loading them in a heavy swell. Also a casualty was Commissioned Torpedo Gunner Grant, Bristowe's deputy, who had been knocked cold by a swinging cargo sling loading the second depth charge and was unconscious for much of the approach.

One engine or two, Bristowe was determined to press on. At first light the French would be receiving torpedo attacks from the carrier's Swordfish. But the *Richelieu* was a big, thickly armoured modern ship; it would not be easy to inflict enough damage to meet the Admiralty's requirement to keep her out of the war for at least a year. This was something extra, something that would take them by surprise and he was determined to make it work. In case the battleship had slipped out, or changed her position in the harbour, he also had a reconnaissance role and had been equipped with a radio which in 1940 was a novel concept on a small boat.

To everyone's surprise, it worked well and he was able to keep *Hermes* informed of his progress.

Bristowe was familiar with the harbour and, having narrowly avoided collision with a French destroyer, navigated its several breakwaters before stopping his engine and sliding his boat's shallow draught, as he always thought he could, over the chain and steel mesh that was the port's defence boom. *Richelieu* was surrounded by several merchant ships which provided good cover as he sneaked towards the battleship at 3 knots. A harbour launch signalled a challenge with a series of red and white flashes but when Bristowe failed to respond did not open fire, presumably unwilling to believe that anything so small could possibly be dangerous.

Bristowe succeeded in getting beneath the high stern of his target and dropping his cargo on the spot where they were most likely to cripple the *Richelieu* by wrecking propellers and flooding stern compartments. As the charges splashed overboard some curious French sailors, who did not appear to be armed, peered over the guard rail on the quarterdeck then disappeared. Below them Bristowe's crew, who had been warned that there would be no attempt to pick up anybody who was blown overboard by the explosions, clung to their cockleshell, bracing themselves for the boiling waters that would erupt as they made their getaway.

Nothing happened. Depth charges required a certain minimum depth for their fuzes to work and the tide was not right for it. As they sped through the still waters of Dakar harbour towards the merchant ships they had to reconcile themselves to the fact that it had been a failure. As if this were not bad enough the next thing to malfunction was their single engine. For twenty minutes they drifted helplessly in the dark before they got it going again, their only consolation being the sound of an explosion which they persuaded themselves must have been the delayed action of at least one of their depth charges. Shortly afterwards they set off, for a while hotly pursued by a French launch which chanced upon them only to become entangled in its own anti-submarine nets.

At about 4 a.m. Bristowe established radio contact with *Hermes* and informed Onslow that he had placed the depth charges beneath the stern almost two hours before. Fifteen minutes later, six Swordfish made night take-offs from the carrier – only three of the pilots had ever done this before – so that they would be over their target with torpedoes at first light, which would minimize the effectiveness of the French anti-aircraft barrage, not only from the *Richelieu* but the other ships in the harbour. All returned safely, two with minor damage. The last aircraft to attack saw four tracks running towards the battleship and two crews reported a column of smoke rising from the *Richelieu*.

But once again, as at Mers-el-Kébir, the Fleet Air Arm had not got its depth and speed settings quite right. Only one of their tinfish found enough water to run true and explode close to *Richelieu*'s propellers which, just like the raiding party, was what they were aiming for. By an enormous stroke of luck this turned out to have been quite enough. Bristowe's depth charges had not gone off. The explosion they had heard while trying to repair their engine was from the *Richelieu* but it was a harmless 'funnel explosion', a maritime version, while trying to work up steam, of a car's backfire only much louder. But in a small-scale copy of what occurred in the second attack on the *Dunkerque* at Mers-el-Kébir, the single torpedo not only hit the 35,000-ton battleship but detonated at least one and probably all four of the depth charges that had been deposited there with so much effort. This blew a hole measuring 500 square feet in the *Richelieu*, ruptured her starboard propellor shaft and caused her to sink her ample stern firmly into the Dakar silt. There were no casualties, her guns were still in working order and from the air, to an untrained eye, the ship looked untouched; but she was not going to go very far until her flooded compartments had been pumped dry and repairs made that the colony was ill-equipped to make.

Bristowe might have expected a Distinguished Service Cross, the navy's equivalent of the army's Military Cross, for his crucial role – Churchill thought it 'most gallant' – in disabling the *Richelieu*. Instead he got the higher Distinguished Service Order and the whole enterprise was greeted in a much more triumphalist manner than the 'more in sorrow than anger' tone generally adopted over Mers-el-Kébir. 'One of the most brilliant exploits of the war on a level with the Battle of the River Plate and the *Altmark*,'* said the BBC Overseas Service, much to the displeasure of parts of the Foreign Office. Sir Hugh Knatchbull-Hugesse, British ambassador to Turkey where he had found the French trading community remained patiently Anglophile, cabled 'not only in worst possible taste, but certain to exacerbate [the] feelings of those Frenchmen who sympathise with us.'

De Gaulle, who had just established his headquarters in Belgravia's Carlton Gardens, was toying with the idea of leaving London to sit out the war in Montreal. 'Mers-el-Kébir was a terrible blow to our hopes,' he said. 'It showed at once in the recruitment of the volunteers.' At a 14 July Bastille Day Parade in Whitehall, Churchill's 'man of destiny' who was about to be sentenced to death in absentia by a Vichy court martial, reviewed some of the best or at least the most presentable of his troops: all 300 of them. Perhaps his only consolation was the presence of a large crowd of Londoners who cheered and applauded and, carried away by the band, attempted to sing the 'Marseillaise'. The parade ended at Grosvenor Gardens where the tall générale, lugubrious-looking at the best of times, laid a Tricolour wreath beneath the statue of Maréchal Foch, commander

* After a gunfight some 300 British merchant seaman off ships sunk by the *Gruff Spee* were rescued from the German tanker *Altmark*, one of the raider's support vessels, by a boarding party from HMS *Cossack* which pursued her into frozen Norwegian waters.

in 1918 of the largest army France had ever put into the field.

Even before Mers-el-Kébir, de Gaulle had been having difficulty recruiting from among the estimated 21,000 French servicemen who had, for various reasons, ended up in England. Some, among them the Narvik veterans who so impressed Auchinleck, had come across the North Sea at the end of the Norwegian campaign. Others had been evacuated from Dunkirk then sent to Cherbourg or St Malo only to be returned to England along with British troops when it was decided that there was not going to be a Brittany redoubt after all. A few had arrived on stretchers from field hospitals in Belgium and northern France or been fished out of the Channel choking on fuel oil from sunken ships.

All for a while were a captive audience and yet, though he had the firm support of Churchill and the British media and 'countless individuals gave our enterprise a warm welcome', de Gaulle encountered opposition from an unexpected quarter. With hindsight, he wrote about it with an empathy for his hosts that he was not always famous for:

> the British High Command, which from one day to another expected the German invasion ... looked with some mistrust upon those allies of yesterday humiliated by misfortune, dissatisfied with themselves and with others and loaded with complaints. What would they do if the enemy gained a bridgehead? Wasn't the most sensible course to ship them away as quickly as possible? And what, after all, was the use of a few battalions without cadres and crews without officers, which General de Gaulle claimed he could rally?

One of the lowest points came after a successful day's recruiting at Trentham Park in Staffordshire where the French Light Mountain Division had been encamped ever since their return from Norway. But after de Gaulle's departure he was astonished to learn that the troops had been addressed by two British officers, one of them the Francophile Tory MP and author Captain Somerset de Chair, who had informed them: 'You are perfectly free to serve under General de Gaulle. But it is our duty to point out to you, speaking as man to man, that if you do so decide you will be rebels against your government.'

To reject the hero of Verdun for an almost unknown brigadier general, perhaps no more than an ambitious scoundrel prepared to be Churchill's puppet, was always going to be a leap in the dark. De Gaulle himself realized this and was obviously fascinated by the sort who rallied to him, describing their motivation with a Conradian relish and exactitude:

> A taste for risk and adventure pushed to the pitch of art for art's sake, a contempt for the cowardly and the indifferent, a tendency to melancholy and so to quarrelling during the periods without danger, giving place to an

ardent cohesion in action, a national pride sharpened to the extreme by their country's ill-fortune and by contact with well equipped allies, and above all, a sovereign confidence in the strength and courage of their own conspiracy.

For some there were, of course, more prosaic considerations such as whether a wife and family awaited in some shattered part of France from where no letter or telegram had reached England for weeks. When this did not apply the decision could be easy. The crew of the French mine-laying submarine *Rubis* had been attached to the Royal Navy and sowing destruction from their base in Dundee since early in the war. Her captain and two of his officers had long since brought their wives over from France and lived with them in rented accommodation. *Rubis* reacted to the armistice with the ballot box: head for Toulon or fight on with the British? All but two, including the captain, chose Dundee and de Gaulle, possibly in that order, for several members of the submarine's young crew were already on the verge of taking a Scottish wife.

Surcouf had about three times as many crew as the *Rubis*, almost a destroyer's complement, but only fifteen of them signed up with de Gaulle. In a typescript report Capitaine Martin, the *Surcouf*'s commander, listed their names, ranks, numbers, marital status and if they had children, how many. By each man's name was written: *déserteur.* Just over half were married and nine were skilled artificer petty officers: electricians, armourers, mechanics to whom the Gaullists usually paid a signing-up fee of £50. An exception was made for their prime catch, Premier-maître électricien Francis Jaffrey who, according to Lieutenant Crescent, was paid £400 – more than enough in 1940 to buy a semi-detached house in any part of southern England. But then Jaffrey knew how to make the *Surcouf* work.

Within twenty-four hours of the British boarding their submarine most of the crew had found themselves, along with hundreds of other French sailors, at a vast tented camp – at one point it would hold about 5,000 men – being set up on Liverpool's Aintree racecourse, home of the Grand National. They had got there after a twelve-hour train journey north packed into locked carriages guarded by some of the Royal Marines who had been in the boarding parties. The Royal Navy had not wasted any time; it was as if they feared that if they did not put some distance between them the French might break out and recapture their ships

Before the *Surcouf*'s crew departed they were briefly allowed back onto the submarine, either in small groups or in the case of the officers one at a time, in order to collect a few items of personal kit for the journey. 'An English sub-lieutenant gave me his word of honour that all our belongings would be packed up and sent to us,' complained Dr Le Nistour. 'Another false word of honour!' Some of the French officers had kept elegant wardrobes – Capitaine de corvette Martin had four dressing gowns on board – and when they failed to turn up they accused the English of looting, a vile calumny according to the senior sailors involved who whispered to the Admiralty that it was the Royal Marines. Both Le Nistour and Bouillaut, the ringleaders of the resistance on the *Surcouf*, eventually submitted lists of all they had lost. Along with a wallet containing 500 francs, 1,000 Gauloises Bleu, two pairs of pyjamas, three sweaters, a service cap, and five books on navigation, Bouillaut included '*1 pistolet automatique (marque MAB police calibre 7.65) et deux chargeurs*.' He had, after all, paid good money for it.

When the others had been allowed back on board the *Surcouf* prior to their departure for Aintree, the lieutenant had been unable to recover any of his personal effects because he was in Plymouth Naval Hospital recovering from his wound. Bouillaut made rapid progress and on 8 July, five days after he had been shot, was judged fit enough for the train journey up to Liverpool where a bed awaited at the city's Walton Hospital because he needed more treatment and convalescence before he could join the others under canvas on the racecourse. 'I must say that I was very well cared for, both at the Walton hospital and the one in Plymouth,' he would report.

Bouillaut's discharge from the naval hospital happened to coincide with the burials of the men fatally wounded on the *Surcouf* including Ingénieur mécanicien Daniel, the single French fatality bayoneted by the dying Leading Seaman Webb. They were all being buried with full military honours at the city's Weston Mill Cemetery where there were already some naval graves from 1914–18. As the only officer from the *Surcouf* left in Plymouth, Bouillaut felt he should attend and the day before the hospital's Chief Medical Officer had informed him this would not be a problem. But when an army lieutenant turned up at the hospital next morning it was with travel warrants for himself and Bouillaut to depart for Liverpool on the next train. 'I protested vehemently, demanding to go to the funeral of my comrade,' said Bouillaut. 'I asked him to telephone the Admiralty in Devonport to clear up what I was certain was a misunderstanding. His orders were confirmed in the strongest terms and we left for Liverpool.'

French outrage at this decision was exacerbated when a few days later they read a newspaper account of the funerals which commented on the absence of mourners from the *Surcouf*. Perhaps if anybody other than Bouillaut had been available the Royal Navy might have relented. He was, after all, the man who had killed two of their own for what could only ever have been a token gesture. The idea of Bouillaut, his lucky wound sling advertising his role in the affair, rubbing shoulders around their gravesides with the widows of the men he had shot may well have been too much. Nor had he for one moment expressed the slightest remorse for it. On the contrary, he wanted his gun back.

In any case, immediately after Mers-el-Kébir, the deaths of three members of the Royal Navy were hardly enough for most of *La Marine Française*. 'The murderous behaviour of the English had made the men angry,' said Crescent. But he noted that despite the discomforts of the tented camp, its outdoor kitchen and washbasins open to England's frequent summer showers and the absence of wine (though Dr Le Nistour thought this beneficial), morale remained high at Aintree and this was not when the defections began.

These started in August following the closure of the racecourse camp and the transfer of the *Surcouf*'s and other crews from the seized ships to Barmouth, a Victorian resort town on North Wales's Mawddach river estuary which had boasted Tennyson and Darwin among its paying guests. Here they were billeted in the small hotels and guest houses that normally catered for those who came to the town for its unspoilt sands and Snowdonia backdrop. 'With rare exceptions they all praised their hosts,' said Le Nistour, who had been provided with a surgery and a little four-bed sick bay. 'The local lady charity workers came to see us to enquire what they could do to make things more comfortable. The state of our health was so good our team scarcely realised what efforts were being made to help them.'

Afterwards the doctor concluded that the British had sent them to Barmouth and its professional hospitality so that they could be softened up for the Gaullist recruiting sergeants who came calling. Since Mers-el-Kébir their task had been made a little easier by the trigger-happy commander of German motor torpedo boat S27. Despite arrangements via the Red Cross to ensure safe passage, off Portland on 24 July S27 had stopped then torpedoed the fully lit French steamer *Meknes* repatriating the first 1,277 of Darlan's marooned sailors. British destroyers rescued almost 900 of them but, including crew, 416 Frenchmen perished and the Gaullists made sure that those intent on taking a similar trip heard all about it. For some waverers it was enough. 'I don't want to be torpedoed on my way to France. I prefer to remain in England,' the *Surcouf*'s Lieutenant Crescent was told by one of his petty officers.

Apart from the *Meknes* factor, Crescent gives several reasons for poor morale. At the top of his list is the lack of mail which he was convinced was an Anglo-Gaullist plot rather than a combination of the collapse of the French postal system, German or Vichy censorship and the inevitable delays incurred when letters had to be forwarded through a neutral country. Whether no news from home made a man more or less likely to want to get back might also depend on distractions nearer at hand. Crescent mentions 'propaganda spread by women' and cites the case of the femme fatale who won Maître armurier Pottier for de Gaulle, though her nationality is not revealed nor whether she was considered a professional or an enthusiastic amateur. But mostly he thought that the Gaullist junior petty officers and seamen who regularly visited Barmouth were the most effective advocates for their cause.

> They presented the following arguments: Maréchal Pétain secretly agrees with de Gaulle; French sailors would never be repatriated and, even supposing they left England, they would be torpedoed like the *Meknes*; our seamen would be really stupid to stay in Barmouth without money or clothing when the Free French forces could provide both.

Nonetheless, by the end of July de Gaulle had, by his own account, recruited no more than a third of the French servicemen in Britain; Mers-el-Kébir and homesickness had turned the rest into ardent Pétainists yearning for repatriation, and only a trickle would come over from those who remained. Even so, de Gaulle knew how to make the best of a poor hand. RAF Bomber Command was persuaded to let a few Free French aircrew participate in an attack on the Ruhr. At this stage of the war the RAF was inflicting little damage with these raids and it is unlikely that this one was any different. But its value to de Gaulle was immense. He was able to announce to the world that at least some Frenchmen had returned to the fight.

In Vichy Colonel René Fonck, a 1914–18 fighter ace with seventy-five confirmed kills, responded to this with the news he had signed up some 200 French aircrew who, in order to avenge Mers-el-Kébir, were willing to join in Luftwaffe air raids on Britain. France, it seemed, would be the only country whose airmen would be attacking ground targets on both sides of the Channel, possibly even passing each other in mid-air. But Fonck's offer was declined.

Chapter Eight

Fonck's attempt to persuade his old Richthofen Squadron adversary Hermann Goering to let his volunteers retaliate for Mers-el-Kébir by flying with the Luftwaffe was typical of Vichy's enthusiasm for a fresh start with Germany. From the beginning it strove to present itself as worthy of its place in Hitler's New Europe: not, as Ambassador Bullitt had predicted, as a vassal state but almost as an equal with the armistice replaced by a proper peace treaty and the government returned to Paris. Only the English, whose pig-headed stubbornness was prolonging the war, were holding this up but they would soon be put in their place.

Meanwhile, the new regime was quick to introduce legislation that was a dream come true for every Frenchman who was anti-Semitic enough to have really meant it when he said, 'Better Hitler than Blum.' First came the announcement that only those who could prove that they had no Jewish blood could be employed by the civil service. Then a commission was appointed to review French citizenships granted under the generous Naturalization Act of 1927 that had encouraged the Russian Jews displaced by the Bolsheviks to settle in France six years before the more prescient of their German co-religionists started to arrive.

Once the initial moves had been made against 'the Déicides', as the Monarchists and Catholic reactionaries of Action Française generally referred to the main civilian victims of Nazi terror, the persecution of the Freemasons began under a law banning all secret societies. As well as introducing new and blatantly discriminatory laws, Vichy also repealed a recent piece of liberal legislation that had put a France a good sixty years ahead of its time as far as the rest of western Europe was concerned. In April 1939 the Marchandeau Law governing newspaper practice had been amended to make it an offence to publish articles intended to incite hatred 'towards a group of persons who belong by origin to a particular race or religion'. The law was scrapped on the grounds that it gave the Jews a special status.

The mechanism to do all this was put into place exactly a week after Mers-el-Kébir, when the full National Assembly – the Chamber of Deputies and the Senate – had convened at Vichy's Grand Casino and voted themselves out of existence. The Third Republic, founded in 1875, was finished and there were no plans for a fourth. Republics had been replaced by *L'État Français* – the French state – which was going to restore traditional values and had started with the national motto, scrapping *Liberté, Egalité, Fraternité* for the moral certainties of *Travail, Famille, Patrie* – Work, Family, Fatherland.

Head of state, with all the executive and legislative powers previously shared between the Assembly, Prime Minister and President, was Maréchal Philippe Pétain who was the only man who could order that the National Assembly be reconvened. To advise him, though he could take or leave their advice, the Maréchal had a twelve-man Council of Ministers. Among them were Baudouin, who remained Foreign Minister, while Général Weygand, the man who had predicted England's neck would be 'wrung like a chicken's' in three weeks, was Defence Minister and in charge of the 100,000 or so troops Vichy was permitted to retain at home and abroad under the armistice.

Much to Weygand's disgust Pétain's deputy and successor, should the octogenarian's health ever take a turn for the worst, was none other than Pierre Laval: *Time* magazine's Man of the Year 1931, the former Prime Minister and one of the shambolic champions of the smoke-filled rooms of the Third Republic's last chaotic decade. As far as Weygand was concerned, Laval was the epitome of all that had brought France to its knees. Pétain shared Weygand's antipathy for the rumpled, chain-smoking Laval whose manners he found deplorable, particularly his generous distribution of the product of his eighty-a-day habit whenever they spoke. Nonetheless, he was deeply indebted to him, admitting: 'I could have done nothing without him.'

When the Paris press had vanished along with its readers, it was Laval's Radio Lyon and provincial daily *Le Moniteur du Puy-de-Dôme* which had derided Paul Reynaud's talk of fighting on from abroad and helped to make the word *émigré* a fashionable insult. It was Laval who persuaded President Albert Lebrun to step aside and allow Pétain a free hand under a changed constitution. It was Laval's charm and advocacy that convinced all but 80 of the 649 National Assembly members who had got to Vichy to vote for its extinction for the good of their country. Pétain had described Laval's performance as nothing less than 'extraordinary'.

Which it was. When he had finished, Laval had proudly informed Monsieur le Maréchal that he now had more power over his subjects than Louis XIV. But he knew that as a puppet master he would have his work cut out, not least because of the old soldier's disconcerting tendency to have his strings pulled by the last minister who spoke to him between his early dinner and bed. Even so, Laval was determined to use this Pétain interlude between the French and the inevitable British armistice to prove to the Germans that he was the best man to take France into Europe's New Order.

Towards the end of the summer, as the Luftwaffe's first assault on England neared its climax, Robert Murphy, the US chargé d'affaires in Vichy, was invited to an informal lunch at the chateau Laval owned in nearby Châteldon, his birthplace and, before the bright son of a local café owner and butcher went into politics, best known for a sparkling mineral water that rivalled Vichy's. Since leaving Paris this was where Laval and his wife lived, and sometimes their only child Josée, whose husband Count René Chambrun was a direct descendant of the Marquis de Lafayette, a lineage that provided honorary US citizenship in recognition of his ancestor's contribution to American independence. The Chambruns had recently acquired a more relevant transatlantic link too. Count Chambrun's American mother Clara Longworth was connected to the Roosevelts through her brother Nicholas's marriage to Alice Roosevelt, daughter of the twenty-sixth President of the United States, Theodore, a cousin of the present occupant of the White House.

After lunch, Laval took his guest for a walk around the grounds which included scaling a small hill where, Murphy was informed, Jeanne d'Arc's army had once defeated the English.

> Then he led me into the great drawing room, one wall of which was covered with an enormous oil painting, showing British soldiers storming the very hill and being repulsed by French defenders. Laval described the French victory of four centuries ago as though it had happened yesterday. Obviously, he had staged for my benefit this little lesson in Anglo-French historical conflicts ... I asked him why he personally was so bitter about the British? Talking very rapidly, he recounted a litany of incidents – financial, political and military – in which the British during his own career had thwarted France and him as Premier and Foreign Minister. During World War One, he declared, the British had let France bear the brunt of the bloodletting, so that France had lost 1,500,000 killed, from which loss the nation never recovered. This time the British had tried the same trick again, he cried, but this time the British and not the French would pay for the war.

Few Frenchmen wished to defend the Anglo-Saxons after Mers-el-Kébir. But it was typical of the dark-skinned Laval that he should go with the flow and accept as well all the new legislation against the Jews, if only to belie old rumours among the anti-Semitic ascendancy that his own business success was due to Sephardic genes. 'Swarthy as a Greek', said a careful *Time* in its 1931 profile. Nor had Laval ever belonged to France's extreme right. His natural habitat was the ruling consensus and his instinct for compromise could make him as reversible as his palindromic surname.

Laval had not worn uniform during 1914–18. Pre-war national service had been shortened by a medical discharge for varicose veins and, in any case, MPs were exempt from conscription though many volunteered. In

1914 he had started the war as a pacifist and a lawyer famous for his defence of militant trade unionists framed as anarchists. At this point he was aligned to the former premier and socialist Joseph Caillaux who advocated a negotiated peace with Germany. By 1918 Caillaux's unfashionable views would see him stripped of parliamentary immunity and in jail facing treason charges of which he was eventually acquitted.* Long before that Laval, calling himself an independent socialist, had with characteristic footwork shifted his allegiance to the successful nationalist Georges Clemenceau. As far as party politics were concerned, he was to remain of no fixed abode for the rest of his career.

With his usual energy Laval now committed himself to finding a way of getting alongside the Germans. He was by no means the only one trying to do this. For the foreseeable future, having influence with their conquerors was obviously going to be the main key to power in Vichy. Laval's rivals all had their own reasons for trying to beat a path to the Nazi camp and they were all irritated that others were doing the same.

Pétain and Baudouin, the man the maréchal had decided should continue to be Foreign Secretary, were both trying through Franco's Madrid to reach Joachim von Ribbentrop, the French- and English-speaking former Hussar officer and wine merchant who had become Hitler's Foreign Minister. Meanwhile in Wiesbaden, at the secretariat of the Franco-German Armistice Commission, Général Huntzinger was trying to talk to Wehrmacht commander Feldmarschal Wilhelm Keitel about the release of over 1.5 million French prisoners of war. Then there was Renée Fonck, Pétain's knight of the air with his access to Goering, not only head of the Luftwaffe but deputy Führer.

Laval tried a different route. Otto Abetz was a Francophile young diplomat – his wife was French – recently returned to Paris as the German Foreign Ministry's liaison with the military. A former Karlsruhe girls' school arts teacher with the blond good looks Hollywood liked for its Nazis, he had just turned 37 and was considered one of Ribbentrop's high-fliers, though it was only three years since he had joined the Foreign Service and with it the Nazi Party. In his teaching days he had been a pacifist dedicated to the idea that Germany and France should never fight each other again and the founder of the Sohlberg Circle, a Franco-German cultural group.

But the eve of continental Europe's third war between its most powerful neighbours in less than a century found Abetz a direct Ribbentrop

* Monsieur and Madame Caillaux both had famous acquittals. In 1914 his second wife and former mistress Henriette shot dead Gaston Clamette, editor of *Le Figaro*, because she feared her husband might die in a duel with him over his threat to publish compromising letters. Clamette took four bullets in an obviously premeditated killing and the guillotine loomed; but it was declared 'an uncontrollable female crime of passion' and she was freed, a gross miscarriage of justice eclipsed by the murder on the same day of an archduke in Sarajevo.

appointee to the Paris Embassy where he funded French anti-Semites of all shades from conservative Catholics to anticlerical Fascists and convinced Hitlerites. Most of his clients were journalists or publishers and Abetz could argue that he had not reneged on his youthful pacifism for one moment: all believed that a war with Nazi Germany would be criminal folly. By the summer of 1939, when the French finally lost patience and expelled him for subversive activities, Abetz's slush fund, which also covered lavish entertaining and trips to Germany, was estimated by the British Embassy at £2,000 a month, enough to buy Laval's chateau with change for a champagne party.

In the first weeks of the occupation Abetz's main task was to search out major artworks and place them in German custody, especially the Jewish-owned. But though he went diligently about these duties they were swiftly taken over by Alfred Rosenberg, the philosopher high priest of Aryan racial superiority, whose Einsatzstab Reichsleiter Rosenberg was hoovering up all it could find. In any case, Ribbentrop had better uses for his protégé. Anxious to play his own role in Franco-German relations, on 5 August 1940 he started by appointing Abetz German ambassador to France though he could not yet be accredited to Pétain's *État Français* as formally a state of war still existed between France and Germany.

By this time Laval had already become the only Vichy minister to have returned to Paris on official business almost two months ahead of Foreign Minister Baudouin. His first meeting with Abetz was on 19 July. It was arranged through the journalist Jean Luchaire, probably the German's closest French friend whose former secretary, Suzanne de Bruyckner, had become his wife. Luchaire had campaigned for closer ties with Germany long before the Nazis came to power and as a young man had been a protégé of the socialist Aristide Briand, 1926 Nobel Peace Prize winner, eleven times French premier and probably the first great democratic statesman to advocate a European federal union of some kind. At one point Briand had subsidized *Notre Temps*, the weekly political commentary Luchaire started and edited; but since Briand's death in 1932 he had discovered another prophet and Abetz was about to fund his latest venture, a Paris evening paper called *Les Nouveaux Temps* that would preach the joys of the New Order and run lots of pictures of Corinne Luchaire, his good-looking film actress daughter.

When Luchaire approached Abetz with Laval's request for a meeting he must have been delighted. A former Prime Minister was certainly an improvement on his pre-war raft of ranters from Paris's political demimonde, some of whom he was busy rescuing from the various stalags and offlags where the fortunes of war had recently marooned them. Among the latest was Louis Darquier, a monocled buffoon, bar-room brawler and phoney aristocrat who called himself Darquier de Pellepoix. Lieutenant Darquier, captured with his anti-tank unit, was president of the Comité antijuif de France and editing proprietor of the fortnightly *La France enchaînée*, which had discovered that Churchill, Eden and Duff Cooper all had Jewish blood or money or both. It had been the only publication to be successfully closed down under the Marchandeau Law but by that time Abetz had got his money's worth. Laval and the new ambassador got on well from the start. 'Neither a thug nor a fool,' recalled the Frenchman. 'At least one could negotiate with him.' Relations were also good with Abetz's senior staff: Ernst Achenbach, his deputy, who had an American wife, and Dr Friedrich Grimm, an expert on international law.

Towards the end of August Laval was back in Paris having a meeting with Grimm which lasted almost three hours as he made his case for the mutual benefits that would accrue from Germany making a lenient final peace treaty. He argued, and this must have been the first time the Germans heard it from one of the Third Republic's major political players, that France's natural partner was no longer Britain but Germany. Of course, it had been France, prodded by the English, who had so unwisely declared war on the Reich and they must expect to pay a penalty for such criminal foolishness. But it would be unfair if their English accomplices, the ones who had led them astray, got off with a lesser penalty. And the more decisive the defeat Germany inflicted on Britain the less severe France's reparation would need to be.

For instance, if France was (once again) required to give up Strasbourg and the rest of Alsace then it might be compensated with one of Britain's African possessions. What was needed, said Laval, was not revenge and a harsh victor's peace like the Treaty of Versailles which he, as was well known, had voted against. What was needed was a reconciliation that would mark the beginning of a new age of Franco-German cooperation: one that would lay the foundations for a powerful and united Europe. It is unclear whether Laval thought the English should be allowed to play any part in this. Certainly, in 1940 he would not have been the only Frenchman to think *La perfide Albion* should be left to contemplate its misdeeds amid the impenetrable fogs and mists of their rainswept offshore island.

But if Laval's words stirred Abetz's embassy they appear to have caused few ripples among the higher echelons of the Reich where France was yesterday's victory and all eyes were on the rainswept islanders in question. On the same day that Laval had his first meeting with Abetz, Hitler made a public offer of peace to the British. 'I believe I can do this not as someone who has been defeated, but as a victor speaking reason,' he had told the party luminaries in the Kroll Opera House. It was one of Berlin's long and sultry July evenings and his speech, which was an enjoyable summary of Germany's war to date, had started shortly after seven. At 9.30 it was still not quite dark when people began to emerge and start looking for cars and chauffeurs, the peace gesture most had been expecting, in many cases dreading, still ringing in their ears, for Hitler knew what to save for the last minutes:

> I feel obliged, in this hour, by my conscience to direct once more an appeal of reason to England ... I see no compelling grounds for the continuation of this war. Herr Churchill may dismiss this declaration of mine, screaming that it is a result of my fears and of my doubts about our final victory. In that case, I have freed my conscience about what is to come.

Six days later German radio was still broadcasting its latest patriotic song: '*Wir Fahren Gegen England*' – We're Going Against England – and the front page of the *Völkischer Beobachter* announced: ENGLAND HAS CHOSEN WAR. 'Everyone had feared that England would grasp the Führer's offer of peace,' wrote Joseph Goebbels in his diary. 'The war against England will be a relief. That is what the German people want.'

Laval too. Churchill's decision to play the match into extra time, however hopeless the score, had given him the chance to unveil his plan for a new European entente to Dr Grimm. And Laval wanted everybody to know that he was the man the Germans spoke to in Vichy. When the American Murphy, a regular caller at his office on the floor below Pétain's quarters in the Hotel du Parc, happened to be present when Abetz's deputy Achenbach telephoned, Laval motioned the US consul to pick up an extension and listen in.

> It developed that Laval had sent the German embassy a list of about ten concessions he hoped the Germans would make to fortify his own position ... Speaking in French Achenbach was very businesslike. He took up Laval's requests one by one replying either 'No' or 'Yes'. Only two minor concessions were granted. But after Achenbach had hung up, Laval turned to me with a satisfied air and said, 'I just wanted you to see how well things are going between us and the Germans.' I thought at first that he must be speaking sarcastically but he was quite earnest ... Adroit lawyer that he was, he apparently had sold himself on his case and was determined to prosecute it to the limit.

Then, towards the end of September, Churchill did something that not only appeared to justify Laval's optimism but even raised hopes that France might get its peace treaty with Germany before the British had been defeated. At the Armistice Commission in Wiesbaden Général Paul Doyen, who had succeeded Huntzinger as chief French delegate, told his German equivalent: 'We find ourselves in a situation without precedent in history. You are making war on England but we are too and yet we are in a state of war with you.'

Chapter Nine

The Gambia, a British colony never more than 30 miles wide, was a deep wound in the bulbous flank of French West Africa following the banks of its eponymous river 295 miles eastward towards its source. Both north and south of this slither of Anglo-Saxon impertinence lay the vastness of Senegal. It was therefore an ideally placed salient from which to insert Gaullist agents into Vichy-held territory and was where, on 20 September 1940, Commandant Hettier de Boislambert and two officer companions, all in civilian clothes, left the colony's Atlantic estuary capital of Bathurst bound for the port of Dakar. They did not go there directly but were put ashore at the fishing village of Fandiougne on the Saloum river estuary from where they acquired motor transport to take them north over uncertain roads to Dakar, which was about 70 miles away.

Once there de Boislambert and his team set to work with a will. Their brief was a simple one: recruit as many officers as they could to their cause; sabotage communications and prepare for the arrival of a Free French contingent who were about to be landed from a large British task force. A blond stocky figure who could easily have been mistaken for an Englishman, de Boislambert was under the impression that key members of the Dakar garrison were ready to defect to the Free French. But he soon discovered this was wrong. Embittered by the slaughter at Mers-el-Kébir, old friends advised him to leave before he found himself facing a court martial. De Boislambert was not the sort of man who gave up easily but, as he admitted later, if he had had a radio he would have urged de Gaulle to call the whole thing off. Since that was not an option, on the eve of the scheduled landing he saw that all telephone links were cut between General Headquarters and the coastal batteries at Cape Manuel and Gorée. Then the three of them went under cover and hoped for the best.

The Anglo-Gaullist expedition to Dakar towards the end of September 1940 was code-named Operation Menace. It was a bold plan in that it involved diverting precious resources from Britain when the German invasion scare was still at its height and the Luftwaffe's aerial assault on the island by no means over, though it was becoming apparent that Goering's airmen were having difficulty defeating the RAF. In many ways it was a consolation prize for the failure to persuade the French to continue the fight from North Africa with all the Mediterranean coastline and warships this would have secured. For the time being these colonies were too tough a nut to crack. Vichy had well over 100,000 troops in Algeria, Morocco and Tunisia, mostly colonial and poorly equipped yet fiercely loyal to their officers. But to the south of them, in the lightly garrisoned outposts of the sub-Sahara, the situation looked much more favourable.

'Remember this, France does not stand alone,' de Gaulle had announced on the BBC back in June. 'Behind her stands a vast Empire.' And shortly afterwards he sent to Africa Commandant Philippe Leclerc, nom de guerre (he feared reprisals against his family) of Viscomte de Hauteclocque, a cavalry officer who had fought under Pétain in the Moroccan Rif Wars. He chose well.

Leclerc, who was almost 40, had already demonstrated great determination escaping to England in the first place despite a head wound and a brief period in German captivity. By the end of August, in a series of almost bloodless coups, he had succeeded in rallying Gaullist support in the Cameroons, a former German colony that had been part of the booty from Versailles, and the French Congo, though both places would need consolidating if they were to withstand a Vichy response. Most crucial of all, he had also helped secure Chad after Félix Eboué, its clever mulatto governor, partly out of revenge for a punishment posting, had declared himself for de Gaulle.

Eboué was born the maternal grandson of a slave – his father was a French gold miner – in Guiana, France's South American colony next door to Brazil, which is mostly famous for its Devil's Island penitentiary where Dreyfus served his time. In 1910 he was accepted by the colonial service and his rise through its ranks showed France at its liberal best when this level of advancement for a non-white was almost unthinkable in the British Empire, not even in India. Most of his career was in Africa, but in 1936 Eboué became governor of Guadeloupe in the Caribbean where his social reforms irritated enough people in Paris to see him transferred to Chad, France's poorest African possession. He was 56 and it should have been the end of his career. Instead it brought undreamed-of honours. Chad might have been a backwater, but for de Gaulle these 500,000 square miles of central Africa were important: Mussolini's Libya lay on the other side of Chad's northern frontier. It was the only colony not in Vichy hands that offered the possibility of the Free French hitting back against one of their Axis occupiers.

All this was good news but Churchill and his War Cabinet were mainly interested in Dakar for the same reasons they were obsessed with the French fleet. They worried that Vichy might allow the port to fall into German hands as a base for U-boats and surface raiders preying on

Britain's South Atlantic shipping. The Americans, always alarmed at any enhancement of German naval power, were also concerned and reopened a consulate in the port they had closed down some nine years before to save money. Thomas C. Wasson arrived on 15 September, about a week before the Royal Navy turned up on the horizon, but the only German speakers the new consul could discover were five Jewish refugees dreaming of US visas.

Initially, de Gaulle was suspicious of British plans for Dakar. Spears, his personal liaison officer with a direct line to Churchill, called it Fashoda complex. 'He could never accept that we had no territorial ambitions at France's expense, always believed we would succumb to the temptation to help ourselves to some tempting morsel of the French Empire.'

Once these suspicions had been set aside, though by no means entirely extinguished, de Gaulle began to question the tactics. Instead of a frontal assault he proposed a landing at Conakry in Guinea, almost 500 miles south of Dakar and only 50 miles north of British Sierra Leone, to be followed by an overland march on the port, gathering support as he went. This was turned down as impractical because it would take too long. Then Churchill asked de Gaulle to come and talk things over. Their meeting took place at Downing Street on 6 August 1940, two days after the anniversary of the opening shots in 1914, a date that had led to speculation among the British High Command that Hitler might think the runes favoured it for invasion day. Above them vapour trail graffiti scratched a mostly blue sky. Goering had briefed his aircrews that the 15th must be Eagle Day, the date by which the Luftwaffe established total supremacy over the RAF. De Gaulle left his own account of how, despite these more pressing matters, Churchill had convinced him of the prospects for Operation Menace, 'colouring his eloquence with the most picturesque tints'.

> Dakar wakes up one morning, sad and uncertain. But behold, by the light of the rising sun, its inhabitants perceive the sea, to a great distance, covered with ships. An immense fleet! A hundred war or transport vessels! These approach slowly making radio messages of friendship to the town, to the navy, to the garrison. Some of them are flying the tricolour. The others are sailing under the British, Dutch, Polish or Belgian colours. From this Allied force there breaks away an inoffensive small ship bearing the white flag of parley. It enters the port and disembarks the envoys of Général de Gaulle. These are brought to the Governor. Their job is to convince him that, if he lets you land, the Allied fleet retires, and that nothing remains but to settle the terms of his co-operation; if he wants to fight he has every chance of being crushed ... During this conversation Free French and British aircraft are flying peacefully over the town dropping leaflets. The military and the civilians, among whom your agents are at work, are discussing passionately

among themselves the advantages offered by an arrangement with you and the drawbacks presented by a battle fought against those who, after all, are the Allies of France. The Governor feels that, if he resists, the ground will give way under his feet. Perhaps he will wish 'for honour's sake' to fire a few shots. But he will go no further. And that evening he will dine with you and drink to final victory.

Thus it was that shortly before dawn on 23 September a large number of ships assembled before Dakar. Not quite the 'immense fleet' Churchill had predicted but impressive enough. The star of the show, on loan from Somerville's Force H, was the *Ark Royal*, still under the command of Hooky Holland who had been so disgusted by the French casualties at Mers-el-Kébir that he had written a letter asking to be relieved of his command but had been persuaded by Somerville not to put it in. Next in line were the old battleships *Barham* and *Resolution*. The *Barham* was recently refitted and it was hoped that the new fire control for her 15-inch guns would prove more successful than her new plumbing which, despite the latitude, refused to provide water that was less than boiling. In their wardroom officers sipped grim cocktails of gin and lime juice served at teapot temperature.

Around the big ships, that would, if necessary, supply the heavy artillery or deliver the air strikes, was a screen of three heavy and two light cruisers, nine destroyers and seven sloops or patrol boats, five of them Free French. Also under their protection were six converted liners carrying almost 6,700 troops of whom 2,400 were French and the rest British, mostly a brigade of Royal Marines. The French were on the Dutch *Pennland* and *Westernland* where de Gaulle's new emblem, the Cross of Lorraine, flew alongside the Netherlands' tricolour.

These ships carried the Narvik veterans of the Foreign Legion's 13th Demi-Brigade, his best troops, sometimes called Brigade Monclar after the alias of its diminutive commander Colonel Raoul Charles Magrin-Vernerey, a tiny terror of a man in wire-rimmed spectacles, seven times wounded during 1914–18 and a Chevalier de la Légion d'Honneur with eleven bravery citations. Apart from carrying de Gaulle, the *Westernland*'s other distinction was that she was the only ship with women on board. These were ten ambulance driver-nurses, six of them British and mostly the kind of adventurous, expensively educated, thirtyish Francophiles who had not been out of France much longer than the Gaullist officers they met when they signed up in Carlton Gardens. Susan Travers, a naval officer's leggy daughter brought up in Cannes and a semi-professional tennis player, had returned to England via Finland where she had gone with the French Red Cross to nurse Finnish soldiers wounded by the Russians.

The presence of these women was the cause of much speculation among their allies and along familiar lines. Soon the British were telling each other that the 'nurses' were not really nurses at all and the hot-blooded French, typically unwilling to accept the communal nature of their calling, were knifing each other over exclusive possession. This apparently explained the large numbers of burials at sea. There was at least one killing or death by misadventure because General Spears happened to trip over the body outside his cabin. Otherwise, *l'amour* was by no means a monopoly of the French. Years later Susan Travers admitted to starting an affair aboard ship with one of Spears's junior British liaison officers though, since they were both sharing cabins, it was not consummated until they got ashore.

The British troop were spread over four ships: the Bombay-registered *Karanja*, two converted P&O liners – the *Ettrick* and the *Kenya* – and the *Sobieski*, a new Polish liner whose dedicated light orchestra had been playing in the salon where the officers dined ever since they left Liverpool. On the *Ettrick*, where he was delighted to discover that Goanese stewards were serving duty-free shots of gin for about the price of a newspaper, was Captain Evelyn Waugh, who was attached to one of the Royal Marine battalions as its intelligence officer while waiting to see whether his application to join the newly formed Commandos had been accepted. The novelist had covered the Italian invasion of Abyssinia as a newspaper correspondent but this was his first campaign as a soldier and, like thousands of others throughout Britain's armed forces, he was ignoring standing orders and keeping an occasional diary.

> Sunday 1 September. [this was the day after Waugh left Scapa Flow] At about 5pm the cruiser *Fiji* next to us in the convoy put up a signal which was variously interpreted to mean, 'I am dropping depth charges at 800 feet' and 'I have been torpedoed and am proceeding to UK'. The latter proved to be correct. She made port under her own power taking with her highly important people ... 7 September. Saturday night at sea observed by hard drinking ... Sunday 8 September. I suggested Lamond [Free French liaison officer] should lecture the officers on French politics: idea treated as shocking. Drunk before luncheon. Sleep. PT under Teeling. Adjutant bottles junior officers for rowdiness ...

The U-boat attack on *Fiji*, which left five dead in a wrecked engine room soon after the convoy entered the North Atlantic, was an unfortunate start. There had already been considerable delay in putting the expedition together. At one point the crews of some of the small Free French cargo ships involved went on strike because it was a long time since anybody had remembered to pay them. Allegations that, even when this was remedied, they refused to sail unless sufficient champagne and foie gras were included in their rations, and that one captain insisted that his mistress accompany him, sound like predictable Francophobe slanders though they are faithfully repeated by at least one French source.

Without doubt there seem to have been some startling lapses of security with Free French officers toasting '*À Dakar!*' over a pre-embarkation dinner at Liverpool's Adelphi Hotel and de Gaulle himself casually informing a London military outfitter that he required tropical lightweights for West Africa. Then at the last moment, when it had got as far as Freetown, it had almost been cancelled altogether after three Vichy cruisers got into Dakar carrying naval gunners to take over from some of the Senegalese crews manning the coastal batteries. En route they had stopped at Casablanca where a British reconnaissance aircraft got close enough to be shot down by French gunners.

At the time London did not know who or what the cruiser squadron was carrying. Nor did they think the additional firepower would make much difference if they came up against the 15-inch guns of the British battleships. What concerned them was that its arrival would greatly improve the morale of the somewhat neglected Dakar garrison and that Operation Menace would not lead to the bloodless capitulation they were banking on. The Admiralty was particularly anxious that they should not risk provoking an all-out war with Vichy by inflicting casualties on a Mers-el-Kébir scale and finding what was left of Darlan's navy, which included the *Strasbourg* and some of their super-destroyers, added to Hitler's invasion fleet.

In an uncharacteristic change of heart, for once even Churchill, whose 'picturesque tints' had so inspired de Gaulle, was among the nay-sayers.

> I had no doubt whatever that the enterprise should be abandoned . . . it was possible however to cancel the plan without any loss of prestige, so important to us at the time, and indeed without anyone knowing anything about it. The expedition could be diverted to Douala and cover Général de Gaulle's operations against the French Cameroons and thereafter the ships and transports could be dispersed or returned home.

Another reason for calling it off was that, even before the cruisers arrived, there had been at least one clear indication that reports of crumbling Vichy morale and a growing Gaullist tendency in the colony were probably at best exaggerated. The Dakar-based coaster *Poitiers*, bound for neighbouring Libreville with railway rolling stock and ammunition, was intercepted by the cruiser *Cumberland* but it took a shot across the bows to persuade her captain to stop engines. By time the British had boarded, opened sea cocks were flooding the holds and her petrol-soaked deck cargo was already well alight. Meanwhile, the crew had abandoned ship and were pulling strongly towards Africa before a close burst of machine-gun fire persuaded them to stop and come alongside, when they greeted their rescuers with cries of '*Vive Pétain!*' and '*Vive Hitler!*'

'There was no mistaking their sympathies,' wrote 18-year-old Roger

Emden in the log all midshipmen were required to keep. Or their prisoners' pleasure when it took sixty-seven shells from the *Cumberland*'s secondary 4-inch guns to sink *Poitiers*, named after the site of a famous Gallic victory over the Moors though better known in England for a battle the Black Prince won there some 600 years later.

Undoubtedly the arrival of the cruisers and the *Poitiers* incident would have ended Operation Menace had it not been for an unusual development. 'It was very rare at this stage of the war for commanders on the spot to press for audacious courses,' Churchill would later admit. 'Usually the pressure to run risks came from home.' By which, of course, he meant from himself.

But in this case the reaction was entirely the opposite. De Gaulle, Admiral John Cunningham who was in command of the ships (no relation to the other Admiral Cunningham who had sweet-talked Godfroy into disarming the French squadron at Alexandria) and Major General Noel Irwin who was commanding the troops, all argued that the operation should go ahead. Their main point was that since the arrival of the cruisers had not significantly altered the military balance its effect on morale should be put to the test. De Gaulle in particular, buoyed by his successes elsewhere in Africa, felt the tide was going in his direction. Churchill changed his mind. 'The men on the spot thought it was time to do and dare.'

Certainly, on the eve of battle there was nothing much wrong with the morale of the men under their command judging from the racket coming out of *Ark Royal*'s aircrew's wardroom where British and Free French officers were swapping rugby songs. 'I learned some very vulgar French words . . . they learned some very vulgar English words,' remembered Sub-Lieutenant Charles Friend, who was an observer on a Swordfish. The English grew particularly fond of the tale of the lubricious monk Frère Le Guillaumet, who was interrogated in monastic plainsong about the secrets of his success with women and the chorus, his stock replies roared out with much refilling of glasses. About twenty French airmen, flyers and airframe fitters had come aboard the carrier at Freetown, transferring from the merchant ship *Pennland*. With them – flown to England in July by escaping French pilots – came two Lucioles, their air force's two-seater communications biplane which was rather similar to the British Tiger Moth trainer but with a slightly better figure.

So as the dawn came up on the 23rd, Cunningham's fleet was arrayed before Dakar more or less as Churchill had promised de Gaulle it would be. Unfortunately, the Vichy defenders were denied this awesome sight. A thick wet tropical fog, which showed no sign of clearing, had descended. When Dakar woke up that morning, feeling nowhere near as sad and uncertain as Churchill envisaged, it could have been any other day. The entire Royal Navy might have been out there or nothing at all. Undaunted, from *Ark Royal* came the sound of aircraft engines starting up.

First to take off were the two unarmed Lucioles manned by the jolly songsters of the night before, a little thick-headed perhaps and wondering why the English could not make decent coffee. Their destination was Ouakam airfield, a fighter base on the Cape Verde peninsula. They were to land there and convince its Vichy aircrew that it would be in everybody's best interests if they rallied to the Free French. This was an important part of the plan because these squadrons flew American Curtiss Hawks, all-metal monoplane interceptors of the same generation as the Hawker Hurricanes currently duelling with Messerschmitts over southern England. *Ark Royal*'s Swordfish biplanes and lolloping Skuas were not in the same league.

The Lucioles landed safely and, as their engines were switched off, the base commander strode up to greet his unexpected visitors, probably assuming they came from one of the smaller landing strips around Dakar and had got lost in the fog. But once their identity had been established this officer made his views on the notorious outlaw Charles de Gaulle quite plain. The Luciole crews responded by tying him up. Then, somewhat optimistically in the circumstances, they proceeded to lay out on the ground some canvas signal panels which indicated to a Swordfish pilot flying low enough to read them that it was safe to go ahead with the next phase of the plan. This was for the Swordfish to land and unload from its cramped cockpits three Gaullist officers whose names were Gaillet, Scamaroni and Soufflet. Having completed his task, the British pilot took off and did a couple of circuits of the airfield and was then intercepted by a single Curtiss Hawk which opened fire and chased the Swordfish away. These appear to have been the first shots fired at Dakar and they were probably not intended to kill.

Other Swordfish crew were flying low over the town taking pictures of the harbour and its defences and scattering Free French leaflets except for the copies they had folded into their pockets as souvenirs. '*Français de Dakar! Joignez-vous à nous pour délivrer la France*,' began a personal message from de Gaulle. There were individual messages for the army and the navy and a general one which began, 'Dakar is threatened by the enemy and famine. We must save Dakar for France! We must resupply Dakar. This is why French forces under my orders have arrived.' The literate minority read this with some astonishment since there was no rationing and little obvious hunger except that which had always existed among the poorest and often the most volatile of Dakar's 100,000 Africans, the black sans-culottes.

Europeans numbered about 12,000 of whom roughly half were military and these were now standing at arms. On the wounded *Richelieu*, which had been painstakingly moved by tug to a safer berth behind a breakwater since Commander Bobby Bristowe's July visit in his blackened motorboat, anti-aircraft gunners opened fire at the circling litter louts at 6.10 a.m.

One aircraft was damaged but all managed to return to the *Ark Royal*, escorted part of the way by some Curtiss Hawks whose main interest seems to have been to get above the fog and discover exactly what was out there. Behind them at their Ouakam airfield base all seven of de Gaulle's emissaries were now the prisoners of the station commander, sprung from bondage by a posse of his irate airmen whose loyalty to the maréchal was as unimpeachable as his own. A thorough search of these treacherous Churchill mercenaries yielded another prize: a list of all the known Gaullist sympathizers in Dakar worth listing. There were fourteen of them, including the mayor and the head of the Chamber of Commerce, and soon most of them had joined the Luciole pilots and the rest in the mosquito-filled cells normally reserved for African prisoners, with stinking buckets in the corner.

There were three code-named contingencies for Operation Menace: Situation Happy envisaged a rapturous reception for de Gaulle where the main danger would be that his troops were overwhelmed by the hospitality displayed by Boisson's garrison in joyous *vin d'honneur*, Situation Sticky imagined the guns on the *Richelieu* and isolated shore batteries making a limited resistance to which there would be a firm but limited response; Situation Nasty was a gloves-off reaction to a complete breakdown in negotiations and determined opposition, in which case the Free French would step aside to avoid fratricidal strife while the British first bombarded then took the port by frontal assault. Throughout, de Gaulle was to broadcast emollient radio appeals from the *Westernland* for Dakar to see reason while always hinting that, although he was talking quietly, he was carrying a big British stick.

By noon on the first day it had become obvious that Situation Happy it was not. The fate of the airmen and the others landed at Ouakam airfield was still unknown. But there was no mistaking the reception accorded to the naval emissary whom de Gaulle had regarded as one of his trump cards.

Capitaine de corvette Georges Thierry d'Argenlieu, brother of a général who had been killed in May 1940 during the first days of the blitzkrieg, was a respected not to say unique figure in naval circles because he was also a monk. During 1914–18 he served in a patrol boat and distinguished himself rescuing hundreds of men from a sinking troopship. Then in 1920, aged 31, he had resigned his commission to become Brother Louis de la Trinité of the Barefoot Carmelites and study theology in Lille. In 1939 he was a mendicant friar doing social work in Paris when, a few days before the outbreak of hostilities, he returned to the navy as a reserve lieutenant. It seems that his religious superiors were under the impression he was going to serve as a chaplain. But when Rommel's panzers captured d'Argenlieu in June 1940 he was helping to defend the Cherbourg arsenal. A few days later the Carmelite leapt from the crammed prisoner train taking him to Germany and, like de Gaulle, got to England via Jersey. It was d'Argenlieu who had given his new commander the idea to adopt as the emblem of Free France the double-barred Cross of Lorraine – about to become part of Germany along with its iron ore deposits for the second time since 1870.

An hour after the Lucioles had landed at Ouakam, two motorboats from the Free French sloop *Savorgnan de Brazza*, which, covered by the fog, had got to within 3 miles of Dakar undetected, reached the harbour's Mole No.2. On arrival one of them tied up while the other, which contained a covering party of a dozen armed men, stayed a little behind with its engine running. Both boats were flying large white flags and Gaullist tricolours. The monk d'Argenlieu was in the first boat heading a delegation that included Capitaine Henri Bécourt-Foch, grandson of Maréchal Foch, and ten others bearing letters from de Gaulle to Boisson and the army and navy commanders. The letters expressed de Gaulle's confidence that he would be able to land his forces so that together they could fight for the liberation of their country but warned that any opposition would incur the intervention of the accompanying Allied forces 'whose mission is to prevent, by all means at their disposal, any risk of the Dakar base falling into the hands of the enemy'.

The first person to greet them was a naval guard commanded by a lieutenant waving a revolver who was shortly replaced by a more senior officer named Lorfevre who announced that he would hand the letters over. D'Argenlieu said that his orders were to give them to the people they were addressed to personally. Lorfevre sent the lieutenant off to get instructions from Amiral Landriau, the Vichy naval commander. While they were waiting, d'Argenlieu, a tall, fine-featured man, looked around the harbour and, trying to break an awkward silence, said, 'You have a nice little fleet here.'

Lorfevre: Yes, and it's ready to defend itself.

D'Argenlieu: We too are a group with a lot of esprit de corps.

Lorfevre: You belong to a religious order and I am myself a believer. We know how to examine our conscience. I have examined mine and I'm absolutely convinced that I've done my duty.

D'Argenlieu: Our duty was first of all to fulfil our obligations to England. [A reference to the Anglo-French agreement not to make a separate peace with Germany.]

Lorfevre: I obey my legitimate orders.

D'Argenlieu: Our superiors have betrayed us.

Lorfevre: What about Mers-el-Kébir?

But before d'Argenlieu could reply the lieutenant was back with a message from the amiral saying that the Gaullist delegation should leave immediately. D'Argenlieu, rather like Hooky Holland at Mers-el-Kébir in July, was insisting that he must be allowed to deliver his important messages when Lorfevre was called away to answer a telephone call at the guard post. When he returned d'Argenlieu detected a change in his attitude, more conciliatory, as if he were playing for time, and he also noticed that the guards were now standing between his delegation and the boats except for a sergeant who had moved closer to him. Towards the other end of the mole there was some commotion and he saw that a score of men carrying rifles with fixed bayonets had appeared and were running towards them. Brother Louis did not hesitate. He gave the sergeant an ungodly kick in the balls and led the rush back to the boats.

A minute later they had all scrambled on board and were following their support craft out to sea, white flags whipping in the wind. D'Argenlieu's instincts had been right. Amiral Landriau had changed his mind and decided to take them prisoner. Nor were their troubles over. The platoon he had despatched to arrest them tumbled into an old tug and attempted to cut them off. A few ineffectual shots were fired from a machine gun mounted on her bows but it soon became apparent that the motorboats were much faster and before long they were well out of range. All that remained was to get past the harbour's outer defences on Gorée Island. It was from here that a well-aimed burst hit the second boat which then veered off into the fog, though not before both d'Argenlieu and a Capitaine Perrin had been wounded.

They were both brought to the *Westernland* where the nurses had set up a casualty station in the dining room of the Dutch liner, while de Gaulle and Spears were on the bridge scanning the shoreline through binoculars. There was a new development: the batteries on Cape Manuel had opened fire and the splashes from their shells were creeping closer to the ships. As usual, to correct fall of shot, the French rounds emitted a coloured smoke on impact with sea or solid. The colour for these coastal guns was yellow. In the dining room the English nurse Susan Travers was attending to Capitaine Perrin, who had just asked her name, when she was distracted by a glimpse through the nearest porthole of a bright flavescent spume of frothy Atlantic. 'Don't be afraid, Susan,' said her patient, who was bleeding in several places. 'They're just bluffing.'

It seems Admiral Cunningham was thinking along the same lines. He sent a polite radio message: 'If fire continues on my ships I shall regretfully be compelled to return it.' Back came the reply: 'If you do not wish me to fire remove yourself more than 20 miles from Dakar.' Not since France's victory at Fontenoy in 1745, when Lord Hay of the Foot Guards foolishly invited the French to fire first, had the two old enemies been so murderously polite to each other.

Almost an hour later the British started to shoot back, the battleships directing their 15-inch guns at the forts and the *Richelieu*. The French ship had been firing at them with almost equal weight from the one 380mm four-gun turret it had working. Both sides were firing blind in the fog without effective aerial spotting or being sufficiently into the century for radar-controlled gunnery. First blood went to one of the Vichy French coastal batteries. A single 9.4-inch shell hit the *Cumberland*, the cruiser that had stopped the scuttled *Poitiers*, killing seven of her crew and seriously wounding two more. It holed the ship about 6 inches above the armour plate on her port side and exploded sufficiently far into her innards to add scalding from a severed steam pipe to shrapnel and blast wounds. As soon as one fire was put out another started up and power failures stopped the boiler room fans so that the stokers could work only ten-minute shifts.

Cumberland limped off to apply what first aid she could, committed her dead to the deep, and was given permission to retire to Bathurst in the Gambia where she arrived battered, scorched and short of drinking water. 'We felt generally fed up,' noted the teenage Midshipman Emden in his log. 'One shell had put us out of action and we had not fired a shot in anger.'

Back at Dakar shots in anger were multiplying and for some of the combatants Situations Sticky and Nasty were already indistinguishable. The destroyer *Foresight* was part of the anti-submarine screen and one of the closest ships to shore. As an additional task, newly joined Midshipman Tony Syms had been supposed to take the ship's motorboat to within loud-hailing distance of the beach with a young Gaullist army officer on board. Fortunately for all concerned, once his passenger's compatriots had made it clear that they were not interested in conversation, this was cancelled.

Syms, not yet 20 and a veteran on the cruiser *Manchester* of the Norwegian campaign, soon found himself admiring the coloured French shell splashes and thinking how useful this marking system would have been when he met up with the Kriegsmarine off Narvik.

> My action station was in the wheel house in charge of the plot. There was no plotting to be done. We knew where we were and the enemy was static. We fired back in their general direction naturally, but more to keep our spirits up than to engage any clearly observed target . . . A-gun was hit and a great sheet of flame [from ammunition] flared up and blew back over B-gun deck towards the bridge. This was the one occasion in the war when I thought I was going to die immediately as I was sure we would blow up. Transfixed, I silently began to count to ten while waiting for the explosion. Number ten came but brought no explosion and the flames subsided. In the wheel house we realised that we might still have a future. The Captain, on the compass platform above, fortunately not bothered with counting to ten, promptly ordered 'Full Ahead' and we accelerated to get clear but not before the shore batteries registered another hit passing through our pendant numbers [destroyers had names and numbers – *Foresight*'s was H68] on the port side and out through our pendant numbers on the starboard side

before exploding but wrecking our wireless office on its way through. Point blank stuff, not to be prolonged.

Four of the destroyer's crew had been killed: a telegraphist, two able seamen and a cook. But though well-holed, the *Foresight* was still able to fight and remained on her patrol line.

Cunningham had twice warned that vessels attempting to leave harbour would be engaged and when the submarine *Persée* tried to sneak out on the surface she was hit by a 6-inch shell from the *Barham* then depth-charged by the cruiser *Dragon*. Most of the submariners were saved. The *Porthos*, among fifty or so merchant ships in the port, received one of the British battleships' 15-inch shells and caught fire. Similar packages fell indiscriminately on the vegetable gardens of officers' wives and ancient courtyards packed with humanity.

The airwaves were also busy with two-way traffic. 'Come, good Frenchmen of Dakar, there is still time. Impose your will on the guilty ones who are firing on Frenchmen,' appealed de Gaulle from the *Westernland*.

'Blood is already flowing and it's your responsibility!' roared a furious Governor Boisson who, being stone deaf in one ear from the same shell that deprived him of his leg, tended to shout down the microphone at the Radio Dakar studio. Nor was his temper helped by his conviction, shared with most of his contemporaries, that he was dealing with a treacherous adventurer and British puppet.

Although de Gaulle did not shout back, he was equally unimpressed and the day was not very old – 10.20 – when he began to take a much firmer line with his unseen adversary. 'The French ships and troops which are accompanying me must enter Dakar. If they meet with resistance, the large Allied forces following me will take the matter in hand.'

But in late afternoon, it was the Free French who attempted to raise the stakes when, with the encouragement of their allies, they began Plan Charles. This was a fallback scheme to go ashore at Rufisque Bay, about 13 miles east of Dakar and well out of range of its heavy guns but less than a day's march away along a good coast road. It was formerly the main outlet for transferring peanut exports from lighters to merchant ships anchored in the bay and had a couple of jetties and a small lighthouse as well as several other good landing places. From Rufisque they could take the port from the rear and de Gaulle decided that the first wave would be some 180 *fusiliers marins*, French marines who had mainly come over to him from the ships seized at British ports, and would be landed from three sloops, two of which had sufficiently shallow draught to get to one of the jetties. Once they had established a bridgehead, preferably without bloodshed, Monclar's Legionnaires would be ferried ashore from the Free Dutch liners in a second wave.

The British arranged to cover the landings with HMAS *Australia*, an

8-inch-gun heavy cruiser that had replaced the torpedoed *Fiji*, and two destroyers, *Fury* and *Greyhound*. It took some time to get all the ships in the right place. This was mostly because of poor radio communications between Cunningham on the *Barham* and de Gaulle on the *Westernland* where cypher operators were often having difficulties decoding messages. Added to this fog of war was the literal fog, still there and sometimes reducing visibility to a couple of hundred yards, though patchy in places. It was through one of these gaps in the goo that a French aircraft spotted the Free French ships heading towards Rufisque. The fast super-destroyer *L'Audacieux* came out to have a better look with the sloop *Surprise* doing her best to keep up but soon falling out of sight. They were followed by the cruisers *Georges Leygues*, *Montcalm* and *Le Malin*, another destroyer that was practically a light cruiser in British terms with big guns – 5.5-inch – on a light hull design.

Australia and her accompanying destroyers spotted *L'Audacieux* shortly after the French ship had emerged through the gate in the anti-submarine net to the east of Gorée Island and opened fire on her almost immediately. The cruiser had been attached to the Home Fleet at Scapa Flow in the twelve months since the outbreak of war and had seen plenty of rough and very cold water but little action. This was the first time the Australians had used their main armament in anger: in the space of sixteen minutes their eight 8-inch guns delivered eight salvos at 4,000 yards, point-blank range for naval gunnery. At least one man aboard had mixed feelings. Eighteen-year-old Pierre Austin's father had been badly wounded at Passchendaele, had married the young woman who had nursed him back to health and taken her home to Melbourne. 'It was a French ship and I had a French mother. It was rather a peculiar position to be in but it had to be done.'

L'Audacieux, her bridge wrecked, soon began to burn in several places. Eighty-one French sailors were killed. By the time her crew abandoned ship she was ablaze from stem to stern and drifting towards the shore where next day, still smouldering, the surf beached her not far from Rufisque's peanut jetties. An attempt by one of *Australia*'s destroyer escorts to pick up survivors was deterred by a coastal battery who were probably unable to see exactly what was going on, but the *Surprise*, though the sloop claimed to have come under British fire, turned up in time to rescue 186, of whom about half were discovered to be wounded in some way.

While the *Australia* was bludgeoning the good-looking super destroyer into a blackened hulk the cruisers *Georges Leygues* and *Montcalm* and *L'Audacieux*'s sister ship *Le Malin* slipped by. They were only about 3,000 yards apart and could hear the sound of the guns but could not work out where it was coming from or what it was about. Had *L'Audacieux* found the ships they were looking for, though there had been no radio message? Or had the British begun a more serious bombardment of the forts? The last thing they wanted was to risk bumping into Cunningham's cruiser and destroyer screen and have them call up the battleships' artillery. So they continued on their south-easterly course confident that, providing the fog held no nasty surprises, they had more than enough firepower to sink the kind of troop carriers and small escorts seen heading towards Rufisque. They had no idea that the defector Charles de Gaulle was on one of them.

Chapter Ten

War gamers subject some moves to the throw of a dice to represent the element of luck which so often determines the outcome of any military endeavour and was the quality Napoléon demanded that his generals have above all else. Certainly, chance played a major role in events at Rufisque Bay on 23 September 1940 and with far-reaching consequences. For had the dice rolled one way instead of another, twentieth century France would have been deprived of its best known and most influential leader and Vichy would have had a stunning triumph.

The dice was the fog, rolling this way and that. Without the fog the landings of the *fusiliers marins* would have been supported by the firepower of the *Australia* and the two British destroyers. Without the fog none of Vichy's warships in Dakar would have dared leave the harbour in broad daylight in the face of overwhelming odds including 15-inch guns that could sink them with impunity. In the fog *L'Audacieux* lived up to her name, did not get the luck she deserved and paid the price.

De Gaulle's first attempt to set foot on French territory since he had fled France with Spears some three months before had suddenly placed him and the nucleus of his little army in considerable danger. But he only became aware of this when Major John Watson, who was General Spears's aide-de-camp, came onto the bridge of the *Westernland* waving a signal from Admiral Cunningham about the two Vichy cruisers that had broken out of Dakar. An *Ark Royal* Swordfish had spotted them less than 2 miles away from the Free French ships and none of Cunningham's fleet was close enough to come to their rescue. If the cruisers found them Spears thought it unlikely, even if it was offered, that de Gaulle would surrender. He envisaged a Free French Götterdämmerung with ships blazing like torches, their flames extinguished only as they sizzled beneath 'a shark-infested sea'.

Fog was only partly to blame for the absence of Royal Navy protection. As the day wore on communications between Cunningham on the *Barham* and de Gaulle on the *Westernland* had grown progressively worse. There was a simple reason for this. The army had provided both ships with a Royal Signals detachment using the very latest equipment: radio telephones coupled with a scrambler device that would leave Vichy wireless monitors listening to a manic warbling garble.

But there was one insurmountable problem. Every time they tried to use them they shut down all the flagship's wireless telegraphy. Cunningham could not speak to his fleet. Wavelengths were changed and antennae adjusted but the end result was always the same. So with great regret the wonderful radio telephones were switched off. Unfortunately, somebody forgot to inform the *Barham*'s own naval operators who had their work cut out taking and deciphering messages from every other ship in the fleet and tended to give the *Westernland*'s messages low priority assuming that all her urgent signals had already been relayed by radio telephone.

Because of this wireless messages were sometimes taking over an hour to be encyphered, tapped out in Morse then decyphered and passed on at the other end. The most crucial example was two requests from Cunningham for the position of the French transports so that he could get the *Australia* and the destroyers to rendezvous with them. The first was sent at 2.15 p.m. then repeated at 3.02. A reply timed at 2.45 giving *Westernland*'s latest position was not received until 4 p.m., hopelessly out of date. In the end, Cunningham despaired and advised that he was cancelling his end of Plan Charles.

But by the time de Gaulle received this message his *fusiliers marins* were already attempting to land. As it turned out it was probably just as well that he did not send his Legionnaires in first because, with their *élan*, they were much more likely to have established a bridgehead and might well have been abandoned on it. There was no such problem with the French marines. Spears described their lacklustre performance as 'pathetic' and accused them of lacking both leadership and training and 'even the minimum required for brave men to dash for an objective'.

He was being too harsh. From the beginning the whole ethos of Operation Menace had been all about bluff and bloodless victory: bouquets not bullets. First of all two of the sloops had come under fire from machine guns and some small 3.7-inch mountain cannon placed near the lighthouse by the peanut lighter jetties. These guns were under a young *aspirant* (a cadet officer) who rather later in his career was adamant that he planned to give up as soon as his position became dangerous.

These pious intentions did not prevent his battery from scoring a bull's-eye on the sloop *Commandant Duboc* which killed three men. The ship, which was not badly damaged, rapidly removed herself, as did the accompanying *Savorgnan de Brazza* which started to return fire with her 5.5-inch guns, demolishing the little lighthouse and sending the *aspirant* and his men running for cover. Next it was decided to put the marines into motorboats and disembark them on what was expected to be a deserted beach further south. They were within 300 yards of the shore when a few rifle shots from some Senegalese troops scared them away, though in less troubled times the askaris' French commander, like the *aspirant*, would insist that he was astonished at this outcome and merely intended a token resistance before surrender.

By now de Gaulle had received the warning about the cruisers on the loose and ordered the sloops and the marines to withdraw. The *Westernland* and *Pennland* were already hastening away through the fog, missing the cruisers by about 1,500 yards as the Vichy ships gave up their search and returned to Dakar. The crippled *Richelieu*, which was acting as the Vichy naval communications centre, had informed them by wireless of what happened to *L'Audacieux* and this must have made them feel that the fog was not necessarily their friend.

'Having begun we must go on to the end. Stop at nothing,' Churchill cabled his commanders at the end of Operation Matador's first day, which could at best be described as disappointing. The messaged revived Admiral Cunningham's flagging spirits. So it was to be Situation Nasty after all: no more pussyfooting around trying to get people to see the error of their ways. 'Desiring Frenchmen not to fight against Frenchmen in a pitched battle General de Gaulle has withdrawn his forces,' it was explained in an ultimatum to Governor Boisson due to expire at 0600 next morning, at which point, if the governor had not agreed that the Free French could land, the Royal Navy would start to exact a terrible retribution. 'Once fire has begun it will continue until the fortifications of Dakar are entirely destroyed and the place occupied by troops who are ready to fulfil their duty.'

Vichy losses included a destroyer and a submarine and exceeded the British but their morale was high. The Anglo-Gaullists had come with their ships and their smooth talk and, when that had failed, they had huffed and they had puffed but they had come nowhere near to blowing down their house. The ultimatum, especially a line that they were obviously prepared to hand Dakar over to the Germans, caused great indignation. Were they expected to collapse because of more threats from these blowhards? Some of the young officers on Boisson's staff, exhilarated by their success, wanted to use the famous single-word reply with which Napoléon's Old Guard were said to have refused English demands to surrender at Waterloo. *Merde*! But this was rejected. It was too poignant a reminder of a terrible French defeat. And Boisson was beginning to sense that this was not going to be a defeat.

Instead he got the navy signallers on the *Richelieu* to send: 'France has entrusted me Dakar. I shall defend Dakar to the end.'

Boisson's reply was picked up at about 4 a.m. Two and a half hours later, well after first light, six Skuas, each carrying a 500-pound semi-armour-piercing bomb, left the *Ark Royal*, flew over the fog and attacked the *Richelieu* and other ships. The results were disappointing: three near misses that might have sprung a few plates, two on the battleship and one on a destroyer. Their crews reported light anti-aircraft fire but Vichy fighters made no attempt to intercept them. Half an hour later another six aircraft, this time Swordfish, bombed the coastal guns at Fort Manual that had put *Cumberland* out of action. Again there was no serious opposition and eight hits were claimed. Photo-reconnaissance of a tight rash of grouped bomb craters was deemed to confirm this, though it is doubtful if any of those looking at them knew exactly where the dug-in and camouflaged Maginot line-style gun battery bunker was supposed to be.

Meanwhile, the aircrew of a second six-strong Swordfish strike on the fort, each aircraft armed with four 250-pound semi-armour-piercing bombs, were sitting in their cockpits with their engines running waiting for the carrier to turn into the wind and allow them to fly off. Among them was the observer Charles Friend who had last been over Dakar scattering leaflets the day before. They all watched as the Duty Boy, a teenager armed with a small blackboard, came down from the conning tower. Once on the flight deck, bracing himself so that no sudden movement of the ship sent him into a moving propeller, he went up to each aircraft and held up his blackboard so that the pilot could see it. Friend saw that on it was chalked: 'Change target to *Richelieu*.' All the pilots acknowledged by giving the Duty Boy the thumbs-up sign then he stepped back from the din and the danger and the carrier completed her turn into the wind and they took off.

In the air they split into two sub-flights of three that, in order to make themselves a narrower target, changed into line astern formation as the harbour came into view. Friend's aircraft was at the rear of his sub-flight. Immediately in front of him, in a Swordfish piloted by 'Aggie' England, was 'Goon' Richardson who had been on the observer course immediately before his. Although they were in the same squadron – 810 – Friend had never learned the first names of these officers any more than he could be sure of the identity of the rating in his rear cockpit manning the Lewis machine gun. In his own aircraft the man sitting immediately behind him with his pans of .303 tracer ammunition was Leading Seaman Huxley. Big black puffs of smoke began to burst around them and Friend thought the French anti-aircraft gunners had judged their height nicely.

> As we lined up to dive bomb the Richelieu I was facing forward looking over Jock's [the pilot's] shoulder and I saw one Stringbag ahead hit by flak and falling out of the line in flames. Then I was startled by a heavy thump on the back from Huxley who was heaving up the rear gun as I looked round. He pointed astern at three or four fighters – one of which was obviously bent on attacking us – Curtiss Hawks. Pointing and shouting were the only means of communicating with the air gunner although I was linked to Jock by the Gosport tube voicepipe. I said to him, 'There's a

fighter on our tail.' 'Christ!' he said. 'Tell me when to turn.' Huxley opened fire just before I saw the flashes of a cannon firing through the Hawk's propeller and said, 'Now!' Next thing, Huxley and I were up on the end of our 'monkey chain' harnesses as Jock turned over to starboard and back. The fighter flew on in a wide turn, unable to follow us round. He, or one of the other Frenchmen attacked the Stringbags ahead and one more of them was shot down before our eyes. Jock jettisoned our bombs over the roadstead outside the harbour and we flew back on our own to land on Ark. Three of the strike were lost, the two I had seen hit and another which fell to the high angle guns. I began to think it was a pretty odd war in which our erstwhile allies the French shot at us from aeroplanes made by the Americans who seemed to be on our side. But I suppose we started it.

Four of the nine missing Swordfish aircrew were killed. The only survivor from Lieutenant Ian England's machine was the observer 'Goon' Richardson. He had great difficulty separating himself from the aircraft which had turned upside down in the water and to which he was still umbilically attached by his flying helmet's connections to the radio and the Gosport speaking tube with the pilot. Half conscious, he surfaced with a broken arm and his mouth tasting of petrol to discover that the aircraft's rubber dinghy had also escaped but was floating bottom up. This made it impossible to get at the flares and fresh water it contained but Richardson was in no condition to right it; all he could do was to haul himself onto its slippery underside and hang on. He was eventually rescued by the Vichy submarine *Bévéziers*, commanded as it happened by a capitaine de corvette called Lancelot, whose crew treated their captive well, as did the Dakar military hospital to which they delivered him.

At this point the *Bévéziers* had become the sole survivor of the three submarines Vichy started with in Dakar. Shortly after 8 a.m. the Asdic operator on the destroyer *Fortune* had detected the *Ajax* about to make a torpedo run on the battleships and dropped a single depth charge which twenty-six minutes later brought *Ajax* to the surface where she immediately showed a white flag. The crew were transferred to the destroyer and the submarine sunk by gunfire though not before a boarding party had gone through her control centre and officers' quarters, snatching all the documents they could find. Their biggest trophy was an order from Amiral Darlan instructing his fleet to use a certain radio code, explaining it could also be read by the Axis powers. Spears was outraged, pointing out to London that it made a mockery of Vichy's insistence that they were neutral because all their reports on the location of British ships were being shared with Berlin and Rome.

But this was the only British triumph of another indecisive day where all the Vichy defenders were required to do was to remain undefeated. The early morning air attacks had been a fiasco. The coastal battery on Cape

Manuel had hardly got dusty. Nor had any of the ships taken a single hit. Even if they had, the 250-pound bombs on the Swordfish were unlikely to have pierced the *Richelieu*'s 8-inch-thick armoured deck plate. 'We might as well have dropped house bricks,' admitted one squadron commander. A change of ordnance brought no more success. In the afternoon nine Swordfish with an escort of three Skuas attacked the two cruisers that had been searching for the Free French forces off Rufisque. The only hits were on the Swordfish with two downed by anti-aircraft fire. This brought the *Ark Royal*'s total aircraft losses up to eight: three Skua monoplanes had also been lost in the earlier attacks, either shot down or too damaged for a deck landing so that their crews had to ditch alongside the carrier then escape their sinking machines before they drowned with them.

None of this would have mattered if the ship-to-shore bombardment, particularly the sixteen 15-inch guns of the two battleships, had been as terrible and awe-inspiring as was expected but little of it was accurate enough to make a difference. The fog had not gone away and the French destroyer *Hardi* did her best to improve on nature by constantly laying smoke screens. Directing fire from the air was becoming increasingly difficult and also dangerous with the French Curtiss Hawks waiting to pounce on any lumbering Swordfish or Skua that dared venture low enough to take a good look.

On the troopships the Royal Marines had barbed-wire entanglements in mind and to blast a path through them were busy assembling Bangalore Torpedoes, the extendable metal tubes packed with fused gun cotton extensively used by British infantry in 1914–18. Few of the marines had any doubt that they would soon be the sharp end of a full-scale amphibious assault on well-defended Vichy positions. The night before, the lieutenants expecting to lead their platoons into action for the first time had been signing bar chits with the abandon of young men with the best excuse in the world.

They could have spared themselves their hangovers. Neither Cunningham nor General Irwin was prepared to risk heavy casualties. There was no intention of attempting a landing on Dakar until most of the coastal batteries were silenced and that was proving far more difficult than they imagined. They were still trying to work out the precise location of all the short-range 5.4-inch guns of the kind that had hit the destroyer *Foresight* when she was operating close inshore the day before. The bigger and slower troop transports would be much more vulnerable.

Dakar was a good example of the old naval maxim that ships should not take on forts that are unsinkable and invariably overlook their sea-level opponents. In his own account of the battle Churchill cites Nelson's view that 'a six-gun battery could fight a 100-gun ship-of-the-line'. If it had not been for the fog, Cunningham's battleships could have kept out of range of all but air strikes and the *Richelieu*, her main firepower reduced to two guns after a fatal accident in her one working turret involving propellant charges. As it was, both the battleships had been obliged to come close enough to be straddled by the French 5.4- and 6-inch guns. *Resolution* led a charmed life but *Barham* was hit four times and was lucky not to sustain any serious damage, while the only fatality was unmourned, being one of the ship's rats. Some of this fire was coming from *Richelieu*'s secondary armament but luckily for Cunningham her brace of working 15-inchers were no more accurate than his own which had succeeded in hitting the *Richelieu* only twice and doing no serious damage. And the British had eight times the firepower. French air strikes on the task force were becoming increasingly troublesome. They had not hit anything yet but there had been several near misses and *Ark Royal*'s Skuas seemed unable to stop them. Nor was Vichy air activity confined to Dakar.

Over Gibraltar that same afternoon forty Vichy bombers from Moroccan airfields flying above high levanter cloud rained an estimated 150 bombs on the fortress, which the Royal Navy had been hastily reinforcing in order to keep its passage through the western Mediterranean open. Although half the bombs fell into the sea it was a much larger affair than any of the essentially hit-and-run Italian raids that had preceded it. The battle cruiser *Renown*, all anti-aircraft guns blazing, made a dash for the open sea and was narrowly missed by two bombs. The dockyards were hit but bad visibility seems to have benefited both sides, for the damage was slight and none of the raiders was brought down.

By the time this Vichy revenge for the attack on Dakar was taking place the British had fired the last of the day's 400 15-inch shells at the port to little avail. Far from terrifying the defenders into surrender it seemed to have stiffened resistance. On the *Barham* the humidity in the gun turrets was so bad that, looking down from the bridge during one of the lulls in bombardment, Admiral Cunningham was startled to see stark-naked gunners sitting on the top of their turret wringing the sweat out of their overalls. Men working in the airless confines of the magazine space below the turrets had been passing out with the heat, been dragged out and revived with buckets of water then gone back to work until they fainted again, when the process was repeated.

While these exhausted nudists stood on the turret savouring the sea breeze, the wireless room had sent Cunningham a translation of an intercepted message from Pétain to Governor General Boisson praising the 'courage and fidelity' of his garrison. 'France follows with emotion and confidence your resistance to the partisan treachery and the British aggression ... The entire mother country is proud of your attitude and of the resolution of the forces under your command.'

After the defection of Eboué, the mulatto governor of Chad and an ingrate if ever there was one as far as his superiors were concerned, Pétain's message made it obvious that Vichy was inspired by Boisson's resistance and that the governor general, basking in the accolades of the hero of Verdun, was unlikely to throw in his lot with 'partisan treachery'. If the Anglo-Gaullists wanted Dakar they would have to be prepared to fight for every inch of it and that was never part of the plan. A lifeboat from the destroyer *Foresight* was sent to fetch de Gaulle from the *Westernland* and bring him to the *Barham* where Spears, who was in attendance, described the conference that followed as resembling 'an old Irish wake at which the participants tried to pretend that the corpse was not dead'.

Throughout the morning de Gaulle had been listening to the 'rather lively cannonade' being exchanged between the British and his countrymen with mounting despair. Nonetheless, Admiral Cunningham and Generals Irwin and Spears would all be impressed by his display of grace under pressure on the bridge of the *Barham* where the consensus was that Operation Menace had become Operation Muddle and Free France had lost. The only sign of any private anguish was de Gaulle's chain-smoking. Most soldiers quickly learned that the Royal Navy's upper decks were as sacrosanct as any parade ground. A fascinated Spears observed the Frenchman flick one butt after another onto timber whitened by daily scrubbing, while the appalled Cunningham silently provided spent anti-aircraft shell cases as ashtrays only to discover his visitor was as bad a shot as his gunners.

While Spears watched the admiral watching cigarette ends 'with all the hypnotised attention of a Wimbledon fan' de Gaulle came up with a face-saving idea: since an opposed landing would lead to the kind of pitched battle between Frenchmen he was trying to avoid, Dakar should be informed that, at his request, they were stopping the bombardment. This was agreed, though another proposal that the British should maintain their blockade of Dakar and deny the Vichy warships freedom of movement was turned down. There were not enough ships: guarding against invasion in home waters, hunting the U-boats trying to starve Britain into surrender in the Atlantic and supporting the army's defence of Egypt and the Suez canal against the Italians by dominating the Mediterranean had to come first. There could be no question of the Royal Navy keeping a permanent squadron off the West African coast.

And that might have brought down the curtain on Operation Menace had it not been for a couple of things. First of all, after de Gaulle had returned to the *Westernland* believing it was all over, late night forecasts indicated that the fog might disperse. The prospect of good visibility tempted the British commanders to inform the Admiralty that they would make another attack on ships and forts in the morning though they added: 'Should inadequate result be obtained we recommend the adoption of de Gaulle's proposals.' Second, this despatch crossed with a querulous message from Churchill who was plainly finding it difficult to comprehend how a puny force of Vichyites could successfully defy a Royal Navy Second Fifteen however arthritic its battleships.

> Why do you not land in force by night or in the fog or both on the beaches near Rufisque and take Rufisque for a start ... ? At the same time, if the weather clears, you could hold down batteries on Goree Island in daylight by long-range sea fire, and if there is fog you would not need to do so. It should be possible to feed force, once ashore, by night. This force, once landed, ought to be able to advance on Dakar ... Pray act as you think best but, meanwhile, give a reasoned answer to these points. Matter must be pushed to conclusion without delay.

Next day was all the weatherman had promised it would be. Clear blue skies had replaced the fog. All night Cunningham's ships had been circling south of Dakar and out of range of French guns. At 6 a.m. they began to move north towards their bombardment positions, the *Barham* and the *Resolution* in the lead. For the first time the French gunners would be able to see what they were up against. Furthermore, the battleships would have their spotters up and be able to shoot straighter. At first light *Ark Royal* flew off reconnaissance and anti-submarine aircraft with Skuas flying fighter cover.

The bombardment plan was for *Resolution* to attack the immobile *Richelieu* while the *Barham* and the cruiser *Devonshire* would take on the forts. Meanwhile, the *Australia*, the other cruiser, would go after her two French equivalents, the *Georges Leygues* and the *Montcalm* which were in Dakar harbour. Spotting for the *Australia* was her own Walrus float plane, an even slower biplane than the Swordfish, whose two-man crew were launched by catapult and their aircraft winched up from a sea landing by crane. It found the cruisers easily enough, lost them briefly under a smoke screen, located them again and had just directed the *Australia*'s fire so that it was straddling the targets when a Curtiss Hawk dived through intense anti-aircraft fire from the battleships and shot it down before crashing itself. None of these three aircrew, French or British, survived.

As more Curtisses began to chase away the Swordfish and Skuas, some badly holed and lucky to get back to the carrier, Cunningham's ships began to find themselves, despite the good visibility, back in the familiar position of firing blind. This gave Pierre Lancelot, commander of the submarine *Bévéziers* which had rescued the wounded Swordfish observer 'Goon' Cunningham the day before, his chance to try to avenge the loss of the other two submarines in his flotilla.

Lancelot was among those French officers who before the armistice had worked closely with the Royal Navy and knew its flag signals. Lurking at periscope depth some 3,000 yards from the two battleships, he saw that Cunningham's flagship *Barham* had hoisted the 'Blue 7' signal instructing

Resolution to 'turn to bombardment course'. He waited until the helmsmen had begun to bring their 30,000 tons of warship around in synchronized turns to starboard then discharged four torpedoes at them. Lookouts spotted the white froth of their tracks almost immediately and the ships began frantic turns back to port in order to get their bows pointing towards the tracks so that they could become a much thinner target and steam between them: a manoeuvre known as 'combing'.

Barham just made it but one of the torpedoes hit *Resolution* amidships, flooding her port boiler room and starting fires. One able seaman was mortally wounded. Speed was halved to 12 knots and she was listing almost 13 degrees to port before the pumps could stop it. With two destroyers attempting to hide her plight in a smoke screen, the battleship tottered away while a third destroyer, the *Foresight*, dashed down the direction of the torpedo tracks and began depth-charging as soon as her Asdic operator thought he heard a telltale ping.

Foresight's captain was convinced he had avenged the four dead from his own ship on their first day at Dakar but he was mistaken: Lancelot had got clean away, the hero of the hour as far as Vichy was concerned, for he had brought Operation Menace to its inevitable end. Half an hour after London had learned what had happened to the *Resolution* Churchill was cabling Cunningham: 'We have decided that the enterprise against Dakar should be abandoned, the obvious evil consequences being faced.'

A crippled capital ship that might never reach dry dock was far more than the Admiralty ever intended to invest in Général de Gaulle; to risk further losses was inconceivable. As it was, Vichy aircraft had just raided Gibraltar for the second time in twenty-four hours and there were a lot more of them. Anti-aircraft gunners claimed to have shot down three but an armed trawler used for anti-submarine work had been sunk alongside the south mole and bombs on shore had killed several civilians, one of them the secretary of Admiral Dudley North. Some British officers insisted that enough bombs had hit the sea to indicate that not all the French flyers had their hearts in it but at this stage of the war people who should have known better still had very exaggerated ideas about the accuracy of aerial bombing.

In Franco's precariously neutral Madrid, France's naval attaché would shortly be making it plain to his British counterpart that they would bomb Gibraltar again if the attacks on Dakar continued. There was not much chance of this in the immediate future. Cunningham's 15-inch gun power had been reduced by half and his ships were returning to Freeport, the *Resolution* towed by *Barham*. 'Bloodshed has been avoided at the cost of honour,' Captain Waugh wrote to his wife Laura from the *Ettrick*. By which he meant Royal Marine blood. In all the British lost about 20 killed, casualties more or less equally divided between the Fleet Air Arm and the sailors. Probably as many were wounded. Vichy lost 166 of whom 92 were

Europeans and the rest African. Wounded totalled 340, almost 70 per cent African, which was hardly surprising after just over two days of heavy naval bombardment with the overs falling into the crush of the urban poor.

'A very gay journey back. Very drunken evenings in the officers' mess. The troops less light hearted about their reverse,' Waugh confided to his diary, notions of lost honour having apparently become less troublesome. In their own bar the warrant officers and sergeants of Waugh's battalion, a professional if mostly untested brotherhood who had been anticipating their battle debut with all the usual feelings of dread and fierce fascination, had composed a new song. In the morning most of them could only remember the chorus:

We went to Dakar with General de Gaulle.
We sailed round in circles and did bugger all.

Chapter Eleven

Vichy lost no time in turning Dakar's defiance into a famous victory. A number of French newsmen, including a cinema newsreel cameraman, had either been in the port from the beginning or got there in time to photograph the defenders artfully arranged amid the ruins. Six weeks later magazines such as *L'Illustration* were still running big black and white pictures of the commander of the destroyer *L'Audacieux* greeting the more photogenic of his wounded crew on a hospital verandah and of their gallant ship herself, beached and burnt out with a couple of respectful camels in the foreground. There was also a trophy: an almost intact Swordfish to which some wit had pinned a piece of cardboard with a '*Communiqué anglais*' dated 24 September 1940 claiming that all British planes had returned safely to base.

In the British press, obliged to accept censorship in its war reporting but still able to bite on its comment pages, contempt for the 'Dakar fiasco' was universal. 'MAJOR BLUNDER! screamed the *Daily Mirror*'s headline over an editorial that spoke of 'the lowest depths of imbecility' and declared the Norwegian campaign now looked like a distinguished naval exploit. 'We have lost a golden opportunity,' observed the *Telegraph*. And the *Daily Mail* warned, 'a fiasco which will discourage our friends and give joy to our enemies'.

None more than Pierre Laval. France had routed the Anglo-Gaullists. The French were no longer on their knees. They had proved they had something to offer. Here was leverage. All Laval's formidable bargaining powers had been roused and Pétain, despite growing reservations about his slippery deputy, knew he was the right man to use Dakar to try to extract concessions out of Germany: allow them to send more soldiers and ships to defend their African possessions. By the evening of the second day of the action, a good twelve hours before Lancelot torpedoed the *Resolution*, Laval was already in Paris and telling Ambassador Abetz, 'France is contributing her modest share to the final overthrow of England.'

For the Germans, the collapse of France had been dreamlike enough. Understandably, the prospect that it would then go to war with England had not entered their calculations. But now things began to move fast.

This was not only because of the Laval-Abetz meetings but due to parallel talks being held between Général Huntziger, who since leaving the Armistice Commission had become Pétain's Minister of War, and Feldmarschal Walter von Brauchitsch, then Commander-in-Chief of the Wehrmacht. 'France and Germany have an armistice, but it is also a fact that France is fighting with Germany against Britain. This anomalous situation must be settled,' Huntziger told him.

Soldier to soldier the two got on well together. This was more than could be said for Brauchitsch's relationship with Laval which had not survived their first meeting. At the end of August Laval had attempted to acquire extra French troops to recapture the new Gaullist enclaves in French colonial Africa by hinting that, if Germany played its cards right, France might declare war against England. 'We don't need your help, which would be practically nil in any case,' snapped the handsome Prussian aristocrat, one of the architects of the summer blitzkrieg and entirely unprepared for Laval's practised insolence. And that was the end of that. Others were less fastidious. When it came to the big breakthrough the former premier, the man who was once getting at least as many column inches in the international press as Adolf Hitler, was Germany's first choice as the obvious go-between for a new understanding with France.

On 20 October 1940 Laval was in Paris when Abetz announced he had arranged a meeting with Ribbentrop but he must not tell anybody. Laval knew he risked an almighty row with Pétain if he met the German Foreign Minister without informing him and persuaded Abetz to let him make a brief return to Vichy for a private chat with the maréchal.

Even at this early stage the Vichy regime was beginning to break up into clearly identifiable camps, the main divide being between Laval's pro-German faction and Foreign Minister Baudouin who, with all his banker's caution, advocated strict neutrality and a policy of *attentisme*: wait and see. On the edge of this group was Général Maxime Weygand, at 73 some ten years younger than Pétain and twice as cantankerous, a xenophobe who disliked the British but disliked the Germans more and felt Churchill's surprisingly prolonged resistance might yet profit France. Weygand had just taken command of the French troops the Axis had allowed to remain in North Africa and, though he agreed it was sometimes tactically necessary to collaborate with Berlin, he had plans to reinforce them secretly so that they might ultimately provide the springboard for liberation. As for Laval, he thought he 'wallowed in defeat like a dog in filth'.

On the morning of the 22nd, the object of Weygand's scorn was back in Paris and meeting Abetz at the German Embassy. As instructed, he was carrying an overnight bag. Accompanying Laval was the aristocratic Fernand de Brinon, a decorated war veteran and right-wing journalist, whom Laval had persuaded Pétain to appoint as Vichy's representative in German-occupied France. De Brinon had long advocated rapprochement with Germany and had been the first French journalist to interview Hitler when he came to power in 1933. A scoop made even more remarkable by de Brinon's marriage to Lisette Franck, a Jewish divorcée and airhead society hostess to whom he was clearly devoted.

Abetz had organized chauffeur-driven official cars and the party, with its accompanying bodyguards and secretaries, left Paris on the road to the south-west following the same route taken only four months before by Prime Minister Reynaud and France's last elected government. Like them they broke their journey at Tours just outside the Vichy zone where Abetz, who had told Laval he did not know the exact venue for the meeting, had to visit the local Wehrmacht headquarters to find out where they had to go next. When he emerged they turned north, back-tracking slightly into the fading greenness of the Loire, for it was now almost dusk. It was about then that Abetz felt the time was right to drop his bombshell. 'I must warn you,' he said, 'that it's not only Foreign Minister Von Ribbentrop you're going to see. It is also Chancellor Hitler.'

'*Merde, alors*!' gasped Laval. It had never occurred to him that they were travelling this fast.

Hitler was going on his private train *Amerika*, two locomotives hauling an imposing composition of comfort and firepower, to keep a rendezvous with Franco on the Spanish border. He hoped to persuade the Caudillo to join the Axis and announce Spain's declaration of war against Britain by launching, with German air support, a surprise attack on Gibraltar. The Führer had decided that on the way he would also make contact with the French and see if, after their surprising performance at Dakar, they too were ready to take the plunge and go to war with Britain in a Continental Coalition alongside Germany and Italy. France, after all, had already gone rather further along this route than Spain and bombed Gibraltar. Between them a united Latin front of Italy, Spain and France should, even without Germany's help, be able to drive the British out of the Mediterranean.

But there was a snag. They all had competing claims to large stretches of North Africa where Mussolini wanted to add French Tunisia to Italian Libya plus a generous slice of Algeria, while Spain demanded French and Spanish Morocco be joined together under Madrid. Vichy was only too aware of its neighbours' ambitions which had long been aired and during Armistice Commission talks at Wiesbaden had made a simple and undeniable response: Gaullist dissidence would always thrive on Axis threats to French colonies just as Anglo-Gaullist aggression, as Dakar proved, bred loyalty to Vichy.

Hitler's meeting with Laval took place at the country railway station at Montoire-sur-le-Loir which was in the occupied zone and until then best known as the birthplace of Pierre Ronsard, the sixteenth-century poet. It was not normally garrisoned but since early morning the pretty little provincial town with its frescoed chapel and stunning bridge had been full of German troops and French police; all the school children had been given the day off and told to stay at home with their parents. Montoire, hardly more than a village, had been chosen as the venue for this initial contact because it was about as remote as you could get and still be on a railway line that could get you to and from the Spanish border. Its other attraction was that its train station came at the end of a tunnel long enough, if necessary, to accommodate the fifteen items of rolling stock carrying *Amerika*' s beds, bathrooms, restaurants, kitchens, conference room, communications centre, SS platoon and anti-aircraft guns. RAF raids on *la France profonde* were hardly commonplace in October 1940; they had far too much else on their plate elsewhere. But if agents of the ubiquitous British secret service did manage to tip them off that Adolf Hitler was paying Montoire a visit *Amerika* could withdraw into a bomb-proof carapace while the RAF wiped the rest of the town off the map.

Laval was no stranger to tyrants. As Prime Minister and Foreign Minister he had had regular meetings with Mussolini and at least two with Stalin. After he got over his shock, his first encounter with Hitler was a brief and businesslike affair during which Laval told him, 'If you offer us a just peace which takes into account our honour and interests, anything may be possible.'

The meeting lasted about forty-five minutes and, as far as its instigator was concerned, its main purpose seems to have been to lay down an agenda – 'a clarification of fundamentals' – for a meeting he proposed with Pétain to take place at the same venue on his return from his discussions with Franco. Hitler lost no time in outlining how he saw the immediate future and France's possible part in it. Laval, in his lawyerly way, took notes.

> Intends mobilise entire continent against England ... Franco-German relations depend on their response to this. If France prepared to gamble on near certainty of imminent German victory when it comes to a proper peace agreement she would not have to pay the kind of financial compensation inflicted on Germany in 1918. But if France hoped for the exhaustion of Germany and played the waiting game and England offered a compromise peace first then she should expect to pay considerable reparations for the mounting costs of this war. 'I will not add to Germany's suffering by sparing France.'

Having enthusiastically accepted, on the maréchal's behalf, Hitler's invitation to meet them at Montoire on 24 October on his return from the Spanish frontier, Laval rushed back to Vichy with the Führer's glad tidings. 'We shall have to endure English reprisals,' Laval warned the following afternoon at a full meeting of the Council of Ministers at the Hotel du Parc. 'But we must take every risk in order to seize this magnificent opportunity.' Anything less, he said, would be 'a crime against France'. Foreign Minister Paul Baudouin, as everybody present expected he would, disagreed, saying he was 'absolutely hostile to a declaration of war against England'. Pétain said he was right and must come along to Montoire with them and tell Hitler. Laval said that Baudouin could not come because his friend Ambassador Abetz would not allow it. Pétain said he must. Laval said in that case they could go to Montoire without him. Pétain climbed down. Baudouin resigned and Laval, while remaining Pétain's deputy, was also made the new Foreign Minister.

At some point during this meeting what a later generation might call a 'photo opportunity' was arranged and the picture released by the American Associated Press which, like other neutral news agencies, had opened a bureau in Vichy along with its rival, United Press. All ten of them are seated around a long table, Maréchal Pétain, Général Huntziger (War Minister) and Amiral Darlan (Minister of the Marine) dressed like their civilian colleagues in suits and ties, the hatless Darlan at the end of the table doffing a rare public sighting of his bald pate. Presumably the photograph was intended to demonstrate consensus and scotch rumours of factionalism but by far the most striking thing about the picture is the way the youngish-looking man with a full head of dark hair seated next to Pétain's white moustache is glaring at Pierre Laval across the table. This is Paul Baudouin, the former Foreign Minister.

There were no Anglophiles in Pétain's Cabinet, the very notion a contradiction in terms. It was Baudouin who had broken off diplomatic relations with Britain but this was in response to Mers el-Kébir when Darlan was demanding blood for blood and the prospect of outright war was first raised. Quite apart from his desire to avoid full-scale hostilities, Baudouin did not think that France's best interests were served by breaking off all communication with their old ally. Vichy's diplomats were not discouraged from cocktail party contact with their British counterparts in Europe's neutral capitals. Madrid saw the most intercourse but it also happened at Lisbon and Geneva. Nor had Baudouin expelled Ottawa's consul in Vichy, a French Canadian named Pierre Dupuy, though his government, like the rest of the British Empire, mostly pursued their war against the Axis under London's guidance. Dupuy, said Churchill, was 'a window upon a courtyard on which we have no other access'. But briefly, and coinciding with the Montoire meetings, there was another.

Professor Louis Rougier, who taught philosophy at Besancon University, which is about 30 miles from the Swiss border in the Jura Mountains, had turned up at Baudouin's office six days before Pétain's Cabinet meeting on Montoire. He announced that he could get to England and was willing to act as an intermediary between Pétain and Churchill. Rougier's motives are uncertain. He was reasonably well known in French academic circles and also abroad: in 1921 his first book – *Philosophy and the New Physics* –

had been published in English translation. By 1940 his views were regarded as mildly eccentric though no more than might be expected of a fiftyish professor of philosophy. His conservative politics – a visit to the Soviet Union had cured him of any faith in planned economies – were certainly in tune with Vichyite thinking and he preached a pragmatism where, as far as government was concerned, what worked was more important than a belief in what ought to work. But presumably he did not, in that Catholic bastion, air his views on religion, which were not merely anticlerical but built on his firm disapproval of the entire Christian dogma.

Rougier's arrival in London and his first talks at the Foreign Office coincided with Laval's first meeting with Hitler and the beginning of the Luftwaffe's intensive night raids on London that had just seen the destruction of the high altar at St Paul's. Among other things, Pétain had asked him to suggest a *modus vivendi* to the British over Africa: Vichy would leave to rot those places that had already rallied to de Gaulle as long as London promised not to encourage the Gaullists to spread their poison in any more loyal Vichy colonies. There was also a request for the BBC to tone down its criticism of Pétain in its French language broadcasts. In this Rougier was pushing at an open door because it had already been decided that insulting the hero of Verdun was about as helpful as calling Joan of Arc a floozie.

Having jumped the first hurdle at the Foreign Office, the next day Rougier met Lord Halifax and the Foreign Secretary was sufficiently impressed to arrange a meeting with Churchill on the 25th, which he would also attend. This was the day after Pétain had met Hitler at Montoire on his way back from a very unsatisfactory meeting with Franco at the border town of Hendaye where the wide-gauge Spanish track met the narrow-gauge French one and the views of the two dictators were as incompatible as their locomotives. It turned out that Franco, though he made all the right noises, was not quite ready to join Hitler's Pan-European alliance against Britain. Spain was wasted by civil war, famine stalked the land, and in the ruins of Madrid there was the start of a typhoid epidemic; in any case, he was by no means convinced that Germany would win. 'The English will fight and go on fighting and never give in,' he told his generals, pointing out that the Admiralty would almost certainly want to console itself for the loss of Gibraltar by seizing Spain's Canary Islands.

Hitler was unaccustomed to Franco's kind of stonewalling. 'I'd rather have three or four of my teeth out than negotiate with that Jesuit swine again,' he confided to Mussolini. Pétain had been much more obliging as Professor Rougier was about to find out. Ushered into 10 Downing Street by Halifax, he was greeted by an angry-looking Churchill brandishing a photograph of Pétain in his full Maréchal's regalia giving Hitler a firm handshake. The Führer was wearing the contrived uniform in which he had been appearing in public ever since the war started: a kind of double-breasted suit with brass buttons and pinned to his left breast the Iron Cross First Class awarded for the courage Corporal Hitler had displayed in the trenches, mostly fighting against the British whose gas temporarily blinded him. Both men were captured gazing at each other with what appeared to be deep mutual respect and at the end of the meeting Hitler had stuck out his hand and the old maréchal instinctively took it. There was hardly a newspaper in the world that had not used the photographic evidence.

Churchill exploded all over the unfortunate Rougier, accusing Pétain of signing a peace treaty with Hitler and threatening to have the RAF, which had recently bombed Hamburg and Berlin though to little effect, visit Vichy and eliminate this nest of traitors. Rougier, of course, had no knowledge of the Hitler meeting, having left France several days before it was arranged and it must have been as much of a shock to him as it was to the British. Somehow he managed to persuade the Prime Minister that he was certain Pétain was merely trying to alleviate the conditions of the armistice and that his regime reflected a variety of views, some pro-British. No doubt his case was helped by Churchill's own reluctance to give up hope of a major defection from the Vichy camp. 'It passes my comprehension why no French leaders secede to Africa where they would have an empire, the command of the seas and all the frozen French gold in the United States,' he had recently written to Sir Samuel Hoare, in 1935 Foreign Secretary and appeaser with Laval of Mussolini's Ethiopian invasion and now Britain's wartime flattery to Franco as ambassador in Madrid. 'Surely the opportunity is the most splendid offered to daring men.'

With this in mind Rougier was given a message for General Weygand in Algiers whom he was visiting via Spain on his way back to Vichy. The minutes of the professor's conversations with the Prime Minister and Halifax had been typed up and agreed by both parties. Across this *procès-verbal* Churchill wrote in his neat hand: 'If General Weygand will raise the standard in North Africa, he can count on the renewal of the wholehearted collaboration of the governments and peoples of the British Empire and a share of the assistance afforded by the US.'

Weygand had been surprised and delighted by England's ability to survive air attacks and last longer than the three weeks he had predicted in the summer. It meant that French North Africa and Darlan's ships remained a wonderful trump card, a guarantee that the Germans would keep their word and not occupy Vichy France for fear of losing these assets to the English. But to 'raise his standard', as Churchill with all his regard for knightly virtue had put it, would require Britain to raise a strong enough army to land in North Africa with the sole intention of using it as a springboard to liberate France. This might take years. 'If they come to North Africa with four divisions, I'll fire on them,' Weygand informed Rougier. 'If they come with twenty divisions, I'll welcome them.'

Weygand regarded the Montoire meetings as further proof, if any was needed, of Laval's chicanery and attached no blame to the maréchal. Pétain, who had overnighted at Tours, was in good spirits during the next day's leisurely return to Vichy via a good lunch with friends at Azay-le-Ferron and streets lined with flag-waving school children in Châteauroux and a couple of other market towns with their inevitable place de Verdun and monument to the fallen. Only when he got back to Vichy to be confronted by the reproachful faces of some of his Cabinet and see, for the first time, the full horror of the photo ambush Dr Goebbels's spin doctors had so easily exploited, did this proud and vain old man realize that he had some explaining to do.

He chose to do it in a live radio broadcast and not one of his best ones, for the weather was getting colder and he was developing a bit of a cough. 'Last Thursday I met the Chancellor of the Reich,' he began. 'I responded freely to the Führer's invitation. I underwent no *diktat*, no pressure from him. This meeting has raised hopes and caused anxieties. I owe you some explanation.'

Then came the sentence in which a Latin-stemmed noun, a word with the same meaning and spelling in both French and English, started its journey into wartime obloquy. 'A *collaboration* was envisaged between our two countries,' he announced. 'I accepted the principle. The details will be discussed later. In the near future, the weight of suffering of our country could be lightened, the fate of our prisoners ameliorated, occupation costs reduced, the demarcation line made more flexible . . . This policy is mine. It is me alone that history will judge.'

As history did. Certainly, calling somebody who worked with the German occupiers a *collaborateur* dates from here. A secret six-paragraph *procès-verbal* was drawn up setting out what had been agreed at Montoire including the Führer's determination 'to see France occupy in the New Europe, the place to which she is entitled, and to have the French people participate in the co-operation of European peoples'. Paragraph two was the nearest Hitler could get to a French declaration of war against Britain: 'The Axis powers and France have an identical interest in seeing the defeat of England accomplished as soon as possible. Consequently, the French government will support, within the limits of its ability, the measures which the Axis Powers may take to this end.'

But even Laval baulked at the prospect of a formal declaration of war against Britain, pleading that the French people were not yet ready for it. What France was prepared to do, he said, was resist *à la Dakar* any English inroads against their colonies. 'But in the beginning, as Maréchal Pétain has pointed out, it was necessary to proceed slowly and with caution.'

In some accounts Hitler is said to have been disappointed by Pétain, though instinctively he preferred the soldier to Laval whom he described as 'a dirty democratic cheapjack politician who doesn't believe what he says'. But Erich Kordt, a former Rhodes Scholar at Oxford whose

Anglophile ways had not stopped Ribbentrop (whom Kordt despised) making him his most senior Berlin based diplomat,* believed that for Hitler the main purpose of the Montoire and Hendaye meetings was to show the British that a sizable European bloc was coalescing in willing coalition around Germany and the odds against them were mounting. How much longer did this isolated offshore island expect to hold out?

If this was the case he succeeded admirably. Both the British and the Americans were rattled. Churchill got George VI to send to Pétain, via the Canadian consul Dupuy, a personal message from one head of state to another pledging Britain's continued goodwill towards France and appealing to him not to endanger its old ally by doing more than the armistice required. President Roosevelt took one look at the Montoire handshake, decided that Vichy were about to put the French fleet at Germany's disposal, and fired off a protest that was much more strongly worded though possibly weaker on syntax:

> Any agreement entered into between France and Germany which partook of the character above mentioned would definitely wreck the traditional friendship between the French and American peoples, would permanently remove any chance that this government would be disposed to give any assistance to the French people in their distress and would create a wave of bitter indignation against France on the part of American public opinion.

Pétain dismissed it all with a massive Gallic shrug, allegedly confiding to a friend: 'It will take six months to discuss this programme and another six months to forget it.' There was some truth in this. Nothing much ever did come out of the Montoire talks. A few days later Hitler became distracted by the prospect of Germany being dragged into an unnecessary Balkan campaign after Mussolini had ignored his advice and started a winter war with the Greek dictator Metaxas. There was no offensive deployment of the French fleet against the British. Nor was there any mass repatriation of the 1.5 million French prisoners of war in German hands – about the population of Marseilles – though a few hundred officers and NCOs were liberated to reinforce Vichy's North African garrisons.

By mid-November, little more than three weeks after his meeting with Hitler, Pétain was confiding to Robert Murphy, the American chargé d'affaires in Vichy that, though he felt no love for the British and would defend French territory against them, 'their victory is much better for France than that of Germany'. Pétain's tendency to tell people what he thought they would most like to hear, a habit uncommon in the elderly,

* Kordt was an anti-Nazi who had risked his life urging Britain to defy Hitler over Czechoslovakia.

was undiminished. And there was no doubt that American sympathy for the defiant British was stronger than ever.

Two days before Pétain's latest meeting with Murphy the Luftwaffe's night bombers had visited the English Midlands and flattened twelve of the armament factories in the old Saxon town of Coventry, killing almost 600 people in the process and demolishing all but the twin spires of its medieval cathedral. Deaths from what Fleet Street called the Blitz were averaging 3,000 to 5,000 a month which Churchill considered an endurable casualty rate, as did the large American press corps sharing the risks in the capital who seemed unanimous in their belief that 'London can take it'. There had also been a major British success against the Axis. Flying off the carrier *Illustrious*, twenty Swordfish fitted with new long-range fuel tanks had made a moonlight attack on ships harboured at Taranto in the south-eastern toe of Italy. All the Fleet Air Arm had learned failing to sink Darlan's fleet at Mers-el-Kébir and Dakar was put to good use and it succeeded beyond their wildest dreams. This time most of the torpedoes ran straight and true and detonated when they made contact. Three Italian battleships, including the new *Littorio*, had been put out of action. Smaller vessels and the docks had been damaged by bombs. Next day almost everything that could still move sailed for Italy's west coast ports where they were safer but not as well placed to intercept Malta convoys. Within the space of a couple of hours, and for the loss of three airmen killed and three captured, the naval balance in the Mediterranean had been utterly changed.

Suddenly the prospects of an eventual British victory were not perhaps as ludicrous as Laval and his supporters liked to believe. At the beginning of December there was more unexpected success for British arms. It had started in August when, against the advice of Brooke and other senior officers trying to prepare for an invasion, Churchill had persuaded the War Cabinet to send half of the best tanks Britain then possessed – the heavy Mark Two Matildas – to Egypt. And that, for a while, was the last most of the War Office had heard of them: the source of some bitterness among those expecting the imminent arrival of a panzer army.

In Cairo the taciturn Archibald Wavell, the poetry-loving general who had been Middle East supremo since 1939, seemed in no hurry to go on the offensive. It looked as though Italy's 10th Army, which had crossed the Libyan frontier in September then dug itself in about 70 miles inside Egypt's western desert at Sidi Barrani, could expect to celebrate New Year there. The nearest British position of any consequence was Major General Richard O'Connor's Western Desert Force almost 100 miles away at Mersa Matruh. In Cairo there were rumours that some of Wavell's forces might be sent to help the Greeks.

Then on 9 December, in a brilliantly executed manoeuvre that had taken weeks of painstaking staff work, O'Connor sneaked forward, slipped his Matildas through a hole in the Italian defences south of Sidi Barrani,

The first three British casualties in the war against the Vichy French, killed in the gun fight aboard the *Surcouf*, lie in a small military section at Plymouth's vast Weston Mill cemetery. Commander Sprague (INSET) and Lieutenant Griffiths are buried almost alongside each other. Leading Seaman Albert Webb is nearby. The body of Ingénieur Mécanicien Daniel, the only French death, was removed to France in 1948.

In the late 1930s the *Surcouf* was the biggest submersible in the world, but it was a white elephant which never lived up to the bold privateer it was named after.

INSET: Admiral James Somerville opened fire on the French ships with great reluctance. Afterwards he referred to himself as an 'unskilled butcher'.
ABOVE: Mers-el-Kébir. The British begin their bombardment of the trapped French ships.

French dead on board the battle cruiser *Dunkerque*. Her maiden voyage was to Britain for George VI's coronation and a naval review at Spithead.

The battleship *Bretagne* on fire and about to capsize.

Almost 1,300 French sailors were killed in about ten minutes. Amiral Marcel Gensoul addresses the survivors at the mass burial of their comrades. 'If there is a stain on a flag today,' he assured them, 'it's certainly not on yours.'

The entrance to the Royal Air Force training station at Habbaniya, which Rashid Ali's rebels besieged with belated support from Luftwaffe planes transiting through neighbouring Vichy Syria.

These burned out trucks, destroyed from the air by the hastily converted training aircraft from RAF Habbaniya, marked the beginning of the end of Rashid Ali's revolt, and of Vichy hopes of a sympathetic regime installed next door to French Syria.

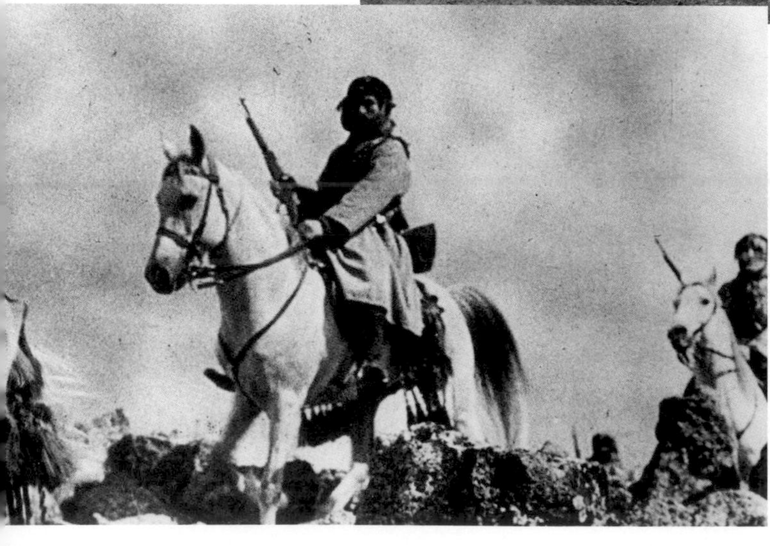

Futile hopes of weak Vichy resistance were raised three weeks before the British invasion when Colonel Alibert Collet's Circassian cavalry followed him across the Lebanon–Palestine border to join the Free French. But half of these Sunni Muslims, originally from the Caucasus, went back.

LEFT: A Free French Marine in Syria carries a British Bren gun. Having joined de Gaulle to fight the Germans, most of the Free French soldiers had little enthusiasm for combat with other French troops.

RIGHT: A forward artillery observer uses a captured periscope in Lebanon's rocky terrain, where snipers on both sides made it pay to keep your head down.

RIGHT: In a shallow tributary of the Litani a Cheshire Yeomanry patrol waters their horses. Much of the hill country in Lebanon and Syria was impassable to wheeled or tracked vehicles and both sides used horsed cavalry for reconnaissance.

LEFT: An officer examines one of the few French Renault-35 two-man tanks to be captured intact. Their thick armour made them impervious to Boys anti-tank rifles and they wreaked havoc among General Jumbo Wilson's infantry.

BELOW: On the first day of the Syrian campaign an Australian wounded in the right hand during the fighting to capture the customs and police post at Khirbe gets a light for his cigarette.

ABOVE: Locals wearing fezzes and smoking hookah water pipes in a pavement café in the port of Sidon must have seemed like something from *The Arabian Nights* for these Australian troops, almost certainly away from home for the first time.

Under fire amidst the ancient ruins of Palmyra, British infantry leap from their slow-moving Bren gun carrier and run for cover.

The fighter aces Pierre Le Gloan (RIGHT) and the Australian Peter Turnbull (LEFT) were the top scorers of the Syrian campaign. Le Gloan, flying a Dewoitine 520, added 7 British aircraft to the 4 German and 7 Italian planes he had downed in 1940. Turnbull's American-built Tomahawk accounted for at least 4 French machines. Both were killed later in the war, by which time they were flying on the same side.

German airfields in occupied Greece were made available to Vichy French as refuelling stops on the way to Syria. This Dewoitine fighter with French and Luftwaffe personnel standing around it was probably in Salonika.

Australian infantry advancing across some of Lebanon's flatter terrain.

A hostage comes home. On 10 September 1941, two months after the Syria ceasefire, a pleased-looking Général Henri Dentz inspects a guard of honour of French Arab troops at Marseille. The British had held Dentz and other senior officers until all the British prisoners sent to France through Greece had been returned.

turned right and right again and surprised them from the rear. It was a rout. Within seventy-two hours the remnants of the 10th Army were out of Egypt, leaving behind 237 intact field guns, 73 tanks and 38,000 prisoners – more than O'Connor's entire command. 'We've five acres of officers and 200 acres of other ranks,' exulted one of the landed gentry who officered the Coldstream Guards. Total British casualties were just over 500, of whom 133 were killed. Churchill's gamble with the tanks had paid off. 'Your splendid victory fulfils our highest hopes,' he cabled the imperturbable Wavell, who had masterminded the entire operation with such secrecy that not only had the Prime Minister been one of the last to know, but until they were almost within sight of the enemy, O'Connor's spearhead had believed they were on a training exercise.

As France entered its sixth month of defeat and occupation Pétain, like Weygand, had to concede that the British had done much better than he had ever imagined they would. The Channel, Churchill and the RAF had denied Hitler his chance to complete his victory in 1940. The winter weather meant that there was no chance of mounting an invasion until the spring of 1941 and by then the Americans would have made sure the British were even stronger. Admittedly, air raids like the one on Coventry, turned into another Guernica by British propaganda despite its munition factories, sometimes took their toll on morale as well as lives; but as yet there had been no reports of the kind of mass panic that had emptied Paris before a bomb had fallen or a German soldier set foot there.

When Pétain told Murphy that a British victory was better for France than Germany it was no more than the truth. An outright British victory would mean a liberated France. Unfortunately, there seemed little chance of a 1918-style German defeat even if the pro-British Roosevelt, who had just enjoyed a landslide victory over the isolationist Wendell Wilkie, did bring America into the war. A separate Anglo-German peace was more likely. In July the English had turned down Hitler's olive branch and for six months withstood the worst he could throw at them and survived. Now they could expect much more favourable terms if they cared to start negotiating.

But the Americans assured Pétain that the illogical Churchill – a drunk with the luck of the devil – was sincere when he said England would never make any kind of peace with Hitler. So they were in for a long war with France, a surrendered non-belligerent, languishing in its painful armistice limbo. Laval would argue that this was all the more reason to take the Montoire route and get closer to Germany before it was too late. But Pétain did not want any more photographs with Hitler. Nor did he want any more of Laval blowing smoke in his face while he announced that he had just done something he should not have done without consulting him first. What the maréchal wanted was to bide his time and see how much he could trade selected acts of collaboration for the release of more of their prisoners. Bringing the boys back home would be another Verdun.

Chapter Twelve

Some Frenchmen were already coming home. These were the last of the overwhelming majority of officers and men, army and navy, who had found themselves in England when the armistice was signed and refused to join de Gaulle. On 21 November 1940 what would turn out to be the penultimate repatriation was about to take place from Liverpool docks, already bombed almost 300 times since the war began. Recent collateral damage included the Anglican cathedral and Walton Jail where twenty-two convicts had died.

Before they embarked on the French ship *Djenné* the returnees were frisked by military police while customs officers searched luggage for anything they considered might be of use to the enemy or in some way contravened Britain's economic blockade on France. Some of this luggage belonged to Lieutenant Bouillaut and his friend Dr Le Nistour who had started the shooting on the *Surcouf* and between them killed the officers Sprague and Griffiths and Leading Seaman Webb.

Both received special attention from a Lieutenant Alders Kaye whom Le Nistour describes as 'the English political officer'. Kaye was one of the French speakers on the staff of Rear Admiral Geoffrey Watkins, a highly decorated 1914–18 submarine captain, who was the senior British liaison officer to all the French naval forces. Both the French officers had met Kaye before and their dislike was evidently mutual.

Le Nistour and Kaye watched as the customs officers emptied his suitcases and shook carefully folded clothes, 'without finding anything'. Then Kaye motioned to a couple of military policemen and they all walked into a side office where the doctor was asked to strip to his underwear.

> I felt insulted, a young woman was present. Kaye accused me of having done everything 'except practise medicine' in England. He claimed to have proof of my anti-British and anti-Gaullist activities. Then he pretended to reflect on the seriousness of my case and decided that he lacked sufficient authority to deal with me. Whilst awaiting orders about me he had me locked up for an hour in an adjacent building.

Le Nistour was eventually allowed to board the *Djenné* after he agreed to sign a statement that the *Surcouf*'s crew had not been treated as prisoners of war or in any way mistreated during their four months in England. 'I told Kaye that this blackmail had no value but he was happy and smiled. I crossed the gangplank with a sigh of relief.'

But, as it turned out, Kaye had by no means finished with the men who started the shooting. Bouillaut was already aboard and had been for over an hour. He had experienced no trouble with the customs and military police searches. Before leaving his last internment camp on the Isle of Man he had taken the precaution of distributing among some of the other officers copies of his account of the *Surcouf* gunfight, written in hospital while recovering from his wounds, so that at least one would get through and he would not have to write it again from a more faded memory. When young Enseigne de vaisseau Massicot was relieved of his copy Bouillaut was not unduly concerned. 'We were all convinced that the British Admiralty knew perfectly well what had happened and had decided not to bother with me.'

This may well have been the case until first Kaye, then Admiral Watkins, read in black and white Bouillaut's full and frank account of his decision to open fire and exactly how he did it. 'No order to resist by force of arms had been given to me but this situation was one of those where one cannot wait for orders ... I took a pace forward and shot at Commander Sprague, Lieutenant Commander Griffiths, the two English sailors and then again on their officers ...' And perhaps most damning of all, the quote from Lieutenant de vaisseau Crescent, the man whose life he believed he was saving: 'I believe you were very wrong to have done that.' As far as Kaye and Watkins were concerned the document was nothing less than a confession to murder.

Bouillaut was promptly removed from the *Djenné* and lodged in a cell in a military detention centre where the only personal possessions he was allowed to keep on him were his pipe and a photograph of the wife he thought he was about to go home to. Dinner was 'a little cheese and some bread'.

> The next morning I was visited by Lieutenant Kaye who asked me to confirm my identity and the fact that I had killed Commander Sprague and Lieutenant-Commander Griffiths. He added that the competent authorities would at some time let me know the fate awaiting me. I immediately wrote several protest letters: to Winston Churchill, to Admiral Sir Dunbar-Nasmith [the Commander Western Approaches at Plymouth who had planned the boarding of the French ships], in which I said that my behaviour on the *Surcouf* was only a reaction to the threats of the English officers and that, in my place, any honourable officer would have done the same had he been able to ... and finally I protested that the measures taken against me

> certainly did not accord with my being an officer. Then I wrote to the French Consul-General in London [the British had allowed him to remain as another conduit to Vichy] so that he could inform our government. I asked my jailers to send off these letters though I had few illusions of the fate that awaited them.

The food got a little better though sleep was difficult because at night he was kept awake by various air-raid noises, some loud and quite close. An old soldier took him out for solitary bouts of exercise in the yard and, according to his prisoner, once whispered, 'Any officer would have behaved like you, sir.'

Rear Admiral Watkins disagreed. As a submariner himself he felt a special affinity for this later generation already suffering enough casualties at Axis hands without having to deal with bloody-minded Frenchmen. Almost all the *Surcouf* boarding party, including Lieutenant Talbot who had found the way in through the conning tower escape hatch, were now dead: killed off the Norwegian coast the following month in the submarine *Thames*. Watkins would have almost certainly known both the officers Bouillaut killed and been unimpressed by claims that French honour was at stake. Now he had the opportunity to make him sweat it out a little: contemplate the awful majesty of English justice and a leather-lined noose at dawn.

But on the fourth day of Bouillaut's incarceration Watkins received a telephone call from the Admiralty ordering his immediate release and repatriation. If he had expected anything else he was sadly out of touch with Their Lordships' desire not to lose the advantage gained at Taranto. Anything that might contribute to Italy's recent losses being made up by Darlan's excellent ships joining the Axis was to be avoided at all costs.

Earlier in the month they had been horribly embarrassed by the sinking off Libreville in Equatorial Africa, where de Gaulle was consolidating his hold, of the French submarine *Poncelot* by the sloop HMS *Milford*. True, the *Poncelot* had started it by hitting *Milford* amidships with a torpedo that should have blown her in twain but merely made a dent having failed to explode. She then surfaced to see what had happened only for the sloop's outrageous run of good luck to continue when a fluke shot from her 4-inch gun made it impossible for her attacker to dive. The submarine then scuttled herself and all the crew were saved except for Capitaine de corvette de Saussine who, by accident or design, went down with his command.

To add the trial and execution of a French lieutenant to Darlan's growing list of grievances against the Royal Navy was not considered appropriate. Since the *Djenné* had sailed the day he was arrested, Bouillaut was moved from his military prison to Liverpool's Stork Hotel to await the next sailing of a Red Cross repatriation ship to France which needed the approval of all the interested parties: Britain, France and Germany. But before he moved into the Stork, Bouillaut was required to report to Admiral Watkins who was determined to have the last word. Their conversation, which was conducted through an interpreter though Bouillaut seems to have known enough English to have had some conversation with his soldier jailers, started amicably enough.

> I was asked not to leave Liverpool for too long at a time so as not to miss the sailing. The Admiral also asked me whether I wanted to be protected by either the army or the navy and have an escort because he thought there were a certain number of English who had little love for me. Naturally, I refused the offer. And then, wanting to have the last word, Admiral Watkins told me that, in his personal opinion, I should not have shot at the English officers sitting in our wardroom without being ordered to do so and that he considered me to be a murderer – which Anderson [the interpreter] nicely translated as 'meutrier' (murderous) instead of 'assassin' (murderer) – and that he would not like to be me when I came before God. I replied that my conscience was completely clear, that I thought I had only done my duty; far from sitting in our wardroom as friends, the English officers were standing, revolvers in hand, threatening the life of one of my comrades. The interview ended.

Dismissed, Bouillaut went to the Stork where he met up with several other French officers who had missed the *Djenné* and the French consul general from Southampton who had been sent there to work out the passenger lists for the repatriation ships. Despite the cold weather there were still about 400 French sailors, some of them merchant seamen, under canvas on the Aintree racetrack. Bouillaut was among those who attended the funeral of a quartermaster from a submarine chaser who had died in hospital of bronchial pneumonia. As the winter nights lengthened, the air raids on and around the docks intensified. On 28 November Liverpool had 200 killed, 164 in a public shelter beneath a school. Behind the blackout curtains at the Stork Hotel its French guests played endless card games, one ear cocked for the closer explosions, and wondered whether the English would have surrendered before they got home.

A few French naval officers had been told they would not be going home for some time. These were five members of the liaison team serving at the Government Code and Cypher School at Bletchley Park, a hideous Victorian stockbroker's pile set in extensive grounds about 50 miles northwest of London. It was here that the abnormally gifted broke wireless codes and produced the intelligence the British called ULTRA.

All but one seem to have taken the news of their enforced stay philosophically enough. The other four either remained at Bletchley or did signals intelligence work with the Free French, though one did at first attempt to sit out the war in an honorary job at the British Museum. The fifth man managed to escape aboard one of the repatriation ships using somebody else's identity papers. It seems he kept his mouth shut because ULTRA was not compromised. In any case, Bletchley Park's operation was in its infancy and its triumphs would not start until the following year.

More worrying for the British was the presence in Vichy of Colonel Gustave Bertrand, former head of the French decrypting service and a man who could claim a founding role in ULTRA. In 1931 a German traitor passed this intelligence officer copies of the manuals for a new Dutch-designed Enigma coding machine the Wehrmacht had just acquired. After the Nazis came to power Bertrand, always Bertie in MI6 reports, shared some of the information with France's Polish and British allies. The first man to break a code set by an Enigma machine was a Polish mathematician. When Poland fell, some of the brightest of its decrypting team escaped to Paris and joined Bertrand who was working closely with the British.

By the time the Franco-German Armistice had been signed some of Bertie's loyal Poles had followed him to Vichy's unoccupied zone. Before long the colonel had soon established a mini-Bletchley of his own though in rather more agreeable surroundings. Code-named Cadix, it was quartered in Languedoc's medieval fortress town of Uzès with its stone architecture and quiet courtyards, a remote place where many of the natives still spoke the old Occitan dialect of southern France. Bertrand was also running a branch office in Algeria but what he really wanted to do was resume contact with the British. Messages were passed, probably through Lisbon which was the more discreet of the neutral Iberian capitals. In them Bertie insisted Bletchley's secrets were still safe with him and they could exchange information.

It was an impossible request, and in his heart he must have known it was, but the British did not want to offend him. The colonel knew what the enemy must never know: he knew that ultimately Enigma did not work. Its codes could be broken. And this information was almost within the Wehrmacht's grasp. All they had to do was become curious enough to charge across the undefended demarcation line and dig the Polish mathematicians and the rest of Bertie's crew out of the cobbled labyrinths of Uzès for interrogation. The Abwehr might have already managed to place an agent into Cadix. As far as Bletchley was concerned, Bertie was a time bomb.

They suggested to the colonel that they could arrange for him to come and see them in London, where no doubt they would have offered him everything except his ticket back; but he would not be led into temptation and suggested Tangiers. Then he called off Tangiers and offered Lisbon instead, but apparently this would take some time. Commander Alastair Denniston, the Admiralty code-breaker in charge of Bletchley since 1939, wondered if it might be a good idea to send Bertie 'some Enigma keys of a minor character' to keep him happy. In some notes on the painful divorce Bletchley was having with its French counterpart, possibly by Denniston himself, their predicament was plainly stated. 'It was felt that if we continued to put the French off they might become discouraged and possibly resentful and, with the information they already have, this state of affairs could be extremely dangerous to us.'

Meanwhile, it was noticeable that not once had Bertie even raised the subject of the fate of the French officers who had remained in England. Presumably he realized he would be wasting his time.

Chapter Thirteen

Bouillaut did get home for Christmas. He arrived in France aboard the Compagnie de Navigation vessel *Djenné* on 14 December. It was an auspicious time for a career naval officer, and one so fully committed to Vichy, to make his return because that evening Pétain made a radio broadcast announcing that he had sacked Pierre Laval. Nothing was confirmed but Amiral Darlan, while remaining Navy Minister, was expected to be his most likely replacement as Petain's deputy.

It had all happened with astonishing speed. For several weeks Laval had spent most of his time in Paris negotiating with the Germans how best they might go about recovering those African colonies they had lost to de Gaulle. This was entirely contrary to the secret agreement Professor Rougier was supposed to have brokered between Pétain and Churchill but the maréchal was fully aware they were going on. For much of the time the talks were also attended by Général Huntziger and Darlan who, according to German records, were both very bullish. As well as a land offensive against Gaullist Chad from neighbouring Vichy territory, Huntziger wanted to attack British colonies. On his itinerary was the capture of Bathurst, that Anglo-Saxon blot on French West Africa, and air raids on Freetown in Sierra Leone and northern Nigeria. Not to be outdone, Darlan had proposed that while Freetown's defenders were distracted by the air attack one of his submarines could take them unaware and wreak havoc in its harbour. Laval stressed that the French public should be prepared for action of this kind by a declaration from Berlin that the Germans had no desire for French colonies. If Germany made such a gesture de Gaulle would be exposed as the 'common English agent' he was.

As it happened, Hitler did have something special in mind to help keep the French happy but it was not the kind of thing that had occurred to Laval or probably anybody else for that matter. Twenty-five years after Waterloo, 15 December was the centenary of Napoléon Bonaparte's state funeral following the return of his mortal remains from mid-Atlantic island exile on Britain's St Helena. As a mark of reconciliation, and a useful reminder that the Führer shared Bonaparte's enthusiasm for uniting Europe, Germany would celebrate the anniversary by sending the body of

Napoléon's only son, the Duke of Reichstadt, for entombment at Les Invalides. Pétain was invited by Hitler to attend the ceremony where the son would be laid to rest alongside his father. The Nazis loved a good funeral.

Since 1832 the duke's body had lain in Vienna, now part of the Reich, where he died of tuberculosis aged 21 and was buried by his mother, the Empress Marie-Louise, who was Austrian. For a while his grave had become a shrine for the wealthier nineteenth-century Bonapartists who could afford the trip. The Parisians of 1940 tended to be less respectful about this celebrity corpse. 'What we want is not bones but meat,' they said. There were food shortages in all the major cities because the summer fighting and lack of manpower that followed had left harvests uncollected and livestock untended. The British blockade, another reminder of things Napoleonic, denied the French imports from their colonies and the combination of a bitterly cold winter and French coal being sent to the Ruhr added to their misery. Contemporary accounts report how thin and tired some people were beginning to look.

Laval suspected that Pétain would be no more enthusiastic about the funeral pomp on offer at Les Invalides than the average Parisian and he was right. But he was determined that the maréchal did not offend Hitler by declining to collaborate in a little harmless theatre when so much bigger collaborations were at stake and knew it would take a face-to-face meeting to convince him. So he rushed off to Vichy taking with him Fernand de Brinon who, as Vichy's ambassador to German Paris, was the bearer of Hitler's official invitation to Pétain to attend the Napoleonic occasion at Les Invalides.

Laval was on a high. He felt that things were going so well with the Germans that they would soon begin to reap the rewards of Montoire. A mass release of prisoners of war would certainly make his position within the Vichy hierarchy unassailable and still only a heartbeat away from the octogenarian at the top. It never occurred to the deputy Prime Minister, busy with affairs of state in Paris and so often away from Vichy where his sharp political nerve ends would have alerted him to danger, that Pétain had already been persuaded to sack him.

But it was not just Baudouin, whom he had replaced as foreign secretary, who was against him. Or Finance Minister Bouthillier, enraged that Laval did not bother to consult him when first he arranged German control of French-owned copper mines in Yugoslavia then agreed that Belgium's gold reserve, entrusted to France in 1939 and stashed in Senegal, should be handed over as well. Or Darlan and Huntziger who had both been quite happy to sit beside him in Paris and compete at telling the Germans how beastly they were going to be to the English but loathed the way Ambassador Abetz obviously regarded him as much more important than themselves. It was also the Justice Minister Raphael Alibert, a monarchist

Catholic fundamentalist of the Action Française. Alibert was a rare anti-Semite – he was the author of Vichy's recently promulgated *Statut des juifs* – in that he appeared to hate the Nazis as much as he did Jews, Freemasons and Protestants, detesting the Anglo-Saxon world as a nest of all three. And perhaps most important of all, it was also Marcel Peyrouton, formerly Resident General in Algeria and now Interior Minister with the Brigade Mobile under his command, a gendarmerie said to include ex-Cagoulard terrorists in its ranks whose newly formed Groupes de Protection guarded Pétain.

Dining alone with Robert Murphy, Peyrouton had confided to the American chargé d'affaires that he was prepared to use his paramilitaries to oust Laval and there might be fighting in Vichy. He had even tried to persuade Pétain that his deputy should be shot as a traitor but the old soldier knew this was not the time to shoot the architect of Montoire for being too pro-German however insufferable his smoke-filled insubordination. As it was, he had felt it necessary to draft a letter to Hitler disclosing his dismissal of Laval and assuring, 'I remain more than ever a partisan of the policy of collaboration'.

Even so, Laval very nearly turned things round. Pétain, as usual, took heed from the last person he spoke to and the Führer's plans for the reburial of Napoléon *fils* had already caused enough ripples in the small pool that was Vichy to make him delay sending Hitler his letter. With the help of Ambassador de Brinon, whose pedigree was so much more to the marechal's taste, Pétain agreed to attend the ceremony on condition that his trip to Paris be made, like his return from Montoire, a triumphal procession with stops where he could shake hands with Verdun veterans and others giving thanks for his leadership.

Unfortunately for Laval, too much time elapsed before the maréchal's departure for others to talk him out of it. The rest of his Cabinet were unanimous: on no account must he accept this ludicrous invitation to Les Invalides. They were certain that if he did there was a real chance the Germans would force him to accept a more docile government under Laval, probably including some of the capital's home-bred Fascists such as Marcel Déat who, judging by the editorials in his newspaper *Oeuvre*, regarded Vichy as no more than an irritating stopgap until the real thing came along. They urged him to stick to Plan A and fire his deputy which, on the evening of Friday, 13 December, he did. 'I hope, *Monsieur le Maréchal*,' Laval told him on his way out, 'that your successive contradictory decisions do not cause too much harm to our country.'

This was not quite the end of it. Laval had intended to clear his papers from his office in the two floors he and his staff occupied in the Hôtel du Parc, collect his wife and daughter Josée from the Laval chateau in nearby Châteldon – Josée had just returned from New York – and return to Paris on a train leaving Vichy at midnight. His chauffeur would bring his baggage and papers up by road together with de Brinon. But he had reckoned without Peyrouton.

If the Interior Minister could not have Laval shot, he would at least hold him incommunicado long enough to ensure that Pétain could make a public announcement of his dismissal and make it a done deal before the Germans could intervene and reverse his decision. All telephone links to Paris were cut and a squad from Groupes de Protection sent to take over Laval's floors at the Hôtel du Parc. At about 10.30 p.m. Laval had a visitor. 'An American journalist, Ralph Heinzen the United Press' correspondent in Vichy, reached my office with difficulty. He had been jostled and roughly handled. Only his repeated statements that he was an American newspaperman had enabled him to force his way up. He told me that my chauffeur had been arrested and the car taken.'

At the reporter's urging Laval looked outside and glaring back at him were a bunch of Peyrouton's finest in their distinctive black leather jerkins and steel helmets and the rare French MAS M38 sub-machine guns which should have gone to the army. 'What swine! And it's Friday the 13th,' said Laval, slamming the door. 'They're out to get me and I've nothing to defend myself with.' Incredulously, Heinzen watched as he searched his pockets and produced a penknife.

Shortly afterwards a senior officer from the National Police turned up and persuaded Laval to let him escort him past the GP squad fingering their weapons outside his office and downstairs to a waiting car. With less than an hour of the 13th remaining on the clock Laval was safely delivered to his family home in Châteldon. There he discovered that he and his family were under house arrest. Their telephone was disconnected and there were police inside the house as well as outside. But they had left or overlooked his radio. Next morning he listened to Pétain's announcement that they had parted ways 'for reasons of internal policy'.

Twenty-four hours later, the Laval family were once again gathered around their set for a report on the homecoming of the young Duke of Reichstadt whose bronze coffin had passed through the high gates of Les Invalides between a line of blazing torches carried by an honour guard. Above them, a kilo of incense smouldering in a giant thurible sweetened the December chill. Pétain was represented by Amiral Darlan who had travelled to Paris with Ambassador de Brinon and Général Laure, a personal friend of the maréchal's whose release from captivity was as yet the only other visible fruit of Montoire. Hitler was not present and it is not clear whether he ever intended to be. Abetz made a speech in which he praised Laval as 'the guarantor of collaboration'. In case Darlan and Laure had missed the point, afterwards he made his disgust at Laval's treatment quite clear and told them that, as far as he was concerned, some of Pétain's ministers were little better than paid British agents. Général Laure returned to Vichy that night and reported that, in a nutshell, Ambassador Abetz was saying: France was free to choose its own government but, if it picked the wrong one, don't expect to reap the rewards of collaboration.

They did not have to take Laure's word for it. Twenty-four hours later Abetz himself turned up in Vichy with a ten-man SS motorcycle escort bristling with weapons, explaining that this bodyguard was necessary to protect him from the notorious 'band of criminals' posing as Minister Peyrouton's special police. Pétain saw him at 10 a.m. the next day. Abetz was usually polite and Pétain too old and distinguished to shout but the meeting, which had started with the maréchal refusing point-blank to reinstate his protégé in any capacity and Abetz threatening to walk out, broke up in disarray when the man himself was released from house arrest in Châteldon and brought in.

The former Prime Minister was accustomed to the ups and downs of political life in the Third Republic but nothing as unexpected, humiliating or briefly as frightening as the virtual coup that had just deposed him. Laval was in a towering rage and, no doubt emboldened by the presence of Abetz, he tore into the maréchal in a manner he was unlikely to have heard since he last earned the displeasure of his drill sergeant at Saint-Cyr. He was, screamed Laval, 'a puppet, a windbag, and a weathercock twirling in every breeze'. Outside the maréchal's closed door Henri du Moulin de Labarthete, his young *chef de cabinet* who had first worked with Pétain when he was ambassador to Spain, could hear every harsh word. For good measure, and in front of the German ambassador, Laval accused him of 'insincerity and double dealing with England'. Abetz, who respected the old soldier, realized Laval's outburst made a swift reconciliation impossible and a decent interval would be required before they could persuade Pétain to take him back. In turn, the maréchal knew that he needed to make some concessions. Peyrouton's Brigade Mobile was disbanded and the minister himself, regarded by the Germans as the muscle behind the ousting of Laval, exiled as ambassador to Buenos Aires where he no doubt did his best to miss mid-winter Vichy in wartime.

Together Abetz and Laval returned to Paris from where the ambassador sent a message to von Ribbentrop extolling Darlan – 'a proven enemy of England' – as Laval's understudy. 'I propose that for the moment we content ourselves with the results achieved and not force the reinstatement of Laval until after Darlan's personal position of power has been strengthened,' he wrote.

Less than a week later, on Christmas Eve 1940, the amiral was granted his first meeting with Hitler. The *Führersonderzug Amerika* was back on French rails again, for its captain was, understandably enough, preoccupied by the English and had been inspecting some newly installed coastal batteries in the Pas de Calais. Operation Sealion, the invasion of England, had been cancelled, though only a few high-ranking Germans knew this or the reason why. On 18 December Hitler had asked the Wehrmacht to prepare plans for a blitzkrieg against Russia. If Germany was to fulfil its destiny and expand eastwards there was no place for a ramshackle, proselytizing giant on its doorstep however convenient the Molotov-Ribbentrop Pact had been when it came to consuming Poland. But the attack on the Soviet Union would have to wait until well after 1941's Russian thaw had dried, at least another five months away.

By then it was hoped that the war between distant cousins in the west would be over. It would be preferable if Germany was not fighting on two fronts at once. As it was, Goering was already whingeing about the losses being inflicted on the Luftwaffe by the RAF's new Beaufighters, which appeared to carry a radar that made them almost as effective at night as the Spitfires were by day. Yet it seemed that the peace he needed with England could only be achieved by the persistent nocturnal bombing of its cities until their inhabitants insisted that Churchill gave in. After a Christmas lull, a massive fire-bombing attack on London was planned for Sunday, 29 December when the Thames estuary was due for a very low tide and it was hoped that water pressure would be further weakened by cracking mains with parachute mines. Meanwhile, Hitler's appointment with Darlan at the railway station in Beauvais, an old cathedral town about 55 miles north of Paris, was his last official business before his return to the Reich and the war's second Christmas.

The amiral was travelling by car from Paris along winter roads and was an hour late for the meeting which did not put the Reich Chancellor in the best of tempers, if only because it reminded him of Franco's tardy arrival at Hendaye. Also present were Abetz and Paul Schmidt, Hitler's French language interpreter.

Darlan had two tasks. The first was to hand over another letter from Pétain reiterating his enthusiasm for the policy of collaboration but stressing that the insults Laval had delivered 'in the presence of Herr Abetz' made it impossible to invite him back into the Vichy government for the foreseeable future. 'Even if I wished it, the improper conduct of M. Laval now being common knowledge,' wrote Pétain, 'I would risk inflicting a dangerous blow to the unity of the empire.' Hitler instantly reacted to this thinly veiled threat that General Weygand's French North Africa might secede to de Gaulle with the accusation that France seemed to be hellbent on 'setting out again on the same road which led it to Vichy'. He also praised Laval's political vision and said that he suspected Weygand was behind his departure.

According to the interpreter Schmidt, Darlan weathered all this 'like a breaker off the oily skin of an old walrus'. No doubt he was thinking of his second task, which was somehow to convince Hitler that he was a worthy successor to Laval and even the maréchal himself. To do this he had decided to play to his strengths. Everybody knew that since Mers-el-Kébir his old irritation with the British had grown into an unbridled loathing. What more could Adolf Hitler wish to hear, what better music to his ears, than his heartfelt desire to join him in his battles against their common foe across the Channel? Or how he had long felt that Germany not England was France's natural ally? How could the little amiral be expected to know that, at this point, the megalomaniac he was addressing remained a reluctant enemy of the British, even something of an admirer? That he yearned for nothing more than to make peace with them so that he could attack a country that might be much bigger but lacked a moat?

'My family have always hated the English,' Darlan confided to the man he sincerely hoped was about to crush them into cowering submission. 'We've been fighting them now for 300 years.' At this point he usually mentioned Trafalgar and his great-grandfather's part in it but perhaps he preferred to give the impression of an unbroken chain of victories. In any case, Hitler was notoriously uninterested in naval occasions.

Soon Darlan found himself, along with Abetz and the interpreter Schmidt, standing on the platform watching *Amerika*'s rear anti-aircraft wagon disappear from view as the the Führer headed first for Berlin and then Bavaria where he and the athletic Eva Braun would spend New Year's Eve and the first weeks of 1941.

PART TWO

War on Land, Sea and Air

Chapter Fourteen

Outside the main gates of Iraq's RAF Habbaniya one of those signposts beloved by the British military abroad informed visitors that they were 55 miles west of Baghdad and 3,287 miles east of London. It was also about 300 miles east of the nearest French airfield at Palmyra in Syria but by the time that was of enough interest to warrant a mention it was too late.

Until the spring of 1941 Habbaniya, built on a bend of the Euphrates close to the large lake from which it took its name, was still very much a peacetime posting. It had a polo field, golf course, swimming pools, cinema, married quarters bungalows dripping with bougainvillaea and eucalyptus-lined streets named Bond, Regent and Tottenham Court Road. Before getting their wings, cadets who had just learned to fly Tiger Moths at one of the RAF's East African establishments went there for their final six months' advanced training at 4 Service Flying Training School. Yet for all its creature comforts, old hands piloting the biplane transports that delivered these pupils delighted in painting doleful tales of the hellhole they were bound for: a desert scorpion colony rarely out of furnace heat.

It could get hot; temperatures of 115°F were not unknown. But this was also part of Mesopotamia's Fertile Crescent, the cradle of civilization. Sometimes the Euphrates brimmed its banks, flooding the huts closest to the river, and the cadets spent a couple of nights under canvas on the nearest high ground, a 150-foot-high windswept plateau about half a mile to the south. But when the mud had dried, roses, stocks and sweet peas flourished around some of its Nissen huts and the little brick bungalows. And if these gardens were well tended it was probably because some of the instructors and administrative staff still had their wives with them. As did the Christian levies of the Assyrian Constabulary who, together with some vintage RAF armoured cars, patrolled its 7 miles of steel perimeter fence and were as loyal to the British as only a persecuted minority could be.

Occasionally Bedouin herdsmen, who disapproved of this infidel carbuncle in their midst, would pass the time by sniping at it from the bluff where the RAF cadets went camping when they were flooded out. Sometimes the Assyrians in their Australian-style slouch hats would send out a patrol under the cover of darkness then come onto the plateau with the dawn and scatter the snipers and their herds, feasting on any four-legged casualties.

Otherwise, sprawling and overlooked, RAF Habbaniya was never intended to defend itself from anything more serious. Apart from a single early model Blenheim bomber and nine Gloster Gladiator biplanes, recently replaced as the Middle East's frontline fighter by the Hurricane, the other aircraft were all trainers. These were not, as some accounts would later suggest, museum pieces but the training aircraft of their day, the majority of them biplanes designed and first built in the early 1930s.

The most common type were thirty pointy-nosed Hawker Audax, not much more powerful than the Tiger Moths the pupils had first soloed in, with the same tandem open cockpits. But unlike the Moths, the Audax was fitted with two .303 machine guns so that pupils could be taught the rudiments of aerial gunnery by firing at the towed canvas wind socks the RAF called drogues. Then there were eight Fairey Gordons, squat light bombers, 10 years old and withdrawn from service just before the war but good for teaching dive-bombing. The only monoplanes, apart from the Blenheim, were twenty-six twin-engined Airspeed Oxfords which looked like scale models of something much bigger, with a closed cockpit and retractable undercarriage. Best of all they had a slow stalling speed so that cadets might survive their mistakes while practising bomb aiming, navigation and gunnery from the Armstrong-Whitney rotatable turrets fitted to the upper fuselage.

In charge of all this was Air Vice-Marshal Reggie Smart, a 50-year-old survivor of the dogfights over the trenches, whose first taste of Iraq was bombing and strafing Kurdish insurgents for which, in 1921, he was awarded the new Distinguished Flying Cross. 'This officer has shown a very fine example to his fellow officers,' read his citation in the *London Gazette*, 'especially during low bombing raids when he has frequently descended among heavy rifle fire to very low altitude to ensure accurate bombing of small targets.'

After that Smart had spent three years on attachment to the Royal Australian Air Force before progressing from one administrative job to another until, just after the outbreak of his second war with Germany, he was back in Iraq as Air Officer Commanding. This made him the most senior military person in the country for there was hardly any army there.

Iraq was a backwater but an important backwater. Habbaniya with its endless days of clear blue skies was not only a training centre but one of the British Empire's important staging posts. The Short flying boats British Overseas Airways Corporation used on its Asian routes through India to Singapore landed on its lake. And in the south, almost on the Persian Gulf, the RAF had another big base at Shaibah near the port city of Basra. Then there was the oil. Pipelines ran from the fields around Kirkuk to two

Mediterranean ports: across Jordan to Haifa in British Mandate Palestine and a little up the coast to Tripoli in French Syria. But after Pétain took over the British told its engineers to turn off the pumps on the Tripoli line.

So for seventeen months while France fell, while the Battle of Britain raged, while the Blitz tore great holes in British cities, Smart drew up his schedules and fought his own battles with the Air Ministry for the spare parts he needed to keep his training fleet in the air. Then came disquieting reports from the embassy the British had maintained in Baghdad ever since Iraq became independent almost ten years before and suddenly there were other priorities. Ground crews began to fit bomb racks to the Audax and the Oxfords and began stockpiling the bombs to go in them. The same went for machine-gun ammunition. Soon his pupils could have shredded every drogue on the establishment a hundred times over. And when Smart entered his Air Headquarters, he found himself eyeing in a thoughtful way the venerable pair of long-barrelled 4.5-inch howitzers with their big wooden farm cart-style spoked wheels which stood in ceremonial guard at its main entrance. They were at least a quarter of a century old, much painted by defaulters from the guard house and a legacy of the last time the British had fought seriously over Mesopotamia.

Iraq was a British creation conceived in 1916 during a clandestine Anglo-French congress to decide how the spoils of Turkey's Ottoman Empire would be divided when the war against its German ally was over. France was to get Syria and Lebanon, where it had historical interests and the British, who had done most of the fighting in the region, would control Palestine, Transjordan and Iraq. Possession of these three countries gave London, for the first time in its imperial history, an overland route from the Mediterranean coast to the Persian Gulf and thence to India.

As well as the air bases, the Anglo-Iraq Treaty gave Britain the right to transit troops through the country by road and rail. Iraq, where oil had been discovered in 1927, had been an independent monarchy since it became a member of the League of Nations in 1932 but the treaty and Britain's determination to maintain its grip on Iraq's foreign affairs provided the main battleground for its often murderous brand of domestic politics with its massacres of the Christian minority, café assassinations and military coups. In Iraqi politics you were either a pro-British monarchist who wished your new country to retain its individual identity or a Pan-Arab nationalist bent on expelling the French and the British from all Arab soil and and uniting its peoples under one flag: an Ottoman Empire but without the Turks.

Baghdad itself was a centre of intrigue and ample proof that Iraqi independence was something more than notional. Haj Amin al-Husseini, the Grand Mufti of Jerusalem, the fugitive leader of the bloodily suppressed 1936–9 Palestinian rebellion against the British over Zionist immigration, had been given sanctuary there and openly walked its streets. When the European conflict started the Iraqi government resisted British pressure for them to declare war on Germany and reluctantly broke off diplomatic relations instead. But when, nine months later, Mussolini entered the war they declined to follow suit and expel the Italian ambassador since by then France's defeat was obvious and the best Britain could hope for was a peace on Germany's terms.

After that the fortunes of Iraqi's politicians tended to follow the ebb and flow of events beyond its borders. Thus in January 1941, when British land and naval victories against the Italians had reached their peak, the Pan-Arabist and pro-Axis Prime Minister Rashid Ali al-Gaylani, a bespectacled lawyer, was gently eased out of power. Then three months later Hitler came to Mussolini's rescue, the British were thrown out of Greece and Libya and a coup by four Iraqi colonels who called themselves the Golden Square restored Rashid Ali. Fearing for his life, Emir Abdullah, the pro-British uncle and regent of 5-year-old King Faisal II, escaped via the US Embassy to RAF Habbaniya and thence to Basra from where he was transferred to the gunboat HMS *Cockchafer.* Meanwhile, the infant King was hiding out in Kurdistan in the arms of his British nanny.

One of the first things Rashid Ali did on resuming power was promise that he would abide by the terms of the Anglo-Iraq Treaty. Newly appointed British Ambassador Sir Kinahan Cornwallis, one of the Arabists who had helped to build Iraq out of its Ottoman wreckage and highly regarded by the Foreign Office if not always by the Arabs, did not believe a word of it. He urged that the Golden Square be overthrown and the Regent restored. At Karachi two British Indian Army brigades were in the process of embarking for Singapore where there were fears that recent Japanese moves onto Vichy France's Indochina airfields were not well intended. But Japan was not yet at war with Britain and might never be. It was decided to divert these brigades to Basra. In addition, also from Karachi, the British Army staged its first ever airlift. Just under 400 men of the King's Own Royal Regiment were flown across the Persian Gulf to reinforce Habbaniya, most of them making their flight debut in the aircraft the RAF called 'the flying pig': Vickers Valencia biplane transports that could take no more than twenty fully equipped infantry and even in good weather lurched through the air in a manner guaranteed to make even experienced fliers yearn for terra firma.

All this was done in the name of the transit rights allowed by the treaty. The British told the Iraqis the brigades, each about 5,000 strong, were ultimately bound for Palestine. Rashid Ali, politely informed, said that it was inconvenient. When the second brigade disembarked at Basra, Iraqi patriots led by the police began sniping at them but this died down after it was announced *Cockchafer* would retaliate with her 6-inch guns. Then the

Iraqi leadership suggested that the matter should be settled through Turkish mediation and the British pretended to consider this option. Neither side was being sincere.

In Baghdad, Cornwallis's embassy had heard rumours of the impending return of Dr Fritz Grobba, one of Germany's most prominent Orientalists and for seven years, until his British-inspired expulsion in 1939, its ambassador to Iraq. Grobba, an energetic Nazi propagandist who had arranged for the Arabic edition of *Mein Kampf* to be serialized in a Baghdad morning newspaper he had bought, was highly regarded by the Pan-Arabists who saw him as the man who would deliver them from British bondage. Baghdad's Italian Embassy, the Axis mission Britain had failed to remove, informed Rome and Berlin what the colonels backing Rashid Ali needed: not just arms and money but the kind of air support that would guarantee them success over the weak British forces deployed against Iraq's army of 60,000. By 25 April it was all agreed: the Iraqis were getting thirty-three warplanes. Germany would supply fourteen twin-engined Messerschmitt 110 fighter-bombers and seven Heinkel 111 heavy bombers. About twenty Junkers transports, including a couple of the big four-engined Ju-90s of the type Lufthansa had used on their pre-war long-haul routes, would bring the ground crews, maintenance equipment and all the munitions the Heinkels and Messerschmitts required. Italy was sending a squadron of twelve of its nippy CR42 biplane fighters which had the same Bristol engines as the RAF's Gladiators. All the German aircraft would carry Iraqi insignia but their crews would be German, the same thin disguise the Luftwaffe's Condor Legion had worn for Franco in Spain.

Vichy France was also asked to play a role and Amiral Darlan was happy to oblige. Now firmly ensconced as Pétain's deputy, he had arranged that the Axis aircraft should be staged through neighbouring Syria rather than fly in directly from Italian bases on Rhodes. More than ever Darlan was determined to win German concessions by showing them how much he wanted to hurt the English.

In recent months the Royal Navy had stoked his Anglophobia with Operation Ration, a tightening of its naval blockade on French merchant shipping bringing colonial imports into Marseilles that the Germans might ultimately get their hands on. Top of the British list were rubber shipments from Michelin's Indochina plantations. 'The Cabinet are particularly concerned that the attention of the French should be drawn to the contrast between the arrival of food ships and the non-arrival of cargoes other than food,' London had informed Admiral Somerville in Gibraltar, who was in overall charge.

Operation Ration had led to several sea chases after French ships striving to get back into territorial waters on sighting British patrols. A fierce exchange of fire between a French shore battery near Casablanca and the cruiser HMS *Sheffield* ended suddenly with an impressive onshore explosion, presumably from a direct hit on a magazine or some kind of accidental misfire with the same result. Afterwards ten Vichy Glenn Martin bombers had caught up with the *Sheffield* and her attendant destroyers about 8 miles outside Gibraltar but in three separate attacks on the cruiser failed to inflict any damage.

Encounters were more often settled by an armed boarding party getting onto the French ship, usually after dire threats of the consequences if she failed to heave to and lower a ladder. For those that did not comply with the last request an Australian ship adapted a Lee-Enfield cartridge so that the rifle could fire a grappling hook with a line attached like a whaling harpoon. On at least one occasion a stubborn refusal to stop and be searched ended in tragedy. On New Year's Day 1941 a Frenchman named Tarte and his 12-year-old daughter, passengers on the liner SS *Chantilly*, were killed and four others wounded when they were hit by what was supposed to be a warning burst from a heavy machine gun on HMS *Jaguar*, one of the Dunkirk destroyers. The British got a doctor aboard and, not surprisingly, found the crew 'in ugly mood'.

'Please at once inform your French colleague and ask him to convey immediately to Vichy our profound regret at this misfortune,' the Admiralty signalled the British naval attaché in Madrid. 'But you should emphasise that it arose out of unjustifiable resistance to a perfectly legitimate operation.'

Chantilly was intercepted off Morocco's Cape Tres Forcas, one of a convoy of four ships whose journeys had begun in the ports of French West Africa with their last cargoes picked up in Casablanca. With the liner were two tankers and the Copenhagen-registered freighter *Sally Maersk* which had fallen into Vichy hands in Dakar and was discovered still to have a detachment of nine French marines aboard. As soon as their jailers were removed the Danish crew, voluntary exiles from their German-occupied homeland since the previous April, had hoisted the Red Ensign of the British Merchant Marine.

All four ships were escorted to Gibraltar, while in Madrid the furious French naval attaché demanded their release 'with the shortest delay if it is desired to avoid very serious consequences'. This was ignored. With Doenitz's U-boats threatening to starve them into surrender the British had an enormous appetite for ships. *Chantilly*, built in St Nazaire in 1922 and big enough to carry 800 passengers, would first become a British troop transport then, painted white, a hospital ship. The fully laden tankers were obvious prizes and for all the innocence of the considerable tonnage of coffee, cocoa and palm kernels found in her holds the Danish *Sally Maersk* – which would be torpedoed off Greenland in September – was considered nothing less than a return to the fold.

Darlan called it piracy. By the time the Germans were asking him for the use of the Syrian airfields his staff had worked out that since July 1940 the British had seized a total of 167 French ships: some 790,000 tons worth. Apart from the Syrian concession he had also decided to offer Rommel's Afrika Korps the use of the Tunisian port of Bizerte which was closer to Sicily than Tripoli and would make his supply ships less vulnerable to air and submarine attack from Malta. And he would discuss the possibility of a German submarine base at Dakar.

The Germans agreed to make Darlan immediate and visible payment for the airfields: by releasing for service in North Africa about 7,000 of their colonial army's professional officer and non-commissioned cadre who had fallen into their hands in 1940; by easing some of the irksome formalities at the crossing points on the demarcation line between the occupied and non-occupied zones; by reducing from 20 to 15 million Reichsmarks a day what Germany charged France for the tediously expensive business of being obliged to occupy the country in the first place. All this was enshrined in a document, the first part concerning Syria signed by Darlan and Ambassador Abetz, to be known as the Paris Protocols.

As far as the little amiral was concerned this was the high-water mark of collaboration. Certainly much better than anything Laval had managed to pull off. It might even revive a French proposal floated during the first days of the armistice that, using Syria as a springboard, France should seize the British controlled Iraqi oilfields at Mosul and Kirkuk and divide the spoils with Germany. It would no doubt have come as a terrible shock to both Darlan and, to be fair, probably the Francophone Abetz, had they known that in return for oil Germany had secretly agreed to support a confederation between Iraq and Syria cleansed of the French. All that Rashid Ali and the colonels of the Golden Square had to do was await the arrival of the Luftwaffe so that they could rid themselves of the British first. They had already seen what a difference a little German assistance could make.

Hitler's decision to come to Mussolini's rescue and intervene in both North Africa and Greece had certainly done nothing to detract from the invincible aura of the Wehrmacht.

During the winter of 1940, the Greek campaign against their Italian invaders in the snow-filled passes of the Albanian frontier had won them worldwide admiration. In Britain comparisons were made between the dismal performance of the French Army earlier that year and the valiant, under-equipped Greeks whose most modern equipment seemed to be the distinctive French helmets they were wearing. Their defiance was a tremendous fillip for British morale. As the Luftwaffe's night bombing was reaching its peak, the chorus of one of the most popular songs on the BBC's Light Programme went:

What a surprise for the Duce, the Duce,
He can't put it over the Greeks,
What a surprise for the Duce, they do say
He's had no spaghetti for weeks!

That the Duce's appetite might well be restored by a German tonic had been by no means unexpected. By the beginning of March, Middle East Command had transferred almost 58,000 men to Greece complete with artillery, a brigade of tanks, lots of trucks and plenty of the little open-topped tracked vehicles known as Bren-gun carriers which comfortably seated four people. This was not a decision that had been lightly taken. A small RAF contingent had already depleted the Desert Air Force and Greek instructors were training Greek pilots at Habbaniya. The desirability of getting some British troops alongside the Greeks had left Churchill agonizing over the risk that it might fatally weaken the army that had inflicted such a gratifying defeat on the Italians in Libya.

After initial reluctance it was Wavell who thought it could be done. He put the Greek expedition under the command of Lieutenant General Sir Maitland Wilson, an enormous bald ball of a man known as Jumbo, who had convinced himself that all would be well because the Greeks had agreed to fall back behind the Aliakmon river, a strong defensive position where they would join together to fight the Germans to a standstill. Instead, the Greeks left it too late and an orderly retreat is always the most difficult of military manoeuvres. By the end of April 1941, harried by the ubiquitous Luftwaffe, it had first become a headlong flight then abject surrender. In Athens the Acropolis was flying a swastika flag. Jumbo Wilson was lucky that the navy got three-quarters of his men back to Egypt or to Crete though most of them, like himself, had got only the clothes they stood up in and their personal weapons.

Disaster had also struck in North Africa. Even as Wilson's expedition was crossing the Mediterranean for Greece, a panzer division under General Erwin Rommel was going the other way and soon unloading in Tripoli. At the end of March 1941 Rommel started his offensive. Two weeks later he had pushed the depleted British forces all the way back to the Egyptian frontier. In the process he captured 2,000 prisoners including three British generals, one of them Richard O'Connor who had started the chain of Italian defeats. The only part of Libya Rommel's Afrika Korps had been unable to restore to Mussolini was the port of Tobruk where Australian infantry with British armour and artillery stood firm.

These then, plus unfinished business with the Italians in Ethiopia and Somaliland, were Archibald Wavell's more pressing concerns when Amiral Darlan decided to add to them by lending a helping hand to Germany's Arab allies in Iraq. On 29 April the fast light cruiser HMS *Ajax*, of River Plate fame, brought Britain's Middle East commander from Egypt to Crete.

Wavell had come for talks with Jumbo Wilson, who had 30,000 of his Greek Expeditionary Force there, and Major General Bernard Freyberg VC, London-born but raised in New Zealand, whose division he was commanding.

Crete is 70 miles off the Greek mainland and Admiral Cunningham's fleet dominated the waters in between. In March it had sunk five Italian warships during a battle off Cape Matapan in which 2,000 Italian sailors died. When Greece fell, total catastrophe for the British had only been averted because the Royal Navy was able to stage a series of miniature Dunkirks. Yet it seemed the campaign was far from over. ULTRA wireless intercepts suggested that the Germans intended to make military history: they planned to exploit their overwhelming air superiority to leapfrog the Royal Navy by using paratroopers, gliders and, once an airfield was taken, Junkers 52 transport planes to capture the island almost entirely by airborne assault.

The New Zealand Division had made a good battle debut in Greece, where they often provided the rearguard, and at Churchill's request Wavell agreed to put the 1916 Victoria Cross winner Freyberg in charge of Crete. The Prime Minister, who loved the brave, thought Freyberg was marvellous. At a pre-war country house weekend he had once persuaded the barrel chested warrior to strip off and reveal his 1914–18 scars and stopped counting at twenty-seven though, as the object of his veneration modestly pointed out, some were from exit wounds.

Jumbo Wilson was considered to have done well during the retreat forced on him in Greece, handing out a couple of bloody noses and keeping his command intact enough for the navy to get most of it out. But his Balkan adventures, for the time being at least, were over. With Rashid Ali in mind, Wavell had decided to make him commander of British troops in Palestine and Transjordan and sent him off with orders that were his usual model of concision: 'I want you to go to Jerusalem and relieve Baghdad.'

Except that in this case appearances were deceptive. Wavell's heart was not at all into sending a relief expedition to Iraq. He felt Middle East Command was far too over-stretched to take on another front, however minor, and the reinforcements that had arrived in Iraq from India were too meagre to make much difference. The mostly British-trained Iraqi Army was quite formidable, with a considerable amount of artillery plus a few light tanks and armoured cars. And even without German help its air force possessed about sixty relatively modern American, British and Italian types that were certainly more than a match for Air Vice-Marshal Smart's trainers at Habbaniya.

Wavell urged London to take up the offer of Turkish mediation. Holding Rommel at the Egyptian frontier was bad enough without risking the consequences of taking on an Arab insurgency with inferior forces. He feared Iraq could easily bushfire into uprisings in his Palestinian and Egyptian rear areas where there was certainly enough dry tinder about.

Three years of full-scale rebellion in Palestine over Zionist immigration had only ended in 1939 and it had taken several thousand troops to do it. The most he wanted Jumbo Wilson to do was rattle any sabres that came to hand in the hope that the noise might contribute to a negotiated solution. As Christopher Buckley, the *Daily Telegraph*'s Cairo-based war correspondent in the Middle East, would write when he was no longer constrained by censorship:

> Our patient and much tried Commander-in-Chief was in the position of the father of a family whose budget cannot cover all the needs of his numerous offspring ... Ever since the preceding June his command had been primarily an affair of making ends meet with totally insufficient resources, and in the months of April and May 1941 it seemed that all the bills were coming in together.

Above all, beyond the Iraqi problem loomed a much larger cloud. Wavell had long suspected that sooner rather than later Churchill would ask him to help the Gaullists take over Vichy Syria. For some time they had been arguing that, with a little English support, Syria (of which Lebanon was then an integral part) would drop into their basket like a ripe fruit. It was far more isolated than Vichy France's African possessions. To its south and east were the British-controlled borders of Palestine, Transjordan and (up to a point) Iraq, while off its west coast were Royal Navy patrols and the crown colony of Cyprus. To the north was aloof and neutral Turkey.

In recent weeks Free France's Levant emissary Général Georges Catroux, a five-star general who had first met de Gaulle in a German prison camp in 1916 and was by far his highest ranking army officer to come over to him, had been hinting at mass Vichy defections if only Wavell would agreed to advance into Syria alongside the 6,000 Gaullist troops they could muster. But the Commander-in-Chief was adamant that they would need far more men than he had available and his opposition to any intervention in Iraq let alone Syria led to an increasingly acerbic exchange of telegrams between himself, Churchill and the Chiefs of Staff.

> *Wavell*: I have consistently warned you that no assistance could be given to Iraq from Palestine in present circumstances and have always advised that commitment in Iraq should be avoided.
>
> *Churchill*: A commitment in Iraq was inevitable. We had to establish a base at Basra and control that port to safeguard Persian oil ... no question of accepting the Turkish offer of mediation. We can make no concessions ... essential to do all in our power to save Habbaniya and to control the [oil] pipeline to the Mediterranean.
>
> *Wavell*: Your message takes little account of realities. You must face facts. I feel it is my duty to warn you in the gravest possible terms that I consider

the prolongation of fighting in Iraq will seriously endanger the defence of Palestine and Egypt. The political repercussions may result in what I have spent nearly two years trying to avoid, namely serious internal trouble in our bases.

Churchill to Chiefs of Staff: I am deeply disturbed at General Wavell's attitude. He seems to have been taken as much by surprise on his eastern as he was on his western flank [a reference to Rommel's offensive] ... he gives me the impression of being tired out.

Chiefs of Staff to Wavell: Settlement by negotiation cannot be entertained ... Realities of the situation are that Rashid Ali has all along been hand-in-glove with Axis Powers and was merely waiting until they could support him before exposing his hand.

At which, a week later, the Commander-in-Chief climbed down, indicating that he was not only willing to take offensive action in Iraq but at least discuss the situation in Syria with the Free French.

Wavell to Churchill: If things go well in Egypt's Western Desert [he had just ordered a tank attack against Rommel] ... we will try to liquidate this tiresome Iraq business quickly ... I am doing my best to strengthen Crete against attack. I discussed the question of Syria with Catroux this afternoon.

Chapter Fifteen

Anyone viewing the first visible evidence of Wavell's new-found resolve to do something about the 'tiresome Iraq business' might have well understood his previous reluctance.

Towards the end of the first week of May, a curious collection of the kind of civilian transport kept alive only by improvisations bordering on genius was gathered near the eastern border of Transjordan to begin a desert journey of some 350 miles to the banks of the Euphrates. Buses, flat-bedded lorries or cars possibly so well born they had started life with roofs, running boards, even uniformed chauffeurs, were piled high with dented tins of bully beef, wooden ammunition boxes and incontinent cans of water and petrol. Next to them stood their almost invariably chain-smoking civilian drivers, most of them Jews from Tel Aviv or Haifa who had been pressed into service with their vehicles.

This was the logistics tail of Habforce, Hab standing for Habbaniya which was where they were bound, for the RAF base was now under siege. Up front at Habforce's sharp end was KingCol, named after its commander Brigadier Joseph Kingstone. Its point included the small 15 hundredweight Morris and Chevrolet trucks of the newly mechanized Household Cavalry Regiment, known as the Tin Tummies to the rest of the army after the breastplates they wore on London ceremonial duties; a battery of nine 25-pounder field pieces; some of the RAF's 1915-pattern armoured cars with their Vickers machine guns; the vehicle mechanics of a Light Aid Detachment who were as important as ammunition; and 200 riflemen of the 1st Essex, a battalion in disgrace ever since their baptism of fire on the Sudanese-Eritrean border six months before when they bolted under Italian bombing.

In his desperation to cobble together an expeditionary force of sorts Jumbo Wilson had also availed himself of a standing offer from Transjordan's King Abdullah, who feared the republicanism afoot in neighbouring Iraq, to make use of his British-officered Arab Legion. Under its commander Glubb Pasha (aka Major John Bagot Glubb, Royal Engineers) 350 of the legion's mechanized regiment, almost entirely Bedouin, would be travelling with KingCol as scouts and sabotage parties. The British troops took one look at them in their ankle-length frocks with crossed bandoliers and ornate daggers and knew what they had to call them: Glubb's Girls.

Behind KingCol came the rest of Habforce. Most of it was from the 4th Brigade of Major General George Clark's 1st Cavalry Division which was mostly close-knit county yeomanry mixed in with regulars such as the Tin Tummies. Habforce's yeomanry came from two regiments, the Warwicks and the Wiltshires, who had each supplied a squadron of about 200 men. Yeomanry were mostly weekend soldiers of the pre-war Territorial Army. Their fathers and older brothers had often fought in the same regiments during Allenby's Palestine campaign against the Turks in 1917–18. The yeomanry had still been horsed when, shortly after the start of hostilities in 1939, they returned to Palestine on internal security duties. Then over the last year the division, regiment by regiment, had begun a process of mechanization that would end up with most of them becoming tank or, in the case of the Tin Tummies, armoured car crews.

The Habforce units had reached the interim stage where, having gone through the heart-wrenching business of shooting some of their horses, they were being used in the old cavalry role of mounted riflemen. In this case their mounts were their small canvas-topped trucks, some of them mothballed in Egypt and Palestine since 1918 and so old they had solid tyres. Kingstone was to lead them across a wilderness the Arabs had for centuries called the Syrian Desert though the map makers at Versailles had placed the biggest part of it firmly in Iraq. For most of the way he was to follow the Kirkuk oil pipeline along which there were pumping stations, usually with a small clinic and other facilities, manned by British civilian engineers. Some of these were believed to have fallen into the hands of the Iraqi Army and KingCol was to recapture them and free any prisoners. Then, shortly before the Euphrates, they were to leave the pipeline and turn south-east to lift the siege on Habbaniya.

It had started on 30 April when Iraqi troops began to deploy onto the plateau above the base with artillery, armoured cars, light anti-aircraft guns and a couple of their small Italian tanks. Rashid Ali had tried to counsel patience but the military had grown tired of waiting for their German air support and decided they must act before it was too late. By blowing holes in some of the dykes along the Euphrates flood waters they had made it difficult for Habbaniya to be relieved by the Indian troops advancing slowly upriver from Basra. But they were well aware that some British infantry had already been flown into the base and were determined that this would not be repeated. From Baghdad one of the last messages out of Cornwallis's embassy before Iraqi police confiscated their wireless and, 'for their own protection', interned them in their own compound was that a large Iraqi force was heading towards Habbaniya. Shortly afterwards, a reconnaissance flight over the plateau by one of Smart's

Audax Harts, still in its bright yellow training livery, confirmed his worst fears.

Yet the shooting did not start immediately. Instead there had been something of a military gavotte with an Arab officer carrying a white flag appearing at the cantonment's main gate to deliver a note explaining they were on a training exercise and must be treated with respect. 'Please make no flying or the going out of any force of persons from the cantonment. If any aircraft or armoured car attempts to go out it will be shelled by our batteries.'

Air Vice-Marshal Smart bade the emissary wait while he dictated a reply. 'Any interference with training flights will be considered an act of war. We demand the withdrawal of the Iraqi forces from positions which are clearly hostile.'

It was a bold answer but the odds were rather less favourable than the last time Smart had been in action in Iraq. In the 1920s the Kurds could rarely take on aircraft with anything better than a Mauser rifle. Sitting above Habbaniya were some 6,000 Iraqi troops trained by a British military mission under a Major General George Waterhouse, presently languishing in the embassy compound in Baghdad. They were well equipped. The abundance of the latest Bren light machine guns in Iraqi hands was the envy of the forces sent to deal with them. They had these and a few larger calibre anti-aircraft weapons to protect the fifty or so artillery pieces that held RAF Habbaniya's airfield, which was actually just outside the perimeter fence, entirely at their mercy.

Smart's ground troops were commanded by Colonel Ouvry Roberts, an Indian Army staff officer who had flown in from Basra for what was supposed to be a brief assessment and had easily been persuaded to stay. Under him were the infantrymen of the King's Own who were perhaps 360 strong; 18 of the RAF's vintage armoured cars which had Rolls-Royce engines but Ned Kelly armour plate; and 1,200 British-officered Assyrian and Kurdish levies who might be good at chasing snipers off the plateau in less turbulent times but had never been tested against more serious opposition. In addition there were about 1,000 airmen of all ranks, mostly ground crew, for whom there were not enough rifles to go round and even those lucky enough to have one had rarely squeezed a trigger since basic training.

Smart ordered slit trenches to be dug all around the base's 7 miles of perimeter which included a stretch of river bank by the airfield. Everybody not immediately engaged in flying or servicing an aircraft was required to man them. This led to some disquiet among those commanding the aircraft, which were the most plausible part of Habbaniya's defence, who toured the perimeter quietly removing essential air and ground crews they were reluctant to risk as infantry.

By this time almost sixty of the training aircraft had been transformed into bombers of a kind but there were not enough qualified crews to fly them. Including the Greek attachment from the Hellenic Air Force, whose foreign language tended to be French or German, there were thirty-five pilot instructors of whom three had seen some air combat. The rest were selected from the more advanced pupil pilots. Air gunners, bomb aimers and observers tended to come from the cadets most recently separated from their Tiger Moth basic trainers or from a pool of ground crew volunteers. Some of the biplanes, which required less take-off space than the Oxfords, were moved to the polo field and the golf course had also been prepared as an emergency landing strip.

By May Day twelve Wellington bombers, badly needed for Wavell's forthcoming offensive against Rommel in the Western Desert, were transferred from Egypt to Basra, from where they could support Habbaniya. On the same day Churchill sent a message to Smart: 'If you have to strike, strike hard. Use all necessary force.'

Whether the necessary force was available was another matter but at dawn on 2 May Smart's twin-engined Wellingtons from Basra made his opening move. Wellingtons carried a bomb load of 4,500 pounds but with a wingspan of 86 feet and a top speed of 235mph they were big, slow and vulnerable and from quite early on in the war whenever possible they were used only in night attacks. For maximum effect they made what, for a Wellington, was an unusually low-level daybreak attack on the plateau from about 1,000 feet and as a result most of them took hits. Fortunately, for all its faults it was an aircraft that could take a lot of punishment. Only one Wellington could not get back to Basra. With both engines knocked out before it had the chance to drop its bombs, its pilot managed to put it down on Habbaniya's airfield gently enough not to explode its cargo though Iraqi gunners were soon doing their best to rectify this. As the crew dashed for the dubious shelter of the hangars, a tractor escorted by two RAF armoured cars sped out to pull the plane to safety. Under fire, the driver got a rope around its tail wheel when a near miss wrecked his tractor and ignited the aircraft. Deafened by the blast, the driver was pulled aboard one of the armoured cars that sped from the scene as the first flames licked the bomb bay.

For the Iraqi gunners the explosions that followed must have been a heartening sight. They returned to shelling the hangars, workshops and barracks areas with renewed enthusiasm, though it was noted that a large red cross painted on the hospital's roof was being respected. But they were close enough for their muzzle flashes to give away their positions and now Smart's second wave took off: thirty-five Audax, Gordons and Oxfords.

The aircraft, which had been lurking between the hangars, shot out of the cantonment's main gate one after the other already doing 30mph before they hit the airfield where the pilots took a deep breath and pulled themselves off the ground some seconds before normal air speed had been attained. Compared with the Wellington the bomb load of these aircraft was pathetic. The Gordons could carry the most, two 250-pound bombs. At the other end of the scale the little Oxfords, even after their practice racks had been modified, could only manage eight 20-pounders. Even so, for the Wellington bombers a round trip from Shaibah to Habbaniya and back lasted four hours, whereas what Smart called his Air Striking Force could take off, bomb and strafe Iraqi positions, and land to be bombed up again in less than ten minutes.

In charge of the Oxfords and the Gordons was Squadron Leader Tony Dudgeon who had recently arrived at Habbaniya with a newly awarded Distinguished Flying Cross and a dachshund called Frankie. Aged 25, Dudgeon, an Old Etonian and Cranwell-trained regular, had already been in the RAF for six years, flown fifty operations against the Italian ports, airfields and troop concentrations in North Africa where he had commanded a Blenheim squadron, and had been sent to the training school as a senior instructor for a rest. It was Dudgeon who had personally made the prototype modified bomb rack for his Oxfords and test-flown it himself to prove it would not crash them. 'One 20 pound bomb carries the same amount of explosive as a 6-inch shell. And 27 Oxfords could now carry 216 of them, which was about a couple of tons of bombs, much better than none at all.'

> We were only too aware that we had nothing, just nothing, which could stop a tank driving up to the front door of Air HQ except our bombs. We knew our very survival depended on knocking out every offensive weapon or vehicle before the Iraqis could bring it to bear effectively. And to keep on and on, without respite until they left ... This drove us into a routine which was to fly, fly, fly in any aircraft we could get our hands on. We bombed and we gunned and looked for other targets. Something had to crack and it was not going to be us. As soon as the aircraft was back on the ground, one of the two crew members would report to the ops room telling the results and suggesting new targets then plot both bits of info on the latest photomap and allot the crewman his next target. While that was going on the other crewman – pilot or pupil acting as bomber aimer – would help reload the machine and make an additional check for any damage which was worse than superficial. 'Superficial' meant any new hole which did not appear to have damaged something important like a main spar, an oil pipe or a control hinge. Usually things would be done with the engines still running. Surprisingly, no-one got clouted by a spinning prop ... the pupils acting as bomb aimers and rear gunners quickly became remarkably accurate even if some of the bombing run corrections were a bit garbled at first. 'Left, left ... right ... RIGHT ... LEFT, LEFT!!! Oh Christ, bomb's gone ... Sir.'

By nightfall the Iraqi artillery fire had noticeably diminished. In total the Air Striking Force had flown 193 sorties during which two of its planes had been shot down with the loss of four crew and four more destroyed on the ground as a result of shellfire and a brief appearance by the Iraqi Air Force. Another twenty aircraft would not fly again without extensive repairs. It was not just the Iraqi anti-aircraft guns that were inflicting the damage but thousands of rounds from machine guns and bolt-action rifles. The flimsy, relatively slow-moving aircraft were quite easy targets for men who were reasonable shots and could keep their nerve, and it seems a good many of the Iraqis had both these attributes. Every machine had taken hits. The record perforation was held by Flight Lieutenant Dan Cremin whose Audax returned after a ten minute sortie above the plateau with fifty-two new bullet holes and a pupil gunner in its rear cockpit in danger of bleeding to death. Cremin was unscathed. Dudgeon mentions several cases of pilots being shot through their thighs and buttocks by bullets that had come straight through their seats. As casualties mounted and the shortage of any kind of aircrew, trained or half trained, became more acute, heavily bandaged young men with what they insisted were superficial wounds often returned to the fray. 'The terms "minor damage" or "flesh wounds" might have been stretched a bit and not assessed in a normal manner,' said Dudgeon. 'But then our situation was far from normal.'

Emboldened, the RAF began to extend its operations, still concentrating on the guns and the armoured vehicles but sending aircraft to attack the Iraqi fighters and bombers parked at Baghdad airport and the nearby satellite field of Rashid on the capital's eastern outskirts. Six twin-engined Blenheim bombers, initially based in Palestine, joined in. It was by no means one-sided. An Oxford trainer's sergeant pilot was killed by a single bullet which severed a main artery and the plane was brought down by the acting air gunner, an aircraftsman normally employed on a target drogue. A Wellington was forced down and its six-man crew captured. More of the flimsy, zippy little Audax were turned into flying colanders. Men survived several missions above the plateau unscathed only to become casualties on the ground either from artillery or Iraqi bombers. Dudgeon had his only experienced bomb aimer killed this way while he was lying beneath his Oxford reloading the racks between missions.

Nonetheless, they began to wear the Iraqis down. Night bombing deprived them of sleep, though some of the half-trained pilots found the return landings in the dark on unlit runways about the most dangerous they were asked to do. Even a little counter-battery fire was introduced after Basra was persuaded to fly in a couple of army gun teams and shells for the headquarters' decorative howitzers, which turned out to be in a remarkable state of preservation.

But if Iraqi morale started to crumble it was not least because the famous Luftwaffe, scourge of the Inglizi, had so far failed to put in a single appearance and their own air force, used in dribs and drabs instead of overwhelming force, had done little better. Yet Habbaniya with its swimming pools and polo pitch and unwarlike ways had produced all these bombing planes. How was it possible? On the fifth day the siege ended with the Iraqis abandoning most of their guns and heading back towards Baghdad pursued not only by Smart's hornet's nest of riddled aircraft but the King's Own and the Assyrian levies, who fought even better than their British officers had ever dared hope.

Fearing something like this might be about to happen the Golden Square had sent reinforcements from Baghdad, a fresh mechanized infantry brigade with towed artillery. They met, heading in their different directions, a few miles west of the town of Fallujah and being unused to the ways of mid-twentieth-century warfare there they parked their vehicles nose-to-tail and got out to talk things over. Which was when about forty of Habbaninya's Air Striking Force found them. At least one account claims 'a solid mass of flame 250 yards long'. These things are often exaggerated* but undoubtedly there was sufficient terror to start a stampede back towards Fallujah.

The defence of Habbaniya was as remarkable as it was unexpected and ultimately it would prove the undoing of Rashid Ali's uprising. Having groped its way through the pipeline's foggy sandstorms, skirmished with an Iraqi police detachment around Rutba's old mud-brick fort, got bogged down in soft sand then rescued by Glubb's Girls, and marked its trail with the exhausted machinery of its civilian baggage train, it took KingCol ten days to get to the RAF base. By that time Habbaniya had managed to relieve itself and be reinforced by Blenheims, Gladiators and even five Hurricanes from Egypt and Palestine. More importantly, it did so seventy-two hours before the first of the German aircraft from Vichy's Syrian airfields had touched down in Iraq in circumstances of such dire misfortune it would seem that their luck could only get better.

On board the Heinkel III was Dr Fritz Grobba, Germany's returning ambassador, and Major Axel von Blomberg, son of a field marshal once close to Hitler but prematurely retired after a messy divorce. Major von Blomberg, a rising star in the Wehrmacht despite his father's indiscretions, had just been appointed overall head of the German Military Mission to Rashid Ali. As they approached Baghdad, the major ordered the pilot to advertise their arrival by flying low and slow, paying particular attention to the army positions on the west-facing bridges across the Euphrates. This was a silly idea and a reflection perhaps of how little the Germans knew of the RAF's heightened presence. The Heinkel's newly painted Iraqi colours did not prevent the inevitable burst of machine-gun fire from the

* Some fifty years later, those of us who witnessed, at the end of what became the First Gulf War, the carnage US aircraft had inflicted on Saddam's retreating army at Kuwait's El Mutla ridge were startled how the tale, already bad enough, grew in the telling.

ground and the pilot scooted off for Baghdad airport. After the aircraft taxied to a halt and Grobba and the crew prepared to get out von Blomberg did not move. It was soon discovered that there was a simple explanation for this: the major had been shot through the neck and was quite dead.

It took RAF reconnaissance one day to spot German aircraft at Iraqi airfields; two days to have their first bloodless encounter with one of them – a Blenheim and an Me110 failing to get on each other's tails over Mosul – and three days to confirm that they were coming through Vichy Syria. At first light on Wednesday, 14 May, a Pilot Officer Watson, flying the long-distance fighter version of the Blenheim, spotted what looked like a four-engined Junkers 90 rising from an oasis airfield at Palmyra, the old caravan stop in French Syria. Later that morning he returned and this time counted four transports plus some smaller planes. Some of them appeared to be refuelling.

Vichy territory was still off limits to the RAF but this was a blatant breach of its neutrality and there seems to have been little agonizing over what to do next. In the late afternoon, Watson with four other Habbaniya-based Blenheims escorted by two newly delivered Curtiss Tomahawk fighters, a low wing monoplane known to its American manufacturers as the P40, bombed and strafed all the aircraft they could find on the Palmyra airfield which included at least two Heinkel bombers. But the RAF was short of incendiary ammunition and the results were disappointing. No smoke and all remained intact-looking. Next day the indefatigable Watson twice revisited the Palmyra field and thought the German aircraft looked to be in much the same positions. On the second occasion he machine-gunned them and again there was no visible sign of damage. But later a reconnaissance by a different pilot revealed one burnt out Heinkel with three more and a Junkers 52 transport looking a little the worse for wear.

The RAF now began a Syrian milk run, delivering regular strikes on those rear echelons of the Luftwaffe's military mission to Iraq which were using Vichy airfields at Palmyra, Damascus's Mezze airport, a landing ground outside the northern textile town of Aleppo, and a French fighter field at Rayak amid the haunted ruins of the Baalbek valley's Roman temples. At the same time, leaving the much patched trainers of Habbaniya's Air Striking Force to harass the Iraqi Army, they hunted down the Messerschmitts and Heinkels that were operating out of northern Iraq, particularly Mosul, and from the airstrip at Rashid near Baghdad.

When they could the Luftwaffe responded in kind. On 16 May three Mosul-based Heinkels inflicted more damage on the aircraft parked at Habbaniya than all the Iraqi Air Force raids put together, killing the engineering officer who had kept Dudgeon's machines flying. But once again they paid a price. Ignoring the bombs, Flying Officer Gerald Herrtage managed to get his Gladiator fighter into the air and, though the biplane was slower, got close enough to Oberleutnant Graubner's aircraft to hit his starboard engine before he was killed by the concentrated fire of the three German tail-gunners. Losing height at the rate of 6 feet a second Graubner left the formation and tried to coax his stricken Heinkel back to Mosul on its one good engine, his crew jettisoning everything that was loose 'except for the guns and a little ammunition'. But they crash-landed in the desert and there was no hope of recovering the aircraft unless Rashid Ali's forces won the day.

The attrition of the German air contingent continued. Next day Herrtage's 94 Squadron, which had been converting to Hurricanes before they were put back into Gladiators at Habbaniya, took spectacular revenge for their first casualty. Sergeant pilots Leslie Smith and William Dunwoodie were patrolling over the Iraqi airfield Rashid when, blissfully unaware of the circling Gladiators, two Messerschmitt Bf 110s took off. They had started to gain altitude when the more lightly armed biplanes, which made up in agility for what they lacked in speed, ambushed them. Dunwoodie got the second one.

> One Me 110 flashed past my port wing, masses of smoke pouring from both engines and Sergeant Smith hot on its tail. A few seconds later I was able to get in an excellent astern attack on the other aircraft, putting a burst right into the fuselage. Almost immediately there was a terrific flash and the Me 110 was a mass of flame and disintegrated in the air. The one that Sgt Smith had shot down blazed furiously on the ground.

Perhaps one Messerschmitt crew survived a crash landing but Leutnant Woerner and his rear gunner Unteroffizier Fischer were killed in the mid-air explosion, probably because they were carrying small bombs as well as full fuel tanks.

The Luftwaffe's mission to Iraq was known as Sonderkommando Junck, after its commander Oberst (Colonel) Werner Junck. It was meant to be a gesture to the strongest and best educated of the quasi-independent Arab states, its oil-fuelled literacy rates and urbanization growing apace, that would give its well-equipped army the heart to take on the threadbare British Empire. Even so, in terms of priority it came a long way below Operation Mercury, the airfleet that was being assembled for the invasion of Crete now scheduled to start on 20 May. Both were eclipsed by the preparations being made for the blitzkrieg against Russia and the need to reconcile the ingredients essential for success: deception, surprise and overwhelming force. Nonetheless, the miniature Fliegerführer Irak's logistics tail had been put together with all the care, efficiency and daring that were so often the hallmarks of Wehrmacht operations, big or small.

Moving short-range warplanes around required constant engineering back-up. As well as fuel they needed bombs, bullets, spare parts, tools and skilled ground crews. Sonderkommando Junck's logistics tail was, in terms of cubic capacity, much bigger than the twenty-one front-line aircraft it was supporting. Initially it included thirteen transport aircraft: ten tri-motored Junkers 52s, three of the big four-engined Junkers 90s of the kind spotted at Palmyra, plus a single-engined Storch spotter and courier aircraft, a small high-winged monoplane. But once they were established ten of these aircraft, which also had to deliver Dr Grobba's large secretariat, were to be returned to Greece for use over Crete, Junkers 52s being needed for the paratroop drop.

Behind them they would leave one of the Junkers 90s and two special Junkers 52s. The latter had been specially adapted for Sonderkommando Junck. One was a communications centre with high-frequency transmitters that would not only keep Oberst Junck in touch with his command's several airfields but also with the Luftwaffe's new advanced headquarters in Athens and even Berlin. The other was a wonderful example of German thoroughness. It was a flying laboratory where technicians could determine which chemicals must be mixed with Iraq's dismally low-octane fuel to refine it to a level suitable for finely tuned Daimler-Benz engines.

All this might have worked had it been in place at the beginning of the Iraqi attack on Habbaniya. If the British garrison had, in addition to bombardment from the plateau, been subject from the start to remorseless bombing and strafing from Messerschmitts and Heinkels, inspiring emulation from the Iraqi Air Force as they did so, then it might well have overwhelmed the makeshift RAF aircrews who saved the base. But Iraqi morale never recovered from the defeat at Habbaniya and the British continued to destroy Sonderkommando Junck in detail both in the air and on the ground.

Inevitably, as the raids against the Syrian airfields continued, Vichy French casualties began to mount. On 19 May, the eve of the German attack on Crete, there was another attack on Damascus's Mezze airfield when, along with a Junkers 52 and a Heinkel, a couple of French aircraft were destroyed or badly damaged. One of them was a twin-engined Potez 630 fighter-bomber which looked a lot like a Messerschmitt 110. Three German airmen and one French soldier were wounded. At first Vichy had seemed to ignore the RAF's intrusion into its air space as if it wished to pretend that neither they nor the Luftwaffe were there. It was several days before the first anti-aircraft fire was noticed, almost a week before Morane fighters were scrambled in pursuit. Then, a bit like an old car starting up, Vichy began to cough and splutter into action.

Both the Armée de l'Air and the RAF flew a twin-engined American light bomber that the French called the Glenn Martin, which was the name of the company that made it, and the British the Maryland. Knowing that Vichy had several Glenn Martin squadrons in Syria, a Maryland borrowed from a South African squadron was sent on a low-level reconnaissance over Aleppo. Two of its three-man crew were Free French, though whether this was in response to Gaullist pressure to participate in operations over Syria or there was an element of deception involving the use of radio or both is unclear. If there was it failed because the Maryland was almost immediately treated as hostile, hit by anti-aircraft fire then pursued nearly all the way back to its Haifa base by Moranes. By the time it landed one of the Free French, Adjutant-chef Contes, had received a bad leg wound and the limb would have to be amputated.

On 28 May the Moranes were in action over Aleppo again and this time their quarry did not get away. Sous-lieutenant Vuillemin shot down a Blenheim, also on a reconnaissance mission, with the loss of sergeant pilot David and his two crew. The dead men belonged to 211 Squadron which was just back from Greece where the RAF had suffered heavy casualties. Later that day the same Moranes were given the task of escorting four Junkers 52s in transit across Syria. This was the first time L'Armée de l'Air had ever done this for the Luftwaffe and was surely another pinnacle of *la collaboration* though somewhat marred by the cautious German rear gunners who, uncertain of these attentive monoplanes, kept them at a safe distance with long bursts of tracer.

Not all German aid to Iraq went by air. Under the Paris Protocols Vichy had recovered 25 per cent of the arms it had been obliged to store with the Italian-administered Armistice Commission in Syria by agreeing that the rest could go to the Iraqi Army whose main arms supplier was Britain. The shipments were made overland to Mosul, mainly by rail but sometimes by road, and overseen by Dr Rudolf Rahn, Ribbentrop's representative on the Armistice Commission in Syria. Starting on 13 May, Rahn sent 12 field guns – 8 of them big 155mm – with 16,000 shells, 15,500 rifles with 6 million rounds of ammunition, 354 machine pistols, 200 machine guns, 30,000 grenades and 32 trucks. Then the British learned what was going on and intervened in what became their first land action against the Levant's Vichy French.

Rahn was using the Taurus railway that was part of the Kaiser's old dream to extend the Berlin–Istanbul leg of the Orient Express east through the Ottoman Empire to Baghdad and then down to Basra, thus securing a German foothold in the Persian Gulf. Eastwards from Aleppo, using a magnificent series of tunnels and bridges, the line hugged Syria's northern border with Turkey until it reached the small Armenian town of Nusaybin. Here it turned south for the last 50 miles to the Iraqi frontier post at Tel Kotchek, which had finally been linked to Mosul a few days after France's surrender when Iraqi engineers completed the last 100 miles of track and thus, wars permitting, made it possible to go by train from Berlin to Basra. On the Syrian side the line's last handsome river bridge was just before Tel Kotchek and this is the one the British elected to destroy to put an end to Darlan's gun-running.

Although it was decided that the operation was too important to leave to the vagaries of aerial bombing, the RAF did play a leading role. For all the unkind things people said about the Vickers Valentia bomber-transport it was a robust machine that could land and take off in spaces more contemporary aircraft would find fatally cramped. Flight Lieutenant Christopher Bartlett, a Canadian already accustomed to bush flying in his native Saskatchewan when he joined the RAF in London in 1937, aged 20, volunteered to land a demolition party of thirteen British Army sappers on what looked like a *possible* landing ground close to the bridge. It was a risky business: the chosen spot might be rougher or softer than it appeared in the photo-reconnaissance pictures and they could crash on landing; it would have to be a daylight raid and they were so slow they would be easy meat for French fighters. Valentias were used for night bombing the Italians in the Western Desert – Bartlett had done it eleven times – but attempting to land on strange territory in the dark was suicidal.

As it happened, Moranes did not intercept them and the ground was as firm as the pictures promised. The Royal Engineers took forty-five minutes, which was perhaps a bit longer than they had estimated, to place and wire up their charges and wreck the bridge beyond easy repair. By this time some outraged locals had managed to get word to the nearest gendarmerie post. Just as the sappers were returning to the Valentia, and the Canadian had started up its Bristol Pegasus engines, a French armoured car appeared, machine gun blazing, but by then Bartlett was making enough dust to coax his lumbering machine into the air before the enemy got close enough to hit it.

This all happened on 24 May 1941, a minor incident in a minor campaign, though it was the first step to bigger and infinitely more bloody things as far as Vichy Syria was concerned. Bartlett got a Distinguished Flying Cross for it and for the sappers who bumped back to Habbaniya in his old Valentia it had no doubt been both exhilarating and frightening enough. On that same day HMS *Hood*, which under Somerville had helped capsize the *Bretagne* and cripple the *Dunkerque*, was sunk by the *Bismarck* when a fluke shot from the German battleship exploded a magazine. Among three survivors from a ship's company of 1,418 was the teenage signaller Ted Briggs who at Mers el-Kébir had so admired the brave attempt to torpedo them by the French gunboat *Rigault de Genouilly*. Briggs, now just 18, had been sucked down by the sinking battle cruiser then shot to the surface on a bubble of escaping air. Three days later the *Bismarck* shared the same fate as the *Mighty Hood*, cornered by British warships while turning helplessly in circles after a torpedo from one of the *Ark Royal's* Swordfish had maimed her steering. Only 115 of the 2,222 German sailors aboard were saved.

In the waters off Crete the Luftwaffe was reaping revenge. A couple of nights after the *Bismarck* went down, French sailors on Godfroy's mothballed Vichy Squadron in Alexandria witnessed a chilling spectacle. As the cruiser HMS *Dido* limped into the Egyptian port a destroyer captain with a sense of occasion ordered his searchlight to seek out the Black Watch piper playing a lament from the cruiser's ruined bridge. In Crete the Black Watch had inflicted grievous casualties on the German paratroopers who had the misfortune of being matched against them at Heraklion, only to be obliged to evacuate by events elsewhere on the island. Before they reached Alexandria two bombs had hit the *Dido*. The first split open a gun turret and the second went through the hole it had made to explode in the between-decks area where, in its enthusiasm to save as many as it could, the Royal Navy had packed its catch like herrings. About 200 were killed.

Yet forewarned by ULTRA intercepts, Freyberg's defence of Crete had started well. Although his over-stretched garrison had little air cover, artillery, radio links or transport, for the first forty-eight hours it looked as if General Kurt Student's Fliegerkorps might suffer Hitler's first major land defeat. But Freyberg, brave rather than brainy as even his best friends would admit, had failed to clinch his victory over the decimated paratroopers. He clung to the belief that the main German threat was a simultaneous seaborne assault in commandeered Greek caiques, though the navy had already sunk some and driven others away. By the time he grasped the significance of losing Maleme airfield and the steady shuttle of Junkers 52s ferrying in fresh troops there it was too late.

A week after the battle started, the navy once again found itself in the evacuation business and eventually removed about 16,500 of the island's garrison, slightly under half, to Egypt. Since the RAF had neither the aircraft nor the bases to intervene the Luftwaffe's dive bombers had a field day. In all they sank three cruisers and six destroyers. Another seventeen vessels, including the battleships *Warspite*, *Barham* and *Valiant*, were damaged. The new aircraft carrier *Formidable*, hit taking aircraft to Malta, which along with Cyprus was also suspected of being on General Student's agenda, was put out of action for six months. According to some statistics, slightly more British sailors died in the Battle of Crete than British soldiers: 1,828 compared with 1,751.

These losses put an end to the British naval ascendancy in the Mediterranean that had been established by the victories over the Italians. Furthermore, they came after a string of defeats that had erased much of the optimism, starting with the Battle of Britain, which had brought in the New Year on such a surge of hope and cast down the Vichy French leadership. Since then setbacks in Greece, Libya and Crete had been matched by the Blitz's worst night raid to date. On 10–11 May, in the space of about five hours, 1,483 Londoners were killed including the mayors of both Westminster and Bermondsey. The debating chamber of the House of Commons had been reduced to its medieval rubble and Big

Ben wore a knowing scar on its face. The raid brought the total number of civilian deaths since the night attacks on ports and cities had started the previous September to about 40,000 with three times as many injured. At this point the British were the most bombed people on earth.

On that same evening Rudolf Hess, who had learned to fly in the First World War, navigated a Messerschmitt 110 fitted with long-range tanks to Scotland and parachuted himself into forty-five years of mainly rigorous imprisonment. The astonishing one-man peace mission of the Nazi Party's weird deputy leader was born out of a determination that Germany should not find itself fighting a two-front war once the invasion of Russia started. At the time Hess did not reveal the real reason for what Churchill called a 'deed of lunatic benevolence'. But one of the things he did display to his interrogators was a sympathy for Arab nationalism. It appeared to be something more than just the normal Nazi desire to exploit their Jew-hating credentials in the Arab world and was presumably the result of spending the first fifteen years of his life in Alexandria where his father was a trader. Any Anglo-German peace treaty, insisted Hess, would be dependent on a British withdrawal from Iraq.

As it happened, this was the only place where things had gone from bad to worse for the Germans. By the end of the month, just as Crete was falling, so was Rashid Ali who fled first to Persia then, rightly fearing that the British might next punish the Shah for his pro-Nazi ways, moved to Turkey before finding sanctuary in Berlin. Despite an effective counter-attack at Falluja when almost twenty of the King's Royal Regiment died under heavy mortar fire, the defence of Habbaniya had set the style and Churchill had been quick to recognize it. 'Having joined the Habbaniya forces, you should exploit the situation to the utmost . . . running the same kind of risks the Germans are accustomed to run and profit by,' the Prime Minister had urged Wavell on 9 May.

Three weeks later, dash, bombs and bluff had done their work, the Iraqi surrender being accelerated by a report that tanks were already on the capital's outskirts and carrying all before them. There was not a single British tank in the country. Wavell needed all he had to try to stop Rommel. The report had been planted by an intelligence officer's Arabic-speaking interpreter via a telephone connection discovered in a newly captured police post. Sonderkommando Junck suffered an ignominious departure by road into Syria having lost all its Heinkels and Messerschmitts and most of its Junkers 52s, the majority to ground attack or destroyed because they could not be repaired*

A squadron of Fiat AR42 fighters might have suffered a similar fate had their arrival not been delayed by hindrances devised in Vichy Syria by

* One Me 110 was salvaged and, until the RAF ran out of spare parts, spent the rest of its war mock dogfighting in Egypt.

French officials who, after Mussolini's mugging of a mortally wounded France, found it hard to stomach any cooperation with the Italians even to please the Germans and annoy the English. Eight out of the twelve Fiat biplanes returned to their base on Rhodes: one was lost in an accident; two destroyed because minor gunshot damage could not be repaired on the Kirkuk airfield they used; and the fourth shot down by a Gladiator and Sottotenente Valentini, who bailed out, was captured at rifle point by the Household Cavalry's intelligence officer, the man who had invented the story about British tanks.

This was none other than Captain Somerset de Chair, Tory MP for Norfolk South-West, acolyte of Churchill and aspiring man of letters who rather inadvisedly published his verse, though his literary tastes were definitely more T.E. Lawrence than D.H. The same de Chair who in England, almost a year before these events, had been discovered by de Gaulle advising the French troops he had just invited to join him to consider that, if they did so, they would be regarded as traitors at home. Along with the rest of KingCol, the MP would shortly be meeting in Syria some of the troops he had encouraged to reject de Gaulle and would find them a very different proposition from the Iraqi Army.

Wavell was the first to admit that he had been wrong about Iraq and Churchill had been right. 'A bold and correct decision, which I really felt I ought to have taken myself.' Even so, there was no doubt that he harboured similar reservations about Syria. How could he not? His command was more over-stretched than ever. Crete had cost him another 15,000 men, about 12,500 of them prisoners and among them some excellent fighting battalions abandoned when too many ships had been lost to rescue them.

To date, as far as Syria was concerned, all that had been done was purely defensive: border bridges in northern Palestine prepared for demolition and horsed yeomanry patrolling the frontier with beer bottles filled with petrol clanking from their saddles, the street fighter's Molotov cocktail and their only anti-tank weapon. '*C'est magnifique mais* ... it's bloody silly,' gasped one astonished officer survivor of the Greek campaign who doubted whether a Vichy tank crew would be as generous as the French general who watched the Light Brigade at Balaclava.

But now, alarmed by the almost casual way the Luftwaffe had used Vichy Syria for their Iraqi adventure, London was determined to take it over before Germany had recovered from its Crete losses and established itself there in a more ambitious fashion. What Churchill could not know, for it was not the kind of stuff that ULTRA picked up, was that Crete had been a kind of triumph after all. As far as Hitler was concerned almost 4,000 dead, the majority from a young and highly motivated élite arm, plus the loss of 151 of the valuable yet so vulnerably slow Junkers 52 transports had been too high a price for what he regarded as a side show.

The Balkans campaign was over, Yugoslavia and all of Greece secured, and unfinished business in the Middle East could wait.

His eye was now fixed on Russia. With amazing discretion 3.2 million men, the biggest army poor blood-drenched Europe had ever seen, was assembling along a front that ran from the Baltic to the Black Sea. Some units were under the impression that they were about to participate in an enormous exercise for the invasion of Britain with only the enemy and a decent water barrier being left to the imagination. Nor had Mussolini been let into the secret. While Soviet border guards were beginning to report 'unusual troop movements' Il Duce was advocating a new airborne operation against Cyprus that would give the Axis a firm foothold in the eastern Mediterranean, hardly 100 miles from the Syrian coast. But all he got were German Crete veterans to help create the Italian parachute division he lacked.

Perhaps London had picked up some of this, because Bletchley Park sometimes broke Italian diplomatic cyphers. By the end of May 1941, with the Iraqi and Crete campaigns drawing to their very different ends, Wavell was beginning to organize his invasion of Syria. To do it he was going to have to weaken his front against Rommel in Egypt's Western Desert, for a major component was to be two infantry brigades, about 10,000 men, of the 7th Australian Division under Major General John Lavarack who belonged to Australia's small professional officer corps.

Lavarack had recently been in command of the besieged Tobruk garrison which was where his division's 3rd Brigade was serving. Otherwise, most of the 7th, which had not been in the Middle East long, were as yet unblooded having spent their short time in the Western Desert in reserve at the port of Mersa Matruh where they had been bombed for the first time but had not as yet seen any kind of infantry fighting. This deficiency was being partly made up with drafts from Australia's scattered 6th Division, veterans of the good days against the Italians in Libya, who had tasted blitzkrieg in Greece then had the luck to get onto ships bound for Egypt rather than Crete though some had got back from there as well.

On 28 May the Defence Committee in London sent Wavell a signal saying that, though victory over Rommel in the Western Desert must remain his priority, he should settle the Syrian problem as soon as he was prepared. Wavell told them he could do nothing before 7 June. It started on the 8th.

Map 4 Lebanon and Syria, 8–21 June 1941 (first phase)

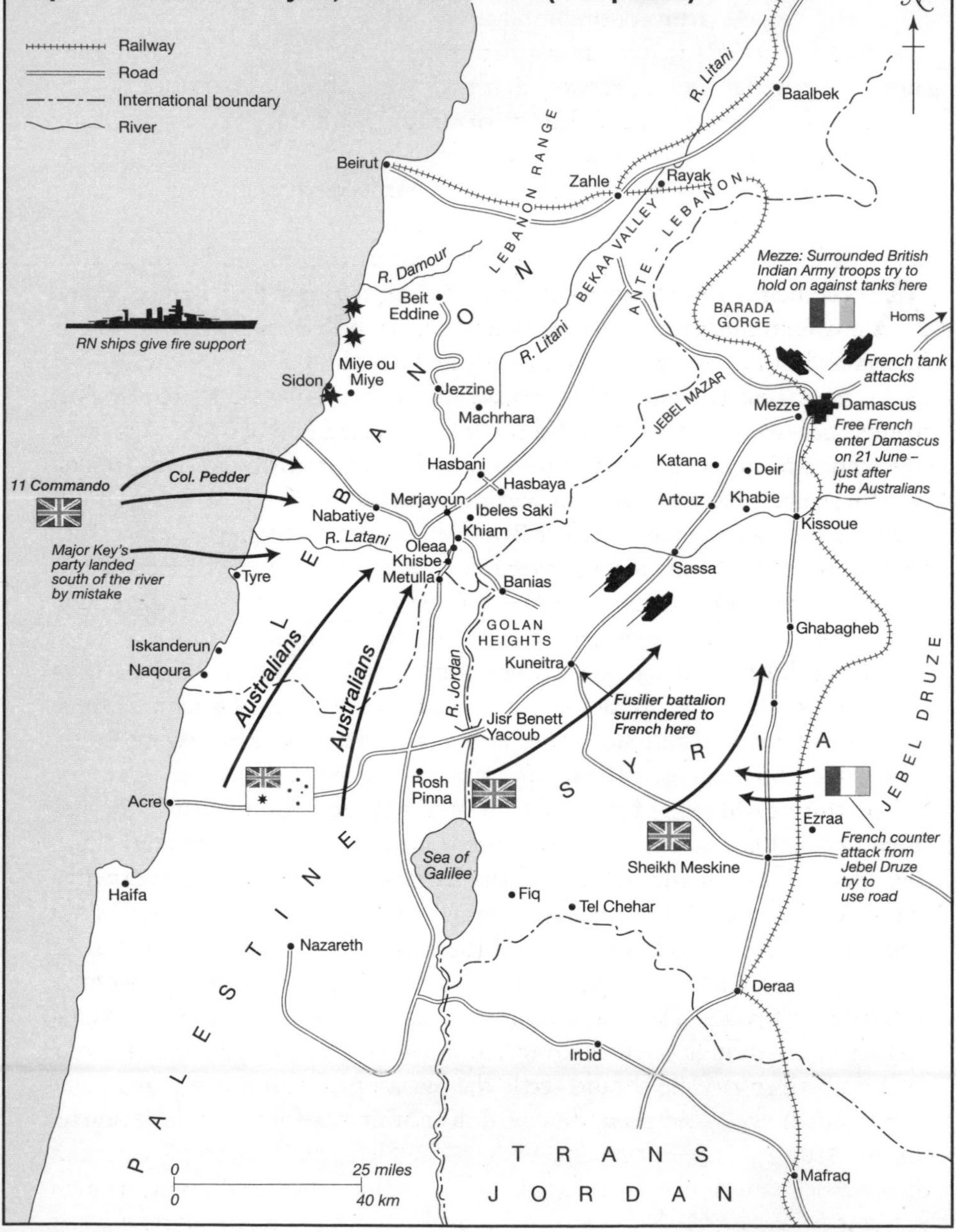

N
Railway
Road
International boundary
River
Baalbek
R. Litani
LEBANON RANGE
Beirut
Zahle
Rayak
BEKAA VALLEY
ANTE - LEBANON
R. Damour
Mezze: Surrounded British Indian Army troops try to hold on against tanks here
BARADA GORGE
Homs
Beit Eddine
RN ships give fire support
R. Litani
French tank attacks
Miye ou Miye
Sidon
Jezzine
JEBEL MAZAR
Mezze
Damascus
Machrhara
Free French enter Damascus on 21 June – just after the Australians
Hasbani
Katana
Deir
Col. Pedder
Hasbaya
11 Commando
Merjayoun
Artouz
Khabie
Nabatiye
Ibeles Saki
Kissoue
R. Latani
Khiam
Major Key's party landed south of the river by mistake
Oleaa
Khisbe
Sassa
Tyre
Metulla
Banias
LEBANON
GOLAN HEIGHTS
Ghabagheb
Iskanderun
Kuneitra
Naqoura
Australians
Australians
R. Jordan
Fusilier battalion surrendered to French here
Jisr Benett Yacoub
SYRIA
JEBEL DRUZE
Rosh Pinna
Acre
Ezraa
Sea of Galilee
Sheikh Meskine
French counter attack from Jebel Druze try to use road
Haifa
Fiq
Tel Chehar
PALESTINE
Nazareth
Deraa
Irbid
TRANS JORDAN
0
25 miles
0
40 km
Mafraq

Chapter Sixteen

At the Beirut headquarters of the Armée du Levant they had suspected it was coming, for the same Arab clans straddled the frontier between British Palestine and French Lebanon and some bits of the intelligence jigsaw were easily acquired. 'Concentration of Australian and English troops in Palestine frontier area north-west of Safad,' Général de Verdilhac reported to Vichy on 28 May. 'Strength 6–7,000 men with artillery, trucks, armoured cars. No tracked vehicles.'

In all, Operation Exporter, as it was called, involved about 35,000 men. Jumbo Wilson, commanding from Jerusalem, had decided on a three-pronged attack. One of the two Australian brigades would take the scenic route along the good metalled coast road with its breathtaking views of the Mediterranean all the way up to Beirut and beyond to the northern city of Tripoli and its port El Mina. The other would enter Lebanon from Palestine's Metulla salient and head north towards the old Greek Orthodox town of Merdjayoun and the serious hill country beyond it.

The third prong was to be a thrust through the Golan Heights started by the 5th Indian Brigade Group which included a UK infantry battalion, the Cockneys of the 1st Royal Fusiliers. Their task was to capture Kuneitra and Deraa and open the door for Gaullist units under Major General Paul Louis Le Gentilhomme to pass through them and capture Damascus. In addition 11 Scottish Commando, presently in Cyprus in case of a German airborne leap from Crete, would assist the Australians' coastal thrust by making an amphibious landing and seizing the arched stone bridge over the Litani river at Qasimiyah. That was the plan.

It was hoped, in some quarters expected, that the French would put up no more than a token resistance. The well-publicized defection less than three weeks before hostilities began of a Colonel Collet, who had dashed across the border with 1,000 splendid-looking Circassian Cavalry, had encouraged the notion that Vichy's Syrian veneer was cracking. But 600 or so of Collet's horsemen returned when they realized their colonel had thrown in his lot with the Gaullist renegades and their English paymasters without a thought for their own pensions. Collet himself was convinced that Dentz and his senior officers would do their utmost to resist an invasion and lost no time telling the British this but his opinion was not widely aired. Instead, the Australians were urged to wear their famous slouch hats rather than steel helmets in the belief that the wild colonial boy was more to current French taste than the Tommy and would win over the floating voters.

Unfortunately for the Anglo-Gaullists once again, just like Dakar, European troops were vastly outnumbered by well-disciplined colonial regulars. Only 8,000 of Dentz's 40,000–strong garrison were estimated to be Metropolitan French. Some of these were army and air force technicians but the majority were the professional officers and non-commissioned officers who commanded France's North African Arabs, Senegalese and mysterious men of the *6ième Régiment de la Légion Étrangère* where English and German speakers served alongside each other and, usually pretending to be Belgian, the only French riflemen could be found.

The allegiance of Arabic-speaking civilians and locally raised home guard units, *troupes spéciales*, was a different matter. And the British had urged the Free French to play what they believed was their trump card. In a bid to win their support, perhaps even create a useful fifth column, Général Catroux made an eve-of-battle broadcast from a British radio studio in Haifa in which, speaking as de Gaulle's Levant representative, he announced: 'This is an important moment in your history. I have just ended the regime of Mandate. France, by the voice of those of its sons who fight for its life and the freedom of all the world, declares you to be independent.'

Zero hour was 2.30 a.m. but on the coastal sector forty-two Australians accompanied by Jewish and Arab guides crossed five hours before this. Their task was to try to secure bridges and disarm demolition charges in those places where the coast road was a ledge carved out of a cliff face easily dynamited onto it.

The Jews were members of the Palmach, the full-time professional arm of the Haganah, the Zionist settlers' underground militia which had recently negotiated a truce with the British in Palestine for the duration of the war against the Nazis. Their leader, three months out of Acre jail, was born in 1915 on a kibbutz near the shores of the Galilee, the son of Ukrainian immigrants from the leftish side of the Zionist dream. His name was Moshe Dayan and he had been in the Haganah since he was 14.

Almost all the Palmach had served apprenticeships in the Special Night Squads founded during the 1936–8 Arab revolt over Jewish immigration by the eccentric gentile Orde Wingate, a Wavell protégé and now a full colonel making life miserable for the Italians in Ethiopia. Dayan was keen that they prove their worth. Since London had decided to review its earlier rejection of the Jewish Agency's plea to allow Jews in Palestine to join its fight against Hitler this was the third time Zionist fighters had been involved in clandestine operations and the first two, through no apparent fault of their own, had both been total failures.

The previous month David Raziel, military leader of Haganah's right-wing rival Irgun Zvei Leumi who had offered his formidable services as a saboteur from prison, had been sent to Iraq with three of his comrades. They got there towards the closing stages of the campaign as the British grip on Baghdad was beginning to tighten. From one of the flooded bunds on the city's outskirts Raziel and a British major escorting him saw off two of his group for a reconnaissance in a small boat. Then they returned to their car and Raziel had just asked for a cigarette when he and the major were killed by a direct hit from one small bomb dropped by one of Oberst Junck's aircraft.

Haganah's casualties had been even more grievous. On 18 May, as it happened the day after Raziel's death, twenty-three of their volunteers accompanied by Major Anthony Palmer, a well-connected young cavalry officer, had left Haifa on the *Sea Lion*, a converted fishing boat carrying a number of small craft for beach landings. Palmer, who was 26 and one of four brothers on active service, was a Royal Dragoon Guards officer who had left its armoured cars for Special Operations Executive, the secret sabotage organization formed for work in Axis-occupied countries.

Palmer's Operation Boatswain, a rapid reaction to the first sighting of German aircraft over Syria, was intended to destroy the French oil refineries in northern Lebanon to which Rashid Ali was pumping the Iraqi oil denied France since the armistice. Employing Palestinian Jews for a raid that could be portrayed as a fanatical Zionist response to a sudden Nazi presence so close to the Yishuv was no doubt an added attraction for the British, who could deny any involvement with a relatively straight face. But there was never any black oil smoke over Tripoli to explain away.

Sea Lion, Palmer and all twenty-three Haganah volunteers, three of them crew, disappeared as if they had never been. Reports that the French had been burying bodies washed ashore on the Tripoli coast were never confirmed. No commander of a ship, submarine or aircraft, whether French, German, Italian or British, ever publicly admitted to sinking a vessel resembling *Sea Lion* in that time or place. The best theory is that they touched off a mine or their demolition charges exploded or both.

For some days afterwards Dayan and his comrades had sat on the flat roof of Haifa's tallest building looking north across the bay with their field glasses, hoping for their first glimpse of the missing boat. In all their skirmishes with the Arabs they had never had casualties like this and these men were some of the best they had. Even the hope that the missing men might have been taken prisoner was sullied by the fear that their fellow Jews might somehow end up in Nazi hands. It was a chilling reminder that the British were not invincible and that the Vichy French might be capable of some nasty surprises.

Dayan was not given much time to brood. After several scouting expeditions into the tobacco fields of southern Lebanon, Operation Exporter began with ten Australians, five Palmach and Rashid Taher, their Arab guide, striding out under a full moon until they reached the ridge above *Iskanderuna*. Here they paused to eat chocolate and take in this coastal village on its silvery edge of sea and the bridges north and south of it they had come to secure.

They had been expecting a fight but when they walked down to it they discovered to their intense relief that there were no guards and the bridges were free of demolition charges. A good start. The Palestine border and the Australian 21st Brigade were 7 miles away. All they had to do now was wait until it reached them. If they were on schedule that would be at about 4 a.m. with a little over an hour left until daybreak. They took up an all-around defensive position around the bridges and then Dayan and the others who were not on sentry stretched out in the roadside ditch and tried to get some sleep. It was a warm night with a gentle sea breeze and Dayan had soon nodded off. 'I awoke to daylight. The sun had already risen, and there was a sound of firing in the distance. I looked around me and was uneasy. The invasion vanguard was nowhere to be seen. But we were very visible indeed. We were in an indefensible position, near the bridge in a deep valley, easy prey to anyone in the hills above.'

The commander of the men Dayan and the others were waiting for was Brigadier Jack Edwin Starwell Stevens, the son of a Scots draper and his English wife who had settled in the small spa town of Daylesford where moneyed Melbourne took the waters. Even by the meritocratic standards of Australia's amateur officer corps Stevens, a small man dwarfed by most of his soldiers, was unusual. He had left school at 12 to work in a cigar factory, joined the Post Office and started weekend soldiering with its militia, then in 1915 had gone off to war as a 19-year-old signaller and returned from France three years later an officer and a gentleman having been commissioned in the field. Back in the Post Office but rather more elevated, married and about to start a family, he had rejoined the militia, whose officers maintained a discreet social cachet, and when he came to the Middle East in 1940 was a full colonel in charge of 6th Division's signals.

In the last five years of peace Stevens had commanded a militia rifle battalion but though he had come under fire often enough in France, he had little experience of infantry fighting let alone directing a large mixed force in battle. Nonetheless, his superiors thought they detected in him leadership qualities that were something more than those required of a good technician and administrator. 'Waspishly aggressive and persistent,' said one. He was switched from signals and put in charge of the new 21st

Brigade: three infantry battalions plus support arms, about 5,000 men in all.

The brigadier had divided his command into two columns. What Dayan and the advance party holding the bridges around Iskanderuna had not been told was that they were almost a diversion. Stevens had decided that the 17 miles of narrow coast road from the frontier to the Litani river estuary were too easy to defend and they were bound to be slowed by broken bridges and landslides blasted out of cliff faces. But there was another way. Two lateral roads ran eastwards from the coast. One hugged the border on the Palestine side. The other started from the ancient port of Tyre, a good 10 miles north of Iskanderuna, then turned south to Tibnin with its Ottoman castle built on French Crusader ruins until, about 20 miles east of the Mediterranean, it came within a mile of the Mandate Palestine border road.

Working by moonlight with picks, spades, axes and a steamroller on loan from Haifa municipality, it took an Australian pioneer company about two hours to bridge this gap with the makings of a short link road that was tamped down by the first traffic to move on it: thirteen of the little tracked Bren-gun carriers, some of the Royal Dragoon Guards' armoured cars, towed artillery, and trucks carrying Lieutenant Colonel Alan MacDonald's 2/16th Battalion. MacDonald was one of Australia's small cadre of regular officers and Stevens thought his West Australians, a number of them British immigrants who had arrived in the 1920s under the Group Settlement Scheme,* the brigade's best battalion. So the name of the column making the dash for Tyre became DonCol after its commander.

Less road-bound were the Cheshire Yeomanry, one of the 1st Cavalry Division regiments still awaiting mechanization. Making a virtue of necessity, they had been attached to the Australian infantry to patrol their flanks and explore country impassable to wheeled vehicles. There were about 500 of these horsemen, each equipped with the 1908 pattern basket-hilted thrusting sword, a weapon which had last been used in anger by the yeomanry regiments that had helped drive the Ottoman Turks out of Palestine some twenty years before. The swords had been blackened, as had cap badges, stirrup irons and anything else that might glisten in the sun and give their position away. As well as the cold steel they all carried Lee-Enfields in rifle boots and dangling from some saddles was a brace of Molotov cocktails in case of tanks. Each squadron also had a few Boys rifles, Thompson sub-machine guns (which few had fired) and a heavy machine-gun section with Hotchkiss guns on mules which also carried the big Number 11 wireless sets for keeping in touch with the Australians.

* Under this scheme settlers worked in small groups to develop fruit and dairy farms and Britain and Australia shared the price of their passage out as well as jointly funding the settlements which were in the south-west of the state.

Two of the Cheshire's three squadrons were to go as far as Tibnin. But when the Australians followed the bend in the road west for Tyre the yeomanry would head due north, riding the ridge lines of the rough country beyond it up to the Litani river and wirelessing back to Stevens's brigade headquarters what they could see of the enemy. It was a wonderful opportunity, proof if any were needed, that there was still a place for cavalry on 1941's battlefield and, in the main, the Cheshire Yeomanry were thrilled. Captain Richard Verdin of B Squadron, a barrister and the son of a former commanding officer, thought their mood resembled 'that of trespassers about to partake in a picnic on forbidden ground'.

Dayan never did have any illusions about picnics. He and the Australians had moved away from their 'indefensible position' by the bridges. According to his own account, this was done at his urging after he had listened to the Arab guide Rashid Taher who told him of a stone-built two-storey French police station about a mile away that was much easier to defend. It turned out that the police post was occupied by *troupes spéciales* under a French officer. But a neighbouring orange grove provided ample cover and after a brief firefight, during which Dayan was much impressed by the courage and marksmanship displayed by the Arab Taher, they stormed the building whose small garrison surrendered. Dayan, who had probably clinched the affair by getting a grenade through an open window, helped carry a captured heavy machine gun and a mortar up to the flat roof.

After a while fresh French troops began to encircle the police station, sniping and closing in. One of the Jews tried to get word back to Brigadier Stevens by swerving through their roadblocks on a motorbike they had found but he was lucky to return with only his tyres punctured. All they could do was hold on until the Australians reached them. On the roof Dayan settled himself behind the machine gun.

> I opened up and drew heavy fire in response. I took my field glasses to try and locate the source of the shooting. I had hardly got them into focus when a rifle bullet smashed into them, splintering a lens and the metal casing, which became embedded into the socket of my left eye. I immediately lost consciousness but only for a moment. I came to and lay stretched on my back. I was also wounded in the hand.

Dayan was lowered to the ground floor in blankets, his face wrapped in the blood-soaked Palestinian keffiyeh worn by Taher. It covered both his eyes and he tried to follow what was happening from what he could hear, though sometimes, in a lull, he was brought up to date by one of the Palmach.

> I must say it required a considerable effort to concentrate. We had no pain killers and my head felt like it was being pounded with sledge hammers. Fearing that I would not survive the loss of blood, one of the Australian officers suggested that I be handed over to the French so that I could receive medical treatment before it was too late. I refused ... We had stout walls and courageous fighters and they kept the enemy at bay. We held out.

By the time Stevens's coastal column had reached them they had even captured several French trucks and their occupants who, understandably enough, had driven up to the police station convinced that it must be the British who were doing the besieging. Dayan and two Australian wounded were sent back in one of these vehicles, an agonizingly slow journey bumping along narrow dirt track detours around stretches that been mined or being pulled over by military police to make way for long convoys heading north. Twelve hours after he had been wounded a surgeon in the operating theatre of Haifa hospital informed Dayan that he would live but had lost his left eye. At this point the Australians, for the cost of about twenty killed and wounded, had taken Tyre and were up to the Litani river.

The Qasimiyah bridge was still intact but not because it was guarded by Commandos. Heavy surf, considered almost certain to capsize blunt-ended flat-bottomed landing craft and drown munitioned and booted soldiery in seconds, had caused the navy to postpone the landing until the weather abated. It had been a last-minute decision taken in the early hours of 8 June after an inshore reconnaissance by the Palestine Police's Marine section who knew the coast well. Eleven packed landing craft had already been lowered from their mother ship HMS *Glengyle* and though Lieutenant Colonel Richard Pedder, their gap-toothed commanding officer, pleaded to be allowed to go on regardless they were ordered back to Egypt.

Eleven Scottish Commando included some of the first men to respond to Churchill's call in the summer of 1940 for volunteers who would terrorize the enemy 'on the butcher and bolt policy'. Not all were infantry or Scots. There were gunners from Scottish Command's anti-aircraft and coastal batteries and a sprinkling of Sassenachs from English county regiments who happened to have a battalion training in Scotland. Lieutenant Eric Garland had won a Military Cross with the Yorks and Lancs just outside Dunkirk and lost his sister Joan, aged 17, to a stray bomb on the family home at Chipstead from where he once commuted, an Imperial Airways management trainee, to Croydon airport. But mostly it was a very Scottish affair with a touch of Scots-Irish from the Ulster plantations.

Pedder, who was 36, was Highland Light Infantry; Geoffrey Keyes, his second-in-command, in the Royal Scots Greys and both regulars. One of the recent civilians now among them was Lieutenant Blair Mayne from

Newtownards, a 6 foot 2 Irish rugby international* and the Irish Universities heavyweight boxing champion who had started as a solicitor with a busy Belfast practice shortly before the outbreak of war. In drink Paddy Mayne, as even the Northern Irish called him despite his impeccable Loyalist pedigree, had an uncertain temper. He had recently been placed under forty-eight hours' open arrest when a dispute over a bill at a Nicosia nightclub resulted in him emptying a pistol around the manager's dancing feet.

The trouble was 11 Commando were bored. Nine months after most of them had volunteered for the special service they were still waiting to go into action. Garland had asked for a transfer to the RAF to fulfil an old ambition to become a fighter pilot. He was not alone. Others were applying to return to their units or to join regiments in action in the desert.

Their frustration was understandable. In Scotland, their naval liaison officer Admiral (retired) Sir Walter Cowan, who was 70 and had won his first Distinguished Service Order commanding a gunboat on the Nile during the Fashoda Incident,† had described their training as 'the most vigorous and ruthless I have ever seen'. For seven months on the Isle of Arran they had honed their military and boat handling skills, constantly weeding out the unfit and otherwise unsuitable and becoming increasingly proficient with their weapons and tactics. Route marches had finished with men stepping off the end of a pier into a freezing sea. They claimed to be the first unit in the British Army to have learned to keep their heads down by having live rounds fired over them.

Yet, through no fault of their own, one operation after another had been cancelled. Then in February 1941 they had sailed to the Middle East with two other Commando units to make up Layforce under Colonel Robert Laycock who would appoint Captain Evelyn Waugh, late of the Dakar expedition, as his intelligence officer. On the trip out Waugh, part of 8 Commando with Churchill's brave but obstreperous son Randolph, found Pedder's unit very different to his own.

* Ireland's rugby team is recruited from both sides of the border. In 1938 Mayne was also selected to play in the British Lions' (as they became known) first tour of South Africa playing in 20 out of 24 provincial and test matches. On his return to Newtownards he had been fêted as a local hero and presented with a gold watch.

† When war broke out in 1939 Sir Walter offered his services 'in any rank' and was appointed as a liaison officer with an Indian Army unit fighting against the Italians along the Libyan coast. In the course of this he was captured, reputedly while firing his pistol at a tank, but within a few months was repatriated in a prisoner exchange after the Italians decided he was 'too old to be dangerous'. On his return Cowan was attached to the Commandos with whom he would win his second DSO forty-six years after being awarded the first.

> Eleven Commando were very young and quiet, over disciplined, unlike ourselves in every way but quite companionable. They trained indefatigably all the voyage. We did very little except PT and one or two written exercises for the officers ... There was very high gambling, poker, roulette, chemin-de-fer, every night. Randolph lost £850 in two evenings.

In another part of the ship, perhaps another planet, Piper Lawson composed his Scottish Commando March with a lyric that ended: 'They'll ken the "Black Hackle", afore we cam hame.' The hackle referred to the feathers Pedder had acquired for their bonnets, the inflated berets worn by some Scots infantry regiments. They were wearing them in Cape Town when they broke their long-way-round journey to Egypt there and, while the other Commandos caroused and shopped, their commanding officer took the 11th on a 12-mile speed march. Waugh accused Pedder of being a 'half mad' martinet whose young officers lived in terror of him. In his novel *Officers and Gentlemen* Pedder became Colonel Prentice, 'a glaring, fleshless figure' who wore his great-great-grandfather's woollen Crimean stockings, decorated the mess dining table with the same ancestor's sabre, and confined his men to barracks until they could swim 100 yards in boots and full equipment. But in his diaries even Waugh, never much interested in being fair about people, conceded that, though Pedder worked his men hard, he 'saw to their welfare'. And if his austere ways and querulous disposition made him a hard man to like, most of his young officers, whose average age was 21, respected him as an excellent trainer and were longing to show what 11 Scottish could do.

Layforce, which was about 2,000 strong, had been created for Operation Cordite: the invasion of Italian-held Rhodes. They were in Egypt and well into their training for Cordite when the German armoured thrust through Greece and the airborne attack on Crete obliged the British to reconsider. Once again the Commandos were told to stand down. Then Laycock was ordered to take about half his men to Crete where they provided the evacuating garrison with its rearguard and Waugh with some of his most perceptive fiction.

Yet for all their keenness the 11th were not included. Just as they had not provided any of the 200 men sent to besieged Tobruk for patrol work and prisoner snatches. Or seen brought to fruition any of the raids that were planned and rehearsed against the enemy's long and vulnerable line of communication along the Libyan coast. Instead Pedder's men were sent from their training camp in Egypt to Cyprus. Morale sank. Garrison duty was hardly Churchill's 'butcher and bolt'. Occasional Italian air raids did not make it any less of a backwater. Wavell's staff fretted that Cyprus might be the scene of another Crete-style airborne assault but for the 11 Scottish it was an island too far and if the Black Hackle was feared anywhere it was the bars and brothels of Nicosia and Famagusta.

Then came the promise of a leading role in the opening act of Operation Exporter, only to have it called off with assault craft already in the water, the enemy coast in sight and Pedder, damning the navy and the surf they were so frightened of, begging to be allowed to go ahead. Few on board the landing ship *Glengyle* doubted that the jinx on 11 Commando had struck again. On the troop deck the latest graffiti had a Churchillian ring:

Never in the whole history of human endeavour,
have so few been buggered about by so many.

Even if the weather improved, the full moon must have made them clearly visible from the shore and lost the surprise the planners had deemed so necessary for success. Famagusta was hardly more than 100 miles from the Litani estuary but to reduce the chances of being spotted they had not travelled the direct route. Instead the Commandos had left Cyprus the week before on a couple of destroyers which took them first to Egypt's Port Said and the waiting *Glengyle*. From there they had doubled back, keeping close to that part of the eastern Mediterranean shore that was firmly in British hands, passing the ports of Gaza, Tel Aviv and Haifa, before the final dash north into Vichy territorial waters. Now the surprise was gone. It was therefore with some astonishment that they heard, within two hours of their return to Port Said, that the weather had improved and, though it must be assumed that the Vichy French were now expecting them, they were going back.

Chapter Seventeen

Nahr al-Litani is Lebanon's biggest river. It is about 90 miles long, its source a little west of Baalbek from where it makes its way south-westwards through the Bekaa valley then turns sharply west to cut a 900-foot gorge through the mountains that stand between it and its entry into the Mediterranean a little north of Phoenicia's Tyre. Near the coast its fast brown waters, which flow between steep banks lined with cypress trees and thick undergrowth, are still at least 60 feet wide and rarely less than 5 deep. In places there are sun-bleached wooden water wheels feeding irrigation systems older than the Book of Genesis.

It is a formidable moat and hardly surprising that between the river and the border with Palestine the Vichy French had decided to fight nothing but delaying actions while concentrating their forces in the south-west behind the Litani. These mainly consisted of a regimental group of the 22 Régiment Tirailleurs Algériens, regulars led by a cadre of dedicated professional French officers amply supported by artillery batteries, big 4-inch mortars, anti-tank pieces and belt-fed Hotchkiss machine guns. In some places they were behind a lot of barbed wire.

Brigadier Stevens had been told that if he manged to cross the Litani before 4 a.m. he was to signal Pedder's Commando that they were no longer required to land by putting up four Very flares. By the evening of 8 June the Australians were up to the river but Stevens had no intention of depriving his brigade of the prospect of a 400–strong raiding party causing havoc in the enemy's rear while they attempted a difficult river crossing. Nor did he want to risk something as complicated as a night attack across a water obstacle. So he timed his assault for 5.30, shortly after first light, when his lead company would try to rush the Qasimiyah bridge. If the French blew it first they would attempt to cross using the British infantry's standard issue canvas assault boats. Once they had a foothold on the other side his engineers would bring up a pontoon bridge they were preparing, capable of carrying trucks, light armoured vehicles and field guns. It did not have to be strong enough for tanks because, though the French were known to have some, Wavell needed all his to deal with Rommel.

Colonel Pedder expected that, by giving the French ample warning the previous night, his commandos would no longer arrive in time to secure the Qasimiyah bridge intact and had modified his plan accordingly. Originally they were going to land on both sides of the river. He had intended to use all 500 of his men by having two of *Glengyle*'s eleven landing craft, which could carry no more than 40 plus equipment', make an extra trip to the beach, a total of 13 deliveries from the mother craft. Now there was no time for that. They would be lucky to get ashore before dawn and the navy wanted the *Glengyle* heading back towards Palestine's RAF umbrella long before the sun and Vichy's bombers were up. The ship was not even lingering long enough to pick up her landing craft, which would have to make their own way back to Haifa. Two troops, about 100 men, would have to remain on board; 395 would land. One of those being left behind offered Lance-Corporal Noble Sproule, a Scots Canadian from Ontario who had left home to enlist in the British Army shortly before the outbreak of war, a month's pay to change places with him. Sproule, who was 19, refused.

In order to inflict maximum disruption deep behind Vichy lines Pedder divided his Commando into three: X Party, 150 men under Major Keyes would land just north of the Litani at a banana plantation called Aiteniye Farm, and try to capture the Vichy positions overlooking the river; a mile and a half to the north Z Party, 96 men and 6 officers under Captain George More, a sapper, were to deny the French the use of the Kafr Badda bridge at the junction of the coast road and the ancient track that ended at the Crusaders' spectacular Beaufort Castle below Merjayun; Y Party, another 150 men under Pedder himself, would land between X and Z parties. Their main objective was a stone barracks, assumed to be used as a command centre, and anything else that came to light by way of artillery or transport. But Pedder also intended that his party would act as a reserve, ready to go to the aid of the other two with whom he hoped to be in radio contact.

The landing craft parted company with the *Glengyle* at about 3.15 a.m. when the ship was still about 4 miles off the coast. 'Waste a lot of time forming up and go in very slow,' recorded Keyes in a journal he was keeping against standing orders. It took well over an hour to get ashore, by which time it was daylight. As they approached, Keyes tried but failed to make out the river mouth which was obscured by a sandbank. He knew the coxswain was using a large white house as his mark, which must be Aiteniye Farm, but as they got closer they could make out several white buildings. They landed shortly before 5 a.m. and ran, trying not to bunch, to the top of the beach in their shorts and boots. It was then that Keyes saw to the left of him the stationary masts of what could only be moored boats and understood that the navy had landed the most important part of the operation south of the river instead of north. At about the same time the French blew the bridge they were supposed to capture.

In 1918 Geoffrey Keyes had been a 1-year-old when his father the admiral led the famous attempt to cork the U-boat pens at Zeebrugge with blockships and to some it seemed that he had spent most of his life trying to prove he was a worthy son. At first sight he did not fit the part. Pedder's deputy at Litani was an acting major about four years older than most of the junior officers – Mayne at 26 was an exception – tall and narrow-chested with an unfortunate clipped moustache, little of his subalterns' natural athleticism and a style that could be irritatingly Bertie Wooster. On the first leg of the operation, the Cyprus-Egypt trip on the destroyer *Isis*, Keyes began his diary entry for 4 June: 'Spent Alma Mater's birthday going 25 knots to Port Said.'* But if this driven Old Etonian was not universally popular, not least because it was assumed that Daddy's influence had secured him second-in-command, it was also recognized that Pedder was too ambitious to tolerate the merely well-connected if they were complete duds. Whatever else he lacked, the admiral's son was possessed of a steely determination to live up to his name.

As far as Keyes was concerned, finding themselves unable to attack from the rear as was intended was no reason to call off X Party's contribution. Although he had already concluded that they were on ground 'likely to be extremely well registered by batteries', Keyes decided to make a frontal assault across the river and get to where he would have been if only the navy had got its navigation right.†

The Commandos were about half a mile south of the river in the flat open scrubland just off the beach. As they advanced they began to meet some astonished Australians belonging to 2/16th Battalion's C Company under Major Albert Caro, an accountant in civilian life. Caro had been expecting them to turn up on the opposite bank and had been ordered to provide supporting fire. His battalion's main crossing was being attempted by A Company at a bend in the river upstream of the demolished stone bridge about half a mile to Caro's right.

In charge of the boat parties here was Captain John Hearman, a London-born immigrant, a large and physically confident man who by the age of 30 had become a successful fruit farmer in Western Australia's Donnybrook area 130 miles south of Perth. His first problem was to overcome the current which was so fast at this point that every man aboard the light

* Eton College celebrates 4 June as its foundation day because it is the birthday of its benefactor King George III.

† The Admiralty's explanation was that the 'abundance of white buildings made comparison with the Army map, on which only one was marked, useless'. RAF photo-reconnaissance was accused of compounding this by taking pictures of the wrong beach. At least one of the Royal Navy Volunteer Reserve sub-lieutenants who commanded the three landing craft realized that they were heading too far south but, according to Lieutenant Garland, turned down the Commandos' entreaties to correct his course on the grounds that he was under strict orders not to break formation with the other landing craft.

assault craft would have to paddle, leaving no fingers free for a trigger. Hearman decided they would pull themselves across on a line and, since nobody had thought to provide them with a rope, had improvised one by cutting and splicing roadside telephone wires. A Corporal Alan Haddy, a brewer's maltster from Perth who insisted he was the best swimmer present, reached midstream with this cable wound around his middle when a mortar bomb exploded on the surface and a fragment grazed his chest. He struggled on to the other side and tried to tie the line to a tree but was obviously weakening when another corporal dived in after him and helped him complete the operation.

Captain Hearman called for volunteers and up stepped eight privates who had all attended the same school in the landlocked desert gold-mining town of Kalgoorlie and seem to have approached the occasion in much the same spirit as a first trip to the seaside. Hearman, who unlike the Kalgoorlie Eight had been in a small boat before, wanted to go with them but they feared his weight would capsize it and, in the Australian way, insolently hauled themselves away. This was a pity because it soon became apparent that it was safer closer to the enemy on the north bank than it was on the south which was coming under bombardment. A single mortar bomb, landing as they always did without the whistling warning of a shell, deprived A Company of all its officers in one bang. Its commanding officer was killed and the other four wounded. The resourceful Hearman insisted on carrying on until he was hit by shrapnel again and evacuated. Nonetheless, by 6.30 about fifty Australians were well into the bamboo thickets on the north bank, hunting the mortars doing the damage.

Keyes was beginning to take even heavier casualties from artillery, machine gun and snipers: 'all firing very accurately'. Shortly afterwards he made some journal notes, possibly even on the spot during lulls. Certainly a generous and unforced use of the present tense lends an authentic air of immediacy. The tone is predictably understated but far from Woosterish. It is an honest enough account of how he conquered his reluctance to get up and move under fire and took command. He also makes it plain how grateful he is for the quality of the men under him, particularly his officers. Yet, though he sings the praises of a few, he is unfairly disparaging about the majority of the Australians for holding back and failing to support the Commandos and obviously had no idea what was going on upstream with Hearman and Haddy and the Kalgoorlie Eight.

> Extremely unpleasant ... snipers in wired post on far side of the river. Very accurate fire. Padbury, Jones, Woodnutt killed. Wilkinson badly wounded, all in one place. Several 3 Troop killed and wounded. George and Eric [Captain Highland and Lieutenant Garland] cool as cucumbers, take most of 3 troop over about 60 yards to right flank ... Four gallant Aussies (the only four) succeed in carrying up one boat ... One killed. [Keyes would

have no doubt been delighted to learn that two of the four, Lance Corporal Charles Dilworth and Private Tom Archibald, had been born in England.

> Very loath to leave for George's position as ground very open and sniped at. Start crawling down minute fold with Ness [his batman runner] level with me. Feels like a billiard table and several bullets very close ... it is completely exposed beyond with a low bank to cross, so decide to run for it. Ness and I start running but I trip up after about three paces as I'm very heavily laden. Fall down on the bank and Ness, the idiot, gets down too, even more exposed. We got badly sniped so I told him to run on to George, which he does safely. I give them about 10 minutes to forget me then do it in two bursts. Inspect Woodnutt and Jones on the way, both dead. George and Eric busy picking off snipers with a Bren and all the men quite cheerful and aggressive. Now about 9.30 and getting very hot on neck and back of knees; we are in a shallow dell which gives good cover.

Garland, with his MC from Dunkirk for rescuing men from an exploding ammunition dump and a particularly risky reconnaissance patrol, was one of the 11th's few subalterns with any battle experience, and so far he was unimpressed with Keyes's performance. 'He was lacking in initiative. I had been under fire before. Keyes had not and it showed.'

The 'shallow dell' Keyes refers to was still about 200 yards from the river but the Australians, who had been watching the Commandos' progress, now came to their aid with some well directed artillery support from a 25-pounder battery about a mile behind them. This enabled the Australian Lance Corporal Dilworth's boat party and six Commandos led by Garland to make a dash for the river where they dived into the cover of a clump of bullrushes between two of the moored boats. Dilworth then carefully arranged Garland and his men in their fragile canvas craft and paddled them across. Their main objective was a well-dug-in Vichy position – Keyes called it a redoubt – on a knoll overlooking the river mouth that had probably been responsible for killing most of the Commandos who died trying to cross the sand bar. It was bristling with machine guns plus a small-calibre pack howitzer and an anti-tank gun.

Once over, they began to use a long-handled wire cutter they had brought to deal with the concertina entanglements they had expected to find on the water's edge. Garland, fair-haired and just under 6 feet, wriggled forward, cutting and parting the wire, while his men covered him with a Bren gun and attempted to lob grenades into the redoubt from a Lee-Enfield rifle fitted with an attachment known as a discharger cap, a poor man's mortar. Sometimes Garland, who liked to carry a rifle as well as a pistol, would pause to start shooting at the sandbagged trenches above him. 'I couldn't really see a target but we were trying to make as much noise as possible and give them the impression that there were far more of us and they were the ones who were outnumbered. Every so often I would shout up to them, "Désarmez!" I hoped it was the right word but if it was I don't remember any kind of reply.'

At first the only discernible response from the native French speakers in command was a noticeable increase in the return fire. Not so much at the Commandos immediately below them, who the Tirailleurs could only see properly by leaving their trenches, but across the river. Like Captain Hearman's Australians upstream, for the moment at least, the nearer the enemy the safer you were. For the next hour and a half Keyes and his companions on the other side of the river found themselves pinned down 'lying almost in the water being bombarded whenever we move'. Machine-gun fire and high explosive set fire to two of the Lebanese fishing boats, the smoke making a marker for the well-trained crew of a 75mm field gun somewhere in the dusty foothills to their right. Unable to find this gun, the Australian battery concentrated on the redoubt and, despite their deep trenches, this eventually had the desired effect for suddenly a white flag was being waved.

Accepting this surrender was not easy. Keyes was desperately short of men. Apart from casualties, almost an entire forty-strong troop reorganizing themselves after coming off the beach had been sent to the rear by Brigadier Stevens in person after the Australian commander had heard that the rest had been almost wiped out. If Garland revealed just how few men he had with him there was always a chance that the Tirailleurs might change their minds and the 75mm, which had a heavy machine gun working alongside it, made it difficult to reinforce him.

But at least the fire from the redoubt had diminished and shortly after midday, some seven hours after they had landed, a total of twenty-one Commandos had crossed and thirty-five prisoners, some wounded, were being escorted down to the river. Keyes counted 'about half a dozen dead men'. At this point his own losses were 14 killed, 20 wounded and 2 missing.

Among the spoils was a 25mm anti-tank gun which interested Garland because in France he had commanded his battalion's anti-tank platoon for a while and the British 2-pounder was similar. They lunched on *singe*, the French rendition of bully beef so-called because a monkey* was the trademark of a popular brand, and *pain de guerre*, a lethal Gallic hardtack. As they ate, the 75mm field gun somewhere to the east of them was back in business shelling the sand bar across the river bank and making it difficult for Caro's Australians to join them. Keyes might not have gone up much in Garland's estimation but his own admiration for what the younger man (21 to his 24) did next is plain.

* Another version has it that after a starving West African garrison was reduced to eating real monkeys all canned meat became the same.

> Eric locates flash of 75mm gun on hillside 1,000 yards away which is shelling Australians at river mouth. It does not seem able to shell us as embrasure does not allow traverse. Gun very well hid from our artillery which is searching for him. We have brain wave and pull up 25mm gun. Eric lays and after three shots ranging puts four through the embrasure. Nice gun and good shooting settles his hash.* Persuade Caro it is safe to cross onto sandbar and come into post from seawards.

The first Australian officer to cross it was a Captain Louis Longworth, a forward observer for the 25-pounders that had been giving them artillery support. Longworth and his wireless operators were aghast at what it had cost the Commandos to get to where they could now walk unmolested. 'Their dead literally littered the beach,' he reported.

On the other side he found Keyes 'nonchalantly perched and in full view of the enemy' staring out at the buildings of Aiteniye Farm, his original objective had he been landed north of the Litani. He no longer had enough men to attack it and must leave it to the Australians. Even so, he had secured Brigadier Stevens an extra crossing point, while elsewhere Pedder's two other landing parties had caused mayhem among the rear echelons of Vichy's Litani line and prevented the arrival of reinforcements. But Keyes's men were not the only Commandos to pay a heavy price.

Captain George More's most northerly party, which had to take the Kafr Badda bridge, came safely ashore but not their two radios which were ruined by salt water after one landing craft hit a rock. Within ten minutes they had captured a Vichy outpost near the bridge, taking about forty Lebanese *troupes spéciales* prisoner in a surprise attack launched from some high ground behind them. An attempt to retake the bridge by French armoured cars and some kind of locally manufactured armoured personnel carrier was repulsed with two captured heavy machine guns and the steel-cored bullets fired by shoulder-breaking Boys anti-tank rifles that inflicted dreadful wounds.

Meanwhile, a patrol under Tommy Macpherson, another of Pedder's boy lieutenants still four months off his twenty-first birthday, rushed a battery of four small mountain guns crewed by Arab gunners under two French officers. The battery was perhaps too well dug in and surprise was complete. The only casualty was a man with a rifle and fixed bayonet in one of the deeper gun pits who Macpherson had not noticed until the man's upward lunge nicked his right wrist and the offender was 'promptly pumped full of tommy gun by Sergeant Bruce'. After this the others

* When Garland visited the site later he discovered that one of their ranging shots had started 'a mini avalanche' that had almost buried the gun beneath a pile of earth from which stuck a pair of feet.

surrendered and their guns were rendered useless by one of the Commando's ex-gunners who broke firing pins and instruments. One of the French officers told them that they had only arrived the previous evening and had not been able to fire a single shot because their field telephone lines to their forward observer had been cut. Not quite four hours after they had landed, having set up a little prisoner-of-war camp and a first-aid post for the wounded, More set off on a motorcycle he had acquired to see if he could locate Pedder and find out how long he would have to wait for the Australians to turn up.

Pedder's party did not have such an easy landing. Over half of them had to swim or wade ashore in water up to their necks when their four landing craft backed suddenly away from the beach after coming under machine-gun and mortar fire. Regimental Sergeant Major Tevendale, a Gordon Highlander with 11 Commando Headquarters, estimated that the fire was coming from a position about 300 yards to their right. There were few casualties and they resented the navy's panic. They could see from the yellow tracer the French were using that most of it was high and soon found cover in what appeared to be a dried-up river bed along which they crawled to the coast road, untying as they went the inflatable navy waist lifebelts they had attached to their weapons so they could swim with them. As arranged, Paddy Mayne, the dancing master of Nicosia, broke away from the rest of Y Force and turned right towards Qasimiyah where it was hoped he would support Keyes with a flank attack and generally kick up a fuss.

Once across the main highway, Pedder's main party, now about ninety strong, started cutting field telephone lines then advanced on the barracks up a deep gully. Before long they discovered ammunition dumps in two separate quarries and began to take sleepy prisoners who had been roused from the deep natural caves where, undecided whether there really was a war on, they had spent the night in their pyjamas. Elsewhere some of the Algerians were only too alert and it took the Commandos the best part of an hour to silence some of their machine gun nests and mortar positions and in some cases they were merely repositioning. Then, at about 7 a.m. Pedder entered the barracks and a Private Adams presented him with the Tricolour he had hauled down.

Not long afterwards came the crack of nearby outgoing artillery and it soon became apparent that they were firing south down the beach towards the Australians' left flank. RSM Tevendale went out into the gully and climbed up its north side. From the top he could see a battery of four 75mm guns with spoked wooden wheels, France's famous field piece of the 1914–18 conflict. The nearest gun had five or six figures throwing grenades at it. Leading this assault was Lieutenant Gerald Bryan, the son of a civil servant from an old Anglo-Irish family now concentrated in Belfast, whom Pedder had poached from another Commando for his rock-climbing skills. Like Macpherson, Bryan was hardly out of his teens, having celebrated his twentieth birthday shortly before they moved from Egypt to Cyprus. This was his first time in action and the men with him happened to include some of the trained gunners who had joined the Commando the previous summer.

> I think I was the first to start throwing grenades at the gun. A corporal was shot through the wrist and was cursing every Frenchman ever born. As he couldn't use a rifle I gave him my Colt automatic pistol and he carried on. We crawled through some scrub to get closer. By then the gun itself was deserted, the crew cowering in a slit trench. We bunged in a few more grenades and then went in. It was rather bloody.

The gun was the right-hand gun of the battery and the other three were between 100 and 300 yards away. One of Bryan's Royal Artillery contingent, a sergeant, started rummaging around the ammunition limber.

> Our gun was pointing away from the battery, so we grabbed the tail piece and heaved it right around so that it was pointing at the nearest gun. The sergeant took over, shoved a shell in and sighted over open sights then fired. The result was amazing. One hell of an explosion and our target flung up like a toy. We must have hit its ammunition. No time to waste. The sergeant traversed onto the next gun, sighted rapidly and fired. There was a pause. Where the devil had the shell gone? Then about half a mile up the hillside, there was a flash and a puff of smoke in the dome of a mosque. A thick Scottish voice said, 'That'll make the buggers pray.'

By trial and error they disposed of the other two guns and, their blood up, shot some of their fleeing crews with a Bren gun. When they had finished the sergeant used a rifle butt to snap the firing pin of the captured gun and they rejoined Pedder's Commando HQ. This involved a sprint of about 300 yards across open ground under fire but nobody was hit. After that their luck began to run out.

Ably led by their French officers, the Algerian Tirailleurs, which literally means skirmisher and implies skill at field craft and marksmanship, began to live up to their name. First they fell back into a wooded area about half a mile above the barracks and overlooking the magnificent Phoenician coast where they set up their machine guns or found comfortable sniping positions among some conifers. Then they waited for the English, who they guessed were advancing up a gully, to emerge onto a bare ridge line some 300 yards below them. Once they had enough of them in their sights they were soon inflicting casualties and had the rest pressing themselves into the flinty slope hardly daring to move. It took Bryan ten minutes to crawl 50 yards to a place where two Bren gunners were doing their best to hit back.

> Every time they tried to fire a machine gun opened up and they couldn't spot it. Suddenly Alastair Coode, the B section lieutenant whose family ran a big engineering firm back in Glasgow, saw it and grabbed a rifle but as he was taking aim he was shot in the chest and went down coughing blood. Then, from a different direction, the Sergeant was hit in the shoulder, so we were being fired on from two fronts. I shouted to my men to make for some scrub about 100 yards away and started crawling towards it. Bullets were fizzing past. The Sergeant, who had been wounded, decided to run for it to catch us up but a machine gun got him and he fell with his face covered with blood. Suddenly I felt what at first seemed to be a tremendous bang on the head but this was shock. When I opened my eyes I saw it was my legs. We were taught this crawl in the commandos where you tried to keep your heels down by keeping your ankles close to the ground. But I was in a hurry to get to the scrub and I suppose my heels were up and it raised my silhouette. I had been hit by a heavy machine gun bullet, something like a .50 I guess, which had gone through my left leg just above the ankle and slap through the tibia and then went on to hit my right leg by which time the bullet had become a kind of dumdum and did terrible damage. The amazing thing was that it completely spun me around and turned me over. Before I was hit I was crawling on my belly towards the scrub. Afterwards, I was lying on my back with my head in the other direction. Anyway, after I got over the shock I decided not to die. I dragged myself into a bit of a dip and tried to get fairly comfortable.

Pedder realized that it was time to get out. He told Captain Farmiloe, commander of 1 Troop, that they would go back down the gully and start heading south, attacking everything they could manage, until they contacted Keyes's party or the Australians. They had hardly begun to move when Pedder himself became the next victim. 'Tevendale, Farmiloe, I'm shot,' he announced, almost as if he had just been declared a casualty by an umpire on a field training exercise back on the Isle of Arran and was curious to see how they would handle this interesting development.

Tevendale, who was about 20 yards away, ran across but by the time the RSM got to him Pedder had died, at least one bullet having passed through his back and chest. It was 0846, about four and a half hours since they had landed. Lying nearby was Private Adams, who had given Pedder the Tricolour. Tevendale lingered long enough in this unhealthy spot to check the colonel's pockets for any maps or papers before he ran after the others moving towards the start of the gully. Shortly afterwards a sniper killed Lieutenant (acting Captain) Robin Farmiloe with a head shot and

Tevendale took over command of the remnants of Command HQ and Number 1 Troop.

There were no officers left standing. In less than thirty minutes three had been killed and Bryan was lying in the dent of earth that was keeping him alive with most of his right calf shot off. Every time he moved one of his sergeants, also wounded, kept yelling at him to keep his head down or he would be killed.

> I was damned thirsty but could not get a drink as I had to show myself to get my water bottle and each time I tried I got about 20 rounds to myself. So I lay there hoping I would lose consciousness. After a while a lot of fire came down and the next thing was about 25 French advancing out of the scrub with fixed bayonets. The four men left in my section were captured. I raised my arm and one of the French came over and gave me a nasty look. I was carrying a French pistol that my sergeant had given me in exchange for my rifle. It had jammed at the first shot but like a fool I held onto it. Anyway, he just looked at me for a while and I was let alone. I had one hell of a drink and felt better. About half an hour later my four men were back with a stretcher.

Bryan was carried to a temporary dressing station where a captured Commando medical orderly gave him a morphine injection. Some time later he was loaded into an ambulance together with two French wounded and two Commando sergeants. One of the sergeants, bleeding copiously from a chest wound, was the NCO who had been shouting at him to keep his head down. On their way to Beirut they stopped at a field dressing station the French had set up at the old Crusader port of Sidon where Bryan's legs were put in cardboard boxes packed with cotton wool. Shortly after they arrived at Beirut's Maurice Rottier Hospital the blood-soaked cotton wool was removed and the young rock climber's mangled right leg amputated below the knee by a middle-aged surgeon named Guillermo who told him: 'You are not our enemy. I served in the last war. You are our allies.' In the next forty-eight hours he would perform sixty-seven operations on French and British wounded.

By the afternoon, about eight hours after 11 Commando had landed, it was apparent that the Australians were not yet advancing and all those who had landed north of the Litani were bound to be overwhelmed if they remained where they were. Tevendale's thirty or so men, mostly all that was left of Commando HQ, were already in serious trouble. They had stirred up such a hornet's nest that they found it impossible to move sufficiently far south to link up with Keyes whom they expected to find with the Australian vanguard. Eventually they dug in on a ridge line about 300 yards from the barracks facing the Litani. The position commanded one of the secondary tracks to the Vichy front line and from it they sniped at the runners the French had to use for communication because the Commandos had cut their field telephone lines. When the enemy retreated before a heavy artillery barrage, Tevendale added to their misery and in temperatures that had hovered around 86°F for most of the day skirmished on until late afternoon. Then at about 5 p.m., some seventeen hours after they had left the *Glengyle*, surrounded, under mortar fire, almost out of ammunition and water and exhausted enough to fall asleep under fire, the French called on them to surrender and they wrecked their weapons and stumbled down from the ridge with their wounded.

At about the same time Captain George More's northern Z Party began to relinquish their hold on the Kafr Badda bridge area. They had held their roadblocks all day against increasingly determined attempts to break through by armoured cars that had mostly been repulsed with Boys anti-tank rifles and captured Hotchkiss machine guns. One of the Hotchkisses was manned by Noble Sproule, the young Canadian who had turned down a month's pay to go on the operation. 'Boy oh boy it was duck soup. They had 200 yards of open flat plain,' he would write to his father. But there were far too few of them and their position was fast becoming untenable. More had been obliged to scatter his 100 or so men over a wide area – his two troops were 500 yards apart – and several of their prisoners had been killed trying to disarm their guards and escape.

As the day wore on some of the Commandos had even come under naval bombardment from a couple of Darlan's Beirut-based heavy destroyers, the *Guépard* and the *Valmy*, which had fired about sixty rounds at them, though the nearest shell landed 200 yards away and there were no casualties. Tommy Macpherson, the subaltern who had been bayoneted in the wrist during the capture of the 6-inch guns, had got his binoculars onto them. 'You felt you were practically looking down the barrels but either their shooting was inaccurate or they had no clear idea where our position was.'

This latter was almost certainly the case, for the French ships soon demonstrated just how good their shooting could be when they were engaged by the four British destroyers *Janus*, *Jackal*, *Hotspur* and *Isis*. Captain John Tothill, a heavily bearded figure, commanded the flotilla from HMS *Janus* which off Crete had participated in one of the Royal Navy's few offensive actions: a night attack in which just over 300 of the Wehrmacht's seaborne invasion force had been massacred in their commandeered wooden caiques. Slower and out-ranged by *Guépard* and *Valmy*'s 5.5-inch guns, Tothill decided there was no time to concentrate his ships and, well in the lead, tried to get close enough to use *Janus*'s 4.7-inch guns.

As usual, the French had attached dye bags to their shells to indicate fall of shot: in this case one ship had green, the other red. They concentrated entirely on the *Janus*, opening fire at 17,000 yards which was long before the British destroyer could reasonably expect to hurt them. It soon became apparent that the green team, probably flotilla leader *Guépard*, were the superior gunners. Her splashes were easily the closest to the target and before long *Janus* received a salvo of three direct hits: one killed or wounded everybody on the bridge except Tothill who was unscathed apart from his beard which had turned a startling green (long after this was remedied he was known as Cap'n Fungus); another penetrated a boiler room and wiped out its entire crew, and the third wrecked Tothill's cabin. Shortly afterwards a fourth shell hit the other boiler room and a fifth was discovered unexploded in a bathroom. Nine of her crew had been killed and *Janus*, though her guns were still firing, was stopped and an easy target. *Jackal*, 4.7-inch guns blazing, caught up and laid a smoke screen around the stricken ship, receiving one hit which wounded a seaman but did little structural damage. *Guépard* followed this up with a torpedo that missed and was in turn hit by a shell, though to little effect.

The French ships now broke off the action, which had lasted just over an hour, and headed back north towards Beirut pursued by *Jackal*, *Hotspur* and *Isis*, which was in the lead and had entered into the spirit of things by flying Nelson's second most famous flag signal: 'Engage the enemy more closely'. This was somewhat optimistic. The engines of much of 1941's Royal Navy were a poor substitute for the days of sail. When it came to obliging Darlan's newer ships to do battle on anything other than their own terms they simply could not keep up and soon *Guépard* and *Valmy* were out of range. More British ships appeared on the scene and the destroyer *Kimberley* began to tow *Janus* back to Haifa at 12 knots while her crew extinguished an oil fire that had started in one of the damaged boiler rooms.

The French were determined to finish off the crippled destroyer and sent ten twin-engined bombers escorted by six Dewoitine 520 fighters. One of the Dewoitines was flown by Sous-lieutenant Pierre Le Gloan, a gifted and experienced pilot – he had joined the Armée de l'Air in 1931 aged 18 – who had already scored twelve victories: four German and seven Italian aircraft bagged in France before the armistice and his first RAF Hurricane shot down over Damascus the day before, when he ambushed Flight Lieutenant J.R. Aldis while he was taking reconnaissance photographs. Three Hurricanes from 80 Squadron RAF, which was just back from Greece and Crete and now based at Haifa, were on a standing patrol and spotted the bombers, six Glenn Martins and four of the more cumbersome Bloch 200s, a slow and ugly-looking high-wing monoplane with the kind of windows in its protruding nose you would expect to find in a railway carriage. The Hurricanes had not noticed the Dewoitines circling above them and concentrated on the Blochs, splashing one with the loss of three of its four-man crew and obliging a second to make a forced landing without serious casualties. Then they were bounced in turn by the Dewoitines which, though they had been hurried into production and had plenty of teething troubles, was France's best fighter and probably a match for a Hurricane. Certainly in the hands of the broad-shouldered Breton Le Gloan it was, for he added two more to his score in about the time it takes to boil an egg: Pilot Officer Lynch died; Pilot Officer Peter Crowther bailed out and was captured badly burnt and taken to the Maurice Rottier Military Hospital in Beirut where he met up with the wounded Commando officer Gerald Bryan.

Three more Dewoitine and three more Hurricanes then joined in the dogfight. No more aircraft on either side were shot down but one of each crashed into the sea after a head-on collision. Their pilots, Sergeant Martin Bennett and Sous-lieutenant Georges Rivory, both bailed out to be rescued by the destroyer *Kandahar.* Bennett was badly burnt. None of the bombers hit the *Janus* though their crews could not be blamed for assuming they had, for a second oil fire, the result of the *Guépard*'s hits in the boiler room, had started. Black smoke was still rising from the ship when she entered Haifa harbour where, to the amazement of the crew, an Auxiliary Fire Service team that came on board with enough foam to smother the blaze turned out to be entirely composed of young Jewish women, a result of Haganah's vigorous civil defence recruiting. It would take at least six months to get *Janus* back into action, a loss the Mediterranean fleet could ill afford after Crete.*

At the cost of one Dewoitine and possibly two Bloch bombers, the French had succeeded in crippling a British destroyer and reducing the RAF's meagre fighter strength by three Hurricanes. Out of radio contact, George More's Commandos were of course as unaware of these setbacks as they were of Pedder's death or the whereabouts of Major Keyes's party. During scouting trips on a captured motorcycle More had got close enough to the Australians across the river to have them shoot one of his tyres out and had been lucky not to meet the French on the bumpy ride back. All he knew for certain was that if the Australians were not coming to them they must go to the Australians.

Dispersal into small groups was very much part of Commando training and one of the reasons why they had more junior officers than the average infantry battalion. The fifty-strong troops were organized into two sections that were further divided into sub-sections of about twelve. They expected to break up and come together again according to events and, given a chance, to be aggressive not merely evaders. All the Commandos still alive and at large north of Keyes's enclave on the northern bank of the Litani,

* The Admiralty reprimanded Tothill for attacking without support, noting that French long-range gunnery was 'significantly superior' to the norm in His Majesty's destroyers.

probably about 150 men, were now heading for the river. Their fortunes varied.

More divided his command into two and took the larger party, which included four other officers, along the coast, keeping to the scrub wherever possible, expecting to meet up with Keyes or the Australians a little north of the Litani's mouth. This left about thirty-five men under Macpherson, who had been told to get to the Litani by a circuitous south-easterly route. Paddy Mayne had taken a similar course with his men and to great effect, bringing about eighty prisoners with him acquired in three different firefights. The most noteworthy of these was the overrunning of a battalion headquarters. Mayne entered first, in his hand one of the US Army Colt .45 automatic pistols most Commando officers were issued and a weapon with which he had become a qualified instructor.

> I called on them to *jetez vers à la planche* but they seemed a bit slow on the uptake; one of them lifted a rifle and I am afraid he had not even time to be sorry. This was the sort of HQ with typewriters, ammunition, revolvers, bombs, and, more to the point, beer and food. While we were dining the phone rang. We didn't answer but followed the wire and got another bull – four machine-guns, two light machine-guns, two mortars and 40 more prisoners. We came back through the Aussie lines. We were rather tired, so the prisoner laddies kindly carried the booty.

Mayne and his haul would cross the river more or less dry shod at 4.30 the following morning on the pontoon bridge the Australian engineers now had in place. His total casualties out of a strength of forty-five were three killed: two when they landed and advanced to the main road and one shot by mistake by the Australians when they first showed themselves at the river.

Macpherson did not have a map, which were in short supply, but marched on a compass bearing with his men following him with what he later admitted was 'an air of unrelieved pessimism and disbelief'. En route they twice skirmished with small units of the locally raised *troupes spéciales* who quickly surrendered. But unlike Mayne, the only prisoner they kept was a French lieutenant. The others were disarmed and freed minus boots, socks and trousers which were cast, together with their heavier or less interesting weapons, over the first suitable precipice.

It was a good decision because where they met the river, some way to the east of the pontoon bridge Mayne had crossed, it was much deeper and faster flowing. Prisoners would have been a burden and five walking wounded were hindrance enough. They moved into the warm water after dark. Macpherson, who was 5 foot 10, found it was up to his armpits and probably just about fordable. But twice the lieutenant, seventh son of a judge and an athletic product of Fettes, Scotland's Eton, had to rescue men who had slipped, panicked and and were being swept away with astonishing speed. One was a former steward on the *Athenia* who had almost drowned on the first day of the war when the transatlantic liner was sunk by a U-boat.

By the time Macpherson got him out his screams had alerted a French post 500 yards downstream which responded with long bursts of machine-gun fire, wild at first then getting onto midstream. It is hard for men in boots, chest-deep in a river and holding aloft a weapon, to move any faster when they are under fire but they will try. One of the wounded stumbled, the man behind him picked him up and the man behind him tripped over the rescuer, gifting 36 pounds of Boys anti-tank rifle to the Litani as he was tugged away by its playful currents. 'I got him out quite a long way down, not without difficulty as he was some four inches taller and three stones heavier than me.'

Macpherson brought all but two of his men back and they had been killed during fighting earlier in the day. His only other losses, for which he would eventually be reprimanded,* were the Boys, a Bren gun and two rifles dropped in the river. After they reached the south bank they walked west until they met up with their first Australians. 'We were warmly welcomed to what appeared to be a continuous beer party.'

More, who had twenty-four of his original Z Party with him, was also close to the Australians. After dark they had gone down to the shore and then waited for two and a half hours for the moon to move behind cloud before, thirty minutes after midnight, heading south towards the Aiteniye Farm buildings, Keyes's original objective. The artillery they had been listening to had subsided but from the direction of the river came the insistent crackle and pop of small-arms fire. Aiteniye still appeared to be firmly in Vichy hands with plenty of intact barbed-wire entanglements going down to the sea. To cross the river mouth to the other side they needed to get through these. They had just managed to cut their way through what sappers called a 'Double Apron', viewed in section a triangular fence, when they were shot at from about 40 yards away with heavy machine guns and some kind of artillery, possibly an anti-tank gun. Then another machine gun fired at them from a different direction and for good measure they came under what seemed like Bren gun fire from the river. Firing back into the darkness and lobbing grenades from rifle discharger caps only made the French fire stronger. Within a few minutes five of the Commandos, including a lieutenant, were dead or dying and three wounded. Stuck in the barbed wire, it became obvious that the French

* He was told he should have used rifle slings to make a line across the river and sent his heavier weapons first. One of his sergeants suggested Macpherson be awarded a George Medal for life saving but this was turned down, possibly because a non-swimming Commando was not quite their public image.

would be able to go on killing them with impunity as long as their ammunition lasted.

'We eventually succeeded in surrendering,' wrote Lieutenant Eoin McGonigal, ex-Royal Ulster Rifles and a close friend of Paddy Mayne, in his report to Keyes, leaving their desperate cries of, '*Cessez le feu! C'est fini*,' and all the terror, anguish and humiliation that went with them to the imagination of the reader. One man, a Lance Corporal Tait, who earlier in the day had distinguished himself against the armoured cars with an anti-tank rifle, somehow managed to crawl out of the barbed wire and abandoning weapon, boots and helmet swam almost naked to the Australian lines.

The French tended to the wounded. There was no chance of getting them to a doctor because the port was virtually cut off. But they had repulsed an Australian attempt to exploit this with a night attack that had fallen back onto Keyes's small garrison in the redoubt in some confusion. 'They all sat in the bottom of the communication trench letting off rifles at nothing,' he noted. 'We make them desist. Then rather bitterly retire to bed, still odd shots landing about the place so have to find uncomfortable spot in trench.'*

It was broad daylight when Keyes awoke and by then all had changed. No shots had been fired in the immediate area since shortly after dawn when Australian Bren-gun carriers, heading north towards Kafr Badda, had rattled over the pontoon bridge and bypassed the Aiteniye Farm buildings. Now some figures waving a white flag were walking towards them from this machine-gun nest that only a few hours before had sent the Australians scurrying back and done such execution among the Commandos entangled in the barbed wire on the beach. As yet Keyes knew nothing of this but as he got his field glasses onto the white flag he recognized, ambling alongside the French officer carrying it, George More. Once they saw the Bren-gun carriers moving behind them, his recent captors had returned his pistol and asked him to negotiate the surrender of their isolated post.

Litani was a costly affair for 11 Commando who lost far more than the Australians. Almost a quarter of the men who landed became casualties: forty-five killed and seventy-eight wounded, some of them so badly that, like Gerald Bryan, their front-line soldiering was over before it had properly begun. As they went about finding and burying their dead and salvaging

* While Keyes is unstinting in his praise of the 'great dash and determination' displayed by Lance Corporal Dilworth and the other Australians in the boat party and admits that he would never have got to the north bank without them, he is less than kind about the performance of Captain Caro and C Company generally. (Dilworth belonged to another company.) But Keyes, the son of a hero, determined to be the same, was dealing with a civilian soldier, an accountant, some twelve years his senior who wanted to do the best by his men in a campaign that had started with excessive expectations of a pushover.

as many of their weapons as they could find, at one point every man on his feet was carrying at least two rifles. The Australians made a great fuss of them delivering hot bully beef stew with fresh bread and whisky to wash it down with, though, much to Keyes's annoyance, while his men slept it off the Aussies spoilt it by purloining some of their precious Brens and Thompsons.

The Commandos would eventually be given a lot of medals for the Litani operation. Regimental Sergeant Major Tevendale, who took over Y Party after Pedder and all the other officers were down, got a Distinguished Conduct Medal. The Canadian machine gunner Sproule, who had calmly dismembered his captured Hotchkiss before departing, and the anti-tank rifleman Tait were among several Commandos to receive Military Medals for their courage. (Like Tait, though at a different time, Sproule had swum to the Australian lines almost naked though wearing his helmet in which he kept his wallet.) Military Crosses went to Keyes and More for exemplary courage and leadership; the wounded Bryan for initiating the successful attack on the 75mm battery and Garland got a bar to the one he won at Dunkirk for his work at the redoubt and an earlier incident when he located and shot a successful sniper by offering himself as bait. Mayne received a Mention in Despatches for bringing all his prisoners south of the Litani, some of them carrying the parts of their own heavy machine guns. Pedder did not receive a posthumous award except from his men, for the regimental march Piper Lawson had composed on the voyage out from Liverpool was renamed 'The Colonel Pedder'.

Twenty-four hours after Keyes had watched More emerge from the Aiteniye Farm the two young officers found themselves in the cooler climes of Wilson's Jerusalem headquarters where they had been invited to tell him and his staff all about it. 'Everyone very kind and interested,' noted Keyes. 'Jumbo asks some shrewd questions then compliments and thanks us.'

Wilson probably felt the need to hear something uplifting. Elsewhere things were not going too well at all.

Chapter Eighteen

Lieutenant General Sir Henry Maitland Wilson, Knight Commander of the Bath, Distinguished Service Order, thrice Mentioned in Despatches and the holder of the Queen's and King's Medals, each with two clasps, was about the same age as the young Commando officers he had just met when he won the last two decorations in South Africa fighting the Boers. Wilson was now 60 and for years friends and contemporaries had used the Jumbo nickname to his face, for he was as fat as he was popular.

'General Wilson has a twinkle in his eye,' noted Hermione, Lady Ranfurly, secretary to the boss of Special Operation Executive's Cairo station, whose husband, Lieutenant the Earl of Ranfurly, had recently been captured by Rommel's newly arrived Afrika Korps along with generals Neame and O'Connor. (Ranfurly was Neame's aide-de-camp.) She first met Wilson over tea at the Wavells. 'He is so large that he looks silly holding a cup and saucer. He puffs when he sits down and he puffs when he gets up again.'

But if his girth and height made the general a Jumbo he was not a Blimp. In the inter-war years he had been on the side of the angels as far as mechanization was concerned, playing a leading role in the revolutionary concept of motorized infantry battalions working alongside tanks. At the time much of this had been notional. Trucks and tanks were scarce in an army that had shrunk back to the size of an imperial gendarmerie. Between jobs and postings a frugal War Office had sometimes put Wilson on half pay. In these reduced circumstances, it was hardly surprising that during his time as an instructor at Camberley Staff College there was some emphasis on the threadbare campaigns waged in Civil War Virginia by the Confederates Robert E. Lee and Thomas 'Stonewall' Jackson, both masters at making a little go a long way. It was a talent Wilson had most recently demonstrated raising the ad hoc Habforce that had ultimately bluffed its way into Baghdad and driven Rashid Ali into Berlin exile.

But in Syria it was beginning to look as if Jumbo might have bitten off more than he could chew. For there was no doubt that Vichy's troops, for a variety of reasons, were determined to resist. 'You thought we were yellow, didn't you? You thought we couldn't fight in France,' a captured

French sergeant told Alan Moorhead, the Australian who had become Fleet Street's leading war correspondent. 'You thought we were like the Italians. Well, we've shown you.'

By the end of the first week the only part of Wilson's three-prong attack to penetrate the Vichy defences to any significant tactical depth had been the Litani crossings staged by the Australians and 11 Commando. In the centre the other Australian brigade had advanced less than 10 miles into the easily defended hill country and was trying to hold onto positions around the town of Merjayoun.

On Syria's Golan Heights, the third prong heading east towards Damascus had started well enough. Near Tel Shehab station, from where the railway branched down to Haifa, there was an important bridge over the Yarmuk river, a tributary of the Jordan. In November 1917 Lawrence had failed to blow it up when one of his Bedouin raiders dropped a rifle and alerted its Turkish guards before they could kill them. Some twenty-four years later Captain Adam Murray and Havildar Goru Ram of the Rajputana Rifles had better luck or were possibly more professional than that strange Englishman who had so mesmerized Murray's generation of schoolboys.

In their case they were attempting to save not destroy the bridge, which the French had prepared for demolition, though their main task remained the same as it had been for Lawrence: remove the sentries. Murray, a Belfast-born regular Indian Army officer aged 24, elected to do this by equipping himself and his havildar (an Indian Army sergeant) with Thompson sub-machine guns fitted with Al Capone-style drum magazines. Then, shortly before 2 a.m., they crawled with infinite patience up to the sandbagged guard post and once they were close enough to make out the shadowy figures within, emptied the best part of 100 rounds of .45 into it. The rattle of these bursts across the night air was the signal for thirty or so of Murray's Rajputs to rush the bridge and start looking for the demolition wires.

Capturing the Shehab bridge was the first act in the advance towards Damascus of some 3,000 men of the 5th Indian Brigade, of whom Indians probably numbered just over half. Their job was to pave the way for the entry into the Syrian capital of the Free French contingent under Général Paul Legentilhomme, the former governor of Djibouti who had fled to British Aden and rallied to de Gaulle. London was anxious to show that this campaign was not, as Vichy was bound to allege, its old imperial rival exploiting France's misfortune to grab an overseas possession..

From the British territories south-west of Damascus there were two roads to the city, both built on ancient caravan trails. One could be reached by crossing the Shehab bridge on Transjordan's north-western frontier with Syria then turning right and picking up the main road that ran due north from the border town of Deraa to the capital 60 miles away. The other began in Palestine's north-eastern corner just above the Sea of Galilee, crossed the border and went through the Golan's important crossroads town of Kuneitra. This route, which is a few miles shorter, is over the flatter, more monotonous, more windswept part of the Golan plateau: better tank country.

Brigadier Lloyd had decided that 5th Brigade's two Indian battalions, the 4/6th Rajputs and 3/1st Punjabis, would make the main thrust to Damascus along the Deraa road. His London infantry, the 1st Royal Fusiliers, would put in a diversionary attack along the northern road to Kuneitra, crossing the river Jordan from Palestine into Syria at Jisr Bennt Yacoub, which means the Bridge of Jacob's Daughter. Allenby's Australian Light Horse had taken the same route in 1918 when they too were on their way to Damascus and their numbers included a symbolic contingent of French cavalry because it had already been agreed that, once the Turks were defeated, Syria would go to France.

By the night of 9 June, as planned, Lloyd had his three battalions astride the approach roads to Damascus. The Fusiliers' Free French liaison officer, a Capitaine Moreau, had advised them to approach Kuneitra from the north and east where it was less strongly defended, something Moreau was in a position to know being a very recent rallier to the Gaullist cause who had served in a Vichy unit there only two weeks before. But the Fusiliers had taken Kuneitra without firing a shot, entering at first light to be informed by its inhabitants that the garrison had declared a curfew then clattered out with its trucks and horses in the middle of the night. Moreau insisted that they establish the officers' mess in the house of the District Commissioner who, it turned out, was justly famous for his wine cellar. Cautiously, hardly believing their luck, the Fusiliers began sending patrols down the road towards Damascus 40 miles away.

Deraa put up a bit more of a fight. A *pourparler* party in a small car flying a large white flag was stopped by an anti-tank shell which wrecked its engine but failed to explode. Abandoning their transport and waving their flag in a determined manner, the shaken emissaries were allowed close enough to deliver a prepared script about the justness of their cause and the foolishness of resisting 'superior forces'. This advice was rejected but an hour later, after bombardment by a battery of twelve 25-pounders, the Punjabis took the town unopposed. Its garrison had escaped by train before the Rajputs, who had made a circuitous march to their rear, were in place to cut them off. Having dispersed with gunfire Arab looters trying to find some profit in this carnage, most of the Indian battalions, accompanied by artillery and a few anti-tank guns, then headed north to Sheikh Meskine.

This hilltop village, where machine gunners and 75mm field guns were hidden among some striking bits of overgrown Roman ruin, was the scene of the Rajputs' first taste of serious French resistance and despite artillery support their initial attack, put in at 4 p.m., was repulsed with losses. But the quality of these Indian professional soldiers, recently returned from an arduous campaign in Eritrea where Italian colonial regiments included a locally recruited warrior elite often as good as themselves, eventually showed. One Sikh naik (corporal), who found himself the most senior man of his platoon still standing, paid particular attention to the shadowy places of archaeological interest then, with three others, was estimated to have killed over forty men.

By 12 June, four days after it started, Brigadier Lloyd had good reason to be pleased with his progress to date. Along both approach roads to Damascus his forward patrols were now within about an hour's drive of the city. His right flank off the Deraa road, the desert flank, was well covered by Legentilhomme's Free French with Colonel Collet's Circassian cavalry, which had both horses and vehicles, on the outer, sandy edge. A Free French battalion, admittedly the same Infanterie de Marine that had put up such a dismal performance at Dakar, was being loaned to 5th Indian. As planned, in preparation for a Gaullist-led entry into Damascus the entire eastern thrust was coming under Legentilhomme and would henceforth be known as Gentforce.

Then three Vichy Dewoitine 520s strafed some vehicles at Sananein on the Deraa–Damascus road and almost scored a bull's-eye. Among the wounded, with a broken arm and flesh wounds, was the Free French commander. Legentilhomme was taken back to a field dressing station at Deraa for treatment where he insisted that a sling and a few stitches should not stop him working. But the doctors were adamant that he needed a rest and Jumbo Wilson put Lloyd in temporary command of Gentforce which continued towards Damascus.

Dominating the main road, 10 miles south of the city, there was a well-defended Vichy position at the village of Kissoué. About an hour before first light on 15 June, Lloyd's two Indian battalions moved through the darkness towards it carrying thirty rough wooden ladders hammered together a few hours before in order to get over the outlying anti-tank ditches. Covering their left flank were the Royal Fusiliers' C Company, about 150 men in all who had been detached from the battalion at Kuneitra along with its anti-tank platoon. As it happened, the French were also fully awake and using the cover of night to rotate most of their garrison. Some of the departing Moroccans were already seated in their transport while the newly arrived Senegalese were moving into their trenches and foxholes. There could not have been a better moment to attack and afterwards many of the Vichy French refused to accept that they were merely the victims of bad luck and not treachery. For over four hours, Kissoué's orchards and gardens saw sudden confrontations with grenades thrown and shouting men with fixed bayonets firing from the hip while, in the lulls, snipers on both sides searched for the white faces in command.

But by 8.30 a.m. it was all over and the Punjabis, who had borne the brunt of it, collected their casualties and rested while 200 or so Rajputs walked through them to complete their victory with an assault on Tel Kissoué, an overlooking hill. Since by now surprise was out of the question this was preceded by an artillery bombardment and by the time they got to the top most of its defenders still able to do so had left. Some of the French professionals who had found themselves at the sharp end and survived expressed admiration, as one officer to another, at the performance of the Punjabis and Rajputs. '*Ce que vous avez fait, c'est incroyable. Vos Indiens sont vraiment formidables*,' one told Brigadier Lloyd.

On the Indians' left the detached company of Fusiliers assisted by the Free French marines had cleared a village and secured that flank. In a few months it would be twenty-three years since Lord Allenby followed his Australian Light Horse into the city and began the delicate business of explaining to the Arabs that France was going to rule there. Now it looked like Lloyd was going to be the man to end that chapter.

Then Raoul de Verdilhac, who had been in the same year as Legentilhomme at St Cyr and staff college and regarded him as a friend, started his counter-attack.

At the end of the first week's fighting the commander of the Armée du Levant, despite the setback at the Litani, had still not committed all his troops. In particular he had made little use of the eighty or so Renault R35 light tanks manned by his European troopers of the Chasseurs d'Afrique. For the first few days de Verdilhac and his staff had been trying to work out which of Wilson's three places of attack were feints and which one – it was assumed it would only be one – the real thing. Initially, the favourite had been the Deraa road push towards Damascus by the Indians, with the Fusiliers at Kuneitra correctly judged an obvious feint and the Australians problematic because they had already been stopped at Merjayoun and the further north you went the easier Lebanon was to defend. Then, as the week wore on, they concluded that they were all feints.

The British, it seemed, had attacked French Syria with an almost insultingly small and under-equipped little army, apparently expecting a show of force and the blandishments of the Gaullists renegades would do the trick. Intelligence reports of armour massing at the border had either been the work of agents who could not tell the difference between a tracked Bren-gun carrier and a panzer or clever British disinformation. All they had by way of tanks were a few Australian manned light reconnaissance models which had no cannon only machine guns and could almost be opened with a tin opener. Nor, according to the Armée de l'Air de Vichy, was the RAF's deployment bigger than theirs. If anything it was slightly smaller and on the defensive. Protecting the British ships bombarding the coast, which were not only being attacked by French aircraft but by the

Germans using Junkers 88s from Rhodes, had reduced their fighter strength above the battlefields.

De Verdilhac chose to hit the British in the three places where they were weakest: the Fusiliers at Kuneitra, the Australians at Merjayoun and the Indians and the Free French by having a bypassed garrison in the rounded lava hills of the Jebel Druse, close to the Transjordan border some 35 miles to their rear, sally out and cut the Deraa–Damascus road. By creating mayhem along the invaders' fragile main supply routes, perhaps even raid the rear of the British baggage train in Palestine itself, he hoped to do two things: throttle the attack on Damascus and buy time to reinforce his eastern desert flank with Iraq from where a British thrust was expected as soon as they judged it expedient to turn their backs on the natives.

As far as the Fusiliers were concerned, the first irrefutable evidence that something nasty was heading their way came in the early hours of the 15th. At the hamlet of Tel El Cham 16 miles north of Kuneitra, their forward company was straddling the Damascus road with orders to harass the French with fighting patrols 'but not to become seriously involved'. Apart from their truck transport, they were accompanied by several of the little Bren-gun carriers and two of the Royal Dragoon Guards' armoured cars, one with a captured Italian 20mm Breda heavy machine gun for which allegedly armour-piercing rounds were available.

Then at 2.30 a.m. tanks, armoured cars and infantry in trucks emerged from the nearest enemy position at Sassa about 4 miles down the road and very nearly overran them. In the dark the Royal Dragoons' Breda gun sought out the intruders and the Bren-gun carriers provided what cover they could but less than half the Fusiliers found their transport and escaped. A head count on their return to Kuneitra revealed more than fifty were missing. At first light the armoured cars went to look for them but 5 miles out of Kuneitra they found that the enemy had moved up overnight and were assembling around the ruins of an old Turkish caravanserai at the village of Khan Arembeh. Most of the missing men had been captured, though a few evaded the French and made their way back to their own lines, often with hair-raising tales of the number of tanks they had seen on the way.

Lieutenant Colonel Arthur Orr DSO was the 1st Royal Fusiliers' third commander in the last seven months. The first had been killed at the beginning of December when the battalion was part of the surprise attack against the Italians in Egypt's Western Desert. The second had lasted until April when he received a bad head wound in Eritrea during the costly mountain fighting around Keren. It had taken them six weeks to push the Savoy Grenadiers off those peaks. On their worst day the Fusiliers had lost 130, killed and wounded. They had expected a rest. Instead, they had gone back to Egypt's Western Desert for a month, kept in reserve digging defences that were never used until Wavell was satisfied that Rommel had been held.

Then, in the middle of May, they had been sent to Palestine where the battalion had been brought up to strength with a draft of 9 officers and 230 men recently arrived from England. Most were conscripts. The 1st Royal Fusiliers, despite a professional cadre, was no longer quite the regular battalion, in India since 1937, where even the dimmest fusilier soon learned that Abhora Day was celebrated because that was the place in Spain where the regiment last put it over the French in 1811.

Orr had arrived eight days before the Syrian invasion, taking over from the major who had led them through the rest of the Keren fighting and now reverted to being second-in-command. This sort of thing often happened and there is unlikely to have been much resentment apart from the initial wariness a new boss brings to any enterprise. And Orr, whose parent regiment was the Royal Scots Fusiliers, had the cachet of a DSO and recent service in the Sudan Defence Force, which the empire regarded as the most exclusive of its frontier policemen, home of the bright as well as the brave. Shortly after they entered Kuneitra Orr had impressed his officers by presiding over a meeting of the town council in Arabic.

The Fusiliers had advanced on Kuneitra supported by a battery of 25-pounder artillery and their own anti-tank platoon's three small 37mm guns made by Sweden's Bofors who were better known for their anti-aircraft wares. Britain's newer and better 2-pounder anti-tank guns were not yet available to the Indian Army. Once they had taken the town, all the guns including their Bofors had been withdrawn because Lloyd wanted them to support the real attack on Damascus by the Indians and the Free French. Orr, with Vichy armoured cars already reconnoitring his defences, sent an urgent message to brigade headquarters asking at least for his Bofors back but to no avail.

The trouble was Kuneitra was not yet under attack and might never be. The tanks down the road could turn out to be a Vichy feint to counter a British feint and draw off scarce resources. Whereas, almost back on the Jordanian border, 5th Indian Brigade was facing an all too real threat. Sheikh Meskine at the southern end of the Deraa–Damascus road was threatened. Verdilhac had ordered a Colonel Bouvier, who commanded a bypassed Vichy garrison lurking in the volcanic fastness of the Jebel Druse, to raid the British rear and cut the road. His first move had been to chase a small detachment of the Transjordan Frontier Force, British-officered bedouin, out of the railway halt of Ezraa. Lloyd, commander of Gentforce while Legentilhomme recovered from his wound, had sent about 150 Free French Senegalese under a Colonel Genin, all he could spare, back south to deal with it. Orr's missing Bofors anti-tank guns would be joining them. There was simply not enough of anything to go round. It was all make do and mend. Some of the commandeered transport in use were Jewish-owned citrus trucks from Palestine 'still slippery with orange peel'.

Meanwhile, on the Kuneitra front the French were taking their time. For all of Sunday, 15 June they built up their tanks and infantry at Khan Ambreh while through their binoculars their scouts watched the Englishmen, in their long shorts and sometimes stripped to the waist, prepare their defences with pick and shovel. The main fruit of the Fusiliers' labours was a horseshoe-shaped anti-tank wall of earth and loose stones about 4 feet high and 3 feet thick which crossed the Damascus Road and took in all the crossroads that made Kuneitra such a nodal point. In the southern part of the Fusiliers' perimeter the horseshoe wall became a ditch considered deep and wide enough to stop a tank.

At regular intervals ten-man platoon section posts covered the anti-tank wall and the ditch from buildings or holes in the ground. Most of the Boys anti-tank rifles were in the blocks that had been set up where one of the four major roads met the defence perimeter. The Damascus highway's northern entrance had the additional firepower of the armoured car with the 20mm Breda, the heaviest gun they had. Four visitors who turned up unexpectedly by car from Middle East Command's Staff College at Haifa took one look at these preparations and declined Orr's invitation to stay, explaining that they were 'only interested in the theory of it'.

Orr had about 475 men under him at Kuneitra, the battalion already reduced by the losses incurred when the French fell on his forward company outside Sassa and the earlier detachment of C Company and the anti-tank platoon. Artillery and air strikes on Khan Ambreh would at least have slowed the methodical French build-up there and, despite their shortages, something could have been managed had there been the will to do it. But Brigadier Lloyd, who does not seem to have grasped how vulnerable his Kuneitra feint had become, was using most of his guns to support the Free French advance on Damascus. And the RAF was busy trying to cut L'Armée de L'Air down to size by attacking its airfields. Allied troops saw so little of them that twice that day they had shot down and killed Hurricane pilots flying low-level reconnaissance, one at dawn and the other at dusk. Flying Officer Holdsworth survived a forced landing in fading light, though not the Free French Senegalese waiting for him. Dewoitines and Hurricanes looked almost identical and both air forces, which had never before been anything other than allies, displayed red, white and blue roundels with the colours in different orders.

Yet despite the air superiority they were enjoying in this, the only war they had got, Vichy made no attempt to harass the British battalion with bombing or artillery fire. Perhaps they simply did not feel the need. For some years, spring manoeuvres had included an exercise in which Kuneitra was attacked from the north with tanks and infantry. Having spent all of the previous day getting ready, shortly before dawn on the 16th their attack was heralded by the insistent and growing roar of 85-horsepower engines as the small two-man Renault R35 tanks of Colonel Lecoulteux's 7th Chasseurs d'Afrique came towards them along the Damascus Road. At first the Chasseurs stayed back waiting for it to get properly light because 1941's tanks, their vision restricted enough once the turret hatch was down, did not fight in the dark if they could help it.

The first glimpse the Fusiliers had of the enemy was not the tanks but small parties of Senegalese infantry coming over a low ridge about 400 yards from their perimeter. When they opened fire on them they went to ground and worked slowly towards them, occasionally trying to snipe from the prone position. Then, at about 5 a.m., the tanks began a cautious advance overtaking the infantry who let them go on unaccompanied. Once they were within range the armoured car with the Breda gun opened fire but after five rounds it stopped and, a few minutes later, withdrew. A vital spring, an essential part of the gun's innards, had snapped and could only be repaired in a workshop. This did not cause great despair. Help was surely on its way.

Meanwhile, before the anti-tank guns turned up, they could probably bag a couple themselves with their Boys anti-tank rifles of which they had about fifteen. This was an elegant-looking weapon, a bit like a match rifle with its long barrel resting on a bipod and a padded butt to take the recoil of its high-velocity .55 bullets. Its overall length was 5 foot 2 inches and it weighed the equivalent of four ordinary service rifles. In France it had rarely been effective against the panzers, but in the early days of the North African desert fighting and in Ethiopia the Boys had coped well with the more lightly armoured Italian tanks. Its huge bullets had drilled neat holes through them then made frightful wounds ricocheting around their cramped interiors exactly as intended by Captain H.C. Boys, the Assistant Superintendent of Design at the Royal Small Arms Factory at Enfield in Middlesex. And even as the Fusiliers were approaching Kuneitra, north of the Litani 11 Commando were wrecking French armoured cars with them. Sometimes it could also be useful against an enemy in rocky ground where a round in the right place made nasty slithers of stone shrapnel. Because of its kick the Australians called the Boys 'Charlie the Bastard' but this was a compliment.

Today, however, the Boys rifles turned out to be all but useless. Renault's R35 light tank, which carried a crew of two, was small (1.87 metres across and 4.02 long) and slow. On a decent surface it could manage no more than 20 kilometres per hour. Its fully laden battle weight was 10.6 metric tons. But some of its armour plate was 40mm thick. That was 10mm more than the panzers had carried when they swept through France. Impressed, the Germans had removed their turrets and converted many of the 843 R35s they had captured intact into mobile anti-tank guns and artillery tractors.

Against the Italians the Fusiliers had never had the chance to use their

Boys for their intended purpose because British tanks or artillery had always been around to deal with Italian armour. Now from turret to tracks they were hitting the squat R35s with shot after shot and all they achieved was screeching ricochets as Renault's most lucrative military contract went remorselessly about its business. Captain Tom Wilson, who had won a Military Cross during the Eritrean fighting, watched as the Vichy tanks shot holes in their anti-tank wall with impunity.

> NOTHING could put these tanks out of action. I found about 80 fired cases of .55 anti-tank rifle ammunition in the nearest post to the Damascus Road of A Company. These had been fired at ranges down to five yards and had had no effect. Molotov cocktails were unsuccessful and grenades also. At first when the tanks came the defenders would jump over the wall and shoot at it from the far side. The French got wise to this however and sent tanks down both sides of the wall simultaneously.

Since his wireless appeals for anti-tank guns had been turned down, as a last resort Colonel Orr decided to send an officer to make a personal appeal to Lloyd who, as acting commander of Gentforce, was at the Free French headquarters at Ghabagheb which the British, who found the Arabic name unpronounceable, called Rhubarb. Orr chose as his messenger a man who had served in the battalion for over twenty years and had been one of its best company sergeant majors before receiving a commission. It was a good 60 miles to Rhubarb and in the immediate vicinity Vichy patrols had to be avoided, for they were attempting to surround Kuneitra by cutting the lateral road that joined the other highway to Damascus at Sheikh Miskine. The officer, who travelled in a small truck with an escort and driver, got through and put his request to Major Bernard Fergusson of the Black Watch, a French-speaking Old Etonian and one of Wavell's aides temporarily assigned as a liaison officer to Gentforce HQ. Fergusson turned him down flat.

> He begged me almost tearfully for some anti-tank guns but I refused to even submit his request and for strong reasons. We would need our four anti-tank guns – all we had – to help blast our way into Damascus and, once we had got Damascus the problems of Kuneitra, I thought, and its garrison would be solved. If we were to detach these precious guns from the Damascus battle and send them lumbering round to Kuneitra by way of Sheikh Meskine, they might well arrive too late to help the British battalion and would be lost to both flanks of the battle at the moment of its climax ... I hardened my heart and in retrospect I am sure I was right; but I felt like a butcher. I had known that battalion all my service and had many friends in it ... The officer looked at me as though I were Judas and set off on his long, unhappy journey to Kuneitra.

It must have soon become obvious to Colonel Lecoulteux, who appears to have had about twenty of the R35s at his immediate disposal, that the English lacked effective anti-tank weapons. Yet he was painfully slow to grasp his prize. For something like three hours, perhaps longer, his tanks cruised the northern part of Kuneitra at will, enforcing a sort of curfew on the Fusiliers who mainly took cover on the floors of its stone houses. Not until 10.45, seven hours after his attack had begun, did Lecoulteux send his infantry and armour in together, though when he did Wilson's description of his tactics indicates that he at last understood that Orr's battalion was entirely at his mercy.

> About five tanks were lined up nose to tail on the Damascus Road and concentrated their fire, both machine-gun and cannon, on one section post. Armoured cars from further out neutralised the fire of supporting sections. Under cover of this fire enemy infantry advanced and took the post. They then made it their base and advanced along the line with tanks threatening both sides of the wall and the infantry on the blind side. They cleaned up our section posts in detail, one by one.

It was by no means a massacre. Most of the Fusiliers, almost 300 all told, had had enough and surrendered. But some seventy men from the rifle companies, among them Captain Wilson, risked the tanks' machine guns finding them in open ground to reach the three adjacent granite houses in Kuneitra's southern end that was battalion headquarters. At about noon an encrypted Morse message from there was received by 5th Brigade HQ's radio operators saying: 'Withdrawing from outer perimeter – situation critical.'

This was undeniable. Even so, reinforced by those Fusiliers who had dared to run the gauntlet of the R35's Reibel machine guns, there were now about 180 men around headquarters. Despite a shortage of .303 ammunition for his rifles and Brens, much of which had been lost when the sections posts were overrun, Orr was determined to hold out until help arrived. Perhaps there was an element of natural selection about those who found themselves with him. A Corporal Harry Cotton, who had won a Distinguished Conduct Medal for a lone charge against a machine-gun post in the Western Desert, brought with him a Hotchkiss machine gun and 1,300 rounds of ammunition he had found when they first entered deserted Kuneitra. Then the Hotchkiss broke down and Cotton was killed stalking a tank with a Boys, probably not the only regular soldier to die that day because he believed that all the anti-tank rifle needed was proper handling. Casualties, which had been light, began to mount. Orr himself crawled out to bring in a mortally wounded Bren gunner who had been taking on snipers. A second lieutenant who had been sticking his neck out all day became the second subaltern to be killed.

The first indication Orr seems to have given that he even considered the possibility that there might not be a happy ending came when he sent away with a three-man escort his battalion's two Free French liaison officers who were likely to be shot as traitors if captured. Major Relanger and the bon viveur Capitaine Moreau, who had led them like a homing pigeon to the District Commissioner's wine cellar, left on foot for the Jordan river bridge at Jisr Bennet Yacoub on the Palestine border some 20 miles away. Evading Vichy cavalry and armoured car patrols they were picked up some way before the bridge by three Australian trucks towing a brace of 2-pounder anti-tank guns towards Kuneitra.

These Australians were part of a force under a Lieutenant Colonel Arthur Blackburn, one of Australia's best known 1914–18 heroes who had been commissioned in the field fighting the Turks at Gallipoli then gone to France and won a Victoria Cross storming German trenches on the Somme. Blackburn, a small, wiry man with an unlikely pair of pince-nez spectacles perched on the end of his nose, was in civilian life a lawyer and Adelaide's city coroner. For his second war he was commanding a machine-gun battalion, a peculiarly British concept that concentrated forty-eight of the old Maxim-style belt-fed and water-cooled Vickers into one unit though they were almost invariably dispersed in four-gun packages as the need arose.

This had already started to happen to Blackburn's battalion, which was part of 7th Australian's divisional reserve in northern Palestine and not intended for the Gentforce expedition to Damascus. But as Orr's radio messages became more desperate he had been ordered to take the rump of his command and, much more appropriately, twelve idle 2-pounders from the Australian 2/2nd Anti-Tank Regiment and secure the Jisr Bennet Yacoub bridge against a possible Vichy raid on Palestine. What those guns might have achieved had they been in place in Kuneitra on the dawn of the 16th must have haunted Orr, when he eventually got to hear about them, to the end of his days.

At his own initiative Blackburn had sent Captain Kennedy, a Tasmanian, up the road with four of his Vickers, which had a very long range, and the two anti-tank guns. The plan was that Kennedy should machine-gun French positions from the outskirts of Kuneitra and lure some of the R35s onto the armour-piercing shot from his 2-pounders. Then Kennedy had met up with the two Free French officers and learned that most of the Fusiliers were already taken prisoner and the rest on the brink of joining them. So he turned back.

Orr's 177 officers and men at battalion headquarters had finally surrendered at about 6 p.m. In the late afternoon, almost as if both sides were observing siesta hours, there had been something of a lull. Senegalese infantry had infiltrated into empty houses when they saw their chance and the tanks cruised about firing at targets of opportunity but these got rarer because many of the Fusiliers, dead beat, were snoozing on the stone floors while sentries eyed their slumbering reliefs and looked at their watches. It had been a very long day. Then at about 5.30 p.m. a Foreign Legion armoured car commanded by a Lieutenant Koshonofski, who was waving a white handkerchief and accompanied by a Fusilier prisoner, had approached Orr's headquarters. Koshonofski had spoken eloquently of how distasteful he found shooting Englishmen – which may have been true for he had closet Gaullist tendencies – and the imminence of their next tank attack. Orr had conferred with his second-in-command and regimental sergeant major, who both stressed the shortage of rifle ammunition, then he had gone off to see Lecoulteux to try to make arrangements for his wounded and the burial of the British dead.

Twenty Fusiliers had been killed and four died later of their wounds. It is not clear how many were wounded but, rule of thumb, it was normally a little under three times the dead. These, though quite enough, were not heavy casualties. The battalion had suffered much greater losses in Eritrea and in appalling conditions, driven half mad by the filth and flies of a long-disputed battlefield where dysentery and desert sores were rife. And there they were the victors.

About forty Fusiliers managed to lie low in Kuneitra until dark, which was only a couple of hours after the surrender, and then made good their escape. Orr and his men were marched to the school yard in the northern part of the town where the 200 or so captured earlier in the day, when the tanks first broke through, had been held for a while before being trucked to Sassa. Officers and men were separated, though the Fusiliers did their utmost to frustrate all attempts by the Senegalese to organize them, convinced that remaining in Kuneitra was the key to rescue.

Tom Wilson, who had watched the tanks line up along the Damascus Road, escaped with a 2nd lieutenant 'due to a very lax sentry on the back door of the school' and they both got back to Palestine. But the next morning, by which time the artillery of a belated British relief force was close enough to start harassing the vicinity, the French had the other officer prisoners put in one truck and the sergeants and the corporals in another, and shipped them out fast. The other ranks, who would be marching to Sassa, raised a cheer as they went by, for the French no doubt one of those incomprehensible *rosbif* moments when the Channel became as wide as the Atlantic.

In all, 374 Fusiliers had been taken prisoner and there would have been more if a company had not been detached, for it was not more men that Orr needed but anti-tank guns. Capturing the best part of an old regiment – in St Paul's their shot-riddled colours from their last encounter with the French (1811) recently removed to the crypt because of the Blitz – was undoubtedly the showpiece of de Verdilhac's offensive. When the news reached London Sir John Dill, the Chief of the Imperial General Staff, was mortified. 'Surely a battalion of the Royal Fusiliers have not surrendered to the Vichy French?' he signalled to Wavell. But they had and from the predominantly Australian sector around southern Lebanon's Merjayoun there was more bad news.

'Those terrible grey horses, how they fight,' Napoleon said of the Scots Greys at Waterloo and years later prints of Lady Elisabeth Butler's famous head-on painting of their charge, wild men on wilder horses, were a popular image of life before the Entente Cordiale. How gratifying for the Emperor it would have been to have witnessed on 15 June 1941 the charge of the 6th Chasseurs d'Afrique at Merjayoun. As their chunky R35s drove all before them in panic-stricken flight, there were the Scots Greys, plucked from the 1st Cavalry Division for use as motorized infantry, doing their dismounted best to out-gallop some of the Australians.

The French chose a good time to attack. The bulk of the 25th Brigade had gone almost 25 miles up the road and taken, after a hard fight, the village of Jezzine. This had been done to provide right-flank protection of the other Australian brigade whose progress up the coast had now reached the port of Sidon which was no more than a couple of hours' drive away. Behind them in Merjayoun they had left the 2/33rd Battalion commanded by Lieutenant Colonel Robert Monaghan, one of Australia's small cadre of regular soldiers and a man who appears to have been better at giving orders than taking them. The previous day he had been given permission to take *one* of his four rifle companies on a reconnaissance in force in the foothills of the Herman range: Monaghan took three.

At least the solitary Australian company remaining in Merjayoun was supported by artillery and anti-tank batteries, the latter demonstrating what might have happened at Kuneitra when three R35s were knocked out almost immediately. It also had alongside them about 200 Scots Greys who unlike the yeomanry element of the cavalry division were mostly regular soldiers and regarded as one of the more illustrious ingredients of Wilson's hotchpotch force. But as Monaghan's mountaineers straggled back despite the initial success of the anti-tank guns Merjayoun's meagre defences began to crumble.

Transport was fast disappearing as men hijacked any vehicle left insufficiently guarded and headed south for Palestine 10 miles away. The War Diary of the Australian 2/5th Field Regiment records a growing conviction that 'tanks had broken through'. One of its officers watched as a troop of the Greys discovered that their vehicles had disappeared and a 'wave of panic set in among some of the men and control, both mass and individual, was lost'. When the gunners' Lieutenant Jack Nagle went forward to investigate he discovered that most of the Australian infantry and almost all the Greys were in headlong flight. 'He endeavoured to rally these troops telling them that the guns would support them but the majority seemed to have no other idea than to get back ... Eventually Nagle got to the south end of the town and held up a trooper carrying his Bren gun to the rear and, on ordering him to stay or give up his gun, the Bren was handed over without ado.'

Nor was his own regiment entirely immune. Four of its vehicles were caught up in the stampede for the nearest Palestinian town of Metulla and it was two days before they returned to their battery by way of Nazareth.

Some of Merjayoun's defenders lingered long enough to be captured having dug themselves in as best they could in rocky ground either side of a road just north of the town. Among them was William Cross, a tall and well-built lance corporal who had joined the Scots Greys from an orphanage as a 15-year-old boy bugler in 1932.

> We were cavalrymen doing an infantryman's job. We hadn't been trained for it, we didn't have much ammunition, and we didn't have much idea what was going on. At about midday we were attacked by Senegalese troops, their legs wrapped in World War One type puttees from knee to ankle, coming through the scrub from the foothills above us. We fired off most of what we had, I don't know whether we hit any, but there were far more of them than us and suddenly they were all around us with bloody great bayonets and these scars on their cheeks, tribal markings I suppose, screaming their ruddy heads off. It was like something out of your worst nightmares. Well it was case of, 'Hands up, credit's up'. Nobody told us to surrender but we would have been dead if we hadn't. As it was, there were a few bad moments when they looked like they were getting ready to shoot us but a French officer stopped them. We were formed up on the road and marched away by some Foreign Legionnaires who had also been involved in the fight. As we moved off one of them, who had heard me talking to a mate, sidled up to me and asked, 'Where you from Jock?' Turned out he was from Glasgow. He told me he had been firing over our heads.

Lance Corporal Cross was a bit sceptical about this but a head count in the truck they were loaded into confirmed that they had suffered no casualties. The Greys were taken via the Bekaa valley and the winding Barada gorge to Damascus where, appropriately enough, their prison was a stone cavalry barracks, a gloomy Ottoman building. They were fed French Army rations. Cross was astonished to be served red wine with every meal including breakfast. 'Of course, the first thing the British soldier misses is his tea. And it was damn cold in that barracks and we wanted something hot.'

Behind them Merjayoun was back in Vichy hands. French close air support had fanned the panic on the roads south of the town with little or no interference from the RAF. For some of the Australians this lack of air cover was Crete all over again. But there was unanimous praise for a Lieutenant Bayliss and his Poms manning a single Bofors gun who stuck resolutely to an exposed ridge line above 'a crowd of struggling vehicles' and picked off a diving Glenn Martin which crashed with a roar of exploding bombs.

For twenty-four hours it looked like the Chasseur d'Afrique's tough little tanks might break into northern Palestine. Even at their slowest speed it was hardly an hour's drive away and, if nothing else, it would have been a marvellous propaganda coup. Then the Australians began to recover and show their mettle. Jezzine, its garrison weakened because a battalion had been sent to help regain Merjayoun, was isolated and virtually under siege but its defenders clung on. This was despite one devastating air attack when seven Lioré et Olivier twin-engined bombers sliced away half of the Hotel Egypt which the 2/31 Battalion were using as a food store and a field kitchen. Among the seventeen dead were four company quartermaster sergeants who were drawing rations. By 18 June this unit had lost thirty-one killed and twenty-seven wounded in the space of forty-eight hours.

On the Merjayoun front itself they fell back to the villages of Khiam and Qleaa, which were near an important fork in the road about 3 miles south of the town, and from there started launching counter-attacks well supported by shellfire. The most feared arm of all the Imperial British land forces was what Rommel called 'the terrible British artillery' and the Australians were no exception. The ideal weapon for lobbing high explosive around steep Lebanese hills was a mortar. The French had quite a lot of them and the Australians very few but their 25-pounder batteries were well served by some daring forward observation officers who were often well ahead of the infantry. Radios were soon discovered to be unreliable, often incapable of transmitting from one valley to the next, and they were almost invariably joined to their guns by a couple of miles of cable for their field telephones which trailed through the rocks and scrub behind them, vulnerable to shellfire and unfriendly eyes. Telephone traffic tended to be two-way and one of the drawbacks was that they came with chirpy bell alarms loud enough to wake the dead or cause you to join them.

'For God's sake don't ring me,' whispered Lieutenant Roden Cutler of the 2/5th Artillery to his battery as the Australian attempt to retake the town hotted up. Together with his signaller, Cutler had managed to insert his 6 foot 5 inch frame into one of Merjayoun's narrow storm drains about 50 yards from the place where the crew of two R35s had chosen to leave their tanks for a chat and a smoke with some Legionnaires. As a result of their presence the 2/5th had been delivering some wickedly well-timed salvos at Vichy convoys coming into town and Butler did not give much for their chances if they discovered the reason why.

Two days before, Cutler had emerged from the ruins of a mud-walled shepherd's hut with Captain Joe Clark, the regiment's senior observation officer, disembowelled and dying, over his shoulder, after two R35s had riddled the building with cannon and machine-gun fire. Cutler and Clark had been sharing the hut with two gunner signallers and a three-man infantry Boys rifle and Bren team when the tanks closed in. Two had been killed outright. Cutler, the only one unscathed, had picked up a Boys and, realizing the R35s armour was too good for it, repeatedly fired at the tracks that also served as their steering mechanism. Gunner Geoffrey Grayson, bleeding profusely from a groin wound, watched with considerable relief as the tank 'slewed around and couldn't fire at us any more'. Then they had staggered downhill into the welcoming arms of the lead infantry company's stretcher-bearers some 200 yards away.

But this time Cutler knew there would be no escape if the Legionnaires discovered, stuffed into what was hardly more than a drainpipe, the reason for the uncannily accurate shellfire they had just endured. Only the dark and the slumbers of an exhausted enemy saved the day. The two men removed their boots, strung them around their necks and tiptoed away to their lines through the marble mausoleums of an outlying Christian cemetery, after which Cutler was nearly shot by an old friend from Sydney University who was commanding a platoon in the most forward Australian position.

There could be little doubt that the Australians would soon be back in Merjayoun. At Ezraa too, the most easterly of de Verdilhac's thrusts, Vichy's success had been short-lived. At first Colonel Bouvier had taken Lloyd by surprise, partly because Collet had indicated that Bouvier shared his own Gaullist sympathies. But Vichy had shown their trust in him, beefing up his small Druze militia, loathed by their mostly Francophobe co-religionists, with Tunisia Tirailleurs, armoured cars and some light artillery. Colonel Genin and his company of Free French Senegalese had not stood much of a chance and poor Genin had died trying to rally them.

Then, against all the odds, Ezraa was recaptured. This was mostly due to the leadership displayed by an Australian-born Hussars officer on secondment to the Transjordan Frontier Force contingent which had been driven out by Bouvier's surprise attack with his armoured cars and Tunisian Tirailleurs. Captain Shan Hackett, a Sandhurst-trained regular from a wealthy Anglo-Irish newspaper family in Perth, took over Genin's counter-attack and turned a disparate collection of about 150 men speaking four different languages into a winning team. Apart from his own Bedouin, he had under his command the remnants of Genin's Senegalese with some junior French officers and about twenty Fusiliers who had missed out on Kuneitra because they had been attached to Lloyd's brigade headquarters. Among them was the crew of one of Orr's missing 37mm Bofors anti-tank guns. Under Hackett's direction this single gun, which was commanded by a Corporal Clark, fired at almost point-blank range at a mud-walled gendarmerie station where some of the Tirailleurs had established a strongpoint. Hackett was wounded in the shoulder and the Tunisians did their best to pick off Clark's crew but the Fusiliers kept punching holes through the mud walls until a white flag went up. Bouvier was among the 200 prisoners and Ezraa was theirs, including the site of a Byzantine church where the Roman knight and England's adopted saint, St George, was believed to be buried.

Perhaps the phlegmatic Welshman Brigadier Lloyd always knew that someone was watching over him. Despite de Verdilhac's counter-attacks, and the painful knowledge of his own contribution to the loss of almost an entire battalion by depriving them of their anti-tank guns, Lloyd had maintained a remarkably cool exterior. Having the enemy sitting on his lines of communication was not allowed to interfere with Lloyd's attack on Damascus which proceeded as if everything had gone according to plan. At Gentforce HQ his staff began to find their battle maps bewildering. 'There had been so many moments when formations of either side had been surrounding each other in concentric circles that my attempts at sketches looked like archery targets,' recalled Major Fergusson of his later attempts to explain what had gone on.

An unexpected bonus for Lloyd was the British failure in Egypt's Western Desert where much to Churchill's distress Operation Battleaxe, the attempt to push Rommel back and end the siege of Tobruk, ended only two days after it began with heavy tank losses. This enabled Wavell to send infantry reinforcements he had been keeping in Egypt, partly as a reserve for Operation Battleaxe if there was a breakthrough and partly to rest them after their experiences in Crete. The first to arrive was the 2nd Queens, which had not quite got to the island having turned back to Alexandria with all the battalion's Bren guns blazing after near misses ignited their ship's deck cargo of 3,500 of the army's notoriously leaky 4-gallon petrol cans. These air attacks caused several casualties and at one point panic below decks when calls for gas masks for the fire-fighting parties were misinterpreted as news that poison gas had been added to their miseries.

After this the Queens' recapture of Kuneitra turned out to be a relatively mild affair when, in extended order with bayonets fixed, they followed the bombardment of a lone 25-pounder into town and took one casualty from the departing Vichy rearguard. De Verdilhac had evidently decided not to risk his precious R35s down a long road where they might be cut off and stranded without fuel. After the Queens came the pince-nezed VC winner Arthur Blackburn's Australian machine gunners with their accompanying anti-tank guns. With them was a scouting screen of about sixty mounted yeomanry of the Yorkshire Dragoons and two of the Palestine Police's locally made armoured cars, which were no more than boiler plate welded to a truck chassis and armed with the same Vickers Blackburn's men used. Their policemen crews were mostly ex-British army.

By 18 June Lloyd, no doubt secretly relieved that his main supply routes had been restored, was ready to launch Gentforce's attack on Damascus. It was to be a two-pronged affair down both main approach roads, no feints. The Free French would be on the right on the Deraa–Damascus road starting from Kissoué, which was about 10 miles away from the city. The Indian battalions would be on the left on the Kuneitra–Damascus road. Their job was to seize the strongly defended village and airfield of Mezze just south-west of the city wall and thus cut its road and rail links to Beirut. Colonel Lionel Jones, normally battalion commander of 4th Rajputana Rifles, was now temporarily in charge of 5th Indian Brigade following Legentilhomme's wounding and Lloyd's elevation to force commander. At Gentforce HQ, where there was considerable foreboding, an apprehensive Major Fergusson watched Jones receive his orders.

> The colonel pondered them, looking at his own map, consulting his pencilled notes. At last he looked direct at Lloyd and: 'I think you're condemning my men to death, Sir.' Lloyd looked back at him and said: 'If you won't do it, I'll have to find somebody who will.' There was a long pause; there was not a sound; my heart was bleeding for the colonel. At last he said: 'In that case, of course I'll do it.'

On the eve of battle most of the Indian infantry were concentrated on the Jebel Madani, some low hills with good fields of fire between the two main roads. Now for the first time binoculars revealed, beyond the green of the Ghouta Gardens, Damascus's minarets dancing in the heat haze. Vichy troops had made three attempts to probe their positions: twice with armoured cars and finally with a cavalry action Lord Cardigan might have arranged involving a couple of hundred Spahis with appropriate musical accompaniment. Fergusson had just finished visiting forward positions when he heard the North Africans' bugles. He dashed back to the skyline in time to view the immediate aftermath of this uncharacteristically unprofessional behaviour.

> The scene was like that of an old print with riderless horses and running men making back for the shelter of the Ghouta and others twitching on the plain, horses and men alike ... It was a spirited performance but they hadn't a hope of reaching their objective even though the Indian troops, unable to believe their eyes, had withheld their fire for an appreciable time. I have never discovered who ordered it – if it was ordered – or who led it.

It was the hottest time of the year, nearly summer's longest day, and well over 100°F at midday. Young men from the Punjab wearing steel helmets sat in sangars of scorching stone and observed Indian Army water discipline never to drink unless their water bottles could be immediately replenished. Then they died of heat stroke. Fergusson recalled 'several cases'.

In the afternoon, having been relieved by the Free French Marines, the Indians came down from their positions, cooled off in the stream at the foot of the hills, prepared and ate some chapatis then sat about drinking sugary tea and smoking while they checked their weapons and primed grenades. The wise tried to grab some sleep. The plan for the assault on Mezze was that they would keep off the road itself and night march for about 12 miles across the country to the west and parallel to the highway. Meanwhile, their towed anti-tank guns and transport carrying ammunition, rations and all the brigade's radios and their operators, which had to stay on the road, would crawl behind them hoping that Mezze would be taken long before the Vichy air force was up.

They set out at about 8.30 p.m. heading more or less into the setting sun. Their first contact with the enemy came some ninety minutes later near the fortified hamlet of Mouaddamiya. In the pitch dark of a wood about sixty Punjabis surprised a mostly sleeping R35 laager, scattered or killed their crews and destroyed several unclosed and unmanned tanks by introducing grenades to their full 37mm cannon magazines. Punjabi casualties, killed and wounded, mounted as the French got over their shock, and fixed positions had to be stormed. 'Only 27 reached the end of the wood but the enemy was obliterated and the main column able to move on,' wrote the novelist Compton Mackenzie in *Eastern Approaches*, his monumental history of the old British Indian Army's war.

Mezze was reached at 4.15 a.m., shortly before dawn and once again surprise was complete. 'There was a French barracks lit up like a Christmas tree,' remembered Frank Caldwell, an attached sapper lieutenant just turned 20 who had won a Military Cross in Libya for the mine clearing that cut the Italians off at Beda Fomm. After just over an hour of hard fighting through its high walled streets, during which a Punjabi subadar led a charge that captured two 75mm field guns, the village was in British hands.

Colonel Jones set up his headquarters in the northern part of the village at Mezze House, formerly the home of the British representative of the Iraqi Petroleum Company. This was a big two-storeyed, double-fronted villa of dark pink stucco with large shuttered windows in its high-ceilinged rooms, built in about half an acre of garden. It was surrounded by a high wall that made it almost invisible. On one side were dense citrus orchards and on the other a street leading directly from its blind drive to the village square. It had running water, there was a pump in the kitchen, beer and wine in its cellar and in the garage a good supply of canned petrol for its missing car. With Jones's brigade HQ personnel were the battalion headquarters of both 3/1 Punjabis and 4th Rajputana Rifles and a rifle company each from both regiments. Assuming by now they were all a bit under strength this would be about 250 men, perhaps a little more. They had ushered some fifty prisoners into the garden.

As planned, two companies of the Rajputs had circumvented the village, beaten off an attack by some Vichy cavalry, secured the place where the road and rail links to Beirut met at a level crossing and began raising merry hell. Reports came back of a train, packed with civilians, sent back to Damascus and the line blown behind it; a seven-truck convoy destroyed. Soon a black column of smoke showed they had added a fuel dump to their score.

At this point Jones may well have been regretting his outburst to Lloyd about 'condemning my men to death'. Casualties were light for what had been achieved. All he was waiting for now was the rest of the brigade to catch up and consolidate Mezze to prepare for the inevitable counter-attack. Two Punjabi companies, including the one that had surprised the tank crews at Mouaddamiya, were clearing the high ground to the west and bringing up the rear were his Bombay Sappers and Miners, the detached Fusilier company that had not been at Kuneitra, and a battery of 25-pounders. There was also the brigade's transport column with their ammunition and rations and, above all, the 2-pounder anti-tank guns. They had lost contact with them, though that was not all that surprising because as they neared their objective they had moved well away from the road. Colonel Jones would have liked to be able to radio Gentforce to confirm that they were on schedule, but the radios and their operators were with them.

According to Fergusson, the first news they had that Jones's transport was in trouble was when a wounded British officer, 'pale and with five bullet wounds', staggered into their headquarters and explained what had happened. Although they thought they were driving slowly enough, they had overtaken the entire column and only come to a halt when their lead trucks had been wrecked by the anti-tank and heavy machine guns of a Vichy ambush. Those vehicles that could still move had gone back and were hoping to find a navigable track through the foothills west of the road.

Meanwhile, de Verdilhac had sent some of his R35s to clear the Rajputs' roadblock on the Beirut road. The Indians had fallen back on Mezze in good order expecting that their anti-tank guns would be in place and the Vichy armour lured onto them. Instead, as the infantry melted into its side streets, the R35s entered the straggling village unheralded and almost unopposed apart from the occasional crack and screaming ricochet made by an optimistic Rajput with a Boys rifle. Caldwell was standing outside the high garden wall at brigade headquarters chatting to two other young officers when the first tank announced its presence with a burst from its Riebel which broke the leg of one of his companions. The sapper crawled over and helped drag him into cover. The siege of Mezze House had started.

Jones was holding a smaller perimeter than Orr had started with at

Kuneitra: the villa and its walled garden, where in places the brick was soft enough to make loopholes, and some of the orange orchards to the rear. One of the retreating Rajputana companies from the Beirut roadblock was cut off in a small house and forced to surrender when the tanks began to dismantle it with cannon fire. But the other got back to Jones who now had almost 400 men to defend his headquarters, and he and his officers, British and Indian, made it plain with every order they gave that help was on the way and there would be no surrender here.

Slit trenches were dug in the garden, Boys rifles sited where it was hoped they might do the most damage. Bed sheets were torn up for bandages in case field dressings gave out. Oranges were gathered from the orchards and a few vegetables from the garden, for it was nearly twenty-four hours since they had last eaten anything. Up from the cellar came the absent oil man's wines and beer, down the kitchen sink went their contents, or perhaps some of their contents. Into the bottles went the petrol from the garage, then the necks were crammed with the doused rags that made the fuse of these crude Molotov cocktails.

As at Kuneitra the tanks were accompanied by West African riflemen. Mackenzie tells how the veterans of Eritrea 'kept the infernal Senegalese from getting close'. But not always. One managed to get a rifle grenade through the window of an upstairs room where Jones was holding a conference. Jones was unscathed but shrapnel mortally wounded Lieutenant Colonel Henry Greatwood, commander of 3/1 Punjabis, leaving Captain John Robertson in charge of those elements of his battalion at Mezze House. Robertson, aged 30, was not a professional soldier but a Darjeeling tea planter who had been wounded at Sidi Barrani during the first flush of victories against the Italians and had missed Eritrea. Now he went round encouraging his men in the Urdu he had learned as a child, making sure the Molotovs were equally distributed and, above all, seeing that they tried to make every shot count. Most of the riflemen were probably about a third of their way through the 160 rounds they had started with and all the reserve ammunition was with their missing transport.

By dusk, which came at about 8.30, there was a lull. Unlike the Fusiliers they had managed to destroy at least one of the R35s with their Molotovs, possibly once their crew had abandoned it after a track had been broken with a Boys. At one point the Senegalese had entered part of the garden and been repulsed with Brens, grenades and a bayonet charge. The well-led Indians do not seem to have been physically intimidated by the larger Africans.

They could hear the sound of artillery and machine-gun fire from Mezze airport about a mile away but there was still no sign of the rest of the brigade. For all Jones knew Gentforce had assumed they had surrendered and decided to concentrate on the Free French sector. Mezze House was more or less encircled and he had two choices: abandon the wounded and try to fight his way out or hold on. Meanwhile, three officers were to try to slip through the cordon and get word of their plight to Gentforce. One was his Gaullist liaison officer who might be able to bluff his way past sentries. The other two were an Indian jemadar and the sapper officer Caldwell.

They left as soon as it was dark, crawling through a hole in the wall at about 8.45. Caldwell had a compass and led the way. Gentforce headquarters was no more than 15 miles away and, with any luck, provided they evaded the Vichy French in the immediate vicinity, they might meet up with a British patrol long before they reached it. As it happened it took all night. They walked every step of the way, getting out of Mezze by way of its flat rooftops, climbing walls, wading steams and, worst misery of all, scrambling through hedges of prickly pear cactus. It was 5.30 before senior officers were being gently woken from their slumbers to listen to the exhausted trio relate the latest calamity to befall 5th Indian Brigade.

Far from shifting the emphasis of the attack to the Free French sector the British were experiencing a good deal of foot dragging on the part of the Gaullists who had begun to display a marked reluctance to fight other Frenchmen. The rot had started with Colonel Magrin-Vernet, the Foreign Legion firebrand who had adopted the nom de guerre Monclar and commanded the Narvik veterans of the Legion's 13th Demi-Brigade. Monclar had resigned as Legentilhomme's overall infantry commander, unable to stomach another clash with old comrades of the 6th Foreign Legion cast by the fortunes of war on the Vichy side. Much to Lloyd's disgust, instead of taking the pressure off the Indians with the planned attack down the Deraa–Damascus road the Gaullists had stayed put at Kissoué. 'It is doubtful whether they can be persuaded to advance against even feeble resistance,' reported one senior British officer.

At this delicate moment Legentilhomme, his arm in a sling, resumed his leadership of Gentforce and Lloyd reverted to command of what was left of 5th Indian Brigade. A relief column was immediately despatched to Mezze under Major Patrick Bourke, a gunner officer who, as an answer to de Verdilhac's tanks, was bringing with him a battery of twelve 25-pounder guns. His command would also include the three infantry companies – two Punjabi and one Fusilier – that were not with Jones plus the missing anti-tank guns.

Now occurred on the battle maps another of Fergusson's puzzling concentric circles. At Mezze House the fighting had resumed at dawn as the thin wisps of wood smoke rose from the fires in the garden where the Indians were brewing tea. It had started a bit like an orchestra tuning up: the crack of single shots followed by bursts from the various automatics, then the heavier sound of the R35's stubby little cannon and afterwards, if the tank had ventured close enough, the soft whumph of a petrol bomb. By noon the battle noise was much fiercer. It had been joined by the sound of Bourke's towed 25-pounders. They were not behind the infantry but alongside them and sometimes even in front of them as they advanced, unlimbered, and fired until they were close enough to do it over open sights. To counter this de Verdilbac sent in fresh troops from the sector facing the Gaullists. These fought back to back with the Senegalese and the tanks trying to finish the stubborn resistance at Mezze House.

Then Lloyd turned up with some reinforcements of his own: Australian infantry of Lieutenant Colonel David Lamb's 2/3 Battalion, an understrength unit that had been in Egypt recovering from Crete and had been sent to replace Orr's Fusiliers. The newly arrived Vichy troops began to fall back. Around Mezze House there was renewed determination to finish the siege and two 75mm field guns, which might well have been better employed against Bourke's battery, started firing down the street from the village square that led directly to the house. A shell collapsed a roof section over one of the shuttered rooms where the wounded were lying and while a rescue party were trying to extract them from the rubble some of the Senegalese dashed through a hole in the garden wall. Robertson emptied his revolver at them and led the bayonet charge that drove out those who could still stand, but to Colonel Jones it was obvious that his exhausted men, short of sleep, food and ammunition, could not hold out much longer.

With Lloyd's relief force no more than a mile away he decided to play for time and sent a captured Vichy officer out with a white flag to parley for a truce so that he could evacuate his wounded and bury the dead in the garden. But as soon as they saw the flag the Senegalese rushed in, shooting two Rajputs who tried to bar their passage with fixed bayonets. Only the hasty intervention of their French adjutant-chef prevented them from killing Jones and the other surviving officers who were gathered in a corner of the garden. It was all over.

Four hours later, at about 6 p.m. Fergusson reached Mezze House with Major Bourke and Brigadier Lloyd.

> One side of the house had collapsed; within the walls were just over 100 bodies. Three burned-out Vichy tanks lay just outside the garden. We found in a hospital afterwards an Indian medical officer who had been left behind with the surviving wounded and he told us the rest of the story ... They had not so much surrendered as been overwhelmed.

Yet, as far as Jumbo Wilson was concerned, this dismal scene marked the turning point of the battle for the city because it had sucked in so many of de Verdilhac's troops. 'It shook the French defence,' he wrote in his memoirs, where he also has Jones's Indians fighting 'to the last man and the last round' which hardly ever happens though, if it did not quite end in a banzai charge, there was heroism almost of that order.

That night Lamb's Australians swept through Mezze, began to capture the forts on the ridge above the airfield and cut the Beirut road a little lower than the Rajputs had two days before. Telephone poles were pulled down for a roadblock and soon they had captured so many vehicles they were complaining of a parking problem. But most of de Verdilhac's garrison, taking their Indian prisoners with them, escaped north to Homs. Some stayed there. Others went, via the northern port of Tripoli, the roundabout way to Beirut then climbed almost back to Damascus to the Barada gorge in Hermon range. Their task was to stop the British descending the winding road from the Syrian capital to the Lebanese coast.

Vichy France quit Damascus on the morning of 21 June. General Legentilhomme, its new military governor, made his entrance in the afternoon though not with all the pomp and circumstance he would have liked. Blackburn's machine gunners, irritated by the lacklustre performance of the Free French forces they had been supporting, were determined that they would be first into the city. Just as the Gaullists were about to get into the limousines provided by the city fathers the Australians, packed into open trucks and waving Digger hats, spoilt Legentilhomme's parade by overtaking it with whoops of triumph and a cloud of dust. The wounded general, his arm still in a sling, made a valiant attempt to interpose his body then leapt aside.

'I didn't have the guts to try,' recalled Fergusson. 'We brushed each other down and got back into the cars. The Vichy troops had fought with skill and courage, and our victory, if it could be so described, was rather hollow; but all the same Damascus was ours.'

The next day, on a front that stretched from the Baltic to the Black Sea, 3.6 million German and other Axis troops invaded Russia with about 3,600 tanks and 2,700 aircraft and the news from Syria fell off the front page.

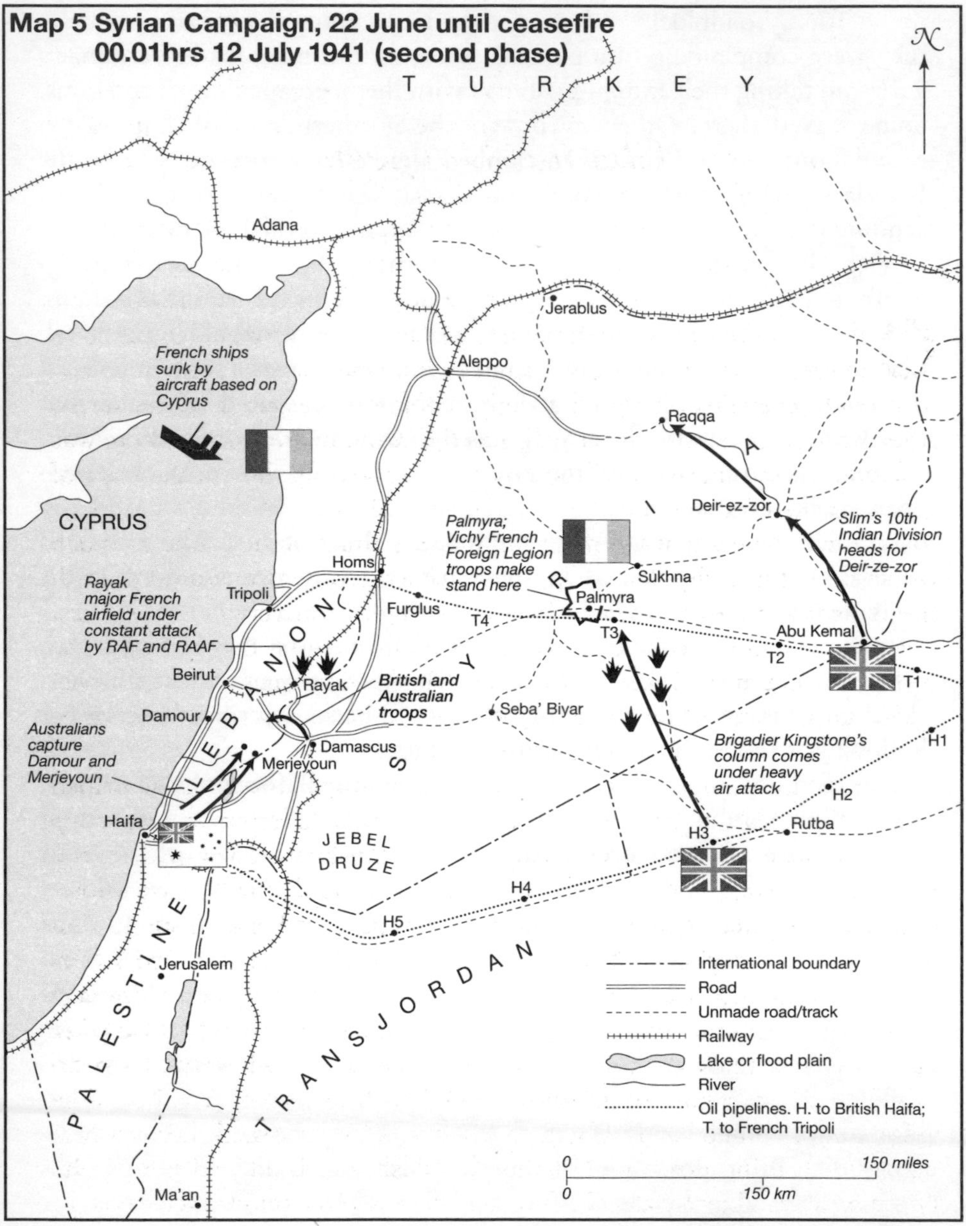

Map 5 Syrian Campaign, 22 June until ceasefire 00.01hrs 12 July 1941 (second phase)
TURKEY
Adana
Jerablus
Aleppo
Raqqa
French ships sunk by aircraft based on Cyprus
CYPRUS
SYRIA
Deir-ez-zor
Slim's 10th Indian Division heads for Deir-ze-zor
Palmyra; Vichy French Foreign Legion troops make stand here
Sukhna
Palmyra
Homs
Tripoli
Furglus
T4
T3
Abu Kemal
T2
T1
Rayak major French airfield under constant attack by RAF and RAAF
LEBANON
Beirut
Rayak
British and Australian troops
Damour
Seba' Biyar
Damascus
Australians capture Damour and Merjeyoun
Merjeyoun
Brigadier Kingstone's column comes under heavy air attack
H1
H2
Haifa
JEBEL DRUZE
H3
Rutba
H4
H5
PALESTINE
Jerusalem
TRANSJORDAN
Ma'an
International boundary
Road
Unmade road/track
Railway
Lake or flood plain
River
Oil pipelines. H. to British Haifa; T. to French Tripoli
0
150 miles
0
150 km

Chapter Nineteen

One of the duties of Beirut police headquarters, that seemed able to maintain an Ottoman sufficiency of informers at small expense, was to provide Dentz's office with a daily report on the mood in the street. After Damascus fell they informed the High Commissioner that there was 'uncertainty and unease' and food prices were soaring though the price of gold remained stable.

But Dentz knew that Germany's blitzkrieg attack on Russia was much worse news for Vichy Beirut. Even the Wehrmacht was unlikely to finish the job in time to rescue them by hitting the English hard enough elsewhere. Certainly, it had put back the prospect of an invasion of England until the spring of 1942 at the earliest. Nor could there be any question of Rommel receiving the kind of reinforcements that would make his entry into Cairo inevitable and even threaten Palestine and Iraq.

Meanwhile, though L'Armée du Levant was not yet throttled, the British were undoubtedly tightening their grip. In a moonlight attack during the early hours of 16 June, Fleet Air Arm Swordfish operating from RAF Nicosia in nearby Cyprus had torpedoed and sunk the French super-destroyer *Chevalier Paul* which was trying to get into Beirut from Toulon under cover of darkness. The Swordfish were off the carrier HMS *Formidable* which towards the end of May had suffered severe bomb damage while getting aircraft off to Malta and was under repair. The *Chevalier Paul* was less than 30 miles from the Syrian coast when the torpedo exploded in an engine room and seven French sailors were killed. The vessel almost immediately began to list but before she sank her gunners managed to bring down one of the Swordfish which ditched nearby. Its two-man crew, Lieutenant Clifford and Sub-Lieutenant Winter, took to their dinghy and were picked up with the 251 survivors from the *Chevalier Paul* by the Beirut-based destroyers *Guépard* and *Valmy*.

The sinking persuaded the French that they must play to their strengths and use transport aircraft. At this point they were still just about maintaining air superiority because one of the Hurricane squadrons was almost constantly employed trying to defend the Royal Navy and Haifa from the Luftwaffe's Junkers 88s on Rhodes. An air bridge was started via Luftwaffe bases at Athens and Salonika with various types pressed into service including some of Air France's long-nosed tri-motor Dewoitine D338s, a slow, noisy aircraft that once flew the Croydon–Le Bourget route. But the carrying capacity of these aircraft was very small. One medium-sized shipload would have been worth more than a month of air bridge.

On land, Jumbo Wilson had at last decided that Iraq was sufficiently pacified to do what Raoul de Verdilhac had expected him to do in the first place and open up a front on Syria's eastern desert border. They would come from two directions. Habforce, as it was still known, though in tranquil Habbaniya the siege now seemed like a bad dream, would start by capturing Palmyra where the first German aircraft bound for Iraq were spotted at its airfield. Once they had Palmyra they were expected to dash west along the Tripoli oil pipeline for Homs. Now that Damascus had fallen, possession of Homs's road and rail junction would make Dentz's Beirut even more isolated, cutting links with Aleppo and the entire northern Syrian hinterland up to the Turkish border.

At the same time this area was to be occupied by newly promoted Major General Bill Slim's 10th Indian Division which had come up from Basra. Slim, the Gurkha officer who had made his name in Eritrea, was to follow the Euphrates to Deir Ez Zor, capture this garrison town and the magnificent suspension bridge the French had built, then proceed north-westwards to Aleppo itself. This would deny L'Armée du Levant all the munitions stored there as well as weakening French air power by reducing the dispersal of their aircraft. Overcrowded airfields were within easy range of the RAF. However, since this had yet to be achieved it all started very badly.

Once again Habforce's vanguard was Brigadier Joe Kingstone's 4th Cavalry Brigade: contingents from the Warwickshire and Wiltshire Yeomanry, the Household Cavalry, the 1st Essex, Squadron Leader Cassano's nine RAF armoured cars, about 350 of Glubb's Girls who had proved their worth in Iraq and some newcomers in the form of a troop of Australian anti-tank gunners who had been in Crete and were looking forward to a campaign without Stukas. There were a few staff cars, ambulances, petrol and water bowsers and signals trucks crammed with wireless equipment, but most people were packed into yellow-painted 3-ton trucks of one kind or another, some of them stolen from the Iraqi Army for, according to the ceasefire, they were supposed to have returned all booty.

The Arabs once thought Palmyra a beautiful place and called it the Bride of the Desert. It was the oasis city whose rebel Queen Zenobia had ended up being paraded in Rome in golden chains and only saved from execution by marriage to a senator. Long after Zenobia's rule it was a caravan stop on the Silk Route to China. Then for almost half a millennium it slumbered and decayed in the casual embrace of Turkey's Ottoman

Empire. Twenty years of French rule had brought a little tourism but in 1941 Palmyra was a small, dusty place with some interesting ruins and half a dozen mostly mothballed hotels.

Kingstone's column set off from the British oil pipeline at pumping station H3 (Haifa 3) and headed north for T3 (Tripoli 3) on the French pipeline which was close to the town. On the meandering camel tracks available, the distance Kingcol had to cover was about 160 miles. Once he got there the brigadier intended to attack the place from all points of the compass. Its garrison was thought to be no more than 500 strong, a mixture of Foreign Legion, air force ground crew, and the 3rd Desert Light Company, French-officered Arabs from the Syrian tribes who considered themselves something of an elite. Somewhere nearby there were two more of these Compagnies Légères du Désert, the first and the second.

The invaders crossed the frontier between British Jordan and French Syria at a point marked by two stone cairns with a short line of boulders either side of them. Shortly afterwards Glubb's Arabs, who were scouting slightly ahead, fell upon an isolated Vichy listening post and took about ten prisoners. Among them were European signals personnel. These may have got a message off before their wireless was smashed, though even if they had not the chances of the force making a surprise attack were slim. Well over 100 vehicles were approaching Palmyra across a pitiless desert plain and their dust was visible for miles from any patrolling aircraft.

Among the vehicles in Kingstone's brigade headquarters, which was in about the middle of the column, was an American left-hand-drive car with its front passenger seat occupied by a French prisoner. He was a broad-shouldered man with a small gingerish beard, wearing a high-crowned, red-topped flat military cap, a khaki shirt and buff-coloured jodhpur-style trousers that ended in bare feet and sandals. This was the sergent-chef who been in charge of the listening post when the Arab Legion fell upon it, vandalizing not only its radio set but also his spectacles, which had been lying nearby.

'He was quite amiable but blinked from the loss of his glasses,' recalled Captain Somerset de Chair, the French-speaking Conservative Member of Parliament and the brigade's intelligence officer, who was at the wheel of the vehicle so that he could gently interrogate their captive. Banished to the back among the rolled maps of Palmyra, Homs and Aleppo were his driver and a Christian Arab available for any Arabic-speaking prisoners Vichy might provide. The sergent-chef had been delivered to the intelligence officer together with all the documents and papers, both personal and professional, scooped up with him. Apart from his radio log, which indicated a boring desert vigil, these included a paperback edition of the French translation of *Mein Kampf* and a letter dated before the British invasion from his brother, a capitaine Merjayoun recently arrived from France and evidently pleased to have 'escaped the Boche'.

De Chair had been instructed by Kingstone to try to discover from his prisoner how many and what type of aircraft were operating from Palmyra airfield. The brigadier, who had been warned from the outset that the RAF lacked the resources to give him proper cover, was only too aware how vulnerable his column was to air attack. But though the sergent-chef seemed happy to talk about the troops at Palmyra, pointing out that since the cavalry officer Colonel Collet's defection they must know all there was to know anyway, he would not or could not give any clue about the French aircraft strength there. However, there soon began a practical demonstration.

> We had been going for some hours now and the Column was again halted. We were in a defile between high sandstone hills. I walked over to Joe [Kingstone] and told him what the prisoner had said . . . I looked up and saw, sharp yellow against the bright blue sky, three aircraft flying down the length of our column towards me. They were not too high up for me to distinguish at a glance the blue, white and red circles under the wings and the twin engines which made me take them for our familiar Blenheims. Even as I watched I saw three bright yellow eggs begin to fall against the blue and my mind, slowly somersaulting to the horrid truth, warned me that there was something quite wrong with the picture. I threw myself down on the hard ground and the bombs burst 75 yards away, blowing the forearm off an officer of the new Australian anti-tank troop.

This was the start of over a week of intensive daylight air attacks against Kingcol. In a single day, Sunday, 22 June, when the eyes of the world were on the news from Russia, the bombers and fighters of L'Armée de L'Air flew a total of 112 sorties against them. And this was only the second day. Vichy's Glenn Martins, Moranes and Dewoitines almost achieved for the Palmyra garrison, which was even smaller than the British suspected, what the Audax and Oxford trainers did for besieged RAF Habbaniya. If Kingcol did not succumb to the kind of rout inflicted on Rashid Ali's army it was probably only because they were much more dispersed.

As it was, the French aircrews turned what the British expected to be a mere bump along the road to Homs into a muddled siege. Most of the Legionnaires and the others in the Palmyra garrison were in a line of concrete pill boxes with plenty of barbed wire around them and excellent fields of fire. Every time Kingstone's formations tried to close with them they were bombed and strafed. Pleas for direct fighter cover were initially ignored because RAF policy at this stage remained one of attacking their airfields where French aircraft were at their most vulnerable.

No doubt this was the right tactical decision but it was not very good for Kingcol's morale. All they had to fight back with were light machine guns and the chances of shooting anything down were slim. When the batman of the Household Cavalry's corporal serjeant major picked up a Bren gun and won a duel with a Morane flown by a Lieutenant Seinturier, who fatally crashed, it was considered sufficiently unusual to merit an immediate award of the Military Medal. At one point de Chair saw the Australian anti-tank gunners, who said it was much worse than Crete, firing their single-shot 2-pounders skywards in what was probably the ballistic equivalent of a lottery ticket. The French aircraft were much faster than the RAF trainers above the plateau at Habbaniya and though some were damaged enough to crash-land at base it did not stop their crews from returning to the fray any more than it had Squadron Leader Dudgeon's men.

When any part of Kingstone's column thought they were about to come under air attack the standard procedure was to slam on the brakes and get well clear of the vehicles. Only then might they engage a low-flying tormentor with whatever small arms they had remembered to bring with them. It was every man for himself. Ambulance crews were expected to abandon their stretcher cases. 'Without them we should have been even worse off,' observed de Chair.

The intelligence officer had just noted how the bomb explosions were black 'tinged with a yellow fringe of sand', when he was wounded standing at the open door of the American car with his phlegmatic prisoner still in the passenger seat. One aircraft had already come low enough for him to feel its slipstream and, for want of anything else to do, he had picked up a camera.

> I should, of course, have seized my prisoner by the arm and shouted, 'Come on, mon vieux', and legged it ... But his calm seemed to freeze my own pride and I remained. Besides, vaguely at the back of my mind, was the idea that he could drive off to Palmyra with all the Brigade secrets. So I turned back, facing the desert, placing a helmet on my head and holding the stupid camera with the other ... My ankle felt a crashing blow, the ground throbbed around me. I looked down at my leg. Blood was pumping out in great gulps, pouring down over my khaki stocking into my shoe and spilling onto the desert. My left hand was also bleeding. I got up on one leg and hopped around the back of the car to the other side. The prisoner was still in his seat, undamaged, while the windows of the car were starred with holes and part of the windscreen was shot away. The Frenchman said, '*Vous êtes blessé alors?*' I took a handkerchief out of the pocket of my shorts and asked him if he could tie it tightly around the wound to stop the bleeding. He sat beside me on the running board and made a tight knot. Then I asked if he could drive me to the ambulance.

De Chair had five injuries, the worst in the left ankle where a lot of the nerves and sinews that control the foot were wrecked. The following afternoon he received two more flesh wounds after the ambulance he and three other stretcher cases had spent the night in jerked to a halt with a screech of brakes and there was nobody behind the wheel when they were strafed by a low-flying fighter. De Chair found himself repeating a childhood prayer and fixated by a tiny metal flake spinning inches from his face around the corner of a shattered window 'until it dashed into my eye socket where it drew blood under my eyebrow'. He also had a bullet graze on his right calf but two of his companions were more seriously injured, one man bleeding from a fresh hole in a foot and the other in a leg which de Chair, easing himself gingerly down from his stretcher, bandaged with a towel. The fourth man had put on his helmet and hopped clear of the vehicle which de Chair discovered to be a total wreck. 'The tyres were all in shreds, the engine holed and bullets through the body. The white circle, with its brilliant red cross, stared reproachfully at the sky. With the vehicle standing still, abandoned by the driver as it had been, the emblem must have been clearly visible at 200 yards, when the pilot fired his burst.'

At 300mph plus, adrenaline up and attacking one vehicle after another, a pilot's ability to recognize and react to a red cross in time is probably as debatable as de Chair's bewildered anger is understandable. One day a French prisoner is bandaging your wound, the next his compatriot is machine-gunning your ambulance. In June 1941 the desert around Palmyra was a bewildering and angry place. One troop of Wiltshire Yeomanry lost thirteen of its seventeen vehicles and thanked their lucky stars that, of the four that remained, one was the water tanker. Thanks to the 'stop and scatter' policy, casualties were relatively low though in some units so was morale. There developed an understandable reluctance to leave slit trenches and drive anywhere in daylight. Among those who became, to use the euphemism of the day, 'bomb happy' and had to be evacuated to Palestine or Iraq was de Chair's Arab interpreter.

Another was Brigadier Kingstone himself, who drove himself hard but was nearing his forty-ninth birthday and, despite his exertions, still carried a few more pounds than suited desert campaigning. After four sleepless days of it the man who had taken Kingcol to Baghdad, and would be awarded a bar to his 1918 DSO for doing so, cracked up and was delivered to a military hospital in Jerusalem. De Chair, who was also mending there, saw the former Sandhurst instructor and commandant of the army's famous School of Equitation at Weedon, 'staring ahead with unseeing eyes', and felt for his humiliation. Kingstone was popular among his officers who were furious that Jumbo Wilson's staff, 'behind the stout defences of their mahogany desks', had so blithely allowed the brigade to go into action without air cover.

The RAF persisted in trying to reduce L'Armee de l'Air by concentrating its attacks on its airfields and, frequent though these were, often found the

French oddly unprepared for them. Roald Dahl, an entirely British product of Norwegian parents long settled in England, had joined the RAF in Kenya where he had just started working for Shell. He was 6 foot 6 and much too tall to be crammed into a fighter cockpit. Nonetheless, he flew Hurricanes in 80 Squadron and had been blooded against the Luftwaffe in Greece. His squadron's main task was to protect the Haifa warships on their shore bombardment sorties up the coast that were sometimes attacked by Junkers 88 from Rhodes and Vichy Glenn Martins at the same time. But one weekend they found themselves switched to a ground attack on the French fighter station at Rayak in the Bekaa valley. They arrived at about lunchtime, sweeping low over the field.

> We saw to our astonishment a bunch of girls in brightly coloured cotton dresses standing out by the planes with glasses in their hands having drinks with the French pilots, and I remember seeing bottles of wine standing on the wings of one plane as we went swooshing over. It was a Sunday and the French men were evidently entertaining their girl friends and showing off their aircraft to them, which was a very French thing to do in the middle of a war at a front-line aerodrome. Every one of us held our fire on that first pass flying over the flying field and it was wonderfully comical to see the girls all dropping their wine glasses and galloping in their high heels for the door of the nearest building. We went around again but this time we were no longer a surprise and they were ready for us with their ground defences, and I am afraid that our chivalry resulted in damage to several of our Hurricanes, including my own.

Nonetheless, they succeeded in destroying some aircraft, though possibly not the five Dahl claimed. Undoubtedly the most successful airfield strike was delivered a few days later by the Australians of 3 RAAF Squadron who were the only pilots over Syria flying the American-built P40s which all the British Commonwealth air forces called Tomahawks. Nine of them took off from a newly rolled refuelling airstrip at the H5 pumping station and raided the French field at Homs, west of Palmyra, where they discovered over twenty Dewoitine 520s parked a little closer than was wise. In ten seconds they had turned five into blazing, broken-backed wrecks, badly damaged six more, and left eleven others in need of minor repairs. Exploding ammunition killed a French pilot and three mechanics. Then they flew to Rayak, which never seemed to be neglected, where they destroyed another Dewoitine, three Potez bombers and holed two more aircraft. Next they found some motor transport to shoot up, though, unlike Kingcol, the vehicles were protected by a Bofors-style light anti-aircraft battery. One of the Tomahawks, flown by a Sergeant Bailie, was badly holed but Bailie managed to keep it airborne long enough to make a belly landing in British Mandate Palestine just north of the Sea of Galilee.

Tomahawks had not been operational for long and they soon acquired a reputation for giving and taking punishment. Yet at first the Australians had loathed them. The squadron had seen six months continuous desert action, chalked up fifty kills against their Italian and German opponents and during the course of it experienced no difficulty in swapping their Gladiators for Hurricanes. Then a few weeks prior to the Syrian invasion they had been sent to an airfield near Tel Aviv for some well-earned rest before they became another Desert Air Force squadron to convert to Tomahawks. This was expected to take these experienced and adaptable pilots a matter of days.

Nineteen crashed P40s later, none fatal and few write-offs but much more than the RAF could afford, they were being reprimanded by Air Vice-Marshal Tedder, the senior air force officer in the Middle East, who told the Air Ministry: 'The Australians are unexpectedly making very heavy weather over the Tomahawks but I have applied a little ginger which, I hope, will have the necessary effect.'

It was not until the end of 1940, shortly after the Battle of Britain was won, that the RAF took delivery of its first Curtiss Wright P40 Tomahawks. They were part of an order for 230 the French government had placed with its American manufacturer that had been lost to the armistice. When they arrived in England their instrument panels were still in French. But by then the Darwinian demands of the summer's fighting over southern England had led to extraordinary leaps of evolution in single-seater fighters as both sides adapted to survive. Continuous improvements to engine power, armament and armour meant that the P40s were not in the same league as the latest marks of Spitfires or Messerschmitts. British fighter pilots also found them difficult to put down because they required a flatter two-point landing whereby wing wheels touch first then the tail wheel rather than the simultaneous contact of a three-point. This was the Australians problem with them. Once test flights confirmed that they were not good enough for Europe they were shipped to the Middle East.

The Desert Air Force learned to love them. They were better than their early model Hurricanes. More important, they were better than the early model Messerschmitts supporting the Afrika Korps. They might have had slow rates of climb, and at high altitudes stagger drunkenly about in stratospheric disarray, but lower down they turned out to be nimble dogfighters and excellent in ground attack. Until, towards the end of the year, the Germans diverted some of their later Messerschmitts to Africa, there was an unexpected interlude of British air superiority in the desert war.

When 3 RAAF Squadron entered Syria they soon discovered that what applied in the desert applied even more in the French Levant. Their Tomahawks were more than a match for L'Armée de l'Air's Dewoitine 520s which looked and performed like Hawker Hurricanes though, since most had led a more mothballed existence, they sometimes had the edge over their sand-sore doppelgängers. On the other side of the ledger, two of the Dewoitine squadron commanded by Sous-lieutenant Pierre Le Gloan, who was emerging as the French ace of the Syrian campaign, had been shot down by tighter turning Gladiator biplanes at no loss to themselves.

Increasingly shrill demands for air cover from Kingcol had led to the RAF reluctantly ordering Tomahawks to pay occasional visits to Palmyra's desert environs though, without the assistance of ground radar, it was realized that the chances of them coinciding with a French sortie were remote. Nonetheless, on the day before their devastating attack on the Homs airfield they had brought down three twin-engined Lioré et Olivier 451s, a good-looking twin-engined bomber, its 300mph envisaged by its designers as being so fast that fighters would pant behind it to be picked off by a 20mm cannon mounted in a rear turret. The Tomahawk was at least 60mph faster. But this interception was regarded as a bit of a fluke. The much greater damage inflicted at Homs twenty-four hours later was held up as sufficient vindication of the policy of targeting airfields to the exclusion of almost anything else.

This was all true. After nineteen days' fighting French aircraft losses exceeded the British by 45 to 16. Vichy attempts to reply in kind were limited to a couple of ineffectual attacks on RAF Nicosia in Cyprus which was mainly used by the Fleet Air Arm's torpedo-carrying Swordfish and Albacores. It was almost impossible to get at the British on the ground because they were operating from such a wide area. The RAF had at least a dozen airfields at its disposal, landing and taking off from strips scattered all over northern Palestine and Jordan. And now the RAF, which had become adept at exploiting newly captured airfields quickly in the roller-coaster Libyan desert war, was beginning to increase its range and endurance by refuelling at Damascus's newly captured Mezze airfield.

So the French continued to concentrate on using their air force in a ground support role, a field in which the RAF did not yet shine as all the British Empire troops involved in this campaign knew to their cost. Certainly the steady attrition of French air power on its airfields was of no immediate comfort to Kingcol where nerves were getting as brittle as melba toast. What they longed to see was L'Armée de l'Air being shot out of the sky. Then on the morning of Saturday, 28 June they got their wish.

Nine Tomahawks had flown up to the newly captured airfield at Mezze to refuel and rendezvous with a flight of Blenheims they were escorting on a raid against the Palmyra garrison. The Australians thought the Blenheims had finished their raid when they noticed the sudden belated eruption of another rash of bomb bursts in the sand. They looked again and saw that it was not the Blenheims that were responsible for this but six other, slightly larger, twin-engined aircraft that were bombing in pairs. These were land-based Aeronavale Glenn Martins of Escadrille 7B, each with a crew of four.

One of the many pleasing characteristics of the P40 was its dive speed. An Australian ace serving with an RAF squadron once described it as 'faster downhill than any other aeroplane with a propeller'. The Tomahawks dropped onto the Glenn Martins like cats. Below them British soldiers emerged from various holes in the ground cheering wildly as, one after the other, all six French aircraft, some trailing smoke and flame, hit the ground. 'A right and left. Another – and another,' screamed one of the young aristocrats who officered His Majesty's Life Guards, watching it through his binoculars and shouting out a commentary for his men like some manic head keeper at a pheasant shoot.

In four of the aircraft everybody died. Two each survived from the remainder though one pair, tended by Bedouin and brought in the next day, were badly burnt. Altogether twenty French aircrew lost their lives. There were no Australian casualties in the action. But afterwards a pilot sergeant was killed by an engine failure on take-off at Mezze where the Tomahawks had, once again, stopped to refuel before returning to their latest Palestinian base near the Arab market town of Jenin.

Despite their losses French aircrews continued to bomb all the advances into Syria across its desert border with Iraq and there was never another success on the same scale as the one the Tomahawks had inflicted on the Aeronavale Glenn Martins. But after that Saturday morning massacre there could be no doubt that the French air attacks on the column grew less intense. And when they did come they came with Dewoitine escorts that no longer added their ground strafing to the bombs but remained high and watched each others' backs.

At the start of the move on Palmyra Churchill had referred in the House of Commons to a 'ring of steel' being placed around the oasis which, to say the least, turned out to be a bit premature. Now that was beginning to come true. Between them the 1st Essex and the Wiltshire Yeomanry had succeeded in capturing the Chateau, the site of an ancient fortress northwest of the town, and Yellow ridge, a tactical bump in the ground with a decent field of fire which at one point the French had recaptured and the Essex recovered.

In the Palmyra fighting both sides used Arab troops to their advantage. The British had Glubb's Girls. The French paid and equipped the Syrian-born Fawzi el-Kawakji and his Palestinian guerrillas. Kawakji had first fought the British as an officer in one of Ottoman Turkey's Arab regiments during the Palestine campaign of 1915–18. Then he went on to play a leading role in the 1930s Arab revolt over Britain's decision to permit limited Jewish immigration there. Now he had attached himself to the will-o'-the-wisp raiders in armoured cars and trucks, they were mainly Légère du Désert, who ambushed supply convoys with the kind of merciless relish

British marauders regularly displayed against Rommel's Libyan baggage train. Survivors from an incident where twenty-two of the Warwickshire Yeomanry were either killed or captured complained they were tricked by a white flag flying from one of his armoured cars. Later, captive French officers insisted that all their vehicles flew them as an agreed identification signal with their air force to ward off friendly fire.

Then George Clark, the general commanding of 1st Cavalry Division from which the Yeomanry and Household Cavalry were drawn and more involved since Kingstone's nervous breakdown, decided to protect their vulnerable lines of communication with Glubb Pasha's Bedouin. Glubb began by occupying two of Vichy's small desert outposts either side of the Tripoli pipeline. First his vehicles rolled up to Seba Biyer (seven wells), about 80 miles south-west of Palmyra, where the French warrant officer in charge promptly paraded his men and declared he had always been a devout Gaullist.

Next Glubb went to As-Sukhna, a mainly Christian village some 60 miles north-east known for its hot springs, which was suspected of being a hide-out for some of the Vichy raiders. All they found there were apprehensive civilians and a deserted gendarmerie post. A Household Cavalry squadron came up to hold the place while the Arab Legion took its trucks on a wide reconnaissance sweep north-westwards towards Aleppo. They drew a blank. Then at about 7.30 a.m. on 1 July Glubb saw fast vehicle dust and quite a lot of it approaching from the direction of Deir Ez Zor to the east. As it came closer and he got his field glass on it he counted six armoured cars and four trucks carrying armed men. Some were flying white flags and Tricolours.

> I was standing on a gravelly ridge with some 30 men and our three home made armoured cars. The rest of our men had moved into a little valley behind our right where there was firewood to make tea and breakfast. About 500 yards from us the column halted and the enemy infantry dismounted from their vehicles and lay down. This was a fatal mistake. We always fought from our vehicles. A man on foot in open desert with a rifle is helpless. I told our armoured cars and our 30 infantry to hold the ridge and dashed off to collect our machine-gun trucks, proposing to bring them round the enemy's flank and surround them. Our 30 infantry and three armoured cars were, however, too impatient to wait and, dashing forward, overran the enemy's infantry. When I appeared with the trucks behind the enemy's flank, their vehicles were already in full flight.

This was far from the end of it. Glubb's Bedouin had their blood up; some of them were irregulars from those Syrian tribes who did not enjoy the favours of the French and loathed them as much as Fawzi el-Kawakji's Palestinians loathed the English. A 60mph chase ensued, with men clinging to their vehicles, firing their rifles in the air and chanting their war song, part of which went: 'Our foes are sick with fear. Pursue them to the death! Abu Haneik! Abu Haneik! Abu Haneik!' Abu Haneik meant 'Father of the Little Jaw' and was their affectionate nickname for Glubb whose lower visage had been foreshortened at Passchendaele when part of his chin was shot away.

In this case their foes might well have been sick with fear. When they had taken on the armoured cars and the scattering of men they had spotted on the gravelly ridge line they had not realized what lay behind them. They were outnumbered by over four to one and excitable Bedouin were not renowned for taking prisoners. In the end, the French troops were cornered in a box valley and Glubb was sufficiently up with his leading vehicles to ensure that their surrender was accepted, though not before one distraught French officer blew his own brains out. They turned out to be the best part of the 2ième Compagnie Légère du Désert: three French officers and eighty Syrian soldiers. All the French armoured cars, trucks and the heavy machine guns that went with them were captured intact. Including the suicide, eleven had died. 'Thereafter there were no more raids on our communcations,' wrote Glubb with pardonable pride. Fawzi el-Kawekji was not among the prisoners or the dead. He had been wounded when his vehicle was hit by a strafing Hurricane and was on his way back to Beirut and thence by air to Salonika, Athens and Berlin where he would spend the rest of the war.

Two days later, there was no more Vichy Palmyra either, now entirely cut off as the Essex and the Yeomanry really did become a ring of steel, its air support dwindling and *sans* raiders to nibble at the English flanks. When at 6 a.m. on 3 July the garrison and its outpost at the T3 pumping station surrendered, there were only 187 men left on their feet. Of these 6 were French officers: 48 air force ground crew who had been working at the local airfield; 87 mostly German and Russian Foreign Legionnaires who, as Hitler's invasion of the Soviet Union neared the end of its second week, had fought shoulder to shoulder for the Legion. There were also 24 Syrians who were all that was left of the 3ième Compagnie Légère de Désert whose comrades had shed their uniforms and melted back into their villages. These men, with the considerable help of their air force, had held up some 3,000 British troops for twelve days.

While the trucks of the Yeomanry and the Household Cavalry at last moved towards the rail junction at Homs, their right flank was being covered by Gurkhas, Indians and the armoured cars of the 13th Lancers. Slim's 10th Indian Division, or at least its 21st Brigade, which had all the petrol and water there was to spare and that was not enough, had advanced north-westwards along the Euphrates and captured Deir Ez Zor and its bridge on the same day that Palmyra fell. Their progress had not been easy. The Indians and Gurkhas found the midsummer heat and dust of the

Syrian desert, which gummed the eyelids of sleeping men, just as unbearable as the Englishmen suffocating in their armoured cars. And, like Kingcol, they had been tormented by the incessant attentions of L'Armée de l'Air operating from the safest airfield Vichy had left in the Levant at Aleppo, Syria's most northerly city. 'While the number of casualties inflicted were not many, the effect on morale of the frequent bombing and machine gunning from the air was serious,' admitted Slim in his report on his division's operations.

Captain John Masters, Adjutant of the 2nd Battalion 4th Prince of Wales' Own Gurkha Rifles, recalled that the rear echelon of his brigade produced three deserters, none of them Gurkhas. One paid an awful price for it.

> An Indian non-combatant cook of Brigade Headquarters couldn't take it and ran away. We found his headless, mutilated body tangled in the reeds by the river the next morning. The Arabs had done us the service of underlining that discipline must hold fast against natural fear. Two Madrassi signallers also decided that they had had enough but, since they were determined in their fear and had a vehide, they succeeded in reaching Basra, 550 miles to the rear. There was considerable confusion everywhere in those days and I believe they got petrol by saying they were carrying urgent dispatches.

Masters longed for the RAF to show the Gurkhas what it could do and, to try to keep the army happy, it did make the occasional patrol with no real expectation of contact. There were simply not enough planes to cover the turf. The Australians had been very lucky over Palmyra. Then one afternoon it happened. Three Lioré et Olivier 451s were making their second sortie of the day to Deir Ez Zor from their base at Tel Abu Danne outside Aleppo. High above them they had an escort of eight Dewoitines. Between the French fighters and the three bombers were two Hurricanes of 127 Squadron flown by a Warrant Officer Pitcher and a Sergeant Adams. This was their third visit to the area that day and now it looked like third time lucky. Below them Masters had spotted the French aircraft, wrongly identifying them all as Glenn Martins. 'Two black dots appeared in the south east. Crouched on the burning sand I pointed up and shouted to those Gurkhas within earshot: "Hurricanes! Now watch!" The Hurricane was at the height of its fame after the Battle of Britain.'

Above the Hurricanes a Lieutenant Legrand in one of the Dewoitines spotted their tracer as they opened up on the bombers perhaps a little too early. He and his wingman, Sergent-chef Maccia, and a Sergent Ghesquière, dived at Adams's aircraft and all three gave it a burst. On the ground Masters watched as, 'A black tree root grew from the leading Hurricane's wing, turned red, expanded. It turned lazily on its side and plunged to earth.'

An air gunner on one of the bombers claimed that, before the remaining Dewoitines were ready to attack, it was he who shot down the second Hurricane flown by Warrant Officer Pitcher. What is indisputable is that, as he went down, Pitcher either collided with or rammed a Lioré et Olivier flown by a Lieutenant Bardollet who nursed his broken machine back to Tel Abu Danne. Its scars were the only damage inflicted by Masters's Battle of Britain fighters and none of them visible to the watchers on the ground. The Gurkhas avoided my eye and I theirs,' he wrote. 'Both pilots had died and we'd bloody well have to put up with the consequences, as they had.'

In terms of aircraft destroyed this was one of the few French successes as the fourth week of operations drew to a close with Vichy losing twenty-one aircraft and the British four. Some of these losses were in transit. Three out of six Morane 406s, all well used in 1940, failed to become operational: one crashed in Rome, another broke down on a Luftwaffe field in Athens and the third burst into flames on arrival at Aleppo killing its pilot. Yet despite these setbacks, and perhaps a growing realization that there was no way they could win this conflict, L'Armée de l'Air and Aeronavale continued to pour in reinforcements. Fighters included a dozen Aeronavale Dewoitine 520s from Morocco. Another Aeronavale contribution was six Late 298 torpedo-bombers, an open-cockpit monoplane seaplane. They were harboured in the northern Lebanese port of Tripoli, presumably with the Royal Navy's offshore bombardment units further south in mind.

The French had just lost one of the submarines they were hoping to use against the British ships. *Le Souffleur*, which had a long history of battery problems, had surfaced to recharge them about 2 miles off the sponge divers' harbour of Khaldé some 10 miles south of Beirut. She was running on one engine and years later local Lebanese recalled she was just visible from the coast.

On deck six men were manning her anti-aircraft guns but the Fleet Air Arm's Cyprus-based Swordfish and Albacores were not about. Instead she was spotted by Commander Michael Rimington patrolling the Lebanese coast at periscope depth in His Majesty's Submarine *Parthian*. Rimington fired a full salvo of four torpedoes. The French lookouts spotted their wakes and *Le Souffleur* turned her narrow bows to comb through them. Three missed. The fourth hit the submarine amidships and almost broke her in two. She sank in just over 100 feet of water with the loss of at least fifty lives including Pierre Lejay, her commander. Four of the men manning the anti-aircraft guns managed to swim ashore where one was captured by an Australian infantry patrol and, according to some reports, later joined the Gaullists.

Renewed attempts to send seaborne reinforcements fared just as badly. At Salonika French troops who had arrived there after a long rail journey through German-occupied territory embarked on two small troopships, the *Saint Didier* and the *Oued Yquem*. The super-destroyers *Valmy* and *Guépard*, both a little scarred from a recent brush with the New Zealand cruiser *Leander*, were also sent to collect troops. Extra fuel oil for them was made available by the Kriegsmarine in Salonika so they would not deplete supplies in Beirut. The ships were to disembark their passengers at the northern Syrian port of Latakia and ordered to 'make use of neutral Turkish waters' in both directions.

The *Saint Didier* went first, clinging to the Anatolian coast as she edged around the north-eastern corner of the eastern Mediterranean where the shores of both Turkey and Syria are washed by the Gulf of Adalia. Nicosia-based Albacore torpedo bombers, possibly acting on wireless intercepts, launched their first torpedoes at the troopship at 7 a.m. on Friday, 4 July. Her master turned her neatly between their wakes while his gunners made some unimportant holes in the biplanes. They did not return until shortly after midday when her helmsman brought the *Saint Didier* through four more attempts to blow her out of the water.

Albacores were being introduced to replace the Swordfish but it looked like the only improvement was its closed cockpit. By late afternoon the troopship was anchored about 400 yards off the Turkish coast, the deepest she had been into neutral waters, and poised to make her dash down the coast to Latakia as soon as it got dark. Why the French thought the British would observe Turkey's territorial integrity any more than they were is unclear. At 5 p.m. the Albacores caught up with the ship and discovered that this time they had a nice stationary target on their hands. They still managed to miss with their first torpedo which took an expensive bite out of a Turkish breakwater and resulted in the kind of practised growls from Ankara that the Foreign Office could have done without. The second, third and fourth all found their mark and the *Saint Didier* sank, though with mercifully small loss of life. Most of those on board, some 500 men, survived to be interned by the Turks. Fatalities totalled fifty-two. But for the British the best result was that the other troopship, the *Oued Yquem*, was ordered to turn back and Vichy ended all attempts to send reinforcements by sea.

John Masters, the clever young Gurkha battalion adjutant with the spear point battalion on the Euphrates, was also having dealings with the Turks. Although the air attacks were unabated, opposition on the ground was weak. They had now reached Tel Abiad, a small town about 100 miles east of Aleppo on the railway line that marked Syria's northern frontier with Turkey. There was a miniature fort there, which Masters thought was exactly like something out of a Beau Geste movie set, that overlooked the town's jumble of mud-brick buildings and dense dark green citrus orchards. Since the fort was such an obvious target they decided to use it merely as a lookout post and made their battalion headquarters in the orange groves.

But Masters persuaded his battalion commander to park some of their most decrepit vehicles, the ones with only a few miles left in them, along the railway tracks and L'Armée de l'Air was lured into strafing Turkey's well-guarded frontier. The gratifying result was the kind of heavy anti-aircraft fire the Gurkhas had been dreaming about and at least one Glenn Martin departed trailing smoke. Afterwards Masters visited the elderly Turkish lieutenant in charge of the aircraft guns and assured him that the British presence on the border was purely temporary and they would never dream of treating Turkish territory in this cavalier French fashion. The next time the Glenn Martins came over, Masters estimated that the Turkish anti-aircraft guns started shooting when they were at least 'two miles inside Syria'.

Later he had a good look around the Beau Geste fort and discovered its last occupants had left them a message on one of its walls. *Wait, dirty English bastards, until the Germans come. We run away now, so will you soon.* 'I love France and it made sad reading, in a way sadder than the actual fighting and that was tragic enough.'

Only the Germans were not coming and the dirty English bastards were winning as everybody knew, in the end, they must, barring a miracle. High Commissioner Henri Dentz had predicted it on 22 June, the first day of the invasion of Russia. His pleasure at informing the buoyant Dr Rahn, Ribbentrop's representative on the Armistice Commission in Syria, that L'Armée du Levant would collapse much faster than Stalin's, is not hard to imagine. It had, after all, been Rahn who had started the whole thing off by providing the Iraqi rebels with military support and the British with a plausible casus belli. Then for four days Dentz had held his breath and wondered whether a miracle had occurred as the air force ensured that Palmyra held out and there was talk of reinforcements coming through Turkey.

But the increasing aircraft losses, the sinking of the destroyer *Chevalier Paul* and the dogged British persistence on the ground soon disabused the High Commissioner of this. He sent two staff officers to Vichy to say that they could not hold out much longer and on the 28th Pétain and Darlan agreed that further resistance in Syria was pointless, but for some reason chose not to let Dentz into the secret.

Then there was a new development. It was a peace feeler from Major General John Lavarack, Australia's senior officer in the Syrian campaign and the first commander of the Tobruk garrison. Ten days into the fighting Lavarack, who had started out commanding the two brigades of 7th Australian Division, was put in charge of all the ground troops – Australian, UK British, Indian and Free French – except for the push into eastern Syria from Iraq which remained under the direct command of Jumbo Wilson in Jerusalem. The most forward Australian positions were now about 10 miles from Beirut almost up to the south bank of the Damour river which, at high summer, was a fordable sluggish brook at the bottom of a deep-sided wadi with thick banana groves at either side. Beyond it, straddling the coast road, was the little Christian town of Damour itself.

But most of Lavarack's command – Australians and UK battalions of the King's Own, Queen's and Leicesters – were much further to the south-east, bogged down among the rocks and sudden clumps of conifers in Lebanon's gruelling mountain country where the mortar tube was king. In some cases the infantry were unable to advance from windy ridge lines they had been sitting on since the fifth day of the campaign. Even the Cypriot muleteers, like the Australians all volunteers, could not persuade their animals to climb to places like the Jebel Mazar. The Australians had to bump their wounded down on stretchers made out of rifles threaded through pullovers which 'sagged so much it was like carrying a man in a bag'.

In other places anonymous hilltops known only by their heights often changed hands several times. Sudden skirmishes were fought between men who sweltered all day then froze by night and were sometimes so short of food and water they took it from the enemy dead. Both sides made promiscuous use of grenades and much of the action was after dark. This seems to have suited the Australians who occasionally used bayonets and often had the advantage of considerable artillery support though this was rarely as effective as well-placed mortar bombs.

Their opponents were usually Senegalese or Foreign Legionnaires. Spanish republicans among the latter sometimes drew the line at fighting for a France so ideologically close to Franco and surrendered. Usually the Legionnaires fought as hard as they did at Palmyra. When the Australian 2/31st Battalion finally took Hill 1284 from elements of the 6th Foreign Legion they discovered twenty-one fresh graves and fifteen unburied bodies. Shortly afterwards the Australians, who had thrown their last grenade, were forced to withdraw, though a small rearguard, which included a Bren-gun team, enabled them to take their wounded with them. Not that they needed to fear for them. L'Armée du Levant were usually scrupulous about observing the Red Cross. In one incident a French stretcher-bearer was killed attempting to rescue an Australian.

Lavarack came to the conclusion that the best way to break this stalemate, which looked like it could go on for some time, was to keep up the pressure while appealing to Dentz to see reason. With Wilson's approval he sent the High Commissioner a message via Cornelius van Engert, the US Consul General in Beirut, a well-regarded diplomat who had worked in the Levant for years.

> General Lavarack, feeling that to both Frenchmen and Australians the idea of comrades of the last war fighting against one another is repellent and

distasteful and a useless waste of good men, suggests that he sends an envoy by air to Rayak or some other mutually convenient airport ... which may lead to a solution of the unpleasant conditions which now exist and thus avoid unnecessary bloodshed.

Unfortunately Lavarack sent his message, presumably through US diplomatic channels in Jerusalem or Cairo, the day after the RAF had decided to end the campaign in a more forthright manner: aerial assassination. In what at this stage of the war was a rare display of pinpoint bombing, at 6 p.m. on Sunday, 29 June four low-flying Blenheims placed fourteen 250-pound bombs on the High Commissioner's Beirut Residency leaving five of his Syrian police guard dead and five wounded and the building's neo-classical edifice severely disfigured. Dentz was not there. Along with the German diplomat Dr Rahn, he had moved several days before to the less bombed Aleppo from where he was making occasional sorties to Beirut. Some of the High Commissioner's staff urged him to retaliate by attacking Jumbo Wilson's headquarters at the King David Hotel in west Jerusalem but Dentz did not want to go down as the man who bombed the Holy City. Seven years later the Zionist terrorists of Irgun Zvei Leumi, who had no such scruples, almost certainly made a much better job of the King David Hotel than any air force would have done.

On the coast the Australians had captured Damour, started shelling Beirut's southern suburbs which were now just within range of their 25-pounders and were advancing between beach and mountain up the flat, straight coast road to Khaldé opposite the submarine *Le Souffleur*'s last resting place. For just over three days the French had fought hard to keep Damour with some dogged resistance from the Legion and a spirited counter-attack by some Algerian Tirailleurs. Among the Australian casualties was the tall Lieutenant Roden Cutler, the daring forward observation officer for the 25-pounders of 2/5th Field Regiment.

At dawn, as the British bombardment lifted, Cutler was on the north bank of Wadi Damour with 2/16th's West Australian infantry, the spear head battalion. At pistol point he extracted from dugouts overlooked by the battalion's vanguard, six possibly shell-shocked Legionnaires. Then, covered by a Bren gunner, he grenaded a persistent machine-gun post, rushed it and accepted another five prisoners, giving a man shot through the cheek a field dressing and his water bottle. Shortly afterwards, while walking back through a banana stand for a field telephone to replace a defective radio, a bullet shattered his right leg below the knee. All around him Vichy snipers were still active. Found after dark then abandoned by a small group of demoralized Australians creeping back to their own lines, convinced in the confusion of the banana groves that their attack had failed, he was not rediscovered until twenty-six hours after he had been shot.

By then his leg had become gangrenous and would be amputated from above the knee. His stretcher party were four of the Legionnaires Cutler had captured, delighted to take a gunner search party to the area where the brave young officer who had handed over his water bottle to their wounded comrade might be found. Somebody took a photograph of them carrying the wounded Australian hero down a long straight road, the stretcher party's *poilu* helmets instantly recognizable, while French shells explode in the background and Cutler's head is inclined in conversation towards Captain Adrian Johnson, his regiment's medical officer who is walking beside him. 'For most conspicuous and sustained gallantry' over a nineteen-day period starting with him, surrounded by the dead and the dying, repulsing the tanks with a Boys rifle at Merjayoun, Lieutenant Cutler, just turned 25, would be awarded the Victoria Cross.

On 8 July, the day before Damour finally fell, High Commissioner Dentz returned to Beirut from Aleppo to call on Consul General van Engert and ask the American if he would enquire about the British terms for a ceasefire. Afterwards he went to inspect the latest damage at his Residency which had been bombed for a second time. The bombing was at the insistence of Air Vice-Marshal Arthur Tedder, newly appointed commander of Britain's Middle East Air Force who, impatient with the army's slow progress, thought he would show them how it was done.

In Sydney a few hours later Sir Frederick Stewart, Australia's Minister for External Affairs, announced that the Vichy French had asked for a cessation of hostilities in Syria and shortly afterwards this was leading all BBC news bulletins. General Lavarack was furious about the leak. Dentz might be talking peace but everywhere the French were counter-attacking. 'Knowledge of the possibility of an armistice will make troops less inclined to do the things which so often mean the difference between success and failure. No man is likely to risk his life unnecessarily if he feels the campaign is virtually over.'

By and large Lavarack must have been right about this. Yet some of his infantry, Australian and UK British, were still fighting as if they had only just begun. Under a crescent moon north of Jezzine in the early hours of 10 July, a company of Australians attacked a French-held ridge they called Bandarane Heights which involved clambering up a series of terraces 2 or 3 feet high. To the right of the ridge Private James Gordon, a 32-year-old farmer of Scots descent who had married shortly before he left West Australia and was the father of a baby boy, was among a platoon pinned down by intense large-calibre automatic fire and grenades. Gordon began a solitary crawl towards the source of this unpleasantness. When he felt he had got slightly behind the enemy, he sprang to his feet and bayoneted and shot four Senegalese he caught lying around a Hotchkiss. This action, which was on his own initiative though not perhaps entirely unexpected, for Gordon had already established a reputation for taking calculated risks, secured the position and resulted in Australia's second VC of the campaign. William Dargie, the war artist who painted Gordon's portrait, described him as, 'Not the smiling, happy-go lucky "Digger" of legend but the slightly older-than-young man with a definite sense of responsibility.'

At about the same time as Gordon was approaching the Senegalese the 2nd Battalion King's Own Royal Lancaster Regiment was forming up for an assault on two rocky and precipitous flat-topped volcanic peaks of the Jebel Mazar, one rising to 1,404 feet and the other about 50 feet taller with a short saddle of land between them. These were part of the tiered French defences commanding the winding highway down to the coast from Damascus with their artillery, mortars and heavy machine guns. Facing the King's Own, the smaller Peak 1404 was to their right nearest the vital road half a mile away and Peak 1455 to their left covering its slightly lower neighbour from that flank. Capturing them would allow Lavarack to augment the Australians' advance on Beirut from the south with an additional one from the east to make it a two-pronged attack. Lieutenant Colonel Barraclough, the King's Own CO, presented their task as an integral part of the ceasefire talks, explaining to his officers that their success would compel Vichy to accept their terms.

It was part of a brigade attack with the King's Own, the Leicesters, the Queen's and the Free French Marines battalion that was attacking a similar position on the Bel Habil on the other side of the road. The only artillery support available was a battery of light mountain guns on loan to the British Indian Army from the Jammu and Kashmir State Forces that was to be deployed according to need once the fight had started. Otherwise, it was decided to make a virtue of necessity and make it a moonlit surprise attack without attempting a preliminary barrage from the mountain guns and mortars. The King's Own started to move off at 3.30 a.m. which was about ninety minutes before first light. But scree rattling underfoot alerted French listening posts and the night was immediately lit up by flares and tracer. 'Rather as though someone had pulled down a main switch,' noted the regimental historian. Bent double, they tried not to bunch and pressed on, ready to throw themselves down if the tracer was anything but a long way overhead. At one point the ground briefly levelled off into a little plateau which led into a narrow re-entry-type dent in the baked earth, the end of which was walled in by a small 20-foot-high cliff. On the ledge above this were the first serious Vichy positions.

In the dark Second Lieutenant Edward Bailey got his men to make the kind of human pyramid beloved by instructors on assault courses, clambered up it and once over the edge was almost immediately heard to be using his revolver while a shower of grenades down the cliff face made it impossible for his men to follow. Later Bailey's body was found next to the Tirailleur he shot as he was impaled by his adversary's fixed bayonet, the causes of death on both sides still gripped in their hands. It was also established that before this happened Bailey had managed to shoot dead the French company commander in this sector.

Dawn found the battalion 'hanging on like flies on a wall' just below the crest of the smaller hill and under machine-gun and mortar fire from three sides. Corporal Tweedale got a Bren gun section within 25 yards of a machine-gun nest and, too close to be mortared, stayed there making his presence felt while ignoring his wounds. Most of the battalion were using bayonets and mess tins to scrape holes for themselves in any soft space between the rocks: entrenching tools, like heavy artillery, were something else they lacked. All Colonel Barraclough could do was ask for the help of the Indian mountain battery. They moved its guns as close as they dared and sent Lieutenant Raizada Madn Lal Vaid, their observation officer, to join the forward infantry. With a linesman unravelling a field telephone cable behind him, Lal Vaid, a Kashmiri aristocrat, managed to get himself and his party across open ground well covered by machine guns and mortars and set to work. Within a short while the mountain guns' well-directed fire was thought to have accounted for at least one machine gun and a mortar and had, quoting the citation for the Kashmiri's Military Cross, 'an encouraging effect on the morale of our own troops'. An additional bonus was that Barraclough now had a field telephone line to his forward company.

For almost two days, while Dentz introduced a new intermediary for the Beirut–Jerusalem correspondence in the form of France's interned Amiral Godfroy on his mothballed battleship in Alexandria, this predominantly North Country English battalion was involved in some of the most bitter fighting of the campaign. French mortar teams could work with impunity from their mountain-top fire bases. The King's Own discovered their own mortars, even when loaded with extra charges that might have exploded the bombs in their tubes, constantly fell short. The mountain guns certainly had the range but their small shells did not always have much effect against an enemy often encased in stone and concrete. At one point six of the Australians' Tomahawks made an air strike. But instead of attacking the peaks they concentrated on strafing the French transport and artillery on the other side of the Jebel Mazar where there were plenty of 20mm flak guns. One aircraft was hit and Flying Officer Knowles was lucky to make his crash landing on the right side of Damascus to get a lift home.

Nonetheless, slowly but surely Barraclough's men closed with the enemy, though officer casualties, as in any good infantry battalion, were high. Two company commanders had been badly wounded, two subalterns killed at the head of their platoons. Barraclough put in a second night attack with his reserve company against Peak 1455, the slightly bigger of the two. It was led by Captain Sam Waring who won a bar to the Military Cross he had earned during Palestine's Arab rebellion, getting his men around some barbed-wire entanglements and capturing a line of sangars. One corporal revved his section in a sudden bezerker bayonet charge and was seen to kill four Tirailleurs himself before they began to collect prisoners.

Then, for the last time in the campaign, the French introduced tanks. This was a shock because nobody had realized that the far side of the Jebel Mazar had slopes gentle and rock-free enough for them to make unhindered progress. But here they were again, the stubby little two-man Renault R35s of the Chasseurs d'Afrique, waddling menacingly towards the British infantry. And this time there was no question of even trying to use Boys anti-tank rifles against them because a Boys was much too heavy to take mountain climbing. All Waring could do was get his company to run away which they did in reasonably good order, taking their prisoners with them and joining the rest of the battalion high up on the smaller peak which was steeper and rockier and definitely not 1941's tank country. They also had the support of Madn Lal Vaid's mountain battery though they lacked armour-piercing ammunition.

The R35s moved off to the 2nd Queen's sector which they found flatter and much more congenial, quickly cutting off and capturing about ninety exhausted men who were almost asleep on their feet. The Queen's had been in continuous action much longer than any other of the UK British battalions, and it was beginning to show. More men were being evacuated with heat stroke than bullet or shrapnel wounds. Among the casualties was their commanding officer Lieutenant Colonel Bevis Haggard, mentioned in despatches and three times wounded in 1914–18, who had collapsed with a heart attack.

Having climbed high enough to shake off the tanks the King's Own spent the rest of Friday, 11 July clinging to the side of their mountain under frequent mortar and artillery fire from the neighbouring peak and sometimes sniped at from the summit of the one they were on. It was a hazy day. Sun spots, those electrical disturbances in the ionosphere that begin with a vortex of gas rising from the surface of the sun, were playing havoc with short-wave radio signals. By midday the outline of the peaks danced in the heat, flies visited the living almost as much as the dead and many water bottles had run dry. Thirst drove men to take the risks the snipers above them were waiting for. Private Pearce, whose platoon was pinned down in a spot devoid of all shade, was killed as he tried to get to the place where water bottles had been dumped by the last man to try to deliver them. Private White, a volunteer from another platoon, was luckier and made the run.

By late afternoon Barraclough was wondering how much longer he could expect his men to put up with this, though one positive development was the arrival of 25-pounder guns with the RAF acting as spotters for them. Then brigade headquarters passed on the plain language signal that Corporal Donald Pickering, the duty senior Royal Signals operator at Jumbo Wilson's Jerusalem HQ, had been trying to transmit through the sun spots for the last two hours. 'All troops in forward areas will cease fire at 0001 hours 12 July. A strict ceasefire will be observed but if fired upon return fire.'

After five weeks the Syrian campaign was over. Or almost over. For it soon became obvious that the French regarded the interval between announcing the ceasefire and its midnight implementation as an opportunity to ensure that none of their ammunition was left unfired. The Leicesters reported that shell after shell was going over their position though most of them were landing harmlessly in a hillside to their rear. The Midlands' battalion had just had a hard time in Crete and this demonstration of pique, if that is what it was, did not win the French any admirers. On both sides it was, after all, a generation brought up on tales about men who had died on 11th day of the 11th month 1918. The Leicesters' regimental history is quite emphatic about it. 'Everyone naturally felt anxious not to be killed a few hours short of the armistice. Whatever the rights and wrong of the case at the time our soldiers, though they despised the Italians and respected the German fighting man, one and all hated these Vichyites who seemed to have occasioned an unnecessary campaign.'

It was a view shared by the Hurricane pilot Roald Dahl. He started the Syrian campaign as one of nine of 80 RAF Squadron who had survived the air fighting in Greece. By the time Dentz surrendered only five were left alive. Years later, when he had become a great and distinguished author, he would write: 'I for one have never forgiven the Vichy French for the unnecessary slaughter they caused.'

Others took a more philosophical attitude. Shortly after the armistice Gerald Bryan, the Commando lieutenant who gained a Military Cross and lost a leg in the Litani action, was surprised to receive a hospital visit from some of the officers belonging to the units that had been fighting him there. They explained, 'slightly apologetically', that they were all regular soldiers and it was their duty to support the government they had pledged allegiance to. 'I explained that I too was a regular soldier and I was prepared to fight anyone my government declared an enemy. We discussed the Litani river battle as if it had been a game of football ... Before they left each officer shook me by the hand and we bade each other au revoir without rancour or recrimination.'

Chapter Twenty

At least 2,000 people were killed in the Syrian campaign, an average of 400 a week. The Vichy French lost slightly more than the Allies. After the war Dentz said that 1,092 French officers and men, most of the latter non-French, had died defending Syria. This would include naval and air force losses and probably locally recruited gendarmerie.

The Australians, who contributed the bulk of the Allied land forces, had 416 killed in action and 1,136 wounded. Total losses among other participants are vaguer because the only available casualty figures have obviously been rounded off, and killed and wounded are lumped together without saying how many died: UK and British Indian Army 600; Free French 300. It would probably be correct to assume that at least 300 of these were killed which, together with some 50 RAF and Royal Navy fatalities, would put the Allied killed at about 800 of whom perhaps 100 were Free French.

Civilian deaths appear to have been quite low. Certainly much lower than those inflicted by the late twentieth-century American munitions used by the Israelis against Palestinian and Lebanese militias defending the same turf and often, having little choice in the matter, from densely populated areas. In 1941 the cities were avoided. The Vichy French tried to hold lines *before* Sidon, Damour and Beirut and Damascus was declared an open city. Anglo-Vichy artillery duels and bombing attacks around Lebanon's hill villages and market towns such as Merjayoun and Jezzine certainly took their toll of innocents who happened to be standing on the wrong map reference at the wrong time. And troops sometimes saw bodies or heard Arabic keening for the dead but nobody was counting. Only in Beirut, which towards the end was receiving a few bombs around the port and the High Commissioner's residence on an almost nightly basis, could Commandant Picard's Lebanese police attempt to cling onto normality and see that a proper record was kept. 'Night of 29 to 30 June. 0010 hrs. Ashrafiyah area (near the Greek Orthodox Hospital) 3 bombs, 2 dead, 5 wounded, 2 houses destroyed ... Rue Lamartine, the courtyard of the Kikano building, Hadji Nicolas Sayegh, a 65-year-old Lebanese, was fatally wounded. Police legal services are taking statements.' Even so, it is hard to imagine that civilian fatalities throughout Lebanon and Syria in the summer of 1941 could have averaged less than three a day: a total of 105.

After two days of negotiations High Commissioner Dentz, according to *Time* magazine looking like 'a provincial druggist in uniform', signed the armistice in the Sidney Smith Barracks at the old Crusader fortress of Acre, Mandate Palestine's most northern harbour. It was Monday, 14 July: Bastille Day. Most of the world's English-language press did not miss the opportunity to point out that signing on the anniversary of the founding of the French Republic was an added humiliation for Dentz. For good measure *Time*'s correspondent gloated that last year the same man, as commander of the capital's garrison, had 'signed Paris away to the conquering Nazis'. (It was not strictly true. It had been declared an open city.)

This year's surrender document was entitled the Armistice of Saint Jean D'Acre, the name the knights of the First Crusade had given their first landing in 1104. The venue, Sidney Smith Barracks, was named after the admiral whose frigates ended Napoléon's Levantine ambitions in 1799. Reporters and newsreel cameramen with a considerable amount of electric cable trailing after them, were allowed in to record the historic occasion which took place after dark in the dining room of the officers' mess.

Unfortunately an Australian photographer, 'somewhat over refreshed' thought Jumbo Wilson, got entangled in one or perhaps several of the leads and fused every light in the barracks. As a result the final signing was lit by hurricane lamps and the headlight of a despatch rider's motorcycle wheeled into the doorway and kick-started into life. Somebody took advantage of the confusion to visit the car being used by Georges Catroux, the leader of the Free French forces in Syria, and remove from one of its seats his général's oak leaf kepi with its generous arrangement of gold thread embroidery on the crown. Catroux suspected the Australians (who vehemently denied it) and, in his memoirs at least, seemed to share the joke though he added: 'When the incident became known to the Vichy delegation the whisper went round that I was a deserving victim of the bad company I kept.'

If it had not been for Catroux's presence Dentz might have been spared the pain of signing on Bastille Day. But he could not stomach the idea of a face-to-face meeting with the Gaullist traitors sitting on the same side of the table as Wilson's delegation and, refusing to attend in person, remained in Beirut until his signature was required. His representative at the negotiations that preceded this awful moment was to be Raoul de Verdilhac, old friend of Legentilhomme, and his adversary in the fighting around Damascus. All his fellow professionals at the table recognized that Général de Verdilhac had conducted a brilliant campaign and, to the very small extent that it had been a civil war, was ending it with all the good-natured aplomb of one of Lee's senior Confederates.

Wilson saw his next task as preparing defences in Syria to stop the ever successful Germans if they should decide to turn south from the Russian Caucasus and enter the Levant through Turkey. With this in mind he wanted to remove all Vichy troops who did not wish to join the Free French as soon as possible. This had contributed to generous terms and infuriated de Gaulle. His response was to pretend that his forces had been an equal partner in the invasion of Syria instead of a failed fig leaf that had not for one moment concealed the naked Britishness of the project let alone procured a single act of mass defection. But having miserably failed to seduce the Armée du Levant on the battlefield, de Gaulle was appalled by how little access his recruiters had to this captive audience now that the shooting was over.

> Everything was going on as though nobody owed us anything. Dentz, with full agreement of the English, had concentrated his troops in northern Lebanon around Tripoli. The units, with their leaders, their arms and their flags, were encamped side by side, showered by Vichy with decorations and mentions in despatches, receiving no information except what came to them through the channel of their hierarchy and basking in an atmosphere of imminent repatriation. Indeed the ships which were to take them away wholesale were already announced from Marseilles, for Darlan was not wasting a day before getting them on their way nor the Germans before letting them leave.

An attempt was made to appease de Gaulle by allowing Free French units to be quartered close to Vichy troops. This led to an election atmosphere with speeches, slogans and banners proclaiming '*Pétain, Maréchal nous voilà*' and '*France Libre – de Gaulle*'. A Gaullist sergent shot and badly wounded a Pétainist officer as he was boarding his ship but overall there was little violence, though the Vichy officers had been allowed to keep loaded pistols. It was becoming increasingly obvious that the Gaullists were losing the election and the British could not fill the repatriation ships fast enough. This led to a serious error when on 16 August 600 delighted German Foreign Legionnaires, who included some of the Palmyra garrison and had been carefully sifted from other nationalities, discovered they were not bound for a POW camp but were a Mediterranean cruise back to France and no doubt the welcoming arms of the Wehrmacht. Churchill was furious. 'I am not prepared to let this lapse be slurred over, or fall into oblivion. More than admonitions are required when 600 German Legionnaires are allowed to go back to France for further use by Germany against us. It might take 600 British lives to deal with these men so casually and incontinently allowed to slip through our fingers.'

Undoubtedly Wilson was ultimately responsible. He was punctilious about keeping to the letter of the Acre armistice which did not discriminate against French troops who happened to be of German nationality. No action was ever taken, partly because it was discovered that the Free French were aware that the German Legionnaires were about to be being shipped out and raised no objection. In return Wilson expected the Vichy French to keep to their word and when they did not took decisive action.

At Acre it had been agreed that there would be an exchange of prisoners. Three weeks after the ceasefire had been signed there was still no sight of sixty-six Australian, British and Indian officers and NCOs who, it had been learned, were no longer in the country. Among them were most of the officers from 5th Indian Brigade captured in the one-sided fights against the Renault tanks at Kuneitra and Mezze. Late in the campaign, presumably with bargaining chips in mind, fifty-three of them had been flown or shipped to Salonika in northern Greece where the German military had allowed Vichy to set up logistics support for their Syrian operation. The other thirteen had ended up in Italian hands on Rhodes, shipped there from nearby Scarpanto where their air transport had made a worrying emergency landing with an engine on fire. Général de Verdilhac had been warned that if these men were not returned by 5 August thirty-five senior Vichy officers, including Dentz and himself, would no longer be free to await repatriation in circumstances that were little different from those they enjoyed as a peacetime garrison. They would be detained until they kept to the agreement.

The arrests took place on the afternoon of 7 August and the hostages were all moved to quarters in Jerusalem where they were held under armed guard. Dentz had at first pleaded he was too sick with dengue fever to travel but eventually, accompanied by his ADC and two servants, was driven there in his own car. Wilson, whose headquarters were nearby, informed them that 'they would not leave for France until our officers set foot in Beirut' and Vichy was apprised of their situation. By the end of the month all sixty-three British prisoners had returned, the last leg of their journey by ship from Toulon to Beirut completed in some style in first-class cabins with waiter service.

They came back with a strange tale of a long but not uncomfortable seven-day rail journey across Hitler's Europe under French guard. After Salonika the first stretch had been through German-occupied Yugoslavia passing through Belgrade and Zagreb. Then, by its Alpine scenic route, they had entered the Reich itself with glimpses of Graz, Salzberg – where they were shocked to see holidaymakers on the platform and no attempt to enforce a blackout – and Hitler's beloved Berchtesgaden before they descended by way of Munich and Ulm and across annexed Alsace to enter the new shrunken France shortly before Dijon. The Demarcation line between the occupied and unoccupied zones had been crossed just north of Vichy itself, after which they had proceeded through Pétain's brittle kingdom to Marseilles and Toulon.

In Salonika the prisoners were held in foul conditions on the merchant ship *Théophile Gaultier* whose master made it quite plain that he considered this payback time, having been interned, along with the crew of the *Surcouf*, at the Aintree camp the previous summer. After the ceasefire was announced the British had expected to be shipped back to Beirut immediately. When they learned they were going to France with the withdrawing Vichy logistics headquarters their disappointment was acute. Despite French assurances that they would remain in their custody the chances of passing through so much German territory without being marched off to the nearest prisoner-of-war camp seemed slim. But they received no harassment from the Germans whatsoever. Twice, at Augsberg then Tuttlingen, they were given comfort parcels by the German Red Cross. Four German soldiers under a Feldwebel who were on the train as a liaison unit to the French were friendly and even serenaded them with the German versions of 'Roll Out the Barrel', 'Tipperary' and 'Pack Up Your Troubles in Your Old Kit Bag'. The sight of guarded working parties supplied by that part of the British Expeditionary Force that did not escape at Dunkirk brought them down to earth. At one point one of these was toiling close to the track when, immune and about to be free, the excited prisoners from Syria rattled past, startling them with their shouted English greetings and thrown cigarettes.

Once in France they had found most of the French they encountered sympathetic though war-weary and not inclined to believe them when they expressed their unshakable belief in ultimate victory. Lieutenant Colonel Percy Calvert-Jones, a Royal Artilleryman captured with his driver going too far forward on reconnaissance, was the Senior British Officer. On his return he reported: 'The resistance put up by the Russians has had a good effect. A British victory against the Germans would have a still greater effect.'

For the moment Syria would have to do. It was not as good as the victory Freyberg had allowed to slip through his fingers in Crete. Or the one Wavell would have needed a miracle to win in North Africa the following month when Rommel lured the British armour onto his 88mm anti-tank gun screen. But the successes in Iraq and Syria had secured the rear areas behind the desert front and given Britain's Middle East defence a lot more depth. On 15 July, the day after the armistice was signed, Churchill explained these gains to the House of Commons.

> If anyone had predicted two months ago, when Iraq was in revolt and our people were hanging on by their eyelids at Habbaniya and our Ambassador was imprisoned in his embassy at Baghdad, and when all Syria and Iraq had been overrun by German tourists, and were in the hands of forces controlled indirectly but none the less powerfully by German authority – if anyone had predicted that we should already, by the middle of July, have

cleaned up the whole of the Levant and have re-established our authority there for the time being, such a prophet would have been considered most imprudent.

Dentz and his officers boarded the ship that took them from Beirut on 10 September while a band played the 'Marseillaise', an Australian honour guard presented arms and the diminutive de Verdilhac was being seen off by several attractive women. This brought the number of French troops who had obeyed the order they had received at the eve of the ceasefire to 'remain faithful to the unity of France and to Maréchal Petain' to 32,032. Only 5,668 had elected to join the Gaullists. Catroux had been hoping to raise another Free French division. Instead he did not have enough to bring the one he had up to full strength. De Gaulle continued to blame the English for indulging the Vichyites and not giving his agents enough time though perhaps they had done as well as could be expected when the only certain thing on offer was exile.

The Vichy loyalists of the Armée du Levant returned to a France riven by violent internal dissent. Since the attack on Russia, the Germans had executed almost 100 hostages – some of them young men picked up for minor infringements of the curfew – as a response to an outbreak of Communist-inspired urban terrorism. At least five members of the occupying forces had been shot dead by hit-and-run assassins including the Feldcommandant of Nantes. Nor were all the victims Germans.

Pierre Laval was in hospital recovering from gunshot wounds after an attempt that had very nearly killed him. Since Pétain had dismissed him in February he had been living mostly in Paris, biding his time, all the considerable political nerve-ends in his being telling him, as they had so often done before, to wait and let others make the mistakes. Darlan had done exactly that, losing Syria for no gain and seeing his Paris Protocols with the Germans come to naught.

Meanwhile, both at home and abroad, Laval had made certain that he did not disappear from sight. Towards the end of May, Ralph Heinzen, the Vichy-based American reporter for United Press who had seen him produce a pocket knife to defend himself on the night of his sacking, was given a long interview which appeared in the *New York Times*. In it Laval rebutted the idea that his country was awaiting liberation from the German yoke. 'France does not want to be liberated,' he told Heinzen. 'She wants to settle her fate herself in collaboration with Germany. Would the United States want to push France into a contrary peace, a peace of destruction and division, by urging her to spurn the extended hand of Hitler – a hand extended in a gesture quite unique in history?'

At home he tried to live by example and do what he could to keep Abetz and Berlin happy. On 27 August 1941 he had been at Versailles inspecting the Légion des Volontaires Français contre le Bolchevisme who were hoping to get to the Eastern Front in time to share in the Wehrmacht's inevitable triumph. As he and the clever French Nazi Marcel Déat (author of the famous eve-of-war article 'Why Die for Danzig?') examined the eager young faces, Paul Collette, a former sailor from Caen who was 21, had stepped from the ranks and started shooting at them with the kind of 6.35mm handbag gun Dr Le Nistour had used on the *Surcouf*.

By the time he had emptied the magazine five people were wounded. Laval was the worst hit with a chest wound which an X-ray revealed was caused by a bullet lodged a quarter of an inch from his heart. An infection set in and with it a temperature of 104°F. For some days it looked as if he might die but he recovered in time to join Déat in successfully petitioning Pétain to reprieve Collette who had been sentenced to death by a French court. According to some accounts Abetz would have liked to see the sentence upheld but Laval did not want to make a martyr. The Germans were already doing quite enough of that.

He spent the autumn and the onset of winter convalescing at Châteldon enjoying its air and its wine and the company of his wife Eugénie. In Russia the Germans were close to Moscow and in the North African desert the British, who were nothing if not obstinate, had gone on the offensive against Rommel again. Only this time they won.

A week before the Syrian ceasefire Churchill had replaced Archibald Wavell with Claude Auchinleck as Middle East Commander-in-Chief and sent Wavell off to be Commander-in-Chief of India with an eye on the possibility of Japan entering the war. Amply equipped with the abundance of tanks made available since Hitler's Russian adventure had scotched fears of an immediate invasion of Britain, Auchinleck's Operation Crusader had begun on 18 November.

After a fifteen-day tank battle on 7 December the 8th Army, as it was now called, had relieved Tobruk. The siege had lasted 242 days. Among the troops fighting their way out to meet them were the King's Own and almost all the UK infantry battalions from Syria which some of them thought had been much harder fighting. Hotly pursued by the British armour, Rommel had retreated another 250 miles to the west, at which point British supply lines were dangerously stretched. In the course of this victory all three of the Afrika Korps's divisional commanders had become casualties. Two were dead and the third, 21st Panzer's General Johannes von Ravenstein, had become the first German general to go into captivity anywhere in the world. But Rommel himself was still at large, having conducted a skilful withdrawal with several stings in its tail. An attempt to capture or kill him, intended as a prelude to Operation Crusader, had gone disastrously wrong.

On 13 November Geoffrey Keyes, accompanied by Tommy Macpherson and some of the other stars of the Litani crossing, had been put ashore by submarine at Beda Littoria some 250 miles behind the German front lines to kill or capture Rommel who was wrongly thought to be there. It turned out to be the quartermaster general's headquarters and Rommel, who was out of the country at the time, celebrating his fiftieth birthday in Rome, was rather hurt that the British thought he would be operating so far behind the front. Nonetheless, Beda Littoria was still well guarded. In a gunfight in and around a darkened building Keyes and four German soldiers were killed. Macpherson tried to walk back to British lines and was eventually captured, though he would later escape from Germany to Sweden and was still only halfway through his extraordinary war. Keyes was awarded a posthumous Victoria Cross and, as the man who had tried to kill Rommel, was briefly more famous than his father. The Germans buried him with full military honours next to their own.

For the politician in Châteldon mending from his closer call with an assassin's bullet, muted news of the British victory in the sand – surely a mere tactical withdrawal on the part of the German maestro? – was entirely eclipsed by the Japanese attack on Pearl Harbor. Unfortunately for Auchinleck this happened to coincide with the relief of Tobruk and the rest of his good fortune. All over Christmas and well into the New Year the Anglo-Americans' Asian dominoes fell, their ships were sunk, their women raped. Towards the end of January, Rommel did indeed go back on the offensive in North Africa and the British lost Benghazi and reeled back 100 miles.

In March 1942 the English had brought the war back to France. On the night of the 3rd, 235 RAF bombers had wrecked a large part of the Renault works at Billancourt near Paris. The factory, on an island in the Seine, was making hundreds of trucks for the Wehrmacht. Civilian casualties were high, twice as many as had yet been killed in any raid on a German city. Most of the 397 dead had been sleeping in the collapsed workers' apartment buildings nearby. There was a national day of mourning with flags at half mast. Admiral Leahy, the US ambassador in Vichy who was finding his tenure increasingly difficult now that Germany and America were at war, noted 'violent anti-British feeling in both the occupied and unoccupied zones'. Darlan, who had been in Paris during the bombing, sent Leahy a handwritten note on the bombing that ended: 'We shall never forgive them. To murder, for political motives, women, children and old people is a method of Soviet inspiration. Is England already bolshevized?'

Then later that month the barbarous English came back. But this time they came by sea to the port of St Nazaire where they destroyed the dry dock originally built for France's magnificent liner *Normandie* which, having languished in New York since the war started, had caught fire and capsized in the Hudson only six weeks before. They did it because the *Normandie* dock, as it was still known, was the only one on the Atlantic coast big enough for the battleship *Tirpitz* and there was nothing the British would not do to deny *Tirpitz* a facility that would make raiding their shipping lanes easier.

HMS *Campbeltown* was originally the USS *Buchanan*, one of the fifty old American destroyers Churchill had got in the crisis summer of 1940 for American bases in the West Indies. Almost two years later frantic British shipbuilding had made her expendable enough to hide a 3-ton time bomb of twenty-four depth charges in her bows, remove her heavy guns to give her the draught for shallow waters, reduce her crew to seventy-five plus Commando demolition parties and send her on her last voyage.

At 1.25 a.m. on 28 March, having bluffed her way up almost the entire length of the Loire estuary flying a false flag and flashing chatty Kriegsmarine Morse signals, the German gunners finally made the right decision. But by now *Cambeltown*, accompanied by a flotilla of seventeen wooden-hulled motor launches carrying more Commandos, was less than a mile away from her target. The destroyer ran up the White Ensign, tore through a steel torpedo net, and despite repeated hits rammed the dock's outer caisson at 20 knots. And there she stuck. The Commando demolition parties took their satchel charges to the machinery selected for destruction, while the men from the launches scrambled ashore to cover them or create diversions. One after another the small craft that had delivered them – little more than stage sets of plywood and mahogany veneer with big-hearted engines – burst into flames. In places it looked as if the Loire itself was alight. Only six of these boats would get back to the open sea, all crammed with dead and wounded.

The time fuzes on the *Cambeltown*'s hidden depth charges did not work properly. They were due to detonate at 9 a.m. Instead they did not go off until 11.30 by which time German engineers, who had still not discovered this enormous bomb, had declared the ship safe. As a result their casualties were much higher than they would have been. The old ship's sloping upper deck was crowded with sightseers: senior officers, administrative personnel, U-boat crews from their bomb-proof pens and, according to most reports, a few female companions. In all about 250 people were killed. More importantly, the *Normandie* dock was wrecked and would never provide a home for the *Tirpitz*.

The raid on St Nazaire, which was entirely in the spirit of Churchill's original concept of butcher and bolt, was probably the most effective large-scale Commando action of the entire war and the most costly. Out of the 622 Commandos and sailors who took part 169 were killed or died of wounds, over a quarter. Another 214 were captured, of whom at least a third were wounded. Five Victoria Crosses were awarded, two of them posthumously. Three were to the navy. Only 27 out of 268 Commandos got back, 22 by sea and the rest overland to Spain and Gibraltar. From the outset these five evaders were helped by French civilians who knew that if they were caught they would face a firing squad. Corporal George Wheeler and Lance Corporal Sims managed to get through St Nazaire and into the countryside beyond. They were discovered, hiding in a haystack, by a farmer. Wheeler spoke some French.

> After I had explained who we were the man brought us food and wine and at about 11pm he took us to the farm house and fitted us out with civilian clothes and gave us 250 francs each. He also advised us to get rid of traces of our identity, to keep to the small roads, and to make for Nantes. We gave him our Colts, which he said he 'might be using one day'.

Wheeler and Sims took his advice and were the first back on 21 May – just under two months. When, passed from one French escape chain to another, Wheeler reached neutral Madrid the corporal told the British military attaché there that 'the propaganda value of the raid was enormous'.

This was not a France that Darlan or Laval knew or wanted to know. By the spring all the former premier's wounds had healed. The one near his heart had been declared inoperable and the bullet would remain in him but, as the momentum to bring him back into government grew, all his old vigour had returned. For this he had a lot to thank the Americans, who had made a tactical mistake. Ever since his interview had appeared in the *New York Times* the US Embassy in Vichy had been hinting that if Laval was restored Ambassador Leahy might well be withdrawn and perhaps all diplomatic ties would be severed.

The Germans seized on this. Suddenly the future of Pierre Laval, a wheeler-dealer politician of the kind Hitler most detested, had been elevated into a trial of strength between the now belligerent capitals of Washington and Berlin. 'By asking Vichy not to compose a collaborationist government the USA has forced Vichy to chose between Washington and Berlin,' lectured the journalist Jean Luchaire in *Le Nouveau Temps* in a piece that was said to have been inspired by the German Embassy, not that Luchaire normally needed much guidance in these matters.

There was never any choice. By mid-April Pétain had formally given in. Laval would return as Chef de gouvernement, a position that had not exactly existed before. He would also be Minister of Foreign Affairs, the Interior and Information and would, of course, choose the rest of his Cabinet. Darlan would still be there as titular head of all the military as well as Pétain's designated successor but the message was clear: he was not the man the Germans wanted.

For Laval, with his unshakable belief in German victory, it was a good time to come back. Almost everywhere he looked the Allies were in disarray. In London the War Cabinet had discussed the possibility of Laval making a formal declaration of war against Britain and ruled that it was not out of the question.

PART THREE
The Island Campaign

Map 8 The six-month campaign in Madagascar, May–November 1942, showing the dates each major objective fell

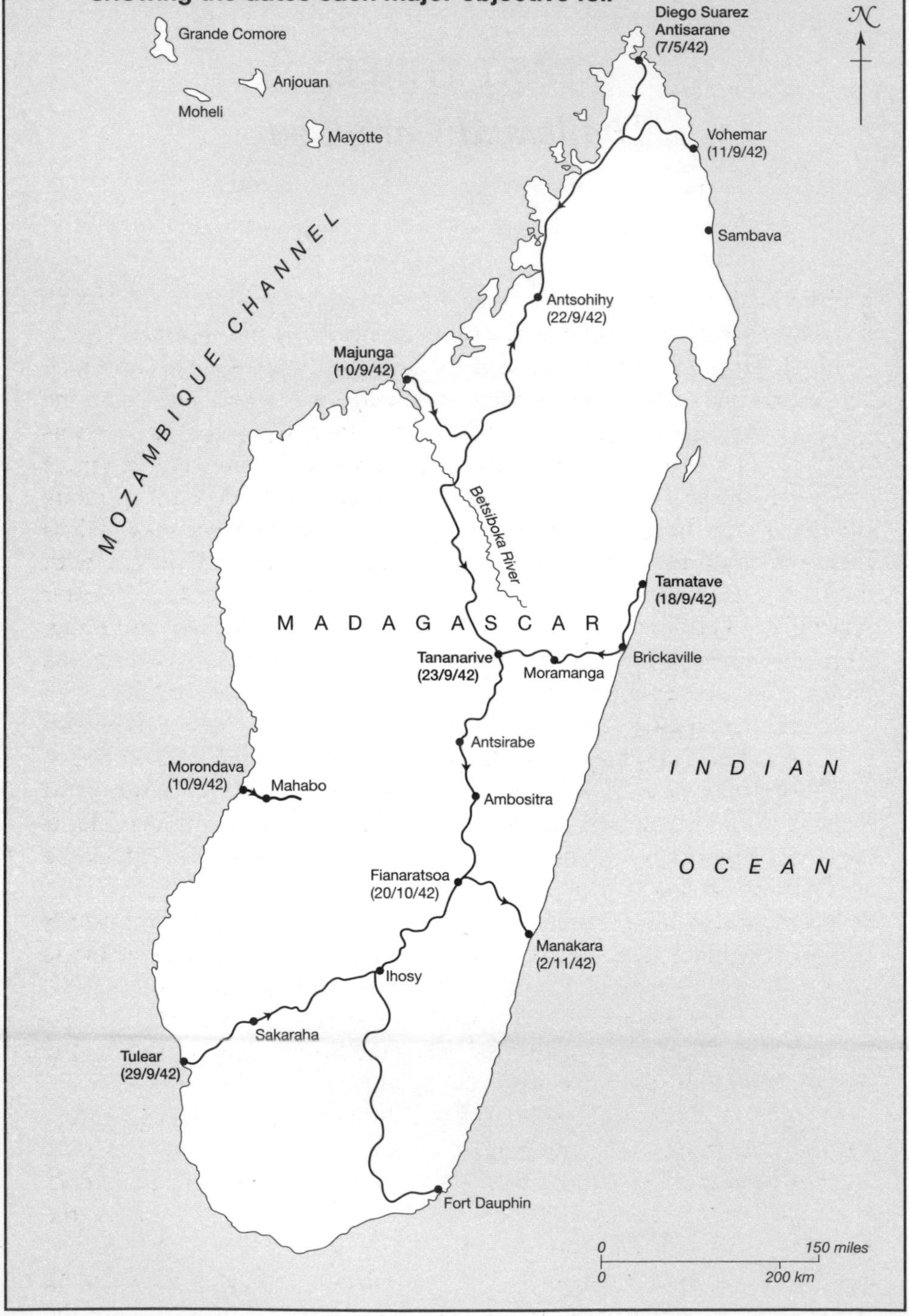

Chapter Twenty-One

In the madness of a world at war Tananarive seemed to be one of its oases of sanity. Visitors had always been struck by the spacious beauty of the Madagascan capital, a pleasing blend of the Franco-Malgache which sat towards the eastern edge of the central plateau and 100 miles from the nearest coast. Surmounted by the palace of its long deposed royalty, it was built around a narrow hilltop some 700 feet above the emerald-green rice paddies of the surrounding plain, its red-roofed houses descending along a series of ridge lines like the legs of a giant starfish. Between these ridges were gardens and sports fields and broad, tree-lined boulevards with churches, restaurants and pavement cafés. At first glance only the poster rash that had erupted on every wall space, the urgent slogans reminding, '*Travaille! Famille! Patrie!*' and '*Vive Pétain!*' gave any hint of the horrors and excitements beyond its shores.

Among the capital's French-speaking elite Berthe Mayer was well known as an accomplished pianist who had studied at London's Royal School of Music. She was the wife of Percy Mayer who, like her, had been born and brought up in the British colony of Mauritius. Mayer's considerable, if now mostly moribund business interests, included being local agent for the Ford Motor Company.

At a time when almost everything, including entertainment, was in short supply in the blockaded Vichy colony and even baguettes were being made from rice, Berthe's musical soirees were popular. Imagine then her friends' surprise had they known that the pianist's fast and assured touch with a Morse key had become equally admired by the British signals personnel at Special Operations Executive's African headquarters in Durban.

At the end of October 1941 Madame Mayer went to her bathroom, extracted her transmitter from behind its false ceiling and began to tap out the most important signal her husband – for mostly she played postman to his spy – had yet to send to Durban. As a result, on 3 November, the Royal Navy captured an entire convoy of five Vichy blockade-runners as they left Madagascar for France. Even with Britain's appetite for shipping it was an enormous meal at one sitting: 40,000 tons worth. Among the prizes were the liner *Compiegne*, the SS *Padaran* and the SS *Bangkok* which in July had delivered six twin-engined Potez 63–11 bombers to the island. The *Padaran*, her engines damaged in an attempt to scuttle, was doggedly towed the 362 miles to South Africa's Port Elizabeth in just under four days. 'A very fine show indeed,' declared Admiral John Godfrey, the Director of Naval Intelligence, in a letter of thanks to SOE.

German reaction was equally predictable. The idea that French lack of security, perhaps even Gaullist infiltration, had allowed Britain to replenish some of its own merchant shipping losses so easily was intolerable. Its representatives on the Armistice Commission, which ultimately controlled all Vichy military movements, forbade Darlan to send any more reinforcements to Indian Ocean waters. By the spring of 1942, when Vichy's Secretariat of Marine was becoming increasingly convinced that the English had Syrian designs on Madagascar, this unexpected bonus of Madame Mayer's timely signal was still in place.

Madagascar is the world's fourth biggest island after Greenland, New Guinea and Borneo. It is as long as New Zealand and larger than France, being 1,000 miles in length and 400 at its widest point. Once heavily forested, by the middle of the twentieth century slash and burn clearance for rice growing and a voracious timber industry greedy for its ebony and rosewood had all but devoured it. An estimated seven-eighths of the island was covered in tall prairie grass interspersed with clumps of bamboo and stands of the tall traveller's tree, a native palm (*Ravenala madagascariensis*) whose huge leaves hold enough water to save a man from dying of thirst and provide excellent house thatch.

In 1942 about 4 million people lived on the island which gave it a population density of five people per square kilometre, one of the smallest in the world. About 3.6 million were native Malagasy who are not of African but mainly Indonesian stock, the descendants of a migration across the Indian Ocean that peaked about the time of England's Norman conquest. Their language has old Austronesian roots though they have mingled enough with their African and Arab neighbours to acquire words from both. About 25,000 resident French were equally divided between the colonial civil servants who administered the island and the *colons* who tried to get rich by exporting its wood, vanilla and the graphite used in electrodes. There were also 10,500 Africans and Asians, among the latter a fairly prosperous community of Chinese traders, some 3,000 Europeans who had the misfortune not to be French and, officially, about 2,000 Métis which, given the reputation of its colonizers, seems like a remarkably small number. On the north-west coast there were small communities of Swahili-speaking Muslims from the Comoros Islands at the northern end of the broad Mozambique Channel separating Madagascar from East Africa.

Unlike the smaller Indian Ocean islands of Réunion, restored to France in 1815 as a post-Waterloo goodwill gesture from its new rulers, and Mauritius, which the privateer Surcouf knew as the Ile de France, Britain and France had never fought over Madagascar. On the contrary, in 1845 an Anglo-French military expedition tried and failed to topple Queen Ranavalona who, riled by the westernization of her realm, had persecuted Christian converts and expelled missionaries. A particular target was the London Missionary Society whose Protestant ministers had considerably increased literacy by devising a Latin alphabet for Malagasy that had only ever been written down in Arabic script.

After Ranavalona's death in 1861, the missionaries were allowed back and French influence, commercial and military, increased, though Madagascar avoided formal European annexation until 1896. For the first ten years there were a series of uprisings, sometimes bloodily suppressed. But by the 1930s coffee, tobacco and cloves crops had been introduced, three major roads and some railways built and bush airstrips cleared. About half its population still practised a lavish form of ancestor worship involving occasional outings for the dead who were returned in new shrouds to tombs better built than most houses. The other half were Christians, though often by no means entirely immune to the old ways, and about equally divided between the Protestant and Catholic churches.

Like Djibouti on the Red Sea, Madagascar was isolated from France's other African possessions, being much closer to the Anglophile President Jan Smuts's Union of South Africa and the British colonies of Kenya and Tanganyika. When France fell Governor Jules Marcel de Coppet, a socialist appointee of the Popular Front not long in office, walked into the studios of Radio Tananarive and made a broadcast that seemed to be advising his listeners to support de Gaulle. For a moment it appeared he might have caught a defiant, anti-armistice mood among the whites. Then along came the casualty lists from Mers-el-Kébir and, though he could have relied on South African military support, the governor dithered and de Gaulle had to accept the loss – for the moment.

In any case, Vichy's National Revolution with its emphasis on hard work, family values and unflinching patriotism was undoubtedly the message Madagascar's *colons* really wanted to hear for, like expatriates everywhere, they had long suspected the old country was going to the dogs. Léon Blum's Popular Front could never be their France. With this went an instinctive Anglophobia, their creed a casual Fashoda complex that left them in no doubt that the English had always lusted after all of French Africa. Nor was the governor's case helped by the unanimous support he received from British missionaries. Vichy replaced de Coppet with his immediate predecessor, the Algerian-born Léon Cayla.

This was a popular choice among many of the Malagasy as well as the whites, for the ebullient Cayla had been Madagascar's longest serving governor – nine years from 1930 to 1939 – and in some circles was considered the man mostly responsible for improving the colony's economy. Then in April 1941 Cayla, who like de Coppet was almost 60, had to retire for health reasons. He was replaced by Armand Annet, previously Lieutenant Governor of Dahomey, before 1919 German Togoland, and at 52 coming towards the end of an unblemished career in the colonial service. Annet was shrewd, hard-working, had all his generation's reverence for Pétain and knew how to please. In a report to his immediate boss, Amiral Platon, Vichy's Secretary General to the Colonies, he obviously delighted in recounting how he had revived an ancient tribute ceremony in which the local aristocracy offered him the first sheaf of their rice harvest. 'I responded that the call to work was one of the precepts of the Marshal. Then I handed a symbolic angady [spade] to each of the sheaf carriers.'

From the start Percy Mayer had regretted the departure of Governor de Coppet and had been anti-Pétain. Both ends of the Indian Ocean were British and, quite apart from any other considerations, Vichy's isolation was not good for a family who thrived on trade. The Mayers, who were of Alsatian and possibly Jewish stock, had long been established in Mauritius. Percy was born there in 1903, a French-speaking British subject of the colony's wealthy and close-knit Eurasian mercantile class who prided themselves on having the best of all worlds: French style, British law, the world's two major languages, a knowledge of wine and a touch of Indian cuisine. Although he had studied engineering in London, there was never any doubt that he would join the family firm Edwin Mayer & Co whose interests included rice and flour mills, a distillery, insurance, and importing refrigerators, radios and bicycles as well as cars.

Clever, energetic and ambitious, in 1934 Percy was appointed the firm's permanent representative in Madagascar and shortly afterwards, because it made things easier in business, acquired French citizenship. As well as being an accomplished yachtsman, he was also a good amateur pilot who had set up an air service to those parts of the island that remained inaccessible by road. In 1938, during a visit to Mauritius, he had married his cousin Berthe Mayer, a striking, raven-haired young woman who had recently returned from her London interlude, and took her back to his well-appointed house in Tananarive and the Steinway piano he had bought her.

Vichy rule gradually severed Madagascar's contacts with its Anglo neighbours. In November 1940 Mayer had arrived in South Africa on the last passenger ship from Madagascar's east coast port of Tamatave and contacted Lord Harlech, Britain's High Commissioner who was based in Cape Town. 'Mayer is ready to put his services at the disposal of the British authorities in order to assist in any way the detachment of the island from allegiance to Vichy,' Harlech reported to London. SOE took a look at Mayer and liked what it saw. 'Great charm, absolutely fearless and clear minded.'

The Mauritian managed to prolong his stay in South Africa for four months. During this time he was given intensive wireless training, learning to use a high-speed Morse key, coding and decoding, and operating a suitcase transmitter. Then he returned to Madagascar with his radio, sailing to the west coast port of Majunga in a small boat he had bought after persuading a Bank Line steamer to put him and his craft down in the Mozambique Channel some 250 miles from the island's west coast. In October 1941 he returned to Durban on a shorter visit, this time going via the neutral Portuguese port of Lourenço Marques where he had been dropped by a Malagasy blockade-runner.

The Treasury agreed to pay SOE an extra £4,000 a year to fund Mayer who, as well as setting up a network of agents, was expected to spend a good deal of it on subversion and propaganda. In addition, Sir Bede Clifford, the Governor of Mauritius, which was the nearest British listening post to Madagascar, had encouraged SOE to set up France Libre d'Outremer, a radio station that made entirely unfounded allegations about the private lives of the devout Catholic Annet and his underlings. In Whitehall it was hoped that their agent, by dint of 'bribery, corruption, murder', would bring the island into the Anglo-Gaullist fold on the cheap and save the blood and treasure of a full-scale invasion.

But it soon became clear that the colony's ability to feed itself, an apathetic civilian majority, and a ruling clique of no more than 100 senior military and civil servants made the chances of an anti-Pétainist coup remote. 'I am convinced, and Mayer confirms, that propaganda alone will never alter the political situation in Madagascar,' Sir Bede reported.

But there was little appetite in London for military intervention, though de Gaulle hoped that his representative in South Africa might persuade Jan Smuts to have a word with Churchill. Then, thousands of miles away from Madagascar, a remorseless series of events began to take its toll. Relations between Japan and the Americans, who were supplying the Chinese military in its war against the Japanese invaders, were going from bad to worse. Talks with a Japanese delegation in Washington about lifting the US trade embargo against Japan had reached an impasse. Tokyo was scarcely bothering to hide its preparations for a wider war. In French Indochina Vichy, without even a token resistance, had allowed Japan to move into naval bases and military airfields in southern Vietnam and Cambodia. A few days before Japan's almost simultaneous attacks on Pearl Harbor, Hong Kong and northern Malaya, the British Chiefs of Staff were already discussing the awful possibility that the French might grant the Axis powers similar facilities on its huge African island.

Britain's main supply route to Egypt avoided running the Mediterranean gauntlet by sailing around the Cape then through the Mozambique Channel between Madagascar and East Africa en route to the Red Sea and the Suez canal. Godfrey's naval intelligence department argued that they would all sleep better at nights if a pre-emptive strike secured for the Royal Navy the port of Diego Suarez on the island's north-eastern tip. Entered through a mile-wide gap in a cliff between Cap Diego and the dockyard town of Antsirane, it was a superb natural harbour almost big enough to accommodate the entire Japanese fleet. In 1935 France had completed new jetties and oil bunkering facilities there and its narrow entrance was commanded by formidable coastal batteries. It would be a foolhardy enemy who tried to get through its front door.

On 10 December 1941 Japanese torpedo-bombers based on Vichy's Indochina airfields took ninety minutes to sink, with the loss of over 800 men, the *Prince of Wales* and HMS *Repulse* which were off the Malayan coast and just in range of the aircraft's new landing grounds. Churchill heard the news in bed and turned his face to the wall in one of his rare moments of utter despair. The *Prince of Wales* was Britain's newest battleship and had been sent to the Far East in the hope that the sight of her awesome profile would keep Tokyo neutral. Shortly after the news of the sinkings was announced, Darlan was seen at an official reception in animated conversation with the Emperor's ambassador to Vichy. As the Japanese blitzkrieg gathered momentum, and in rapid succession the Anglo-Americans suffered defeat after defeat, preparations for the Madagascar operation gathered apace. On 23 December, forty-eight hours before the Christmas Day surrender of Hong Kong, Major General Robert Sturges of the Royal Marines was appointed commander of Force 121: the land element of what would be Britain's first major amphibious landings since Gallipoli where Lieutenant Sturges had heard his first shots in anger and whose mistakes he was determined to avoid. Its code-name was Ironclad.

The nucleus of Force 121 was to be Brigadier Francis Festing's 29th Independent Brigade Group. This was an obvious choice because for over a year it had been in Scotland undergoing the kind of intensive training for combined operations normally confined to the Commandos. Its men had spent months living on ships and getting in and out of landing craft and to all intents and purposes were marine infantry, though the Commandos sometimes tended to be a bit sniffy about their boat-handling skills. Instead of an infantry brigade's usual three battalions the 29th had four: 1st Royal Scots Fusiliers; 2nd Royal Welch Fusiliers; 2nd South Lancashires; 2nd East Lancashires plus an independent artillery battery, the 455th Light, with four 3.7-inch howitzers and two 25-pounders. There was also an anti-aircraft troop of four Bofors.

For Operation Ironclad, Festing's brigade was strengthened by the attachment of two other units. One was 5 Commando, 500 men who had been training even longer than 11 Scottish had been when they went into action on the Litani and were just as keen, though their hard-drinking commanding officer was nowhere near as good as Pedder. The other was the Royal Armoured Corps' Special Service B Squadron with its twelve tanks: six Valentines and six Tetrarchs.

The latter was a small, fast, but thinly armoured tracked reconnaissance vehicle named after one of the essential four parts of an ancient Macedonian phalanx. Like the heavier Valentine, it was armed with a 2-pounder cannon as well as a machine gun but this did not stop it being any more than a mini-tank.

In the early part of 1942 about twenty of them were shipped to the Soviet Union where they were treated with the kind of curiosity an élite cavalry unit might reserve for a troop of Shetland ponies. No tank has ever been spacious but perhaps only certain Japanese models ever required the same Houdini-like contortions as the Tetrarch and the men who commanded them seemed, at best, to look back on the experience with a kind of exasperated affection.

> It was like looking through a bloody periscope, shaving, riding a bike, reading a map, talking on the wireless and doing ten other things at once. The gunner had an amusing act as well. He had a seat which went up and down; to his right was the big two pounder gun and to the right of that a machine gun. He had two triggers – left hand for the two pounder and right hand for the machine gun. By moving his shoulder up and down against a pad, and bumping his seat up and down, he could move the gun. His eye was glued onto a periscope with a brow pad that held his head steady while his left hand turned a handle which traversed the turret, and with his left foot he cracked walnuts!

All these tank crews were volunteers for special operations abroad involving landing armour on a defended enemy beach, then a novel concept. Some had just spent a frustrating six months confined with their Tetrarchs in the cramped and sticky accommodation of a fleet auxiliary tanker at Sierra Leone, poised to invade Spain's West African island of Fernando Po should Hitler persuade Franco into the war. But a year after they were founded this was the nearest the squadron had come to seeing any action.

Most of them were regulars who had already fought in France in 1940 and felt the Germans were not as good as they were cracked up to be. Second-in-command Captain Peter Llewellyn Palmer of the 10th Hussars, a popular officer, had been delighted to discover men in the squadron eager to 'continue where we left off'. Among them was Llewellyn Palmer's gunner, and devoted unofficial batman, Lance Corporal Clegg, who had served out a pre-war enlistment with the 10th Hussars and been a reservist working for the General Post Office when he was recalled to the colours. In the interest of esprit de corps all ranks had received the same training as the Commandos in unarmed combat until, according to a clearly mystified Clegg: 'We were considered good enough to look after ourselves should we become involved in a pub brawl.' More relevant, as things turned out, they polished their small arms skills, not only with Brens and Thompson sub-machine guns but also with the .38 revolvers all tank crews were supposed to carry.

But by the beginning of March 1942, almost three months after it had been decided to seize Diego Suarez before the Japanese did, Clegg and his comrades along with the rest of General Sturges's Force 121 were still in Scotland. Britain, in what Churchill later called its 'worst disaster', had surrendered Singapore and the Americans were in the process of losing the Philippines. India itself, the jewel in the crown, was threatened and in London opinion was sharply divided about whether Madagascar was important enough to divert precious resources that should be going further east. The divisions were on familiar lines: Churchill was for it. 'If the Japanese walked into the island, our inaction would take a deal of explaining away.' And Wavell, now India's woefully accoutred Commander-in-Chief, was as against it as he had been to the Iraq and Syrian interventions. 'Sheer madness,' he warned. 'Unless War Cabinet considers Ironclad of greater strategical importance than Ceylon.' Alan Brooke, the new Chief of the Imperial General Staff, backed him, saying there was, 'Little to gain by it.'

Then the American ability to break the Japanese diplomatic cypher revealed that Berlin was encouraging Tokyo, which already had a carrier task force in the eastern part of the Indian Ocean, to occupy the island and cut the 8th Army's supply line before Rommel launched his next offensive. On 12 March the War Cabinet agreed to go ahead with Operation Ironclad and named South African-born Rear Admiral Neville Syfret as its Combined Commander. In addition, it was decided to learn the lessons of Syria and apply the kind of overwhelming force that would assure a swift and decisive victory. The 5th Division was being rushed out to India but en route two of its three brigades, about 12,000 men including six infantry battalions, would go via Madagascar. Neither the British nor the Germans consulted their respective 'friendly French' about their plans for the colony. In London the political advantages of a Gaullist fig leaf were outweighed by memories of the loose talk that preceded Dakar, the reluctance to fight other Frenchmen in Syria and the need for maximum security.

Ironclad was not an easy operation to keep secret, though the army did its best by issuing some of the troops involved with the kind of Arctic clothing that might suggest a large-scale raid on Norway. Festing's 29th Brigade was travelling with the entire 5th Division which would be loaning two-thirds of its infantry to Ironclad before it saw Bombay and expected to get them back in the state they left them. When their convoy set out it was the biggest to leave Liverpool since the war began and Doenitz's U-boats were at the peak of their success.

But Operation Ironclad got off to a good start and on 5 April all the ships arrived safely at Freetown in Sierra Leone. At this point, out of the 7,000 or so soldiers, sailors and airmen aboard, only Admiral Syfret, General Sturges and perhaps a dozen or so others knew where they were going. On the *Winchester Castle* Bombardier Frederick Bailey, a driver with 455 Independent Battery, took a mournful first look at the muddy waters and red earth of Africa. After a year's strenuous training for amphibious landings Bailey, a London lorry driver called up in 1939 shortly before his twenty-second birthday, assumed their destination must be Egypt and the nearest they were going to get to a beach was the Western Desert. It was not until they reached Durban, where most convoys stopped en route for Egypt or India, that Bailey found the port 'alive with rumours that we were going to attack the French in Madagascar'. Then orders to waterproof their vehicles tended to confirm that Rommel probably had the good fortune not to be facing 455 Light Battery in the near future.

They were back at sea, watching the flying fish play as they headed north up the Mozambique Channel, when commanding officers gathered their men and the scuttlebutt was confirmed: they were going to capture Madagascar's Diego Suarez harbour. D-Day was set for 0400 hours, 5 May. There was a spate of last letters home before they were separated from the navy's postal links, in this case one of the fleet's auxiliary ships to the British Forces Post Office in Durban. Often there was no time to scribble more than a couple of lines of love and reassurance. 'Please don't worry, you are more than ever in my thoughts at this time,' concluded Corporal Roland Moss, one of the 2nd South Lancashires best footballers, to his wife Catherine who had been working in a cotton mill in Stockport when he met her. Their son, also Roland, was almost 2 and they were expecting their second child. The only action Moss had seen to date was during basic training when he had been sent to help civilians caught up in the Liverpool Blitz.

'Operation Ironclad is on. I wonder what sort of battle it's going to be?' Captain Joseph Patterson, the Medical Officer for 5 Commando, asked himself some twelve hours before zero hour. Patterson, who was 32, had volunteered for the Royal Army Medical Corps at the outbreak of war, seen action in France and joined the Commandos shortly after being evacuated from Dunkirk. He was keeping a diary for the wife he had left behind at Windermere in the Lake District where he ran a general practice.

> I don't feel scared, only rather tired and a little bit excited. I must try and get some sleep. This [the diary] must be packed with the rest of my kit. Breakfast is at midnight. The situation in Burma is bad. I should be feeling more nervous if it were Japs or Germans we were up against. There is really no reason why we should lose this battle but I dare say we shall have a fair number of casualties, especially on the beaches ... *Ramilles*, *Illustrious* and *Indomitable* are all in a row on our port ... It was amusing yesterday on

the BBC to hear that the *Illustrious* had just arrived in a British port after being repaired in America. I could see her through the porthole as they said it and we were somewhere off the south coast of Madagascar.

There were two aircraft carriers: the *Illustrious* and the *Indomitable*. The *Illustrious*, which had undergone major surgery in a US dockyard after being badly damaged by dive bombers off Malta, was back in action for the first time in over a year. The *Indomitable*, recently based in Ceylon, was borrowed from Admiral Somerville's new command, the much depleted Far East fleet, which was currently playing hide and seek with superior Japanese forces in the eastern half of the Indian Ocean.

Including the merchant navy vessels carrying the landing forces and their equipment, Syfret now had over fifty ships under him. Accompanying the aircraft carriers were the old and rather slow 15-inch-gun battleship *Ramillies*, two cruisers, eleven destroyers, four minesweepers, and eight of the little U-boat hunters the navy called corvettes. These wore green, white and blue zigzags of camouflage paint with splashes of red and, according to Patterson, 'look very pretty nipping around us'.

The *Ramillies*, launched in 1913 and one of the few British warships named after an old victory over the French (albeit a land one), was flying the admiral's flag. For Syfret to have done otherwise was still unthinkable. Yet his carriers provided at least as much firepower. Their eighty-six aircraft included twenty American-built Grumman F4 Wildcats, which the Fleet Air Arm insisted on calling Martlets, as well as Sea Hurricanes and Fulmars. Albacores and Swordfish biplanes would deliver bombs or torpedoes.

The French had a little over thirty aircraft of which the best were twenty Morane 406 fighters and seven Potez 63–11 twin-engined bombers that had arrived the previous summer on some of the ships that, thanks to Percy and Berthe Mayer, had been intercepted on their way back to France. There were also a few old Potez 25s, biplanes that had mainly been used for courier work. On the ground, Vichy forces in Madagascar totalled about 8,000 of whom perhaps three-quarters were native Malagasy and the rest Senegalese or French, most of the latter being in the navy. All the infantry were French-officered Africans, either local or West African, and so was most of the artillery, the exception being the coastal batteries which were manned by the navy. According to surviving Vichy documents the Diego Suarez garrison seems to have been no more than 3,000 strong at most, consisting of a three battalion brigade group, the 2 Régiment mixte malgache; an artillery regiment of a dozen or so 75mm guns, some mule-drawn; five coastal batteries, some with large-calibre battleship guns; a battery of 90mm anti-aircraft guns and eight anti-tank guns of 65mm and 75mm calibre.

Defending Diego Suarez had always been a simple proposition for the French. Since its narrow entrance and covering batteries made the harbour almost impregnable to a hostile fleet, the majority of their troops were facing the western side of the island's northern isthmus where the most obvious landing places were two neighbouring bays, Courrier and the smaller Ambararata. These waters were full of reefs and shoals and the three safe passages through them were well mined. For anything that survived the mines, both bays were covered by a single coastal battery. Its fire was directed by field telephone from an observation post overlooking the beaches on the summit of a 1,300-foot rocky volcanic plug that rose suddenly from the flat ground. The French, no doubt with a certain irony, called this protuberance Windsor Castle and its use dated from Maréchal Joffre's tenure as Fortress Commander.

In 1909, five years before Joffre saved Paris from the Kaiser when his fame rested on a desert crossing and the conquest of Timbuktu, he passed his time laying the foundations for Diego Suarez to protect itself from some jealous maritime power with nearby bases. One Fashoda was quite enough and the British, Germans and Portuguese all had East African colonies. Windsor Castle was Joffre's most visible contribution to the Diego Suarez defences. But the most important was 2 miles of trenches and pill boxes he built on some rising ground about 2 miles south of the Antsirane dockyards. At either end was a low loopholed stone and concrete redoubt, one named Fort Caimans and the other Fort Bellevue. This line, which was on the narrowest part of the Antsirane peninsula, covered the three main red-dirt roads into town. From both flanking forts the land fell down scrub-covered slopes to mangrove-fringed shore lines. In between the terrain varied: rocks and scrub near the roads then not far off them tall stands of pampas grass and some woodland.

Over the years, parts of the Joffre line had been neglected: scorpions nested in its crumbling pill boxes, its diggings became clogged and overgrown until it was hard to find them in places. But in recent months, as fears of invasion increased, the scorpions had been evicted and loopholes fitted with wire netting to prevent their return, the trench system traced and re-dug though in places the vegetation that hid it was left. About half a mile in front of it unhappy civilian forced labour dug a formidable anti-tank ditch as broad as it was deep, which was well over 6 feet. Some navy-crewed 75mm guns were moved into the forts. Exercises were held whereby a mobile reserve supported by most of the available anti-tank guns could be rushed into place. Thirty years after it was built, the Joffre line was being treated exactly as a treasured heirloom should be and restored to working condition.

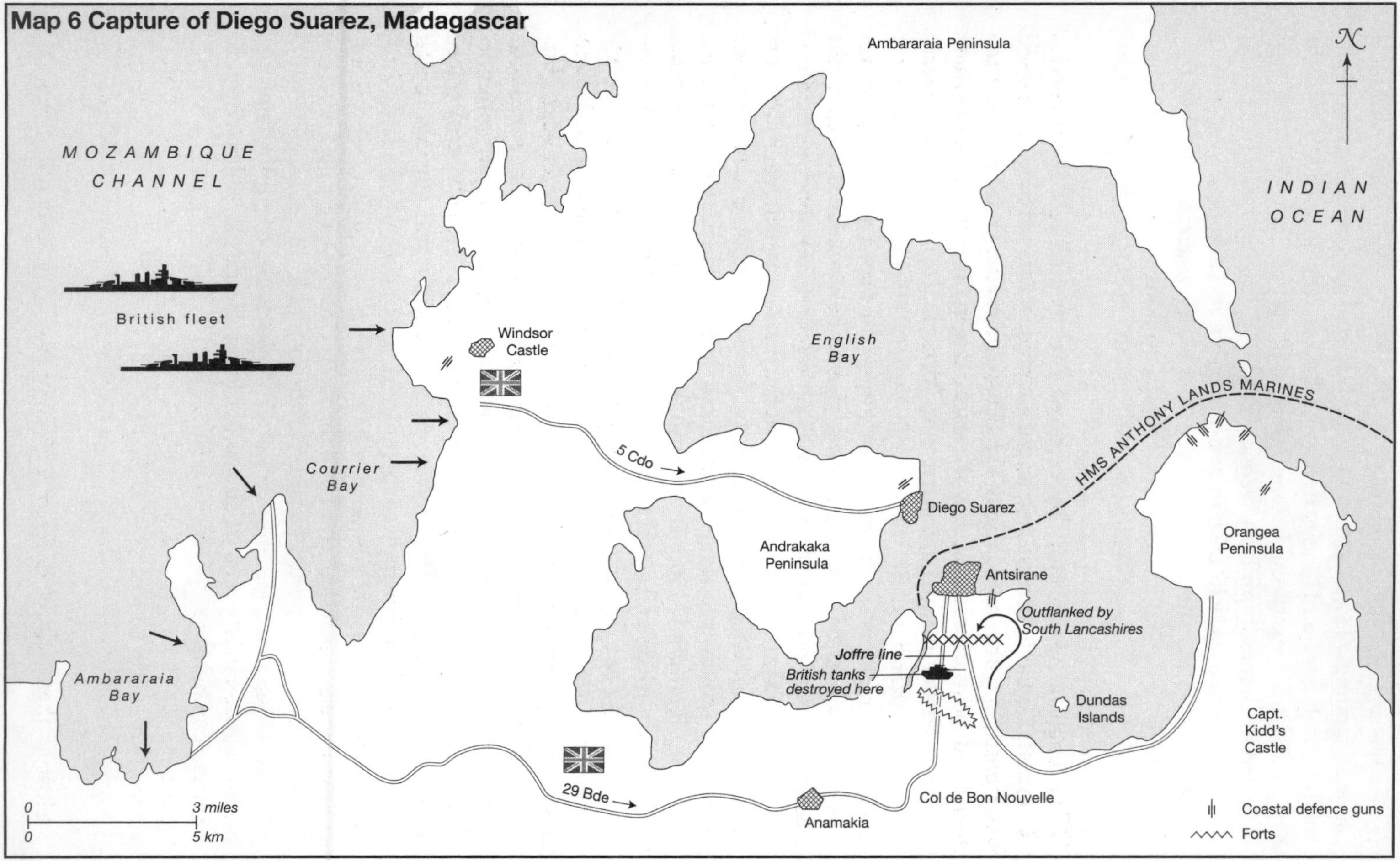
Map 6 Capture of Diego Suarez, Madagascar
Ambararaia Peninsula
MOZAMBIQUE CHANNEL
INDIAN OCEAN
British fleet
Windsor Castle
English Bay
HMS ANTHONY LANDS MARINES
5 Cdo
Courrier Bay
Diego Suarez
Andrakaka Peninsula
Antsirane
Orangea Peninsula
Outflanked by South Lancashires
Joffre line
British tanks destroyed here
Dundas Islands
Capt. Kidd's Castle
Ambararaia Bay
29 Bde
Anamakia
Col de Bon Nouvelle
0 3 miles
0 5 km
Coastal defence guns
Forts

Chapter Twenty-Two

The English did land on the west coast of the island's northern tip exactly as the French suspected they would. But what they envisaged was a costly daylight assault with the defenders gradually falling back to their fixed positions having already inflicted demoralizing losses. What they were unable to imagine was an invader capable of putting a large force ashore after dark.

'Firing at night is not contemplated, the entrance to the bay being considered impossible,' read part of the standing orders discovered by delighted Commandos at the Windsor Castle observation post above Baie du Courrier. Instead Syfret's ships, operating under the uncertain light of a waning moon, had astonished the French by first sweeping then marking a safe channel with green lighted buoys. In the process fifty-seven mines were lifted. It was the kind of naval trick the English were supposed to excel at and their opponents should have known better.

Not even the accidental detonation of the last two mines to be collected in the clearing gear of the minesweepers spoilt it. As the orders 'let go kedge anchor' and 'fix bayonets' announced that they were about to hit the beach, 5 Commando's first wave were convinced that the explosions must have brought triggers to first pressure and they were only waiting for them to get closer. But much to his delight Captain Bill Knight, one of the two attached Royal Artillery forward observation officers sent to each landing beach, found himself stepping onto a silent shore. Behind him, with wireless and Morse lamps, came the three navy signallers who were his link to the 4.7-inch guns on the destroyer HMS *Laforey*.

> We moved up to the gun position which we could see quite clearly in the moonlight. Strangely enough, all was quiet and deserted, no sentries posted and no sign of life at all. We removed the breech blocks from the guns and put them in a place apart just in case of a counter attack and could not help wondering what had happened. As dawn broke we saw some buildings nearby and went to investigate. There we found the gunners all in bed.

Most of them were Malagasy with French officers and *sous-officiers*.

Only the French fought. A Commando was stabbed through the arm and one of the Frenchmen took a burst from a Thompson sub-machine gun. Another grabbed a bayonet and charged at Lieutenant 'Dopey' Rose, so called because his brother officers insisted he looked remarkably like that member of the Seven Dwarfs. But Dopey proved fast enough with a Colt .45 automatic and brought his assailant down with a single shot through his forehead. A horrified Knight, who had celebrated his twenty-first birthday shortly before his convoy left Liverpool, could not help noticing how much bigger the exit wound was.

> That was the end of the opposition. One elderly French officer was clearly enraged by these events and shouted at me, '*Ce n'est pas bon ça*', and then observing my badges of rank coupled with my tender years he went on, '*Vous êtes trop jeune pour capitaine.*' No doubt I was but it was none of his business. I expect promotion prospects were bleak in a colonial backwater like Madagascar.

Dr Patterson, who was not feeling his best with 'bad bellyache' from a bout of gastroenteritis that had been going through his troopship since before Durban, treated the bayoneted Commando then examined the Frenchman who had taken the Tommy-gun burst. He discovered that the man had a broken thigh, a shattered arm, and three bullets through his belly. He did what he could for him and got him stretchered down to the beach for evacuation to one of the ships if he survived that long. To his amazement his patient would make a complete recovery.

By now a white flag was fluttering from the observation post on the top of Windsor Castle and Patterson watched as some of the Commandos under a Captain 'Chips' Heron started their way up to take the surrender. 'It was beginning to get hot and I didn't envy them the climb.' But once Heron's party had neared the top there seems to have been a change of mind, for somebody dropped a grenade on them which wounded Chips in the leg. Once he was back down, Knight and his signallers got busy and *Laforey*'s guns 'knocked the concrete off the top of the hill, complete with inmates'.

'The battery at Courrier Bay was unable to fire a single shot,' noted the official postmortem, which would not be circulated around the Vichy War Office for another four months. 'They were taken by surprise and overwhelmed.' The gunners were asleep when the Commandos arrived. Surprise was achieved because they did not believe a night landing was possible and the last-minute telephone call from Windsor Castle which might have woken them up did not arrive. The man responsible for this was the SOE's Percy Mayer.

Some 500 miles north of his home in the capital, the remote and security-conscious naval base around Diego Suarez did not offer much in the way of commercial cover for Mayer. But two weeks before the invasion the inventive and well-connected Mauritian came up with an excellent reason to spend an awful lot of time there.

Diego Suarez was getting short of rice which was the staple diet of most of the troops defending it, Malagasy and Senegalese. Deliveries by both road and ship had been severely reduced by the fuel shortage brought on by the British blockade. A small amount was getting in on dhows but wind and tide often made this impossible. Mayer persuaded the authorities that he might have the solution.

Let him explore the possibility of bringing the rice up the coast in chains of barges towed by wood-burning tugs and unloading it (where else) at Ambararata Bay. From there he proposed to find sufficient dirt road, even if he had to do a little road building himself, to truck it up to Diego Suarez. Obviously, considerable reconnaissance of the overland route would be necessary. The military could not do enough to accommodate him, starting by allowing him to ship his own car to Ambararata and providing all the petrol he required.

For the two weeks preceding the invasion, based in Antsirane's Hôtel François, Mayer had mixed freely with both the Diego Suarez garrison and its civil authorities. He had called on District Commissioner Garrouste whose enthusiasm for his rice transport was unbounded. He had visited Courrier Bay and met a lonely and garrulous French sergeant who claimed to command its defences and invited him to go fishing with him the following Sunday. 'We had a drink and he then showed me all over the defences, position of machine-guns, signalling gear, gave me the number and composition of troops etcetera.' There had been an informative lunch with Colonel Édouard Clarebout, who was in charge of the army at Diego Suarez, and a guided tour of the harbour where he had been shown over the submarine *Bévézier* and noted alongside her *Le Héros* preparing to go out on patrol. Above all there was a meeting with Capitaine de vaisseau Paul Maerten, the naval commander.

Mayer and Maerten, who often visited the capital, were already well acquainted and had, to say the least, an ambivalent relationship. Six months before, Mayer had decided that Maerten was ready, if the bribe was big enough, to allow the British to take over Diego Suarez without a fight. But when he had broached with him the hopelessness of the Vichy cause, Madagascar's isolation and the need for a strong man to seize his opportunity, it appeared he had made a terrible misjudgement. Capitaine Maerten, it seemed, might enjoy the good things in life but he was as Pétainist as the next man and if he had to tighten his belt he would. He found this kind of treasonable talk appalling. Yet not, it seemed, quite appalling enough to turn Mayer in. During his recent meeting Mayer had suggested that perhaps a better place for unloading the rice would be Courrier Bay. Maerten had told him that this would be a very bad idea because the navy had just mined the place and Mayer had departed with another trophy.

Passing on these gems to the attention of the approaching fleet was not so easy. It would have been far too risky to bring his suitcase transmitter to Diego Suarez and there was little he could tell Berthe in a lightly coded conversation over an open telephone line when his hotel operator was able to get a call through to the capital. The best communications SOE could lay on were through the *Lindi*, one of SOE's wooden-hulled dhows with sails and an old Perkins diesel engine which operated out of Dar Es Salaam in Tanganyika. The *Lindi* was engaged in mapping and sometimes buoying channels to the invasion beaches and had a powerful transmitter as well as sonar aboard.

On 29 April, a week before D-Day, the spy kept a rendezvous at Ambararata Bay with a landing party off the boat. It was through this meeting that Syfret received the latest list of Vichy ships operating out of Diego Suarez: the converted liner *Bougainville*, ugly with guns and grafts of armour plate and considered an auxiliary cruiser; *D'Entrecasteaux*, an anti-submarine sloop with lots of depth charges and the same calibre guns carried by most British destroyers; and the submarines *Bévéziers*, *Le Héros*, *Monge* and *Le Glorieux* with the last two thought to be out on patrol. The only other vessel of interest was a small German merchantman, the SS *Wartenfels*, which had arrived there in March in a dash from neutral Portuguese East Africa where she had been stuck since the beginning of the war. There was speculation that there might be a German naval wireless team on board monitoring British merchant traffic in the Mozambique Channel for the U-boats.

The French submarines posed the main and most obvious threat to Syfret's ships unless a Vichy bomber could get through the fighter screen. And from Diego Suarez harbour itself, the two surface vessels, particularly the sloop with her shallower draught, could move alongside and harass any troops moving towards them along the isthmus that shielded them from the invaders, though they could fire over it. It was decided, in the first strike anyway, to let the Fleet Air Arm deal with all the enemy shipping. Mayer also brought them up to date on troop deployments including the latest refurbishment along the Joffre line, where he had visited an officer who lived in a hamlet the French called Joffreville.

Mayer had arranged for another meeting with a landing party off the *Lindi* in three days' time and set about preparing maps and notes to update his latest report. But out of a mixture of muddle and faint-heartedness, the *Lindi*'s crew failed to keep this second rendezvous, leaving the Mauritian to spend hours pacing the shore before he accepted that they were not going to turn up and drove back to his hotel. Apart from being unable to hand over his notes and sketches he had been curious to receive some written instructions for the knockout drops he had been given at their last encounter.

The idea was that, on the eve of the invasion, Mayer would throw a party at the François with the best black-market booze the SOE could buy. It would be a classy affair for *de tout* Diego Suarez from which Maerten and Clarebout, sipping their adulterated drinks, would awake a day older to find that their confused and leaderless command had surrendered and they were themselves prisoners of war. The problem was that the man from the *Lindi* who had delivered the drops, and had no idea what was planned, was under the impression that they lasted no more than the three minutes an agent might need to escape an embarrassing situation. If this were true they were useless and Mayer had been seeking clarification.

As it was, on the night in question Mayer was not entertaining but had come up with a rather more certain way to serve his cause. General Sturges would call it 'the finest bit of Fifth Column work he had ever heard of'. He spent most of the day at Ambararata talking about the construction of landing stages for the rice he was never going to bring in. Then at around dusk Mayer drove to an isolated spot he had long marked and cut the telephone line that ran from the observation post at Windsor Castle to Maerten's headquarters in Diego Suarez.

Afterwards, he drove back to the beach hoping to be there to greet the British troops when they landed and hand over the sketches and notes he had made to the first senior officer he could find. But at 10.30, wondering whether the date had been changed since he was last in touch with Durban, he gave it up and drove back to his hotel.

Relieved to be woken at 4.30 a.m. by the sound of guns, he waited until it got light and then walked down towards the harbour and watched the Fleet Air Arm bombing the ships. At about 7, strolling back to his hotel with breakfast in mind, Mayer was arrested by a police patrol, among them a Frenchman in civilian clothes. At the central police station he was caught trying to destroy the notes (written in English) and sketches he was going to hand over and these were painstakingly restored. By the end of the day he had been questioned by Colonel Clarebout at Defence Headquarters and from there sent to Maerten's office where he was interrogated by a Commandant Melin. Afterwards he was told he was charged with espionage, warned that he would probably face a firing squad and placed in a cell in Antsirane's naval barracks where he was asked if he wished for the comfort of a priest.

For all the risks Mayer had taken the most important information came from the crew of the *Lindi*, some of whom had not been inclined to take many risks at all. During their peregrinations off the western coast they had discovered that Anambo Island, the mark for entering the Nosi Fati shoal, was not where it appeared on Admiralty charts. It was $1\frac{3}{4}$ miles further west. Had this not been corrected, and to make sure *Lindi* put a lamp on the island's western shore, Syfret's night approach would have been a catastrophe. Those vessels not lost to mines might well have run aground.

As it was, at first everything worked like a dream. About 700 men in all – 5 Commando plus one company of East Lancs – landed in Baie du Courrier, captured the coastal battery and Windsor Castle then pushed on along the Col du Courrier, across the narrow isthmus of Andrakaka towards Diego Suarez. On their right flank, in the smaller Baie du Ambararata, Festing's 29 Brigade also came ashore without any major problems. More than four times stronger than the Commando and the detached East Lancs, and with all Operation Ironclad's land artillery and tank support, Festing was making the main thrust to Antsirane 15 miles away. His brigade's first shots came from the revolver of a lieutenant in the Royal Welch Fusiliers who, wading through water he could not see, heard splashing from something large and close by. At the time he thought it might have been one of the sharks they had been warned about. Later, when he had got to know the country better, he decided it was probably a crocodile. Elsewhere small groups of the enemy showed fight and sometimes paid the price. A Tommy gunner in the East Lancs and another private killed three and captured a man they had wounded after they had come under machine-gun fire from a low ridge.

Meanwhile, at first light the Fleet Air Arm were in action over Diego Suarez harbour and Arrachart airfield just south of Antsirane. In order not to jeopardize the element of surprise their orders were to stay at least 7 miles offshore until fifteen minutes after the 0430 zero hour set for the landings. Then they circled around and attacked from the direction of the east coast where the cruiser *Hermione* was staging a diversion by bombarding and firing illuminating star shells over the hinterland of Baie du Ambadavahibé. This was about as far from the harbour as the west coast landing places and the only plausible alternative. The Fleet Air Arm contributed to this deception by dropping dummy paratroopers, a British innovation and rather less than life-size but they did divert troops to where they were not needed and two years later were used in the Normandy landings.

Armed with either bombs, torpedoes or depth charges, eighteen Swordfish off the *Illustrious* attacked in three waves of six. They quickly sank the armed merchant cruiser *Bougainville*, hit by two torpedoes, and the submarine *Bévéziers*. Over 100 died. But the sloop *D'Entrecasteaux* bore a charmed life and, when the waters around her had subsided, emerged with only superficial damage.

The third Swordfish wave under Lieutenant Robert Everett, the son of an admiral, first dropped leaflets before going on to bomb a gun battery and the *D'Entrecasteaux*, again without significant result. Sailors who picked up these leaflets were astonished to find them addressed to '*Camarades de la Marine Française*' and decorated with the flags of both nations.

On one side it explained why Britain felt compelled to do what it was doing: 'On Hitler's orders, Japan has brought the war to the Far East.' On the other it explained what the Royal Navy wanted them to do:

> To avoid any untoward incident, we ask you not to move whilst the operations are under way, nor to load your guns. We have already mined the entry channels. If there should be fascists or enemy agents among you, you doubtlessly already know who they are and will stop them from taking any provocative action. Those of you who want nothing to do with all this, remember that in Saigon French officers have to salute Japanese other ranks.

Also fluttering slowly to earth was the full text of the message Syfret had already radioed Annet. It assured him that His Majesty's Government 'did not covet an inch of French territory' and urged His Excellency to avoid bloodshed and assist this pre-emptive strike against Tokyo with an 'unconditional surrender'. A couple of hours later Annet got round to sending his reply: 'We shall defend ourselves to the last.'

By then Lieutenant Everett and his two crew had become prisoners of war. Their Swordfish's engine was hit by anti-aircraft fire and Everett managed to ditch the smoking biplane in shallow water off a beach. This was the only British aircraft lost on the first day. Five Morane fighters were destroyed and four more aircraft damaged, two of them Potez light bombers, when Albacores – the Fleet Air Arm's newer biplane – surprised the best part of the Groupe Aerien Mixte on the ground at Arrachart airfield. Among those killed was the detachment's commander. In one stroke Vichy air strength on the island had been reduced by almost a quarter. Later in the day another Morane was lost. Sergent Ehret was flying one of two fighters that strafed the beachhead at Baie du Courrier then failed to return to his airstrip at Anivorano some 50 miles south of Diego Suarez. No British claims were made, no wreckage ever discovered. It seems that Madagascar or its surrounding sea had swallowed Ehret whole.

On the ground all went well until about 9.30 a.m., five hours after the landing. Things started to unravel when the motorcycle scouts of the Royal Welch Fusiliers, which was the vanguard of 29th Brigade's advance from the beach, captured a car containing a French naval officer and three ratings. General Sturges had made a standing order that the first captured officer should be released and sent back to Diego Suarez or Antsirane with a letter to the governor repeating Syfret's demand for his surrender. This was duly done.

But before he was allowed to drive back into Antsirane in his own car the prisoner was taken back to battalion or even brigade headquarters to be given the letter he was to deliver. He was not blindfolded and probably it was considered no bad thing that he should see what they were up against: scores of tramping infantry in long columns along the sides of the road, a terracotta army coated in the thin red African dust churned up by the Bren-gun carriers, towed artillery and even a few tanks all heading down the unmade road to Antsirane. If so it failed to intimidate, though it certainly gave the game away. It was obvious that this was the main axis of the British attack and not the Commando push towards Diego Suarez. Shortly after the officer got back to his own headquarters, Annet started to put his mobile reserve and their anti-tank guns into the Joffre line with a screen of skirmishers in front of them to buy a little time while they got into position. 'The despatch of that letter was, I fear, a great error,' Sturges later admitted.

By about 11.15 French skirmishers, who had brought up machine guns, were in the scrubs, rocks and elephant grass either side of a saddle of land where the road passed through a slight ridge line. It was called the Col de Bonne Nouvelle, the good news for the weary traveller presumably being that Antsirane and journey's end was a couple of miles up the road. The Joffre line was even closer.

The first British units to reach this col were the Royal Welch Fusiliers. Brigadier Festing, a tall man with ginger hair and armed with a stout walking stick, had attached his own open-topped Bren-gun carrier and part of his headquarters to the Fusiliers' lead carriers. When the French fired their first burst at them his driver was shot through the hand and he helped him steer the machine off the road into the cover of some trees. Shortly afterwards Major Jocelin Simon came along in a Valentine tank accompanied by another Valentine and one of the lighter Tetrarchs. There was still some small-arms fire coming in and all three tanks had their hatches down. Festing hammered on the top of Major Simon's turret with his walking stick until he opened up.* The brigadier, pointing his stick towards the enemy, told him what had happened and ordered the tanks to put a stop to it and make a hole he could push his infantry through. And so at last the Special Service Squadron, trained to perfection, went to war.

Even before they reached the Col de Bonne Nouvelle Simon's gunners located the enemy and began to engage them with their 2-pounder cannon and Besa machine guns. Some of the skirmish line evidently decided it was time to go because when the lead Valentine got right into the saddle about ten riflemen were caught out of cover and, according to Simon, more casualties were inflicted. 'But owing to the rocky nature of the ground the tanks could not get right in and, as the carriers had not followed up, the position was not mopped up.'

This was not the way the Royal Welch Fusiliers remembered it at all. As far as they were concerned, the Tirailleurs simply went to ground, let

* Soon tanks would have telephones attached to their exteriors so that accompanying infantry could communicate.

the tanks go on down the road at the Valentine's top speed of 15mph, then had another go at them and this time with more effect. Two officers, one a captain and a company commander, were shot dead by snipers with the nerve to wait until they could be reasonably sure of their target's rank. The captain's killer was close enough to die from a lucky pistol shot by the lieutenant who took over. By 3 p.m. the Vichy screen had withdrawn to the Joffre line and the exhausted Royal Welch, who some twelve hours earlier were being seasick in a landing craft before marching 15 miles in 80°F to kill and be killed in a bit of a battle, dumped their packs and slumped under whatever shade they could find on Col de Bonne Nouvelle.

Ahead of them they had for some time been hearing machine-gun and some sort of artillery fire and hoped that the tanks were doing their next job for them. Since Festing had rapped on Simon's turret the armour had been steadily reinforcing and, with the exception of a tank stuck on the beach because salt water had got into its electronics, the entire squadron was now engaged. First another two Tetrarchs, these light reconnaissance machines instantly recognizable by their size and their speed, had dashed through to join the three tanks under Simon which were now almost 2 miles ahead of the main column. Then, a couple of hours later, the infantry's occupation of Col de Bonne Nouvelle and the ground a little beyond it had been consolidated by the arrival from the Baie du Courrier landing of the rest of the squadron. This consisted of four Valentines and two Tetrarchs under its second-in-command Captain Llewellyn Palmer, who would have been with Simon's party but his Valentine had slipped a track in soft sand and it had taken a couple of hours for the squadron's fitters to get it back on. Shortly afterwards Palmer's tanks were joined by one of the Tetrarchs from Simon's spear point detachment commanded by a Lieutenant Astles. Its return from enemy territory had been accompanied by a captured French motorcycle and sidecar team who rode closely behind while Astles covered them with a Bren from his open turret. But what Astles had to tell them was nowhere near as good as this looked.

When Major Simon, having decided that his tanks had silenced the machine guns that were doing the damage, had continued towards Antsirane he was blissfully unaware of the existence of the Joffre line. So was Brigadier Festing. So was General Sturges. The blame for this lay mostly with the South African Air Force. At the risk of giving away their intentions Sturges had insisted on aerial reconnaissance but somehow the SAAF's overlapping camera shots had just missed Vichy's most formidable inland defences. Yet even this, which was mostly bad luck, should not have mattered. Percy Mayer's network, indeed the energetic Mayer himself, had provided a good description of the mini-Maginot that awaited the unwary. But somewhere along the line this had slipped through the hands of the right members of Sturges's planning staff. As so often with intelligence failures, people had risked their necks to get what was needed only to see it wasted. If there was ever an inquiry this too appears to have vanished, lost perhaps in some chasm between competing desks.

Simon's tanks had gone down the road in single file. In the lead was a Valentine under 2nd Lieutenant Whitaker followed by Simon's own Valentine, for the leader did not ride point. Behind them were the three Tetrarchs with their lighter and more vulnerable armour. These, in order of march, were commanded by a Corporal Watkins and Lieutenants Carlisle and Astles. Both types of tank had a crew of three: commander, gunner and driver. It was a little past midday. Under their armour plate the men were sweltering and it was tempting to keep the turret and driver's hatch open as much as possible. There was a good deal of dust. Nonetheless morale was high. In Lieutenant Carlisle's Tetrarch there was a large Union flag he was carrying to fly from the highest point in Antsirane.

After Col de Bonne Nouvelle the road bent left to the north as it entered the little peninsula where Antsirane's whitewashed buildings, church spires, barracks and dockyard could be found at the tip. About 3 miles south of it the lead Valentine shuffled around a slight bend to find its gun sights filled by a truck that must have come off a side road. It was carrying a small mountain gun and its crew. The Valentine shot them to pieces.

Almost immediately the French gunners on the Joffre line, loading solid-shot armour-piercing rounds, returned fire with their 75mm guns. One of their first shots killed Whitaker's driver and knocked off a track. Then more hits ruined the turret's rotating mechanism and the Valentine was effectively disarmed because it was impossible to shoot in the right direction. At this point Whitaker and his gunner bailed out, though by the time they had scrambled into cover the gunner had been wounded by machine-gun fire.

Jocelin Simon, who was about 50 yards or so behind Whitaker's Valentine, had worked out that there were two guns that were really doing the damage: one firing directly down the road and the other from the Fort Bellevue blockhouse on the right. The major ordered his driver to get off the road in the same direction and at the same time opened fire with the 2-pounder though he could not actually make out a target. But when the driver tried to leave the road he discovered there were too many boulders so he turned back. Then they were hit in the front where, at almost 3 inches, the armour plate was at its thickest. The French solid shot could not penetrate but made a large area of the hull glow dull red inside. It also knocked the driver senseless though hands and feet still operated the controls.

As the Valentine advanced relentlessly towards the enemy, Simon was screaming down the intercom at him to get off the road. Another hit damaged the gear-change mechanism and the tank slowed but did not come to a complete stop. Then a round jammed the turret ring which meant they could no longer traverse their guns. Simon told his crew to get out. The driver, who had come round, struggled head first through his forward hatch but he was obviously still concussed. Once he had extracted himself, instead of rolling clear, he somehow fell face down onto the soft red earth in front of the tank so that one of its still moving tracks rolled over him as casually as if he had been a log. Crushed and broken and screaming in agony he begged Major Simon to shoot him and this may have happened. In any event, he died.

Horror piled on horror. Next the three Tetrarchs behind the Valentines moved forward and began to lay down covering fire. Simon was delighted by their 'great gallantry' but, since there were no longer any roadside boulders to stop them, expected them to move off the road to the right where the ground dropped and would lower their profile, exposing no more than their turrets. Instead they stuck to the road and came straight on.

At least the Valentines had not caught fire. Within seconds the first two Tetrarchs had burst into flames. Corporal Watkins was killed and his gunner so terribly burnt he would die in a naval sick berth a few days later and be buried at sea. Their driver could just about walk away from the flames but was also badly scorched. Behind them in Lieutenant Carlisle's machine both the driver and gunner were wounded. But Carlisle himself was more or less unscathed and Simon saw him first help his driver out of the smouldering wreck and then, 'disregarding the fire from the 75s and machine guns and rifles', he detached the Tetrarch's Bren gun from its anti-aircraft mounting and ran over to the rest of them.

Astles's Tetrarch bore a charmed life. Partly covered by the broken or burning tanks in front, it expended a lot of ammunition in the general direction of the enemy, whose exact positions were hard to spot, until Simon ran over and ordered him back to brigade headquarters. En route Astles surprised the motorcycle and a truck-load of reinforcements on their way to those western outposts of the Joffre line around the Col de Bonne Nouvelle. He shot up the truck and claims to have left most of the men on it dead or wounded but took the officers in the motorcycle and sidecar team prisoner. Perhaps they had the opportunity to surrender.

Simon watched the Tetrarch depart then began to organize his shipwrecked crews who were lying in the long grass and scrub about 20 yards off the road. Lieutenant Whitaker and Sergeant Grime, his gunner, led a scavenging party that crawled back to the four knocked-out tanks and, despite some sniping, retrieved another Bren, a Thompson sub-machine gun, ammunition, water and first-aid kits with morphine for the burn cases who were placed in the best of the available shade. At this point there were ten of them of whom half were wounded. Then the sound of a motorcycle engine was greeted by a renewed crackle of rifle and automatic fire as, from the direction Astles had gone, there came towards them a small and apparently unstoppable cloud of high-speed dust. It contained the squadron's liaison officer with brigade HQ, an anxious Royal Marines captain named Belville who was wondering if there was anything he could do to help. A badly burnt lance corporal was put on Belville's pillion and managed to cling on while his rescuer ran the gauntlet with him back to a British field dressing station.

Simon was under no doubt that their liaison officer had probably saved the life of a man 'who would otherwise have had to remain in the open under fire for three-and-a-half hours'. During that time they had three times beaten off attacks by Senegalese riflemen while they waited in vain for their own infantry to rescue them. It was a nerve-racking business, for concealed in the long grass they could sometimes hear the 'low jabberings' of the Africans before they tried to rush them with fixed bayonets. Once Simon saw some Bren-gun carriers appear down the roads and thought they were about to be relieved 'but owing to heavy machine gun fire they were unable to approach'.

> The enemy then made a third sortie, employing the same tactics. They managed to approach quite close, but were held off by fire from the Bren guns, Thompson sub-machine-gun and pistols. The Tommy and pistol ammunition was, however, by now almost exhausted. Finally 2nd Lieutenant Whitaker, who had been manning the Bren gun on the right flank with great determination and accuracy, was fatally wounded.

In the North African desert, bailed-out tank crews from both sides would try hard to get back to their own lines but rarely attempted to avoid capture by fighting it out on foot. There seems little doubt that Simon's Special Squadron really were a bit special and their training with the Commandos, particularly weapons handling, had imbued them with a fighting spirit that almost made them welcome dismounted action, and it showed. It would hardly be surprising if some of the Africans were in no mood to take prisoners and probably had a good idea who had done the most damage.

Simon's concise 1,600-word after-action report of this epic stand was routinely classified secret and lodged in the War Office's basement filing depository. Dated eight days after it took place, the style is almost comically impersonal. His own role is rarely referred to and then always in the third person as 'the squadron commander' or the 'tank commander'. 'The tank proceeded down the road under its own power, without the tank commander being aware that the driver was not in control.' That same driver's terrible death is not mentioned though it is reliably sourced elsewhere. And while Simon makes it plain that Lieutenant Whitaker was good with a Bren gun and played a crucial role in prolonging their defence, perhaps with next of kin in mind, it does not say how he received his fatal wound.

A little more detail is supplied in an account that appeared some years later in the regimental magazine of the 9th Lancers who lost three men in the fight. It says that Whitaker died 'in a hand-to-hand fight with a Senegalese and it was only the intervention of a fine spirited French officer which saved the rest of them from a similar fate'. Perhaps for 'hand-to-hand' we should read 'bayoneted'.

Certainly, the 'fine spirited French officer' matches Simon's brief description of what happened immediately after Whitaker's death when the eight survivors, including the badly burnt gunner who died of his wounds, surrendered. 'The enemy then advanced and at approximately 1545 hours captured the party. Only three of the tank crews were then unwounded. The prisoners were treated by the enemy with great consideration.'

All Palmer knew from Astles, and probably confirmed by the liaison officer Belville, was that his commanding officer had lost four tanks in fewer minutes, had some badly wounded men with him, and when last seen was trying to hold out until help arrived. For Brigadier Festing there was some profit in Simon's losses, for at least he had become aware of these formidable Vichy defences before his infantry learned about them the hard way. Now he had to work out how to deal with them.

As a first step, once Col de Bonne Nouvelle was secured, Festing personally ordered Palmer to go forward and 'locate the precise positions' of the guns that had just reduced his tank strength by a third. 'A most difficult but necessary task,' admitted the brigadier who came to see them off. Nonetheless, Palmer appeared to welcome it, perhaps thinking he might be able to rescue Simon and the others, though by then it was at least half an hour too late. Two years after Dunkirk, he was also anxious to get back into action.

As the seven tanks moved out they were shelled. There were no casualties but the French must have suspected something was stirring. They were close enough now to spot each other's dust. Shortly afterwards the four Valentines and three Tetrarch slipped off the main Antsirane road, and began to go through the scrub and sugar cane to the right of it until they came to some long grass high enough to cover the tanks. Then they stopped and dismounted for a briefing.

Palmer's plan, as he outlined it to his men, was simplicity itself. Using whatever cover was available, they would advance until they discovered a hull-down position, the tank commander's tactical eldorado where they could see and shoot with only turrets above the parapet. Then they would fan out into an extended line and all open up together, carefully noting where the return fire was coming from. But the Hussar officer confided to his own crew that they were going to do a bit more: he and the sergeant major were going to take their tanks back towards the road and get the French to reveal their positions by deliberately drawing their fire. This part worked magnificently. Even Lance Corporal Clegg, Palmer's devoted gunner, was a bit taken aback. 'It was another Balaclava. As soon as we were clear of the pampas grass all hell descended on us. The crack of the shells as they flew over the turret and around us sounded as if the artillery was on our hull. We made for the cover of a wood to our right but Sergeant-Major Allen's tank, another Valentine, had been hit.'

Allen's tank had a track broken, its main gun jammed in the half-coil position and all three crew members were wounded. Palmer's machine had also taken several hits and he and his driver were hurt though Clegg was unscathed. Both crews bailed out and four managed to get into cover; but Palmer noticed that Allen's driver was still struggling in his hatch. Despite his own injury, and the French artillery's evident determination to prove that practice makes perfect, Palmer went over and got the wounded driver out. He was helping him towards the other tanks, which had found a reasonably hull-down position, when a shell-burst killed both of them. Clegg saw it happen. 'One moment they were there, as if held motionless, and in that terrible flash they were gone.'

For a while the remaining five tanks, now under a Lieutenant Harwood, duelled with Fort Bellevue's artillery but by 6 p.m. the light was fading fast, which was probably just as well. They withdrew with a slightly better idea as to where the French guns were but hardly one that could be called precise and certainly not worth the price the squadron had paid in their two brief encounters with them. In less than twenty-four hours their unit strength of 6 officers and 39 men had been reduced by over a third: 7 were dead, 8 wounded and their commanding officer was among 3 unwounded prisoners. They had also lost half their tanks, though a couple might be repairable. Brigadier Festing would recommend Palmer, who had died because he went back for the wounded driver, for a posthumous Victoria Cross but it was turned down. Instead he got a Military Cross for the leadership he had displayed before he was killed.

In its small way, the Joffre line was showing what in 1940 the Maginot line could have accomplished had the Germans been sporting enough to attack it head-on instead of sneaking around it. The navy might have put Sturges's men into the ring but, against all odds, there could be no doubt who had won the first round of the land battle.

Chapter Twenty-Three

Brigadier Festing welcomed the dark. He knew that he lacked the artillery and now the armoured support to break through these Vichy defences in daylight. It would have to start with a night attack. By noon he had all four of his infantry battalions ashore, the last to arrive at Ambararata Bay being Lieutenant Colonel Michael West's 2nd South Lancashires, the brigade's reserve.

At 11 p.m. West was attending a conference at Festing's HQ which had been set up in a Chinese-owned trading store known as Robinson's Hotel, its proprietor being well disposed to the British who had come to deliver him from the Japanese. This was at the village of La Scama which was also the site of Antsirane's abattoir and a meat canning factory. It was well forward for a brigade headquarters, easily within rifle shot of the Joffre line's outposts and there was a considerable amount of sniping. The Royal Welch Fusiliers, who had spent the day as spearhead battalion and were now in reserve, were deployed around it though it was not much of a rest.

At this conference West learned that his South Lancs, being the freshest battalion, had been given the star role in Festing's plan of attack. The Vichy defences spanned the three approach roads into the Antsirane peninsula but ended where the land crumbled steeply into its mangroved coast, an area that could only be protected by foot patrols. Taking advantage of the moonlight, West's men were to make a night approach and get behind the enemy's left flank (British right) by going over the broken ground that skirted the east coast's Baie des Français. Once firmly installed behind the Joffre line they would attack from the rear while the 1st Royal Scots Fusiliers and 2nd East Lancs attacked from the front. Zero hour was set for 5.30 a.m. and would be preceded at first light by air strikes from the Fleet Air Arm's Albacores and Swordfish. There would be additional fire support from the six 3.7-inch howitzers of the brigade's 455 battery.

'Speed and savage hearts in the attack. Tolerance in victory,' General Sturges had signalled his troops, though how many got the message is uncertain. Wireless communications, as the general would soon learn, were bad and some company headquarters were loath to be lumbered with heavy sets that would not work. Festing's abiding memory of that night was of a 'fierce heath fire raging around my brigade's perimeter'. It had been started by his own troops to smoke out snipers and the flickering flame gave the place a sinister edge. The East Lancs were delighted when a bunch of South Lancs, not yet adjusted to the sounds of battle, prostrated themselves when one of its Bren gunners fired a burst.

At 2 a.m. the newcomers set off to turn the enemy's flank in three columns some 50 yards apart. Colonel West, carrying a heavy Thompson sub-machine gun with a Capone-style drum magazine, was with B Company which was part of the column on the extreme right. He was 37 and his contemporaries suspected he was destined for great things if he lived long enough.

At first they kept their moonlit march to order with company commanders halting every few hundred yards to wait for the tail to close up, a painfully slow business. Two sentries encountered in some mangroves were shot without raising the alarm. But it was hard going. The mangrove swamps made every step an adventure and the mosquitoes could not believe their luck. Soon they had little more than two hours to get to the Antsirane cemetery from where they were supposed to arrange themselves to deliver a battalion attack at 5.30. Now the gaps were no longer being closed and before long entire platoons had gone astray.

At first light it was discovered that parts of C Company from the left column were inextricably merged with B Company from the right. With the minutes ticking away to zero hour West knew they had no chance of making their rendezvous at the cemetery even if they were entirely certain where it was. They had brought no wireless sets. The ground was hard enough going for men with rifles and West had left the sets behind with his rear companies whom he hoped to be in touch with by runner. As far as he was concerned this was a large-scale raid and they needed to be light on their feet. West had already briefed his officers that, if they got lost, they must share their confusion with the enemy by attacking whatever offered a reasonable chance of success. Now he ordered Major Northcote, who commanded B Company, to split it into guerrilla bands of ten – all infantry platoons divided into three sub-sections of this number – and 'do the maximum damage possible'.

At 5.00 a.m. the Swordfish and Albacores began bombing the Joffre line and half an hour later, to coincide with the troops' zero hour, some Martlet fighters machine-gunned the same positions at spectacularly low altitudes. As the 2nd East Lancs and 1st Royal Scots Fusiliers went forward they saw an aircraft burst into flames and were relieved to see a parachute open. But no British planes had been lost. The man at the end of it was a Lieutenant Héloise, the observer and sole survivor of one of two Potez 63-11 light bombers shot down by the Martlets as they headed for Syfret's ships. Two wounded French airmen survived the crash-landing of the other bomber, making a total of three prisoners and three killed. Héloise said that his pilot, Adjutant Dietsch, had stuck with the plane and died to give him the chance to jump.

There was Gallic heroism on the ground too, though not under the same flag. Peter Reynier, a subaltern in the Royal Scots Fusiliers, was the son of a Finnish mother and a French wine merchant who had flourished in London where Reynier was born at the family home in Pimlico in 1916. Shortly after the outbreak of war Reynier had volunteered for the British Army and served for a while in the Commandos before being commissioned into the Scots regiment. He spoke fluent French; after leaving school he had spent some time learning the family trade in Burgundy and Bordeaux, and given the usual dearth of interpreters and translators could easily have got a headquarters job. But that was not what he wanted any more than his elder brother Roderick who was also commanding a platoon in Madagascar in Hugh Stockwell's Royal Welch Fusiliers.

Unlike his brother, who had served in France, Peter Reynier had not seen action before he got to Madagascar and this second morning was certainly noisier than the first. The battalion had breakfasted at 2 a.m. and spent the last hours of darkness edging closer to the Joffre line. By zero hour they were already forward of the line's anti-tank ditch and awaiting the end of the air strike. It looked impressive enough; the pilots were so low it was hard to believe the French could miss them, but when they got up to advance it did not seem to have reduced by one iota the amount of artillery and machine-gun fire coming their way. 'Further, the defences remained undisturbed by any intervention from the rear by the South Lancashires,' notes the regimental history. 'Casualties mounted rapidly.'

For a short while the Scots Fusiliers' 3-inch mortars set up 200 yards behind the anti-tank ditch hit back and they thought they had scored a direct hit on one machine-gun post. But they rapidly ran out of its heavy ammunition, all of which had to be hand carried, and the officer in charge died trying to replenish it. Stuck between the anti-tank ditch and the Joffre line, it seemed that the Scots had walked into their own little Somme. There was scant cover and most of those nearest the Vichy defences crawled into shell holes where they were pinned down. Half a dozen men under D Company's Sergeant Knox would remain in one for sixteen increasingly thirsty hours. 'We tried several times to get out but the snipers were too hot for us so we waited until darkness.'

Reynier and his platoon seem to have been in a similar position though perhaps even closer, for they were almost in striking distance of a loopholed concrete emplacement in a sector of the line the French called Rue Placers. It was still not long after first light when Reynier decided there was a good chance he could open the way for his men to rush it. Armed with mills grenades and his revolver, and using every dusty shrub and dent in the ground he could find, he belly-crawled patiently towards it. Gripped tightly in his right hand was the spring-loaded safety lever of a mills bomb, the safety pin already removed.

In overall command of his target, which consisted of riflemen and a 75mm gun behind sandbags on the roof with a section of machine gunners inside, was Lieutenant Bande of the 3rd Company, 2 Régiment mixte malgache. Reynier had got within 20 yards of it when one of Bande's roof lookouts spotted him and squeezed off a shot which hit him in the side of his mouth. Springing to his feet, Reynier dashed forward and received a second bullet wound in the left arm just as he threw his grenade with great accuracy at one of the loopholes of the pill box. It came straight back.

Fortunately for its occupants, and perhaps even with this eventuality in mind, they had left their anti-scorpion mesh in place. The grenade exploded close enough to Reynier to leave him stunned and bleeding copiously from head and other wounds. And there he might have bled to death if Bande and a couple of his men had not risked leaving their cover to drag their fallen enemy inside and set to work with field dressings. Bande, a regular soldier, was so impressed by Reynier's courage and delighted to discover he was half French that, at his first opportunity, he sent a letter about it to Lieutenant Colonel Jamie Armstrong, the lieutenant's commanding officer. Armstrong appended it to his successful recommendation for a Military Cross, a rare occasion when the most relevant part of a gallantry citation came from the enemy.

'He told us, and it is certainly the truth,' wrote Bande, 'that he had wanted to carry out an assault on the gun and open a path for your men. That action is one of a brave man. I believe I can tell you that, for you can be sure that the French can pick one out.'

Certainly, thanks to Maréchal Joffre's prescient planning, the French could fairly claim to be facing fearful odds with unbowed heroism. If it was allowed to go on much longer there was a danger it would eclipse the considerable British naval achievement of bringing so much so far with so little fuss.

The East Lancs had fared no better than the Royal Scots Fusiliers. Lieutenant Brian Wood, a platoon commander in C Company, found himself advancing over ground that was 'flat and open with only a few straggly bushes'. They passed by some dead oxen and a smashed truck containing corpses. Then a shell wounded five of his men, the most seriously a private who had a grenade detonated in one of his pouches 'blowing away most of his right elbow and side'. When their carrier platoon went forward to support them with some extra Bren-gun fire they travelled over the same stretch of road Simon's tanks had used with the same result. Three out of eight carriers returned, though some of the four-man crews, often wounded, straggled back on foot.

Nor did they find it any safer in the brigade HQ area in La Scama village where Lieutenant Wood and the rest of his company had been ordered to retire.

> Our position was most unhealthy. We were collecting all the ricochets and overs fired at the forward companies, as well as direct sniping and machine-gun fire which zipped through the bushes a few feet over our heads. The cry of 'stretcher bearer' here and 'stretcher bearer' there began with monotonous regularity and the stretcher bearers never hesitated. Who would be next on their list? One buried one's face towards the ground and, in a lull, turned on one's side or back and dozed or smoked.

Doing their best to give the French some of their own back was Bombardier Bailey and the other gunners of 455's Light Battery. Their neat little 3.7-inch pack howitzers, an accurate gun popular with the British Indian Army for keeping Waziristan in order, had been unlimbered by the meat canning factory and there was a brief period when they seemed to have quietened the French down. Then suddenly the .75s were onto them and two of their signallers became the battery's first casualties, killed as they tried to get an abandoned Peugeot started.

The gunners, like everybody else, were desperately short of wheeled transport. Force Eight winds continued to delay its unloading and among the late deliveries were 455's two 25-pounders and their towing tractors, which were heavier than the pack howitzers and fired a shell almost three times as big. Twelve more 25-pounders, a battery attached to 17th Infantry Brigade which was beginning to come ashore, should have been up with them but HMS *Bachaquero*, a converted Lake Maracibo tanker, had had enormous difficulties landing them.

Bachaquero was supposed to be one of those innovations that would make all the difference but she had proved a great disappointment. She had been designed and operated by a British company that needed a tanker that could transport oil from the Venezuelan salt lake over a sand bar to the South Atlantic's oil terminal on Aruba Island. Her shallow draught and sturdy nether parts proved irresistible to the Royal Navy who requisitioned her and two sister ships. A Clyde shipyard had fitted bow doors and a ramp and turned the *Bachaquero* into the world's first Landing Craft Tank.

Because even the Valentines were light enough to load onto an ordinary infantry landing craft, for her debut it had been decided that instead of tanks the former oil shuttle would carry the guns plus fifty-four vehicles for various units including the battery's towing tractors. But when the great moment arrived for the *Bachaquero* to deliberately run her strengthened bows aground, open her vast doors and watch her cargo drive away with a menacing growl it had taken an entire awful day.

Admittedly, an uncharted reef and uncleared mines meant that over three hours were wasted trying to land on the 29th Brigade's beach at Baie Ambararata before, at her top speed of 8 knots, the ship chugged round to neighbouring Courrier, where 5 Commando had landed. There she made repeated attempts to get far enough up the beach to land her cargo. Eventually two of the guns with their tractors were tugged and pushed onto dry land by gunners of 19 Field Battery, some of whom nearly drowned doing it. Then at dusk, on a rising tide and two guns lighter, her captain made one last attempt and the *Bachaquero* was finally beached in water sufficiently shallow to disgorge totally.

The guns should now have been rushed up to the La Scama front and would have been had it been possible in the dark to find a way over rough ground that would connect them to the road there. In the end, they did the next best thing and followed the Commandos' route to Diego Suarez and onto the Andrakaka peninsula from where, shooting across the water, the Joffre line was well within range. It was not ideal because they had nobody to tell them where their shot was falling but it was better than nothing. There was one more delay. On the way there the sloop *D'Entrecasteaux*, which was lurking in a cove after a second air attack had failed to finish her off, took a few pot shots at them as they drove by, killing one man and wounding several more. Eventually, they were ready to contribute at about the time the British had concluded that the attack had failed and were calling it off.

Major General Sturges, unhappy Gallipoli veteran full of foreboding, turned up at Brigadier Festing's headquarters at 7 a.m. and his worst fears were confirmed.

> It was quite clear the attack had failed. The only artillery, 455 Light Battery, was withdrawing. It would have been folly to have done anything else. Isolated infantry were creeping back with their rifles pointing in all directions. The whole of 29 Brigade was deployed or being deployed, and with the disappearance of many of the leading troops in the dawn attack, assumed to be casualties, units were considerably under strength. A good deal of most irritating enemy sniping and unaimed rifle fire was going on. To this was added shelling from .75s which was a good deal more terrifying than effective. The shelling set fire to the bush ... These fierce and rapidly spreading bush fires caused no serious casualties but resulted in serious confusion and loss of equipment. Very little artillery had as yet come into action owing to the failure of the *Bachaquero;* and what there was in action, had great difficulty in obtaining observation.

At La Scama Captain Hector Emerton, 29th Brigade's Royal Artillery spotter for naval fire support, was on the top floor of the canning factory where management kept offices with panoramic views. Below him 455 Light were beginning to pull out. For a while he had been in the ludicrous position of having no communication whatsoever with these gunners, who were practically in hailing distance, while trying to keep in contact with ships whose guns were now out of range. With his field glasses he could spot the smoke and sometimes the muzzle flash of the French artillery which he estimated at less than 2,000 yards. It was an ideal observation post, though at a price. 'The trouble was, it was the only two-storey building in the area and an obvious place to site an OP. Consequently, I was intermittently shelled. At one time, while I was in occupation of an upstairs room, a shell landed downstairs. I went to the aid of a soldier who had been grievously wounded but he died in my arms.'

There was no doubt that for the moment the British were outgunned and even the navy could not help. The Joffre line was a good 20 miles from the west coast. This made it out of the question for the *Ramillies* to join in the bombardment with her 15-inchers because she did not have a shallow enough draught to get in range. The same applied to the cruisers with their 8- and 6-inch guns. Only the destroyers could navigate the shoals and get close enough to fire with their 4.7-inch guns.

Emerton had started off with the eight 8-inch guns of the county class cruiser HMS *Devonshire* at his disposal, which would have made a devastating contribution had the enemy been obliged to make his stand closer to the west coast. Now he had to share the destroyer HMS *Laforey* with Bill Knight, brother Royal Artillery officer who had gone ashore with the Commandos at Courrier Bay. Knight and the *Laforey* worked well together. That second morning ashore, following *D'Entrecasteaux*'s surprise attack on the artillery convoy from the *Bachaquero*, he had directed the blind fire over an isthmus, which left the defiant sloop beached and burning with most of the survivors captured by Commandos.

But calling in fire on a ship close to shore was an easy target, especially when you were not under fire yourself. From his precarious post, almost staring into the cannon's mouth, Emerton could only hope that he got the French artillery before they got him. As it turned out, it seems neither side achieved anything that could be counted as conclusive, though the observation officer was lucky to get out in one piece. Later in the day the Fleet Air Arm reluctantly, because they preferred a more offensive role, provided the destroyers with Swordfish spotters and this was more effective.

Yet considering the size of Rear Admiral Syfret's fleet, the French must have been relieved not to find themselves under much greater bombardment. The main reason for this was *Prince of Wales* syndrome. After the loss of Britain's best battleship and the *Repulse* off the Malayan coast there was a great reluctance to risk capital ships. Syfret could have sent his big guns around to the east coast, where they would have been easily in range of the Joffre line, but he feared they would be easy meat for the coastal batteries protecting the entrance to the main anchorage there. So far he had risked only one ship on that coast when the cruiser *Hermione*, famous for having once rammed and sunk an Italian submarine, had staged a D-Day diversion, and that well south of the coastal guns in question. But now Syfret was going to take a bit of a chance though, in one of those awful calculations admirals and generals have to make, he had already decided that the men and the ship involved were expendable.

In the early afternoon of 6 May Major General Sturges, having endured a bone-rattling Bren-gun carrier ride back to the beach from La Scama then a soaking in a landing craft in a choppy sea, was welcomed by Syfret aboard his flagship *Ramillies*. According to his host, who had just finished his lunch, Sturges looked: 'Hot, begrimed and unhappy. Things were not going well.'

Sturges was not quite as down as he looked. He had a new plan. On his way back the road had been full of fresh-looking troops, some of them wearing solar topees instead of steel helmets and marching to the sound of pipes. These were Brigadier Rupert Tarleton's newly landed 17th Brigade: 6th Seaforth Highlanders, 2nd Northamptons and another battalion, the 2nd, of Royal Scots Fusiliers. 'New heart was put into everyone,' recalled the weary Lieutenant Wood of the 2nd East Lancs. 'What an effect they had on tired troops.'

Since they had so few tanks or artillery Sturges had decided to make a virtue of a necessity. Between dusk and the rising of the almost full moon at 11 p.m. Tarleton's brigade would make a surprise attack, what he called a 'silent night advance and assault'. There would be no covering barrage to alert the enemy that they were coming. Just dark shapes edging nearer then a sudden rush of men at about the time the defenders should be settling down for the night. Sturges had calculated that 'provided they could stick the heat, dust and sniping' most of these reinforcements could reach the forward area by 6 p.m. 'I ordered zero hour for 20.00 hours – later postponed until 2030 – and arranged for the maximum harassing fire from artillery and the air during the remainder of the day.'

Now he had come to see Syfret, who as Combined Commander was his senior, to ask a favour. He wanted the navy to stage a diversion. Originally it been intended that 5 Commando, having captured Diego Suarez, would seize whatever small boats were available to cross the narrow strip of water and be hammering at Antsirane's back door while 29th Brigade was kicking in the front. But Commando HQ had insisted that they could not find anything suitable. Patterson, the Commandos' medical officer, was incensed. He knew that two serviceable boats had been located and blamed the alcoholism of their commanding officer – 'too dithery from being without a drink for 12 hours' – for their failure to act.

When the facts came out the culprit was eventually sent home in disgrace, a rare thing in the British military where heavy drinking was often tolerated as a good man's fault.* At the time all Sturges knew was that he needed another diversion and, being a Royal Marine himself, he turned to his own corps. 'I wished to try and arrange for a destroyer to force the entrance of the harbour and land a party of Royal Marines in the dock area, thus making direct assault on the town from the rear. This, even if the destroyer was lost, would draw the enemy's fire, create a diversion and give the main night attack the best possible chance of success.'

Syfret immediately agreed to provide the destroyer HMS *Anthony* and fifty marines from the contingent aboard the *Ramillies* where they helped to crew the 15-inch guns and provided the band which in action doubled as stretcher-bearers. But, as he later admitted, his outward show of enthusiasm disguised deep forebodings. He thought that Sturges's hastily planned night attack against a strong position with troops exhausted from an 18-mile march in full kit, however fresh they were when they started, offered no more than a 10 per cent chance of a breakthrough. However, this had to be balanced against recent Japanese and German successes and the desperate need for the troops and ships under his command to be elsewhere. 'Prolonged operations, which we so much wished to avoid, was the unpleasant alternative ... The *Anthony*'s chance of success I assessed as about 50 per cent, my advisers thought 15 per cent and, of the Royal Marines, I did not expect a score to survive the night. The next few hours were not happy ones.'

On top of these concerns was a nagging fear for the safety of his ships. Not only were two Vichy submarines still unaccounted for but intelligence reports indicated that Japanese U-boats based in newly captured Penang Island off the Malayan coast were moving towards the western half of the Indian Ocean. Then, in the course of the day there were developments, not always immediately known to the Combined Commander, that made the prognosis look a little less gloomy.

First of all another battery of 25-pounder guns was found. They were the other half of 9 Field Regiment, the Royal Artillery unit attached to 17th Brigade. Instead of being shipped on the revolutionary roll-on-roll-off *Bachaquero* they had travelled on the troop ship *Mahout* with the expectation that they would be unloaded once Diego Suarez port was captured. But since there was a gun shortage, the sea was calmer, and somebody was feeling lucky, they had been lowered onto bobbing landing craft and brought into action at La Scama at about the time Sturges was boarding the *Ramillies* to request his diversion.

A dozen more 25-pounders were certainly a valuable addition to the harassing fire the general had ordered. But the best news came a bit later in the day. Surrounded by a small and admiring coterie of his men, who

* After much soul searching Dr Patterson, having told the Commando's second-in-command what he was going to do, had informed Brigadier Festing who acted immediately.

insisted that their colonel had personally accounted with his Thompson for at least thirty-five of the enemy, the South Lancs' Michael West had walked back into British lines. This marked the beginning of the return of the half of his battalion that had gone missing. They had quite a story to tell.

Two of his companies had been stopped well before Fort Bellevue where they had never lost touch with Festing's headquarters and simply dug in there not far out of La Scama as his brigade's right flank. But the other two, plus West's battalion headquarters, some 400 in all, had been out of contact for at least twelve hours, vanished as if they had never been. West had tried to send messengers but none of them had got through and Festing feared they had been cut off, surrounded and surrendered.

This was far from the case. By sniping, ambushing and stampeding a grazing herd of pack horses and mules for the French 75mm guns, West's soldiers had created the kind of uncertainty that makes men who are not losing believe that they might be. Not only in Vichy's rear echelons, but also on the Joffre line itself where sentries staring one way found themselves being shot at from the other. Men who had been disarmed and released were walking back into Antsirane and saying that the English were everywhere and all was lost.

It was not done without cost. An early attempt to send back about a hundred or so prisoners under a ten-man escort was stopped by French artillery fire which killed thirty of their own and wounded five of the guards who were all captured. In all seventeen South Lancs lost their lives and about forty were wounded. Among the dead was the footballer Roland Moss from Stockport who died staring at a photograph of his baby son which he had asked to be removed from his shirt pocket and placed in his hand.

Because West had failed to get word of their exploits out, Brigadier Festing was unable to exploit the South Lancs' success as quickly as he would have liked. But Sturges was under no illusion about the contribution they had made. 'The effect of this penetration on the morale of the enemy command and troops was later found to have been very great,' he wrote.

It was not until late afternoon that the brigadier and some of his officers began to sense that the enemy's grip on the Joffre line might be weakening. Festing, 'Frontline Frankie' to his troops, made a personal reconnaissance in a Bren-gun carrier and then sent out a fighting patrol of Royal Scots Fusiliers who returned with fifty prisoners. This was followed by a probe by the surviving tanks, though not before they came under artillery fire while the crews were being briefed and one of the two Valentines left was disabled. Nobody was hurt but it indicated that a French Forward Observation Officer was somewhere close enough to see them and at the end of a field telephone.

The remaining four set off with orders 'on no account to commit themselves against the French guns'. After a while they discovered some hapless Malagasy infantry trying to hide in a swathe of sugar cane and, when they failed to surrender, used their machine guns on them. Behind the tanks, deafening bangs at the headquarters of 1st Royal Scots announced that they were being mortared. Two were killed and the twelve wounded included the second-in-command and the adjutant. Weakening they might be, but finished the French were obviously not. It was shortly after 5 p.m. and the heat was going out of the second day.

Map 7 Royal Marines raid on Antsirane

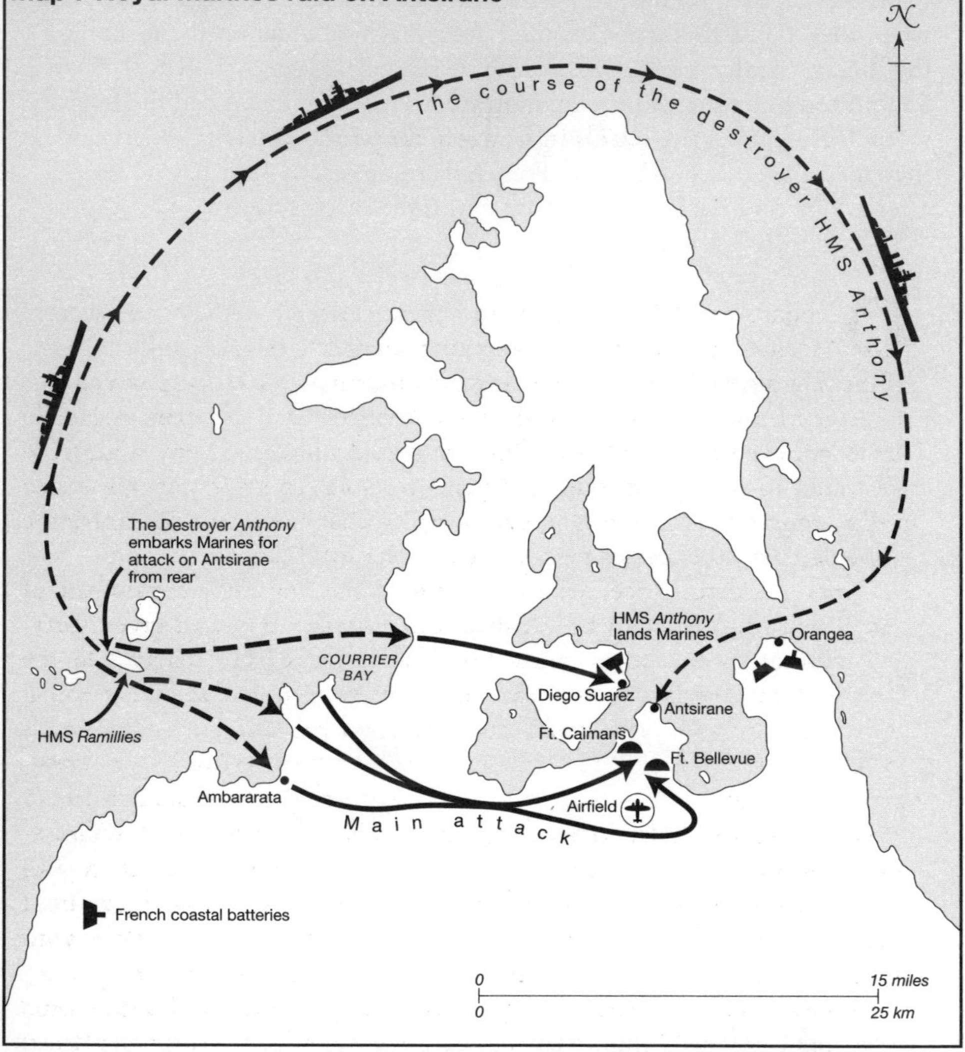

Chapter Twenty-Four

On board the *Anthony* most of the Royal Marines were being seasick. Marines rarely served on anything smaller than a cruiser and some of them had never been to sea in anything less than a battleship which was a lot gentler on the stomach than the bronco ride a destroyer usually provided, even in a mild sea. This one was distinctly choppy and, from west coat to east coast, they had just over four hours to cover the 120 miles around Madagascar's northern tip so that their raid on Antsirane coincided with the army's night attack on the Joffre line.

Captain Martin Price, who commanded the flagship's contingent of 160 Royal Marines, had been called into Syfret's cabin and given forty-five minutes' notice to organize his fifty-strong landing party. On the *Ramillies* the marines' main shipboard task was to man the 15-inch guns in X turret and the starboard 6-inch gun battery, part of the ship's secondary armament. Price decided to take all the 6-inch gun crews with him, reasoning that Syfret would probably prefer his main armament to be fully manned. The only exception was X turret's Sergeant Willmott who doubled as the admiral's valet. Willmott pleaded so passionately to be allowed to go that Syfret gave in. Given his private misgivings about their chances, it must be assumed that it was a decision taken with heavy heart.

Almost all Price's party were regulars trained to man guns, board enemy ships, fight ashore as infantrymen, guard prisoners and protect the Royal Navy's officers from mutinous seamen, though this last issue had not come up for some time. They were not Royal Marine Commandos, who would not exist for another year. They shared the same regard for a bulled boot, a ramrod back and a good band as the Brigade of Guards and generally despised new notions of military athleticism. On the parade ground they had declined to follow the army's new drill manual, introduced just before the war, and march in columns of three instead of the four that had been good enough for Nelson and the Iron Duke. They were sartorially conservative too. Royal Marines went into action in Madagascar with their lightweight khaki drill trousers swaddled by the knee-to-ankle cloth puttees of 1914–18. As it happened, this made them the envy of the army who wore shorts. There were some fatal strains of malaria on the island and some men were literally being bitten to death.

By 8 p.m., it was dark and three hours away from moonrise and HMS *Anthony*, her speed reduced to 13 knots, was feeling her way by echo sounder and radar for the mile-wide break in the cliffs that was the entrance to Diego Suarez harbour. When the water became calmer they knew they had got through it. The destroyer was one of the ships that was normally based in Gibraltar and Syfret had almost certainly chosen her because she was one of the older ones, launched in 1927, her two funnels dating her like last year's hemline. Like so much of the navy she had been in almost continuous action in the thirty-two months since the war began. She had brought 3,000 men home from Dunkirk, was part of the destroyer pack around the sinking *Bismarck*, had been bombed, shot at, combed torpedoes and dropped depth charges from Malta to Murmask; but she had never been asked to do anything quite like this.

The whole point of landing on the western side of the isthmus and marching across to the anchorage entered from the east coast had been to avoid its well-sited coastal batteries which contained a score of guns of various calibres. Now Lieutenant Commander John Hodges was praying that the darkness, the smallness of his ship, which was his first command, and the sheer impertinence of it all would enable him to slip the *Anthony* in and out of this 8-mile gauntlet of coastal artillery. It seemed a very tall order, almost like one of those stunts against Napoléon's navy the author C.S. Forester dreamed up in the Hornblower books to be found in most 1940s wardrooms.

Hodges, who would be 32 in three days' time, had already warned his crew that if they had to abandon ship they must try to head for the northern shore that was occupied by the Commandos. Behind him the *Hermione*, which since the operation began had always been on this coast to make her diversions and keep the French guessing, had been joined by the *Devonshire*, another cruiser. The two had closed up within 6 miles of the harbour entrance to support Hodges with their 8-inch guns. They particularly had in mind the searchlights whose startling beams they had sometimes noticed dancing around these silent waters.

The biggest and most feared guns was a battery of 330mms at Orongea Point, the same type of Modèle 1931 found on the Dunkerque class battle cruisers. But the destroyer, her speed now up to 22 knots, had penetrated the harbour and was half a mile to the west of these before the French spotted her and opened fire. Soon all the batteries had joined in but Hodges, who had been on destroyers for four years, was keeping much closer to the shore than they realised and in the dark the French gunners were not depressing their barrels enough and shooting high. When one of their searchlights tried to help, the *Devonshire* doused it with her second salvo.

On the *Anthony* Ordinary Seaman Yule, whose action station was on the stern by the depth charges, was convinced that it was the 'prompt and efficient shooting' of their own port Oerlikon heavy machine gun mounted on the bridge that had snuffed the light out. The port pom-pom had also joined in as had their aft 4.7-inch gun; the other two, which were forward of the bridge, could not be brought to bear. Then the destroyer was coming alongside the jetty.

Even at this late stage it had been hoped that 5 Commando might at least have been able to get a small party over to Antsirane, seize the deep water quay and be there to take a line from the *Anthony*. Not only was there no welcoming party but in the darkness Hodges, with Price's men prepared to disembark over the port side, overshot the jetty. He was obliged to turn his ship round so that the marines then had to rush over to the starboard side but once again the landing party was disappointed. Strong offshore winds were preventing the destroyer from coming alongside.

By now these parking manoeuvres were attracting the attention of the French who for the first time had a firm idea where their target was and began to subject the *Anthony* to rifle and automatic fire, though the pom-pom and Oerlikon soon diminished it. Coastal batteries, even if they could depress their barrels enough, could not shoot at the ship for fear of hitting the town. An artillery officer named Clavel decided that the answer was to get some of his men to manhandle one of their 75mms onto the jetty and fire at the ship at point-blank range.

At about the same time Hodges also had an idea: instead of trying to berth alongside he would back into the jetty and stay there long enough for the marines to scramble ashore over the low stern. It worked. Ordinary Seaman Yule had helped get the gangplanks down for the marines and was counting them off when he noticed some movement on the jetty. 'Figures could be discerned about 100 yards away to the left wheeling a field gun into position.'

Then the petty officer in charge shouted up to the bridge, 'All Marines ashore.' They had started to pull the gangplanks in when Capitaine Clavel, who had never imagined it would get quite as point-blank as this, gave the order to fire. As they hit the deck Yule and his party heard the swoosh of the shell above them. Clavel stood there staring at his target which still looked oddly intact. Then he reluctantly concluded that this was because it was. He had actually succeeded in missing a destroyer with a field gun at a hundred paces. He could have hit it with his revolver. But there was no time to dwell on this, for some menacing figures were bearing down on him, his crew had fled and he had no choice but to follow them.

Anthony was already pulling away from the jetty, all guns blazing and her five battle ensigns catching the night breeze as every man aboard wondered whether their luck would hold and they would run the thoroughly alerted gauntlet a second time. At first the French shooting was just as wild and inaccurate and there was no help from their searchlights. But once off the Orongea headland the crews on the 330mm batteries almost immediately started to land their shot 'rather close'. The little ship groaned and shook and was covered by their spume. In their thrumming engine room the lights flickered and the artificers looked up at the hatches closed for action stations. Probably the best place to be was behind one of *Anthony*'s three open 4.7-inch guns where constant loading, aiming and firing left little time to dwell on the unfair advantage coastal gunners enjoyed over ships. Then suddenly the entire crew felt the unmistakable swell of an open sea beneath their feet and knew that Hodges had done it. He had threaded them back through the gap in the cliffs and the chances were they had survived.

Behind them they had, as planned, left Price and his marooned Marines to their own devices without the slightest prospect of retreat. Their last memory of the *Anthony* was a departing burst of tracer from her pom-pom that passed about 6 feet over their heads and vanished into the all-consuming darkness. It was pitch-black. Only in the dockyard was there a faint flickering provided by the fires started by the Fleet Air Arm earlier in the day. As they moved away from the wharf somebody's shore-serviced boots stumbled over abandoned metal cooking pots with a ghastly clatter and this drew some fire though none of it was close and Price was not unduly concerned. 'They were obviously firing at the patter of little feet which seem to have grown several sizes larger than usual.'

Price had been briefed, probably as a result of information Percy Meyer had supplied, to try to establish a strongpoint in the headquarters of the Artillery Commandant. But both he and Lieutenant Powell, his deputy, only had a vague idea where this was and in the darkness it was hard to get their bearings. For a while they wandered rather aimlessly around the port area. Rolling artillery rumbles of the distant thunder kind and faint bursts of automatic fire could be heard from the Joffre front 2 miles to the south. From nearer by came the occasional sharp crack of rifle fire but if they were aimed at them they were bad shots. Otherwise, Royal Marines had known noisier Wednesday nights in Portsmouth.

Price had made sure they all had plenty of grenades and, conscious that they were supposed to be making a diversion, he decided to 'advertise our presence' by throwing a few around the buildings that had already suffered from the air raids. But unless they exploded in confined spaces grenades could sound rather feeble and if the French heard them they refused to take the bait. They seem to have decided that if there was something nasty in the night their best policy was to stay indoors. To say the least it was all a bit anticlimactic.

Then the marines discovered a gap in a wall that led to a high bank, almost a cliff, on the top of which was a brick wall topped by a close-meshed fence. It appeared to be the back of something important. Using hands as well as feet as it got steeper, they scaled the bank, employed their bayonets to hack a hole through the wire and entered a compound where a slum of live cows, goats and pigs were being kept in their own filth as emergency rations. Beyond them a large Tricolour hung over an imposing gateway on which there was a brass name plate. Price produced his torch. On it was written: Direction d'Artillerie. They had found it.

Shortly afterwards Lieutenant Powell became involved in a brief skirmish with some Malagasy guards. There were no British casualties and it ended in a shower of grenades and a few bursts of Bren-gun fire after which, to Price's astonishment, the French commandant marched out carrying a large white flag with a Malagasy bugler a respectful few paces behind him. Price allowed Powell to take the surrender. The marines crowded round, some with their rifles slung, glad it was all over so easily. Suddenly the colonel muttered something to the bugler who began to play a call at once so startling and insistent that there was only one possible meaning. Aghast at this treachery, a khaki scrum fell on the musician and his instrument and soon neither was in any condition for an encore. It is unclear at what point the commandant managed to convince his captors that he had merely ordered the sounding of the *cessez-le-feu*. According to the Royal Marines, profuse apologies were not only made but accepted. Whether this included the unfortunate bugler is not recorded.

Inside the Direction d'Artillerie, which was a fairly large barracks, Price discovered about fifty British prisoners, among them the tanks' commander Jocelin Simon with the two officers captured with him and a three-man Swordfish crew. Most of the other ranks were infantry who had become cut off in the attack on the Joffre line which had petered out some fifteen hours before. There were enough confiscated French weapons to arm all the freed prisoners, which meant that Captain Price had just doubled the strength of his command, which he now began to deploy as a stronghold capable of withstanding an infantry counter-attack.

While the marines were exploring their gains, alerted by the ringing of telephones which were obviously being picked up and answered, they came across what appears to have been an operations centre. Its occupants also surrendered their supper, for the landing party had not eaten much more than boiled sweets and chocolate since the majority of them lost their lunch during the start of *Anthony*'s dash through rough waters. In its retelling this incident became gold-braided senior officers interrupted at *une grande bouffe* though it was more likely men in shirtsleeves with cold cuts and, if they were lucky, a couple of bottles of wine.

The delay in uncovering this switchboard played into British hands. It enabled its occupants to continue to spread alarm and despondency about the attack on their rear which was by no means unexpected though, like General Sturges, they thought it would come from the Commandos across the water in Diego Suarez itself. Nor could they be blamed for thinking that the marines were a small part of a much larger force. There was a general perception in Antsirane itself that the British had broken through, which dated from the the South Lancs turning the Vichy flank and their subsequent raiding. By the time the 'hot and begrimed' Sturges was asking for the marines to stage their diversion there was already a feeling among some senior French officers that the game was up.

None knew this better than the spy Percy Mayer. On the night of 5 May he had considered himself a condemned man, sleepless on a hard palliasse, wondering whether the dawn would bring a priest and a firing squad or the British Army. Instead it had brought a return visit from Commandant Melin, the naval Chief of Staff who informed him that it had been decided to grant him parole on condition that he did not leave the confines of his hotel. Before they parted Melin, who had become noticeably friendlier, told Mayer that the invasion had surprised them and he believed the English had already broken through.

Twelve hours later Sturges's night attack on the Joffre line was a total success. Advancing on a front 600 yards across, by 11 p.m. moonrise the two lead battalions, the Seaforth Highlanders and the Northamptons, were both firing their Very light success signals. With great good luck they had gone straight between the flanking French forts that were so camouflaged that the British were not quite sure where they began or ended. But it had hardly been a walkover. The trenches and pill boxes between the forts were manned by some very tough and determined Senegalese and Malagasy troops whose French officers had convinced them that they were winning.

To get through them the Seaforths – some fuelled on a mixture of army-issue Benzedrine* and navy rum they had taken for the 18-mile route march that preceded the attack – found themselves screaming the regiment's Gaelic war cries and delivering a bayonet charge. One of these was Sergeant Jim Stockman, a regular soldier who had fought in France but like almost everybody else had never stuck a 17-inch bayonet into anything more unpleasant than a bag of straw. Nine hours had elapsed since Stockman, a God-fearing man troubled by killing, had taken, as well as his own, an additional three unwanted pep pills and washed them down with 'four or five' tots of rum. When he stepped into the landing craft he had felt 'ready to take on anybody'. Now the grog and bennies were wearing off but, if not one of the bezerkers, he seems to have been in a dreamlike state filled with a kind of cold resolution.

* Used by pre-war long-haul pilots to stay alert, Benzedrine was handed out by all three British services though some infantry battalions thought it affected marksmanship and barred it, while individuals often refused the drug because it could have hallucinogenic side effects. Others thought it kept them alive.

> We just kept moving, driven by some inexplicable group momentum yet feeling strangely introspective with fear and confusion. I recall Lieutenant Penny, my platoon officer, together with Major Lowe and other officers all shouting at us to keep on moving in order. And this with men dropping left, right and centre ... As I kept going I suddenly came across this huge Senegalese coming at me. For a moment I panicked, hesitated. Then, on thankful impulse, stopped him in his tracks by thrusting forward and shoving the bayonet right through him until it emerged on the other side. At first, I did not realise the ferocity with which I stuck him and then found to my horror that I could not pull it out again. I had to fire a round, twist savagely then pull to disengage it.

Covered in the African's blood and vomiting, a shaken Stockman stumbled further into the Vichy positions. At one point he exchanged his rifle for the Bren gun of a wounded friend, using it until the ammunition ran out. Another Seaforth had lost part of an arm and was insisting that it had been bitten off by an enraged African. A French grenade exploded close enough to pepper Stockman's own right arm with shrapnel. He picked up a discarded rifle that would not fire and used the bayonet. Then he was flattened by the blast of a mortar bomb which left him crawling to a field dressing station with shrapnel wounds in his back and buttocks. Loaded with other stretcher cases onto the back of a truck on the first stage of their journey to a hospital ship, a medical officer handed an indignant Stockman a revolver saying that, since he could still sit up, he could look out for snipers. 'As if I still had the energy!'

He was one of eighty-seven wounded Seaforths. Another seventeen died, including three officers. All this was in less than three hours and by far the heaviest casualties of any of the British infantry battalions since the landings started. Five of its officers, all injured, won the Military Cross.

The Seaforths' bayonet charge was almost the last act in the capture of Antsirane and with it all the other strongpoints that went to make up the Diego Suarez anchorage. Long before dawn on 7 May elements of both the 17th and 29th brigades, with Festing in overall command, were well into the town where the Royal Welch Fusiliers had their last fatalities when they lost another officer and his batman at a roadblock. By 1 a.m. they had got to the docks and met up with Price's marines. But their later insistence that they were in time to welcome an unopposed landing must be seen as a mischievous response to Admiral Syfret's irritating claim that the marines' feint was the 'principal and direct cause of the enemy's collapse'.

Seeing that Distinguished Service Orders went to Lietenant Commander Hodges and Captain Martin no doubt reflected Syfret's gratitude for the cold-blooded professionalism that improved the chances of his outrageous gamble not ending in tragedy. But if the *Anthony* and her passengers had been blown out of the water, the South Lancs would still have got behind the Joffre line, the Seaforths still made their charge and Sturges still have in reserve the fresh 13th Brigade which was just coming off the ships. Bluffing with bumps in the night and inserting a mere fifty marines, while it could not be anything else must have contributed to Vichy's disarray, but as it turned out, it was a needless risk.

Anyway, the Royal Welch refused to be impressed and D Company commander Henry Jones rushed off to the Defence Headquarters with Lieutenant Roddy Reynier and his platoon. On the face of it this half-French officer, fluent in his father's native tongue, was the obvious choice. But Reynier had just heard from the Royal Scots Fusiliers that his younger brother Peter was missing believed killed and was in no mood to indulge in the military courtesies normally afforded senior enemy officers. When Capitaine de vaisseau Paul Maerten, the Vichy naval commander who Percy Mayer tried to suborn, and Colonel Pierre Clarebout, head of the military garrison, insisted on surrendering to officers of equivalent rank they were frog-marched out of the building.

Brigadier Festing wasted no time getting there, publicly reprimanded Jones and Reynier for the unchivalrous treatment of their prisoners and saw that they were made fit for public viewing at a ceremony Sturges was planning. Maerten was sufficiently mollified to draw Festing's attention to the contents of his wine cellar before it was discovered by the rapacious soldiery. Not long afterwards Reynier came across his heavily bandaged brother alive if unwell in a French military hospital where he had obviously been well cared for. Years later he would still be picking particles of his own grenade shrapnel out of his scalp, but he otherwise made a full recovery.

In the air and on the sea the fighting spluttered on for another twenty-four hours. As the British infantry were consolidating in Antsirane, three Morane fighters on a first light reconnaissance patrol clashed with four of the Fleet Air Arm's Martlets doing the same thing. In the ensuing dogfight a Martlet pilot with 20mm cannon shells in his engine ditched off a remote beach and took two days to get back to his ship. All three Moranes were shot down. One pilot, Capitaine Assollant, was killed. The other two, one of whom bailed out, escaped with superficial injuries.

At about the same time one of six Swordfish off the *Illustrious* flying anti-submarine cover, spotted *Le Héros* on the surface at the northern entrance of the Baie du Courrier and straddled her with depth charges at the beginning of her crash dive before she was properly submerged. Three hours later fifty survivors were picked up by the destroyer *Pakenham* and the flower class corvette *Jasmine*. That evening, after four minesweepers had ensured that the entrance channel and harbour were free of mines, Syfret took the *Ramillies* into Diego Suarez, followed by the cruiser *Hermione* and the destroyers *Paladin* and *Lightning*. It was scarcely sixty hours since the initial landings and a proud moment for the rear admiral. But Darlan's navy had not yet finished with him.

By daybreak on the 8th the submarine *Monge*, which had returned to Madagascan waters from her island hideout on Réunion, had placed herself in an excellent position to exact revenge. In the expectation that more of Syfret's ships would soon be joining him, she was cruising at periscope depth some 7 miles east of the entrance to the Diego Suarez anchorage, opposite the gap in the cliffs the Royal Navy called the Orongea Pass. She did not have long to wait. Shortly before 8 a.m. along came the aircraft carrier HMS *Indomitable* with forty or so aircraft aboard. Lookouts spotted the telltale trails from the *Monge* and, with agonizing slowness, the top-heavy carrier tried to turn to starboard in order to face the torpedoes and sail between them. She just made it. The wake of the nearest torpedo was seen to be 50 yards ahead of the carrier's bow. The *Monge*, named after Gaspard Monge the eighteenth-century mathematician who became the Revolution's Navy Minister, did not get a second chance. *Indomitable*'s destroyer escorts were already in sonar contact and soon their depth charges were bringing to the surface a large amount of oil in which were mixed pieces of men and machinery. There were probably sixty crew on board and, unlike *Le Héros*, there were no survivors.

By then the ground fighting had been over for almost twenty-four hours. After a brief and bloodless bombardment by the 15-inch guns of the *Ramillies* the coastal batteries on the Orongea peninsula had put up a white flag, though not before they had spiked their guns by burying the breech blocks somewhere. Final negotiations with these gunners were conducted by Hugh Stockwell, debonair commander of the Royal Welch Fusiliers, who was said to have started them off with a white flag, a bugler and two bottles of gin.

Some of Captain Price's marines, dog-tired though they were, were shipped back to the *Ramillies* to change into their white tropical uniforms in order to inject what Sturges hoped would be a soothing ceremonial ingredient. Their main task was to mount guard with the marine band outside the residency where Capitaine de vaisseau Maertens was listening to the British terms for the capitulation of the naval base that was Madagascar's most visible military asset. There was no word from Governor Annet who, as far as anybody knew, was still 500 miles away in the capital.

At one point a marine platoon was diverted to one of the Joffre line forts where it was required to turn out a guard and present arms to a garrison that declined to surrender without being granted full honours of war. Price himself was bemused by the final-whistle approach both sides brought to the ceasefire. 'It was as though we had won a hard game of rugger and neither team appeared to have any ill-feeling.'

Overwhelming force had inevitably won the day but the French had inflicted more casualties than the British had really expected, most of them incurred during their frontal assaults on the Joffre line. In two and a half days' fighting they had lost 105 killed, 15 of them officers, and 283 wounded of all ranks, some permanently disabled. French losses were 145 killed and 336 wounded. Of these 129 of the dead were metropolitan French, all but 18 of them navy, though some of the naval casualties would have been gunners killed in the land fighting.

After almost two years of British naval blockade drugs were in short supply in Madagascar. Most of the more seriously wounded on both sides were eventually sent to the hospital ship *Atlantis*, a converted cruise ship, where there were not only medicines but proper facilities. On shore Frenchwomen volunteers, usually the wives or daughters of officers and non-commissioned officers, were helping out in makeshift wards. To feed a *sous-officier* unable to swallow because of a throat wound from a bullet which had exited through the back of his neck, 5 Commando's Dr Patterson improvised with a contraceptive douche 'shyly proffered by one of the French ladies in response to my inquiries'.

Three days after the capitulation the British staged a victory parade. The marine band was back in action once again. So were the pipers of the Royal Scots Fusiliers. French-speaking members of the SOE's signals team off the schooner *Lindi* tried to assess local reaction from a pavement table at the town's main café where the only drink available was a rather poor local rum. They decided it varied from 'the silently apathetic' to the openly disapproving. 'They add insult to injury,' an elderly gentleman was overheard saying. 'First they take our town, then they play the bagpipes at us.'

Chapter Twenty-Five

Within a few days Sturges's soldiers were behaving just as they would have done in any other garrison town. All the infantry battalions made an effort to get back to 'real soldiering'. Boots were shone and webbing scrubbed and never mind the scarlet dust which made both these pastimes as silly as top hats and gave Madagascar its second name: Red Island. At sunset the drum and bugle bands of the various regiments competed at beating the retreat. And the same Michael West who had toted a Tommy gun and preached guerrilla fighting when he took his South Lancs behind the Joffre line, introduced a polished swagger stick inscribed 'Madagascar 1942' for the briefly immaculate soldier most often chosen as 'Stick Orderly' during the inspections that preceded guard mountings. Late afternoons were for sport. The Commandos won the 29th Brigade football final, beating the East Lancs 3–1 'after a good fight by the Lancs'. In Festing's brigade there was also a concerted effort to exploit the comfort of warm waters and teach the non-swimmers, of whom there were a lot, to swim. The officers organized a drag hunt and steeplechase meetings.

Most evenings there were cinema shows sometimes replaced by communal singing when the electricity failed. Naturally, the Royal Welch had their own choir and boasted that they 'taught Diego Suarez how to sing'. These distractions were welcome. Provision for drink and sex was not up to the normal standards of a French colonial town, certainly nothing like Beirut's thriving bordellos or, for that matter, the British officers' 'club' known as Mary's in Alexandria until it was hit by an Italian bomb. Medical officers reported low rates of VD though considerable malaria. For the first few weeks of the occupation, after which some trade with South Africa had been restored, the only alcohol available was the weak rum or the moonshiners' astonishingly strong *carburant*, which also served as the blockaded island's main petrol substitute.

Officers congregated for al fresco dinners in the courtyard of the Hôtel François where the occasional bottle of hoarded wine supplemented the gin and navy rum smuggled ashore from Syfret's ships. Sometimes they would be joined by a group of war correspondents, desperate men offering outrageous bribes to the wireless operators to get their copy back to Fleet

Street ahead of their colleagues. They had arrived from Mombasa to write about what Churchill, groggy from the Japanese avalanche, would later admit was the 'only sign of good and efficient war direction of which the British public were conscious'. A British victory, however humble, was a story in itself.

Despite this the Prime Minister was anxious to move on. It had never been his intention to try to occupy all of Madagascar, merely seize the strategic port at its northern tip, and five days before the landings he had made this plain to the Chiefs of Staff. 'A principal object must be to get our best troops forward to India and Ceylon at the earliest moment, replacing them with garrison battalions from East or West Africa. Getting this place is meant to be a help and not a new burden. The true defence of Madagascar will be the Eastern Fleet, when based with adequate air support on Colombo.'

Eight days after the fall of Diego Suarez nothing had changed as Churchill's telegram to Admiral Syfret makes clear:

> your problem is one of holding the place with the least subtraction from our limited resources. It may well be that you will think it better to let matters simmer down and make some sort of modus vivendi with the French authorities. Money and trade facilities should be used. The way you can help the war best is to get the 13th and 17th Brigades on to India earliest and the 29th Brigades within the next two months. Everything else is subordinate to this, except of course holding Diego Suarez, which must on no account be hazarded.

Then three weeks after the invasion, on 27 May, Governor General Annet sent an emissary to see the British at Diego Suarez. Lionel Barnett was an Englishman who had lived and worked in Tananarive for some years as the representative of the Standard Vacuum Oil Company of South Africa. He was also loosely connected with Percy Mayer's Special Operations Executive network in that he sensed Mayer had something to do with British intelligence and had passed on enough that was useful, mostly concerning the effects of the blockade, to earn an SOE code-name: DZ14. Now DZ14 had shown commendable initiative.

He had convinced Annet to allow him to go to Diego Suarez as a spokesman for the island's commercial interests, hoping to persuade the British to lift their blockade of all the island's ports including those still firmly under Vichy control in the south. Annet had agreed to this on condition that Barnett asked the British to 'save further bloodshed' and settle for an agreement whereby a neutral Vichy French sovereignty would be recognized over all but Diego Suarez. Unstated seemed to be the offer that Vichy would accept that the anchorage on the island's northern tip had temporarily become a kind of Madagascan Gibraltar. Barnett's own impression was that Annet was playing for time and would probably like to start a dialogue he could drag on until November when the seasonal rains would make further campaigning difficult.

General Smuts, who feared that Vichy might invite the Japanese to do mischief from some of its southern ports, also had the Madagascan monsoon in mind. Ever since Churchill had first confided the Ironclad plan to him he had urged that the whole island be occupied and offered to contribute a South African brigade. Now the chances of doing this were improving. On India's eastern border with Burma the situation could be said to have stabilized. A British Indian Army under Bill Slim (last seen as a divisional commander chasing Vichy out of northern Syria) had just regrouped there after a horrific fighting retreat. And even the Japanese had at last reached the end of their frugal ration train and were consolidating.

But Churchill remained adamant about the need to reinforce India before the small men with the long rifles were on the move again. Diego Suarez was quite enough of Madagascar. The 13th Brigade, which had hardly been engaged in the fighting, was already on its way and the Seaforths and the rest of the 17th were getting ready to go. The navy too was much reduced as Admiral Somerville, hunted by Japanese aircraft carriers and short of everything except trouble, demanded that his destroyers rejoin him off the Seychelles. The only ships left for anti-submarine duties were the corvettes *Thyme* and *Genista*.

This was not a matter of great concern because the chances of an underwater attack on the Diego Suarez anchorage seemed low. All the known Vichy submarines in Madagascan waters had been sunk. German and Italian U-boats, hunting British ships avoiding the dangerous Mediterranean route by supplying its forces in Egypt the long way around the Cape, tended to attack them in the South Atlantic off West Africa. Sinkings in the smaller waters of the Mozambique Channel and the Red Sea were comparatively rare.

At the beginning of the war the German ace Gunther Prien, later lost with all his crew, had entered the British anchorage at Scapa Flow and torpedoed the battleship *Royal Oak*. But of the three Axis navies, the one that had given the most thought to submarine attacks on defended harbours was Japan's.

They had developed two-man midget submarines launched from *Surcouf*-sized mother ships. These Ko-Hyoteki class midgets carried two torpedoes and could go down to 100 feet. They were 78 feet long but at 10 feet high and 6 feet across were almost as cramped as a coal face. Five of them had been used at Pearl Harbor though only one might have done any damage and even that was disputed by Japanese aircrews. None of them returned to their mother ships: two were definitely sunk, two disappeared, and one ran aground. Her petty officer drowned but the lieutenant in command swam ashore to become America's first Japanese prisoner of war, thus missing out on the Hero God status bestowed by the Emperor on all his dead comrades.

Certainly the usual Japanese preference for death before even honourable capitulation applied to most of these volunteers who were not official kamikaze but accepted that their chances of survival were slight. Nothing more was heard of the Ko-Hyoteki until the Australian evening of Friday, 29 May when three of them managed to slip into Sydney harbour though they did not remain undetected for very long. Two cornered crews had killed themselves by detonating their 300-pound scuttling charges, one after their craft became enmeshed in an anti-torpedo net. The only pair that managed to hit something and return to their mother ship missed with the torpedoes they fired at the US cruiser *Chicago*, which instead sank a nearby floating barracks killing twenty-one Australian sailors.

About the time this was happening at one end of Japan's military endeavour there had been a portent for Admiral Syfret that something nasty was about to occur at the other. At 10.30 p.m. on the 29th, a small and silent seaplane had glided down from under Madagascar's moon and seemed for a moment to be about to settle near the *Ramillies*. Then its engine had coughed abruptly into life and, banking steeply, it vanished into the darkness, flashing some unintelligible reply to an enquiring Aldis lamp challenge just long enough to keep the pom-pom crews off their triggers. Identification books were consulted but, though the little Glenn seaplane that operated as a scout from the larger Japanese submarines was in them, nobody was sure. It could have been Vichy, Japanese or German.

Syfret ordered extra vigilance. Next day, long before dawn, *Ramillies* started steaming up and shortly after sunrise had anchored at a new position in the lee of the Antsirane lighthouse. A newly arrived South African Air Force squadron equipped with Marylands and Beauforts took a good look at the western fringe of the Indian Ocean which appeared as innocent as their day was long. The two remaining corvettes increased their patrols of the Orongea Pass but the gap they guarded was a mile wide and a Ko-Hyoteki had a beam of 6 feet.

Saturday, 30 May was a beautiful evening. Like a paper lantern an almost full tropical moon hung above the anchorage. At Antsirane's Hôtel François the usual crowd were gathered around their tables in the courtyard when at 8.25 a heavy explosion rocked the ground beneath them. Quartered nearby in an old stone-walled French barracks, where the bed bugs were driving him crazy, Bombardier Bailey of 455 Light Battery thought it was an earthquake. But the diners at the François were close enough to know differently and some were already running towards the harbour. About half an hour later Dr Patterson had found himself a good position on a bandstand overlooking the water from where the moonlit silhouette of the battleship *Ramillies* had now developed an obvious list.

> Corvettes were chasing about. I saw depth charges going up all over the harbour. A tanker was moving broadside to me and watching her I saw an almighty flash just forward of the engine room and, before the noise reached me, she clearly settled by the stern and the well deck was awash. This was 40 minutes after *Ramillies* had been struck, so the sub was still alive. A corvette tore past the sinking tanker and threw out a fan of depth charges. They went up with a colossal thump and after a few seconds there was a monstrous bubbling and boiling.

Two men were responsible for all this. Lieutenant Akeida Saburo and Petty Officer Takemoto Masami of the Imperial Japanese Navy had sneaked into the anchorage in a midget launched by its mother ship I-20 from a position about 9 miles east of the Orongea Pass. A little further out I-20's flotilla mate I-16 sent a second midget which does not appear to have played an active part in the attack. A body that could be identified as a member of the Imperial Japanese Navy was eventually cast up in a remote cove near the island's northern tip and the submarine is presumed to have foundered long before she reached the harbour entrance.

But the first submarine had navigated Mozambique's shoals and sudden sand bars well. Her first torpedo blew a hole 20 feet in diameter in the *Ramillies* port bow under her forward 15-inch gun turret. The loss of half her ordnance and shock waves from the explosion played havoc with the trim of the lightened submersible. Before they knew what was happening Akieda and Takemoto found that they had bobbed to the surface. Their conning tower was spotted by a lookout on the nearby tanker *British Loyalty* which was manned by Indian seamen, mostly from Bombay, under British officers. Somebody got to an anti-aircraft gun in time to give it a burst but the Japanese managed to submerge before he got his eye in. On the *Ramillies* all the interior lights had gone out. Some magazine compartments were flooding and the old battleship had taken on a list of almost five degrees before watertight doors and pumps stopped her going any further. Then the lighting came back on and it was discovered that nobody was seriously hurt.

The Royal Navy's reaction was painfully slow. The *Ramillies*'s own picket boat, a large motor launch armed with depth charges though without sonar detection gear, was already in the water but had strayed some way from the ship's new location. It took her fifteen minutes to get to the vicinity where the gunner on *British Loyalty* had spotted the submarine and start dropping her drums of amatol. Shortly afterwards she was joined by the two corvettes depth-charging as guided by the sonar pings from their British Asdic systems. Possibly there was too much depth-charging and not enough listening. In any case, Asdic was far from perfect and, in the shallower waters of an anchorage, all that pinged was not a submarine.

At 9.02 p.m., the Ko-Hyoteki was still sufficiently intact for Akieda and

Takemoto to come up to periscope depth and fire their second torpedo at the *Ramillies*. Compared with conventional submarines their main weapon was of a narrower circumference with a reduced warhead – 772 pounds instead of 1,213. Even so, one more might well have been too much for the battleship's old frame. Instead it hit the *British Loyalty* which strayed into its path while manoeuvring slowly astern as a first step to making herself a moving target. Five of the Indians working in the engine room were killed. The rest of the crew abandoned ship and the tanker sank slowly by her stern into almost 70 feet of water so that only the tip of her funnel was showing. At about the same depth Akiedo and Takemoto headed back towards the open sea. Above them the sky was filled with tracer as one anti-aircraft gunner after another swore he saw something break the surface. On shore some drunken Commandos arrested and beat up a drunken Frenchman who had dared to break the curfew.

Ramillies moved to shallower water so that if she did sink she would settle on the bottom and her top deck and superstructure would remain dry. But it soon became apparent that prompt action had made this unlikely. Her own shipwrights and electricians worked around the clock to make her seaworthy again. Eight portable pumps arrived from Durban which, to improve anti-submarine defences, also sent three Asdic-equipped converted trawlers. Two destroyers dashed back from the Maldives. A corvette arrived from the South Atlantic. All they lacked was something to depth-charge.

It was still unclear who was responsible for torpedoing the *Ramillies* or even that the culprit was not a conventional submarine, for the lookout on the *British Loyalty* had caught only a moonlit glimpse of her conning tower and could be no judge of her size. Then, two days after the attack, an excited Malagasy came rushing up to some of 5 Commando who were patrolling the coastal area north of Diego Suarez. He spoke heavily accented French and appeared to think he knew something they would be willing to pay for.

It turned out that he came from the nearby village of Anijabe where, at about eleven o'clock that morning, two dishevelled Chinese gentlemen had turned up asking for food and water. They were different from any Chinese people he had seen before in that they both had pistols in their belts and one carried a curved sword. They explained that they were friends of the French people and wished to avoid the English who were their enemies. They had just sunk one of their ships.

After they left the anchorage Akieda and Takemoto had headed in a north-westerly direction for their rendezvous with I-20 off Cape Amber, Madagascar's northern tip, where it would wait for two days. But the battery of their Ko-Hyoteki had run down and the submariners beached their craft on a small island where they were kindly treated by the local Malagasy who paddled them across to the mainland. By the time the

Commandos had them cornered at Amponkarana Bay on the morning of 2 June they had covered a total of forty-eight miles on foot and were not far from the pick-up point.

They were called on to surrender but took cover and there was a short gunfight. Then two single shots announced that, as required by the cruel medieval code most of the Japanese military aspired to, these brave men – both married with children – had killed themselves rather than submit to capture. Among the personal possessions recovered was Akieda's samurai sword, a watch, Imperial Japanese Navy-issue cigarettes and a short report to the commander of the I-20 submarine recounting all they had done in Diego Suarez. The next day, some forty-eight hours after the rendezvous deadline had expired, the I-20 surfaced off Cape Amber and tried once more to contact her missing offspring by sending radio signals and firing flares. It was a loving and irresponsible thing to do, jeopardizing over 100 men to any passing British plane loaded for submarines. Then around dusk she submerged with the sinking sun and went on her way.

It was several days before the Royal Navy could get anyone to Madagascar with enough Japanese to be capable of reading Akieda's papers. Not that there was any longer any doubt who had holed the *Ramillies*, now Durban bound and facing several months of repairs. As salvage divers set about raising *British Loyalty*, which became a fuel storage tank in the Maldives until a passing German U-boat torpedoed her again, Smuts seized his chance and cabled Churchill that these losses proved his case for occupying all of the island.

> Attack must have been made by Vichy submarines or by Japanese submarines acting on Vichy information and advice. It all points to eliminating Vichy control completely from whole island as soon as possible. Appeasement is as dangerous in this case as it has proved in all others, and I trust we shall soon make a clean job of this whole business.

Of course, as Smuts knew full well, it had nothing to do with appeasement. Churchill's reluctance was about scarce resources and his unwillingness to squander them against the Vichy French when the Germans, Italians and Japanese raised more pressing issues. Then the Japanese submarines gathered around Madagascar started sinking the ships supplying the army trying to halt Rommel's advance into Egypt.

Commodore Ishizaki had under him five big ocean-going craft of which three had carried Ko-Hiyoteki midgets (the third had been unable to launch) and two Glenn scout planes. One of these had been the aircraft making the moonlight reconnaissance of Diego Suarez before the *Ramillies* was torpedoed. There were also two well-armed support ships, the *Aikou Maru* and *Hokoku Maru*, which carried their munitions and supplies. In the space of thirty-five days, between 5 June and 10 July 1942, Ishizaki's squadron sank twenty-three merchant ships. Doenitz's U-boats had rarely matched figures like these. Most were torpedoed in the Mozambique Channel. The I–10 was the top scorer with eight. The I-20, Akeida and Takemoto's mother ship, was runner-up with seven. East of Madagascar even his supply ships joined in sinking one ship and capturing two more. There was little the British could do to halt this massacre. Short of the number of escort ships and aircraft needed to even the odds, they advised ships' masters either to hug the coast or go east of the island and chance the long way around.

Ishizaki's rampage had been of great benefit to the Afrika Korps. Then it stopped as suddenly as it began. Off Midway Island in the Pacific the US Navy had ended six months of Japanese victories by sinking four of their aircraft carriers for the loss of one of its own. Tokyo felt that it had done its German ally enough favours and, though its confidence in final victory was undiminished, wanted most of its assets closer to home. But as far as Madagascar was concerned, the sinkings had begun to persuade Churchill that, one way or another, Smuts was right: they needed to make a clean job of it.

There was another, almost equally pressing, reason why the British were coming round to the idea of taking the rest of the island. Within days of Japan entering the war de Gaulle, realising that Madagascar was a French card he could play in this new theatre, had proposed that his Free French be landed on the island. Confronted six months later by the fait accompli of an exclusive British action, his outrage had been compounded by what he perceived as Churchill's new-found willingness to try to make deals with Vichy functionaries such as Annet. There were even threats to transfer Free French headquarters to one of its African bastions, Chad or the Cameroons, which must have been worrying news for those kepied staff warriors who already found the French pub in Soho exile enough.

Anthony Eden was sympathetic. Churchill's Foreign Secretary wanted to 'clear out the rot' and install a Free French governor in Madagascar without delay. As a first step Laurence Grafftey-Smith, a First Secretary at the British Embassy in Cairo, was sent to Diego Suarez where he was styled Chief Political Officer and charged with keeping the military from making any embarrassing accord with Annet. By now neither London nor Vichy wanted any kind of deal with each other over Madagascar. At the beginning of July Annet made a plaintive request for 'modern aircraft to unsettle the warships at Diego Suarez' and asked: 'Is it not possible to execute reprisals, especially on English colonies on the East African coast?'

What sort of reprisals he had in mind and where they might be staged from is unclear. The nearest Vichy base was French Somaliland under Governor Pierre Nouailhetas, which had British-occupied territory on all its land borders and the Royal Navy patrolling its Red Sea coast. It is possible that Nouailhetas possessed a few aircraft that might have staged a hit-and-run raid on British-occupied Addis Ababa or even Nairobi but there would have been sharp retaliation. The Vichy Foreign Ministry clearly did not consider Annet's question merited a reply. Instead he was urged to resist any British advance into the south 'by using guerrillas, scorched earth etcetera'.

And so the stage was set for the completion of the British conquest of Madagascar, though during the high summer of 1942 it did not seem anywhere near as certain as this. Not to Armand Annet, sitting in his hilltop home in Tananarive sipping a drink and watching the sun go down over the rice fields and wondering about guerrillas and a scorched earth. Or a bit further down the hill to Berthe Mayer, relieved to have heard from Lionel Barnett on his return from Diego Suarez that Percy was safe and well but wondering how long it would be before Annet's police came for her. Sometimes there were local power failures and people said it was the Deuxième Bureau working with the electricity company to locate a secret transmitter by discovering which district was switched off when it went off the air.

Yet, apart from the power failures the city appeared to be quite untouched by the war. There were all sorts of rumours. But as Berthe Mayer and anybody else with quite an ordinary radio set could testify, they were rarely as depressing as the contents of the average BBC news bulletin. There was no doubt that the war was going badly for all the Allies and particularly the English. There had even been a 'no confidence' vote in the House of Commons over Churchill's leadership. Admittedly it had been defeated by 475 votes to 25 but it was startling to think that it had ever happened in the first place.

On the heels of the Japanese whirlwind, June, July and August had brought fresh humiliation from the Germans. First 33,000 men had surrendered at Tobruk, most of them white South Africans under General Klopper. After this the Afrika Korps had chased the British right back into Egypt's Western Desert. They had not stopped running until they reached the coastal railway stop of El Alamein. Nor was there any comfort from the Russian front where Kleist's First Panzer Army had crossed the Don and threatened the Grozny oilfields and the Caspian Sea, while further north another armoured pincer was on the Volga and nearing Stalingrad.

Partly to take the pressure off the Russians, in August there had been the disastrous Operation Jubilee. This had been a large-scale raid on the northern French port of Dieppe. It was much bigger than the one on St Nazaire but with ill-defined objectives. Most of the infantry were a Canadian division, in Britain for two years and yet to fire a shot in anger and among them the Fusiliers Mont Royal, volunteers from French-speaking Quebec despite the strong Pétainist sympathies there. The rest were British Commandos who successfully suppressed two German gun batteries that would have made the slaughter even heavier. As it was, in less than three hours the Canadians had over 900 men killed. Not because they were green but because it was a stupid plan. At Madagascar there had been much better preparation against a much weaker enemy. Well over half of the 6,000 men who went ashore at Dieppe failed to return, most of them captured when they were pinned down on the beach or not far off it.

Afterwards Maréchal Pétain had congratulated the German Army for 'cleansing French soil of the invader', a remark he would come to regret. Then, referring to what he called 'the most recent British aggression', he asked that French troops might be allowed to garrison coastal defences alongside Germany's soldiers. All this was music to the ears of collaborators like Fernand de Brinon who reported that in Vichy the talk was all about manning 'a French crenellation in the Atlantic wall'. Not suprisingly the Wehrmacht did not share their enthusiasm. Instead, as a reward for not providing the Canadians with an instant fifth column, not that there had been much opportunity, Berlin radio announced that Germany was releasing 750 sons of Dieppe held captive in Germany since 1940. But by far the best propaganda were the Dieppe pictures of the Calgary Regiment's brand-new Churchill tanks knocked out on the beach and lines of crest-fallen men in British battledress and soup-plate helmets with their hands up, a *promenade des anglais*.

Against this dismal backcloth it was not hard to believe that the British might well have better things to do than occupy the rest of Madagascar and would settle for the 'Gibraltar solution' of holding Fortress Diego Suarez at its strategic tip. And for four months this is what happened.

The 13th and 17th brigades went off to India, which was ablaze with anti-British rioting over the arrest of Gandhi, and eventually to Burma to fight the Japanese. Their replacements were the 22nd East African Brigade, three battalions of white-officered King's African Rifles from Kenya, Tanganyika and Nyasaland with Ugandan gunners, and the mostly Afrikaans-speaking whites of 7th South African Motorised Brigade Group. Smuts had promised Churchill this formation when he had been pressing for the capture of the entire island. It included a squadron of twenty Marmon-Herrington armoured cars, built in South Africa by welding locally made armour plate onto the chassis of a 3-ton Ford truck. Armed with a variety of weapons including 2-pounder cannon, they were as fast as Jocelin Simon's Tetrarchs but thicker skinned.

Festing's 29th Independent Brigade Group, the amphibious landing specialists who had done most of the fighting, were still there, though at any one time a large number of them were in hospital with malaria. Nonetheless, their presence was a good indication that the British had at least retained the option of 'going south', for they would be the best troops to capture the island's two other main ports: Majunga on the west coast and Tamatave on the east, with its rail link up to the capital. Meanwhile,

There were no holds barred in the propaganda war. 'A frog he would a-wooing go . . .' was the *Daily Mirror*'s caption to this cartoon of a distinctly amphibian Pierre Laval, which appeared after he and Pétain met Hitler at Montoire (RIGHT).

ABOVE: Laval after being shot in the chest with a small calibre pistol at Versailles. He later successfully appealed for the life of the young man who tried to kill him.

RIGHT: Charles de Gaulle in 1940.

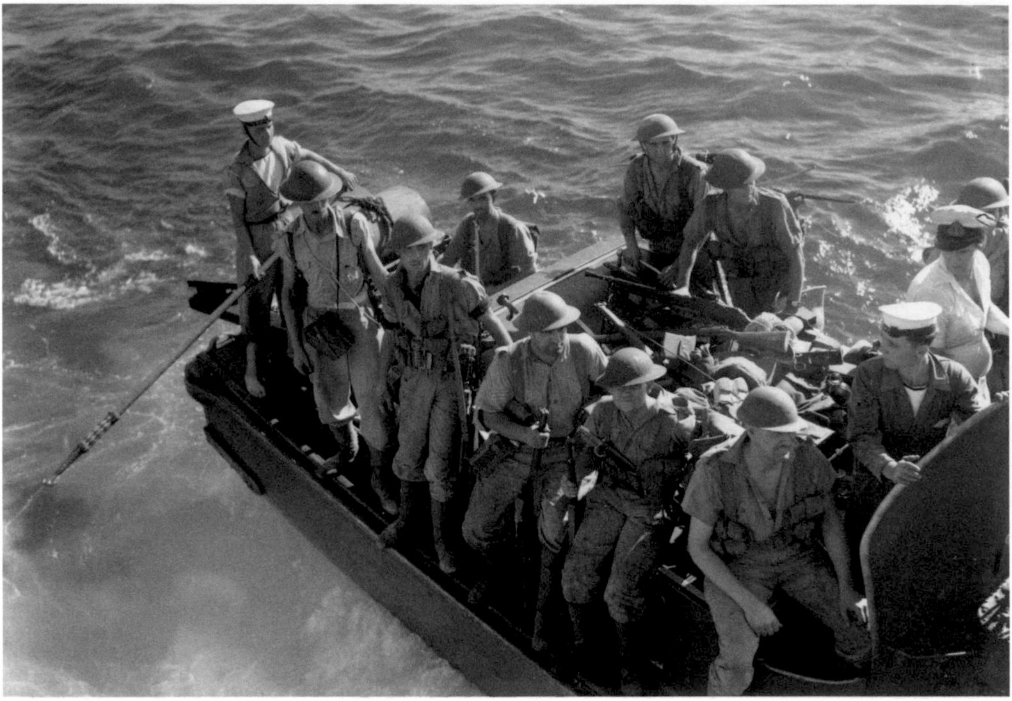

Royal Marines returning with their souvenirs to the battleship *Ramillies* after their successful raid on Madagascar's Diego Suarez. Note the hilt of the French bayonet tucked into the webbing of the second marine from the right.

Under the stern gaze of Maréchal Pétain – one of the thousands of images of him that adorned Madagascar – British and French officers discuss ceasefire terms at Antsirane.

LEFT: In Madagascar, local French surrender terms often stipulated being granted full honours of war. Here British soldiers present arms to a Vichy naval contingent which had been manning a coastal battery.

RIGHT: Part of the Diego Suarez Joffre line, which was missed by air reconnaissance and inflicted heavy casualties on British tanks. A French 75mm gun muzzle is visible in the blockhouse on the left.

BELOW: In Madagascar's misty hill country a Commando officer uses his Gurkha Kukri to point out a French position to a Bren gunner resting his weapon on a rock.

A morose looking French officer – Colonel Passerou – who was captured in the closing weeks of the Madagascar campaign.

ABOVE: Red umbrellas were issued to British troops as ground recognition signals to keep out the RAF's hard rain – with any luck.

BELOW: A wrecked bridge in southern Madagascar. As the campaign dragged on towards its inevitable end the French could do little more than apply a scorched earth policy and destroy key sections of the island's hard-won road system.

BELOW: Lt-Colonel Alston Robert West, battalion commander of the 2nd South Lancs, led his men in a daring night attack around the Joffre line and secured Diego Suarez.

ABOVE LEFT: Some of West's men travelling in style in a Madagascan railway freight car after what had often been a hard marching campaign. When they left the island most of them went to Burma to fight the Japanese.

General Mark Clark (INSET) is canoed ashore from the British submarine *Seraph* off Cherchell in Algeria for his secret meeting with Général Mast and the other dissidents which ultimately sealed the success of the Anglo-American North African landings. *Seraph*'s conning tower can be seen to the right of the picture.

8 November 1942. Almost a year after America came into the war the US Army participated in its first major land attack: the Anglo-American invasion of French North Africa codenamed Operation Torch. This landing on a beach 20 miles east of Algiers was almost unopposed. Others were not so lucky.

The enormous anti-aircraft barrage put up by British ships in Algiers harbour after Luftwaffe night bombers based in Rhodes and Sicily tried to interfere with the landings and sank several ships.

HMS *Walney* capsized in Oran harbour after a foolish attempt to emulate what the Royal Marines got away with at Diego Suarez. Over half *Walney*'s crew were killed or wounded when French ships and shore batteries open fired at point blank range during a night attack.
INSET: War correspondent Leo 'Bill' Disher, a survivor of the *Walney*, receiving a Purple Heart – the US medal awarded to those wounded in action. Disher won his several times over. He was hit 26 times: 15 from shell fragments and the rest from bullets. The crutches date from an ankle broken on passage from England to Gibraltar but Disher refused to abandon his assignment.

Amiral Darlan and his wife Berthe Morgan, who was partly of English stock, taken at their villa in Algiers shortly before Darlan was assassinated on Christmas Eve 1942.

November 1942.
RAF reconnaissance pictures of French warships burning in Toulon after La Marine Française kept its promise to destroy its ships rather than allow them to fall into German hands.

October 1945. A defiant Laval in a Paris court room after being accused of treason.

Laval's execution at Fresnes prison on 15 October 1945. He had to be brought back to consciousness after attempting to poison himself. He refused a blindfold. 'Aim at my heart,' he told the firing squad, 'Vive La France!'

there were still a few nearby Vichy outposts to be dealt with.

In a bloodless operation Mayotte Island, an old pirate lair in the northern part of the Mozambique Channel, was seized by a company of King's African Rifles and thirty Commandos who scaled a cliff and, since it was shortly before dawn, captured its governor in bed. Later the same day the neighbouring island of Pamanzi, which had an airstrip, was taken. Both islands would become a base for RAF Catalina flying boats hunting for submarines.

South African-crewed Marylands built up a photographic map of the areas around the capital and the ports the British would have to use to get to it if they were to take the rest of the island with its abysmal lack of roads. The South Africans were obviously determined that there would be no more missed Joffre lines and dozens of missions were flown. At this point Annet's forces had only one serviceable Morane left, though their anti-aircraft fire had its successes.*

One day a Monsieur Minot, president of the Planters' Association in Tananarive, turned up in Antsirane and spoke with the diplomat Grafftey-Smith. His message was a simple one: most of the French in Tananarive wanted a deal with the British but Annet would incur great displeasure in Vichy if he made one. If Britain wanted all of Madagascar it must exhibit enough force to make surrender an entirely honourable proposition.

The British had already begun to prepare for their administration of the island. A few days before Millot's visit Lieutenant General Sir William Platt had been told that from July the French colony would become part of his East African Command along with Mauritius and the Seychelles. Platt, who had been knighted for his long and hard-fought campaign against the isolated Italian forces in the Horn of Africa, would retain Sturges as commander of land forces in Madagascar. But the weeks rolled by and nothing changed. In Diego Suarez, the British infantry continued to beat the retreat, polish their boots, learn to swim, play football and, if they were a Royal Welch Fusilier, perfect their rendition of 'Men of

* One Maryland crew shot down on the east coast made an enterprising escape. Major Ken Jones (the SAAF used army ranks) and his four companions had walked away from a crash-landing taking with them the Vickers K machine gun from their rear turret. It was carried by Navigator 'Bull' Malan, the biggest member of the party and younger brother of the RAF fighter ace Sailor Malan. On a narrow path through thick bush the South Africans heard what turned out to be a French officer and eight Malagasy riflemen approaching. Jones told his crew to hide and remained where he was.

'You are my prisoner,' announced the Frenchman in English.

'No, no, Monsieur le capitaine. You are my prisoner,' replied Jones, who then broke into Afrikaans, '*Bull – los maar 'n paar skote* (Fire a few shots)', at which Bull obliged with a brisk overhead burst with his Vickers.

'Monsieur, I am your prisoner,' agreed the sensible French officer and they adjourned to a nearby lighthouse where the keeper was persuaded to radio the Royal Navy in Diego Suarez which sent a minesweeper to collect them all.

Harlech'. Meanwhile, in Delhi, Wavell was awaiting the arrival of Festing's brigade which General Slim needed for an amphibious operation he was planning in the Arakan.

Then on 20 August it looked like it was all over. Festing's men departed Diego Suarez, packed into two old rust buckets called the *Empire Pride* and the *Ocean Viking* with the troops complaining that their meals were pig swill and the overcrowded mess decks colonized by cockroaches. Even so, few were sorry to say goodbye to malarial Madagascar. First stop was Kenya where a draft of a couple of hundred reinforcements from the United Kingdom brought all the infantry battalions up to strength, their numbers depleted by sickness as much as battle casualties. After that, with a certain amount of foreboding, they expected to be on their way to India and Burma where they sincerely hoped that the Japanese had not established anything like the Joffre line.

On 30 August the brigade were the main participants in Exercise Touchstone, an authentic-looking assault on Mombasa's port defences which were found wanting. This and the renewed waterproofing of their vehicles started a new crop of rumours. Perhaps it was not going to be Burma after all. Perhaps they were going to attack Dakar and wreak revenge for the 1940 fiasco there? Or make a landing behind the Axis front line at El Alamein, recapture Tobruk or Benghazi? Rommel had just started another offensive but for the moment the new British commander Bernard Montgomery was holding him at the Alam el Halfa Ridge.

It was not until 5 September when, re-embarked on the rust buckets, Festing's brigade learned that they had been involved in an enormous feint. They were going to finish the occupation of Madagascar by starting with a surprise attack on the port of Majunga. By then they had rendezvoused with a fleet of almost seventy ships under the recently promoted Rear Admiral William Tennant who was flying his flag on the aircraft carrier *Illustrious* with her new American Wildcat fighters. Surrounding the carrier was a screen of five cruisers, one of them a dedicated anti-aircraft vessel, plus sixteen destroyers and minesweepers. Tennant must have been comforted by the protection he had against an enemy estimated to be down to its last half-dozen bombers. His previous command had been the old battle cruiser *Repulse*. There had been no such umbrella for him off Malaya in February when the Japanese Mitsubishis, based on the Vichy airfields they had seized in French Indochina, had first sunk his ship and then the *Prince of Wales*.

Chapter Twenty-Six

The plan was to capture Tananarive in three operations: Stream, Line and Jane. Stream was a surprise attack on Majunga which was what Mombasa's Exercise Touchstone had been all about. Line was the insertion into the captured port of the motorized 22nd East African Brigade and most of the South Africans' armoured cars that would seize vital bridges and dash down the road towards Tananarive, 270 miles away. Jane would involve 29th Brigade getting back in their ships and sailing around Diego Suarez and the island's northern tip to the east coast to seize the Indian Ocean port of Tamatave and advance on the capital from the other direction.

These three successive hammer blows were poised to crack a very small nut indeed. Over 3,000 Vichy troops had surrendered in the Diego Suarez area. Général de brigade Guillemet had at most six formed infantry battalions left – perhaps 4,800 men – supported by sixteen artillery pieces, some of them manufactured just too late for the Franco-Prussian War, and five aircraft. After the bloodshed on the Joffre line it looked like Annet was about to receive the overwhelming force the planter Millot had indicated he would require to make an honourable surrender.

In addition there were various feints and diversions designed to alarm and confuse and suck in troops that might have been better employed elsewhere. A 600-strong South African column called Getcol after its commander Lieutenant Colonel David Getcliffe, supported by the remaining armoured cars and artillery, would work its way south from Diego Suarez and link up with the East Africans at Majunga. Some forty Commandos were to be landed at the harbour of Monrondava 300 miles south of Majunga from where there was also a road to Tananarive, making it a plausible landing place. Their task was to start the kind of rumours whose investigation might draw away from the capital at least a reconnaissance in force.

Operation Stream, the initial assault on Majunga, took place at dawn on 10 September and was over about two hours later after attacks from the landward and seaward sides. At one o'clock that morning the East Lancs and Royal Welch Fusiliers had been landed on a beach 10 miles north of the town and stumbled south through the bush and clouds of mosquitoes in time for them to take the defenders from the rear shortly after first light. At about the same time the landing craft of 5 Commando and the South Lancs, accompanied by a destroyer, had rushed the harbour where they came under some machine-gun fire from a building and a barge secured to a jetty. One of the first ashore was the Commando doctor Patterson.

> The tide was well up and we scrambled out among the bullets and up a low wall about four feet high and I crouched down by the houses with my chaps before following the troops towards the Point de Sable along the front. There was quite a lot of shooting going on and one fellow behind a heap of coal at the petrol store was being a nuisance and shooting at me. However, Buckland (my batman) made him keep his head down with a few accurate shots and we got under cover. A white head on the coal heap gave Buckland a mark. He was very excited. I thought he would shoot me at any moment and decided I would be a lot safer behind him so I made him go in the front. I was pleased with his aggressiveness but he was very trigger happy. As we moved up the town I saw a hand-pushed dust cart pulled in under some palms on the open left side of the road. Slowly, over the top of the cart, up came a floppy white hat on top of a silly looking black head. The dustman was having a shufti. Buckland immediately put up his rifle to shoot him but I roared at him to desist, which he did, and the white hat slowly sank behind the cart again.

Patterson got into an empty building and set up a field dressing station. One of his first patients was a South Lancs sergeant 'shamefully deserted and almost dead from loss of blood' with a large hole in the hollow behind a knee. But most of the casualties were either locally recruited Vichy troops or people who had shown themselves at the wrong moment. 'I patched up a few French and Malgache too. One poor innocent civilian came running and staggering into my aid post riddled by bullets all down one side, his left arm shattered. Another trigger happy warrior's victim I'm afraid.' Later, concerned by the casualties among the non-combatants, he got into the operating theatre of the municipal hospital and was appalled by what he saw.

> Flies and blood and filth were everywhere. A gloomy French doctor was rootling with his finger inside the chest of a little black child who was being held up by the feet by a nurse. There was another doctor with a bottle of chloroform standing around but not doing anything particular. Perhaps he had noticed that the kid was already dead. There was no noticeable asepsis. The instruments were all in a tin bucket of water. There were other casualties lying around, victims of our shooting, and all seemed to be civilians. I was not popular and small wonder.

While Patterson did what he could to help, Michael West's South Lancs had surrounded French headquarters and procured the surrender of Colonel Didier Martins, the commander of the Majunga garrison, who wanted to know if his men had fought well. West assured him that they had. The capture of Majunga had cost the British twelve dead.

Two cars, each containing a French and a British officer and bedecked in white flags, then toured the port calling on both sides to stop shooting. Within a short time the gunfire had died down and the only combatants left were some forty or so Commandos who had gone up the Ikopa river in small boats to seize a bridge. They were using their grenades to keep a tribe of hungry crocodiles at bay. More fortunate were the detachment landed at Monrondava to make a diversion. As expected they were unopposed, the only occupants of its small harbour fort being the families of the French officers who had gone north with their men. Hoping to excite Vichy air reconnaissance, a Union flag replaced the fort's Tricolour which was rescued by the commandant's wife who, eyes blazing, encased her body with it, daring the Commandos to do their worst.

Operations Stream, Line and Jane all went about as according to plan as any military operations ever could. Stream ended with the successful capture of Majunga. Line began with the white South Africans and the East African askaris bounding down the main road towards Tananarive. Jane put Festing's 29th Brigade back in their ships and brought them around to the east coast port of Tamatave which on 18 September surrendered after a three-minute bombardment. The race to capture the capital was now on.

From the south-east, sometimes using the railway, came the 29th Brigade with West's South Lancs in the lead. From the north-west under Colonel John Macnab, who had made a name for himself in Italian Somaliland and Abyssinia, came the 1st (Nyasaland) King's African Rifles supported by six armoured cars. Both columns were delayed by blown or damaged bridges and a steeplechase of roadblocks, mostly felled trees, boulders and loose stone walls that were sometimes defended but more often not. On 23 September, five days after the 29th Brigade had landed at Tamatave, the South Lancs were still a day's march away. Macnab and his African riflemen won the race.

On its 4,000-foot-high plateau Tananarive, with its convenient ridge lines and magnificent view of the surrounding plain, was a natural fortress and the British had been approaching it with some foreboding. But Annet and Guillemet had slipped away with a couple of thousand men heading for the island's vast southern hinterland where other loyal regiments were waiting for them. Madagascar's stunning capital was hardly defended at all and therefore spared the shells and bombs that would have been used to break into it had British troops met another Joffre line. All Macnab's men had encountered was a small rearguard above the city's military airfield where a Sergeant Walasi won a Military Medal when his platoon captured two gun crews before they had begun the harassing fire they had planned.

Shortly after this Macnab met the Chef du District who informed him that the French Army had left. But there seems to have been more than one authority at work, for a more flamboyant emissary was on his way to meet the British advance. Peter Simpson-Jones, a brave if sometimes accident-prone Royal Navy lieutenant in Special Operations Executive, had delivered a transmitter to an agent in Réunion and been captured after his dinghy capsized in shark-filled waters while trying to return to an SOE launch. A companion drowned.* Kitted out by his captors in a new white summer uniform and a chauffeur-driven Renault with a flag to match his clothes, he had been released with instructions to find General Platt and bring him back to the Tananarive Mairie where the mayor was waiting to surrender his city. Being the enterprising fellow he was this is exactly what Simpson-Jones did, finding Platt at the head of a long convoy of military vehicles and not amused to find his progress blocked by a young man in a Renault, dressed for sundowners in Shanghai and purporting to be an officer in the Royal Navy.

The next day, the 24th, Platt took the salute at a victory parade. But the vanquished were not being buried or herded into prisoner-of-war camps. They had disappeared. Governor General Annet was now at Fianarantsoa which was about 150 miles south of the capital and the last big town in Madagascar that was still in Vichy hands. From there, knowing full well it would be picked up by British wireless intercepts, he sent a telegram to the Colonial Ministry in Vichy: 'Although Tananarive has been occupied, our available troops are preparing to resist every enemy advance in the other sector of the island with the same spirit which inspired our soldiers at Diego Suarez, at Majunga, at Tananarive and other places, where each time the defence became a page of heroism written by "La France".'

While the defence of Diego Suarez's Joffre line had undoubtedly been a spirited affair, the rest of his message, as Annet knew full well, was arrant nonsense. But by now the governor general had a very clear picture of what Laval expected of him. A few days earlier he had been firmly rapped over the knuckles for even daring to suggest that he should remain in Tananarive to negotiate its surrender with Platt while his Chef de bureau

* Charged with espionage, his court martial had been presided over by Général de bridgade Guillemet, Annet's Commander-in-chief. Before sentencing him to five years' hard labour Guillemet summed up the case for the defence. 'Lieutenant Simpson-Jones, as I understand it, you arrived in the island because your ship caught fire and you had to abandon it and land as a survivor. When you tried to leave the island you chose a boat which leaked so much that it sank and you had to be rescued by fishermen who brought you ashore and, just at the moment we were arresting you, you managed to fall into a gold fish pond. Don't you think that in the next world war you might do better to join the artillery?'

Claude Ponvienne and a team of civil servants went south with the troops to administer what they continued to hold. In a reply that, judging by its tone, had spent some time on Laval's desk, this was arrogantly rejected for 'reasons of general policy which may escape you but which outweigh your arguments'.

For Laval the Madagascar campaign was a godsend, an opportunity to demonstrate to the Germans France's willingness to fight the British however hopeless the circumstances. Unlike Syria there would be no surrender. Vichy Madagascar would fight to the finish, thereby tying up thousands of British troops that could be better employed elsewhere. Annet must be Vichy's symbol of resistance to an English army of occupation. This indeed was collaboration.

It was Chef de bureau Ponvienne who remained behind to greet Platt who decreed that the French flag would continue to fly over Tananarive and asked local officials to remain at their posts under temporary military government which would 'respect local customs'. But this was not enough for Ponvienne who refused to collaborate in any way and urged others to do the same. Eventually he was interned, thereby ensuring that his credit remained high in Vichy which presumably was all that mattered.

At this point, with the campaign almost won and Guillemet's remnant of no more than nuisance value, the obvious solution should have been to install a Gaullist administration while Platt got on with what was left of the fighting. In London on 6 September, four days before Madagascar's second round started at Port Majunga, this is exactly what Foreign Secretary Anthony Eden had promised Maurice Dejean, de Gaulle's Commissioner for African Affairs. But plans for major developments elsewhere had meant that the offer had to be put on hold just as Eden was hoping that Anglo-Gaullist relations were about to start running a little more smoothly.

That they had recently gone through a bumpy patch was undeniable. In early May, de Gaulle, recovering from a serious bout of malaria after inspecting some of his Equatorial African possessions, had been enraged to discover that Free France had not been invited on the Madagascar expedition. But in June there was reconciliation and even tears of joy, rare for de Gaulle who unlike Churchill was not much given to lachrymose display. The occasion was the Prime Minister's fulsome tribute to the 3,700 Free French troops under Général de brigade Marie-Pierre Koenig for the stand they had made against Rommel at Libya's Bir Hacheim. Shortly afterwards Churchill had spoken of his vision of them both being back in France together 'perhaps next year'.

Then in August the Churchill-de Gaulle roller coaster had taken another dip. This time it was over Lebanon and Syria. British insistence that Général Catroux honour his pre-invasion pledge of independence for their Arabic-speaking peoples was suspected, perhaps rightly, of being an Anglo-Saxon ploy to turn the French Levant into another of its beholden client states. British diplomacy had already forged the Hashemite kingdoms of Iraq and Jordan. Now Glubb Pasha was about to ride roughshod over the ghosts of Fashoda.

The prompt insertion of a Gaullist administration in Madagascar would have undoubtedly gone some way towards smoothing over this latest tiff. But something much bigger than this sort of political knitting was afoot, a plan that was such an ambitious contribution towards the waging of war against Nazi Germany that nothing was going to be allowed to jeopardize it. As much as Churchill and Eden would have liked to start handing over the running of Madagascar to the Free French it was no longer quite the right time to do it. The trouble was, they were not yet in a position to explain a word of it to de Gaulle.

France's best overseas possessions were its closest: Algeria, Morocco and Tunisia with their deserts and mountains, superb Mediterranean and Atlantic coastlines and volatile peoples. The most important was Algeria. Quite apart from being by far the biggest of the three it was different from the others because it was neither a colony or a protectorate. It was an integral part of France which, in happier times, elected deputies to the French parliament. Some 9 million Arabs and Berbers had about 1 million Europeans living among them. Some were the descendants of Alsatians displaced by the result of the 1870 Franco-Prussian War. Others came from the kind of hardy and enterprising peasant stock that used to go to Canada before the English got hold of it. At least half were not originally French at all but of Spanish, Italian and Maltese descent.

This was where, if Churchill's deepest wishes had come true in 1940, Free France would have taken root with Weygand's army and Darlan's ships. There would have been no Afrika Korps because, long before the Germans had time to send reinforcements, the French and British armies would have attacked Mussolini's Libya from either end and met in the middle. There would have been no siege of Malta because the Anglo-French fleets would command the Mediterranean. Another Anglo-French force under somebody like Koenig, certainly no braver but perhaps a bit brighter than Freyberg, might have won the Battle of Crete and inflicted the first land defeat on the unstoppable Wehrmacht.

Now an Anglo-American army was going to try to do at least some of the things an Anglo-French one might have accomplished two years before. The United States was in almost its twelfth month of war against Nazi Germany and the nearest it had come to a land action in Europe was allowing fifty of its Rangers, who had been training with the Commandos, to accompany their mentors on August's disastrous Dieppe raid. President Roosevelt was only too aware of this. In order to take the pressure off the Russians, whose losses seemed increasingly insupportable, he wanted to open a second front. The most obvious place to strike was at the limit of Hitler's westwards expansion across the English Channel. At the very least the Americans wanted to establish a bridgehead in somewhere like Brest or Cherbourg and then break out of it the following spring.

This sort of talk frightened Churchill. He knew that they were not yet strong enough for it. Dieppe had been lesson enough. The army was of the same opinion and mass demonstrations in Trafalgar Square demanding help for Uncle Joe Stalin with chants of 'Second Front Now' were worrying. 'Many of them seemed to think that the Russians had come into the war solely for our benefit,' Brooke, the Chief of the Imperial General Staff, had noted in his diary. 'A premature Western Front could only result in the most appalling shambles.' And since any such attack would have to be launched from Britain with mainly British forces, on this the British had the last word.

The Prime Minister was, of course, all for striking the Axis elsewhere. But his suggestion that they mount a joint expedition to seize French North Africa and attack Rommel in the rear was not at first received with much enthusiasm. The US Army agreed with the crowds in Trafalgar Square. They wanted Berlin or Bust. Less than 600 miles from the French coast to the German capital, and flattish most of the way, did not seem all that far for an American. Then Roosevelt tired of the bickering. He wanted to get on and do something before the year was out. 'Here is your true Second Front of 1942,' Churchill had said in a message to Washington dated 8 July, and by the end of the month the decision had been made. It was to be called Operation Torch.

As it happened, the Americans had already done a lot of the spadework for Operation Torch. Roosevelt's decision to maintain diplomatic relations with Vichy France, a grace-and-favour Nazi client state that Hitler could close down at the click of a switch, had been castigated by the liberal press who wanted America to back de Gaulle. But now it looked like it was going to pay dividends. The diplomat Robert Murphy, for the last eighteen months US Minister to French North Africa living mainly in Algiers and reporting directly to Roosevelt via the US Embassy in Vichy, had been building up an extensive network of Allied sympathizers. Some were serving officers, others influential civilians, and between them they had the makings of the kind of fifth column that might well make Operation Torch a bloodless affair.

But Murphy's conspirators, while united by a common desire to defeat Germany and liberate France, often had little else in common. Many were Pétainists who had convinced themselves they were only doing what their maréchal secretly desired. Others were royalists who dreamed of restoring their heir apparent, the Count of Paris, to the throne. A growing number were Communists who felt that the valour of the Red Army was living proof of the innate goodness of Stalin. By necessity they were almost all pro-American but few were pro-Gaullist. De Gaulle was rightly seen as Churchill's creation. Few knew or cared about the difficulties Churchill was having putting his genie back in the bottle. And generally the British were much more disliked in North Africa than they were in metropolitan France. At Mers-el-Kébir the regiment of graves and the rusting wrecks in the harbour were hard to miss. And since then there had been Syria and Madagascar. Delicate discussions were taking place between Murphy and his contacts, assurances demanded that French North Africa remained French North Africa. This was why it was not a good time for the Americans' British allies to be seen to be installing a Gaullist administration in Tananarive.

So while Annet and Guillemet dragged the campaign on into the malarial mush of the island's rainy season the Madagascan capital remained in Platt's military limbo. South of the capital the main problem was road-blocks. Some had become almost major feats of engineering. One stretched for 2 miles. The South African armoured car crews, which were normally in the lead, had to make gaps through twenty-nine stone walls of which the widest measured 18 feet across. Another had consumed 800 felled trees in the space of half a mile. Alongside the roads the undergrowth was so thick it was usually impossible to go round these obstacles.

Annet was almost killed when a Fleet Air Arm Fulmar strafed his car near Fianarantsoa. By then his own air force had been reduced to three biplanes and a single Morane fighter. The Morane astonished a column of King's African Rifles, who had never known aircraft that were not their own, when it appeared to want to share the same muddy track with them then started machine-gunning. One man was wounded. Over the next week South African-crewed Beauforts and Marylands sniffed out the Vichy aircraft on their bush landing strips and destroyed them parked and unmanned on the ground. But the Morane was still at large.

Some of the Africans followed the railway line from Tananarive south-east into the temperate climes and misty mornings of the line's terminus at Antsirabe, a spa town with thermal springs 4,000 feet up the island's second highest peak. In the 1920s its optimistic developers advertised it as the 'Vichy of Madagascar'. As they approached, the King's African Rifles had one of their white officers killed and five men wounded by a mortar bomb but the town itself was not heavily defended. One account refers to 'a little light sniping', though sniping light or heavy can ruin any man's day. Defended ridge lines invited artillery and air attack but were almost invariably deserted by the time the infantry got up to them. Sometimes they discovered machine guns and mortars too heavy to carry away in a hurry.

Then Guillemet lost his last two 75mm field guns when the East Africans cut off and captured 700 of his men, among them almost 200 Europeans who probably included some sailors and marines from Diego Suarez. The British-officered troops suffered no casualties. After that, delaying actions rarely delayed very long. Malagasy morale started to crumble and they began to desert in droves. 'The French shoot us if we run away in battle so better to desert before,' one told K.C. Gandar Dower, *The Times*'s correspondent. When they had run out of bombs aircrews sometimes hurried the battle-weary along by dropping empty beer bottles which emitted a ghastly shriek followed by a puzzling silence. It was obviously close to the end. Yet on 23 October Annet remained at large and some of his men still had enough fight in them to keep their nerve and put up enough fire to kill the observer when one of the Fleet Air Arm's Albacores put in a low-level attack. Then the last Morane was destroyed on the ground. In Vichy, Laval's Foreign Ministry at the old Hôtel de L'Angleterre released daily bulletins to the German Armistice Commission drawing their attention to the 'heroic resistance of the French troops' in Madagascar.

But the only people who noticed were the British and then only with irritation, all the grudging admiration the Joffre line had induced long since evaporated by this Quixotic defiance so irrelevant to the rest of the world conflict. In Russia two enormous armies were beginning to square up to each other at Stalingrad. In Egypt's Western Desert Montgomery started his long awaited offensive against Rommel at El Alamein and some half a million men with thousands of tanks and artillery were locked in a 1914–18–style battle the like of which the desert war had not seen before. And aboard His Majesty's Submarine *Seraph*, a mile out from the heavy surf off the Algerian coast, a trouserless American general, whose recent adventures ashore Churchill had backed with 'the entire resources of the British Empire', was celebrating his success with a mug of navy rum.

Mark Clark was the London-based deputy of Dwight Eisenhower, the lieutenant general who had been made the supreme commander of the 112,000 American and British troops involved in Operation Torch. A tall man, Clark was the product of Pennsylvania and Romania. He had inherited some of the dark good looks and slightly aquiline nose of his Bucharest Jewish mother and the physique of his Episcopalian father Colonel Charles Clark, a veteran of the Spanish-American War. At 6 foot 2 inches the general was not the best size for small British submarines – he kept banging his head – and even less for canoes. But what he had just done was going to be a valuable contribution to Operation Torch and possibly of even more benefit to Mark Wayne Clark who was clever, brave and at times the most egotistical American commander since George Armstrong Custer. Only luckier.

In four two-man foldboat canvas kayaks, all but one coxed by a British Commando officer, Clark and four staff officers had got ashore easily enough the night before. A strong offshore wind had made coming back a different matter. But shortly before dawn they had eventually succeeded in riding the incoming surf and returning to the *Seraph* after a long and fruitful meeting with Murphy's star recruit. At a clifftop seaside house near the town of Cherchell 65 miles west of Algiers, Murphy and Clark had spent almost a day in talks with a French Army delegation headed by Général Charles Mast.

Mast was the mouthpiece of Général Henri-Honoré Giraud. Up until 16 April 1942 Giraud, who had been captured in the third week of the Blitzkrieg when his headquarters was overrun, had been the most senior French officer in German captivity. Then in the early hours of the 17th he had lowered himself down a 150-foot rope to escape from the old Saxon fortress of Königstein on the Elbe. Ten days later, having passed through Switzerland, Giraud was lunching with Pétain in Vichy. Laval was furious and wanted the distinguished escapee to give himself up to the Germans but the maréchal would not hear of it. He had sanctuary.

Giraud, who was 63 and slightly lamed by an old wound, was perhaps what Conan Doyle had in mind when he invented Brigadier Gerard, the Napoleonic Hussar: immensely tall, magnificently moustached and, if not always all that bright, a man of unquestionable gallantry and integrity. His departure from Königstein was his second escape from German capture, his first being in 1914 when, wounded, he got out of a military hospital to neutral Holland. Perhaps not all that surprisingly, with these considerable attributes went the same views on who was mostly to blame for the defeat in 1940 – the British – and the general decline in France that preceded it – Léon Blum and the Popular Front – as every other ardent Pétainist. De Gaulle was, at the very least, misguided and Giraud wanted nothing to do with him or his English paymasters. He differed in only one important respect from most of the senior French officers who welcomed him in Vichy: he was utterly convinced that Germany was going to lose the war and France must make a pact with the Americans and renew hostilities.

During the Allies' Black Spring of 1942 this was, to put it mildly, an unusual point of view that would have found some secret doubters in London, Washington and Moscow let alone Vichy's Hôtel du Parc. Pétain thought the younger man sadly out of touch and advised him to go under cover. Vichy intelligence had been tipped off that Heinrich Himmler, the head of the SS, was trying to persuade Hitler to let him arrange Giraud's assassination. Giraud could not have gone very far under cover for, not long after Roosevelt decided on Operation Torch, Murphy had no difficulty in getting in touch through one of his agents, a peanut oil king who practically commuted between Algiers and the south of France.

It soon became clear that, though the général did indeed want to get his country back into the fight, some hard bargaining lay ahead. Two of Giraud's demands were totally unacceptable: simultaneous American landings in France as well as North Africa and that all troops involved in the latter, American as well as French, should be under French command. Murphy accepted that this was not because Giraud, whom he came to like and respect, was a vainglorious idiot but because he was a French Arabist who knew the importance of demonstrating American acceptance of French sovereignty to the Arab and Berber population. An insistence that it should be an exclusively American operation, without any British involvement, could be finessed though it could never be more than cosmetic. Most of the ships were British. Excluding de Gaulle could be done, at least in the short term. It was just a matter of making sure the British understood how important it was not to tell him anything before the deed was done.

Once initial contact with the Americans had been made, Giraud started to communicate through what he told Mast in notes hand-carried to Algiers by trusted army couriers. In the 1930s he and Mast had fought the Rif rebels in Morocco. Then in 1940 they had found themselves in Königstein together. Mast was released after the failed Anglo-Gaullist attack on Dakar when Vichy persuaded Berlin to allow them to increase their North African garrison.

Now here was the lanky Clark and the stocky Mast sizing each other up over coffee and cigarettes after a breakfast at which the Americans had been surprised to discover sardines. Above them the three Commando officers, warm proof of British collusion, were decently out of sight in a bedroom where they had seized the opportunity to catch up on some sleep. This was to be a Franco-American occasion.

One of the first things Mast asked was whether the latest Allied intelligence indicated an imminent Axis takeover of French North Africa. Clark replied that it did not. This was the right answer because neither did Vichy's intelligence, though from time to time Murphy, in the hope of eliciting an invitation for American intervention, had hinted that, at the very least, it was under active consideration. Having established this entirely false note of candour Clark started, in his own words, 'lying like hell'.

In September 1939, when Germany invaded Poland and the war started, the US Army was nineteenth in size in the world: a little bigger than Bulgaria's and slightly smaller than Portugal's. Long before Pearl Harbor Roosevelt had started to rebuild it. Among the British tanks at El Alamein were 300 brand-new Shermans removed in toto from a US armoured division and shipped out. But the US Army was still nothing like as strong as it was going to be. Mast's main concern was to establish the strength of the forces the Americans proposed to land. German propaganda had built up Dieppe as a failed attempt to establish a bridgehead rather than a raid. Going to the assistance of anything as feeble as that would see them all hanged. Would there be enough of them to do the job?

Clark did not hesitate. 'I tried to keep a poker face while saying that half a million Allied troops could come in and I said we could put 2,000 planes in the air as well as plenty of United States Navy. Mast was pretty impressed.'

Whether Mast was so easily impressed as Clark imagined is hard to say. Perhaps he merely divided by half and was impressed enough. In which case the 112,000 coming ashore was still slightly less than half of what he was expecting.

Clark made it clear that 'logistical problems' made it impossible to make a simultaneous landing in the south of France, which did not quite fit with another claim he made that the shipping was available to land half a million men. Mast let this pass. But he did point out that the obvious Wehrmacht response to an Allied presence in North Africa and a threat from across the Mediterranean would be to put an end to Pétain's unoccupied France and place it firmly behind the concrete and steel of Festung Europa.

Mast relayed a request from Giraud that arrangements should be made for an American submarine to pick him up as soon as possible and, though Clark knew it would have to be a British boat, this was agreed. 'What I could not tell Mast, and had to be careful not to reveal by any slip of the tongue, was that Torch had actually gotten anywhere beyond the planning stage. And this with the leading elements of our armada actually at sea.'

Mast had to return to Algiers well before lunch which Clark describes as 'chicken with a hot Arab sauce served with red wine and some oranges'. It was prepared by Lieutenant Jacques Teissier whose father Henri owned the house along with considerable other lands and properties. Teissier and most of the other staff officers stayed on as briefings continued well into the afternoon, their visitors filling page after page of their notebooks as almost every aspect of the landings were discussed. Clark was delighted. 'They gave us locations of strengths of troops and naval units, told us where gasoline and ammunition were stored, supplied details about airports where resistance would be heaviest and information about where our airborne troops could land safely.'

In return the Americans had promised the swift delivery by submarine of 2,000 British Sten guns and ammunition that had been requested so that armouries and headquarters and other key positions could be secured by small groups of picked men.

Then in the late afternoon the meeting came to an abrupt end. Teissier received a telephone call from somebody he knew in the local gendarmerie warning him that they were about to receive a visit. Later it would turn out that the household's Arab servants, told to absent themselves for a couple of days, suspected some large-scale smuggling enterprise was afoot and had informed the police in expectation of the reward money on general offer. All the French officers except Teissier fled, some of them changing into civilian clothes as they went. 'One would have thought that 50 dead skunks had been thrown on the table,' recalled Clark. 'I can't say I blamed any one of them for their lives would certainly have been in jeopardy if caught.'

One of the Commando officers was sent into some nearby woods with the experimental walkie-talkie radio they had been issued, a tremendous leap in wireless technology, to contact the submarine and tell them they were in trouble. The rest of them disappeared into the pitch-dark of a wine cellar, its trapdoor entrance closed above them and covered with a rug. There was no time to remove the boats which were in a locked storeroom.

They were all armed to the teeth with Colt .45 automatics, Thompsons and the neat new M1 carbine Winchester had just provided for the US Army which everybody wanted for hunting after the war though it would prove no better at killing deer than it was people. General Clark, 46, and in action for the first and last time in 1918 when a shell had removed him from that war just a few hours after he caught up with it, took command of his six men.

> I knelt at the foot of the stairs with a carbine in my hands.* It was my intention, if they came down, to try and fight our way clear without shooting; but all of us were prepared to shoot if it were necessary. I whispered that no-one was to fire unless I did. It might be hours before we were able to get through the surf to our submarine ... Poor Courtney [Captain Godfrey 'Jumbo' Courtney, the British Commandos' canoeing expert who had started badly by capsizing his own boat as they left the *Seraph*] was seized with a coughing fit. He coughed and spluttered in the darkness and whispered, 'General, I'm afraid I'll choke.' I said, 'I'm afraid you won't.'

Eventually Clark attempted to soothe Courtney's cough by passing on his well-worked wad of chewing gum. Courtney complained that British chewing gum was much sweeter. Above them they could hear the rattle of poker dice, the clinking of glasses and the slurred voices of Teissier and Robert Murphy who began to sing some mournful Irish dirge full of Celtic loathing for the Anglo-Saxon. Clark thought this was overdoing it a bit, though Murphy, for years a man of irreproachable public persona, obviously felt it was a talented contribution. 'I posed as a somewhat inebriated member of a raucous social gathering,' he wrote in his memoirs. 'Fortunately the police were not looking for military conspirators but for smugglers.'

Having failed to get much sense out of these well-connected people the gendarmes left, muttering that they would be back when they had consulted senior officers. As soon as it was dark enough Clark and his party returned to the beach. To cut down on the weight the canoes were carrying, most

* According to one of the Commandos Clark caused some concern by fiddling with the firing mechanism and asking, 'How the hell do you work this thing?'

of the weapons were handed over to Lieutenant Tiessier who knew people who might soon have more need of them.

Clark also divested himself of a heavy money belt packed with gold Canadian dollars that had been procured in London from the Bank of England. He had them in case they failed to make a rendezvous with the submarine and it became necessary to buy a boat and crew. Fearing that the weight of the coins might drown him in the undertow he had parcelled the belt in his trousers and stowed them well into the forward part of the boat where he could feel them with his feet. When, during his first attempt to get through the waves, the kayak capsized Clark managed to retain his paddle but not his parcel which is why the general arrived on the *Seraph* without his trousers.

In Madagascar Annet finally surrendered on 5 November, forty-two days after the capture of Tananarive, having sent his aide-de-camp Capitaine Louis Fauché and a Norwegian clergyman to ask for terms. He was informed they were exactly the same as they had been six months before. The ceasefire came into force at one minute past midnight on 6 November which was exactly six months, to the day if not the hour, after the campaign started with the British air strikes on Diego Suarez. Fauché is widely reported to have done this because a minimum of six months' hostilities were required to qualify a French soldier for a campaign medal and even certain cash rewards. If this was true, like many Vichy projects, it was doomed to disappointment.

Total British casualties for operations Stream, Line and Jane starting with the attack on Port Majunga on 10 September are put at 142 killed or wounded. On the French side reliable figures are unavailable but allowing for the British superiority in artillery and aircraft it is reasonable to suppose it must have been at least twice that. Annet was transported to South Africa and comfortably interned in Durban where he began work on his memoir, *Aux heures troublés de l'Afrique française*. Later he would be handed over to the Free French.

In London de Gaulle and Churchill were dancing one of their by now well-choreographed reconciliation minuets. The first steps were taken by the Prime Minister.

Major Sir Desmond Morton, a pale and mysterious former artillery officer said to have survived a shot through the heart, was one of Churchill's intimates on his personal staff at Number 10. His main duties were to liaise between the PM and the secret services, and at one point he was official deliverer of the ULTRA decrypts from Bletchley. But because he spoke good French, and in 1918 had been aide-de-camp to Field Marshal Haig, he had from the outset also had a liaison role with the Gaullists.

On Friday, 30 October, Morton called on de Gaulle at his headquarters in Carlton Gardens. Ostensibly, the reason for his visit was to congratulate him on the recent exploits of the Dundee-based Free French submarine *Junon:* a fjord penetrated and Commandos put ashore for a raid that closed down a Norwegian aluminium plant; an Oslo-bound freighter torpedoed. All such a contrast to the performance of the mammoth *Surcouf*, seized at the same time as the *Junon* though in distinctly bloodier circumstances. Never a happy or effective boat and without a single sinking to her credit, in February *Surcouf* had been lost with all hands in the Caribbean after a night collision with an American freighter.

De Gaulle responded to Morton's praise for his submarine with kind words about General Montgomery's efforts at El Alamein, though it was still far from certain that the British were winning. Morton said that it was a terrible thing that relations had been allowed to reach such a low ebb and it was about time there was 'a more favourable evolution'. Madagascar was coming to an end and perhaps the général might consider who he would like to appoint as its new governor. By 5 November de Gaulle had told Churchill that he wanted Général Le Gentilhomme, who had taken over Damascus after the Vichy French moved out, to do the same thing in Madagascar.

D-Day for Operation Torch, the Anglo-Saxons' next and biggest incursion into French territory without a Gaullist imprimatur, was only three days away on 8 November. Churchill planned to tell him just before it happened. 'As some means of softening this slight to him and his Movement, I arranged to confide the trusteeship of Madagascar to his hands.'

But when Churchill informed Roosevelt of his intentions the President was concerned. Any suggestion that de Gaulle had been consulted was seen as a threat to 'our promising efforts' to bring the Vichy French forces in North Africa over to the Allied side. 'I consider it inadvisable for you to give de Gaulle any information subsequent to a successful landing. You would then inform him that the American commander of an American expedition with my approval insisted on complete secrecy.' For good measure Roosevelt pointed out that de Gaulle's announcement that he was about to send his own governor general to Madagascar 'will not be of any assistance to Torch and it should be sufficient at the present time to maintain his prestige with his followers'.

Churchill did what he was told and made arrangements to have lunch with de Gaulle on the first day of Operation Torch. Now he had the time bomb ticking away at Carlton Gardens to worry about as well as the success of the landings. Axis Gibraltar-watchers in Spain had already noted part of the invasion fleet gathering around the British bastion. Luftwaffe and Regia Aeronautica reconnaissance flights confirmed them. The Rock's airport, with its newly extended runway created by the spoil Canadian mining engineers had tunnelled out while improving its defences, also seemed to be a bit busier than usual. But when the reports and the aerial photographs were analysed in Berlin, Rome and Vichy they got it wrong.

By 7 November Hitler in particular became convinced that, after Montgomery's indisputable victory at El Alamein, the British were planning to cut off Rommel's retreat with a landing at Tripoli or Benghazi. U-boats moved hundreds of miles in the wrong direction – eastwards – to be ready to intercept them.

Shortly after midnight on 8 May General Pug Ismay, Churchill's Chief of Staff, telephoned General Pierre Billotte, his opposite number at Carlton Gardens, and told him that in about three hours' time the Americans would be making landings along the French North African coast. De Gaulle, who had just returned from a reception at the Soviet Embassy, was asleep and Billotte needed his own. He told him at six next morning when de Gaulle's reaction was entirely predictable. 'I hope these Vichy people are going to throw them into sea,' he said, and much more.

But by the time he was taking lunch with the Prime Minister he had calmed down. Rather than rage over Free France's exclusion, another insult to the Cross of Lorraine with the ink on the Madagascar ceasefire hardly dry, he had decided to celebrate and exploit the landings. 'You'll see. One day we'll go down the Champs Elysées together,' a much relieved Churchill told him at the end of their meal. On leaving it was noted that his guest was smiling. This was not what was expected.

From lunch de Gaulle went directly to Portland Place and made a live broadcast on the BBC French language service. He started by praising the British for their success against Rommel, and the Russians for their stubborn defence of Stalingrad. Then he urged his countrymen in North Africa to rise up and embrace the opportunity the Allied landings offered. 'Let us return through you to the line of battle and there it will be: the war won – thanks to France.'

None of his listeners had been given the slightest reason to believe that the news of this extraordinary opportunity was as much a surprise to him as it was to them. On the contrary, it might well have been his own idea.

PART FOUR

Operation Torch and the end of Fighting Vichy

Chapter Twenty-Seven

Poliomyelitis is an acutely infectious viral disease which is no respecter of diet, hygiene or generations of healthy genes. Most people make a complete recovery and may have thought they had had nothing more than a bad dose of flu. But about 20 per cent of its victims suffer varying degrees of incurable paralysis. In 1942, some twenty years before the Salk vaccine started to eradicate the worst effects of polio in the western world, it was almost as capricious as the bombs that so casually consumed streets full of non-combatant innocents. With utter impartiality and devastating suddenness, it entered the homes of rich and poor alike.

It is sometimes called infantile paralysis, which is a misnomer. While it is true that it has a predisposition for children and young adults, people considered to be in the prime of life were by no means immune. Roosevelt – the world's most famous victim – contracted it in August 1921 when he was 39 and on vacation at New Brunswick. Alain Darlan, a reserve lieutenant in the French Navy and only son of the amiral and commander of all Vichy's military forces, was 29 when he caught it on a business trip to Algiers in October 1942. In doing so he set in train a series of ineluctable events that helped change the course of history.

Darlan *fils*, often accompanied by his wife Annie, had been making regular visits to Algiers where he represented a consortium buying foodstuffs for Vichy France and perhaps for Germany and Italy. No doubt his father's contacts were useful when it came to arranging shipping. The young couple usually stayed at Villa Sidi-Allowi. This was the bougainvillaea-covered shore quarters of Amiral Raymond Fenard, senior naval officer in Algiers and Darlan's intermediary to the American diplomat Robert Murphy just as Général Mast had become Giraud's.

Then Alain also became a go-between. Murphy would be invited to dinner and afterwards, when the women had retired to admire Madame Fenard's petit point, the men would sit around the fireplace, smoking, sipping their drinks and talking, one way or the other, about the war. Murphy thought young Darlan seemed 'ardently pro-Allies' and, together with Fenard, the lieutenant had been doing his best to assure him that his father had become the same. Sometimes, he explained, it had been necessary to make 'minor concessions' to the Germans but only in order not to have to make bigger ones.

These overtures had been going on for the last six months, ever since Laval had returned to power. In the course of them, Fenard had informed Murphy that Darlan wished the United States to regard French North Africa as willing, when the time was right, to renew hostilities but not before America had enough strength 'to outmatch the Germans there'.

Murphy was cautious. He could understand that North Africa was Vichy France's 'last high trump'; that they were terrified of losing it through some feeble Anglo-Gaullist Dakar-style expedition that would give the Germans the chance to establish a permanent military presence. But Darlan was so vehemently anti-British it was hard for the Americans to trust him. However piqued he was at being usurped by Laval would he ever believe the moment was right for North Africa to secede from Vichy? Was he just playing for time, hoping the Allies would make a compromise peace with Hitler that would restore France's sovereignty and leave Germany to deal with Russia?

This was, after all, still Pétain's official deputy speaking, the man who had not hesitated to provide the Luftwaffe with transit rights in Syria and was rightly suspected of being prepared to see Dakar become a South Atlantic U-boat base. After Laval was reinstated Ambassador Leahy had been recalled to Washington to become Roosevelt's Chief of Staff, leaving a chargé d'affaires at Vichy's US Embassy. But before that there had been plenty of time for Darlan to confide in Leahy the necessity for 'minor concessions'. Over dinner at Villa Sidi-Allowi Murphy had asked his son why he had not done this.

> Alain explained that his father did not believe the Americans could keep secrets. If Darlan talked to the Germans he could be sure that nothing would leak out in Berlin. The reverse was true in Washington ... While I let his remark pass without comment, I had to admit to myself that there was some truth in it. I had been embarrassed when some of my own confidential reports got into newspapers and broadcasts.

Then on Friday 9 October, Alain Darlan was back in Algiers with a message for Murphy from his father proposing a larger-scale Franco-American operation into southern, unoccupied France but cautioning against the risk of premature and therefore ineffectual strikes elsewhere. But he could not deliver it immediately because Murphy, who had been away in Washington and London being briefed on Operation Torch, was not expected back for another forty-eight hours. Nor was Darlan getting much else done. He was beginning to suffer from some of the headache, sore throat, nausea and high fever that mark the onset of poliomyelitis and had taken to his bed. By Sunday afternoon the naval doctor attending him at Sidi-Allowi was almost certain what was wrong and Alain had been delivered by ambulance to the Maillot Hospital for a second opinion. On arrival his condition almost immediately worsened and he began to develop respiratory problems.

Even if Alain had been in any condition to deliver his father's message it would not have made the slightest difference: an invasion of mainland France had been ruled out and Operation Torch was far too advanced for any second thoughts now. Ever since Darlan first made contact with him in May Murphy had sent Washington detailed reports of these vague feelers; but it would be four months before any interest was shown in them. Then in September the diplomat attended an Anglo-American Torch planning conference being held under tight security at Telegraph Cottage, Eisenhower's mock Tudor country quarters in the Kingston-upon-Thames stockbroker belt. Only then, and for the first time, had there been some discussion on what was seen as the 'Darlan problem': should they accept help from a man the Anglo-American press had been encouraged to vilify as a Nazi stooge?

The answer was that Torch was a tough one and its planners would accept help from the devil himself. And both Churchill and Roosevelt had covetous eyes on the idle French warships in Toulon. 'If I could meet Darlan, much as I hate him, I'd cheerfully crawl on my hands and knees for a mile if it would bring that fleet of his into Allied forces,' the Prime Minister had told Eisenhower shortly before he left London for Gibraltar where the British had set up Operation Torch's advance headquarters.

Not that the chances of the amiral making a 180-degree turn were considered all that likely. Admiral Leahy, who had got to know him probably better than anybody else in the Allied High Command during his time as US ambassador in Vichy, had established, despite his limited French, an affable enough sailor-to-sailor relationship with him; but he could not bring himself to trust Darlan and described him as 'ambitious and dangerous ... a complete opportunist'.

Instead, the Operation Torch planners continued to put their trust in Giraud, escapee extraordinaire and clearly as an officer and a gentleman, the man most likely to rally France's North African garrison to their cause. Arrangements to pick him up by submarine and bring him to Gibraltar were already well advanced. In the Rock's labyrinth of cold tunnels where Eisenhower and his team lurked it had been decided that Giraud's code-name would be Kingpin. He was to be picked up off the Côte d'Azur by HMS *Seraph*, the same boat that, under Lieutenant Norman Jewell, had put Mark Clark and his party ashore at Cherchell for their meeting with Mast and brought them home again. Only this time *Seraph* would be nominally commanded by the US Navy's Captain Jerauld Wright, one of the Cherchell party who had shared Clark's canoe on the return trip. Wright was considered an essential American seasoning to make the English ingredients in Giraud's latest escape more palatable.

On 20 October Darlan had left Vichy on a ten-day inspection of most of its African possessions, starting in Dakar. By now he had become much more concerned about the likelihood of an Allied incursion there rather than in North Africa, probably because he thought it would be easier and of more immediate benefit. The German submarine campaign was hurting more than ever. In the South Atlantic Dakar would be an asset for either side. Flying on to Morocco, in Rabat he met General Oskar Vogl, the head of the German Armistice Commission and the man who had originally asked him if the Luftwaffe could transit through the Syrian airfields. He assured Vogl that France would defend its West African territories and to prove how seriously he was taking this put Dakar on a war footing by ordering the repatriation of all the French women and children in the garrison's married quarters.

By the 28th he had reached Algiers and for the first time was able to visit Alain in hospital. His wife was already at their son's bedside. Berthe Darlan had arrived on the 17th accompanied by the family physician who wanted their only child transferred to the Institut Pasteur in Paris, which had achieved remarkable things with some polio cases. On the same day Darlan took the opportunity to catch up with the latest clues Murphy had seen fit to drop regarding America's local intentions.

All he learned seemed to confirm Darlan's hunch that the Americans were not planning to intervene in North Africa in 1942. 'You have nothing to fear on our part,' Murphy had assured Major André Dorange after promising massive American assistance should the Axis ever invade. 'We will not come unless you summon us.' Dorange was the Chief of Staff of Général Alphonse Pierre Juin. Like Mast, whom he outranked, Juin had been released from captivity the previous year to become overall commander of the French forces in North Africa.

Before first light on Friday 30 October, Darlan had started his journey back to Vichy in the Aeronavale version of the twin-engined Glenn Martin bomber he used as his private transport. His inspection tour of North Africa was over and he did not expect to see Algiers again before New Year 1943. He had many other responsibilities, his mothballed fleet in Toulon for instance, and in any case it was probably unwise to turn his back on Laval for too long. At this point the latest news from El Alamein indicated a bloody stalemate. It seemed that Rommel had been away when the battle started and now he had returned. Darlan was mostly preoccupied with making the arrangements necessary to move Alain to Paris.

Then, on 4 November, scarcely four days after his return, Darlan's Glenn Martin was heading back to Algiers. He had just received an urgent message that his son's condition had deteriorated and it was feared he had only a few more hours to live. For the next seventy-two hours Alain clung to life in his private room at the Maillot Hospital while his distraught parents kept a bedside vigil. His coffin had already been ordered. But some time on Friday 6 November, their most fervent prayers were answered. Their son's fever subsided and soon, though he was still weak and had no feeling in his legs, he was breathing normally for the first time in almost a week.

Twenty-four hours later, though the paralysis in the legs remained, Alain's remission was in full spate and Darlan left Berthe and daughter-in-law Annie at the hospital to join Fenard and General Juin at dinner at Villa Sidi-Allowi. His pilot was put on stand-by to fly him back to Vichy next day. Juin brought him up to date with the latest news from El Alamein, which was that the British had broken through and Rommel was in full retreat. It was now the eve of the landings. As Darlan and the others dined, an Anglo-American armada of some 700 ships was converging on nine designated beachheads in French North Africa. The war had not yet seen anything quite like it.

Approaching three places on the Moroccan coast, having come directly across the Atlantic from Norfolk, Virginia, was a fleet of 102 vessels under Admiral Henry Kent Hewitt. For the past two months most of it had been assembling at Hampton Roads, where the port's brass band had never tired of playing the 1917 favourite 'Over There'. Few involved knew whereabouts over there they were bound, only that the Yanks were coming with as much force as they could muster. About seventy of Hewitt's fleet were warships including one aircraft carrier, four smaller escort carriers – usually converted oil tankers – and the new American battleship *Massachusetts*. The rest were transports carrying 35,000 men from parts of three US divisions: 2nd Armoured, 3rd and 9th Infantry. Their commander was a major general whose habitual foul-mouthed truculence masked a capacity to charm and a certain erudition. Visitors to George S. Patton Junior's cabin were astonished to find, as perhaps they were meant to be, that along with the ivory-handled revolvers and the kind of thrillers most officers read, was an English translation of the Koran.

Patton's troops were part of Western Task Force and their job was to capture Casablanca. Centre and Eastern Task Forces, which contained the ships the Axis had noticed forming up around Gibraltar, were heading for beaches around Oran and Algiers respectively. Almost all the ships in these fleets were British, as were about a third of the troops.

The commander of Centre Task Force was Commodore Thomas Troubridge who was flying his flag on HMS *Largs*, a combined operations headquarters ship crammed with wireless communications. Until November 1940 the *Largs* had been France's *Charles Plumie*. She had been launched at St Nazaire in 1938 for the Jamaica banana run, converted on the outbreak of war to an armed cruiser then captured by British destroyers en route from Dakar to Marseilles and brought into Gibraltar: one of the 'acts of piracy' that so fuelled Darlan's Anglophobia. To protect the 28 transports and 19 landing ships carrying the 39,000 American soldiers, Troubridge had 2 escort carriers, 2 cruisers, an anti-aircraft cruiser, 2 submarines (which would surface and show seaward lights as navigational marks), 13 destroyers, 6 corvettes, 8 minesweepers, 8 converted trawlers, 10 motor launches, 2 sloops and 2 cutters.

These cutters, which were Lend-Lease former US Coast Guard boats designed with Prohibition's rum-runners across the Great Lakes in mind, had been renamed HMS *Walney* and HMS *Hartland*. They had an important role to play and their mission had been given its own code-name: Operation Reservist. Commanded by Canadian-born Captain Frederic Thornton Peters, a daring and highly decorated 1914–18 destroyer commander, their job was to wait until troop landings either side of Oran had encircled the city and then crash through the harbour boom and land almost 400 American infantry who would secure the port for the disembarkation of tanks and artillery. Some senior American naval officers on Eisenhower's staff had questioned the wisdom of entering a port that was both well defended by coastal batteries and whatever French warships happened to be in it. But the British, whose plan it was, had assured them that it had worked very well when the destroyer HMS *Anthony* did something similar with a Royal Marine landing party at an equally well-defended Vichy port in Madagascar. And the Americans, as they knew they must, had bowed to their experience.

The Eastern Naval Task Force, the one bound for Algiers, was commanded by Rear Admiral Sir Harold Burrough. It also had two of its warships laden with American troops and earmarked for charging into the harbour before it could be blocked with scuttled ships or have all its port machinery wrecked. In this case it was called Operation Terminal and the ships involved were not cutters but the old destroyers HMS *Malcolm* and HMS *Broke*. Like Commodore Troubridge, the admiral's flagship was another headquarters ship, a floating electronic communications centre. His was called *Bulolo*, Glasgow-built in 1938 for Australia's Brisbane-based Burns Philip's shipping company and like the *Largs* thickly forested with radio antennae. Also aboard was the British Lieutenant General Kenneth Anderson, a taciturn Scot, who would be leading an Allied sortie into Tunisia. This was anticipated to be a race against an Axis attempt to do the same from Sicily which was only 150 miles away.

Algiers was Operation Torch's most important objective. Not only was Algeria's capital the biggest city in North Africa but the landings here were nearest – about 500 miles – to the Tunisian-Libyan border and the rear echelons of the retreating Afrika Korps. Once the Anglo-Americans were there Rommel would have Allied forces to both the east and west of him and, with the Royal Navy dominating the Mediterranean coast, be practically surrounded.

Packed onto seventeen landing ships and sixteen transports, Burrough had 33,000 troops of whom at least half were British. But the initial amphibious landings in the Algiers sector would be made by American troops under Major General Charles W. Ryder. It was expected that Ryder, the commander of the US 34th Infantry Division, would be more acceptable to the French than Anderson, though the Scot happened to speak their language well which Ryder did not. Once a bridgehead had been firmly established the British would come ashore, make a smart left turn and, with a few American reinforcements, spearhead the dash for Tunisia. By this time they would be known as First Army and be under Anderson's command.

At first Admiral Burrough would be putting fewer men ashore than Troubridge's Centre Task Force was landing around Oran; but he had more firepower to cover them. Along with 2 aircraft carriers, 3 cruisers, 3 anti-aircraft ships, over 40 anti-submarine vessels, including 13 destroyers, he had been allotted the monitor HMS *Roberts*. This carried a single pair of the kind of huge 15-inch guns normally only found on battleships yet had a draught shallow enough to let her get as close inshore as a destroyer.

Nor was this the end of it. Behind them, under Neville Syfret, whose ships had navigated with such precision at Madagascar, both task forces were covered by Gibraltar's enlarged Force H with all the heavy artillery on the battleships *Duke of York*, *Rodney* and *Renown*. In addition there were the three carriers *Formidable*, *Victorious* and the old *Furious*, which once flew Sopwith Camels off her flight deck against the Kaiser, plus three cruisers, seventeen destroyers and various auxiliaries. Operation Torch was a formidable display by the world's two greatest sea powers with the US Navy, already heavily committed in the Pacific, supplying 105 warships and the Royal Navy 196 despite the effect the missing destroyer escorts was bound to have on the safety of Atlantic and Russian convoys.

Allied Naval Commander for Operation Torch was Admiral Sir Andrew Cunningham, scourge of Mussolini's navy. In the dark days of the Stukas over Crete, when a ship's captain complained that fighting the Luftwaffe was like banging his head against a wall, Cunningham had famously told him: 'You might just loosen a brick.' He had recently returned from four months in Washington DC as the Admiralty's representative at the newly set-up Combined Chiefs of Staff, the highest Anglo-American military authority, where the inevitable politicking had got him down. Not that he had anything against Americans. In Gibraltar he got on well with Supreme Commander Eisenhower and his deputy Mark Clark and the goodwill was mutual. 'One of the finest individuals I've ever met,' was Eisenhower's assessment. 'Vigorous, hardy, intelligent and straightforward ... He believed that ships went to sea to find and destroy the enemy. A real sea-dog.'

After considerable prevarication by Giraud, it was Cunningham who made the arrangements to try to extract him from Vichy France and get him at least as far as Gibraltar in time for operation Torch. There was one bad moment when the French général (the nimble abseiler from Castle Königstein) fell into the sea while trying to board the submarine *Seraph* from a pitching rowing skiff in the dark. The 63-year-old was hastily retrieved by his son and another young officer who were travelling with him as aides-de-camp, the only visible damage being to the herringbone suit he was wearing and his cavalry moustache, neither of which were intended for full saline immersion. The général retired to the captain's bunk, which was not quite long enough for him, and tried to get some sleep.

Next morning, in order to get Giraud to Eisenhower as soon as possible, an RAF Catalina flying boat rendezvoused with the *Seraph*, making a landing close to the submarine despite a choppy sea. South African-born Squadron Leader James Louw, one of Coastal Command's stars with a sunk U-boat on his log book, managed to get his American-built aircraft within 30 yards of the *Seraph*. Yet it still took an agonizing eighty-five minutes to transfer by paddled rubber dinghy Giraud, aides-de-camp, Captain Wright USN (his guarantee of the Americanness of the occasion) and the French-speaking former US diplomat Colonel Holmes. There were also various items of luggage. While this was going on an aircraft began circling them at, Louw estimated, 'about two miles distance'. They were some 700 miles from the nearest RAF base and it was unlikely to be friendly. But the luck that had been with Giraud ever since he descended from Königstein on 60 feet of untested prisoner-plaited rope held and the mysterious aircraft flew away. Three hours later Kingpin, after a bumpy take-off in sea that was getting choppier by the minute, was safely delivered to the British Empire's most British of fortresses, the Rock of Gibraltar.

For Giraud it was not a happy landing. With great expectations he went almost immediately into conference with a much relieved Eisenhower and Clark who were receiving visitors down a dank 500–yard tunnel bored deep into Gibraltar's Jurassic innards. Both sides were almost immediately disappointed in each other. Clark in particular felt that Giraud simply did not look the part. 'He was a tall man with wrinkled civilian clothes – a man with dark cheeks and a dark growth of beard straggling across his face but with a beautiful handlebar moustache, which also seemed to be drooping. At first glance he hardly seemed a figure that would fit easily into the important niche in history that might be awaiting him.'

This seems a little unkind from a man who had lost his trousers during his own recent submarine adventures and, even if he had not heard all the details of Giraud's eventful journey, was fully aware that he had not come in on the Pan Am Clipper. According to his memoirs Clark eventually came to admire Giraud's patience and dignity. At this first meeting the quality that stood out most was his stubbornness.

Zero hour for Operation Torch was about eight hours away. By now Giraud should have been smuggled into Algiers and be poised to emerge at the head of Général Mast's joyful *résistants*, a commanding and heroic figure calling for a return to arms against Germany. This would be Washington's superlative answer to London's controversial de Gaulle who, as the end of the Syrian campaign had proved, most French officers would not serve under. But time had run out. Giraud's arrival would have to wait until they had captured an airport. A battalion of American paratroopers flying non-stop from Cornwall was earmarked for this very task. Meanwhile, for the moment, what he could do was authorize a short radio broadcast to French North Africa, to be transmitted under his name, urging French troops to cooperate with the Allies and save their bullets for the Axis. It was to be transmitted as soon as it was confirmed that the initial landings were successful.

Since time was of the essence, Eisenhower and Clark had taken the liberty of writing it for him. Giraud was invited into the small office they shared where the glow of an exterior red light above their door indicated that they should not be disturbed for anything less than a poison gas attack. The interpreter Colonel Holmes translated it into French. The gist of it was that the United States, in order to thwart an Axis plan to seize Morocco, Algeria and Tunisia, had decided to act first and called upon all officers and men of L'Armée d'Afrique du Nord to join them in the fight against the common enemy. Of his own role in all this, Giraud was scripted to say no more than, 'I resume my place of combat among you.'

Kingpin was unaware of his code-name but he knew that the Allies did not risk their submarines and aeroplanes for people they did not value. He drew a deep breath. 'Now let's get it clear as to my part,' he said. 'As I understand it, when I land in North Africa I am to assume command of all Allied forces and become the Supreme Allied Commander in North Africa?'

'I think there must have been some misunderstanding,' said Eisenhower. Clark describes his tone as 'cautious'.

> I thought Ike had never been so shocked and showed it so little. Giraud got a stubborn look on his face ... There was no question in my mind that he was stating what he believed to be in the agreement. Furthermore, he was under the impression that there would be an almost immediate Allied effort to invade France proper to forestall German occupation of Vichy territory. Just how he had gotten this impression I was never able to clear up. In conversation with General Mast I had particularly not promised that Giraud would have top command. Murphy had been in the position of wanting to offer almost anything because it was of such importance to have a man of Giraud's calibre to prevent French resistance ... All I could ever figure out was that there had been some exaggerated promises made to Giraud in

> order to make sure that he joined us. Mast, for instance, may have told him not to worry about the command; that it could be straightened out; and since such messages had to be taken to Giraud by courier it is not difficult to see where he might have got the wrong impression. I am sure, at any rate, that Giraud, when he discovered the situation, was as shocked as Ike and I. As we talked it over, it became obvious that we were in for some serious trouble.

Clark was right. At the end of three hours Giraud's signature was still not on the statement the Americans had told London to expect for the BBC's French language service. They agreed to disperse for dinner and try again later. Clark, who knew they had a long night ahead, had camp beds moved into the office and arranged to eat there. Decrypted messages on the flimsy paper the British liked to use for classified material were already beginning to pile up from London, Washington and some of the units involved. Giraud or no Giraud Operation Torch was on.

Admiral Cunningham took Eisenhower, whom he thought looked 'desperately tired and worried', off to dinner at the Mount, the living quarters of the Royal Navy's senior staff. Giraud dined separately with the governor of Gibraltar, General Sir Noel Mason-MacFarlane, at his official residence The Convent. 'MasonMac', as he was known to his contemporaries, had spent most of the inter-war years in central European diplomatic posts as a military attaché and their lingua franca was German. The governor had just returned from a well-publicized trip to Malta, all part of the deception operation to make the enemy believe that the ships gathered around the Rock were about to lift the siege of the island and he was there to coordinate their movements. The German Navy had not fallen for this. They were still advising Hitler that the most likely intention of this British fleet was an attack on Rommel's rear by landing troops between Tripoli and Benghazi. If not there, Sicily was their next choice. After that came Sardinia, then somewhere on the Italian mainland. French North Africa was on their list of possibilities but it was last.

Under a setting sun some 6 miles off the Algerian coast Sergeant Stamford Weatherall was worried that some playful dolphins were about to capsize them. He could see the school's phosphorescent wake as they charged towards their canoe, veering away at the last second. Sitting in front of him, navigating with a hand-held compass, was Sub-Lieutenant John Harris of the Royal Naval Volunteer Reserve. They had shipped far too much water when they were launched into a choppy sea from the submarine HMS *Ursula*. Weatherall estimated their lee board at no more than 2 inches and, since he could not find find the bailer, he was trying to stay afloat by scooping the water out with his green beret. They had already jettisoned the rucksacks containing their spare clothing and a twenty-four-hour ration pack, though the sergeant had retained his boots – they wore plimsolls in the canoe – and his weapons: a Tommy gun in a waterproof cover, a Colt automatic and a kukri, the curved miniature machete that was the Gurkha fighting knife.

The pair were one of several canoe teams belonging to the recently formed Combined Operations Pilotage Parties whose personnel were drawn from the army and the navy. Weatherall, a Dunkirk veteran from Nottingham who had recently celebrated his thirtieth birthday, was a Commando in No. 2 Special Boat Squadron. In theory their task was first to reconnoitre a hostile beach then guide in landing craft at night by setting up infra-red beacons visible through an adapted molecular glass. In practice, on this their first operation, they had been forbidden to reconnoitre the Operation Torch beaches. After some reflection it had been decided that the dangers of any chance contact with the enemy giving the game away far outweighed the advantages of knowing more about where they were going.

At 9.15 p.m., over two hours after they left the submarine, Harris and Weatherall, cold and wet and with the sergeant now using one of his boots as a bailer, got through the surf and landed. They thought they had arrived at the place the planners called Z Beach which was west of Algiers. Actually they were at least 5 miles further west than they should have been, something they might have realized had they been allowed to make a reconnaissance. The American first wave was due to arrive at 1.05 a.m. They had plenty of time to set up the infra-red gear, visible for miles out to sea, which the Royal Navy coxwains would spot through their molecular glasses and use as their mark. This done, they cursed the loss of their dry clothing and did their shivering best to keep warm, not daring to move about too much in case the beach was patrolled.

At the Villa Sidi-Allowi *les* amirals Darlan and Fenard and *Général* Juin were on their main course. Juin, who was almost as small as Darlan, used only the fork, in his left hand, his right arm limp at his side as it had been since 1915 when he lost the use of it on the Western Front. But since, even then, Major Juin was considered an officer with a great future ahead of him he was not given a medical discharge. Instead he was granted special permission to salute with his left hand.

Juin was born the son of a colonial gendarme at Bone, one of the most picturesque of the old Phoenician ports, in Algeria's north-eastern corner close to the Tunisian border. Between the wars he had served under both Pétain and Giraud in the campaigns against Arab insurgents in Morocco's Rif Mountains. In 1940 he was captured commanding the 15th Motorized Division during the French stand at Lille which bought time for the Dunkirk evacuation. For Juin, being released from Königstein and replacing Maxime Weygand as Commander-in-Chief in North Africa had been a dream posting, a return to his *pied-noir* roots and a world away from defeated France.

Weygand, as he subsequently admitted to Murphy, had accepted the North African post as soon as Britain proved its ability to withstand air attacks. His desire to use his fief as a launch pad for the eventual liberation of France had always been transparent. In the end, his departure in November 1941 had been as a direct result of an ultimatum from Berlin that it would occupy all of France unless he did so. To become his replacement Juin had been required to make a solemn promise that he would never take up arms against the Germans again. In recent months he had made it plain to Murphy that, at the right moment, he wished France to re-enter the war. But the American always felt that Juin would feel honour-bound to inform his superiors in Vichy if he confided in him that they intended to intervene, whereas the escapee Giraud was under no such obligation. Otherwise Murphy would have told him because he liked Juin.

On the eve of Darlan's scheduled return to Vichy, once due mention of Alain's remarkable recovery had been made, the main topic of conversation over dinner at Sidi-Allowi was the usual one. Who would invade French North Africa first: the Axis or the Allies? A good case could be made that the British success at El Alamein had increased the risk from the Axis because Rommel's defeat could be partly blamed on the number of oil tankers British submarines and aircraft had sunk. The obvious remedy was to shorten the Mediterranean crossing by occupying Tunisia and shipping supplies to Bizerte, hardly 100 miles away from Sicily, instead of Tripoli or Benghazi. Or would the Allies move first to prevent this?

Towards the end of their meal they received a visitor who was now firmly of this opinion. An excited Contre-amiral Jacques Moreau, commander of the fourth naval district at Algiers, turned up to report what he obviously regarded as a disquieting development. The ships they had thought were heading for Malta, Moreau informed them, were now ideally deployed to turn back towards Oran and Algiers and land whatever troops they had aboard before first light.

Moreau was advised to calm down and get some sleep. Nothing was going to happen. Not for the first time that evening Darlan cited Murphy's comment about not coming unless they were summoned. 'I have assurances,' he said. Then, after bidding Juin goodnight, he took his own advice and went to bed. He had an early flight back to France in the morning.

Shortly before midnight Murphy, listening to the BBC French service on his short-wave radio, heard what he had been waiting for. It came amid the list of 'personal messages' the announcer gave out after the news summary, each read out twice and carefully enunciated, like a language teacher giving a pupil a new phrase. '*Allo, Robert*,' said London. '*Franklin est arrivé*.'

This oddly transparent message to Robert Murphy from Franklin D. Roosevelt was the signal that the Operation Torch landings were about to begin. If everything went on schedule American troops would be in the city in two hours. In the interim Murphy's first task was to see that Mast's insurgents had been alerted and had taken over the key positions that would ease the Americans' passage into the city. Britain's Special Operations Executive had failed to deliver the arms Clark promised at the Cherchell meeting. On several occasions, dates had been set and men left standing on lonely beaches flashing their insistent Morse at an empty sea until they ran out of darkness. Murphy thought the SOE had let them down because the British had no faith in the American ability to judge who was worth the risk of a ship. If so, SOE were sadly mistaken. Despite their ill-assorted weaponry, and well within the allotted time, the insurgents had acted. Police posts and power stations had been seized, as had most communication centres for radio and telephones. They also began to encircle some military headquarters as well as cordon off the residences of several senior officers.

On what had now become Z Beach, where Sub-Lieutenant Harris and Sergeant Weatherall had been keeping their cold vigil, the coxes landed the first wave of Americans at 1.15 a.m. – ten minutes late. Weatherall noted in the log he was keeping that they made 'a perfect landing without any opposition'. At least they were only an hour's march or so from where they should have been. Some of the Americans were put ashore even further from Algiers than was intended and none of them, wherever they were landed, managed to get to the city as quickly as they were supposed to.

French North Africa was neutral. There was no blackout. An American submarine commander surfacing that same night 7 miles off Casablanca said it was 'like coming up in the centre of Times Square'. At about the time Z Beach's Combined Operations Pilotage Party were introducing themselves to the first wave of Americans to set foot in French North Africa, Murphy, accompanied by US Vice-Consul Kenneth Pendar who was to remain in the car, was being driven along the well-lit, jacaranda-lined streets of el-Biar district. He was about to make an unannounced call on Général Juin at Villa des Oliviers, official residence of the army's Commander-in-Chief. This was not the way it was supposed to happen. According to the script he was supposed to have accompanied Giraud to Juin's house as living proof of Franco-American collusion. But Giraud was missing and there had been no message from Eisenhower explaining why.

It was now about 1.30 a.m. and Juin, having returned from his dinner with Darlan and Fenard, was fast asleep. Mast's fifth column had not yet arrived here and the security of Villa des Oliviers was still in the hands of a detachment of tall Senegalese askaris who Murphy had to talk his way through.

> After some difficulty I was admitted and persuaded a servant to wake the *général*. He came to the drawing room in pink-striped pyjamas, tousled and sleepy. My news snapped him awake. I told him, as calmly as I could, that an American expeditionary force of half a million men was about to land all along the coasts of French North Africa. According to my instructions, I multiplied the size and made no mention of its British components.

'I wish to tell you about this in advance,' explained the American, the words well rehearsed, 'because over the last year our talks have convinced me that you desire, above all else, to see the liberation of France which can only come about through co-operation with the United States.'

'But you told me only a week ago that the United States would not attack us,' protested a clearly incredulous Juin.

'We're here by invitation.'

'From whom?'

'Giraud.'

'Is he here in Algiers?'

'We expect him momentarily,' murmured Murphy.

The général began to pace the room. His visitor repeated that they had always been confident of his support when the time came.

Suddenly Juin found his way out of this dreadful dilemma. 'If the matter was entirely in my hands I would be with you,' he said. 'But, as you know, Darlan is in Algiers visiting his son. He outranks me and no matter what decision I might make, Darlan could immediately overrule it.'

'Very well,' said Murphy, taking a deep breath. 'Let us talk with Darlan.' And so the die was cast.

In Gibraltar Giraud was being as stubborn as ever. Well after their dinner break he was still insisting that a Frenchman must be in overall command of an Anglo-American expedition into French territory. Left unsaid were all the European colonial concerns that, French or British, so deeply irritated the Americans who could not care less if Arabs and Berbers, already emboldened by Germany's recent colonization of their colonizers, would regard a purely US intervention as another important step towards independence.

With so little time left for even a radio statement from Giraud to be of any use at all, Eisenhower decided to play good cop, bad cop. Clark was bad cop.

'Tell him,' bad cop said to Colonel Holmes, 'that we would like the honourable general to know that the time of his usefulness to the Americans and the restoration of the glory that once was France is NOW.'

'But what would the French people think of me? What about the prestige of Giraud? What about my family?'

Clark repeated that they were more than happy to see him commanding all the French forces in North Africa but they were not prepared to give him anything more.

'Then I shall return to France,' said Giraud.

'How are you going back?'

'By the same route I came here.'

'Oh no you won't,' said Clark. 'That was a one-way submarine. You're not going back to France on it.'

The Americans then told Giraud that he must not let personal ambition come before the best interests of France but perhaps he sensed they did not really mean it, for he shrugged off the insult. Finally Clark turned to Holmes and said, 'Tell him this. Tell him if you don't go along with us, General, you're going to be out in the snow on your ass.'

Colonel Holmes, late of the US State Department, looked imploringly at Eisenhower who decided they were all exhausted and ought to try to get a couple of hours' sleep while they still could.

In Algiers Darlan was not mincing his words either. 'I have known for a long time the British are stupid,' he told Murphy. 'But I always believed Americans were more intelligent. Apparently you have the same genius as the British for making massive blunders!'

The American and Juin had not gone to see him at Fenard's villa where Darlan, his bag packed for his dawn flight back to Vichy, was sleeping. When Juin had woken him with his call he had been told to stay put. He and Fenard would come there. Vichy's senior officer, the man in charge of all the army, navy and air force the Germans had allowed France to keep, had arrived in a red-faced fury. All the joy his son's recovery had brought had obviously evaporated.

For the first fifteen minutes Darlan had found it impossible to keep still. Instead, he had paced up and down the marbled floor of Juin's main reception salon, puffing so hard at his pipe that the smoke seemed to be rising from the balding head he so rarely uncovered. Dancing alongside him was the tall Murphy, doing his best to shorten his stride and keep in step with the smaller man while making various soothing noises and reminding him of the time he told Ambassador Leahy that if the Americans ever came in force he would welcome them.

'That moment has now arrived!' declared Murphy with all the fervour of a revivalist preacher. But even as he said it he found himself wondering whether by some ghastly mistake he had got the date wrong. A glance at his watch showed that it was now long after 2.30 a.m. The deadline set for American troops to reach Algiers from their landing places and take control had come and gone.

Map 9 The Anglo–American landings in North Africa, 8–10 November 1942

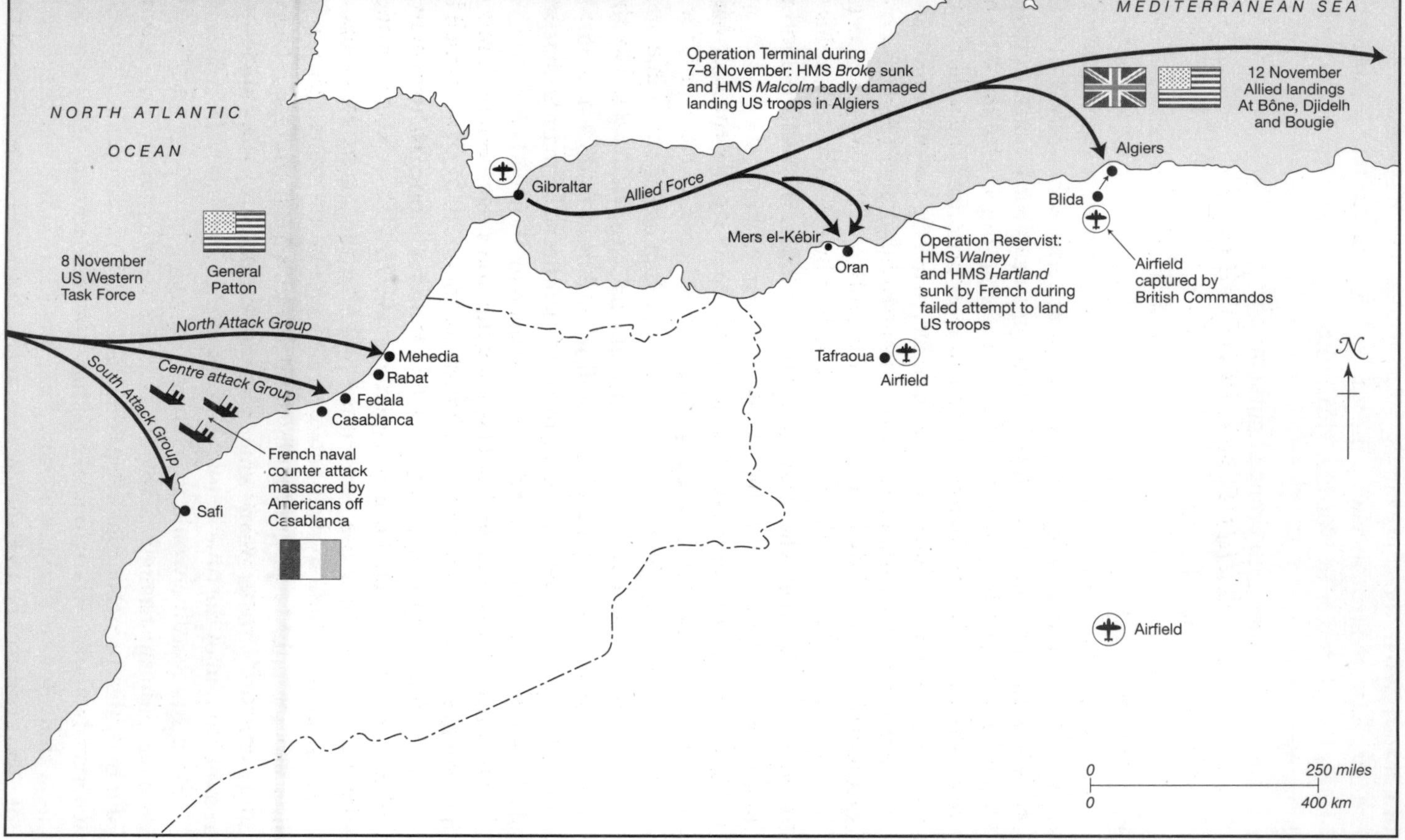
MEDITERRANEAN SEA
NORTH ATLANTIC
OCEAN
Operation Terminal during
7–8 November: HMS *Broke* sunk
and HMS *Malcolm* badly damaged
landing US troops in Algiers
12 November
Allied landings
At Bône, Djidelh
and Bougie
Algiers
Gibraltar
Allied Force
Blida
Mers el-Kébir
Oran
Operation Reservist:
HMS *Walney*
and HMS *Hartland*
sunk by French during
failed attempt to land
US troops
Airfield
captured by
British Commandos
8 November
US Western
Task Force
General
Patton
North Attack Group
Centre attack Group
South Attack Group
Mehedia
Rabat
Fedala
Casablanca
French naval
counter attack
massacred by
Americans off
Casablanca
Safi
Tafraoua
Airfield
Airfield
0
250 miles
0
400 km

Chapter Twenty-Eight

At that moment the nearest United States soldiers to Murphy were the 634 officers and men of the 3rd Battalion 135th Infantry Regiment aboard the two old destroyers HMS *Malcolm* and HMS *Broke* which were about a mile off Algiers harbour and approaching fast. The 135th was a Minnesota regiment with a roll call of Scandinavian names and a few Scots with relatives in Canada. Commanding its 3rd Battalion was Lieutenant Colonel Edwin T. Svenson, recently the assistant warden of Minnesota State Penitentiary, who liked telling British officers that his top sergeant was the man who could beat him in a fist fight though behind this pugilistic exterior lurked a thoughtful soul.

After Gettysburg the 135th had adopted the motto 'To the Last Man'; but Svenson's battalion liked to call themselves 'The Singing Third' for the soldiers' songs they had learned by heart, some of them British compositions of a brutal bawdiness, during their last six months in Northern Ireland. Their favourite was 'There's a Troopship Now Leaving Bombay' with its joyful chorus: 'Fuck 'em all Fuck 'em all, the long and the short and the tall.'*

The British warships they had boarded in Belfast had been built just too late for the last German war though both, particularly *Malcolm* which had sunk a U-boat, had more than made up for it in this one. To give them the added weight they might need in order to crash through the harbour boom, the ships' hollow bow compartments had been given a concrete filling, and armour plate welded to their exterior. And around the upper deck, where the crouched American infantry would be packed in the final stages of their approach, there was a 3-foot-high screen of ¾-inch-thick bulletproof steel plate.

By 3.30 a.m. the destroyers were getting their first close look at Algiers which, to the amazement of their lookouts, was still lit up by its peacetime quota of illumination. And although, a few miles either side of the city, the flicker of gun flashes could plainly be seen there was no fire from the port's

* 'Bless 'em all', a sanitized version, became quite a hit and was sung by Gracie Fields, among others.

batteries themselves. Then, apparently at the flick of a switch, came total darkness swiftly broken by searchlight beams from the Isle de Marine and Batterie des Arcades which began a teasing kind of dance around the two destroyers that was never quite consummated.

Once the Algiers street lights went off it was difficult to find the right way into the harbour that, in the normal way, had been made more sheltered and the entrance narrower by having jetties built from either side. And when the destroyers did find it they knew they would have to work up to something approaching full speed in order to give their reinforced bows the momentum to cut through the boom – heavy chains on thick wooden floaters – intended to wrap itself around an intruder's propellers.

The first time they tried it they realized they had missed it altogether and were heading directly for the reinforced concrete of the Jette de Mustapha, which would certainly have held its own against the armour-plated cement implants coming its way. The second time *Broke* went first, missed the entrance again, and scooted off seawards under fire from two batteries, though the searchlights failed to hold the destroyer long enough for the guns to do their work. Then *Malcolm* had a go. Once again Commander Archibald Russell, decorated for destroyer actions at Dunkirk and in the Atlantic, was unable to find the entrance and was obliged to make another tight turn back to sea. But this time the shore batteries spotted her phosphorescent trail and scored several hits, putting three of her four boilers out of action and reducing her speed to 4 knots.

Ten crew were killed and at least another twenty on the ship wounded, including some of the American infantry amidships where fire had broken out among the pasteboard cases of mortar ammunition. One of Svenson's youngest officers, 2nd Lieutenant William L. Muir of L Company, started picking up the burning boxes and throwing them overboard. This encouraged others to do the same and possibly saved the ship, which limped away and took no further part in these or any other proceedings until repairs were completed in early 1943. The Lords Commissioners of the Admiralty granted Muir a Mention in Despatches 'for your bravery on passage to North Africa', the first of several awards he would get before he died of malaria in Italy the following year.

Aboard *Broke* was Lieutenant Colonel Svenson and the other 300 or so of his battalion. With his command reduced by half, the colonel rapidly rewrote his plan, reducing the area of the harbour he would hold until reinforcements reached them. On the bridge Lieutenant Arthur Layard prepared to make his third attempt to put them there. This proved no more successful than the last, the entrance to the harbour remaining as elusive as ever. Dawn was now coming up. All hope of a surprise attack under cover of darkness had gone. But for his fourth attempt Layard could, for the first time, just about make out where he was going. The downside was that the French gunners were also enjoying the benefit of first light and they had already proved with the hits inflicted on *Malcolm* that they could shoot accurately enough in the dark.

At least *Broke* could now return fire with some hope of keeping her opponents' heads down and the crews manning the fore and aft 4.7-inch open gun turrets, which on later destroyers had been replaced by fully closed ones, were firing as fast as they could. Above them fluttered the Royal Navy's White Ensign and the Stars and Stripes flying in tandem for the first time in their history as joint battle flags. Most of the French coastal batteries were 8-inchers, almost twice as big as the ship's guns. For a moment it seemed that the destroyer might miss the entrance again. Then Layard spotted the buoys that marked the route between the jetties and ordered a slight change in course and full speed ahead. *Broke* sliced through the boom as if it were a thread of cotton. According to Svenson's report there was 'hardly a sensation of hitting' and for a moment it seemed as if all their troubles were over.

But as the ship slowed and approached the empty Quai du Falaise on Môle Louis Billiard, a small patrol boat moored only a few feet away from the intruder raked it with heavy machine-gun fire and caused several casualties. *Broke* was too close to depress her 4.7-inch guns enough to blow her tormentor out of the water with cannon fire. Instead, Layard had to use his Oerlikon anti-aircraft guns. Before it finished, this escalated into a prolonged and deafening close-quarters duel that must have sounded something like a contest between competing choirs of road drills with occasional high notes from ricochets. Eventually the patrol boat was silenced and for the first time the Americans could hear the steady crack-crack of rifle fire and occasional bursts of some kind of light automatics coming from the buildings behind the port.

Almost to a man the Singing Third had never been shot at before. Already drained by a sleepless night of cold, seasickness and regular soakings from near misses they were, according to their own account, 'quite shaken and a little slow in getting underway to disembark'. But by 5.20 a.m. the landing had been completed and Svenson had begun to deploy his men around a seaplane base and behind barricades of wood, sand and baled straw near a warehouse on Môle Louis Billiard.

At about eight o'clock two civilians accompanied by a couple of gendarmes approached them and explained they wanted an American emissary to accompany them into Algiers and make arrangements for taking it over. These probably came from Général Mast's insurgents. But while this was being discussed one of Layard's officers from *Broke*, who appears to have ventured further into the city centre than anybody else, returned with some bad news. A French major with whom he had attempted to parley had politely informed him that, Americans or British, they were about to be surrounded and annihilated.

*

At Oran this had almost happened. Operation Terminal had at least put men ashore in Algiers. The almost identical Operation Reservist, where the former US Coast Guard cutters HMS *Walney* and HMS *Hartland* were supposed to land almost 400 American troops, had been an unmitigated disaster.

Twenty-six months had elapsed since Somerville's ships had killed almost 1,300 French sailors at neighbouring Mers-el-Kébir. Since then that port had not been much used and what was left of the Vichy French fleet in North African waters operated out of Casablanca or Oran itself. In the early hours of 8 November, as well as a few armed trawlers and submarines, Oran contained three decent-sized warships. These were the two super-destroyers *Epervier* and *Typhon* with their 5.7-inch guns and *La Surprise*, a large and well-armed minesweeper completed only four months before the armistice. They could hardly be expected to make much difference against the enormous firepower at the disposal of Commodore Troubridge's Centre Force. But this was waiting outside the harbour while *Walney* and *Hartland*, each flying large American flags and accompanied by two wooden-hulled launches with smoke-laying equipment, tried to bluff their way in. When that bluff was called the French ships proved a deadly supplement to the port's fixed defences.

The *Epervier*, which had served alongside the British off Norway and then at Dunkirk where she had rescued an RAF pilot, was commanded by Capitaine de frégate Paul Laurin. For the last five months the destroyer had been in dock for a major refit and Laurin had been unable to do any training. His crew was thirty-three men short of what it should have been and he had just detached another twenty-seven under Enseigne de vaisseau Schillte for guard duties on the quays. At 3 a.m., almost two hours after the initial beach landings, he was ordered to put his ship into a state of readiness. Boilers were started up and the anti-aircraft guns manned but not the heavy 5.7-inchers because Laurin lacked the gunners.

For about an hour all was quiet. Then a searchlight on Oran's Santas Cruz bastion briefly illuminated an unknown ship. On the *Epervier* they heard the sound of machine-gun fire followed by the swoosh of French red alarm flares. Laurin ordered his men to action stations and mustered scratch crews for the 5.7-inch guns. On shore Enseigne de vaisseau Schillte, whose machine guns were covering the main entry channel into the port, heard the 8-inch battery on the Môle Ravin Blanc open up. Soon *La Surprise* and *Typhon*, which were berthed nearer the sea than the *Epervier*, had joined in. The surface of the channel began to fill with the white vapour of a smoke screen the intruders were laying which, for a while at least, did its job well. But while Schillte could not see anything through it he could distinctly hear the panting noise a ship's engines make when somebody wants more revs out of them.

Schillte was listening to HMS *Walney*'s oil-fired American Babcock and

Wilcox boilers bringing her up to her top speed of 16 knots. *Hartland*, her sister ship, was a little behind on her starboard side. In Gibraltar these neat little single-funnel craft, 250 feet in length and designed for nothing more lethal than making life miserable for Prohibition's Lake Erie rum-runners, had embarked Lieutenant Colonel George F. Marshall and his 3rd Battalion of the 6th Infantry Regiment. Marshall, a 31-year-old West Pointer from Florida with a high forehead and a strong jaw, was travelling on the *Walney* with Captain Peters who, until the soldiers got ashore, was in overall command of Operation Reservist.

'Fritz' Peters DSO, DSC and bar, the Canadian-born destroyer hero who had won his Distinguished Service Order in January 1915 helping to sink the battleship *Blücher* during the Battle of the Dogger Bank, had just turned 53, thinning on top and thickening below. He was born, the son of a prominent lawyer and politician, on Prince Edward Island in the Gulf of St Lawrence that after the American War of Independence had provided a new home for loyalist refugees. In 1905, aged 15, Peters had gone to England and joined the Royal Navy. But despite his 1914–18 successes, in 1920 he asked to be put on the Reserve list and returned to Canada where his mother wished to see more of her surviving son. Her youngest two had been killed in France in 1915 and 1916. He never married and was back on active service almost immediately after the second German war started.

In July 1940, for his 'good work' commanding an anti-submarine flotilla of armed trawlers in the North Sea, Peters received a bar to the Distinguished Service Cross he had been awarded in 1918 for another destroyer action. Then came a complete change. For the next two years he was first with Naval Intelligence, then commanding officer of Brickendonbury Hall near Hertford, a training centre for the paramilitary Section D of the Secret Intelligence Service, MI6. Kim Philby, the Communist traitor who was at the school at this time, held Peters in high regard.

This was by no means uncommon. 'The mist, like rain, darkness and secrecy followed him. And he would have one or the other, or all of them with him to the very last,' wrote Leo S. Disher, an American news agency reporter who had been assigned to the *Walney* to cover the landings. Like all the journalists covering Operation Torch he was required to wear uniform. The only thing that distinguished Disher from anybody else in an olive drab combat jacket was the brassard he wore on his left arm which bore the letter C for Correspondent.

It was an assignment Disher, who worked for what later became United Press International, could have honourably avoided because on the way out he had slipped on a pitching deck and broken his left ankle. Once the ship got to Gibraltar the US Army, to whom he was accredited, wanted him off the ship. Disher added a broken heart to his injuries. This was the biggest story he had ever been asked to cover. And he had endeared himself to everybody on board by acquiring a pair of crutches and refusing to leave the ship.

Long John Disher was soon hobbling about the *Walney* with increasing expertise, though the tall, good-looking young man with his swashbuckling Errol Flynn moustache and slicked-down hair combed straight back from his forehead found it more tiring than he made out. As the lights of Oran became visible he had somehow managed to climb the ladders up to the bridge and wedged himself into the passageway behind it, his back pressed against one bulkhead and the crutches against the other, leaning on them with his forearms. He had a life jacket on his chest and another lashed around the several pounds of plaster of Paris covering his lower left leg, the brainwave of one of Marshall's company commanders, convinced he would sink like a stone without it. And tucked into his belt was Colonel Marshall's personal .45 automatic. The colonel had a Tommy gun and it had bothered him that Disher was sticking so close to the action without anything to protect himself. Correspondents, like medics, were considered non-combatants and not supposed to be armed but Disher thought he did not have to use it so he took it. 'I didn't want to offend the colonel.'

From his wedged-in position the reporter could look along the bridge to where Peters, Marshall, Lieutenant Commander Peter Meyrick, an admiral's son who commanded the *Walney* (Peters was in charge of both ships) and the other officers were standing. He could make out the shapes of their bodies but not their faces which they had covered in black camouflage grease. Among them was Disher's new friend – they were both in their twenties – Lieutenant Paul Duncan, a yachtsman from Cardiff with a French mother who in 1935 had joined the Royal Naval Volunteer Reserve and was teaching French in London when war broke out.

Peters had made Duncan his Chief of Staff and lighter of the little black cheroots he chain-smoked. But tonight Duncan had a starring role and was costumed for the part in US Army combat garb with a brace of revolvers in open western holsters on his hips. In his right hand he clutched a bullhorn through which he would shortly be calling on the hidden listeners of the night to stop firing at their American friends. This would all be in the American-accented French he had been trying out on Marshall and his officers, whose forbearance did them credit.

'I think we've got a good chance of carrying out our mission without firing a shot,' Peters said at his last officers' conference in the wardroom. As they closed with the shoreline and, one by one, the chains of amber lights that beaded the slopes above the port were snuffed out, Disher overheard Meyrick pass on a message from the command ship *Largs* that seemed to confirm their commander's prediction. 'It says landings up to now have been carried out without shooting. Don't start a fight unless you have to.' Everybody on the bridge laughed. So they were the hard men who had to be kept on a short leash. En route to Gibraltar, over the nightly drinks in the wardroom, Peters had made sure that Disher understood that he was a man who loved to smell the powder, once confiding to him that he only felt properly alive when he was being shot at.

Then briefly a searchlight got onto them before darting off in another direction as if its operators had been too confused to examine what they were doing. But somebody had a good idea where they were. First lazy blobs of red tracer arched slowly towards them followed by the clang of a coastal battery. Disher felt the ship shudder from near misses: once, twice. Orders were shouted and the *Walney* began to turn away. *Hartland* followed. Once again a beam was briefly on them then lost and they were heading back towards the open sea and the safety of Troubridge's big ships. Then Disher heard Peters say something to Meyrick. He failed to catch the actual words though he soon realized what they meant because Admiral Meyrick's middle son – the eldest was a destroyer captain and the youngest on cruisers – was ordering his helmsman in a loud, clear voice: 'Turn her, we're going back in.' Peters was going to sniff the powder.

Just like Algiers there was a harbour boom defence to get through. This one was a chain followed by tethered line of what looked like coal barges. The two accompanying motor launches began to lay the smoke screen that had blinded the *Epervier*. Everybody except the carefully braced Disher was lying flat, as they had been trained to do, in anticipation of a crash that would knock them off their feet. But a prow meant for Great Lakes ice had no more problem with the boom than a good knife on a wedding cake, parting it with a gentle crunch. Even so, it was no bad thing to be lying down because the *Walney* was beginning to take a few hits, though at this point the most terrible sound was a grinding crash as they hacked the bow off one of the smoke screen launches disorientated by its own work. The craft, still able to steer, bumped back towards Troubridge's ships for first aid.

Not long after this a gentle offshore wind began to disperse the smoke screen and both cutters started to take heavy punishment. One of the first casualties was Captain Michael Bolitho, of the Coldstream Guards, who was standing by the forward 3-inch gun when it took a direct hit. Bolitho, whose mother was from Jersey's prominent Anglo-French Lemprière family, was part of a small Special Operations Executive explosives team who were on board to defuse any mines and booby traps on the port's installations. The SOE team were to be delivered to their targets by Commando canoeists. After the destruction of the forward gun the next shell to hit *Walney* wrecked her engine room and she was no longer under power. Disher recalled the 'sudden quiet' as they began drifting, temporarily unmolested, into the harbour past a breakwater wall on which, illuminated by one of the flares the French were putting up, he read in stencilled capitals: LA BELLE FRANCE.

A little behind them the *Hartland*, caught in searchlights, had one of her gun crews wiped out by heavy machine-gun fire then started taking shell hits, first from the 8-inch guns on Fort Laumone, then the destroyer *Typhon*'s 5.7-inchers and then from *La Surprise* and almost every other ship, launch or submarine with something that could reach her. On the bridge was Lieutenant Commander Godfrey Billot who was 36 and, like the older Peters, had rejoined the service from the Royal Naval Reserve having taken his discharge as a lieutenant in the early 1930s when the navy was looking for cuts.

Billot had just been temporarily blinded in one eye by shrapnel, which may account for the *Hartland* missing by a few feet the gap *Walney* had made in the boom and ramming a pier. Bouncing back on his buckled prow, Billot did not make the same mistake twice but by the time they entered the harbour both his ship's 3-inch guns were out of action and she was on fire. On deck the hoses needed to put it out were covered by mounds of dead and dying Americans. Engine room steam pipes cracked and hissed and scalded screaming stokers to death, while in the wardroom's makeshift dressing station the wounded were being wounded again. When Billot gave the order to abandon ship the flames were almost funnel-high and he could hardly stand from fresh wounds in his legs, but he got into the water.

On the drifting *Walney* Peters and his officers could see that the *Hartland* was in serious trouble but there was nothing they could do about it and they were busy trying to save themselves. On the bow Colonel Marshall and one of his company commanders were throwing grenades and firing bursts from their Tommy guns at a submarine that had manned her deck gun, while from the bridge, Lieutenant Duncan RN was letting them have it in what he fondly imagined was American French: '*Ne tiray pas! Noo sarmes vos armis. Noo sarmes Americaine. Ne tiray pas! Noo sarmes Americaine.*'

The only response Duncan got was a burst of machine-gun fire, which killed him. He fell against Disher who noticed how 'strangely soft' his friend's body felt, nothing like the stiff muscles of a man merely thrown off balance. The next shell mortally wounded two doctors toiling in the wardroom dressing station, one American the other British. Then the harbour current tugged them towards the *Epervier* whose dark bulk was intermittently illuminated by moon and gun flashes.

Peters saw it as his salvation. Casualties were mounting but he still had at least 150 fully armed infantry at his disposal eager to get out of this hell and kill somebody. He would make fast alongside her – they had been supplied with grappling hooks with that very purpose in mind – and Marshall's men would storm over the side in a good old-fashioned boarding party. Once she was in their hands he would launch his canoes and the Commandos would dart across the harbour, silent as snakes, attaching limpet mines to those ships that had the temerity to fire at them.

They were now less than 100 yards away. Suddenly the ship put a searchlight on them. Some of the Americans and Peters's surviving anti-aircraft crews started shooting at her. The light went out and the French, hesitantly at first, started shooting back with heavy machine guns. Paul Laurin, the captain of the *Epervier*, had been taken by surprise. At first he had thought this ghost vessel drifting silently towards them was a French ship. But, as it drew closer, Laurin realized that he did not recognize her shape and told his searchlight crew to give him a better look at her. As soon as he saw the large American flag flying from her stern, he ordered his light switched off.

> By this time the American ship started firing at us. We replied with the Browning machine-gun starboard of the bridge and the starboard Hotchkiss. I ordered the 5.7-inch and the 37mm guns to open fire. The order was not immediately executed. The navigating officer rushed to the 37mm and the gunnery officer to the 5.7-inch guns. The gunnery officer loaded gun No. 5 and fired at the enemy ship which was about 50 metres from us. The other rear guns also opened fire.

The last time the French had fired at British ships at this range – Laurin put it at 50 metres – the cannon had been Napoleonic. By 1942 a couple of 5.7-inch shells were probably the high explosive equivalent of the average Trafalgar broadside. According to Laurin's report the *Epervier* fired seventeen of them altogether with 'many rounds of 37mm and 13.2mm'. It was as one-sided as Mers-el-Kébir though without the preliminaries. Both *Walney*'s 3-inch guns were out of action and Colonel Marshall was killed leading by example and trying to get his men to do what they could with rifles, Thompsons and grenades.

The French concentrated their fire on the bridge which had already had some of its thin armour-plating shot away. So far its most senior casualty had been the Anglo-French Lieutenant Duncan, cut down in mid-spiel. It probably took only one other 5.7-inch shell to kill or maim most of the rest on the bridge who appear to have numbered almost twenty people including signallers and lookouts. Among them was Meyrick, the *Walney*'s captain. There were at least two survivors. One was Peters, who had a shoulder wound and, like Billot on the *Hartland*, had lost the sight in one eye. Somehow he managed to reach the quarterdeck where, despite his injuries, he got some men around him and tried to organize the lowering of an anchor. The other was Disher who had lost his crutches and it seems, for a bit, his mind as he crawled about the bridge, choking on the thick smoke and fumes rising from the fires on deck, trying to orientate himself.

> The blasts were so loud they hurt, seemed solid ... I was the only living

> person moving. I crawled to the starboard bridge ... Some fire was blazing below and in its glare I saw a piece of broken, floating wreckage. I could see nothing else. I lifted the Colonel's pistol and slowly fired shot after shot at the wreckage. I can't explain. It just seemed the thing to do ... There was a triple crash of shells. The blast caught me, hurled me back on the bridge with wounds in my legs. Once more I began crawling. Then behind me appeared a figure. A voice yelled, 'Is that you Captain Peters?' 'No, it's Disher.' He started to say something else. A shell exploded near us ... I must have been knocked unconscious for, when I was thinking again, I was crawling in the blackness over bodies, over glass and pieces of metal. And as I crawled I thought this is it, this is the end.

Total casualties, dead and wounded, for Operation Reservist exceeded 90 per cent of all those involved. Marshall and 189 of his men were killed. Another 157 soldiers needed medical attention. Some would never soldier again. On the *Walney*, which only doused her fires when she capsized, 82 British sailors died and *Hartland* lost another 32 including Lieutenant Jacques de Bourgeois, her French-Canadian surgeon. Among the wounded 86 were Royal Navy and of about 20 attached US Navy personnel, including marines, 5 died and 7 were hurt. At least one member of SOE, Bolitho, was killed. As far as the French were concerned they had been fish in a barrel and their own casualties had been light. On the *Epervier* Laurin had one dead and four others in his sick bay. All the survivors, wounded and unwounded, appear to have been captured, though perhaps a couple of evaders got to the beaches on which the main landings had taken place.

Peters was picked up by Enseigne de vaisseau Schillte and his shore party when he came into the docks with thirteen others on a Carley float, one of the canvas and kapok life rafts used by both the British and American navies. Schillte had them all locked up in the dock canteen until daybreak when they were escorted to naval headquarters.

Despite his lack of crutches Disher found his way off the bridge, climbed down a ladder being licked with flames, removed his helmet and fell into the sea through a broken guard rail before he was quite ready for it. He was a strong swimmer but almost drowned. Shrapnel had punctured the inflated tubular British life belt around his chest but the one that had been secured to his leg cast was still intact and this was bringing his feet up and keeping his head below water. Choking and spluttering, the reporter managed to get rid of it and 'with infinite weariness' began swimming until he got between a swaying merchant ship and a pier. Here he found a dangling mooring line and began to pull himself up.

> I got my elbows over the pier rim. Then the full weight of the cast on my leg caught me and I knew I couldn't make it. I began to lose my grip. A

single hand groped down and braced me. I swung my good leg up and it caught. Then the hand from above began to pull and I rolled over the edge with open, gasping mouth pressed against the stone surface of the pier. I could see the man who had pulled me as a hazy, unreal figure swaying near me. He had only used one hand because the other had been shot away. I never knew his name, never even knew his nationality because just then a bullet struck my injured foot. I was sprawling in the dirt, crawling again.

Disher took cover behind a pile of timber where perhaps the same sniper wounded him again, this time in the buttocks. Later another group of survivors named the men they claim to have seen being machine-gunned in the water. 'Lieutenant George Lawrence of Cadiz, Kentucky was killed as he swam,' Disher would write in a piece for *Collier's*, then at the peak of its popularity and selling over 2.5 million copies a week. 'And so died Lieutenant Charles D. Buckley of Princeton, New Jersey and Lieutenant C. Browning of Bowling Green, Kentucky.' Perplexed and grieving parents, who imagined their sons had gone off to fight the Germans, were left to wonder whenever this cruel war with France had started.

Once they were face to face with the French the survivors were almost invariably well treated. After a long moment, when weapons were cocked and they were dazzled by flashlights, the men on the pier were picked up by a foot patrol. One of them managed a fireman's lift and single-handedly carried the broken and bleeding Disher to a field dressing station. Later, in a long ward of mostly Allied casualties, a French nurse placed a cigarette between Disher's lips while a doctor examined the reporter's twenty-six wounds: eleven from gunshots and the rest shrapnel. When these had been dressed he was put into a bed and tried to get some sleep but found this difficult because Oran's forts were now coming under close bombardment from the 15-inch guns on the shallow-draught monitor HMS *Roberts* with the battleships *Rodney* and *Duke of York* occasionally joining in from further out. The whole building shook though they were assured they were well out of danger. A visiting French officer told the Americans and British in the ward: 'Soon we shall all be your prisoners.'

The survivors of the late Colonel Marshal's battalion (his body was never found) did not feel much like they were about to become victors. Nor in Algiers did Svenson's Singing Third, the majority of whom were being marched into captivity. The exception were fifteen killed and about sixty who had managed to scramble back aboard HMS *Broke* which had hung around the harbour being intermittently shelled by the overlooking clifftop batteries without much effect until 9.20 a.m. when she was hit by a salvo of five 8-inch shells.

Badly listing and on fire, she staggered back out to sea with nine crew killed and about twenty wounded, including her surgeon who had lost an arm and was taking morphine while instructing the surviving sick berth attendant on amputation. The destroyer HMS *Zetland* rushed up to provide cover with her 4.7-inch guns, put down a smoke screen and take *Broke* under tow. But a heavy sea came up and it was obvious that the old destroyer was never going to reach Gibraltar. Once the wounded had been transferred GIs and sailors jumped onto mattresses and hammocks spread onto *Zetland*'s forecastle which then put *Broke* out of her misery with a couple of shallow-fused depth charges.

When Lieutenant Commander Layard had blown the agreed recall signal on *Broke*'s siren, on shore Colonel Svenson had not been too downhearted that he and most of his men had been unable to fight their way over open dockland to the ship. Almost everything that could go wrong had gone wrong. Half his command had never got ashore when the damaged *Malcolm* had withdrawn; another sixty had departed with the *Broke*. And it was only too apparent that the batteries above the harbour had certainly not been dealt with, as planned, by Commando parties coming from the beaches. Nor did the landings either side of the city appear to have drawn defenders away from the harbour as one rosy British scenario they had heard in Gibraltar had suggested. But he still had over 200 men with him on the Môle Louis Billiard and, though he suspected the French outnumbered them by at least twice that, they contented themselves with sniping or sneaking close enough to throw a grenade. Furthermore, the British Fleet Air Arm had given him some support and bombed at least one battery into silence.

There was still a good chance, he thought, that any moment the good old 168th Infantry Regiment, part of the Iowa National Guard, would arrive from their beach landing. There would be a flurry of shots and there they would be, large as life and twice as ugly, and they would all be joshing and laughing and saying, where the hell have you boys been? What Svenson had not expected were tanks. They were the ubiquitous Renault R35s, the same little two-man machines with the thick armour, 37mm cannon and Riebling machine gun that had made such inroads into the British infantry in Syria.

Some American battalions had been given the new Bazooka, the world's first hand-held rocket-propelled anti-tank weapon but this only seems to have applied to Patton's infantry which had come directly from America. Certainly the Singing Third were not among the Bazooka-blessed. All they had were a few rifle grenades, a cumbersome weapon shot from a special discharger screwed into the muzzle. Some of these rifle grenades were allegedly armour-piercing but so was the British Boys rifle and neither could make a hole in an R35. When they had used them all up, and the tanks and the infantry were getting closer, Svenson gave the order to fix bayonets. Then he came to his senses and surrendered. It was 12.30 p.m. over three hours since the *Broke* sailed away and he had thirty-three wounded men on his hands. In the course of patting their prisoners down for hidden weapons Senegalese soldiers removed watches, cigarette cases and lighters until Svenson complained and their French officers made them give them all back.

Thanks to the British attempt to emulate the Royal Marines' success in Madagascar, the Allies' first public appearance in French North Africa was in the guise of dazed captives, some half-naked survivors covered in oil and blood. A less public humiliation was the total failure of Operation Villain, the war's first American airborne operation and the longest reach ever attempted by any of the combatants – the record being held by Germany with its 1941 leap from Greece to Crete.

From the beginning the British had been as vehemently opposed to Operation Villain as the Americans had been to Reservist and Terminal, saying that it was a waste of valuable resources better employed trying to get to Tunisia before the Germans. But Clark, who favoured an all-American act of derring-do, urged Eisenhower to go ahead. And shortly after 9 p.m. on Saturday, 7 November, 556 American paratroopers in thirty-nine twin-engined United States Army Air Force C-47 transports (Dakotas to the British) left RAF airfields near Land's End and headed due south for a dropping zone over 1,000 miles away.

They were commanded by Lieutenant-Colonel Edson T. Raff whose orders were to secure two Vichy air bases south of Oran: La Sénia and Tafaraoui. Originally they had been going to leave four hours earlier to be in time to drop at first light. But they had been wrongly informed that there would be no resistance and the drop time had been put back four hours to give them a more friendly time of arrival.

Their night flight would take them over Franco's neutral Spain but long before they got there strong winds over the Bay of Biscay scattered a formation flown mostly by pilots and navigators not long out of training. This might have been righted if a signal pad error on somebody's part had not resulted in a British anti-aircraft cruiser, which was 35 miles off Oran, being instructed to transmit a prearranged homing beacon on the wrong frequency. Even worse was the frustration of one of Murphy's American agents who had succeeded, at considerable risk to himself and his French accomplices, in planting a 9-foot-tall beacon antenna almost on Tafaraoui airfield itself. Unfortunately, he had not been informed about the decision to put back the original zero hour by four hours. When, well after dawn and after a cold and sleepless night spent ensuring that the wireless beacon was working, the paratroopers had still failed to arrive, the mast had been dismantled and its operators returned to Oran.

By now none of Colonel Raff's battalion were where they should have been though some had done better than others. Four of the C-47s, lost and running out of fuel, had put down on the first runway they saw which left over 100 men interned in Spanish Morocco for the next three months. Two more landed at Fez which was at least French Morocco. One aircraft, its crew glad to be alive after a bumpy and vomitous night, looked down, saw Gibraltar and stopped for coffee and directions. Most ended up making forced landings somewhere in Algeria and usually quite close to the airfields that were their objective, three having been convincingly shot at while flying over La Sénia. Some crew and soldiers were captured and taken to Oran's Fort Philippe where they met the survivors, American and British, from the *Walney* and the *Hartland* and learned how much worse it could have been. Six Dewoitine fighters caught another three of the defenceless C-47s in the air, followed them down to where they had hastily landed more or less intact then continued to machine-gun them on the ground leaving five dead and fifteen wounded.

Raff, whose aircraft was flown by the mission's senior pilot, had rounded up nine of his scattered herd and was looking for more when he spotted a dozen or so parked C-47s huddled by the side of a dry lake. Steadily approaching them were several menacing columns of dust which the Colonel rightly assumed to be made by tanks. Raff informed the other aircraft by radio that a parachute diversion was required. He jumped first, landed hard, cracked a rib and, as some 120 men and their weapon containers floated down beside him, discovered that the tanks were American Stuarts making for the same airfields they were supposed to capture. They followed their tracks. Operation Villain was over.

Operations Terminal, Reservist and Villain were all costly and unnecessary frills. The spectacular failure of the first two might have given the French so much encouragement it could have been the undoing of Operation Torch or at least brought about the kind of prolonged resistance seen in Syria. It was as well for Murphy that he was unaware of these failures. As it was, isolated at Général Juin's Villa des Oliviers with his imagination running riot for twelve nerve-racking hours, Torch certainly did not seem the almost sure thing it had done after the Clark-Mast meeting at Cherchell. 'Giraud is not your man,' Darlan said to him at one point. 'Politically he's a child. He is just a good divisional commander, nothing more.'

At about 3 a.m. his relations with Darlan and the others, which had become quite cordial, had been badly undermined by the unexpected appearance at the villa of about forty of the white arm-banded insurgents commanded by an *aspirant*, a ranker who had been selected as a potential officer cadet. Since the SOE had failed to deliver they were armed with a variety of weapons, some of possible interest to collectors. Nonetheless, the Senegalese guards were disarmed and the occupants of the house informed that no-one would be allowed to leave apart from the US Consulate General whom they were there to protect.

So now the two most important men in Vichy French North Africa were prisoners. Murphy thought the insurgents' leader a 'courageous youth' – *aspirants* were rarely more than 21 – but he was unable to convince Darlan and Juin that he had been no more aware that this was going to happen than they were. Largely ignored by the French officers, the American was left to pace miserably up and down. On both sides the smoking was industrial.

Then at about 6.30 a.m. there were sounds of commotion and a couple of shots outside and at first the diplomat thought the US cavalry had at last arrived and went out to welcome them. It turned out to be another changing of the guard. About fifty Gardes Mobiles, well-armed para-military police, had arrested or chased away the *aspirant* and his men who, like the rest of French Algeria's Cinderella underground, had been assured that the Americans would replace them long before the dawn revealed they were not properly dressed for the ball. Murphy and his deputy Keith Pendar, who was hoping they would not find the pistol he was carrying, were roughed up then shoved at gunpoint into a hut the Senegalese, who had magically reappeared, used as their guard post.

The Gardes had been led by Major Dorange, Juin's aide, who was incensed that his général had been taken prisoner and arrived brandishing a large old-fashioned revolver and threatening to kill 'that cochon Jean Rigault', the former journalist who was the best known of the underground leaders. Rigault may have been a handy whipping boy but it seems that most of Dorange's immediate anger was aimed at Murphy, the man who had abused his friendship and trust by pledging, 'We will not come unless you summon us.' Truth is, of course, often cited as war's first casualty and this carefully planted piece of disinformation, which had been swallowed whole by Darlan, had been of enormous help to the Allied cause. 'Dorange and I had been good friends,' Murphy admitted in his memoirs. 'But he was understandably aggrieved to be caught unawares by the Allied landings and he told me sternly I was under arrest.'

Dorange had already had a small measure of revenge. He was responsible for the manhandling the American diplomats had received when his rescue party arrived. Uncertain of the Gardes' loyalty, Dorange had briefed them that the Axis had invaded Tunisia and that Général Juin was about to be kidnapped by German agents. After a few minutes people began to calm down. Amiral Fenard saw to it that the diplomats were released from their hut in the grounds. Darlan, also newly liberated now that the *aspirant* and his followers had disappeared, instructed Fenard to keep an eye on them while he and Juin went to army headquarters at Fort L'Empereur to find out what was happening. Darlan's parting shot to the Americans was that he had 'grave doubts' about their story. Murphy, deeply troubled by the continued absence of US troops in his life, did not blame him.

Then, not all that long after they had left, Fenard received a telephone call from Juin. It was all true. The Americans were landing in force up and down the Algerian and Moroccan coasts.

Chapter Twenty-Nine

Around Algiers alone, on the landing beaches west and and east of it, some 35,000 Allied troops were ashore. True, some had not landed as close to the city as they were supposed to and a few had drowned or been cast up by the surf *sans* rifles after their landing craft capsized. Six of the flat-bottomed vessels, 2 miles off course and carrying British Commandos, drifted up to Ilot de la Marine, a little Ottoman fort joined to the rest of Algiers harbour by a causeway, and at least three were sunk. Among the dead was a major who had distinguished himself in the raid on Vaagso in Norway in December 1941. Others were taken prisoner.

But this kind of bad luck was rare. Along the beaches the French had been badly outnumbered and had none of the advantages they had enjoyed at Algiers harbour when the *Walney* and the *Hartland* tried to bluff their way in. Resistance had been at the most disjointed and often, thanks to Mast's band of conspirators, nonexistent. 'Gentlemen, you are late,' Major Pierre Baril greeted the Iowans of the 168th Regiment when they came ashore at Fort de Sidi Ferruch, in 1830 the same place Amiral Guy-Victor Duperré had chosen to start the French conquest of Algeria. The 168th were the second wave. Two hours earlier Major Baril had handed over the fort to some Commandos only to have them press on to Blida airfield after General Mast had turned up in person to urge them to get there fast. His man at Blida needed some support and the airfield was important. Apart from denying it to L'Armée de L'Air it was where Giraud was supposed to fly in. At this point Mast's scruples about dealing with *les anglais* appear to have vanished.

Infantry battalions from the Northamptonshires, Lancashire Fusiliers and East Sussex had been landed at the village of Castiglione about 6 miles away from Sidi Ferruch where they discovered that another congenial French officer had made certain that his Tirailleurs would do nothing to hinder them. With their artillery and logistical support, most of which had yet to land, they numbered 7,230 men and were part of Major General Vyvyan Evelegh's 78th Division. Evelegh's main job was to try to get to Tunisia before the Germans did. Dealing with the French would be left to the Americans who would be providing most of the Allied army of occupation in the rest of French North Africa only they could not, of course, call it that.

When Darlan returned to Juin's house at about three o'clock his mood had changed considerably. The first thing he did was to ask Murphy to find Major General Charles Ryder, senior American officer in the Algiers sector, and bring him to Fort L'Empereur to discuss the terms of a local ceasefire with himself and Juin. Presumably, he had learned Ryder's name from the signed leaflets the Fleet Air Arm were dropping, announcing that the Americans had come as friends. Darlan told Murphy that he believed Ryder could be found on or near a beach about 10 miles west of Algiers and he would provide the diplomat with General Juin's car and his driver to get there.

By now the neighbourhood was getting dangerous. There was what Murphy called 'a volume of brisk small arms fire' around the house as elements of the 168th, running, taking cover and firing, finally skirmished their way into town half a day overdue. Their casualties were not so much heavy as significant: the 1st Battalion had just lost its commander, Lieutenant Colonel Edward Doyle, shot in the back by a sniper at the entrance of the governor's summer palace where a po-faced Arab gate-keeper was refusing admission on the grounds that His Excellency was 'at the beach'. A French Red Cross ambulance was touring the streets, its crew picking up wounded on both sides. And gathered on balconies were groups of *colons* still in their Sunday best, though the main morning mass was long over and some had not dared go out to it. Certainly, they would never see another Sunday like this one.

Before they drove off Murphy walked out of the gates of Villa des Oliviers and saw some American soldiers 'hugging the wall and firing in our direction'. The diplomat went back to the car, which was flying a French Tricolour and a large white flag, and told Juin's chauffeur to drive slowly towards them. The soldiers stopped firing and waited, some aiming at the car.

> I came up to them, introduced myself, maintained a respectful distance as ordered by the young lieutenant in command and shouted an explanation of the circumstances. The lieutenant asked me to repeat the story slowly. Then, apparently convinced that it was not a ruse, he allowed me to walk up to him. I asked his name and he replied, 'Lieutenant Gieser.' I could not help but smile and say, 'You're the best looking geezer I've seen for a long time.' That seemed to convince him that I was a bona fide American. He detailed one of his men to accompany me and we went down to the landing beach without further incident.

At the beach the first person Murphy met, dressed in US Army Ranger uniform, was the brave, intelligent and drunken (though possibly not on this occasion) Captain Randolph Churchill, only son of Britain's Prime Minister and close friend of the almost equally drunken Evelyn Waugh. It was just over two years since Churchill and the novelist Waugh had made their military debut in the humiliating attempt to replace the Vichy French with de Gaulle in Dakar. During that time Churchill had served with a Commando detachment at Tobruk and, more usefully, as the press officer when Britain followed up its success in Iraq by invading Persia and toppling its pro-German Shah. Now he was the intelligence officer in a Commando brigade that was the most composite Anglo-American unit in Operation Torch in which US Rangers trained by the Commandos were going into action with them. After the Allies had gone to enormous lengths to make Operation Torch as American as possible, nobody seems to have disputed the wisdom of risking a Churchill becoming a captive of the French.

Much to Murphy's delight, the famous son greeted him effusively. 'He seemed to know about me and said something to the effect that the British diplomatic service could do with a few like me. I considered that quite a compliment.' These pleasantries over, he led Murphy through the beach-head's bewildering mass of shouting men and revving vehicles to where Major General Charles Wolcott Ryder, commander of the 34th US Infantry Division, was sitting on a rock trying to dictate a despatch. The general's words were coming out slowly and in the wrong order and he kept having to start again. Ryder, who was 50, was exhausted. He explained to Murphy that he had not slept properly for a week, a condition with which the diplomat had some empathy, and would need to finish his message for Eisenhower and get into a fresh uniform before he met any French officers. Luckily Murphy was as tall as most generals and had a commanding presence. 'I took him by the arm, gently but firmly and we were in the car and on our way to Fort L'Empereur.'

At the fort, solid nineteenth-century symbol of colonial rule, the French had laid on a little military pageant as if they were determined to show these Americans the way real soldiers behaved. Even before Ryder had arrived a French bugler blowing the *cessez-le-feu* had mounted the running board of the borrowed car he and Murphy were travelling in. And when they halted outside the fort they were greeted by a staff officer whose role was to surrender to Ryder the sword he was wearing for the occasion. It was proffered hilt first. Vice-Consul Pendar, who was also in attendance, was reminded of paintings he had seen of sixteenth-century sea captains surrendering their dismasted ships.

Once inside, they were ushered into a kind of great hall decorated with trophies of both chase and battlefield: the magnificent curved horns on the severed heads of the Nubian ibex which must be stalked in the high slopes of the Atlas Mountains, Arab and Berber armour and weaponry, the Spahis' crossed and pennoned lances. Darlan and Juin, the latter in full dress uniform with a red sash about his middle, were standing at the end of a large table that had been covered in green baize. Around them stood about fifty French officers. As the Americans entered the room bombs from another Fleet Air Arm strike seemed to land quite close by in a long, rumbling explosion.

'How wonderful!' gasped Ryder, rumpled but gun-dog friendly. 'This is the first time since 1918 that I've been under fire.' No doubt the general thought it a good moment to remind the French that they had once all been brothers in arms but his audience looked about as receptive as the heads on the wall.

'A moment of icy silence followed,' recorded Murphy. Then, in his indomitable way, he proceeded to break this *froideur* by introducing Ryder to Darlan and Juin just as if nothing untoward had been said before getting on with the business of interpreting terms and conditions.

Within a remarkably short time it was agreed that Ryder would assume responsibility for law and order in Algiers, providing the local gendarmes came under his control. French troops would return to barracks but be allowed to retain their arms. All prisoners would be released immediately. Most of them were Colonel Svenson's Singing Third and those British Commandos who had survived the sinking of their landing craft when they strayed too close to Ilot de la Marine. Allied forces would enter the city centre at 8 p.m. A short document was drawn up and there was some delay while it was typed out. Then Juin and Ryder signed as respective commanders of the ground forces and Darlan and Murphy witnessed it.

It was a local ceasefire. There had been no more than a tentative agreement on the part of Darlan and Juin to try to expand it to the rest of French North Africa. For the moment it did not apply to Oran or Casablanca around where there were soldiers and sailors on both sides who would be looking at their last sunset that evening. Nonetheless, it was a good start.

Certainly, back in Gibraltar General Giraud thought so, for when he heard the news he stopped demanding Eisenhower's job, agreed to settle for the American terms and become commander of the French military in Algeria, Morocco and Tunisia. On the morning of Monday, 9 November General Mast arranged for a French aircraft at Blida airfield to pick him up in Gibraltar and bring him back there. Eisenhower heaved a sigh of relief. 'It can be expected that his presence there will bring about a cessation of scattered resistance which is tragic among soldiers who have the same enemy,' the supreme commander announced in a wildly optimistic press statement. Not that anybody could blame him for hoping that the wish might fulfil the deed. Privately he was telling people, 'these Frogs are driving me mad'.

Vichy Radio responded by calling Giraud 'a rebel chief and a felon' who had broken his oath as an officer for, it emerged, after his escape and reception in Vichy he had been persuaded to write a letter to Pétain promising never to do anything to embarrass him. The broadcast insults had been attributed to the maréchal himself though the vocabulary sounds much more like Laval.

The Prime Minister, holder of the portfolios for both foreign and internal affairs, had arrived in Vichy from his home in nearby Châteldon at 4.15 on the morning of the invasion. The rest of the Cabinet were also assembling and, for once, glad to see him. The first decision they made was not to wake Pétain before 7 a.m. He was obviously in for a long day. Next on the agenda was replying to a message from Roosevelt explaining that the invasion was for 'the liberation of France and its Empire from the Axis yoke'. Under Laval's direction, they had drafted a reply in a fair pastiche of the maréchal's style.

> It is with stupor and grief that I learned during the night of the aggression of your troops against North Africa ... I have always declared that we would defend our empire if we were attacked. You knew that we would defend it against any aggressor whoever he might be. You knew I would keep my word. France and her honour are at stake. We are attacked. We shall defend ourselves. This is the order I am giving.

Once he was up and about, Pétain approved the draft and shortly after 9 a.m. received Pinckney Tuck, the career diplomat made US chargé d'affaires following Ambassador Leahy's departure. Tuck was handed a copy of the message to Roosevelt. But when he rose to leave the maréchal shook him warmly by the hand, looked at him 'steadfastly and smiling', escorted him to the antechamber then, as the bemused Tuck later reported to Washington, 'turned briskly back to his office humming a little tune'. Hardly the action of a man consumed by 'stupor or grief' but typical perhaps of the false trails laid by this vacillating old soldier who could not bring himself to part from anyone on less than amiable terms.

It would be the chargé d'affaire's last meeting with the hero of Verdun. Later that day Vichy broke off diplomatic relations with Washington and Tuck was packing his bags and hoping he would get out of town and across the Spanish border before the Germans arrived. All the resident diplomats in Vichy knew that the chances of Pétain's kingdom maintaining its distinct and separate entity as an unoccupied zone free of Axis troops now hung by a thread. There could only be one German response to the loss of a neutral French North Africa and that was to occupy the south of France and ensure that the Côte d'Azur came under the firm embrace of Festung Europe. The terms of the Franco-German Armistice Agreement of July 1940 may have lasted longer than the Munich Agreement but now they were unravelling fast.

At 12.15 a.m. on Monday the 9th, not quite twenty-four hours since the Torch landings began, Berlin had delivered an ultimatum to the French delegation at the Armistice Commission in Wiesbaden. It gave them one hour to agree to allow Axis aircraft the use of bases in Tunisia to attack the Allied build-up in neighbouring Algeria. Just before the time expired Laval telephoned Wiesbaden and instructed them to say yes, a formality it would have been useless to deny. There was no way the lack of a Vichy French permission would have been allowed to cause a threat to Rommel's rear. As it was, U-boats and Luftwaffe units based on Sicily and normally employed against Malta were already beginning to inflict casualties on the massive Allied fleets assembled for Operation Torch. Among their victims would be the monitor HMS *Roberts* whose twin 15-inch guns were silenced when she was hit by two 500–kilo bombs in a Stuka attack and had to retire from the fray for extensive repairs.

By the late afternoon of the 9th, Laval was on his way to Munich having been summoned to meet Hitler there at 11 p.m. En route he was to break his journey at the Dijon préfecture where he would be meeting Ambassador Abetz from Paris who was to accompany him.

Laval had mixed feelings about this meeting. Apart from Doriot and the other French Nazis in Paris with their mystical yearning to be swallowed whole by the New Order, he had always been the most ardent exponent of collaboration. On 22 June, the first anniversary of the start of the war against Stalin's Russia, he had, in a broadcast speech, gone further than he had ever gone before, declaring: 'I desire the victory of Germany, for without it, Bolshevism would install itself everywhere.' The shock waves had gone round the world and made it even harder for Roosevelt to maintain diplomatic relations with Vichy and keep Robert Murphy in place for Operation Torch.

On previous occasions Laval had always welcomed encounters with Hitler as opportunities to try to convince him to make a permanent peace with France which would include the kind of economic and political concessions that would make its citizens welcome it. Even now, there was some consolation in knowing that France and its empire had, if only momentarily, eclipsed Russia in Berlin's immediate priorities. Otherwise, he knew that these were dire circumstances and the repercussions could be grave.

Would Hitler believe that Darlan, as appeared to be the case, had accidentally found himself in Algiers at the eve of the Anglo-American action? Even worse, that when he did find himself there he was incapable of rallying the troops for even twenty-four hours before calling for a local ceasefire? A ceasefire that might well prove to be contagious and deliver the whole of French North Africa into the enemy camp? 'What price would Hitler force France to pay for the desertion of an army whose chiefs and officer cadres had, for the most part, been released from the German prison camps?' wrote Laval in an account of his thoughts before this meeting.

And there was another problem. Shortly after he heard the news of the landings Laval had suggested to Baron Krugg von Nidda, German consul general in Vichy, that Germany should respond by declaring its recognition of all French territory, whether overseas or metropolitan France with the exception of the disputed provinces of Alsace and Lorraine which the Germans would never give up. It was not long before von Nidda was back with a reply.

Chancellor Hitler wanted to know whether, 'in view of the latest Anglo-Saxon aggression', the French government was now disposed to fight the Allies on Germany's side? Merely breaking diplomatic relations with Washington would not be good enough. What was needed was a clear-cut commitment. If it got that, said Hitler, Germany was prepared to 'march side by side with France through thick and thin'.

But Laval did not exactly want to march with Germany. What he envisaged, and what he thought France would accept, was to march behind it. Be part of its prosperous baggage train, a well-disposed neutral cheering it on rather like the Americans had done for Britain before Pearl Harbor, though instead of supplying the tools France would donate its skilled labour. Of course, there would always be small groups of Frenchmen such as the Légion des Volontaires Français contre le Bolchevisme fighting alongside the Germans just as some neutral Americans had flown with the RAF. What there would not be, could not be, was any question of France becoming a co-belligerent, the fourth member of the Axis. The French people were simply not ready for it and Laval knew he was unpopular enough already.

His reply to von Nidda had been evasive. He was, of course, grateful for the Führer's generous offer, would do his best to persuade the maréchal etcetera, but there would certainly be problems with the rest of the Cabinet. When Abetz met Laval at Dijon on the afternoon of the 9th the German ambassador expressed surprise and concern that there had not been an outright acceptance of Hitler's offer. Abetz acted as if he would somehow get the blame for not being persuasive enough in the past. They had known each other for almost two years now and were almost friends. But this cast a shadow on their journey.

At dusk they entered the Black Forest. The trees already held a little snow and were pleasing to look at. Laval, chain-smoking as usual, was worrying what sort of reception he was going to get. How offended would Hitler be at the French failure to jump at his offer to become a fighting ally? Or had Darlan made it irrelevant by already making an unconditional surrender of the rest of French North Africa to the Anglo-Americans? Pulled the rug from under his feet? Darlan had been sent a message saying: 'As the head of government is at present away no negotiations must take place until he returns.' But Laval did not trust Darlan. After all, he was virtually a prisoner. As soon as they got into Munich he would have to call his office for an update and risk sharing the information with the German telephone monitors.

Then they ran into the first serious blizzard of the year and the drivers of the two cars, hardly able to see and fearful of a skid, slowed to a crawl and sometimes stopped altogether. Laval and Abetz, travelling in the same car for company, leaning away from each other in the back seat, overcoats buttoned and belted, tried to sleep, then gave up, smoked and talked about the Jewish problem. At the end of June Himmler had decreed that all French Jews must be deported. By September 27,000 had gone, 9,000 from the unoccupied zone. Laval was trying to avoid deporting the zone's French Jews by rounding up all the foreign ones, the pre-war asylum seekers. 'Every time a foreign Jew leaves our territory it's one more gained for France,' he had told a private meeting of prefects, all from the south of France. Abetz warned him the numbers leaving the unoccupied areas were not enough to satisfy the SS. Couldn't they strip some of the more recently nationalized French Jews of their citizenship? Laval pointed out that he was already making up the numbers by insisting that the children of the foreign Jews go with them. This was not required but he didn't think children should be separated from their parents. He had told an American Quaker protesting at the deportations that 'these foreign Jews had always been a problem'. He was grateful that the Germans were giving them a chance to get rid of them. Laval was under the impression that the Germans were 'setting up a Jewish state in Poland'. This is what he said.

They eventually got into Munich at 5 a.m., six hours after the meeting was scheduled. Abetz was informed that Hitler would see them at 8 a.m. Count Ciano, Mussolini's Foreign Secretary and son-in-law, would also be there. They would not have much time to catch up on any sleep.

Laval called his office in Vichy. He learned that Darlan had not extended the ceasefire to Oran or Casablanca and Pétain was about to send him another telegram. The contents were read out to him and anybody else who happened to be listening. 'I issued orders to resist the aggressor. That order still stands.'

'Tell the maréchal that he has once again saved France,' said the Prime Minister. Then he went to see Hitler.

Off Oran the ships that had so severely punished the old US Coast Guard cutters *Walney* and the *Hartland* for their impudent scheme had resisted the aggressor for the last time. At 9.22 a.m. on Monday the 9th Capitaine de frégate Laurin was told to take the *Epervier* and *Typhon* to sea immediately and 'sailing as a group make for the most favourable port in Metropolitan France'. His orders came from Amiral Jacques Moreau, the man who had interrupted Darlan's dinner with Juin and Fenard with alarmist talk of an armada gathering offshore.

Laurin called on board Capitaine de corvette Abgrail, the commander of the *Typhon*, and they confirmed the plan which, expecting these orders, they had discussed over dinner the night before. Both men knew that the odds were against them. Their best hope was that a haze on the horizon would reduce visibility and keeping close to land would blur their outline. If it did they might just be able to show the English a clean pair of heels.

In 1940 the *Strasbourg* had got away with something similar when she made her famous dash from Mers-el-Kébir and a battle cruiser was a much bigger target. But then Admiral Somerville had had nowhere near as many ships at his disposal. And *Strasbourg* had all her boilers firing. Only two of *Epervier*'s four were working because the others were waiting for parts from France. All the fuses had been removed from the depth charges on their sterns to reduce the chances of them being detonated by a lucky shot, the fate of the *Mogador* at Mers-el-Kébir. Laurin made it clear that, as far as he was concerned, it would not be a suicide mission. If they were blocked by superior forces they would break off contact and return.

They left Oran at 10 a.m., the *Epervier* in the lead, heading steadily due north through a Mediterranean beginning to wear its brief winter greyness with useful fog banks here and there. Their luck held for almost an hour. Then three Fleet Air Arm Fulmar fighters and an Albacore flew over them, also on a northerly bearing, presumably returning to their carrier and too low on fuel to make a closer investigation. Nonetheless, they had to assume they had been spotted and plotted and Laurin ordered a change in course to the west.

Shortly afterwards his lookouts began to report ships on his port, seaward side but some distance away. They were heading towards the *Epervier* on a parallel course. By 11 a.m., with about 16,000 yards between them, they were identified as a mixed force of cruisers and destroyers. A Walrus seaplane, a type the Royal Navy used as gunnery spotters, flew around them in long, high circles well out of anti-aircraft range. Laurin again changed course, this time to the east, and his ship began to work up to as many knots as half her boilers could produce. It was not the 36 knots her full complement of four might have yielded; but slowly she began to lose the cruisers, which showed no interest in matching their change of course, and faded into the haze on their port side.

The relief this must have brought was short-lived. At 11.20 a.m. Laurin had just ordered a resumption of their northern course when the bridge was informed that a British light cruiser was astern of them starboard and closing fast. No Vichy French ships had radar and the lookouts had failed to spot the stalking cruiser coming from the landward side, her outline broken up by black and white zigzag camouflage stripes. For Laurin this was a very nasty shock indeed. It meant that they were almost surrounded. He decided to get back to Oran before they were cut off. *Epervier* and *Typhon* leaned into the kind of tight U-turns destroyer captains only dream about in peacetime, sending men and everything else not tied down flying.

At 11.23 the cruiser, now on their port side, opened fire. Laurin, in a report written five days later, could appreciate another professional. 'The enemy's first salvo (12 rounds) was perfectly grouped but overshot us by about 100 metres. The second salvo was about 50 metres short, the third bracketed us. The enemy guns were perfectly fired with only a weak dispersion.'

The French ships had come up against HMS Aurora, flagship of Captain Sir William Gladstone Agnew who, at not quite 44, was the commander of Force K. This was a mixed force of cruisers and destroyers that terrorized Axis transports to Africa. Exactly a year ago to the day Agnew had sunk in a night action an entire Italian-German convoy of seven ships plus one of its destroyer escorts. In one blow Rommel lost 18,000 tons of fuel oil, 35,000 tons of munitions and over 700 new vehicles. Agnew gained an instant knighthood, a reflection of the contribution he was considered to have made to the Afrika Korp's (temporary) departure from Tobruk and the rest of Cyrenaica. The Italians eventually got their revenge with a clever mines ambush. Force K lost a cruiser and a destroyer and *Aurora* had been badly damaged. She was now not long out of dry dock in Liverpool where she had acquired her distinctive fresh coat of zebra war paint.

Naval gunnery was Agnew's main maritime passion: he had been a senior instructor in it. What better way to celebrate the first anniversary of his greatest triumph than balancing the books against La Marine Française who, in the last twenty-four hours, had sunk three of the Royal Navy's ships and damaged a fourth at no loss to themselves? Within twenty minutes *Aurora*'s 6-inch gun had almost reduced *Epervier* to a hapless hulk. One engine was knocked out, most of her guns out of action, her torpedo platforms wrecked, the officer in charge of them among the dead on the demolished gunnery bridge. From the port side HMS *Jamaica*, Agnew's other cruiser, and the destroyer *Brilliant* had closed in and engaged the *Typhon*, which was trying to keep them at bay with her 5.7-inch guns. *Epervier*'s gun crews had also been busy but they had been taking such violent evasive action there had been little chance of hitting the cruiser.

By now Laurin had given up all hope of getting his ship back into Oran harbour and decided to beach her below the cliffs at Cap de l'Aiguille where coastal batteries offered some protection. *Epervier*'s stern was well alight and small explosions were coming from the storerooms located there. The fire crew who had been trying to deal with it were among the latest casualties though the *Aurora*'s fire was becoming less accurate because the *Typhon*, which seemed to bear a charmed life, had managed to hide her crippled companion in a smoke screen. Even then, seconds before her keel scraped the beach, a shell stopped her last working engine. 'As we ran aground the ship was completely disabled,' reported Laurin. 'No engines, no steering, no electricity, no boilers and the fire was spreading forwards.'

Agnew edged a little closer to take a look but came under fire from a shore battery and withdrew. (There were probably few Royal Navy captains who could not recite Nelson's dictum: 'A ship's a fool that fights a fort.') Partly covered by her own smoke screen *Typhon* slipped away and back into harbour despite another encounter with the cruiser *Jamaica*, which at last did some serious damage. With most of his guns and engines out of action Capitaine de corvette Abgrail was ordered to scuttle his ship in the harbour's best navigable channel. Sharing the seabed not far away was what was left of the minesweeper *La Surprise* which was sunk along with her captain and about fifty crew when the destroyer *Brilliant* had hit her magazine.

Twenty-one had died on the *Epervier* but by the time she was beached Laurin's surviving crew could find only twelve of them. The other nine were either in those parts of the ship that were too hot to get to or had been blown overboard. Laurin got his dead and thirty-one wounded off then began to behave as if he were already on a hostile shore by seeing to it that anything that was salvageable was rendered useless. Wireless equipment and anti-aircraft machine guns were thrown overboard, firing pins removed from the 5.7-inch guns. Anything that might be of value to the Allies or, even worse, the dissident Gaullists was wrecked.

When they had finished Laurin decided that the *Epervier* deserved a final ceremony of the lowering of the colours. Petty officers arranged a flag party which stood stiffly to attention on her bows, the only habitable part of the ship. As the fire crept towards this last parade, its smoke already wafting around them, the colours were lowered then handed to her captain who carried them ashore. 'I made this decision because I did not want any enemy coming by land to take my flag as a trophy,' explained Laurin. 'I must make it clear that this ceremony was performed out of view of any enemy ship.'

For the moment Darlan was not going to be seen striking his colours either. In Algiers the local ceasefire was holding, the harbour open, and Allied troops and their equipment pouring in. But Murphy's hopes of swiftly enlarging this into a wider armistice that would embrace all of French North Africa had to be put on hold.

For all of the second day of the invasion, Monday, 9 November, while ships were sunk and men died in a dozen hard-fought little battles around Oran and Casablanca, Darlan could do nothing but wait and see what came out of Laval's meeting with Hitler in Munich. It was obvious that the politician would try to barter his permission for the Wehrmacht to move into as much of Tunisia as they needed – not just use its air bases – for a German promise that Vichy France itself remained an unoccupied zone. Darlan doubted whether it would succeed. It was hard to imagine Berlin would continue to leave the security of France's Mediterranean coast in the hands of its unreliable natives. He was surprised Hitler had not moved immediately. Darlan's last call to the Admiralty in Vichy before overseeing the Algiers ceasefire between Juin and Ryder was to enquire whether there was any sign of the panzer grenadiers yet.

Since he now regarded the Wehrmacht's arrival in the free zone as inevitable, Darlan must have been disappointed to be told there was no change. It would have left him free to negotiate a general ceasefire with the Allies because the Germans had broken the 1940 armistice. Nor would he be open to accusations that he had lost unoccupied France because he had failed to fight the Anglo-Americans hard enough. Instead he found himself in limbo and a limbo prolonged by bad weather across Europe.

In Germany's Black Forest Laval and Abetz were stuck in a blizzard and becoming hopelessly late for their appointment with Chancellor Hitler. General Clark was also late for a meeting with Amiral de la flotte Darlan. He was supposed to have left Gibraltar for Algiers soon after Giraud so that they would arrive there within minutes of each other and start talks with Darlan and Juin. But Giraud's aircraft was the last to take off that morning before gale-force Atlantic winds and rain closed down the Rock's airstrip for the next five hours.

Clark's second coming to North Africa was hardly any more comfortable than canoeing through the Atlantic breakers on Cherchell beach. At dusk *Red Gremlin*, his personal B-17 Flying Fortress, closely followed by another B-17 called *Boomerang*, at last touched down at Algiers's La Maison Blanche airport. On board the aircraft were all Clark's staff, the signallers and clerks manning his communcations centre, a defence platoon and a US Army film unit commanded by Colonel Darryl Zanuck, the Hollywood producer who for the first time in his movie career was shooting without a script. In case they were intercepted by the Luftwaffe the B-17s had been escorted by a squadron of Spitfires and crossed the Mediterranean from Gibraltar at a height that never exceeded 700 feet.

But after an uneventful flight this aerial caravan arrived just in time for the city's first air raid of the war. Murphy was waiting for Clark at the Hôtel Saint-Georges, a large and elegant *belle époque* establishment with a magnificent view of the bay. He estimated that about twenty-five German and Italian aircraft were involved and had watched as the pyrotechnics from the British fleet's combined anti-aircraft barrage 'threw the Arabs into a frenzy of excitement'. As an added treat a couple of Spitfires got behind a Junkers 88 and started to set it on fire.

Shortly afterwards Clark and some of his staff turned up at the Saint-Georges which, thanks to a very recent deal Murphy had struck with the *colon* millionaire who owned it, was about to become Allied Forces Headquarters. They had travelled from the airport in open-topped, tracked, British Bren-gun carriers which were the only vehicles with any armour plate available to bring them down from the airport. They were a little shaken up. Shortly after they had landed and disembarked from the *Red*

Gremlin a stick of three bombs exploded within 100 yards of the parked B-17's tail. This was followed by a burning Junkers in a near vertical death dive which seemed bent on taking them and their Bren-gun carriers with it. 'Our legs were over the sides and we were looking desperately for cover when the plane exploded into thousands of pieces in the air,' recounted a thankful Clark.

Then, as soon as Murphy had Clark to himself in his suite and stiff drinks were being poured, he started telling him about his negotiations with Darlan and Juin and dropped another kind of bombshell. 'How ironical it was, I remarked, that while Clark was arguing with Giraud in Gibraltar, events in Algiers were already rendering obsolete his Giraud agreement.'

Clark jumped. 'This really messes things up,' he said. And he proceeded to tell the diplomat about the statement Eisenhower had released that morning, saying that Giraud's presence would ensure 'a cessation of scattered resistance' and the excessive expectations it would arouse. The Supreme Commander was going to be made to look ridiculous. 'We've got to put Giraud back in the business right away.'

But Murphy knew that Kingpin was in no hurry for the Americans to restore him to his crown. Giraud's landing at Blida had been a miserable anticlimax. Instead of the conquering hero's welcome Mast and others had promised, he was received by a few furtive conspirators who, fearing he would get shot, spirited him away to the Arab quarter home of Jacques Lemaigre-Duibreuil, the peanut oil millionaire who had been the link between him and Murphy. Had the Americans arrived in Algiers and Oran in time to link up with the partisans' takeover of key points it might, in the initial euphoria successful revolution normally brings, have been different. But tentative contacts with senior soldiers, some of them old friends, had revealed to Giraud's astonishment that he was regarded at best as a dupe of the Anglo-Saxons and often no better than Vichy Radio's 'rebel chief and felon'.

Yet Giraud was not as bitter about this reaction as he was probably entitled to be. He empathized entirely with his brother officers' obsession with legality and chain of command, their fears that they would lose unoccupied France to the Germans and French North Africa to the Allies. Much to Murphy's relief, he fully understood how beneficial Darlan's accidental presence could be. Already he had expressed the hope that the amiral would consent to become something like North Africa's High Commissioner while he became overall commander of its French troops.

Murphy explained all this to Clark and also pleaded with him to make a bigger show of force in Algiers. There were fears that the more ardent Pétainists, realizing that the Allies were still weak in the city and heartened by the Axis air attacks, might renege on the local ceasefire. 'Run your tanks through the main streets. Give them a big parade.'

Clark promised to have all three of his tanks drive around town as soon as he could find them. Then he announced he would see Darlan in the morning, was going to get a good night's sleep and advised the diplomat, who was clearly in need of it, to do the same. Murphy later discovered that Clark's belief in the benefits of sleeping on a problem entailed posting a sentry close to wherever he was getting it with orders that he was only to be roused if the enemy was at the gates. But Murphy was not so fortunate. He had a lot of old friends in town who wanted to know if it was true the Americans were dealing with the arch-collaborator Darlan and not the hero Giraud.

> Having no such guardian or sensible rule of life, I stayed up that night of the 9th of November, my fourth successive night with little sleep. I conferred endlessly with our assorted French helpers who were excited and worried about the unexpected turn of events. I had to soothe them while trying to piece together from radio reports a coherent account of what was happening. Darlan also stayed up the whole of that night, in conferences and studying radio reports. He was hoping for some word from Pétain before his meeting with Clark, but no word came.

Laval had got nothing out of Hitler. The Führer had kept him waiting for two hours in an antechamber, trying to keep awake on ersatz coffee and tobacco, before calling him in and when he went through the door he saw that Count Ciano was still there. The interpreter was also a familiar face. Paul Schmidt had first translated for Laval in 1935 when he had visited Berlin as Minister for Foreign Affairs.

Much to his relief Hitler made no direct mention of his offer of an alliance with Germany. He started by announcing – with 'great vigour' according to Laval – that Germany and Italy intended to 'chase the Anglo-Saxons out of North Africa' and were going to do it quickly. (The Germans, and the Vichy French too, often referred to the Anglo-Americans as Anglo-Saxons, presumably inspired more by common language than genetic make-up.) This was followed by some sharp words about the apparent ease with which Général Giraud had been able to leave Vichy France and place himself at the disposal of the Allies.

'You must know that France, from this day forth, will be permitted to keep only those parts of her Empire which she is able to defend,' pronounced Hitler. So much for Laval's hopes that Germany might be prepared to guarantee all of France's borders, home and abroad. He had responded to this, perhaps it was lack of sleep, with a rambling discourse on his favourite theme: Europe's New Order, an entire continent organized for peace under German hegemony which would create 'a suitable atmosphere' by its just treatment of France. But though Hitler was not always averse to discussing the forthcoming National Socialist nirvana this was not the right day for it and Laval was reminded 'time was pressing'. They went on to the main business of the meeting: Tunisia.

'Is it possible to provide safe ports for disembarkation of Axis troops in Tunis and Bizerta? If it was not possible collaboration was over.'

Laval tried to exclude the Italians. The one thing that united the French regardless of their politics was that they all loathed the *macaronis* because in 1940 they had put the boot in after the Germans had wrestled the French to the ground. The politician in him surfaced like a cork and he carefully pointed out that a problem might arise about the inclusion of Count Ciano's people. Since the armistice, and even before, Italian press and radio had conducted a persistent campaign for the annexation of Tunisia, Corsica and Nice. Not surprisingly, France rejected all these demands and Laval said that, before it had been discussed in Vichy, he would not want to be accused of encouraging Italy's irredentism by allowing Mussolini's troops to enter French territory.

Hitler was unimpressed. In August he had told Dino Alfieri, Italy's ambassador to Germany, that the main difference between de Gaulle and Laval was that 'the former is simply trying to obtain by force what Laval seeks to get by cunning'. A judgement that would probably have stunned both parties. Now he was determined not to be taken in by this parliamentary hack and his crude attempts to divide the Axis. Who did he think he was? Before he left, Laval had agreed that Germany would deliver an ultimatum regarding their entry into Tunisia. The wording of Pétain's protest would be agreed with Berlin in advance.

Afterwards Laval, who was taking Ambassador Abetz's advice and spending the night in Munich in case Hitler wanted to see him again, called Vichy and told the navy what had been agreed about the Tunisian ports. Orders not to resist a German takeover were relayed to Amiral Derrien, the French commander at Bizerta by Amiral Gabriel Auphan, Minister of State for the Navy. 'Please believe me that I'm only thinking of France's ultimate benefit,' he told him. So now it was official. The French were resisting the Allies but not the Axis.

Darlan had arrived at his first meeting with Clark at the Hôtel Saint-Georges with a pantalooned ceremonial guard of Zouaves and flanked by four admirals and four generals. To greet them thirty or so helmeted American infantry had been stationed around the hotel. Unshaven and gum-chewing, with white salt water stains on their unshone boots, they were certainly not as smart as the Algerian soldiers, though perhaps the grenades clipped to their webbing and the obvious modernity of the fast-firing weapons they carried made them look a bit more useful. 'I was charged with fighting a war, or more specifically, with preventing a war against the French and getting on as rapidly as humanly possible with the war against the Axis in Tunisia,' said Clark. 'I wanted everybody to know that we meant business and I adopted a formal attitude.'

Formal was the last word Murphy, who was interpreting, would have chosen to describe Clark's negotiating technique as Eisenhower's deputy took his place at the head of the table in a small room off the hotel foyer. Most of the participants had a good view of the hotel's terraced garden with its flowering shrubs and palms. Inside, the atmosphere soon became anything but tranquil. Often Murphy had no need to translate.

> Clark didn't pretend to understand French politics, so he found a simplified view of French-American relations easy and rode roughshod over delaying tactics. In his reports to Eisenhower he made frequent use of their code word YBSOB: yellow bellied sons of bitches. In his opinion, any Frenchman who did not immediately support the Anglo-American expedition deserved this appellation. In like manner, Clark punctuated his negotiations with frequent table thumpings and colourful epithets in English, a language most of the French officers knew to some extent.

During one lull in the storm Darlan whispered to Murphy, 'Could I ask you a favour? Would you mind suggesting to Major-General Clark that I am a five star admiral. He should stop talking to me like a lieutenant junior grade.'

Why had Pétain's chosen successor, by his own description the Vichy dauphin, voluntarily submitted himself to this kind of humiliation? He could have remained aloof, allowed himself to be taken prisoner or fled to Morocco whose governor, Général Auguste Noguès, had rallied his troops and was making it plain to Patton that his Atlantic crossing would not end in a walkover. And from there he could, had he chosen, have slipped across the border into Spanish Morocco and returned to Vichy through Tangiers and Madrid.

Why now this softening towards the Allies? It was not six months since Darlan had dropped Laval a private note describing as 'moving and courageous' the bombshell planted in the Prime Minister's 22 June speech declaring his desire for a German victory. Before that, during his time as Laval's replacement, there had been his own more public toadying to Hitler, his obsessive Anglophobia, the German aircraft transiting through Vichy Syria on their way to bomb the British in Iraq. On 24 August 1942 *Life* magazine had listed Darlan as one of France's leading traitors. Yet by then his son Alain was assuring Murphy that this was all a front and he was convinced that the Allies would win. Even after the Torch landings, with Britain's church bells about to break the two-year silence imposed by their invasion warning role and ring out for El Alamein, the turn of the tide was not all that obvious to those caught up in the ebb and flow of events. Other British desert victories, admittedly not on the scale of El Alamein, had proved ephemeral. And if Russian resistance had stiffened at Stalingrad the Red Army had stiffened before only to be broken.

How much had really changed in the five months since Darlan congratulated Laval on his courageous speech? Or was it simply that he wanted to ensure that all doors remained open, the arch-opportunist guarding his opportunities? Clark points out that the Americans were not all that surprised to find Darlan in town and it is true that two days before the invasion Murphy notified the White House that Darlan had returned to Algiers to visit his dying son. The message was passed on to Roosevelt by Admiral Leahy, the former Vichy ambassador who was now his Chief of Staff. Once he learned what was wrong with Alain, Roosevelt asked Leahy, who had probably seen more of Darlan than any other living American, if he thought a personal letter to him from the President of the United States might be useful. Leahy thought it was a nice idea. But nothing was done immediately to exploit the Alain polio link. As far as the Americans were concerned, at that point Giraud was their man.

'It is quite possible that Darlan knew enough of our plans to be in Algiers at the right time,' Clark suggested later but this seems unlikely. Murphy, who knew the French North African scene better than anybody, certainly never seems to have thought so. As far as he was concerned it was a fluke, pure serendipity. As Darryl Zanuck was finding out, war was full of these unscripted moments Hollywood could not make up.

Darlan himself, never a very religious man or given to great modesty either, unhesitatingly put his presence down to divine intervention. 'My son nearly died and this is why I was in Africa on 8 November,' he would write to Leahy. 'Is God's hand to be seen in that? It is my deeply held conviction that it is.'

Undoubtedly, having his wife and his only child with him was an advantage. He was unused to the long partings of seagoing sailors. There were comfortable quarters in Toulon they would miss and a family home in Nérac. But whatever happened he and Berthe would be together to look after Alain. To that extent he had already left Vichy.

Nonetheless, it soon became apparent that Darlan, thinking on his feet, had a firm idea of what he wanted to achieve. His priority was to discover a modus vivendi whereby he could preserve the Pétainist hierarchy in French North Africa and weed out all the dissidents Murphy had suborned. Général Mast for example. This would be a military government uncontaminated by the likes of Laval. He would probably also be able to bring over Dakar and the rest of Governor Boisson's French West Africa. Whether he could get hold of the fleet in Toulon he did not really know, though he was trying to give the Americans the impression that he could. In any event, they would have a much bigger army and, with any luck, navy than de Gaulle who would be left to wither on the vine in London with his British paymasters. Whereas he would have the support of the Americans who, up until two days ago, still had diplomatic relations with Vichy France.

To achieve all this Darlan had to give Clark the ceasefire he needed to pursue the war in Tunisia. The trouble was that Pétain was already obviously none too pleased with the local truce Darlan had overseen in Algiers. His last order was to 'resist the aggressor' and was likely to remain so as long as he thought that a determined defence in North Africa would ensure that unoccupied France would remain unoccupied. In one of his messages to Vichy Darlan had gently pointed out that 'it may be wondered whether the occupation of France's Mediterranean coast will take place in any case'. But Pétain had not reacted to it.

Which meant that Darlan was stuck. He had nothing like the maréchal's personal following. Nobody had. He needed Pétain. He needed to speak in the name of the grandfatherly figure with the well-trimmed moustache whose portrait and wise sayings were in most public places and many private ones. For nowhere had the Pétain cult taken root more firmly than among L'Armée d'Afrique du Nord where, in the misery of France's defeat, its officer corps had chosen to emulate the sacred chieftain worship of their Fascist conquerors. Darlan knew he had to give the Americans what they wanted but until Hitler tore up the 1940 armistice and marched into Vichy France all he could do was stall. This made Clark deeply unhappy with the 'stubby, ingratiating little man with watery blue eyes and petulant lips' seated on his left.

Clark (Murphy interpreting): It is essential that we stop this waste of time and blood.

Darlan: I sent a résumé of the terms to Vichy. Laval was away. There will be no reply until the Council of Ministers meet this afternoon.

Clark: What you propose is not possible. I will end this conference in 30 minutes.

Darlan: I understand what this means and I will tell my government of what has happened.

Clark: This is impossible. It will be necessary to retain you in protective custody. I hope you understand.

Darlan: I am giving my opinion that it is stupid to continue hostilities here. I urged acceptance of the terms. I am confident Pétain will agree.

Clark: That is fine, but do you understand that we can't sit here while governments agree and ministers debate? If the Admiral will not call for the cessation of hostilities, I will go to General Giraud.

Darlan: I am not certain the troops will obey.

Clark: If you think that Pétain will agree with you that hostilities will cease, why can't you issue the order now?

Darlan: I'm bound by an oath of fidelity to the *maréchal*. I can't take the responsibility of giving an order to cease hostilities.

Clark: What you are doing now means the killing of more French, British and Americans. This all boils down to one question: are you going to play with Vichy or go with us?

While this drama was unfolding the loud, bloody and wasteful noises offstage that Clark had alluded to continued in Oran with success for the Allies. A pincer movement by the 1st US Infantry Division took Algeria's second city by noon on Tuesday the 10th. From the west came 5,000 men who had come ashore among the cabanas of a beach resort. They were led by a man who, within hours of landing, had unseated a French cavalryman with a shot from his Winchester carbine and used a jeep stencilled Rough Rider. Brigadier General Ted Roosevelt was indeed the son of Theodore, twenty-fourth President, hero of the Rough Riders' charge at Cuba's San Juan Hill during the 1898 Spanish-American War and distant kinsman of the incumbent Franklin D.

From the east came the rest of the division under its equally pugnacious and certainly harder drinking commander, Major General Terry de La Mesa Allen. ('Even his name swaggers,' observed one fan. His Spanish maternal grandfather had been a Union colonel under Sherman.) After two days of failing to capture St Cloud, a vintners' market town straddling the highway some 15 miles from Oran, Allen had realized that he possessed the men and *matériel* to risk bypassing the town. It left a strong enemy force across that side of his lines of communication but it worked.

During a freezing night of sleet and biting winds – American troops were shocked to find date palms with weather like this – the two prongs had converged on Oran and were ready by first light. The battleship HMS *Rodney* and the cruisers *Aurora* and *Jamaica* duelled with coastal batteries. But in the city itself resistance was patchy. After the massacre of the American infantry during Peters's attempt to force the harbour Général Robert Boisseau, who commanded in the Oran sector, had concluded that the Allies would not risk another frontal assault. He had concentrated his limited resources at St Cloud and for a while it had worked well. It had never occurred to him that Allen would simply walk around it.

Oran itself was thinly defended and what they had was often taken by surprise. In one instance a 75mm field gun battery was overrun by Stuart light tanks before their crews had a chance to fire them. Whites in the local branch of the Service d'Ordre Légionnaire, the militia of the Paris-based French Fascist Joseph Darnand, picked off the unwary or the plain unlucky with their sniping. Then shortly before midday Boisseau decided that it had gone on long enough and sent out his emissaries for a ceasefire. Some of the Stuarts went down to the harbour in time to thwart a French plan to fill it with fuel oil and set fire to it. Others clattered around the town until they ran out of gas. One of the crews of these was approached by a gentleman in a suit, wearing a black fedora hat and carrying a large white flag who eventually managed to convey that he was the mayor of Oran and offering its surrender.

Many of his fellow citizens had decided that they were not being conquered: they were being liberated. Bottles of wine were produced. Young women in dresses that were unseasonably thin threw flowers, blew kisses, kissed. Fort Philippe disgorged its American and British prisoners from Operation Reservist including an eye-patched Peters who was borne off in triumph on the shoulders of a laughing, cheering, singing crowd of Gaullists or at least anti-Vichyites.

In three days Peters would be dead. He was killed on Friday, 13 November when the RAF Sunderland flying boat returning him to Britain from Gibraltar for treatment on his damaged eye crashed in bad weather while attempting to land in Plymouth Sound. In May 1943 it was announced that for 'an enterprise of desperate hazard at Oran harbour' he had been awarded a Victoria Cross. Although nobody denied Peters's courage, senior US officers questioned his judgement in continuing once it was obvious that the French were ready to fight. 'I hate to serve under the British,' wrote Major General Orlando Ward whose division had provided Peters's infantry. 'They have misused my troops enough already.'

American critics of operations Reservist and Terminal were right. They had been a disgraceful waste of lives and perhaps a clear indication of how lucky Admiral Syfret had been in Madagascar to get away with the Royal Marines' Diego Suarez raid that inspired them. The most that can be said for them is that in Algiers the French had been so pleased with the way they had repulsed the British destroyers that they had not bothered to sabotage harbour installations. And in Oran, confident that there would not be another attempt to test his seaward defences, Boisseau decided to make his stand 15 miles down the road at St Cloud, which had ended up making things easier for Allen.

With both ports now firmly in Anglo-American hands it was obvious that the Allies were on the verge of controlling all of Algeria. Just in case he had not heard the good news Clark told Darlan about the fall of Oran over the conference table at the Hôtel Saint-Georges. But Darlan was well aware that Général Auguste Paul Noguès was still resisting in Morocco and their wrangling over a general ceasefire continued with Murphy wincing as Clark pounded the table and repeated his latest threat: the imposition of US military government over all French North Africa. 'I tried to imagine what would happen if Americans undertook to fight the Germans in Tunisia and simultaneously govern 20 million assorted civilians in a vast territory without knowing any Arab dialects or even, in the case of most Americans, the French language.'

For the moment the Americans were far from done with fighting the French. In Morocco the invasion had started with a gentle coup by Major

General Marie Émile Antoine Béthouart, Noguès's deputy and army commander who like his immediate boss had his headquarters at Rabat, the Moroccan capital. Béthouart had been recruited by Mast and was a good catch. A lean mountain warfare expert in his early fifties who had distinguished himself in the Norway campaign with his ski-trained Chasseur light infantry, he was held in great esteem by his staff.

Unfortunately, Béthouart lacked one talent: conspiracy. On the eve of the Moroccan landings he had made his move a few hours too soon and the wiley Noguès, officially the French protectorate's Résident-général to the Sultan's court, had soon turned the table on him. Béthouart was arrested as were several of his officers, one of them Noguès's nephew. Béthouart was told he had been duped. The Americans were not coming. There was talk of firing squads.

One of the reasons Noguès had acted so promptly was that his friend Amiral François Michelier, who was also in his mid-sixties, had assured him it was 'technically impossible' for such a large force to sneak up on them unawares. This was a bold assertion, for the French did not, unlike the Allies and the Germans, have radar, and fuel shortages had grounded their reconnaissance planes for days. When at first light Admiral Hewitt's armada, having crossed the Atlantic on schedule, speckled the horizon like a nasty rash Michelier had remained quite unabashed. He simply ordered the eighteen warships he had at his disposal – eight of them submarines – to action stations.

These were all at Casablanca, 70 miles south of Rabat and a much better port than the capital's silted-up old harbour. The Americans were well aware of this and it was exactly where Hewitt's 122 vessels were heading. The *Jean Bart*, France's newest and uncompleted battleship which had fled to Morocco in June 1940, soon got involved in a duel with the even newer but totally finished USS *Massachusetts*. Four 15-inch guns versus the American ship's eight 16-inchers: silent orange flashes, express train noises, splashes taller than a lighthouse. *Jean Bart* should have had eight heavy guns too but there had been no time to fit her second forward four-gun turret before she made her dash from Brest in the last days before France's surrender. Her other disability was that she was immobile, encased in a concrete berth while her engines were being worked on. The French ship got off seven shots then the *Massachusetts*, a splendid example of the speed of American shipbuilding, had silenced her with hits on or around her turret which was covered with concrete rubble from a neighbouring jetty. A little later photo-reconnaissance revealed *Jean Bart*'s guns pointing skywards at oddly splayed angles as if rigor mortis had set in.

Coastal batteries joined in the fight and soon the sky above Casablanca's port and docks area was raining American shells. Off Algeria, Cunningham's fleet was divided between Oran and Algiers. All Hewitt's ships were concentrated against a single target. Among the civilian casualties were some of the service wives and families Darlan had ordered out of Dakar a few weeks before in order to prove to the Germans how serious he was about defending West Africa against Allied aggression. The three ships that had brought them there en route for Marseilles were among ten merchant vessels and two submarines sunk at their quays.

Seven French warships and five working submarines in the port were not seriously damaged. They had three choices: surrender, scuttle or try to fight their way out, perhaps as they did so wreaking a little extra hell among the seasick soldiery bouncing through the breakers in their flat-bottomed landing craft. Surrender was no longer an option for Michelier and Noguès who seem to have been exhilarated by the plaudits their defiance was earning them from Vichy. 'You saved France's honour,' Pétain would shortly be telling the Résident-général. Scuttling smacked of defeatism (though, done properly, it might have denied the Allied ships use of Casablanca for months). So it was decided that they would fight.

Senior sailors who make stupid decisions sometimes earn a measure of redemption by including themselves among those in peril on the sea. Not a year ago Britain's Admiral Tom Phillips had drowned off Malaya with his battleships *Prince of Wales* and *Repulse* after refusing to break radio silence and call the RAF fighters which might have saved them. But Michelier did not sail with his ships. That honour would go to Contre-amiral Gervais de Lafond who commanded what was designated a 'Light Squadron'. Since his flagship, the cruiser *Primauguet*, was in the middle of minor repairs on her engines and guns, he departed on the super-destroyer *Milan*, leaving the *Primauguet* to put herself together and catch up. She was commanded by Capitaine de vaisseau Léon Mercier, who was unusual in that he made no secret of his belief that only an Allied victory would save France. As Lafond's ships went out the squadron's chaplain was spotted standing on the tip of the last breakwater, the wind snatching at his soutane, making the sign of the cross and mouthing a silent blessing.

It took the Americans a little over three hours to sink or ruin all but one of their attackers, which were mostly destroyers and submarines with scant cover in shallow waters. At first, especially when the pounding of their own guns jarred fragile radar mountings, they had found the French ships difficult targets. Lafond cleverly hugged the coast, put down smoke which mingled with blacker stuff from burning oil tanks ashore and most of Hewitt's sailors, firing west to east, were already squinting into the sun. 'Like trying to hit a grasshopper with a rock,' reported Lieutenant Commander Samuel Morison aboard the cruiser USS *Brooklyn*.

It was not long before they got their eye in. The destroyer *Fougueux* was the first to go down, sinking by the bows, her stern gun firing to the last. *Boulonnais* tried to avenge her, circling the *Massachusetts* for a torpedo strike but was straddled by one of the battleship's full eight-round 16-inch salvos and rolled over with the loss of almost all hands. *Frondeur* and *Bestois*, filling rapidly and with heavy lists, staggered back to port and even got alongside a jetty but both snapped their mooring cables and capsized before they could be pumped out. To add to the squadron's misery Grumman Wildcats from the carriers USS *Ranger* and *Suwanne* started to strafe Lafond's desperate sortie. The stubby Wildcats, called Martlets by the British who in 1940 had taken over a French purchase and were also flying them from their carriers off Algeria, had four heavy .50 machine guns which jammed almost as often as they worked but were awful when they did. Stuck in their mothballed neutrality, Vichy French ships had not had the chance to develop their anti-aircraft capability the way the Allies had and the Wildcat was well armoured. Almost with impunity American pilots came in low and concentrated their fire on the ships' bridges where they knew the officers would be.

Capitaine de frégate Martinant de Preneuf of the *Albatross*, his ship already badly holed, was killed. On the super-destroyer *Milan*, where shellfire had already removed part of her bow and put one of her guns out of action, the Wildcats hit every man on the bridge. Lafond, who was wounded in the leg, had the ship run onto the beach at the ominously named Roches Noires and the hurt hurriedly evacuated. They would come back for their dead. The *Albatross* did the same.

It was about now that the light cruiser *Primauguet*, Lafond's forsaken flagship, caught up with them in time to be neatly cornered by the heavy cruisers *Augusta* and *Brooklyn* in the north and the *Massachusetts*, *Tuscalooa* and *Wichita* and several destroyers in the north-east. Seen from a Wildcat it must have looked about as fair as the end of the *Bismarck*. Before long *Primauguet* was holed below her water line and half her engine room crew were dead. Capitaine Mercier gave the order to drop anchor near *Milan* but as they did so the Wildcats caught up with the cruiser. When they had finished the ship was on fire and Mercier lay dead among the wreckage of his bridge. 'We may all be thankful if our lives have not been rent by such dire problems and conflicting loyalties,' wrote Churchill some time afterwards, moved by the dilemma of an officer who yearned for Allied victory yet died so uselessly for Vichy.

Almost 500 French sailors were killed at Casablanca on 8 November and another 1,000 wounded. They were the worst losses La Marine Française had suffered in a single day since Somerville attacked their ships at Mers-el-Kébir in 1940. US casualties were three killed and twenty-five injured. At least one of the American dead was aircrew. There had been several dogfights over Casablanca in which the Wildcats claimed to have shot down seven Dewoitines or Moranes for the loss of five of their own, several of the downed Americans being taken prisoner. Only one French destroyer, the *Alcyon*, managed to return to port more or less intact, having picked up some survivors. Others walked back from their beached ships. The wounded Lafond, leaning on a stick, reviewed those of his men still able to fight, thanked them for what they had done, then saw them issued with a rifle and five rounds of ammunition and sent off to join the infantry.

Forty-eight hours later, as Operation Torch went into its third day and Clark reached new heights of exasperation with Darlan at the Saint-Georges, the Moroccan front's guttering flame continued to symbolize Vichy's will to oppose an Allied presence in French North Africa. Patton had landed almost 30,000 troops but he was far from satisfied with the zeal displayed by his green infantry when they came ashore at Fedala, Casablanca's seaside playground and also its horse-racing track. 'As a whole the men were poor, the officers worse,' he noted. 'No drive. It is very sad.' Nor was the general's temper improved by the flavescent changes to his appearance wrought by a splash from a French naval shell tinged with yellow dye which had narrowly missed the *Augusta* just before he left her. It would not have been the colour of his choice.

As it happened, in some places the Americans had done rather better in Morocco than Algeria. At Safi, a sardine fishing port some 130 miles south of Casablanca that the French had been dredging before the war to facilitate phosphates exports, they had seen the only successful storming of a defended harbour. The secret of their success was complete surprise and the accuracy of the ten 14-inch guns on Hewitt's oldest battleship, the USS *New York*, launched in 1914. Unlike Oran and Algiers no nearby landings had taken place to alert the defenders. The first they knew about it was when two destroyers, not much younger than the battleship supporting them and each with 200 US soldiers on board, had bluffed their way into the port shortly before dawn. By mid-afternoon, having stopped a counter-attack led by three circa 1918 Renault FT-17 light tanks with more contemporary armour-piercing rifle grenades, the port was theirs. This had cost the Americans four killed and twenty-five wounded. All the docks were intact and the first cargo Patton had unloaded there were fifty-four Shermans, the heavy tank the British had just made good use of at El Alamein. Some of these reached Casablanca's southern suburbs by Tuesday the 10th.

Despite this, Patton had decided that the only way he was going to capture the town was to blast a path through the Vichy defences with Hewitt's ships and aircraft plus as many of his own batteries as had been landed. He should have had his own air support by now. Almost fifty P-40s presently languishing on the carrier *Chenango* were supposed to be tearing the heart out of the enemy from the airfield at Port Lyautey, which was a good 80 miles north of Casablanca and a little above Rabat.

Brigadier General Lucien Truscott, who had come ashore with 9,000 men at the fishing port of Mehdia on the Sebou river estuary, had been expected to secure the airfield on the first day. Two senior air force officers, one of whom had served as a US military attaché in Athens and Cairo, had gone boldly forward in a jeep flying French and American flags as well as a white one. Then they vanished. Later it transpired that the former attaché had been killed by a nervous machine gunner and the other officer taken prisoner. An apologetic French colonel had explained to him that he simply did not have the authority to implement a ceasefire. Resistance stiffened. Half a dozen Stuart light tanks Truscott had landed found themselves matched against Renault R35s that had the same cannon but thicker front armour. Honours appear to have been about even. Otherwise, Truscott was not enamoured with the fighting quality of most of his men and concluded with a candour typical of some US commanders at this early stage of America's war that the landing would have been a disaster against 'a well armed enemy'.

Eventually the airfield, which was about 12 miles upstream along the bends of the oxbowing Sebou, was captured at about the same time as the Shermans were approaching Casablanca. As long planned, bombs and aviation fuel had then been delivered by the shallow-draught Caribbean banana boat *Contessa*, commandeered from the Standard Fruit Company along with her British skipper who had found some of his crew among seamen nursing hangovers in Norfolk county jail. (The *Contessa* and her explosive contents, chemical and human, had crossed the Atlantic somewhat to the rear of the rest of Hewitt's ships that were not companionable.)

Securing the airfield had cost Truscott almost 300 casualties, 79 of them dead. But Patton was not prepared to wait another twenty-four hours for the P-40s to become operational. Casablanca was still firmly in Vichy hands and had teeth. On Monday the 9th, a military police company sent to sort out traffic snarl-ups on the Fedala beachhead had strayed into its port when the lead coxswain of four American landing craft got lost. Some of the twenty-eight killed died convinced it was all a terrible mistake, shouting, 'We're Americans.' Most of the forty-five the French pulled out of the water were wounded. Two boats got away. Next day French sailors brought two of *Jean Bart*'s big guns back to life, astonishing the *Augusta* by bracketing her with six near misses when Hewitt thought his flagship was safely out of range of all that was left intact. Shortly afterwards, she was. After the evasive action came the American response. Unlike the *Augusta*, the French battleship did not have anywhere to run to and this time Dauntless dive bombers off the *Ranger* made sure with two direct hits that the *Jean Bart*'s guns would never fire again.

In the afternoon Patton went out to the *Augusta* to see Hewitt. He drank some medicinal bourbon with him, for senior officers tended to feel their age and need a tonic on dry USN ships, and discussed the final details of the Götterdämmerung he planned for Casablanca for Armistice Day, 11 November. Zero hour was set at 0730 hours.

Afterwards the admiral saw Patton down to his boat for the return journey to Fedala and his suite in the resort's Hôtel Miramar where on his bedside table rested his first trophy of the campaign: a spiked *pickelhaube* helmet with its gold Prussian eagle, the ceremonial headgear of General Erich von Wulisch, head of the German Armistice Commission to French North Africa. Von Wulisch had occupied the same suite in the Miramar shortly before his hurried departure for Berlin via Spanish Morocco. Not all his staff had been quick enough and several became the US Army's first German prisoners of war since 1918. At dinner Patton had amused Charles Codman, the lieutenant colonel who was his senior aide-de-camp, by striding in with the *pickelhaube* on his head and announcing he would be wearing it the day they all entered Berlin. Afterwards, his staff officers had returned to their immediate plans to turn a large number of Casablanca's mud-brick buildings into a pile of rubble.

Shortly before 2.30 a.m. Codman was knocking insistently at the general's door. Patton knew he would not be disturbed unless it was important and dressed quickly. Waiting for him downstairs was a French major who had just been driven through the American lines under a flag of truce. He handed Patton a short note pencilled on flimsy paper which he read by candlelight, for either by design or some accident of crossfire Fedala was without electricity. Darlan and Noguès had agreed to a general ceasefire with the Allies throughout their country's North African possessions. Not only were there no more contested areas to fight over but, even if there had been, very soon Vichy would not have the forces to do so. In years to come the American most associated with Casablanca would not, after all, be the soldier George Patton, who might certainly have made a lasting local impression, but the Hollywood actor Humphrey Bogart. The eponymous wartime film with its opportunistic Vichy police chief ('I blow with the wind, and the prevailing wind happens to be from Vichy') had just been completed. It was about to be released a little earlier than planned to exploit the publicity generated by the fighting in Morocco in which some 400 Americans died.

Patton staged a stylish armistice ceremony at the Miramar with an Honour Guard for Noguès and Michelier, champagne toasts to gallant adversaries and another one to 'our future victory over our common enemy'. Amirals Michelier and Hewitt agreed that they both had their orders and there were no hard feelings. It seems nobody thought to ask Michelier why he had wasted the lives of his sailors on such a futile gesture. Patton said the party was 'worth every Goddam cent'.

And on this convivial note all Vichy French hostilities against the Allies ceased. England's last war with France, undeclared and unacknowledged, had briefly become America's first one and then faded into the footnotes of history almost as if it had never been.

Chapter Thirty

It did not end tidily. There was no official announcement, no appointed hour for the guns to fall silent, for officially Britain and France had never been at war. Hitler, having made sure that Axis troops could land unopposed in Tunis and Bizerta, ended the existence of an unoccupied France on 11 November, the twenty-fourth anniversary of the 1918 armistice. In Munich, Ambassador Abetz woke Laval with a 4 a.m. call to tell him the news. Laval told him it was a terrible mistake. 'It's a decision of the Führer's,' said Abetz. 'There's nothing to be done.' The only consolation he could offer was that Germany would continue to recognize Pétain's administration as the legitimate government of a totally occupied France.

In Vichy Baron Krug von Nidda presented Pétain with a personal letter from Hitler that, after some preliminary remarks about his puzzlement that France and Britain should ever have declared war against Germany in the first place, got down to the business at hand.

> *Monsieur le Maréchal*, I have the honour, and at the same time the sorrow, to inform you that in order to avoid the danger which threatens us I have, in agreement with the Italian Government, been compelled to give the order to my troops to cross France by the most direct route in order to occupy the Mediterranean coast, and second, to take part in the protection of Corsica against the impending aggression of Anglo-American armed forces . . .

It was called Operation Anton. In overall command was General Johannes Blaskowitz, a Lutheran pastor's son, who had once incurred Hitler's displeasure for his outspoken criticism of SS atrocities in Poland. Blaskowitz had inherited contingency plans first drawn up by the Wehrmacht only five months after the 1940 armistice and later coordinated with a project for Italy's simultaneous seizure of Corsica. At about the same time that Patton learned of the ceasefire at Fedala's Hôtel Miramar, Germany moved into what Vichy normally referred to as the Free Zone. In all, it involved over 200,000 men with tanks and artillery. In addition the Italian 4th Army advanced into all the territory Mussolini coveted: Nice and the rest of the French Riviera plus Corsica where they had been instructed to behave like liberators rather than conquerors. By the evening of the 11th, Blaskowitz's panzers had reached the Mediterranean coast.

In the course of this eventful day Feldmarschal von Runstedt, who commanded all the German forces in western Europe, called on Pétain who made the expected protest against 'a decision incompatible with the armistice agreement'. This denunciation was repeatedly broadcast by Vichy Radio though, one maréchal to another, Pétain confided to von Runstedt that he had only done it 'on account of public opinion in France'.

In Algiers Amiral Darlan had declared that Pétain, the most distinguished victim of this gross violation of the armistice, must now be considered a prisoner. As his deputy, he was entitled to give orders, such as his endorsement of the ceasefire, in the maréchal's name dismissing all attempts by Vichy to question his authority as bogus, having been made under duress. A delighted Churchill would soon be explaining to a secret session of the House of Commons: 'In fact, if Admiral Darlan had to shoot Marshal Pétain he would no doubt do it in Marshal Pétain's name.'

The Allies were hoping that for his next trick Darlan would deliver them the French fleet still at anchor at Toulon, which the Germans had agreed should remain a Vichy stronghold and be defended against 'all enemies of the *maréchal*.' Arrangements were already in place for the Royal Navy to cover their dash for Gibraltar and a return to the war. Surely all that remained was for Darlan to give the word? But it was not as simple as that.

When, in 1940, Pétain elevated Darlan to his Cabinet the command of the High Seas Fleet went to Contre-amiral Jean de Laborde, who was of aristocratic demeanour (if not exactly lineage) and an unswerving Catholic. His nickname in the navy was Comte Jean, his manner authoritative and monosyllabic, but like Darlan he was an enthusiastic modernizer. Laborde also shared all Darlan's views about de Gaulle and the English. 'I'm not Anglophobe,' he liked to tell people. 'I'm Anglophage. I eat 'em.' Despite these enthusiasms he had little liking for his clever and conceited superior, almost three years his junior but with the unchurched background that had made him so acceptable to Léon Blum's Popular Front. Now his turncoat behaviour had confirmed what he always suspected of the Godless parvenu: Darlan believed in Darlan and little else.

On the 12th, pressed by Clark and Admiral Cunningham, who had now turned up in Algiers, Darlan did his best to persuade Laborde to bring the fleet over, revealing in his argument all the effortless sophistry that had enabled him to sound as convincing in his new role as he had in his old one. In his message he was careful to make no mention of British involvement.

> The Armistice is broken. We have our liberty of action. The *maréchal* being no longer able to make free decisions we can, whilst remaining personally loyal to him, make decisions which are most favourable to French interests. I have always declared that the Fleet would remain French or perish. The occupation makes it impossible for the naval forces to remain in metropolitan France. I invite the Commander-in-Chief to direct them towards West Africa. The American Command declares that our forces will not encounter any obstacles from Allied forces.

'*Merde*', replied Comte Jean, consistent in all things. Others were more sympathetic. There were signs of unrest among some of the 12,000 sailors at Toulon. Demonstrations on the *Strasbourg*, Laborde's own flagship, had spread to the cruisers *Foch* and *Colbert* and the super-destroyer *Kersaint*. They had started after orders had been given for the boilers to be shut down. Men had assembled on the fo'c's'le deck demanding with cries of '*Appareillage!*' that they set sail for Algiers immediately. This was followed by chants of '*Vive Darlan! Vive de Gaulle!*' which scarcely twenty-four hours before would have been a ludicrous combination devoid of any serious political content. Now it made a kind of sense.

For five days Laborde had kept his boilers fired, starting the day before the Torch landings when, quite coincidentally and for the benefit of men and machinery, he took his ships out on a short constitutional cruise along the coast and back. When it was learned that the Anglo-Saxons had 'done another Mers-el-Kébir' at Oran and Casablanca, their continued state of readiness had fanned welcome rumours among their crews that they were about to intervene. Nor was this entirely fanciful. Laborde had indeed volunteered to take the fleet out, perhaps eat some English pirates for breakfast, only to have Amiral Auphan, Vichy's Secretary of State for Maritime Affairs and close to Darlan, order him to stay at his moorings.

But on the mess deck there were cigar box radios with a bit of lead ore for an oscillator and some clever wiring to a single earphone quite capable of picking up the BBC's French language service. The gradual realization that Darlan had joined the Americans had changed the mood of the more politically aware. They were no longer all that interested in going out and tearing out the heart of the English. What they wanted to do was join Darlan and the Americans and use their excellent ships to fight the Boche. Laborde had clamped down. Ringleaders were arrested. Ashore, liberty men got into fights in their favourite bars with snoopers from the Service d'ordre légionnaire, about to be renamed the Milice, paid to drink and move in on Gaullist troublemakers inciting mutiny. Meanwhile, Laborde decided to confront the issue of Darlan's defection head-on with an Order of the Day that left nobody in any doubt as to who he was talking about.

> At such time that those in high command lose their sense of duty, you must show that Honour is not measured by gold stripes and Admiral's stars. Unflinching discipline and correct service behaviour are the ultimate duty of all. I myself have guaranteed your loyalty to the *Maréchal* who has directed me to say that he is counting on you to save the unity and honour of France . . .

As far as Laborde was concerned North Africa might be lost but the fleet was still something Vichy could bargain with to maintain a measure of genuine self-government, certainly more than all the other occupied countries had, even Quisling's Norway. To an extent the German Navy had fostered this illusion. In June 1919 the German Grand Fleet, having surrendered to the Royal Navy at Orkney's Scapa Flow some six months before, had scuttled itself there when it looked like the talks at Versailles would deliver every one of them to the British. Grosseadmiral Erich Raeder, the head of the Kriegsmarine, was in no doubt that Laborde and his officers would keep their word and do exactly the same rather than let any of the belligerents take their ships.

In order to reassure Hitler on this point Raeder sent one of his aides, Kapitänleutnant Ruault von Frappart, to see both Laborde and Amiral André Marquis, the *préfet maritime* who commanded the 135 vessels in various states of repair and readiness that were not in Laborde's High Seas Fleet. Frappart, an Austrian of French descent, procured word-of-honour promises from both of them that their ships would never be used against Axis forces and that Toulon would be defended against any Anglo-American aggression. 'If you undertake that no German will come into our docks I will give my word,' Laborde told him. And Frappart had agreed.

Toulon, it seemed, was to be the last bastion of Vichy's armed neutrality unlike the much bigger port of Marseilles where the newly appointed Gauleiter had just confiscated all those merchant ships not needed to victual Italian-occupied Corsica. But within days it became plain that Germany's army was not as comfortable as its navy with this arrangement. It had pointed out that, with the connivance of its garrison, the Allies might use the port as their bridgehead into continental Europe. A barracks was taken over, the last of the French Army on French soil disbanded. Tanks began to turn up. Soon there was hardly a road leading to the port not jammed with a line of them, crews in black overalls sitting on their turrets smoking and listening to Lale Andersen on German forces' radio.

In the end Hitler, as he usually did, came down on the side of the army. If the idea of the Allies turning Toulon into a bridgehead was a bit fanciful the risk of French ships slipping out of Germany's reach was not. After their North African success it was obvious that the Anglo-Americans would try to gather them in. Any doubts on that score would have been settled by German radio intercepts. Darlan's invitation to Laborde was probably sent via Auphan in a code based on a key in a pocket dictionary they had been using since the landings. (Darlan had falsely claimed that Pétain, in an *accord intime*, had passed on approval of the ceasefire in it.) It is unlikely that the Germans had failed to crack this simple cypher with the content so easy to guess; but even if it remained unbroken any contact between the defector and Vichy would have caused alarm.

Laborde's slogan-shouting dissidents were more cause for concern and had every reason not to feel alone. Following the Axis takeover of the Tunisian ports, Général Georges Barré, the French Army commander in Tunisia, had rallied to Darlan and the Allies. So had Governor Boisson in Dakar, bringing with him his huge West African territories. Isolated French Somaliland on the Red Sea, where in Djibouti Governor Pierre Nouailhetas would not surrender until shortly before Christmas after 101 days of British blockade, was the only French African colony that remained loyal to Vichy. In Algiers Général Giraud, who Darlan had put in charge of all the French military in North Africa just as the Allies had always wanted, declared in the name of the maréchal that as soon as Tunisia was finished he would attend to the liberation of metropolitan France.

It was four days after Boisson's defection and well before first light when, on Friday, 27 November, the first tanks finally rolled downhill towards the port at Toulon. At 4.30 a.m. Krug von Nidda, who had been waiting in his car outside the front door of Laval's home at Châteldon refusing to come in until precisely that hour, handed to the prime minister a copy of Hitler's second letter to Pétain in sixteen days. (There seems to have been a convention that the old gentleman himself should not be disturbed at these ungodly hours.) It got quickly to the point. 'French generals and admirals have broken their word of honour by their intention to open to the Anglo-Jewish warmongers metropolitan France as well as North Africa. I have given orders to occupy Toulon at once and prevent the ships from leaving port or to destroy them.'

Operation Lila promised the ships to Italy, which had lost so many of its own in their Mediterranean campaign against the British. Hitler was uninterested in acquiring more surface vessels. Soon the defeat of the battleship *Hipper* and destroyers by a Royal Navy escort that stopped her sinking any of an important Russian-bound convoy would result in Raeder being replaced by the U-boat supremo Doenitz. In any case Hitler expected the French to scuttle their fleet, a choice he wished they had made in 1940, though this was among many secrets he never shared with Mussolini. 'I fear the French fleet will not come to us intact,' he wrote to Il Duce when he notified him that Operation Lila was about to take place. 'But if this does happen Italy is the only lawful possessor.'

As it happened, the Germans very nearly pulled it off. Despite the blatant building up of their forces they managed to achieve a large element of surprise. Their first move was to enter the outlying La Valette police post, cut its telephone lines and kidnap one Gendarme Le Moigne who was made to sit on a tank and direct them to Fort LaMalgue where they knew they would find Amiral Marquis. But here things began to go wrong. LaMalgue was a much built upon, rabbit warren of a place, old when Admiral Hood had made it his headquarters during the English occupation of Toulon in 1793. German officers, sometimes deliberately misdirected, got lost stomping around its endless corridors in search of command centres.

None of this would have mattered had they made it a priority to cut the telephone lines as they had done at La Valette when they picked up Le Moigne. As it was, senior staff officers had the opportunity to alert Laborde on the *Strasbourg* who, reluctant to believe that von Frappart's promise had been so casually broken, even had time to call LaMalgue back and check. 'Hello, yes the Germans are all around me,' whispered a voice he recognized as belonging to an Amiral Robin. 'Please don't call back.' Then the line to the fort went dead.

At this point Laborde knew that, unless he immediately gave the order he had always dreaded giving, his ships would soon be flying a different flag. *Sabordez la flotte! Sabordez la flotte!* It went out by radio, Morse lamp and despatch boat while slowly descending parachute flares, released by a Luftwaffe squadron that had wakened the whole town with its engines, lit up the still darkened harbour. Once the Junkers could see the ships were still there they flew further out to sea to lay magnetic mines a little beyond its entrance in case they tried to make a run for it.

Without Laborde's knowledge five submarines did just that. Diesel engines were much faster to start up than the ships' boilers and, as the Germans came down their quay, they slipped mooring lines and were off. In the dark, their low profiles were difficult targets for small arms and they were soon out of range. The captain of one of them, the *Venus*, was merely making sure he scuttled his boat in waters deep enough to make her hard to recover. But the other four wanted to join Darlan and persuaded the tug manning the steel anti-submarine net to pull open the gate for them. Two had enough fuel to go directly to Algiers, the *Casablanca* being the first to arrive on 30 November. The other two put into Barcelona to refuel where they were promptly interned by Franco's navy though one of them, *Glorieux*, eventually managed a second escape. Only two surface vessels got to North Africa. One was a tug, possibly the one that opened the gate for the submarines. The other was the *Leonor Fresnel*, which is usually described as a buoy tender.

Otherwise every French warship in Toulon did her best to destroy herself just as Gensoul had promised Somerville they would when the war between Britain and France began twenty-eight months ago. It was intended to render them utterly inoperable so it was not just a matter of opening the seacocks and allowing them to settle into the harbour mud. Explosives were attached to most machinery, weaponry, bridges packed with all their navigating tools, engine rooms and fuel tanks. By tampering with the gauges the tanks usually contained far more oil than the Armistice Commission permitted, easily enough to have got them to Algeria if Laborde had been willing to do it. None of the big gun magazines appear to have had charges set, probably because there were fears that not everybody would be able to get off in time, and there were few large explosions. In most cases there appears to have been a sharp series of bangs leading to varying degrees of billowing, black oil smoke followed by a slow subsidence, almost imperceptible at first, until the main decks were well awash.

Laborde's flagship, the 8-year old fast battle cruiser *Strasbourg* that was at the Milhaud jetty, was the first to go. In her engine rooms the splendid Rateau turbines, the machinery that in July 1940 had produced over 30 knots to escape HMS *Hood* at Mers-el-Kébir, were blown into twisted scrap. Soon, brown harbour water was lapping around their broken blades. Outside, the first Germans had arrived on the quay, a young officer interpreter speaking through a bullhorn and demanding in passable French that they hand over the ship intact. 'Too late,' Laborde shouted back. 'The ship is sinking.' There was a pause while this was digested. Then the same voice came back: '*Amiral*, my Colonel orders me to say he admires you.'

Strasbourg's siren started up, the agreed and appropriate keening signal for mass suicide in the unlikely event that there was a ship's captain in the Toulon basin who was unaware. Only one man hesitated. Capitaine de vaisseau Amiel commanded the *Dunkerque*, Strasbourg's slightly older sister ship and the template of the class, which was the vessel that had been left for dead at Mers-el-Kébir. First she had been crippled by the *Hood*'s 15-inch shells then holed when a Swordfish's torpedo detonated a clutch of spilt depth charges from another casualty. Eighteen months later the British had turned a blind eye when the patched-up battle cruiser crept across the Mediterranean and into intensive care at Toulon's dry dock for the best ship surgery that could be provided in France's straitened circumstances. After nine months' work the battle cruiser was still only partly recovered but undoubtedly beginning to bear a greater resemblance to the ship that had once starred at the Spithead review for King George VI's coronation.

Amiel demanded confirmation in writing to do the foul thing he was being asked. Then, at Laborde's prompting, the captain of the cruiser *La Galissonnière*, which was berthed nearby, assured him he had seen written orders and a tight-lipped Amiel, as he probably always knew he would do, went ahead. Holes in the hull Somerville's ships and aircraft had made, their temporary dressings ripped out, put the ship down quickly once her dry dock was flooded. The turrets and bridge of the battle cruiser were then destroyed by carefully placed explosives. For good measure *Dunkerque*'s tomb was sealed by *La Galissonnière* scuttling herself across the entrance of the battle cruiser's dock.

Around the cruiser *Foch* there was an exchange of fire between tanks and some of the men manning the cruiser's anti-aircraft guns who were trying to keep the Germans at bay long enough to complete demolitions. There were one or two other incidents like this and perhaps the sailors were mainly firing warning shots. Total German casualties were one man wounded. The French had twelve killed and twenty-six wounded though some of these might have been caught up in their own explosions.

For the most part the Wehrmacht's reaction was typified by the colonel who saluted Laborde through his interpreter while the *Strasbourg* sank at her moorings. In some instances the Germans stood at the end of a gangplank asking politely if they might come aboard and when told they might not remained where they were as the ships sank and fires took hold. Some burnt for several days and were well photographed by RAF reconnaissance. In all, counting tugs and auxilary supply vessels, in the region of 130 ships were put out of action including 3 battle cruisers (*Strasbourg*, *Dunkerque*, *Provence*), the old seaplane tender *Commandant Teste*, 4 heavy and 3 light cruisers, 16 destroyers, 13 torpedo boats and 15 submarines.

In Algiers Darlan heard the news while he was in the middle of writing a letter of thanks to Admiral Leahy. Alain had just been flown in a US Air Force plane from Algiers to Rabat in Morocco on the first stage of his journey to the clinic President Roosevelt had founded for the treatment of poliomyelitis at Warm Springs Spa in Georgia. 'I am just told that part of the French fleet in Toulon has been scuttled,' he wrote. 'But fortunately the French Empire still stands.'

Later that day Darlan made a broadcast that blamed Laborde for failing to save the fleet and called upon Frenchmen to 'crush Germany and Italy'. It was a most extraordinary volte-face from a man who not so long ago had been assuring Hitler that Britain was always his traditional enemy.

> Germany's aim is now clear. That is to wipe out France. We shall have no mercy for all those who, deliberately or not, serve the designs of our eternal enemy. No one of us must any longer hesitate to do his duty which is to crush Germany and Italy and liberate the country. French Africa is the only place in the world where our flag flies freely, where the army has its weapons, the navy flies its ensign and the air force uses its wings. We are the sole hope of France, let us show ourselves worthy of her.

It was a blatant attempt to put himself on at least an equal footing to de Gaulle and possibly supplant him altogether. In his letter to Leahy Darlan had emphasized that only he could have brought North and West Africa over to the Allies. 'I certainly could not have done it had I been a "dissident". I think that, when time has passed, all those differences between Frenchmen will be smoothed down, but for the time being the dissidents and ourselves must follow parallel roads, ignoring each other. Besides, many Frenchmen were Gaullists only from hatred of the Germans and not because they felt sympathetic to that movement's leader.'

In London de Gaulle bided his time, predicting: 'Soon the retching will begin.' He was right. Before the month was out Darlan's usefulness was coming towards an end and he knew it. 'People are saying I am but a lemon which the Americans will drop after it is crushed,' he protested to Mark Clark on 23 November. Clark showed the letter to Eisenhower who had just moved his headquarters to Algiers from Gibraltar. Ike told the amiral it would help if he had 'an enlightened liberal government in action'. But enlightened liberals were about as likely to join a Darlan-led government as dance the hokey cokey with him.

Once Darlan had arranged the ceasefire that had allowed the Allies to consolidate their presence in French North Africa there was little else he had to offer. He had failed to deliver the fleet or keep the Axis out of Tunisia's ports until Anderson's British spearhead had reached them with the result that a gruelling campaign had now begun there. Instead 'the Little Fellow', as Clark had taken to calling him, had become an enormous embarrassment, a political hot potato.

Initially, realpolitik dictated that Churchill and Roosevelt greet Darlan's presence in French North Africa with open arms, a welcome alternative to the disappointing Giraud. But from the beginning there was considerable indignation over this in both Britain and America where an almost unanimous press made sure it stayed that way. Why, they asked, were the Allies making deals with a man who for the last two years had been vilified as a Nazi stooge? Especially one who was still surrounded by all the trappings of a Fascist state including anti-Semitic by-laws and strutting militias such as Service d'Ordre de la Légion. The *New Yorker*'s A.J. Liebling, a Francophile, took a look at Oran's café society.

> Members of uniformed fascist organisations had left the city or at least hidden their *sturm* duds when the Americans marched in. They had sniped at our people all through the battle and might have legitimately expected to have been backed against a wall and shot. But in a couple of weeks they had reappeared in the cafés wearing their capes, monocles and high boots and talking loudly about the day of revenge, not against the Germans but us ... They had not really collaborated with the Nazis: the Nazis had come along belatedly and collaborated with them.

Churchill, as he readily admitted, had been 'somewhat contemptuous' of this criticism of the Darlan deal, finding it small-minded considering the Allied lives it had saved and the gains a successful Operation Torch had brought so close on the heels of the victory at El Alamein. Then he changed his mind. 'I understood what was troubling them and felt it myself.' He wrote to Roosevelt about it.

> We must not overlook the serious political injury which may be done to our cause, not only in France, by the feeling that we are ready to make terms with local Quislings. Darlan has an odious record. It is he who has inculcated in the French Navy its malignant disposition by promoting his creatures to command. It is but yesterday that French sailors were sent to their death against your line of battle at Casablanca and now, for the sake of power and office, Darlan plays the turncoat.

The President was of the same opinion and included in his reply a statement he had just made at a press conference emphasizing that 'the present arrangement in North and West Africa is only a temporary expedient justified by the stress of battle'.

It seems that other stresses now dictated that the Anglo-Americans dump Darlan.

But as Christmas 1942 approached Darlan was still in place though, thanks to mild Allied pressure, some improvements had been made. The bully boys in the high boots were not quite as blatant, a few of the more prominent leftists and Gaullists picked up after the coup for which the Americans had arrived too late had at last been released from detention. Others had not. 'Jews and Frenchmen who had publicly expressed satisfaction at our landing were now serving jail sentences for their bad taste,' reported Liebling. *L'Oran Républicain*, voice of the Popular Front, had kept going through two years of Pétainist censorship with intriguing white spaces bleached in its pages. Now its editor was incensed to find that, while the Allies got on with their war in Tunisia, the same censor was still able to remove a pro-American editorial with impunity.

Nonetheless, the old certainties were crumbling. Algiers, its economy improved by a large army's rear echelons, had become a febrile place, gently smouldering on rekindled French politics, a dormant volcano coming back to life. There were four main factions. These were the Darlanists, the Gaullists, the Communists and the Monarchists plotting to restore the Orléanist dynasty by putting Henri, Count of Paris, on the throne. In Algeria the Gaullists and the Monarchists, the latter being well financed though without popular support, had a fragile alliance. Despite this the Communists were making headway by exploiting fears that the Anglo American accommodation with Darlan meant there was little point in supporting the Gaullists who were obviously being sidelined. This was also happening in France itself where the Communists were vying for control of the Resistance and, exactly as Churchill had feared, winning recruits with the argument that London and Washington had gone to bed with a Quisling.

The European quarters of Algiers and Oran were awash with small arms and there were plenty of young men willing to use them. All the parties had their own gunmen. Some of them were becoming well trained too. Both the Special Operations Executive and America's Office of Strategic Services were recruiting French speakers for operations in Tunisia, the south of France and Corsica. Several training schools had been set up. The OSS had established one on the coast east of Algiers at the village of Ain Taya run by Carleton S. Coon, a portly Harvard anthropologist who was good with guns and explosives.

Among Coon's pupils was Fernand Bonnier who had been born in Algiers where his father was a well-known *colon* journalist who wrote for the *Oran Républicain*. Bonnier, who was now 20, had been at the Lycée Stanislas in Paris when France surrendered. In 1940 he demonstrated at the first 11 November remembrance day of the occupation when, to indicate their sympathies, students turned up at the Arc de Triomphe carrying fishing rods which in French are called *gaulles*. The following year he smuggled himself across the demarcation line and into Vichy France where in Marseilles he was eventually able to find passage on a boat home to Algiers.

But once there it was not the Gaullists he fell in with but the Monarchists who had sponsored several young men to attend OSS and SOE 'finishing schools' such as the one at Ain Taya. Bonnier always appears to have been something of a loner. A fellow pupil at the Normandy boarding school he attended before he went to Paris recalled that he was an unpopular boy with attention-seeking ways including suicide attempts of dubious authenticity. At some point, perhaps when he fell in with the Monarchists, Bonnier began to use the suffixation 'de la Chapelle', an aristocratic affectation indicating his father's birthplace in the south of France.

In the wet and cold of the Algerian winter Bonnier de la Chapelle, as he preferred to be remembered, was training hard and anxious not to be excluded from anything. He had missed out on the excitement of the 8 November coup when, for reasons he could not understand, his friends had not invited him to participate. Since then he had remained close to Abbé Louis Cordier, confessor and secretary to Henri d'Astier de la Vigerie, an aristocrat highly regarded by the Orléanist pretender. It was Abbé Cordier who had arranged for the young men to train with Coon. The priest, a sinister figure, was known to the OSS as 'Necktie', widely believed to be the abbe's chosen instrument for disposing of Axis agents after first forgiving them their sins.

On 24 December Bonnier de la Chapelle put two bullets into Darlan from an old Spanish automatic pistol of a type produced in its thousands for the French Army during the First World War. The shooting took place at Darlan's office, which was in a compound known as the Summer Palace, shortly after he returned from a late Christmas Eve lunch. Abbé Cordier had arranged to get his assassin into the building by providing Bonnier with a letter and other forged papers, which showed that he had an appointment with a civil servant on the floor below Darlan's office. Cordier knew that the man would not be there and Bonnier would have plenty of time to go up the stairs to the next floor and wait in its narrow corridor for his target to return from lunch. Before they parted the abbé heard the young man's confession and gave him absolution for what he was about to do plus 2,000 US dollars and a forged passport to get him to Spanish Morocco where he was to stay until things cooled down.

But Bonnier did not escape. After shooting Darlan in the corridor the plan was that he should get away by jumping through an open window of the low building into the courtyard below. It turned out that the window was barred. Cornered, the gunman fired several more shots with his .32 automatic, one of which wounded one of Darlan's aides in the thigh, before he was overpowered and badly beaten up by guards.

Darlan, who had been shot in the chest and the jaw, was taken to the Maillot Hospital, where Alain had been treated, and died in the operating theatre. The fatal bullet had gone through a lung and lodged in the lower part of his heart. Berthe Darlan arrived at the hospital a few minutes too late.

Forty-eight hours later his killer was dead, shot at dawn on 26 December by a French firing squad after a Christmas Day trial. A confession stating that he had acted alone, motivated solely by the love of his country, had been presented before a military judge who immediately passed sentence. There was no right of appeal. It was, of course, preposterous to imagine that a young man found with 2,000 dollars on his person, a fortune anywhere in 1942 let alone French Algeria, had been acting alone. And as the hours before his execution had slipped away Bonnier had assured his father, who visited him, guards and a priest that he had powerful friends who would not allow him to die. At the last moment the priest persuaded him to say some prayers but he was shot before he could finish them. The haste of Bonnier's trial and execution, without even a Christmas postponement, inevitably led to speculation of a cover-up though some said it was merely Giraud, who was now in charge, determined to demonstrate to the Anglo-Saxons just how efficient the French could be. 'Darlan's murder,' admitted Churchill, 'relieved the Allies of their embarrassment for working with him and left them with all the advantages he had been able to bestow.'

From the moment he was shot Darlan never properly recovered consciousness though one account has him gesturing feebly to somebody who was trying to give him encouragement. Certainly, he never recovered the ability to speak. But this was not good enough for Vichy Radio who thought it would be wasteful not to give the man who had once been Pétain's chosen successor some suitable last words. It was decided that he had been heard to whisper: 'Nothing more can be done for me. England has attained her goal.'

EPILOGUE

April in Paris 1944. Outside Notre Dame on the 26th of that month, cheering people were giving Philippe Pétain a rapturous reception as he emerged from a requiem mass for French civilians who had been killed in allied air raids. Most were paying homage to the victor of Verdun. They were indifferent to the now almost defunct Vichy government whose major preoccupation had become the savage civil war its Milice was waging against the Resistance, mostly in the old free zone area of southern France. Nonetheless, German propaganda made the most of it and news pictures of Pétain acknowledging his applause and people singing '*Maréchal nous voilà!*' were widely distributed.

Forty-two days later the Anglo-Americans landed on the Normandy beaches and Pierre Laval made a national radio appeal for people to conduct themselves as neutrals. 'We are not in the war,' he told them. 'You must not take part in the fighting. If you do not observe this rule you will provoke reprisals the harshness of which the government would be powerless to moderate. Those who ask you to stop work or invite you to revolt are the enemies of our country.'

But the brave minority willing to take on the Germans did not require an invitation and were certainly not going to listen to Laval. The Resistance, now more or less united under the leadership of de Gaulle (who in 1943 had moved his main headquarters to Algiers), rose en masse with their parachuted British weapons and instructors. Bridges were blown, railway lines cut, convoys ambushed. An entire SS panzer division, the Das Reich, was delayed for two vital weeks on its way from the south of France to Normandy. Among those involved were the two Litani River veterans Paddy Mayne and Tommy Macpherson. Colonel Mayne, whose raids on desert airfields had become legendary, commanded an SAS regiment and was one of the most decorated soldiers of the British army.

The kind of terrible reprisals Laval had predicted failed to diminish the appetite of the Forces Françaises de l'Intérieur, as the Resistance now called themselves, for guerrilla warfare. Less than three months after the Allied landings the street barricades were up in Paris and behind them men and women wearing FFI brassards. The Wehrmacht, outflanked by the Allies, were already withdrawing and the partisans awaiting the arrival of Général LeClerc's Free French 2nd Armoured Division to link up with their uprising and complete the capital's liberation.

When de Gaulle arrived in Paris on 25 August elements of the German rearguard and a few Milice snipers were still at large. There is a famous photograph of a welcoming crowd, looking no more or less Parisian than the one that greeted Pétain almost exactly four months before, suddenly trying to find cover in the Place de la Concorde. De Gaulle, refusing to crouch and apparently unafraid, strode into the old War Ministry building on the rue Saint Dominique. Shortly afterwards he left to address the crowd gathering outside the Hôtel de Ville (town hall). Introduced as 'Charles de Gaulle, President of the provisional government of the French Republic', he then made his second most remembered speech since 1940's 'France has lost a battle but not the war'. It contained these words:

> Paris stood up to liberate itself and knew how to do this with its own hands ... Paris! Outraged Paris! Broken Paris! Martyred Paris! But liberated Paris! Liberated by itself, liberated by its people with the help of the French armies, with the support and the help of all France, of the France that fights, of the only France, of the real France, of the eternal France! ... France returns to Paris, to her home ... bloody, but resolute.

This was the new truth and, like all cosseted seedlings, it swiftly took root. Paris had liberated itself. Later in the speech there is passing reference to 'our dear allies' but the driving force behind this victory was 'all France' which was Gaullist. Vichy had been an aberration invented by the Nazis. Certainly not an administration that, for well over two years and in some cases much longer, most of its citizens regarded as the legitimate government of France. Who cared to mention Pétain's last April in Paris now? Certainly not those who had been singing *maréchal nous voilà*. History was not only being made. It was being rewritten.

Pétain and Laval both spent the last eight months of the war in what virtually amounted to German custody, briefly at Belfort in eastern France and then at Sigmaringen Castle, once the seat of the Hohenzollern kings, at Württemberg on the Danube. On 24 April 1945 Pétain had his eighty-ninth birthday there. Two weeks later, he made his way through the rubble of Nazi Germany to Switzerland and thence to France. By the end of July, charged with treason, he was on trial for his life in a hot, stuffy courtroom in the Palais de Justice where he sat, saying little, 'dignified but dumb' according to the the *New Yorker*'s correspondent. As expected, de Gaulle commuted to life imprisonment the sentence that he be shot by firing squad. Pétain died in 1951, aged 95, on the bleak fortress island of Ile d'Yeu off the Atlantic coast. By then, without the stimulation of affairs of state, he had become quite senile.

One of the witnesses at his trial, called by both the prosecution and the defence, was Pierre Laval. In the last week of the European war he and his wife Eugénie had got away to Spain, landing at Barcelona airport in a Junkers 88 bomber on 1 May. Laval had been trying to persuade the Spanish to grant them asylum for the last two weeks along with the Swiss and Liechtensteiners. 'It is a tired and worn out old man who is writing to you,' Laval, just turned 62, had told Spanish Foreign Minister José Felix de Lequerica, an old friend, asking if they might 'enter Spain and await better days'.

Granting asylum to Vichy's most wanted man was not something the Franco regime was prepared to do in the delicate aftermath of the universal triumph over Fascism everywhere but on the lonely Iberian peninsula. The Spanish allowed Laval to stay for three months but made sure he did not receive a letter from Général de Chambun, his son-in-law's father, urging him not to come back but try to get his visa extended or go somewhere else. On 31 July, their three months expired, the Lavals found themselves back on an aircraft, this time bound for Linz where they were met by the Americans who took them to Innsbruck, which had become part of the French zone of the occupied Reich and where LeClerc's soldiers were waiting to receive them. Next day the Lavals were in separate cells in Paris's Fresnes prison. 'I don't know why my wife was arrested,' he told one of his lawyers. 'She's always been an Anglophile and a Gaullist.' Some eight weeks later Eugénie Laval was released without charge. This was nine days before her husband's trial began on 4 October.

It lasted for five days and by the end of the third day Laval was refusing to attend. So were his lawyers and the trial proceeded without the accused or defence counsel. 'Scenes which can only be described as scandalous led to this state of affairs,' reported the *Manchester Guardian*'s correspondent. The trial of one of France's most senior politicians for treason, a man accustomed to holding high office since the early 1930s (twice Prime Minister and Foreign Minister) should have been a solemn affair. But at this point Laval was probably the most detested man in France. Far more than Pétain, his fawning collaboration had come to symbolize all the humiliation of the occupation. Pierre Monibeaux, the president of the court, could not resist playing to the gallery or controlling others who wanted to do the same.

Laval gave as good as he got. 'His superior brain guided even the cheapest gibes,' observed the *New Yorker.* Prosecuting was the newly appointed *Procurateur général* André Mornet who in 1917 had been on the legal team that had the spy Mata Hari shot. At one point Mornet, who had a notoriously short fuse, remarked that a quick bullet as soon as Laval fell into French hands at Innsbruck 'would not have been a judicial mistake'.

'That would have deprived me of the pleasure of hearing you,' snapped the prisoner. But this set the mood. Long before all the evidence had been heard, several of the jurors found it impossible to conceal their prejudice any longer. 'The swine hasn't changed!' said one. 'Twelve bullets for him,' shouted another.

'The jury, before judging me, it's fantastic,' gasped Laval, suddenly very much the lawyer he had once been. And an editorial in the *Voix de Paris*, deploring the 'unimaginable lack of proprietary' of the jurors, noted 'the astuteness of Pierre Laval, that old warhorse quick to exploit any situation'.

Sentenced to death, put into leg irons and transferred to the condemned cell, he instructed his three lawyers not to ask for a reprieve but a retrial. De Gaulle granted them an audience – one of them had been in the Resistance – and listened to what they had to say. Their main point was that, guilty or not, the execution of a Prime Minister after such an appalling trial was a banana republic image unworthy of France. As they left they saw an aide bringing a copy of a French law book into the room they had just left and this made them hopeful.

But forty-eight hours later they were informed that the sentence would stand. The execution by firing squad was set to take place at Fort Châtillon in Paris at 9.30 a.m. on Wednesday, 15 October 1945. Laval was told the news the night before and his lawyers found him composed, even cheerful. Next morning at 8.45, as French law requires, *Procurateur général* Mornet, accompanied by Laval's lawyers, turned up at his cell to read him his death sentence. Next day the *Manchester Guardian* published an account of what followed which was obviously based on a conversation with one of Laval's lawyers.

> Without replying, he put his head under the blankets. His advocates thought that he had had a moment of weakness and one of them raised the blanket to ask him to master himself, but saw at once from Laval's appearance that he must have taken poison. He was already losing consciousness. He had in fact drunk from a bottle of cyanide of potassium which he still held, but in his hurry he had not drained the bottle and had not shaken it before drinking.

The poison, as Laval explained in a note he left, was 'a little packet of granules which no search has discovered'.

> I do not accept the sentence. I do not accept the stain of execution; it is murder. I intend to die in my own way, by poison, like the Romans ... I hope it will not have lost its strength for it has often had to change hiding place. The inside pocket of my fur coat sheltered it and my briefcase, which was always respected, sometimes received the packet when it was better wrapped. To execute is the duty of soldiers but today their duty is ques-

tionable. They are obliged to commit murder. Thanks to me they will not be the accomplices, even involuntary, of those who, from their very high positions, have ordered my assassination. They will not have to fire on a man who must die because he loved his country too much.

But Laval was denied his Roman death. A prison doctor and a stomach pump were summoned and within an hour he was deemed conscious enough to face execution. Meanwhile, the firing squad had been brought from Fort Châtillon and the venue changed to one of the courtyards in Fresnes prison. Laval had put on one of his trademark white ties and wrapped as a scarf around his neck the tricolour sash that was the symbol of office of the mayor of Aubervilliers. Still bringing up the water he had been given for the terrible thirst the cyanide had brought on, he was helped to the execution stake where he managed to croak out a few last words. 'I pity you for the work you have done,' he told *Procurateur général* Mornet. Then, refusing a blindfold, he turned to the firing squad and said, 'I pity you for having to execute this crime. Aim at my heart. *Vive la France!*'

De Gaulle, in his memoirs, conceded that Laval 'died bravely'.

In May 1979 *Victor*, a boys' comic, published in a series of true-war stories an account of how the half-French Peter Reynier won his Military Cross in Madagascar and was lucky to survive his own grenade. The now defunct *Victor* was a product of the flourishing Scots firm DC Thomson of Dundee, which at the beginning of the twenty-first century still counts the veterans *Beano* and *Dandy* among its most popular publications. It is a business with strong local ties. Their decision to include the story of the Royal Scots Fusiliers' lieutenant among the more predictable accounts – Desert Rats, Dam Busters, Chindits and Cockleshell Heroes – probably came about because the publishers had lost at least one of their employees among the three Scots infantry battalions that served in the almost forgotten campaign in Madagascar.

Otherwise, on both sides of the Channel, memories of Vichy and battles fought within living memory between the English and the French quickly dimmed to the point where an entire generation, possibly two, grew up almost entirely unaware of it. Perhaps more so in Britain which knew nothing as awful as the ten minutes of sudden death meted out by a recent ally at Mers-el-Kébir. Then occasionally, like grass through concrete, it surfaces.

In January 2004 the *Daily Telegraph* carried an obituary of the Highland broadcaster and farmer Ben Coutts who had been horribly disfigured by shrapnel at Tobruk and, after a year of plastic surgery, was being shipped home for more. On 12 September 1942 Coutts was aboard the *Laconia*, which was carrying 1,800 Italian prisoners-of-war as well as about 80 women and children, when the liner was torpedoed and sunk off West

Victor's *account of Reynier's heroism*

Africa. Once the Germans realised so many of their Italian allies were aboard, U-boats flying red cross flags did their best to rescue or at least provision all the survivors including the British. This came to an end when an American air attack killed some of those in the water and obliged the submarines to dive. Next on the scene were Vichy warships out of Dakar but, as the *Telegraph* reported, the badly wounded Coutts did not arouse universal compassion.

> The French sailors, Coutts remembered, treated them with wonderful kindness; their officers, with memories of the destruction of the French fleet at Mers-el-Kébir in mind, did not. As Coutts, unable to walk, crawled from his berth to the heads, a French officer kicked him violently on the backside. Thereafter, Coutts decided to urinate where he lay.

British civilians among the *Laconia* survivors were sent to a desert internment camp where conditions apparently left much to be desired. In June 2005, in its *People's War* website series, the BBC quoted Mrs Ena Stoneman, who at one point had been taken inside one of the U-boats along with her small daughter. Mrs Stoneman, the wife of an RAF sergeant, made some unflattering comparisons between the kindly German sailors and the treatment she received at the hands of the Vichy French at Sidi El Ayachia camp in Morocco until the Allied invasion brought her captivity to an end.

> The French were rotten. That's the only way to describe them. We ended up thinking of them as our enemies and not the Germans. They treated us like animals most of the time. It's quite impossible for me to describe the filth of the place. We were infested with lice and fleas and almost everybody suffered from dysentery. We were a burden to the French and they made it quite clear they hated us.

All a great contrast from the usual treatment of military prisoners, Coutts excepted, as the former Commando officer Gerald Bryan makes clear in his 2008 account of a hospital visit by Madame Dentz, wife of Syria's Vichy High Commissioner. Bryan, who had lost his right leg from below the knee during the Litani operation, was sharing a room with Pilot Officer Tommy Livingstone, a Hurricane pilot shot down in a dogfight with one of Le Gloan's Dewoitines over Rayak, where he bailed out wounded.

> I am afraid that Tommy and I were not very polite and did not give her a great welcome. She asked us if we had any complaints and I said, 'Yes.' We were about to complete one month as prisoners of war and under the Geneva Convention we were entitled to the pay of corresponding rank in

> the French Army. I would be glad if she would arrange for me to be paid accordingly. To my astonishment two days later I received a relatively small sum of money but it was sufficient to allow me to acquire a wrist watch with luminous hands. This made an enormous difference to my life because I no longer woke up in the middle of the night with no idea what the time was or how long it would take for day to break. It is impossible for me to explain adequately the enormous improvement this made to my morale.

In 1944, unfit for active service, Bryan transferred to the Colonial Office and by the early 1960s was Governor of the much fought over and still francophone Caribbean sugar island of St Lucia, which by 1814 had changed hands between the British and the French five times. Among his official duties was to make a New Year's Day broadcast in French, including a greeting to neighbouring Martinique which had been staunchly Vichy. Another, every 11 November, was to lay a wreath on St Lucia's French war memorial.

Memorials for England's last war against France are few and far between. The epitaphs in Plymouth's Weston Mill cemetery of the three British sailors killed on board the *Surcouf* give no indication who they were fighting. 'Greater Love Hath No Man', says Commander Sprague's tombstone. The cemetery at Mers-el-Kébir where Amiral Gensoul's men lie, and where the remains of Darlan were reinterred in 1962, has recently been desecrated by Islamic fanatics. In Madagascar goats graze on the overgrown graves of the 171 French servicemen who lie in Diego Suarez, their neglect made more reproachful by the neat contrast of the nearby British war cemetery where the casualties from the Joffre line are to be found. In Damascus there is a French cemetery with about 800 graves, Vichy and Gaullist, with an inscription over its gate that reads: '*Morts pour la France*'.

ACKNOWLEDGEMENTS

In 2005 Oxford's Bodleian Library republished a school-masterish booklet about France and the French that, in the spring of 1944, the War Office issued to every British serviceman about to take part in the Normandy landings. It was written by Herbert Ziman, a *Daily Telegraph* journalist and 1914–18 veteran, then serving as an officer in the Intelligence Corps. Apart from some useful advice about sex, alcohol – 'don't drink yourself silly' – and remembering that the French tend to be much politer than we are, it included a chapter entitled 'What do the French think of us?' which starts: 'It is fair to say that in 1940 we and the French parted on pretty bitter terms. They felt that we had not sent them a large enough British Expeditionary Force and that we had left them in the lurch at Dunkirk. Few of them believed we should carry on the war long after the evacuation.'

Over the last three years I have come to feel considerable admiration and sympathy for Ziman, confronted by his iconoclastic task in the face of almost four years of relentless contemporary propaganda. It took me much longer to write about this forgotten war within a war than I thought it would. The more I got to know about it the more important it became to put it all into context and explain what led up to these 'bitter terms'. It would have taken me even longer had it not been for the help of a number of people.

Murray Wrobel, who served against the Vichy French in Syria in 1941 and to whom this book is dedicated, looked at the kind of military documents he last translated as a 21-year-old lieutenant in the Cairo branch of the secretive Combined Services Detailed Interrogation Centre. His ability to sort out the wheat from the chaff – 'now it gets interesting' – was always invaluable and saved me months of work. Most of these papers came from the archives kept in Paris at the Château de Vincennes by the Service Historique de la Defense whose staff were unfailingly helpful to the Englishman come among them probing sensitive areas of the national psyche. For over a year, the leads they provided me with were followed up by the indefatigable Caroline Huot who unearthed one little scoop after another then mailed the copies to me in Nicosia where I live.

Other documents came from Britain's National Archives at Kew, the Royal Marine Museum at Southsea, the Templer Research Centre at the National Army Museum and the Greenwich Maritime Museum. Original material also came from the Imperial War Museum's Department of Documents where Roderick Suddaby and his team preside over a treasure trove of diaries, letters and unpublished manuscripts. All published sources are mentioned in the bibliography. While very effort has been made to trace copyright holders, if any have been inadvertently overlooked the publisher will be happy to acknowledge them in future.

I also had the luck to meet or correspond with some of the people caught up in these events. In Guernsey the late Patrick Whinney talked to me about the Darlan he had known in 1940 as an RNVR lieutenant in the British liaison team at the Château de Maintenon near Chartres where the French navy had its operational HQ. On the same island I also met Major General Frank 'Griff' Caldwell who, then a young sapper officer, made an arduous trek through the Vichy lines at night to try to get help for the besieged garrison at Mezze. I was able to talk to three of the young officers involved in 11 Commando's action on Lebanon's Litani river. Over lunch at his home in Berkshire Gerald Bryan relived for me how he had lost his right leg below the knee after he and his troop had captured and destroyed a French artillery battery. Sir Thomas Macpherson and Eric Garland, who both went on to have extraordinary wars, patiently did their best to answer my questions over long international telephone calls.

At the Royal Hospital in Chelsea four Pensioners who fought the French also shared their memories with me. Bill Cross of the Scots Greys told me how he and his mates were captured at bayonet point at Merjayoun by Vichy's Senegalese Tirailleurs. Donald Pickering and Walter Offord, both Royal Signals, recalled the way sun spots interfered with Jumbo Wilson's ceasefire signal and despatch riding with the Australians. Frederick Bailey, a gunner with 455 Independent Battery, told me about his experiences in Madagascar with its sudden casualties from pinpoint French counter-battery fire and a bewildering Japanese submarine attack in Diego Suarez harbour.

My thanks to Alan Samson at Weidenfeld & Nicolson for his enthusiasm for this project and editor Keith Lowe (author of the excellent *Inferno* – the story of the Hamburg fire bombing) who did his best to keep me on the straight and narrow. And to Beatrice Hemming, who took over the book in its final stages and demonstrated great persistence unearthing some of the photographic evidence. In London I owe, as usual, a great debt to my good friends Martin and Mori Woollacott for all their hospitality and encouragement. In Paris Charles Glass shared some of the research he was doing for his own book on the Americans who remained in Paris throughout the German occupation. For providing me with a small library, some of it privately published, on the Australian contribution to the Syrian campaign, I am greatly indebted to David and Susan Balderstone of Melbourne and Kakopetria. In Nicosia Lakis Zavallis, another close friend, constantly came to the rescue of this poor technophobe, a habit he first got into during the Turkish invasion of Cyprus in 1974. My wife Sylvia, whose native Guernsey suffered the same fate as France, sparked the idea for this book and though, as the years rolled by, she might sometimes have wished otherwise, she was, as ever, my most loyal supporter.

SOURCE NOTES

IWM Imperial War Museum
NA National Archive
VA Vincennes Archives

PROLOGUE

1 'Each of us fights': Robert and Isabelle Tombs, *That Sweet Enemy*, William Heinemann, London, 2006, p. 262.
1 'All of us hoped to continue the fight': Le Nistour, Vincennes Archives (VA).
2 'Are we prisoners?': ibid.
3 'It would be better to permit the existence of a French government': William L. Langer, *Our Vichy Gamble*, Knopf, New York, 1947, pp. 48–9, quoting Graziani papers on the Hitler–Mussolini meeting at Munich, 18 June 1940.
5 the martyrdom of the général's English exile began: Edward Spears, *Assignment to Catastrophe*, William Heinemann, London, 1954, p. 620.
6 'No more perceptible than a crack in crystal': ibid., p. 248.

CHAPTER ONE

9 'French cooks are so fond of cutting up joints into morsels': *Belfast Newsletter*, 6 April 1903.
10 'We are prisoners of an army': Thomas Pakenham, *The Boer War*, Weidenfeld & Nicolson, London, 1979, p. 110.
11 about 2,000 bottles of claret, champagne: Tombs, *That Sweet Enemy*, p. 428.
12 'We were confronted with the fact that a 'friendly Power' had, unprovoked': Winston Churchill, *The River War*, Standard Publications, Inc., New York, 2007, p. 319.
12 'An explorer in difficulties upon the Upper Nile': ibid., p. 320.
12 'Great Britain was determined to have Fashoda or fight': ibid., p. 319.
13 'Before they left a *sous-officer*': ibid., p. 323.
13 'his own brooding boyhood shame at this national humiliation': Charles Williams, *The Last Great Frenchman: A Life of General de Gaulle*, John Wiley, London, 1997, p. 19.
17 'The Great Asparagus': ibid., p. 42.

18 'My heart bled': Charles Williams, *Pétain*, Little, Brown, London, 2005, p. 138, quoting his memoirs.
19 'A Paladin worthy to rank': Max Egremont, *Under Two Flags*, Weidenfeld & Nicolson, London, 1997, p. xi (preface).
20 'red rosettes pinned to their uniforms': ibid., p. 56.
20 'It is wholly unnecessary to mount huge attacks with distant objectives': Williams, *Pétain*, p. 110.

CHAPTER TWO

22 About 743,000 of these came from the United Kingdom: all the British Empire casualty figures come from Martin Gilbert, *First World War*, Weidenfeld & Nicolson, London, 1994, p. 541.
23 The Americans had suffered 50,300 battle deaths: Gary Mead, *The Doughboys*, Penguin, London, 2001, p. 349 (Gilbert says 48,000).
24 'Deep fear of Germany': Winston Churchill, *The Second World War*, vol. i, *The Gathering Storm*, Penguin, London, 1985, p. 6.
24 'This is not peace': ibid., p. 10.
25 'Ties that the passing years can never weaken': Piers Brendon, *The Dark Valley*, Jonathan Cape, London, 2000, p. 505.
25 'No more wars for me at any price!': Robert Graves, *Goodbye to All That*, Penguin, London, 1966, p. 240.
26 'The English gave way': Tombs, *That Sweet Enemy*, quoting Desagneaux.
26 16,000 prisoners and more than 400 guns: Heinz Guderian, *Achtung Panzer!*, Weidenfeld & Nicolson, London, new edn, 1999, p. 121.
26 'old timers like us relive that feeling of impending doom': ibid., p. 121.
26 Life belts and rafts from cross-Channel ferries: Gilbert, op. cit., p. 646.
26 Exploiting a foggy dawn, nine North Staffords: privately published Staffordshire Regimental history available in the Templer Research Department, National Army Museum.
26 'I lost all my earthly faculties and fought like an Angel': quoted in C.D. Lewis's introduction to *The Collected Poems of Wilfred Owen*, Chatto & Windus, London, 1971, p. 23.
27 'genius and premature death': ibid., Edmund Blunden, memoir, appendix, p. 147.
27 'No celebration since the Armistice has aroused such deep feeling': Brendon, op. cit., p. 50.
27 Waiters clad in the ornate livery, powdered wigs: ibid., p. 503.
28 caviar, quail stuffed with foie gras, and Périgord truffles: ibid., p. 506.
28 'Let's not be heroic': ibid., p. 508, quoting Georges Bonnet.
28 a public appeal was started to buy Chamberlain a house: Duff Cooper, *Old Men Forget*, Rupert Hart-Davis (ed), London, 1954, p. 243.
29 'Anything, even the cruellest injustice': Simone de Beauvoir, *Prime of Life*, Gallimard, Paris, 1956, p. 268.
29 'I know how you have struggled to avoid war,' he said. 'You were right; we would have been beaten': Williams, *Pétain*, p. 290.

29 'Another few seconds please Mr Executioner': Williams, *The Last Great Frenchman*, p. 204.
29 'Disfigured the smiling landscape': Cooper, op. cit., p. 101.
30 'a pious one-eyed, one-legged war veteran': Adam Nossiter, *Algeria Hotel*, Houghton Mifflin, Boston, New York, 2001, p. 104.
30 'a cunning talmudist': Wikipedia, from judaisme.sdv.fr/perso/lblum/lblum.htm
31 'union tyranny': Brendon, op. cit., p. 498.
31 'Who said this man has no French blood?': ibid., p. 497.
33 'Thank God for the French army': Roy Jenkins, *Churchill: A Biography*, Macmillan, London, 2001, p. 268.

CHAPTER THREE

34 'The only great army on the side of decency': Orville H. Bullitt, *For the President*, Houghton Mifflin, Boston, 1972, p. 333.
34 'his great-grandfather Antoine Darlan': George E. Melton, *Darlan: Admiral and Statesman of France*, Praeger, Westport, Connecticut and London, 1998, p. 5.
35 'into a meritocratic family with a strong belief': ibid., pp. 5–6.
35 'I don't have any special respect': ibid., p. 27.
35 a spell in the British Ypres-Passchendaele sector: ibid., p. 9.
36 'the Battle of Trafalgar; on the other, Waterloo': ibid., p. 17, quoting *Service Historique de la Marine*, Vincennes Archives (VA), 1BB2 EMG/SE, Carton 208.
36 'A vast fabric of stupidities': ibid., p. 17.
37 The only bad note came at the coronation itself: ibid., pp. 50–51.
39 'HOPE THAT WE MAY HAVE': VA
39 Hooky to his navy friends: author's interview in Guernsey, 2002, with Patrick Whinney who was an RNVR lieutenant on Holland's staff when the British naval attaché worked out of the French Navy's operational HQ at the Château de Maintenon near Chartres.
40 'An infinitely courteous': 1–TS, VA.
40 *Amis de Darlan:* Melton, op. cit., p. 47.
40 failed to explode: Churchill, *The Second World War*, vol. i, p. 592.
40 'surprise, ruthlessness and precision': ibid., p. 532.
41 They informed their rescuers: ibid., p. 531.
41 'worth all the rest of the blockade': Jenkins, *Churchill*, p. 566.
41 'harebrained': Major General Sir John Kennedy, *The Business of War*, Hutchinson, London, 1957, p. 48.
42 'use bluff and good humoured determination': ibid.
44 almost half of Britain's oil imports: *Oxford Companion to World War 2*, Oxford, 2000 p. 821.
44 'Some of our finest troops, the Scots and Irish Guards': Churchill, op. cit, p. 582.
44 'By comparison with the French, or the Germans': Roger Parkinson, *The Auk*, Granada Publishing, London, 1977, p. 55.
45 'as great a disappointment': Bullitt, op. cit., p. 484.

45 almost universal agreement among its chattering classes that *they* would have done much better: author's conversation with Patrick Whinney, Guernsey, summer 2002.

45 'All I need to sit at the peace conference': Alistair Home, *To Lose a Battle: France 1940*, Macmillan, London, 1969, p. 631.

45 Three French divisions: ibid., p. 63.

CHAPTER FOUR

47 shortly before dawn on Wednesday, 3 July 1940: Lieutenant de vaisseau Crescent, report after repatriation from England, dated Toulon 12.12.40. Vincennes (VA), Document 267c.

47 had ordered all but one of *Surcouf*'s four deck hatches to be battened down: ibid.

47 torpedoes had been disarmed, their fuses and firing pins removed: ibid.

48 the flotilla's flagship was called the *Entente Cordiale:* NA ADM 199/822.

48 'All men who had fired a rifle were included': from a report by Colonel Noyes lodged at the Royal Marine Museum, Southsea, Hampshire.

48 a typewritten sheet of four French phrases: James Rusbridger, *Who Sank Surcouf?*, Random Century, London, 1991, p. 38.

49 'The French Nation has fought gallantly to a standstill': Admiral Dunbar-Nasmith's letter, NA ADM 119 822.

49 'Any resistance can only cause unnecessary bloodshed': ibid.

49 'arms and ammunition readily available': ibid.

49 'Cayol was naturally very distressed': ibid.

49 'he had considered the question of scuttling': ibid.

49 'ran along the casing for'ard': from Talbot's report on the capture of the *Surcouf*, NA ADM 199/822.

49 its catches looked similar to the new ones on British conning tower hatches: ibid. Talbot described the hatch as 'of the D.S.E.A.[Davis Submarine Escape Apparatus] type and thus could be opened from outboard'.

50 'I ordered him to close the last hatch': Crescent's report, VA, Document 267c.

50 engine room artificers . . . refused to budge: Talbot's report, NA ADM 199/822.

52 'I took a pace forward': Lieutenant de vaisseau Bouillaut, from his report to Capitaine de corvette Martin commanding the submarine *Surcouf*, dated Walton Hospital, Liverpool, 25 July 1940. VA, Document 284c.

53 not kneeling but lying on his stomach: from Talbot's description of what he could see of the gunfight from the Command Post. NA ADM 199/822.

53 squeezed off one ineffectual shot as he fell: Crescent's report, VA, Document 267c.

53 hanging onto the ladder to the Command Post: Talbot's report, NA ADM 199/822.

53 travelled down the inside of his right arm, entered his chest: from *Copie de certificate d'origine de blessure du Lieutenant de Vaisseau Bouillaut*, Le Nistour papers, VA.

53 'there were no English capable of fighting left': Bouillaut's report. VA, Document 284c.

53 Bouillaut had heard more shots: ibid.
53 'Things are getting hot': Le Nistour's report on the evacuation from Brest and his stay in England. (In colloquial French the expression is, '*Ça va barder*!') VA.
54 'The English sergeant [Webb] rushes towards us with his fixed bayonet': VA, Document 267c. Le Nistour was convinced Webb was a soldier or a marine, not a sailor, and insists he was wearing khaki. He was probably confused by the khaki webbing holding his ammunition pouches.
55 'we can't let them do this to us': Bouillaut's report, VA, Document 284c.
55 saying, 'Finis': Talbot's report, NA ADM 199/822.
55 'the impasse was resolved by Crescent suggesting': Crescent's report, VA, Document 267c.
55 'I told them to wait': Le Nistour's report, VA.
55 '25 minutes before the doctor reached Commander Sprague': Talbot's report, NA ADM 199/822.
56 'seven separate bullet wounds': surgeon commander's report, NA ADM 199/822.
56 'An English officer, bareheaded very agitated': Dr Adrian Carré, VA, Document 1406.
56 'How sad, how sad': ibid.

CHAPTER FIVE

57 thinking about the day's sporting activities: Bezard papers, IWM, Misc 2, Item 38.
61 'The more I see the nakedness of our defences': Field Marshal Lord Alanbrooke, *War Diaries 1939–45*, Weidenfeld & Nicolson, London, 2001, p. 90.
62 'We had to shoot them down a second time': Churchill, *The Second World War*, vol. ii, *Their Finest Hour*, p. 203.
62 'The addition of the French Navy to the German and Italian Fleets': ibid., p. 205.
63 'I felt that I should be failing in my duty': Somerville's report on Operation Catapult, NA ADM 399/192.
63 'a) Sail with us and continue to fight for victory': ibid.
64 'THE BRITISH ADMIRALTY HAS SENT CAPTAIN HOLLAND': NA ADM 199/391.
64 dogged by a French awareness that theirs was the smaller fleet: author's interview with Patrick Whinney, Guernsey, 2002.
64 'The first time, they sent me a Vice Admiral': Philippe Masson, *La Marine Française et La Guerre* 1939–45, Paris, p. 143.
64 completed by dusk: NA ADM 199/391.
64 'I refused to receive Captain Holland': Gensoul's report to Darlan dated 9 July 1940, No.154 E.M.3, *Service Historique de la Défense*, VA.
65 'In no case will French ships': ibid.
65 'any time, anywhere, any way': Holland papers, Greenwich Maritime Museum, London.

65 'French ships will use force to defend themselves': Donald MacIntyre, *Fighting Admiral: The Life of Admiral of the Fleet Sir James Somerville*, Evans, London, 1961, p. 67.
65 'three fair offers': ibid.
65 'this veritable ultimatum': Gensoul's report, No.154 E.M.3, *Service Historique de la Défense*, VA.
66 decrypts of German naval codes: F.H. Hinsley and Alan Stripp, *Codebreakers: The Inside Story of Bletchley Park*, OUP, Oxford, 1994, p. 2.
66 'I tackled him on the question of Admiral Darlan's hands being tied': Force H war diaries, NA ADM 119/391.
66 'the first shot fired against us': ADM 199/391.
66 'They're mad – absolutely mad': Jean Boutron, *Mers-el-Kébir à Londres*, Plon, Paris, 1980, p. 26.
67 'But we are not beaten': ibid., p. 14.
67 'unacceptable ultimatum': ibid., p. 28.
67 'The bloody Armistice, we haven't finished paying for it': ibid., pp. 42–3.
68 great doorsteps of sandwiches: Alan Coles and Ted Briggs, *Flagship 'Hood': The Fate of Britain's Mightiest Warship*, Robert Hale, London, 1988, p. 76.
68 a man who was not about to wait much longer: ibid., p. 78.
68 'I HAVE NO INTENTION OF PUTTING TO SEA': Gensoul's report, No.154 E.M.3, *Service Historique de la Défense*, VA.
68 'PASS TO GENSOUL': Coles and Briggs, op. cit., p. 79.
69 'AM PREPARED PERSONALLY': Gensoul's report, No.154 E.M.3, *Service Historique de la Défense*, VA.
69 'it was my intention to use force if necessary': Somerville's report, NA ADM 199/391.
69 'to gain the advantage of darkness': Gensoul's report, No.154 E.M.3, *Service Historique de la Défense*, VA.
70 'If God judged that my salvation': taken from the statement made on the death of Grall by Ingénieur mécanicien Albert Borey at Cherbourg on 4 January 1945 in support of his citation for a posthumous Croix de Chevalier de la Légion d'honneur. VA.
71 'You – priest – fuck off – now!' (and above): Boutron, op. cit., pp. 92–3.

CHAPTER SIX

73 'tantamount to a declaration of war': Holland's report to Somerville, NA ADM 199/391.
74 'I explained most carefully to him': ibid.
74 'Admiral Gensoul however remained stubborn': ibid.
75 'IF ONE OF THE BRITISH PROPOSALS': Somerset's report to Somerville, NA ADM 199/391.
75 'CAN GET NO NEARER': Holland's report, NA/ADM 199/391.
75 '1. The French Fleet cannot do otherwise': ibid. Original note in pencil.
75 'if they had anything to communicate': Holland's report, NA/ADM 199/391.
75 They would all be massacred: Boutron, *Mers-el-Kébir à Londres*, p. 101.
76 'There is a sudden loud explosion close by': ibid p. 102

77 Ingénieur mécanicien en chef Egon, Xavier Grall, another ingénieur mécanicien named Quentel: Borey's report on Grall's death included in Amiral Ortoli's recommendation for a posthumous award. VA.

77/78 'All the men in that section were shredded': VA. The damage report is Appendix One of *Contre amiral* Ortoli's recommendations, dated Paris, 12 February 1945, for posthumous awards for Grall and others, to which he added the note: 'If one considers that, in the Breton village where Mr Grall's widow lives, public opinion has not shown this officer the respect due to those who died for their country, one would understand why Madame Grall, now wonders if her husband's sacrifice was but a cruel delusion.'

78 'men come up onto the deck and jump into the water': Boutron, op. cit., p. 106.

79 'give the French an opportunity to abandon their ships': Somerville's report, NA ADM 199/391.

80 'a fire extinguisher in his hands' and all description of the damaged *Mogador:* from Bezard, IWM Misc 21, Item 38.

80 'the water suddenly stirred': ibid.

80 'The *Volta*'s done for!' ibid.

80 'planned to double back with *Le Terrible*': ibid.

81 'the conditions required by the English were being met': Gensoul's report, No.154 E.M.3, *Service Historique de la Défense*, VA.

81 'UNLESS I SEE YOUR SHIPS SINKING': Somerville's report, NA ADM 199/391.

82 shell splinters had blinded an able seaman: letter home from Able Seaman Bernard R. Williams, IWM 92/27/1.

82 at least 100 of the smaller 4-inch and 6-inch shells: ADM 199/391.

83 'At about 1910, while at 12,000 feet, 9 French fighters': ibid.

84 waiting for the first bomb to be dropped: ibid.

84 'It was a fine sight': de Winton papers, IWM 85/44/1.

86 'One or two hits were possibly obtained': ADM 199/391, quoting Hodgkinson's report.

86 its track was spotted by *Poursuivante:* Gensoul's report, No.154 E.M.3, *Service Historique de la Défense*, VA.

86 'the possible loss of British ships was justified': NA ADM 199/391.

86 'I would not have any of my destroyers sunk': MacIntyre, *Fighting Admiral*, p. 69, quoting Somerville papers.

87 'At about eight o'clock the first of the rescuers': Borey's statement supporting a citation for the Légion d'honneur for Grall, dated 4 January 1945, Cherbourg. VA.

88 After various malfunctions in the shallow water: Arthur Marder, *Operation Menace: The Dakar Expedition and the Dudley North Affair*, Oxford University Press, London, 1976, pp. 257–8.

88 'the unskilled butcher of Oran': MacIntyre, op. cit., p. 189.

CHAPTER SEVEN

89 'If there is a stain on a flag today': Gensoul papers, No.154 E.M.3, *Service Historique de la Défense*, VA.
89 'The impression which emerges from these conversations': Bullitt, *For the President*, p. 481.
90 'Headstrong, spoiled, spectacular, something of a nabob': *New Yorker*, April 1938.
90 'I am fully prepared to pay for them myself': Bullitt, op. cit., p. 455.
90 'Every precaution should be taken to avoid publicity': ibid.
91 threatening to shoot the trespassers: ibid., p. 477.
91 'a very foul specimen of double crosser': NA FCO 371.
91 'one of the most remarkable and revealing documents in the entire annals of this great war': Langer, *Our Vichy Gamble*, p. 69.
91 'Darlan went on to say': Bullitt, op. cit., pp. 484, 486.
92 'even some of the *Amis de Darlan* were unprepared': Melton, *Darlan*, p. 85.
92 'soft silky manner': Churchill, *The Second World War*, vol. ii, p. 159.
92 'Little stands between French acts of war against the British': Bullitt, op. cit., p. 481.
92 French naval officers informed Murphy: Robert Murphy, *Diplomat Among Warriors*, Collins, London, 1964, p. 78.
92 'no prior knowledge of the naval attack and deplored it': ibid., p. 78.
92 'a tragic blunder': Cordell Hull, *The Memoirs of Cordell Hull*, Macmillan, New York, 1948, p. 798.
92 'Even if there was only the remote possibility': Marder, *Operation Menace*, p. 282, quoting Francis Charles-Roux's *Cinq mois tragiques aux affaires étrangères*, Gallimard, Paris, 1947, p. 130.
92 had been urging Bullitt: Bullitt, op. cit., p. 306.
93 'the British mean to win': Raymond E. Lee, *The London Journal of General Raymond E. Lee, 1940–41*, Hutchinson, London, 1972, p. 12.
93 Approval, often mingled with astonishment, was widespread: NA ADM 199/192. Foreign Office telegrams were copied to the Admiralty. The quotes from the Swiss press were sent by the British consul in Berne.
93 'still has the ruthlessness of the captains and pirates': Marder, op. cit., quoting *Ciano's Diary* 1939–43. Edited by Malcolm Muggeridge.
94 'stir up the heavy dough': John Lukacs, *The Duel: 10 May–31 July 1940: The Eighty-Day Struggle Between Churchill and Hitler*, Bodley Head, London, 1990, p. 32.
95 'The Prime Minister expects': Churchill, op. cit., vol. ii, p. 211.
95 tears of joy: Jenkins, *Churchill*, p. 625, quoting Harold Nicolson's diaries.
95 'a scene unique in my own experience': Churchill, op. cit., vol. ii, p. 211.
96 painted a matt black for the occasion: NA ADM 234/318.
96 'meet attacks from the English enemy with the utmost ferocity': Churchill, op. cit., vol. ii, p. 210.
98 'One of the most brilliant exploits of the war': NA ADM 199/822. From Knatchbull-Hugessen's 10.7.40 Ankara-Foreign Office despatch copied to the Admiralty.

98 'Mers-el-Kébir was a terrible blow to our hopes': Charles de Gaulle, *The Call to Honour,* Collins, London, 1955, p. 97.
98 attempted to sing the 'Marseillaise': Williams, *The Last Great Frenchman*, p. 121.
99 'looked with some mistrust upon those allies of yesterday': de Gaulle, op. cit., p. 94.
99 'You are perfectly free to serve under General de Gaulle': ibid., p. 94.
99 'A taste for risk and adventure': ibid., p. 98.
101 '*1 pistolet automatique (marque MAR police calibre 7.65) et deux chargeurs*': Bouillaut papers, VA, Document 287c.
101 'I protested vehemently': ibid.
102 'I don't want to be torpedoed': Crescent report, VA, Document 267c.
103 'They presented the following arguments': ibid.
103 'a few Free French aircrew participate in an attack on the Ruhr': de Gaulle, op. cit., p. 86.

CHAPTER EIGHT

104 a dream come true for every Frenchman who was anti-Semitic enough: Michael R. Marrus and Robert O. Paxton, *Vichy France and the Jews*, Stanford University Press, California, 1995, p. 3.
105 the word *émigré* a fashionable insult: Patrick Marnham, *The Death of Jean Moulin*, John Murray, London, 2000.
106 'Then he led me into the great drawing room': Murphy, *Diplomat Among Warriors*, pp. 82–3.
108 estimated by the British embassy at £2,000 a month: NA FOHX1.
109 the only publication to be successfully closed down: Carmen Callil, *Bad Faith: A Forgotten History of Family and Fatherland*, Jonathan Cape, London, 2006, pp. 185–6.
109 'Neither a thug nor a fool': Alexander Werth, *France 1940–1955*, Henry Holt, New York, 1956, p. 79.
109 Towards the end of August Laval was back in Paris: Robert O. Paxton, *Vichy France: Old Guard and New Order 1940–44*, Columbia University Press, New York, 2001, p. 60.
110 'I see no compelling grounds for the continuation of this war': Lukacs, *The Duel*, p. 190, citing *Der grossdeutsche Freiheitskampf: Reden Adolf Hitlers, vol.* ii, Munich, 1941.
110 'It developed that Laval had sent the German embassy': Murphy, op. cit., pp. 84–5.
110 'We find ourselves in a situation without precedent': Paxton, op. cit. p. 70.

CHAPTER NINE

113 'He could never accept': Edward Spears, *Two Men Who Saved France: Pétain and de Gaulle*, Eyre and Spottiswoode, London, 1962, p. 144.
113 'Dakar wakes up': de Gaulle, *The Call to Honour,* p. 121.

114 he had written a letter asking to be relieved of his command: Holland papers, National Maritime Museum, Greenwich, London.
114 her new plumbing which, despite the latitude: Marder, Arthur, *Operation Menace: The Dakar Expedition and the Dudley North Affair*, OUP, London, 1976.
115 the 'nurses' were not really nurses at all: papers in Royal Marine Museum, Southsea, Hampshire.
115 Susan Travers admitted to starting an affair: Susan Travers, *Tomorrow to be Brave*, Bantam Press, London, 2000, pp. 50–51.
115 playing in the salon where the officers dined: papers in Royal Marine Museum, Southsea, Hampshire.
115 'At about 5pm the cruiser *Fiji* next to us': *The Diaries of Evelyn Waugh* (ed. Michael Davie), Weidenfeld & Nicolson, London, 1976, pp. 479–80.
115 refused to sail unless sufficient champagne and foie gras were included in their rations: Philippe Masson, *La Marine Française et la Guerre 1939–45*, p. 203.
116 'I had no doubt whatever that the enterprise should be abandoned': Churchill, *The Second World War, vol.* ii, p. 427.
116 'There was no mistaking their sympathies': Emden papers, IWM 86/59/1.
117 'I learned some very vulgar French words': Friend papers, IWM 86/37/1.
118 '*Français de Dakar! Joignez-vous à nous pour delivrer la France*': ibid. (Friend lost his own copy when the *Ark Royal* was sunk in 1941 but remembered the headline.)
120 'You have a nice little fleet here': Marder, op. cit., p. 112, quoting *Histoire de la France outre-mer, 1940–45*, Paris, 1949, pp. 112–13.
121 He gave the sergeant an ungodly kick in the balls: ibid., p. 113.
121 Amiral Landriau had changed his mind: ibid.
121 'If fire continues on my ships': ibid., p. 118.
122 A single 9.4-inch shell ... holed the ship about 6 inches above the armour plate: Emden papers, IWM 86/59/1.
122 'We felt generally fed up': ibid.
122 'My action station was in the wheel house': IWM 61/39/1. From 'Five Years of My Life' privately published autobiography of Commander James Anthony Syms, DSC.
124 'It was a French ship and I had a French mother': Christopher Somerville, *Our War*, Weidenfeld & Nicolson, London, 1998, p. 57.

CHAPTER TEN

126 'a shark-infested sea': Spears, *Two Men Who Saved France*, p. 201.
127 'even the minimum required for brave men to dash for an objective': ibid., p. 200.
127 he planned to give up as soon as his position became dangerous: Marder, *Operation Menace*, p. 125.
128 intended a token resistance before surrender: ibid., p. 126.
128 'I shall defend Dakar to the end': Irwin papers, IWM 139.
129 'As we lined up to dive bomb the *Richelieu*'; Half conscious, he surfaced with a broken arm and his mouth tasting of petrol: Friend papers, IWM 86/37/1.

(Richardson told Friend his story when, both civilians, they bumped into each other in London shortly after the end of the war.)

132 Over Gibraltar that same afternoon: Raymond Dannreuther, *Somerville's Force H*, Aurum, London, 2006, pp. 48–9; also Marder, op. cit., p. 175; other details of the air raid from Gibraltar sources.

132 'courage and fidelity': Marder, op. cit., p. 135.

133 'an old Irish wake': Spears, *Assignment to Catastrophe*, p. 205.

133 'rather lively cannonade': de Gaulle, *The Call to Honour*, p. 131.

133 Spears observed the Frenchman flick one butt after another onto timber: Spears, op. cit., p. 208.

134 'Why do you not land in force by night or in the fog': IWM 139. Full text of Churchill's message contained in General Irwin's report on the Dakar expedition.

134 *Australia*'s fire so that it was straddling: first-person account by Midshipman Mackenzie J. Gregory, Naval Historical Society of Australia.

135 'We have decided that the enterprise against Dakar': IWM 139. Churchill's message is appended to Lieutenant General Irwin's report on Dakar. The Admiralty received the news of the *Resolution*'s torpedoing at 12.45 p. m. on 25/9/40 and the Prime Minister's reply, which would have been sent a few minutes after he wrote it, was timed at 1.27 p. m.

135 sunk alongside the south mole: Dannreuther, op. cit., p. 48, and other details of Vichy's second air raid on Gibraltar.

135 'Bloodshed has been avoided at the cost of honour': *The Diaries of Evelyn Waugh*, edited by Michael Davie.

136 'A very gay journey back': ibid.

136 'We went to Dakar with General de Gaulle': Marder, op. cit.

CHAPTER ELEVEN

137 some wit had pinned ... a '*Communiqué anglais*': *L'Illustration*, 2 November 1940.

137 'modest share to the final overthrow of England': Geoffrey Warner, *Pierre Laval and the Eclipse of France*, Eyre and Spottiswoode, London, 1968, p. 228, citing German Foreign Ministry archives.

138 'France is fighting with Germany against Britain': Paxton, *Vichy France*, p. 70.

138 'We don't need your help': Warner, op. cit., p. 224.

138 'wallowed in defeat like a dog in filth': Langer, *Our Vichy Gamble*, p. 84, quoting Raymond Brugère's *Veni, Vidi, Vichy*, Paris, 1944.

139 'it's not only Foreign Minister Von Ribbentrop you're going to see': Warner, op. cit., p. 232.

139 'Merde, alors!': ibid.

140 'if you offer us a just peace': ibid., p. 233.

140 'I will not add to Germany's suffering by sparing France': from Josée Laval's compilation of her father's surviving papers, *The Unpublished Diary of Pierre Laval*, Falcon Press, London, 1948, p. 75.

140 'We shall have to endure English reprisals': Warner, op. cit., p. 234.

142 'The English will fight and go on fighting': John Toland, *Adolf Hitler*, Ballantine Books, New York, 1977, p. 870.
142 'I'd rather have three or four of my teeth out': Ciano's Diaries, op. cit., p. 402.
143 'If General Weygand will raise the standard': NA FO 370/2769.
143 'If they come to North Africa with four divisions': Langer, op. cit., p. 86, quoting Louis Rougier's *Les Accords Pétain–Churchill*, Montreal, 1945.
144 'A *collaboration* was envisaged': Paxton, op. cit., p. 77.
144 'The Axis powers and France have an identical interest': Langer, op. cit., p. 95.
144 'it was necessary to proceed slowly and with caution': Warner, op. cit., p. 237.

CHAPTER TWELVE

148 'I felt insulted, a young woman was present': VA. Le Nistour's report to the Médecin Général Director of Health Services, 3rd Maritime Region, dated Toulon, 8 December 1940.
149 'I told Kaye that this blackmail': ibid.
149 'The next morning I was visited': Bouillaut papers, VA, Document 287c.
150 except for Capitaine de corvette de Saussine: mentioned by de Gaulle in his memoir, *The Call to Honour*
151 'I was asked not to leave Liverpool for too long': Bouillaut's report on his stay in England, VA, Document 287c, dated Toulon, 27 December 1940.
151 Liverpool had 200 killed: www.liverpool.gov.uk/archives/
153 'with the information they already have, this state of affairs could be extremely dangerous to us': NA HW 50/10.

CHAPTER THIRTEEN

155 'What we want is not bones but meat': Werth, *France 1940–1955*, p. 12.
156 Dining alone with Robert Murphy, Peyrouton had confided: Murphy, *Warrior Among Diplomats*, p. 98.
156 'I remain more than ever a partisan of the policy of collaboration': Langer, *Our Vichy Gamble*, p. 110.
156 judging by the editorials in his newspaper *Oeuvre:* Werth, op. cit., p. 110.
156 'I hope, *Monsieur le Maréchal*': Warner, *Pierre Laval and the Eclipse of France*, pp. 255–6.
157 'An American journalist': Laval, *Unpublished Diary*, p. 84.
157 'What swine! And it's Friday the 13th': Warner, op. cit., p. 256.
158 'a puppet, a windbag, and a weathercock twirling in every breeze': ibid., pp. 263–4
159 'Even if I wished it, the improper conduct of M. Laval': ibid., p. 266. Quoting DGFP Series D, Vol. XI. The text of the letter was forwarded to the German Foreign Ministry on Christmas Day 1940.
159 'setting out again on the same road which led it to Vichy': Melton, *Darlan*, p. 101.
160 'My family have always hated the English': David Irving, *Hitler's War*, Hodder & Stoughton, London, 1977, p. 193.

CHAPTER FOURTEEN

163 streets named Bond, Regent and Tottenham Court Road: Roald Dahl, *Going Solo*, Penguin, London, 1988, p. 92.
163 delighted in painting doleful tales of the hellhole: ibid., p. 91.
163 a couple of nights under canvas on the nearest high ground: ibid., p. 93.
164 Air Vice-Marshal Reggie Smart, a 50-year-old survivor: all details on AVM Smart from www.rafweb.org/biographies.
164 'frequently descended among heavy rifle fire': *London Gazette*, 28 October 1921.
167 his Anglophobia with Operation Ration: Paxton, *Vichy France*, p. 116.
167 'The Cabinet are particularly concerned': NA ADM 223/678.
168 a direct hit on a magazine: ibid.
168 an Australian ship adapted a Lee-Enfield cartridge: Marder, op. cit.
168 a Frenchman named Tarte: NA ADM 223/678.
168 'Please at once inform your French colleague': ibid.
168 'with the shortest delay': ibid.
169 It might even revive a French proposal floated: Paxton, op. cit., p. 59.
171 'I want you to go to Jerusalem and relieve Baghdad': Field Marshal Lord Wilson, *Eight Years Overseas*, 1939–1847, Hutchinson, London, 1949, p. 109.
172 'Our patient and much tried': Christopher Buckley, *Five Ventures*, HMSO, London, 1946, p. 45.
172 'I have consistently warned you': the exchange of telegrams between Wavell, Churchill and the Chiefs of Staff are an edited version of those quoted by Churchill in his wonderful history, *The Second World War.*

CHAPTER FIFTEEN

176 'Please make no flying or the going out of any force': article by Kelly Bell, *Aviation History*, May 2004.
176 'Any interference with training flights': ibid.
178 'One 20 pound bomb carries': Anthony Dudgeon, *Hidden Victory*, Tempus, London, 2000, p. 45.
178 'We were only too aware that we had nothing': ibid., pp. 59–60.
179 with fifty-two new bullet holes: ibid., p. 59.
179 'The terms "minor damage" or "flesh wounds": ibid., p. 60.
180 'a solid mass of flame 250 yards long': Christopher Shores, *Dust Clouds in the Middle East*, Grub Street, London, 1996, p. 176.
180 to advertise their arrival by flying low and slow: Dudgeon, op. cit., p. 63.
182 'except for the guns and a little ammunition': Shores, op. cit., p. 186.
182 'One Me110 flashed past my port wing': Thomas Andrew, *Gladiator Aces*, Osprey Publishing, London, 2002
183 a communications centre . . . a flying laboratory: Dudgeon, op. cit., p. 111.
184 Adjutant-chef Contes, had received a bad leg wound: Shores, op. cit., p. 191.
184 Sous-lieutenant Vuillemin shot down a Blenheim: ibid.
184 same Moranes were given the task of escorting four Junkers 52s: ibid.

184 Rahn sent 12 field guns – 8 of them big 155mm – with 16,000 shells: Buckley, *Five Ventures* (Iraq–Syria–Persia–Madagascar–Dudecanese), HMSO, London, 1954.

186 the second went through the hole: Bernard Ferguson, *The Black Watch and the King's Enemies*, Collins, London, 1950, pp90–91.(On German casualties at Heraklion, Ferguson quotes the commander of a parachute battalion who was later captured by the British in North Africa.)

186 1,828 compared to 1,751: Antony Beevor, *Crete: The Battle and the Resistance*, Penguin, London, 1992, Appendices, p. 346.

188 Sottotenente Valentini, who bailed out: Shores, op. cit., p. 195.

188 captured at rifle point by the Household Cavalry's intelligence officer: Somerset de Chair, *The Golden Carpet*, Faber & Faber, London, 1945, p. 77.

188 'A bold and correct decision': John Connell, *Wavell: Supreme Commander*, Collins, London, 1969, p. 446.

188 '*C'est magnifique mais ... c'est* bloody silly': John Verney, *Going to the Wars*, Collins, London, 1955, p. 83.

CHAPTER SIXTEEN

191 'Concentration of Australian and English troops in Palestine frontier area': VA, Cipher No. 524 A 526/DE 2200 hrs 28.5.41.

192 'This is an important moment in your history': VA. Catroux's proclamation dropped by the RAF as a propaganda leaflet.

193 Raziel had just asked for a cigarette: J. Bowyer-Bell, *Terror Out of Zion*, Avon Books, London, 1977, p. 70, quoting Yaacov Tarazi who survived the air strike.

193 one of four brothers on active service: Hermione Ranfurly, *To War with Whitaker: Wartime Diaries of Countess Ranfurly 1939–45*, Heinemann, London, 1994, p. 76.

193 Palmer and all twenty-three Haganah volunteers, three of them crew, disappeared: Allied Special Forces Association, Hereford. www.alliedspecialforces.org (The fate of the *Sea Lion* is one of the more enduring mysteries of the Second World War. Nothing in the surviving British, French, German and Italian archives has ever been unearthed that sheds any light on it.)

194 paused to eat chocolate: Moshe Dayan, *Story of My Life*, Weidenfeld & Nicolson, London, 1976, p. 48.

194 'I awoke to daylight': ibid., p49.

196 much impressed by the courage and marksmanship displayed by the Arab Taher: ibid.

196 'I opened up': ibid., p. 50.

196 'I must say it required a considerable effort': ibid.

198 emptying a pistol around the manager's dancing feet: ibid., pp. 33–4.

198 In 1938 Mayne was also selected to play [ftn]: Hamish Ross, *Paddy Mayne*, Sutton Publishing, Stroud, Gloucestershire, 2003 p. 31

198 'too old to be dangerous' [ftn]: *Chambers Biographical Dictionary*, quoting L. Dawson's *Sound of Guns*.

199 'Eleven Commando were very young and quiet': *The Diaries of Evelyn Waugh*, p. 493.
199 accused Pedder of being a 'half mad': ibid., p. 512.
199 'saw to their welfare': ibid.
199 most of his young officers, whose average age was 21, respected him as an excellent trainer: author's interviews and correspondence with Gerald Bryan, Eric Garland and Sir Thomas Macpherson, June – July 2008.
200 'Never in the whole history of human endeavour': Julian Thompson, *War Behind Enemy Lines*, Sidgwick and Jackson, London, 1998, p. 47.

CHAPTER SEVENTEEN

202 One of those being left behind offered Lance Corporal Noble Sproule: www.combinedops.com/
202 not even lingering long enough to pick up her landing craft: NA DEFE 2/349.
203 could be irritatingly Bertie Wooster: Ross, *Paddy Mayne*, p. 46, quoting interview with Sir Thomas Macpherson.
203 'Spent Alma Mater's birthday': Keyes's journal, NA DEFE 2/349.
203 'likely to be extremely well registered by batteries': ibid.
203 London-born immigrant: Gavin Long, *Greece, Crete and Syria*, Halstead Press, Sydney, 1962, p. 309.
204 had improvised one: and other details of the 2/16th's river crossing, Jim and Trigellis Smith, Syd McAllester, *Largely a Gamble*, Commonwealth of Australia, Canberra, 1995, pp. 62–6.
204 'all firing very accurately': Keyes's journal notes on Litani operation, NA DEFE 2/349.
204 'Extremely unpleasant ... snipers in wired post': ibid.
205 'I couldn't really see a target': Eric Garland, author's telephone interview, 7 July 2008.
207 'Eric locates flash of 75mm gun on hillside': Keyes's journal, NA DEFE 2/349.
207 'Their dead literally littered the beach': R.L. Henry, *The Story of the 2/4th Field Regiment*, Melbourne, 1950, p. 100.
207 'nonchalantly perched and in full view of the enemy': Long, op. cit., p. 364.
207 An attempt to retake the bridge: papers of Colonel Sir Thomas Macpherson CBE MC TD DL, IWM 05/73/1 and author's telephone conversations.
207 'promptly pumped full of tommy gun': ibid.
208 'Tevendale went out into the gully and climbed up its north side': ibid. From Regimental Sergeant Major Tevendale's 'Brief Account of the Action Taken by No 1 Troop and Commando HQ in action on Monday 9th June, 1941', included in Macpherson papers.
209 'I think I was the first to start throwing grenades': Gerald Bryan. Author's interview at his home in Binfield, Berkshire, 10 June 2008. Also mentioned in his autobiography, *Be of Good Cheer*, Wilton 65, Windsor, Berkshire, 2008.
209 'Our gun was pointing away': ibid.
210 'Every time they tried to fire': ibid.
210 'Tevendale, Farmiloe, I'm shot': from the account by RSM Tevendale DCM, op. cit.

210 'one bullet having passed through his back and chest' ibid.
211 'I was damned thirsty': author's interview with Gerald Bryan.
211 'You are not our enemy. I served in the last war. You are our allies': ibid.
212 'Boy oh boy it was duck soup. They had 200 yards of open flat plain': Noble Sproule, quoted in Combined Ops website, www.combinedops.com/
212 trying to disarm their guards and escape: Lieutenant E. McGonigal's report on the action of no. 4 Troop in the Litani river engagement (Macpherson papers), IWM 05/73/1.
212 'You felt you were practically looking down the barrels': Macpherson papers, IWM 05/73/1.
213 'had turned a startling green': George Stitt, *Under Cunningham's Command*, Allen and Unwin, London, 1944, p. 105.
213 *Guépard* followed this up with a torpedo: Commandant Pierre Guiot, *Combats sans Espoir: La Guerre Navale en Syrie (1941)*, La Couronne Littéraire, Paris, 1971, p. 68.
213 'Engage the enemy more closely': Stitt, op. cit., p. 86.
214 Crowther bailed out and was captured badly burned: author's interview with Gerald Bryan who was in the same ward as Crowther.
214 Their pilots, Sergeant Martin Bennett and Sous-lieutenant Georges Rivory: Shores, *Dust Clouds in the Middle East*
214 composed of young Jewish women: Stitt, op. cit., p. 91.
214 'significantly superior' [ftn] : Christopher Langtree, *The Kelleys: British J, K, and N Class Destroyers of World War Two*, Chatham Press, UK.
215 become a qualified instructor: author's interview with Gerald Bryan.
215 'I called on them to *jetez vers à la planche*': Ross, *Paddy Mayne*, p. 42, quoting a letter from Blair Mayne to his younger brother Douglas.
215 His total casualties out of a strength of forty-five: Macpherson papers, IWM 05/73/1.
215 'an air of unrelieved pessimism and disbelief': ibid.
216 'I got him out quite a long way down': ibid.
216 'a continuous beer party': ibid.
217 'They all sat in the bottom of the communication trench': Keyes's journal, NA DEFE 2/349.
217 It was broad daylight when Keyes awoke: ibid.
218 purloining some of their precious Brens: Keyes's journal, NA DEFE 2/349.
218 shot a successful sniper by offering himself as bait: Keyes's citation for Garland in his official report of the action, Macpherson papers, IWM 05/73/1.
218 'Jumbo asks some shrewd questions': Keyes's journal, NA DEFE 2/349.

CHAPTER EIGHTEEN

219 'General Wilson has a twinkle in his eye': Ranfurly, *To War With Whitaker*, p. 91.
219 'You thought we were yellow': Alan Moorehead, *African Trilogy*, Hamish Hamilton, London, 1944, p. 165.
221 an anti-tank shell which wrecked its engine: Compton Mackenzie, *Eastern Epic*, Chatto & Windus, London, 1951, p. 109.

222 paid particular attention to the shadowy places: author's interview with Major General (rtd) Frank Caldwell, Guernsey, 6 September 2005.
222 killed over forty: Mackenzie, op. cit., p. 110.
222 then three Vichy Dewoitine 520s: Shores, *Dust Clouds in the Middle East*, p. 125.
223 '*Ce que vous avez fait, c'est incroyable*': Buckley, *Five Ventures*, p. 90.
223 the favourite had been the Deraa road push towards Damascus: telegram from de Verdilhac's HQ to the War Ministry in Vichy. VA, signal reference 7465 and 7466 ('the major effort appears to bear on the Axis Deraa axis').
224 'but not to become seriously involved': statement by Captain T.P. Wilson MC 1st Battalion, Royal Fusiliers, concerning the action at Kuneitra, NA WO 169/1722.
226 'still slippery with orange peel': Bernard Fergusson, *The Trumpet in the Hall*, Collins, London, 1970, p. 102.
226 about 4 feet high and 3 feet thick: NA WO 169/1722.
226 with the 20mm Breda: ibid.
226 'only interested in the theory of it': C. Northcote Parkinson, *Always a Fusilier*, Sampson Low, London, 1949, p. 86. (Parkinson, best known for *Parkinson's Law*, was a pre-war TA officer in the regiment and during 1939–45 served in training or administrative posts. For his regimental history, published in 1947, he interviewed or corresponded with many of the participants but rarely attributes quotes. However, it is certainly among the more readable regimental histories.)
226 Orr had about 575 men under him: Captain Wilson's statement on Kuneitra, NA WO 169/1722.
226 though not the Free French Senegalese waiting: Shores, op. cit., p. 224.
226 manoeuvres had included an exercise in which Kuneitra: Fergusson, op. cit., p. 108.
228 'NOTHING could put these tanks out of action': Wilson's post-action report, NA WO 169/1722.
228 'He begged me almost tearfully': Fergusson, op. cit., p. 108.
231 'driven half mad by the filth and flies': Parkinson, op. cit., p. 80.
232 'Surely a battalion of the Royal Fusiliers have not surrendered to the Vichy French?': Dill, quoted by Robert Lyman, *First Victory*, Constable and Robinson, London, 2006, p. 206, citing NA PREM 3/309/5, 17 June 1941.
232 'He endeavoured to rally these troops': war diary of 2/5th field regiment, quoted in Long, *Greece, Crete and Syria*, p. 399.
233 'We were cavalrymen doing an infantryman's job': author's interview with William Cross, Chelsea Hospital, June 2007.
233 'Of course, the first thing the British soldier misses is his tea': ibid.
234 'a crowd of struggling vehicles': Long, op. cit., p. 399. (The Bofors gun team who distinguished themselves were from 171 Light Anti-Aircraft battery, Royal Artillery.)
236 'There had been so many moments when formations of either side had been surrounding': Fergusson, op. cit., p. 102.
236 panic below decks when calls for gas masks: papers of H. Atkins, a sergeant in the battalion's motor transport pool, IWM 92/28/1.

236 no more than boiler plate welded to a truck chassis: Edward Home, *A Job Well Done: The History of the Palestine Police*, Anchor Press, Tiptree, Essex, 1982,

237 'The colonel pondered them': Fergusson, op. cit., p. 111.

237 'The scene was like that of an old print': ibid.

238 'Only 27 reached the end of the wood': Mackenzie, op. cit., p. 116.

238 'There was a French barracks lit up like a Christmas tree': author's interview with Major General (rtd) Frank Caldwell, Guernsey, 6 September 2005.

239 'pale and with five bullet wounds': Fergusson, op. cit., p. 111.

239 the first tank announced its presence with a burst: author's interview with Caldwell.

242 'One side of the house had collapsed': Fergusson, op. cit., p. 113.

242 'to the last man and the last round': Wilson, *Eight Years Overseas*, p. 116.

243 'I didn't have the guts to try': Fergusson. op. cit., pp. 113–15.

CHAPTER NINETEEN

247 marked by two stone cairns: de Chair, *The Golden Carpet*, p. 185.

248 'We had been going for some hours now': ibid., pp. 187–8.

249 flown by a Lieutenant Seinturier: Shores, *Dust Clouds in the Middle East*, p. 232.

249 sufficiently unusual to merit an immediate award: de Chair, op. cit., p. 194.

249 slam on the brakes and get well clear of the vehicles: ibid., p. 198.

249 'I should, of course, have seized my prisoner': ibid., pp. 190–91.

250 'The tyres were all in shreds': ibid., p. 198.

250 One troop of Wiltshire Yeomanry lost thirteen: ibid., p. 195.

250 'staring ahead with unseeing eyes': ibid., p. 207.

251 'We saw to our astonishment a bunch of girls': Dahl, *Going Solo*, p. 193.

251 In ten seconds they had turned five into blazing, broken-backed wrecks: Shores, op. cit., pp. 238–9.

254 'A right and left. Another – and another,' screamed one of the young aristocrats: de Chair, op. cit., p. 208. (This was the 9th Duke of Roxburghe, a lieutenant known to his friends as Bobo.)

254 Altogether twenty French aircrew lost their lives: John Bagot Glubb, *The Changing Scenes of Life*, Quartet Books, London, 1983, p. 127.

256 'Thereafter there were no more raids': ibid.

256 there were only 187 men on their feet. Of these 6: all figures Long, *Greece, Crete and Syria*, p. 477.

257 'An Indian non-combatant cook': John Masters, *The Road Past Mandalay*, Michael Joseph, London, 1961, p. 48.

257 'Two black dots appeared': ibid., pp. 47–8.

257 a Lieutenant Legrand in one of the Dewoitines: Shores, op. cit., pp. 249–50 *et passim.*

258 'The Gurkhas avoided my eye': Masters, op. cit., p. 48.

260 *Wait, dirty English bastards:* ibid., p. 56.

261 'sagged so much it was like carrying a man in a bag': Long, op. cit., p. 509.

261 discovered twenty-one fresh graves and fifteen unburied: ibid., p. 458.

261 a French stretcher-bearer was killed: ibid., p. 486.
261 'General Lavarack, feeling that to both Frenchmen and Australians': ibid., p. 511.
262 placed fourteen 250-pound bombs on the High Commissioner's Beirut Residency leaving five of his Syrian police guard: Police Information Bulletin, 30 June 1941, VA.
263 'Knowledge of the possibility of an armistice': Long, op. cit., p. 512, letter to Blamey.
267 'All troops in forward areas will cease fire': author's interview with Chelsea Pensioner Donald Pickering at Chelsea Hospital, July 2007.
267 'Everyone naturally felt anxious not to be killed': Brigadier W.E. Underhill, ed., *The Royal Leicestershire Regiment 1928–1956*, Underhill, Plymouth, 1956
267 'I explained that I too was a regular soldier': Bryan, *Be of Good Cheer*, p. 47.

CHAPTER TWENTY

268 'Night of 29 to 30 June': Police Information Bulletin, VA.
269 'a provincial druggist in uniform': *Time* magazine, 21 July 1941.
269 'signed Paris away to the conquering Nazis': ibid.
269 'When the incident became known': Georges Catroux, *Dans la bataille de Méditerranée*, Gallimard, Paris, 1949, p. 150.
270 'Everything was going on as though nobody owed us anything': de Gaulle, *The Call to Honour*, p. 201.
270 This led to an election atmosphere with speeches, slogans: Wilson, *Eight Years Overseas*, p. 72.
270 'I am not prepared to let this lapse': NA PREM 3/422/4.
271 a strange tale of a long but not uncomfortable seven-day rail journey across Hitler's Europe: all the details of the British prisoners' journey through occupied Europe are taken from files at the UK's National Archives at Kew, London. Also from Parkinson's *Always a Fusilier.*
272 'If anyone had predicted two months ago': Hansard, 15 July 1941.
273 'remain faithful to the unity of France and to Maréchal Petain': in General Order 14, dated 13 July 1941 and signed by Général Pierre Arlabosse, commander of troops in Lebanon, VA.
274 shooting at them with the kind of 6.35mm: details from Warner, *Pierre Laval and the Eclipse of France*, p. 281.
274 an X-ray revealed was caused by a bullet lodged a quarter of an inch: ibid.
275 twice as many as had yet been killed in any raid on a German city: Patrick Bishop, *The Bomber Boys*, Harper Press, 2007, pp. 87–8.
275 'violent anti-British feeling in both the occupied and unoccupied zones': Admiral William D. Leahy, *I Was There*, Whittlesey House, New York, 1948, p. 82.
275 'To murder, for political motives, women, children ... Is England already bolshevized?': ibid., quoting letter from Darlan, p. 83.

277 'might be using one day': Wheeler quoted in James Dorrian, *Saint-Nazaire*, Pen and Sword, Barnsley, Yorkshire, 2006, p. 180.

277 'the propaganda value of the raid was enormous': M.R.D. Foot and J.M. Langley, *M19: Escape and Evasion 1939–1945*, Bodley Head, London, 1979, p. 85.

CHAPTER TWENTY-ONE

281 known as an accomplished pianist: E.D.R. Harrison article in the *English Historical Review*, 1999, quoting SOE files HS 3/9, HS 3/14 and HS 3/7.

281 from behind its false ceiling: ibid.

282 towed the 362 miles to South Africa's Port Elizabeth: NA ADM 1/11709.

282 'A very fine show indeed' 'SOE Operations in Africa', NA HS 3/14.

284 'Great charm, absolutely fearless': Harrison, op. cit.

285 agreed to pay SOE an extra £4,000: ibid.

285 France Libre d'Outremer, a radio station: ibid.

285 'bribery, corruption, murder': ibid.

285 'I am convinced, and Mayer confirms': ibid.

287 'It was like looking through a bloody periscope': Keith Flint, *Airborne Armour*, Helion Publishing, UK, 1991, p. 11.

287 'We were considered good enough to look after ourselves': Sergeant (as he became) Clegg quoted in *Guidon*, journal of the Royal Hussars, 1990, p. 152.

288 'If the Japanese walked into the island': Harrison, op. cit., quoting *The War Against Japan* by Major General S. Woodburn Kirby, GB Cabinet Office, *Principal War Telegrams and Memoranda*. NA WO 208/1518.

288 'Sheer madness': ibid.

288 issuing some of the troops involved with the kind of Arctic clothing: Jonathan Riley, *The Life and Campaigns of General Hughie Stockwell*, Pen and Sword, Barnsley, Yorkshire, 2006, p. 74.

289 perhaps a dozen or so others knew: ibid., p. 75.

289 the nearest they were going to get to a beach: author's interview with Chelsea Pensioner Bombardier Frederick Bailey at the Royal Chelsea Hospital, London, 2006.

289 alive with rumours that we were going to attack the French in Madagascar: ibid.

289 watching the flying fish: papers of Captain J.H. Patterson (1910–81), IWM 05/49/1.

289 'Please don't worry, you are more than ever in my thoughts': BBC's World War 2 People's War: Roland Moss and Operation Ironclad in Madagascar by David Moss.

289 'Operation Ironclad is on. I wonder what sort of battle': papers of Captain J.H. Patterson, IWM 05/49/1.

290 'look very pretty nipping around us': ibid.

291 2 miles of trenches and pill boxes: Buckley, *Five Ventures*, op. cit.

CHAPTER TWENTY-TWO

293 'Firing at night is not contemplated, the entrance to the bay being considered impossible': RN Battle Summaries, NA ADM 234/331.
293 fifty-seven mines were lifted: ibid.
293 accidental detonation of the last two mines: ibid.
293 'We moved up to the gun position': papers of Captain William Knight, R.A., IWM 97/7/1.
294 through his forehead: Patterson papers, IWM 05/49/1. (Patterson examined the body and attributed the sharp shooting to somebody else but Knight was an eyewitness.)
294 how much bigger the exit wound was: Knight papers, IWM 97/7/1.
294 'That was the end of the opposition': ibid.
294 'knocked the concrete off the top of the hill': ibid.
294 'The battery at Courrier Bay': report on the Diego Suarez battle compiled in Vichy and dated 17 October 1942, VA.
294 'taken by surprise and overwhelmed': ibid.
295 'We had a drink and he then showed me all over': Marcus Binney, *Secret War Heroes*, Hodder & Stoughton, London, 2006, p. 182, quoting PF 859/1011/7, Meyer's personal file with SOE.
298 the revolver of a lieutenant in the Royal Welch Fusiliers: Riley, *The Life and Campaigns of General Hughie Stockwell*, p. 81. (Lieutenant Ray Simmons commanded the leading platoon of A Company.)
298 A Tommy gunner in the East Lancs: 2nd East Lancs war diary, NA WO 174/30.
298 their orders were to stay at least 7 miles offshore: RN Battle Summaries, NA ADM 234/331.
299 'To avoid any untoward incident': British propaganda leaflet dropped at Madagascar, in the archives of Royal Marine Museum, Southsea, Hampshire.
299 'did not covet an inch of French territory': RN Battle Summaries, NA ADM 234/331.
299 'We shall defend ourselves to the last': Vichy Colonial Ministry files, VA, 5.5.42. ('Have received the following telegram from the Governor of Madagascar ... Diego Suarez attacked this morning by British aircraft – Naval forces of unknown strength are off shore ... ultimatum demanding unconditional surrender replied to ... ')
300 'The despatch of that letter': from a copy of Major General Robert Sturges's after-battle report lodged in the Royal Marine Museum, Southsea, Hampshire.
300 'But owing to the rocky nature of the ground': Major Jocelin Simon's after-battle report on B Special Service Squadron RAC, NA WO 218/156.
301 The blame for this lay mostly with the South African Air Force: Buckley, *Five Ventures*
301 somewhere along the line this had slipped through the hands: ibid.
303 'great gallantry': Simon's report, NA WO 218/156.
304 'who would otherwise have had to remain in the open': ibid.
304 'low jabberings': *Guidon*, journal of the Royal Hussars, 1982, p. 158.

304 'The enemy then made a third sortie': Simon's report, NA WO 218/156.
305 'in a hand-to-hand fight with a Senegalese' *Guidon*, op. cit., p. 158.
305 'The enemy then advanced': Simon's report, NA WO 218/156.
306 'One moment they were there': *Guidon*, op. cit.

CHAPTER TWENTY-THREE

308 'do the maximum damage possible': War Diary, 2nd South Lancashire Regiment, NA WO 274/31.
308 saw an aircraft burst into flames: War Diary, 2nd East Lancs, NA WO 174/30.
308 The man at the end of it was a Lieutenant Héloise: Shores, *Dust Clouds in the Middle East*, p. 28.
309 Peter Reynier, a subaltern in the Royal Scots Fusiliers: biographical details from *Times* obituary, September 1999.
309 had breakfasted at 2 a.m.: Colonel J.C. Kemp MC, *The History of the Royal Scots Fusiliers*, Maclehose, Glasgow, 1948, Chapter V.
309 thought they had scored a direct hit on one machine-gun post: ibid.
309 'We tried several times to get out': ibid.
309 sector of the line the French called Rue Placers: ibid.
310 Lieutenant Bande of the 3rd Company, 2 Régiment mixte malgache: ibid.
310 Armstrong appended it to his successful recommendation: ibid.
310 'you can be sure that the French can pick one out': ibid.
310 'flat and open with only a few straggly bushes': War Diary, 2nd East Lancs, NA WO 174/30. C Company's report on capture of Antsirane by Lieutenant Wood.
310 'blowing away most of his right elbow and side': ibid.
311 'Our position was most unhealthy': ibid.
311 two of their signallers became the battery's first casualties: author's interview with Frederick Bailey.
311 Force Eight winds continued to delay: RN Battle Summaries, NA ADM 234/331.
312 'It was quite clear the attack had failed': Archives of Royal Marine Museum, Southport, Hampshire. From General Sturges's report on Ironclad, p. 14.
313 'it was the only two-storey building in the area': papers of Captain Hector Emerton, IWM 96/42/1.
315 'I wished to try and arrange for a destroyer': Sturges's report, Archives of Royal Marine Museum, Southport, Hampshire.
315 'Prolonged operations, which we so much wished to avoid': NA 'RN Naval Summaries NA ADM 234/331'.
316 seventeen South Lancs lost their lives and about forty were wounded: War Diary, 2nd South Lancashire Regiment, NA WO 174/31.
316 'The effect of this penetration': Sturges's report, Archives of Royal Marine Museum, Southport, Hampshire.
317 'on no account to commit themselves against the French guns': Report of B Special Service Squadron, R.A.C., NA WO 218/156.
317 two were killed and the twelve wounded: Kemp, op. cit.

CHAPTER TWENTY-FOUR

320 if they had to abandon ship: papers of Ordinary Seaman A.L. Yule, IWM P-1–3.
321 'Figures could be discerned': ibid.
321 'All Marines ashore': ibid.
321 Clavel stood there staring at his target which still looked: General Sturges's report, Royal Marine Museum, Southsea, Hampshire. (Sturges evidently met or was told about Clavel after the end of hostilities and wrote: 'A French 75mm manned by a Capitaine Clavel failed to register a hit, a fact that this officer still disbelieves.')
322 felt the unmistakable swell of: RN Battle Summaries, NA ADM 234/331.
322 'They were obviously firing at the patter': Captain Martin Price DSO quoted in a wartime pamphlet, *The Royal Marines 1939–43*, by the journalist Owen Rutter, HMSO.
324 'ready to take on anybody': Jim Stockman, 'Madagascar 1942', *British Army Review*, 1986, no.83.
325 'We just kept moving': ibid., p. 93.
327 a white flag, a bugler and two bottles of gin: Emerton papers, IWM 96/42/1.
327 'It was as though we had won a hard game of rugger': Rutter, op. cit.,
328 had lost 105 killed, 15 of them officers: Buckley, *Five Ventures*, p. 187
328 French losses were 145 killed and 336 wounded: VA. (From a report datelined Vichy, 17 October 1942 from the Lieutenant General Secretary of State for War on 'the operations at Diego Suarez on 5, 6, & 7 May 1942'.)
328 'shyly proffered by one of the French ladies': Patterson papers, IWM 05/491.

CHAPTER TWENTY-FIVE

330 'A principal object must be to get our best troops forward': Churchill, *The Second World War*, vol. iv, *The Hinge of Fate*, p. 205, quoting his 30 April 1942 memo to General Ismay.
330 'your problem is one of holding the place': ibid., p. 208.
331 'only ships left for anti-submarine duties': RN Battle Summaries, NA ADM 234/331.
332 where the bed bugs were driving him crazy: author's interview with Frederick Bailey.
333 'Corvettes were chasing about': Patterson papers, IWM 05/49/1, op. cit
334 beat up a drunken Frenchman: ibid.
335 'Attack must have been made by Vichy submarines': Smuts message quoted in Churchill, op. cit., vol. iv, p. 210.
336 'clear out the rot': John Grehan, *The Forgotten Invasion: Madagascar 1942*, Historic Military Press, Storrington, West Sussex, 2007, p. 115, quoting Harvy.
338 'a French crenellation in the Atlantic wall': Paxton, *Vichy France*, p. 305.
338 750 sons of Dieppe held captive in Germany: ibid., p. 306.
339 One day a Monsieur Millot, President of the Planters' Association: Grehan, op. cit., p. 125.

CHAPTER TWENTY-SIX

342 'The tide was well up and we scrambled out among the bullets': Patterson papers, IWM 05/49/1
342 'I patched up a few French and Malgache': ibid.
342 'Flies and blood and filth': ibid.
343 cost the British twelve dead: Riley, *The Life and Campaigns of General Hughie Stockwell*, p. 93.
343 'encased her body': Grehan, *The Forgotten Invasion*, p. 137.
344 'Lieutenant Simpson-Jones, as I understand it' [ftn] : interview with Peter Simpson-Jones, Audio archives, IWM 15320.
347 'that the Russians had come into the war solely for our benefit': Alanbrooke, *War Diaries*, 30 March 1942, p. 243.
349 'heroic resistance of the French troops': Grehan, op. cit., p. 165, quoting Hytier.
350 'Ten days later, having passed through Switzerland': Langer, *Our Vichy Gamble*, p. 277.
351 'I tried to keep a poker face': General Mark W. Clark, *Calculated Risk*, Harper, New York, 1950, p. 69.
352 'What I could not tell Mast': ibid., pp. 68–9.
352 'One would have thought that 50 dead skunks': Langer, op. cit., p329; Clark, op. cit., p. 70.
353 'I knelt at the foot of the stairs with a carbine': Clark, op. cit., p. 71.
353 'I posed as a somewhat inebriated member': Murphy, *Diplomat Among Warriors*, p. 153.
355 'As some means of softening this slight to him': Churchill, *The Second World War*, pp. 542–3.
355 'I consider it inadvisable for you to give de Gaulle any information': ibid., quoting Roosevelt's message.
356 'I hope these Vichy people are going to throw them into the sea,' Williams, *The Last Great Frenchman*, p. 196, quoting Pierre Billotte, *Le Temps des Armes*, Plon, Paris, 1972, p. 29.
356 'You'll see. One day we'll go down the Champs Elysées': ibid., quoting Jacques Soustelle, *Envers et contre tout*, vol. 1, Laffont, Paris, 1947, p. 452.
356 'Let us return through you to the line of battle': ibid., quoting Charles de Gaulle, *Discours et Messages*, vol. 1, Plon, Paris, 1970, p. 250.

CHAPTER TWENTY-SEVEN

360 'Alain explained that his father': Murphy, *Diplomat Among Warriors*, pp. 147–8.
361 'If I could meet Darlan': ibid., p. 152, quoting Eisenhower's *Crusade in Europe*, Doubleday, New York, 1948.
366 'He was a tall man with wrinkled civilian clothes': Clark, *Calculated Risk*, p. 81.
367 'I thought Ike had never been so shocked': ibid., p. 82.
368 'desperately tired and worried': John Winton, *Cunningham: The Greatest*

Admiral Since Nelson, John Murray, London, 1998, p. 281.
368 If not there, Sicily was their next choice: Thaddeus Holt, *The Deceivers*, Scribner, New York, 2004, p. 269.
368 Sergeant Stamford Weatherall was worried that some playful dolphins, et seq.: Weatherall papers, IWM 76/143/1.
370 the American always felt that Juin would feel honour-bound: Murphy, op. cit., p. 163.
370 'I have assurances': Melton, *Darlan*, p. 167.
370 '*Allo, Robert*,' said London: Murphy, op. cit., p. 162.
371 Murphy thought the SOE had let them down: ibid.
372 'After some difficulty I was admitted': ibid., p. 163.
373 'I have known for a long time the British are stupid': ibid., p. 165.
373 'got the date wrong': ibid., p. 167.

CHAPTER TWENTY-EIGHT

375 recently the assistant warden of Minnesota State Penitentiary: Rick Atkinson, *An Army at Dawn*, Abacus, London, 2004, p. 97.
375 Their favourite was 'There's a Troopship Now Leaving Bombay': ibid., p. 96.
377 'quite shaken and a little slow in getting underway to disembark': History of 134th Division, US Army's Historical Department, Pentagon, 1943
380 'I didn't want to offend the colonel': Leo Disher, *Springboard to Berlin*, Thomas Y. Crowell, New York, 1943, p. 115. (Disher was one of four United Press correspondents who contributed to the book with his account of the disastrous assault on Oran harbour.)
380 'a good chance of carrying out our mission without firing a shot': NA ADM 196/52, quoting Peters.
380 'It says landings up to now have been carried out without shooting': Disher, op. cit., p. 116.
381 confiding to him that he only felt properly alive: ibid., p. 93.
381 he read in stencilled capitals: LA BELLE FRANCE: ibid., p. 118.
383 'By this time the American ship started firing at us': Laurin's report dated 14 November 1942, Oran, VA.
383 'many rounds of 37mm and 13.2mm': ibid.
383 'The blasts were so loud they hurt': Disher, op. cit., pp. 120–22.
384 'I got my elbows over the pier rim': ibid., p. 123.
385 this time in the buttocks: Jo Alex Morris, *Deadline Every Minute: The Story of UPI*, Random House, New York, 1963
385 'Soon we shall all be your prisoners': Disher, op. cit., p. 125.
388 'Giraud is not your man': Murphy, *Diplomat Among Warriors*, p. 167.

CHAPTER TWENTY-NINE

390 a major who had distinguished himself in the raid on Vaagso in Norway: Hilary St George Saunders, *The Green Beret*, Collins, London, 1950, pp. 130–31.

391 'a volume of brisk small arms fire': Murphy, *Diplomat Among Warriors*, p. 168.
391 'hugging the wall and firing in our direction': ibid.
391 'I came up to them': ibid., pp. 168–9.
392 'He seemed to know about me': ibid., p. 169.
392 'I took him by the arm gently but firmly': ibid.
393 'How wonderful!': ibid.
393 'these Frogs were driving him mad': Atkinson, *An Army at Dawn*, p. 120.
393 'a rebel chief and a felon': ibid.
394 'It is with stupor and grief': Warner, *Pierre Laval*, p. 322.
395 Laval telephoned Wiesbaden and instructed them to say yes: ibid., p. 316.
395 'What price would Hitler force France to pay': Laval, *Unpublished Diary*, p. 145.
397 'Every time a foreign Jew leaves our territory': Laval and the Jews, all from Warner, op. cit., pp. 305–6.
399 'The enemy's first salvo (12 rounds)': Laurin's report dated Oran, 14 September and headed *Engagement du 9 novembre à la mer*, VA.
400 Twenty-one had died on the *Epervier*: VA. All casualty figures from Laurin's report.
400 'I made this decision because': ibid., p. 5.
401 Darlan's last call to the Admiralty: Melton, *Darlan*, p. 174.
402 'Run your tanks through the main streets. Give them a big parade': Clark, *Calculated Risk*, p. 88.
403 'Having no such guardian or sensible rule of life': Murphy, op. cit., p. 174.
404 'I was charged with fighting a war': Clark, op. cit., pp. 89–90.
405 'Clark didn't pretend to understand': Murphy, op. cit., p. 175.
407 'it may be wondered whether the occupation of France's Mediterranean coast': Warner, op. cit., p. 329.
407 'stubby, ingratiating little man': Clark, op. cit., pp. 89–91.
407 'Clark (Murphy interpreting): It is essential that we stop this waste': Edited Clark. Darlan dialogue from shorthand note taken at the time. Clark, op. cit., pp. 91–2.
409 was borne off in triumph on the shoulders of a laughing, cheering, singing crowd: *London Gazette*, May 1943. Mentioned in his VC citation.
409 'an enterprise of desperate hazard': ibid.
409 'I hate to serve under the British': Atkinson, op. cit., p. 279.
409 'I tried to imagine what would happen': Murphy, op. cit., p. 176.
411 'Like trying to hit a grasshopper with a rock': Atkinson, op. cit., p. 133, quoting Commander Samuel Morison, the naval historian, who was on board the *Brooklyn*.
412 'We may all be thankful if our lives': Churchill, *The Second World War*, vol. iv, p. 556.
414 'We're Americans': Atkinson, op. cit., p. 139.

CHAPTER THIRTY

416 'It's a decision of the Führer's': Warner, *Pierre Laval*, p. 336.

416 '*Monsieur le Maréchal*, I have the honour': *Keesing's Contemporary Archives*, p. 5447.
417 'on account of public opinion in France': Warner, op. cit., p. 337.
417 'In fact, if Admiral Darlan had to shoot Marshal Pétain': Churchill, *The Hinge of Fate*, p. 575.
417 'I'm not Anglophobe': *Marine du Levant* No.9, October 1942. Information bulletin of 3rd Maritime Region.
418 'The Armistice is broken': Warren Tute, *The Reluctant Enemies*, Collins, London, 1990, p. 268.
419 'At such time that those in high command lose their sense of duty': ibid., p. 288, quoting Amiral Laborde's address to his sailors in Toulon.
420 'French generals and admirals': Warner, op. cit., p. 355, quoting German Foreign Ministry files 110/115212–24.
420 'I fear the French fleet will not come to us intact': ibid., p. 356.
421 'Hello, yes the Germans are all around me': *Marine du Levant*, op. cit.
422 '*Amiral*, my Colonel orders me to say he admires you': Tute, op. cit., p. 293.
423 'I am just told that part of the French fleet in Toulon has been scuttled': Leahy, *I Was There*, p. 559.
423 'Germany's aim is now clear': Tute, op. cit., p. 294, quoting *L'Affaire Darlan* by A.J. Voituriez.
424 'I certainly could not have done it had I been a 'dissident': Leahy, op. cit., p. 558.
424 'Soon the retching will begin': de Gaulle, *The Call to Honour*, p. 352.
424 'I am but a lemon which the Americans will drop' Clark, *Calculated Risk*, p. 105.
424 'an enlightened liberal government': ibid., p. 106.
424 'Members of uniformed fascist organisations': A.J. Liebling, *The Road Back to Paris*, Michael Joseph, London, 1944, pp. 188–90
425 'We must not overlook the serious political injury': Churchill, op. cit. p. 568.
426 known to the OSS as 'Necktie': Melton, op. cit., p. 209.
426 'Darlan's murder,' admitted Churchill, op. cit., p. 578.

EPILOGUE

428 'We are not in the war': Warner, *Pierre Laval*, pp. 396–7.
430 'She's always been an Anglophile and a Gaullist': ibid., footnote, p407.
430 'Scenes which can only be described as scandalous': *Manchester Guardian*, 8 October 1945.
431 'Without replying, he put his head under the blankets': ibid., 16 October 1945.
431 'I do not accept the sentence': Laval, *Unpublished Diary*, p. 220.
434 'The French sailors, Coutts remembered, treated them': *Daily Telegraph*, London, 3 January 2004.
434 'The French were rotten': BBC WW2 *People's War*, contributed by Jo Challacombe, June, 2005.
434 'I am afraid that Tommy and I were not very polite' Bryan Gerald, *Be of Good Cheer*, op. cit., p. 46.

BIBLIOGRAPHY

Alanbrooke, Field Marshal Lord, *War Diaries 1939–45*, Weidenfeld & Nicolson, London, 2003

Baldick, Robert, *The Siege of Paris*, New English Library, 1964

Beevor, Antony, *Crete: The Battle and the Resistance*, Penguin, London, 1992

Bierman, John, *Napoleon III and his Carnival Empire*, St Martin's Press, New York, 1988

Bierman, John and Smith, Colin, *Alamein: War Without Hate*, Viking, London, 2002

Binney, Marcus, *Secret War Heroes*, Hodder & Stoughton, London, 2006

Bishop, Patrick, *The Bomber Boys*, Harper Press, London, 2007

Blumenson, Martin, *Mark Clark*, Congdon and Weed, New York, 1984

Boutron Jean, *Mers-el-Kébir a Londres*, Plon, Paris, 1980

Brendon, Piers, *The Dark Valley*, Jonathan Cape, London, 2000

Bryan, Gerald, *Be of Good Cheer*, Wilton 65, Windsor, Berkshire, 2008

Bullitt, Orville H., *For The President*, Houghton Mifflin, Boston, 1972

Callil, Carmen, *Bad Faith: A Forgotten History of Family and Fatherland*, Jonathan Cape, London, 2006

Chair, Somerset de, *The Golden Carpet*, Faber and Faber, London, 1945

Churchill, Winston, *The Second World War*, vols. i–iv, Penguin edition, London, 1985

Churchill Winston *The River War*, Standard Publications Inc, New York, 2007

Ciano, Galeazzo, *Ciano's Diary, 1939–43*, Malcolm Muggeridge (ed), Heinemann, London, 1947

Clark, General Mark W., *Calculated Risk*, Harper, New York, 1950

Coles, Alan and Briggs, Ted, *Flagship 'Hood': The Fate of Britain's Mightiest Warship*, Robert Hale, London, 1988

Colville, J.R., *Man of Valour*, Collins, London, 1972

Cooper, Artemis, *Cairo in the War 1939–45*, Penguin, London, 1995

Cooper, Duff, *Old Men Forget*, Rupert Hart–Davis (ed), London, 1954

Dahl, Roald, *Going Solo*, Penguin, London, 1988

Dannreuther, Raymond, *Somerville's Force H: The Royal Navy's Gibraltar-based Fleet, June 1940 – March 1942*, Aurum, London, 2006

Dayan, Moshe, *Story of My Life*, Weidenfeld & Nicolson, London, 1976

Dear, I.C.B. and Foot, M.R.D. (eds.), *The Oxford Companion to the Second World War*, OUP, Oxford, 1995

Deighton, Len, *Blitzkrieg*, Jonathan Cape, London, 1979
Dorrian, James, *Saint-Nazaire*, Pen and Sword, Barnsley, Yorkshire, 2006
Dudgeon, Air Vice-Marshal A.G., *Hidden Victory*, Tempus, London, 2000
Egremont, Max, *Under Two Flags: The Life of Major General Sir Edward Spears*, Weidenfeld & Nicolson, London, 1997
Foot, M.R.D., *SOE in France*, Frank Cass, London, 2004
Foot, M.R.D. and Langley, J.M., *M19: Escape and Evasion 1939–1945*, Bodley Head, London, 1979
Gaulle, Charles de, *The Call to Honour*, Collins, London, 1955
Gildea, Robert, *Marianne in Chains*, Pan Books, London, 2003
Graves, Robert, *Goodbye To All That*, Penguin, London, 1966
Grehan, John, *The Forgotten Invasion: Madagascar 1942*, Historic Military Press, Storrington, West Sussex, 2007
Guiot, Commandant Pierre, *Combats Sans Espoir: Guerre Navale en Syrie (1941)*, La Couronne Littéraire, Paris, 1962
Horne, Alistair, *The Price of Glory*, Mcfadden-Bartell, New York, 1964
Horne, Alistair, *The Fall of Paris*, Reprint Society, London, 1967
Horne, Alistair, *To Lose A Battle: France 1940*, Macmillan, London, 1969
Horne, Alistair, *Friend or Foe: A History of France*, Weidenfeld & Nicolson, London, 2004
Horne, Edward, *A Job Well Done: The History of the Palestine Police*, Anchor Press, Tiptree, Essex, 1982
Hull, Cordell, *The Memoirs of Cordell Hull*, Macmillan, New York, 1948
Jennings, Eric T., *Vichy in the Tropics*, Stanford University Press, 2004
Johnston, Mark, *Fighting The Enemy: Australian Soldiers and Their Adversaries in World War Two*, Cambridge University Press, Sydney, 2000
Kedward, Rod, *La Vie en Bleu*, Allen Lane, London, 2005
Kennedy, Major General Sir John, *The Business of War*, Hutchinson, London, 1957
Kitson, Simon, *The Hunt for Nazi Spies: Fighting Espionage in Vichy*, Chicago University Press, 2007
Laffin, John, *British VCs of World War Two*, Sutton Publishing, London, 1997
Langer, William L., *Our Vichy Gamble*, Knopf, New York, 1947
Leahy, Admiral William D., *I Was There*, Whittlesey House, New York, 1948
Lee, Raymond E., *The London Journal of General Raymond E. Lee, 1940–41*, Hutchinson, London, 1972
Liebling, A.J., *The Road Back to Paris*, Michael Joseph, London, 1944
Long, Gavin, *Greece, Crete and Syria*, Halstead Press, Sydney, 1962
Lormier, Dominique, *Mers-El-Kébir*, Calman Lévy, Paris, 2007
Lukacs, John, *The Duel: 10 May – 31 July 1940: The Eighty-Day Struggle between Churchill and Hitler*, Bodley Head, London, 1991
Lunt, James, *Glubb Pasha*, Harvill Press, London, 1984
Lyman, Robert, *First Victory*, Constable & Robinson, London, 2006
Lyman, Robert, *Iraq 1941*, Osprey Publishing, London, 2006
MacIntyre, Donald, *Fighting Admiral: The Life of Admiral of the Fleet Sir James Somerville*, Evans, London, 1961
Mackenzie, Sir Compton, *Eastern Epic*, Chatto & Windus, London, 1951

Marder, Arthur, *Operation Menace: The Dakar Expedition and the Dudley North Affair*, OUP, London, 1976
Marnham, Patrick, *The Death of Jean Moulin*, John Murray, London, 2000
Marrus, Michael R. and Paxton, Robert O., *Vichy France and the Jews*, Stanford University Press, California, 1995 (First published 1981 by Calmann-Lévy, Paris, as *Vichy et les Juifs)*
Masters, John, *The Road Past Mandalay*, Michael Joseph, London, 1961
McCullough, Colleen, *Roden Cutler VC: The Biography*, Random House, Sydney, 2001
Mead, Gary, *The Doughboys: America and the Great War*, Penguin, London, 2001
Melton, George F., *Darlan: Admiral and Statesman of France, 1881–1942*, Praeger, Westport, Ct, and London, 1998
Mockler, Anthony, *Our Enemies the French: Syria, 1941*, Leo Cooper, London, 1976
Murphy, Robert, *Diplomat Among Warriors*, Collins, London, 1964
Nossiter, Adam, *Algeria Hotel*, Houghton Mifflin, Boston, New York, 2001
Parkinson, C. Northcote, *Always A Fusilier*, Sampson Low, London, 1949
Paxton, Robert O., *Vichy France: Old Guard and New Order 1940–44*, Columbia University Press, New York, 2001
Ranfurly, Hermione, *To War with Whitaker: Wartime Diaries of Countess Ranfurly 1939–45*, Heinemann, London, 1994
Riley, Jonathan, *The Life and Campaigns of General Hughie Stockwell*, Pen and Sword, Barnsley, Yorkshire, 2006
Ross, Hamish, *Paddy Mayne*, Sutton Publishing, Stroud, Gloucestershire, 2003
Rusbridger, James, *Who Sank the 'Surcouf'?*, Random Century, London, 1991
Shamash, Violette, *Memories of Eden*, Forum Books, London, 2008
Shores, Christopher, *Dust Clouds in the Middle East*, Grub Street, London, 1996
Somerville, Christopher, *Our War*, Weidenfeld & Nicolson, London, 1998
Spears, Major–General Sir Edward, *Assignment to Catastrophe*, William Heinemann, London, 1954
Thomas, Andrew, *Gladiator Aces*, Osprey Publishing, London, 2002
Tombs, Robert and Isabelle, *That Sweet Enemy: The French and the British from the Sun King to the Present*, Heinemann, London, 2006
Tute, Warren, *The Reluctant Enemies*, Collins, London, 1990
Verney, Sir John, *Going to the Wars*, Collins, London, 1955
Vinen, Richard, *The Unfree French*, Penguin, London, 2007
Warner, Geoffrey, *Pierre Laval and the Eclipse of France*, Eyre and Spottiswoode, London, 1968
Watt, Donald Cameron, *How War Came*, Heinemann, London, 1989
Werth, Alexander, *France 1940–1955*, Henry Holt, New York, 1956
Williams, Charles, *The Last Great Frenchman: A Life of General de Gaulle*, John Wiley, London, 1997
Williams, Charles, *Pétain*, Little, Brown, London, 2005
Wilson, Field Marshal Maitland, *Eight Years Overseas, 1939–1947*, Hutchinson, London, 1949

Winton, John, *Cunningham: The Greatest Admiral Since Nelson*, John Murray, London, 1998

Yung–de Prévaux, Aude, *Jacques and Lotka*, Bloomsbury, 2000

Ziman, Herbert David, *Instructions for British Servicemen in France, 1944*, Bodleian Library, Oxford, 2005

Index